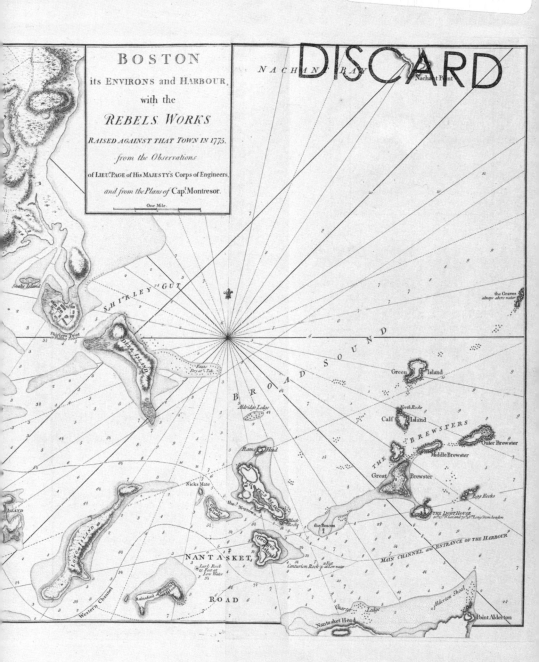

BOSTON

its ENVIRONS and HARBOUR,

with the

REBELS WORKS

RAISED AGAINST THAT TOWN IN 1775,

from the Observations

of LIEU.ᵗ PAGE of His MAJESTY's Corps of Engineers,

and from the Plans of Cap.ᵗ Montresor.

One Mile.

NACHANT BAY

Nachant Point

SHIRLEY GUT

BROAD SOUND

the Graves *always above water*

Snake Island

Shirley's Point

DEER ISLAND

Fort
Dep.ᵗ at Tide.

BROAD SOUND

Green Island

Midridge Ledge

North Rocks

Calf Island

THE BREWSTERS

Outer Brewster

Rams Head

Middle Brewster

THE

Nicks Mate

SPECTACLE ISLAND

Great Brewster

the Narrows

Egg Rocks

Calf Island

Black Rocky

THE LIGHT HOUSE

NANTASKET

GEORGES ISLAND

the Beacon

MAIN CHANNEL and ENTRANCE OF THE HARBOUR

LONG ISLAND

Lark Rock
15 Feet at
Low Water

Centurion Rock 9 Feet
at Low water

Rainsford Island

ROAD

Western Channel

Quarse Ledge

Alderton Shoal

Nantasket Head

Point Alderton

Igniting THE AMERICAN REVOLUTION

1773–1775

DEREK W. BECK

sourcebooks

Published by Sourcebooks, Inc.
P.O. Box 4410, Naperville, Illinois 60567–4410
(630) 961–3900
Fax: (630) 961–2168
www.sourcebooks.com

Library of Congress Cataloging-in-Publication Data

Beck, Derek W.
  Igniting the American Revolution : 1773–1775 / Derek W. Beck.
     pages cm
  Includes bibliographical references and index.
  (hardcover : alk. paper) 1. United States—History—Revolution, 1775–1783—Causes.
I. Title.
  E210.B39 2015
  973.3—dc23
                              2015016941

Printed and bound in the United States of America.

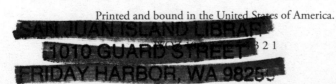

321

To my dear wife Vicky
You have sacrificed much in supporting this book.
Thank you.

CONTENTS

PREFACE

This volume covers the crucial events between 1773 and 1775 that set in motion what would ultimately become the American War for Independence. In writing on this subject as an American, and one who has served in the U.S. Air Force, I am predisposed like all American historians toward a pro-American bias. Yet I have strived to paint the events in this book with accuracy and objectivity, avoiding such bias to the best of my ability. One consequence of this is that I have generally avoided the word *patriot*, even though it is today a commonly used term in other history books to describe the colonists.

While we can call the Americans *patriots*, can we not also call the British *patriots*? For what is a patriot, in the true sense of the word, but a lover of one's country? The British believed they were fighting a civil war, and were fighting to maintain—and for the love of—their empire. The Americans were equally fighting for the love of a land they understood and appreciated in a very different way than their British brethren across the sea. Were they not all patriots in their own right?

The logical result of this attempt at an unbiased approach is that in some cases throughout the book, the British may appear to be the "good guys" and the Americans the "bad guys". At other times, the British may seem like "tyrants", just as many American stories love to paint them. Rather than attempting to steer readers one way or another, I have worked to embrace these shades of gray and present as real and authentic a portrait as possible based on the extensive research I have conducted of both sides. America's Founding Fathers were not all super-heroes. Nor were the British all murderous oppressors. They were all real people, imperfect people—like the rest of us.

My intent and my hope is that this book provides an honest look at the events that began the Revolution, warts and all. Some readers may prefer to adhere to the perspective of older history books that paint the Americans as superheroes. These readers may not like this more honest perspective and may even call me an Anglophile. But I think my con-tinued honorable service in the modern American military refutes any such claims. Rather, I would prefer to be called a lover of truth. (Sadly, I can find no word for this: veritophile?) Truth is where real history is to be found.

Author's Note: This volume employs "logical quotations", meaning the only punctuation appearing inside quotation marks is also in that position in the original as well. So, a quotation ending with a comma inside the quotation marks, such as "quotation," indicates the comma was there in the original, while one with the comma outside the quota-tion marks, such as "quotation", indicates the comma is not part of the original. This style is observed for emphasis or scare quotes as well. See the bibliography for more.

ACKNOWLEDGMENTS

First, thank you to two of my biggest supporters of this project, my mother, Katherine Esber, and my father, (Maurice) Mo Beck, who have both given years of encouragement—even after I quit a successful full-time career in the Active Duty U.S. Air Force to pursue writing this.

I wish to express my sincere gratitude to my longtime friend Jonathan Varoli for introducing me to his sibling literary agent and thus getting this whole thing off the ground. I also wish to express equally sincere gratitude to my literary agents, Doug Grad and Jacqueline Varoli Grace, for becoming champions of the book and exhibiting great patience with my many questions and concerns throughout the publication process. And last but certainly not least, I am so very thankful to my editor, Stephanie Bowen of Sourcebooks, for taking a chance on this first-time author, and for her great passion for Revolutionary Boston, which has made our partnership so refreshing and enjoyable. Thank you all sincerely for believing in this book and making it a reality.

Just as important to the success of this book are my many friends and colleagues who helped with the research along the way, and I thank them all. In particular, my trusted colleague and avid supporter Dr. Samuel A. Forman kindly read through my manuscript and offered many useful suggestions, and has long been a source of encouragement for the project. John L. Bell of the blog *Boston 1775* has also been a longtime supporter. He patiently responded to all of my many queries on various minutiae during the research process and even helped to spread the word of my project on his popular blog. Todd Andrlik gave me frequent encouragement as well. He pushed to have my agents contact Sourcebooks and has also published several of my articles in his *Journal of the American Revolution*. And Benjamin Smith and David Paul Reuwer of the *Patriots of the American Revolution* magazine were the first to ever publish any of my historical writings. Lora Innes also was a source of encouragement and shared advice on branding and all things social media. And Thomas Fleming read my manuscript at two different stages, provided feedback and encouragement, and kindly offered an endorsement.

Several friends also helped me in random ways. David and Sarah Garner let me crash at their Boston home when I needed to research there, and Christophe and Souri Gaillard let me crash at theirs when I needed to research at the Clements Library in Ann Arbor, Michigan. Brian Raimondi shared his access to the University of California, Los Angeles's (UCLA) digital databases for my research. David Silver donated a rare book on Ticonderoga to help aid my research (and it now appears in the bibliography, by A. French). Sandro Catanzaro ran out and bought me copies of the *Boston Globe* and shipped them to me when they noted my research on Dr. Joseph Warren.

I am also much indebted to the many people at the 614th Air Operations Center and 9th Space Operations Squadron at Vandenberg Air Force Base, California (where I serve as an Air Force Reservist), as well as the many folks at the American Flyers flight school in Santa Monica (where I was a pilot instructor), all of whom allowed me tremendous flexibility to write and research this book while at the same time keeping me gainfully employed.

Authors and seamen Rif Winfield and John Harland shared many email discussions with me on various naval matters. Judy Anderson shared much information on Marblehead, Massachusetts. Peter Ansoff, former president of the North American Vexillological Association (NAVA), helped me decipher flags and their use. Sean Rich of Tortuga Trading gave me advice on colonial-era weaponry. My friend and fellow history enthusiast Joyce Kelly of the Watertown Historical Society has long encouraged the project. William M. Welsch has corresponded with me on many random subjects, including the rank of Gen. George Washington, and also has been a longtime fan.

Finally, thanks to the many people who helped me at the research facilities. Janet Bloom, Brian Leigh Dunnigan, and the staff of the William L. Clements Library at University of Michigan; Caitlin Corless, Elaine Grublin, and the staff of the Massachusetts Historical Society; Thomas Knoles and the staff of American Antiquarian Society; Jessica Murphy and the staff of Harvard's Countway Library and the Center for the History of Medicine; Tim Salls of the New England Historic Genealogical Society; Mark Vassar of the Cambridge Historical Society; Jean-Robert Durbin, Mary Robertson, Olga Tsapina, and the staff of the Huntington Library; Lee Spilberg, Megan O'Shea, and staff of the Manuscripts and Archives Division of the New York Public Library; and Michael St. John-McAlister of the British Library.

The UK National Archives is, lamentably, the only archive I worked with that was unwilling or unable to provide research copies by correspondence. However, Alexander Poole came to my rescue. And so, for his generous help in researching and collecting for me documents from the UK National Archives, I am greatly indebted.

PART 1

Ratcheting Tensions (1773 to 1774)

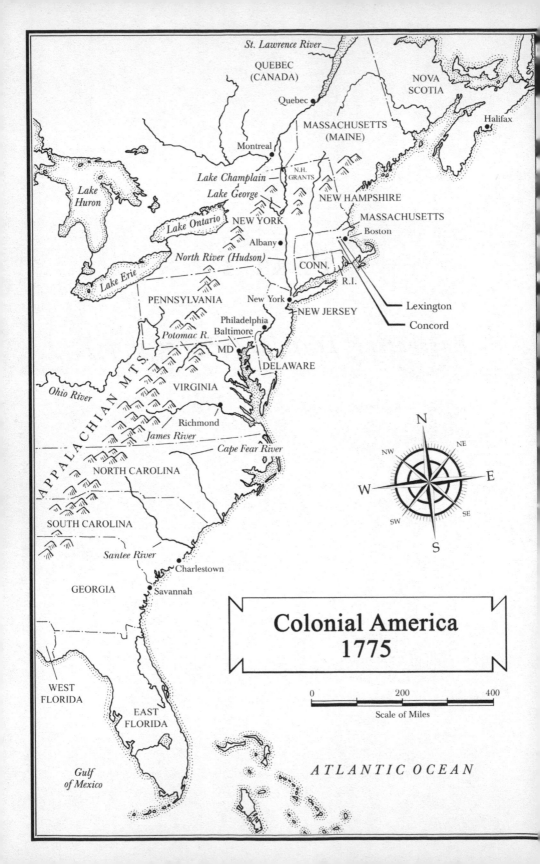

Colonial America 1775

CHAPTER 1

DAWN OF AN EPOCH

It began in late 1773.

December 16 was a dark, dank night, the thin crescent moon having at first been obscured by showery overcast, only to pass below the horizon just as the drizzle tapered off.[1] The waters in the harbor were calm as the waves lapped softly against the sodden wharves. Except for the gentle wooden creaking of the various sail ships against their hemp moorings, all was eerily quiet in the little New England town of Boston.

Splash! The stillness of the night was shattered only for a moment, then instantly silent once more. *Hack! Smack!* The tranquility was broke once more, this time from the cracking of hatchets into hollow wooden crates. This hacking echoed across the harbor, followed by another heavy splash. Then more hatcheting. *Splash!*

These sounds came from Griffin's Wharf on the southeast side of Boston, where the two transports *Dartmouth* and *Eleanor* were docked, each holding 114 chests of detested East India Company tea onboard. Moored nearby was the brig *Beaver* with another 112 chests. Altogether, the shipment was 92,616 pounds of dutied tea (about 21 million cups of tea), worth about £9,659 then, and more than a million U.S. dollars today.[2]

All along the wharf, a large but hushed crowd of spectators, including Bostonians and curious folk in from the countryside, watched as an extraordinary event unfolded. Parties of men dressed as "Mohawk

Indians" worked to hoist the tea chests onto the decks of the three ships, while more worked to hatchet those chests open, pulling the loose-leaf tea from within and then tossing the tea and the chests overboard into the harbor.[3]

For several years, the East India Company had been suffering financial problems, due in part to its own poor business practices, resulting in overdue loans to London banks and a massive surplus of unsold tea amounting to nearly three times its annual turnover. By December 1772, company officials had determined they could safely reduce their inventory to one year's worth of tea and sell off the remainder to inject some much-needed income, for some ninety percent of the company's profits came from tea.

But selling this surplus in Britain would mean unfavorable tax liabilities as well as restrictions to sell only at wholesale. If the company instead sold the surplus in Europe, that would depress the tea market there and encourage smuggling of the cheaper tea back to England, thus undercutting the company's sales at home. So the company ultimately devised a plan to sell the surplus tea at a steep discount in America. The problem was that, by law, the company had never before been permitted to export to America; that was a service provided by various merchants serving as middlemen. Consequently, the proposed plan had to be laid before the British Ministry, which had already deemed the company too powerful to let it founder and was even now moving to take some degree of control over it.[4]

There was one important nuance to this scheme that seemed irrelevant at the time. Upon import to America, the tea would be subject to a tea duty of three pence per pound—the only remaining import tax left from the otherwise repealed Revenue Act of 1767, which the colonists had vehemently opposed. But ever since that partial repeal, American protestations had almost disappeared. In their place, colonists had returned to their avid consumption of tea, especially in Boston, where tea imports reached near-record highs. The British Ministry therefore had little reason to worry about this remaining tax on what was to be otherwise discounted tea.[5] After all, it was expected that the colonists should be delighted to pay *less* for their tea.

Of the various teas the East India Company offered, their primary product was consumer-grade Bohea black tea, grown in the Bohea Hills (now Wuyi Shan) of Fujian Province, China.[6] The company determined to sell this bestselling Bohea leaf at a steep discount of two shillings per pound, which included the tax. Though such a low price would still not undercut illegally smuggled Dutch tea—the primary supply for New York City and Philadelphia—the East India Company could expect a significant profit from the Boston market, whose primary source was legally imported tea from England. The Tea Act of May 10, 1773, made the scheme official.[7]

Initially, the American response was mild. The first reaction came from New York, where smugglers and conspiring merchants worried that strong enforcement of the new act would cut into their considerable illicit profits. They justified their opposition by warning colonists that the East India Company would create a monopoly in America, squashing small merchants and businessmen. Philadelphia soon followed suit, then went further by demanding that its local East India Company consignees resign, which, after considerable public protest, they did. American merchants also worried about the implications of this huge government-backed monopoly and the precedent it could set for more government controls in other industries.

Slowly, the American resistance grew and reshaped itself into a defensible and legitimate argument: the Tea Act was a renewed effort by the British Ministry to force-feed America a tax it had never consented to. Despite the fact that Americans had accepted the tea tax left over from the former Revenue Act, public sentiment was soon roused against this new massive tea shipment. From their perspective, Parliament appeared to once again be forcing overt recognition of its claim to tax America. And so the Tea Act rekindled the flames of antipathy between the colonies and the mother country.[8]

Boston, however, was slow to respond to the mounting crisis. Instead, radicals there were preoccupied with another issue: that its governing authorities might soon be paid directly by Parliament, thus stripping the colony of fiduciary control over its crown officers and thereby eliminating the colony's balance of power with its local government and violating its colonial charter. (John Adams allegedly admitted years later that, had there not been resistance led elsewhere, Boston would probably have accepted the tea, duty and all.) But when Boston saw the response of her sister seaports, she soon responded with a kind of mob violence that had grown typical for the town over the past decade when protesting tax-related acts of Parliament.

It began with harassment and threats, with Boston radicals demanding that once the tea arrived, the East India Company's local consignees send it back to England. The consignees stalled for weeks until the radicals set a town meeting and demanded the six consignees attend to resign their commissions. When the consignees failed to attend, a mob stormed one of their stores, where the consignees were known to be meeting. The consignees rushed to a secure counting room and there remained until the mob at last dispersed, and then spirited themselves to the safety of the secluded island fortress of Castle William in Boston Harbor, having never agreed to the mob's demands.[9]

Amid this turmoil, on November 28, 1773, the transport *Dartmouth* came up Boston Harbor, carrying with it the first of the detested, dutied tea.[10] *Dartmouth* first moored under the sixty-four protective guns of the HMS *Captain*,[11] the flagship of Rear Admiral of the Blue John Montagu, fleet commander in North America.[12] But when *Dartmouth*'s Capt. James Hall came ashore, the Sons of Liberty, an organized group of radical protesters led by Samuel Adams, either induced or coerced him to bring his *Dartmouth* up to the town and dock it at Griffin's Wharf instead. There the Sons of Liberty could guard the ship and ensure the tea was not off-loaded, which would weaken their goal to get the tea sent back to England.[13] That position also meant the Royal Navy could not intervene, in case the radicals turned aggressive, for if the Navy dared fire at *Dartmouth*, they would also be firing into the town.[14]

The second transport, *Eleanor*, arrived on December 2, and her captain also was ordered to moor at Griffin's Wharf, this time by the year-old Committee of Correspondence. This committee acted on behalf of the popularly elected General Assembly, which had gradually grown more defiant against the royal governor because of his perceived support of all the recent controversial acts of Parliament. (Akin to the modern state's house of representatives, the General Assembly was the people's only direct representative at the colonial level.) A third tea ship, the brig *Beaver*, was observed in Massachusetts Bay on December 7. But with her tea, she also brought smallpox, and so she remained to the south for cleansing and smoking before she sailed within sight of the other tea ships on the fifteenth. (A fourth, the brig *William*, had blown ashore on the back side of Cape Cod and was totally destroyed, but her cargo was salvable and later brought to Castle William.)[15]

Now that the tea had arrived, the transport captains were in a quandary. They cared little about the political debate surrounding their goods, but worried greatly about their business. First, they offered to deliver their cargo, but the consignees refused to accept it, citing the resolves and fury of the townspeople. The ships' captains thus had no one to deliver the tea to.

Worse, per a parliamentary act of 1696, customs officials could confiscate a ship's lucrative cargo if duties were not paid within twenty days after the ship's arrival, and for *Dartmouth*, this was December 17. If this happened, the captains would owe the East India Company for the loss. For Boston radicals, confiscation was just as unacceptable as having the tea properly landed. The customs officers would then sell the confiscated tea at a discount, and radical leaders knew well that the tea-drinking populace would not remain so obdurate if discounted tea became widely available.

Nor could the transport captains simply return to England, because trade laws dictated that cargo once exported, if returned to the mother country, was subject to confiscation by authorities there. Not that it mattered. Castle William stood guard over the only water approach into and out of Boston, and both it and the Royal Navy had long-standing orders to seize or destroy any departing vessel without a pass—which Boston customs officers were refusing to issue to the tea ships until the duties were paid. Even Royal Governor Thomas Hutchinson refused to issue a pass, judging it a matter for the customs officers. As it was, the transport captains were stuck, and the bureaucracy of the local officials turned a bad situation worse.[16]

On December 16 afternoon, the eve of the twentieth day for *Dartmouth* (the other transports still had a few days more), more than five thousand people from the town and neighboring countryside descended on Boston to see how the quandary would be resolved.[17] The still-standing two-story, redbrick Old South Meeting House, with its tall, white steeple adorned with a massive clock, had for decades served both as a public gathering place and a church. Though it was the largest building in town, it could not hold the throng, which spilled onto the street. There the people heard radical leaders preach firmness and resolve against the encroaching powers of Parliament.[18] Among them were fifty-one-year-old Samuel Adams (only his enemies called him

PORTRAIT OF SAMUEL ADAMS (C. 1772) BY JOHN SINGLETON COPLEY (1738–1815). PHOTOGRAPH © 2015 MUSEUM OF FINE ARTS, BOSTON.

Sam), thirty-six-year-old John Hancock, and young Josiah Quincy Jr., just twenty-nine.

At length, Francis Rotch, acting on behalf of his father, Joseph, the owner of the *Dartmouth*, was sent by the boisterous town meeting to call on the governor at his countryside home in Milton and plead for a pass to allow his ship's departure along with her tea. But Governor Hutchinson remained resolute, claiming that permitting the ship to sail without clearance from customs would be a violation of the Acts of Trade.[19]

Boston had already grown dark at quarter till six, when the disheartened young Rotch returned more than two hours later to Old South and gave his pitiful news.[20] To this, the crowd erupted, "A mob! A mob!" Some spectators began to slip out to the streets. *Eleanor* owner John Rowe asked, "Who knows how tea will mingle with salt water?"[21] To this, the applause intensified. But order was quickly restored as radical Dr. Thomas Young reminded the crowd that Rotch had endeavored to comply with the town's demands.

The meeting's moderator Samuel Savage then asked: would Rotch send away his vessel, tea and all, under the present circumstances? Rotch answered he could not possibly comply, for doing so would completely ruin him. When asked if he would then land the tea, Rotch said he would not, unless forced by the government.[22] At this, Samuel Adams said he could "think of nothing further to be done…for the Salvation of their Country".[23]

As even more spectators slipped away, the meeting continued with some final formalities for several minutes.[24] Then, "hideous Yelling…[came from the street] as of an Hundred People, some imitating…[war whoops] of Indians and others the Whistle of a Boatswain, which was answered by some few in the House": "Boston harbor a tea-pot tonight!" "Hurrah for Griffin's Wharf!" "The Mohawks are come!"[25] Cheers erupted in Old South as many more poured onto the streets. As one witness wrote, "What with that, and the consequent noise of breaking up the meeting, you'd thought that the inhabitants of the infernal regions had broke loose."[26] Samuel Adams tried to stay the crowd by declaring the meeting not yet done, and Dr. Young gave a speech on the (dubious) ill health effects of tea for maybe fifteen minutes before a crowd that had shrank to less than a hundred. But in truth, Young's speech was a ruse; Adams and his radical colleagues desired an alibi while events began to unfold outside.[27]

Meanwhile, the crowd outside parted to reveal upward of one hundred disguised men thought to resemble Mohawk Indians, their faces smeared with grease and soot, some in rags, others "cloath'd in Blankets with the heads muffled, and copper color'd countenances, being each arm'd with a hatchet or axe, and pair pistols". They spoke in code to one another, but "their jargon was unintelligible to all but themselves."[28]

These men knew they were about to commit a crime, and though their fervor had obliged them to participate on moral grounds, they feared retribution. They pulled off their incognitos so well that one participant noted, "[we] should not have known each other except by our voices. Our most intimate friends among the spectators had not the least knowledge of us."[29] Most would take their secret involvement to their graves, but the most famous participant may have been Paul Revere.[30]

These "Mohawks" quickly formed ranks and marched off through the parted crowd toward Griffin's Wharf, the spectators following closely behind. As they reached their destination, they split into three parties.[31] Two groups boarded the tea ships *Dartmouth* and *Eleanor* moored at Griffin's Wharf, aboard which they found customs officials and forced them ashore. The other went by boat to the nearby *Beaver*, commandeered her, and warped her alongside the other two vessels.[32]

As *Beaver* hauled in, "Mohawks" on the other two ships began their work silently and without fanfare. Some dropped into the hold and secured the blocks and tackles to the heavy tea chests. Others hoisted the chests onto the spar deck. The rest put their hatchets to work, staving in the wooden chests to reveal the aromatic Bohea black tea, only to then pour the loose-leaf overboard, into the water, before finally heaving over the shattered chests themselves.

Aboard one of the ships, a padlock secured the hold. The Americans broke the padlock open, but they were so careful not to damage private property that they afterward replaced the lock. (Their sole objective was the tea.) *Dartmouth* and *Eleanor* had already disembarked all of their other private goods, so only their tea remained. But the *Beaver* still had aboard other cargo and private goods, some of which were stacked atop the tea chests. The "Mohawks" rearranged the ship's private cargo to get to the tea, careful not to damage those other goods.[33]

Much of Boston Harbor area turned to mere mudflats at ebb tide, so the water that night was only a few feet deep. As the Americans continued to pour more and more tea overboard, the leaves began to accumulate in heaps well above the water line. Several times the "Mohawks" had to shovel and strew the tea to ensure all of it was ruined before they continued to dump more.[34]

All the while, the crowd remained silent as the spectacle unfolded. The only sounds were the chopping and breaking of the wooden chests, the tea splashing into the water, and the larger splashes of the chests themselves.

The crowd continued to grow, and the Boston radical leaders who had lingered at Old South may have joined them. Calling themselves Whigs because of their support for the pro-liberty Whig Party in Parliament, these leaders included Samuel Adams, the fervor behind the Sons of Liberty; the wealthy John Hancock, who bankrolled the radical efforts; and an able doctor and political protégé who was still a rather obscure figure outside of Boston.[35]

That doctor was Joseph Warren III, noted as a handsome man, just thirty-two, with blue eyes and light-brown hair. Though he was a successful doctor, leading the advocacy for smallpox inoculations in a Puritan society that objected to the procedure as dirty and unholy, he had slowly taken to politics, spurred by the Stamp Act crisis some eight years earlier. He had also become a leading member of the Freemasons, where, despite his young age, he quickly rose to become Grand Master of all of North America.[36] Earlier that year, in April 1773, his dear wife Elizabeth had died, leaving him alone to raise their four young children, Elizabeth (nicknamed Betsey), Joseph (Josey), Richard (Dicky), and Mary (Polly), all under the age of ten. (Mere days after Warren's loss, the thirty-eight-year-old Paul Revere also lost his wife, a commonality that led to a bond between the two. Unlike Warren, Revere soon remarried.)

To cope with his anguish, Warren plunged himself into the politics of the day, finding solace in public service. Faced with the need to care for his children and continue his medical business, while also wanting to engage in politics, most men of that era would have immediately sought a second wife to serve as a caregiver, if not a lover. Warren appears to have instead placed his children under the eager care of his widowed mother, Mary, who was able to provide a comfortable home at the family farm in nearby Roxbury, the very house in which Joseph himself had grown up. And yet, about this time he became interested in the affections of Mercy Scollay and, throughout the next year, would begin a courtship for her hand.[37]

On this night, as Warren watched the "Mohawks" dump tea into the harbor, he grew certain the present course of action was a necessary

PORTRAIT OF DR. JOSEPH WARREN (C. 1772, UNFINISHED) BY JOHN
SINGLETON COPLEY (1738–1815). ADAMS NATIONAL HISTORICAL PARK.

one. Months later, he would write, "Vigilance, activity, and patience are necessary at this time: but the mistress we court is LIBERTY; and it is better to die than not obtain her."[38] Little did he know, the events unraveling before him would skyrocket him to become one of the most famous men in all America.

Americans were not the only spectators to this "party". Royal Navy warships stood idle just a few hundred yards away. Surely, their captains were aware of what was transpiring, yet they received no orders to intervene. The fleet commander, Adm. John Montagu, was also well aware of the tea destruction underway. In fact, he was lodging ashore at the nearby home of a Loyalist, and from there he could overlook the entire scene from a window.[39]

At nearby Castle William, Lt. Col. Alexander Leslie, commander of the 64th Regiment of troops stationed there, was also aware of the affair, because the customs commissioners and the tea consignees had fled to his island fortress for safety. Leslie later wrote to his superior in New York, Maj. Gen. Frederick Haldimand, Acting Commander in Chief for British forces in North America:[40] "I had the regiment ready to take their arms if they had been called upon."[41] Yet just as no call was sent to the Royal Navy, no call was sent to the King's men on Castle Island.

The man who might have called for their support, native-born Governor Thomas Hutchinson, was unavailable. Frustrated with the constant mobbing and the vituperative attacks against his character after the unauthorized publication of some of his opinionated private letters on the radical politics in Boston, he was eager to escape the harassment and turmoil brewing in town and so had secluded himself at his country estate in nearby Milton. There, he was out of touch with what was happening that night, and he imagined the tea would merely be seized by customs the following day. Thus, he never called for the military to intervene.[42]

Lt. Gov. Andrew Oliver was also at his country home, in distant Middleborough. Oliver was so greatly stressed by the constant backlash against him and his association with Hutchinson that a few months later he would suffer a fatal stroke.[43] (And to the discredit of the Whig movement, Samuel Adams and his radicals would attend Oliver's funeral only to cheer as his body was committed to the earth.[44])

The only authority left in town was the Governor's Council (akin to the modern state senate), but unlike the councils of other American provinces, which were selected by the Crown, the Massachusetts Council was locally chosen by the popularly elected General Assembly, and thus mostly reflective of the burgeoning antitax political views of the general public.[45] In other words, the council would not intervene. Thus, Boston was left that evening without any legal authority willing to enforce the British Parliament's tea duty or suppress the "Mohawks" from illegally dumping the dusied tea.[46]

So the Destruction of the Tea, as John Adams initially referred to it, continued unmolested for three hours.

While most "Mohawks" worked honestly to stave the chests and dump the tea, a few dishonest ones could not resist the opportunity for easy booty of their beloved brew, despite precautions to prevent such. One participant, Charles O'Conner, "had ript up the lining of his coat and waistcoat under the arms" and surreptitiously stashed handfuls of the succulent loose-leaf in the lining, nearly filling it up.[47] He thought himself clever and unnoticed, but his former master cobbler George Hewes spotted him in the act. Recognizing his old apprentice, Hewes reported the thievery to their captain, Lendall Pitts.

Pitts drew the attention of the other "Mohawks" by shouting, "East Indian!" He and Hewes then moved to seize the looter, while others swarmed to block his escape.

O'Conner recognized his old shoe master and in desperation yelled that he would complain to the governor and so reveal at least one of the disguised "Mohawks". But Hewes was undaunted and yelled back, "You had better make your will first!" Hewes then seized O'Conner by his coat, but the thief squirmed free, tearing his coat off as he did so.[48] O'Conner then leaped onto the dock and scurried through the angry crowd. But each way he turned, spectators kicked or punched him, knocking him a few times to the ground. Trying to block the blows, he frantically plowed and crawled his way through the mob and made his escape. He "was handled pretty roughly. They not only stripp'd him of his cloaths [coat], but gave him a coat of mud, with a severe bruising into the bargain; and nothing but their utter aversion to make *any* disturbance prevented his being tar'd and feather'd."[49]

Another participant, an old man, "had slightly slipped a little [tea] into his pocket, but being detected, they seized him, and taking his hat and wig from his head, threw them, together with the tea…into the water. In consideration of his advanced age, he was permitted to escape, with now and then a slight kick."[50]

Finally, around nine o'clock, the "Mohawks" accomplished their deed. Three hundred forty broken chests floated in the harbor, their contents soiled and scattered in the salty tide, which was just beginning to flood back in.[51]

With their mission a success, the "Mohawks" swept the decks and repositioned any private property they had moved. On each of the transports, they then called the ship's first mate on deck to report whether they had left everything as they had found it—except for the tea, of course.[52]

Fearing that any evidence left behind could link them to their criminal act, Captain Pitts commanded the "Mohawks" to pull off their boots once they had disembarked the three vessels to ensure no loose-leaf was hidden inside.[53]

Satisfied, Captain Pitts drew upon his militia experience and ordered his party to form up, shoulder their "arms" (hatchets, shovels, and the like), and then to march. As the "Mohawks" marched forward, the crowd parted again, allowing them to pass. Admiral Montagu watched with indignation as they approached his window to depart the wharf. Finding the opportunity irresistible, he slid up his window and called out, "Well boys, you have had a fine pleasant evening for your Indian caper—haven't you? But mind, you have got to pay the fiddler yet!"[54]

"Oh, never mind!" shouted Pitts, "never mind 'Squire! Just come out here, if you please, and we'll settle the bill in two minutes!" A few in the crowd cheered as one "Mohawk" drew out a fife and began to toot a lively tune. Incredulous at the affront, Montagu merely slammed his window shut. Pitts probably smirked as he continued to march his "Mohawks" away.[55]

The next day, townspeople observed that the current and tides had formed a clumpy, windy path of floating tea that stretched from the wharves all the way to Castle Island in the harbor. One participant later wrote, "to prevent the possibility of any of its being saved for use, a number of small boats were manned by sailors and citizens, who rowed them into those parts of the harbour wherever the tea was visible, and by beating it with oars and paddles so thoroughly drenched it as to render its entire destruction inevitable." With that, the tea was thoroughly scattered, almost none of it salvable.[56]

This Boston affair was not an isolated incident. In Charlestown (now Charleston), South Carolina, the inhabitants were yet unaware of the events in Boston when the transport *London* arrived on December 22. They landed the tea and stored it in a warehouse, duties unpaid.[57] In Philadelphia, the ship *Polly* was returned to England along with her loose-leaf. In New York, weather delayed their ship's arrival until late March, by which time Boston's response was well known. When the transport *Nancy* finally arrived, New Yorkers also succeeded in sending back their tea.[58]

Then on March 6, 1774, another brig, *Fortune*, arrived in Boston. Among its large and varied cargo were a mere twenty-eight half-chests of tea. This was private tea, unrelated to the East India Company, and though the owners were surprised to discover it onboard, they immediately expressed willingness to send it back. Nevertheless, when the custom officials again refused to grant a pass, Bostonians again destroyed the tea, this time not waiting for the twenty days to expire. Throughout the continent, various other towns held their own anti-tea demonstrations, but none was as flagrant as that of Boston.[59]

The continent's initial response to the tea parties was one of solidarity. However, most Americans held private property sacred, and neither the East India Company nor its tea was government owned.[60] When George Washington learned of it, he wrote to a friend, "the Ministry may rely on it that Americans will never be tax'd without their own consent[,] that the cause of Boston...now is and ever will be considerd as the cause of America (not that we approve their cond[uc]t in destroy[in]g the Tea)".[61] In truth, the dumping of the tea was tantamount to theft and vandalism, not an act of civil disobedience, and some began to call for Massachusetts to offer restitution to the company. But the debate over repayment would soon become irrelevant.[62]

Decades later, Boston's Destruction of the Tea would become known as the Boston Tea Party. It was not boisterous; it was not obnoxious. It was a silent and careful affair. John Adams wrote of it in his diary, "This is the most magnificent Movement of all. There is a Dignity, a Majesty, a Sublimity, in this last Effort of the Patriots, that I greatly admire. The People should never rise, without doing something to be remembered—something notable And striking. This Destruction of the Tea is so bold, so daring, so firm, intrepid and inflexible, and it must have so important Consequences, and so lasting, that I cant but consider it as an Epocha in History."[63]

Events would soon unfold to prove how prophetic these words really were. For the Tea Party marked the beginning of the end.

CHAPTER 2

COERCIVE MEASURES

January 29, 1774, was undoubtedly a frigid, wintry day in London. But if Benjamin Franklin trembled when he stepped outside his house on Craven Street, it was probably due not to the cold, but to the trepidation he felt as he walked the short distance to his important legal summons in front of the King's Privy Council. Portly and balding, Dr. Franklin—as he was fondly called in reference to the honorary degree given him in 1759 by Scotland's University of St. Andrews— had spent the better part of the last fifteen years in London, and had just recently turned sixty-eight.

Now he made his way along the possibly snow-covered cobblestones, perhaps accompanied by a small entourage that included his legal counsel. Franklin was to serve this day as agent for Massachusetts, though he also officially represented the interests of three other provinces.[1] As such, he appreciated that his job would prove more difficult than usual, given the news of the Tea Party just then arriving in London.[2]

Soon he came upon the octagonal two-story Cockpit, one of the only buildings that remained after a fire a century earlier had destroyed the adjacent great Palace of Whitehall. The Cockpit drew its name from the barbaric entertainment of cockfighting it once featured, long forbidden by the time of Franklin's visit. Instead, the Cockpit now featured the more civilized sport of politics. But the spectacle that was to transpire this day would seem remarkably similar to an actual cockfight. Franklin was walking into a trap, and perhaps he knew it.[3]

Inside, politicians, nobility, and other spectators crowded the entryway into the small chamber. Of note, in attendance were the Prime Minister, Lord North; the Archbishop of Canterbury; the Whiggish and influential Lord Shelburne (a future Prime Minister); and the most outspoken friend of America to be found in the House of Commons: the Whig Edmund Burke. Burke noted there were thirty-five Privy Council members in attendance—a number he claimed was without precedent. At the head of the Council and behind the podium sat Lord President Granville Leveson-Gower. The spectators who packed the remainder of the floor and the balcony above included Franklin's good friend Joseph Priestley and Lt. Gen. Thomas Gage, Commander in Chief of the British Army in North America, temporarily on leave in England.[4] Excitement and whispers filled the room as the crowd watched Franklin and his entourage enter center stage.

Lord President Gower called the room to attention, and the hearing began with the reading of a letter and its two enclosures from Franklin to William Legge, second Earl of Dartmouth, Secretary of State for the Colonies. The most important enclosure was a petition from the Massachusetts General Assembly to the King requesting the removal of the colony's Royal Governor, Thomas Hutchinson. (The other enclosure gave the assembly's Resolves on the matter.)[5] This petition made the serious allegation that Hutchison had undermined all attempts at peaceful resolution between the colony and the mother country; that this one mischievous man charged with managing Massachusetts on behalf of the benevolent King was in fact the central cause of the present conflict.

As proof of Hutchinson's treachery, the Massachusetts petition provided thirteen private letters, mostly written by Hutchinson and Lt. Gov. Andrew Oliver to an unnamed recipient in England. The letters had since been intercepted and published in America.[6] These were now read before the packed crowd at the Cockpit.[7]

The letters themselves were in fact quite mundane, and several even had words expressing Governor Hutchinson's sorrow over the troubles in Massachusetts. But because Hutchinson was the Crown-appointed leader who had dutifully supported parliamentary efforts to tax

Massachusetts over the past decade, he became the easy scapegoat for Boston radicals, and they wanted to see him ousted.[8]

To make their case, the radicals had latched on to the very few lines of those private letters that sounded most tyrannical, the most damning of which, written in the wake of violent mobbing and riots in Boston, was: "There must be an abridgement of what are called English liberties... I wish the good of the colony when I wish to see some further restraint of liberty, rather than the connection with the parent state should be broken; for I am sure such a breach must prove the ruin of the colony." Radicals ignored that in the same letter, Hutchinson added, "I never think of the measures necessary for the peace and good order of the colonies without pain."[9]

Rather, the two most incendiary comments were found in two letters not authored by Hutchinson at all, though they were included among the rest and read aloud in the Cockpit hearing. One was by Lt. Gov. Andrew Oliver, who stated, "if [crown] officers are not in some measure independent of the people (for it is difficult to serve two masters), they will sometimes have a hard struggle between duty to the crown and a regard to self".[10] This was a hotly contested issue in America, because such a law would strip the people of fiduciary power over their governing officials, allowing their leaders to become unbridled despots.

But the most offensive letter was by neither Oliver nor Hutchinson, but by Custom Commissioner Charles Paxton, who penned, "Unless we have immediately two or three regiments, 'tis the opinion of all the friends to government, that Boston will be in open rebellion." In other words, Paxton was calling for Boston to be placed under military occupation.[11]

After the letters were read, the hearing turned to Franklin himself, for the famed American was not merely in attendance as a representative, but also as a defendant, having played a part in the publication of the Hutchinson letters. Defending him were prominent British lawyer John Dunning and a young American lawyer in London, Arthur Lee, who together began describing the events leading up to this moment.[12]

As they explained, Franklin had obtained the private letters months earlier from a secret informant sympathetic to the colonies. How they came into his hands remains a mystery,[13] but Franklin forwarded them to the Massachusetts General Assembly for its members' consideration.

The one stipulation, imposed by Franklin's secret informant: they were not to be copied or printed.[14] The General Assembly at first published only an announcement of the general implications of the letters. But then, after some debate, they had all the letters printed in the *Boston Gazette*. When the public read them, those few comments in the letters led to outrage.[15]

Franklin probably expected the letters to be published from the start, and perhaps hoped they would be, but he could never encourage it, per his informant's instructions. But once his role became public, Franklin later justified himself to the newspapers: "They were not of the nature of *private* letters between friends. They were written by public officers to persons in public stations, on public affairs, and intended to procure public measures; they were therefore handed to other public persons, who might be influenced by them to produce those measures. Their tendency was to incense the mother country against her colonies…which they effected."[16]

All of this was discussed before the Privy Council and the many spectators there at the Cockpit, while Franklin himself remained silent as his counsel "acquitted themselves very handsomely".[17]

Finally, it was the opposition's turn. Hutchinson and Oliver were still attending their duties in Massachusetts, but their agent Israel Mauduit stood nearby with his legal counsel, the haughty forty-year-old Scotsman Alexander Wedderburn, the solicitor general, infamous for his venomous sharp tongue. Wedderburn had been impatiently looking forward to his moment in center stage, and now this political predator was free to feast on his prey.[18]

The anxious spectators drew to the edge of their seats. They knew the real show was about to begin.

Dressed in a suit of spotted velvet, Franklin stood in the center of the room, conspicuous not only because he was perhaps the only balding man present—for the rest wore wigs or powdered their hair white—but because he represented the rebellious American colonies.[19] Some of the ladies there gazed at Franklin with great attraction, strange as that

Benjamin Franklin Appearing before the Privy Council, 1774 —
ENGRAVING BY ROBERT WHITECHURCH (1814–C. 1880), C. 1859, BASED ON
A PAINTING (C. 1859) BY CHRISTIAN SCHUSSELE (1824–1879). ENGRAVING
COURTESY OF THE LIBRARY OF CONGRESS. (ORIGINAL PAINTING IN THE
HUNTINGTON ART COLLECTIONS, SAN MARINO, CALIFORNIA.)

may seem, for the portly sixty-eight-year-old Yankee carried an aura that
drew their fond fascination. But Wedderburn, as if to savor the moment
before the kill, gave Franklin only a steely gaze before he pounced.

The solicitor general began with a biased history of the events so far,
as if to prime his audience for some tragic Shakespearean play, the fallen
hero to be Governor Hutchinson.[20]

Whatever Wedderburn's version of this history, the roots of the turmoil
had begun with two events. First was the accession in 1760 of George III
as King of Great Britain and Ireland, and the King's move to strengthen
the monarchy into one that led Parliament, instead of merely serving as
its figurehead.[21] The second was the Seven Years' War, fought in Europe
and North America, with the American campaign known as the French
and Indian War. It pitted the British against the French for the right to
the undeveloped expanse west of the coastal British colonies. Action on
the American front ended by 1760, the war itself in 1763, and the French
ceded New France (Canada and claims east of the Mississippi) to Britain.

But Britain also gained a massive debt—£122,603,336 in January 1763, plus an annual interest rate of about 3.6 percent, compounded further by the greater costs of managing an enlarged empire.[22]

So, Britain looked to the prosperous and untapped colonies as a lucrative source of taxation to help refill its depleted coffers. After all, had Britain not expended most of its treasure to protect the American colonies from French and Indian threats along its western borders? The first attempt was the Sugar Act of 1764, but it had unintended consequences that drove the British economy into a postwar depression when it effectively killed the lumber, iron, and rum trades.[23]

Next, continued Wedderburn, was the Stamp Act of 1765, which required an inexpensive stamp to be affixed to a wide array of legal and trade documents, newspapers, newspaper advertisements, and even playing cards and dice, effectively ensuring that all classes of society would somehow be burdened by the new tax.[24] Americans were outraged—politicians rallied to "no taxation without representation", and extralegal mobs calling themselves the Sons of Liberty led days of riots, the greatest of which were in Boston, led by Samuel Adams.[25]

When Parliament repealed the Stamp Act in 1766, Americans were too busy celebrating to pay attention to the Declaratory Act of the same year, which affirmed that Parliament had "full power and authority to make laws and statutes of sufficient force and validity to bind the colonies and people of *America*, subjects of the crown of *Great Britain*, in all cases whatsoever."[26]

Parliament then passed the Revenue Act of 1767, which applied various import duties (a more discreet form of taxation), but also explicitly earmarked those revenues to pay for crown officers in the colonies.[27] This latter stipulation re-enraged the colonists, who "thought they read their own annihilation", believing it would give civil officials unbridled control and turn the populace into abject slaves.[28] With such wholesale governmental restructuring, the Revenue Act singlehandedly changed the face of the political debate. No longer was the argument over taxation, though it would remain so on the surface. Now the debate became one of constitutionality, liberty, and self-determination. Even the oft-repeated phrase "no taxation without representation" became not about taxation, but about the authority of

Parliament. That the British continued to simplify the debate to that of taxation is what led in part to the great divide between the mother country and her colonies.[29]

As Wedderburn reminded his audience, to fight the Revenue Act, the American colonies began an unprecedented nonimportation agreement, first only on the dutied goods listed in the Revenue Act, then on all British goods and all tea from any source whatsoever.[30] Boston was at the center of it all, and Lt. Gen. Thomas Gage, the British Army commander in chief then serving in New York, sent two regiments of troops to Boston to help control the mobs.[31] This led to still greater tension that culminated on March 5, 1770.

When an angry Boston mob violently harassed a handful of British troops, shots were fired, and five townsmen died, with another six wounded. Paul Revere famously engraved a gross misrepresentation of the affair, and the Sons of Liberty absurdly called it the "Boston Massacre." In response, Massachusetts's Governor Hutchinson reluctantly withdrew all British troops to Castle William in the harbor.[32] On April 12, 1770, the Revenue Act was mostly repealed, except for a lingering duty on tea.[33] The nonimportation agreement was then abandoned, and a tentative peace returned to the colonies.

Then there was the Tea Act of 1773.

Throughout Alexander Wedderburn's biased version of the history, he painted Governor Hutchinson as a benevolent man of service, a struggling keeper of the peace, not the villain.

The theatrical solicitor general next turned his oration to the Hutchinson Letters Affair and the resulting allegations brought against Hutchinson and Oliver. "My Lords, they mean nothing more by this Address, than to fix a stigma on the Governor by the accusation... The mob, they know, need only hear their Governors accused, and *they* will be sure to condemn." "There is no cause to try—there is no charge—there are no accusers—there are no proofs."

Indeed, Wedderburn was right. Boston radicals had manipulated public opinion to ensure Hutchinson's condemnation. (True, Hutchinson had proved himself a poor leader in failing to resolve the conflict leading to the Tea Party, but news of this was just arriving in England.)[34] Wedderburn then persuaded the lords that it was not

Hutchinson, nor his predecessor, that had brought troops into Boston; it was the insolence of the colonists themselves.[35]

Content he had sufficiently exonerated his clients, Wedderburn then used his cunning tongue and carefully contrived argument to shift his entire examination from Hutchinson and Oliver onto Benjamin Franklin. "Dr. Franklin…stands in the light of the first mover and prime conductor of this whole contrivance". This was surely one of those times that the audience chuckled, as Wedderburn probably punctuated "prime conductor" in reference to Franklin's experimentation with electricity. He continued, "[H]e now appears before your Lordships to give the finishing stroke to the work of his own hands. How these letters came into the possession of any one but the right owners, is still a mystery for Dr. Franklin to explain."[36]

By now, Wedderburn was playing more to the room than the Privy Council. "I shall now return the charge, and shew to your Lordships, who it is that is the true incendiary, and who is the great abetter of that faction at Boston".[37] The solicitor general danced about the center of the room, stoking the fervor of the crowd and bashing the "wily American" Franklin for nearly an hour, and soon his oration shifted from haughty to scathing. "The letters could not have come to Dr. Franklin by fair means… I hope, my lords, you will mark [and brand] the man, for the honour of this country, of Europe, and of mankind… Men will watch him with a jealous eye; they will hide their papers from him, and lock up their escrutoires [writing desks]." Wedderburn must have then paused to enjoy the cleverness of his next statement. "He will henceforth esteem it a libel to be called *a man of letters* [an intellectual]; *homo trium literarum!*" This was fancy Latin wordplay, but it translated simply: Wedderburn had just called Franklin a thief![38]

Throughout the ordeal, Franklin "stood *conspicuously erect*", keeping his "countenance as immovable as if his features had been made of *wood.*"[39]

Finally, Wedderburn turned his attention from his excited crowd to the Privy Lords and delivered his final words with utter condescension: "But if a Governor at Boston should presume to whisper to a friend, that he thinks it somewhat more than a moderate exertion of English liberty, to destroy the ships of England, to attack her officers, to plunder their goods, to pull down their houses, or even to burn the King's ships of war, [it is] he [that] ought to be removed[?]"[40]

Wild applause erupted. Wedderburn had practically hypnotized the Privy Council with his snake tongue. It is no wonder then that days later, Hutchinson and Oliver were absolved of all charges against them, the Massachusetts petition for their removal rejected. Lt. Gen. Thomas Gage, who had watched the entire affair, rejoiced at Hutchinson's victory, thinking the practice of prying into others' mail was a "damn'd villainous" one. But the fair-minded general also lamented Franklin's humiliation.[41]

Though the great philosopher remained stoic throughout, Franklin was deeply wounded by this betrayal of his government. He had previously been working in earnest to temper both sides of the ideological dispute, urging compromise and understanding between the mother country and her colonies. He had even served His Majesty directly as postmaster general for America, though that office would be stripped from him in the coming days.[42] The dejected Franklin would soon make plans to at last return home to Pennsylvania, though he would not in fact make the trip until 1775.

The Hutchinson Letters Affair was symbolic, for it not only represented Franklin's rift from his fealty to the English government, a division that would send him into the company of American radicals, but it also paralleled the rift British America would soon undergo from her parent state. The Hutchinson Letters Affair was thus the beginning of the Revolution in miniature.

———◆———

On February 4, 1774, shortly after having watched the Hutchinson Affair at the Privy Council, Lt. Gen. Thomas Gage received the honor of an audience with His Majesty King George III. These two men, whose decisions and measures would shape the fate of a country across the ocean, met in the court at St. James Palace in London.

At just thirty-five, George III was still a young king. Lord Waldegrave, a court official during George's earlier years, wrote of him before he ascended the throne: "He...will seldom do wrong,

PORTRAIT OF KING GEORGE III (1771) BY JOHANN ZOFFANY
(1733–1810). ROYAL COLLECTION TRUST © HER MAJESTY
QUEEN ELIZABETH II, 2015/BRIDGEMAN IMAGES.

except when he mistakes wrong for right; but as often as this shall
happen, it will be difficult to undeceive him, because he is uncommonly indolent and has strong prejudices".[43] Indeed, the American
problem would be one instance where the King would mistake wrong
for right.

On this day, His Majesty was anxious to have Gage's valued opinion
on the present crisis, because the fifty-four-year-old lieutenant general
was very familiar with life and politics in the thirteen colonies. Gage
had served admirably under British Maj. Gen. Edward Braddock in
the last war against the French and the Indians and had fought in 1755
at the devastating British defeat known as the Battle of Monongahela
near modern Pittsburgh. There, Gage witnessed firsthand the heroic
efforts of Braddock's aide-de-camp to organize the retreat and bear the

mortally wounded Braddock from the field. That aide-de-camp was the little-known Virginian named George Washington.

Later in the war, Gage had married a well-to-do American woman from New Jersey named Margaret Kemble. And since 1764, following the end of the war, Gage had served as commander in chief in North America, spending most of his time in New York, though now on temporary leave in England.[44]

Honored to give his advice to his King, Gage expressed "his readiness[,] though so lately come from America[,] to return at a day's notice if the conduct of the Colonies should induce the directing coercive measures". Gage thought the Americans would be "Lyons, whilst we are lambs", but if government took "the resolute part they will undoubtedly prove very meek", and he thought four regiments earmarked for New York would be sufficient to keep order in Boston while its inhabitants were punished for

PORTRAIT OF FREDERICK, LORD NORTH, LATER 2ND EARL OF
GUILDFORD, (DATE UNKNOWN), BY ALLAN RAMSAY (1713–84). PRIVATE
COLLECTION/PHOTO © CHRISTIE'S IMAGES/BRIDGEMAN IMAGES.

their conduct.[45] Such a haughty boast! But this was how many Britons saw the Americans, as spoiled children in need of proper discipline.

These words were unusually aggressive for the otherwise mild-mannered Gage, but while he had faith in his forces in America, he never claimed they could maintain order in Boston under all circumstances. King George III, however, was much more aggressive, writing later to his prime minister, Lord North, "once vigorous measures appear to be the only means left of bringing the Americans to a due Submission to the Mother Country…the Colonies will Submit".[46]

It took a few weeks to gain momentum, but soon Parliament and the British Ministry were indeed demanding vigorous measures. First were the calls to bring those involved in the Destruction of the Tea to trial in Britain, which was considered for a time, but soon "the project was dropt", for there was no hard evidence by which to implicate anyone.[47] Then it was decided that if the instigators could not be identified, perhaps the whole colony should be punished. By the end of February, the Ministry was calling for coercive measures against all of Massachusetts.

The first proposed measure was to close the Port of Boston. The King had in his authority the power to issue orders to Admiral Montagu there to effect the blockade, but John Pownall, assistant to Colonial Secretary Lord Dartmouth, suggested the port be closed by law instead. This way, King George could save face, maintaining his reputation as a benevolent sovereign while Parliament became responsible for the coercive measures.[48]

On March 14, 1774, Lord North rose before the House of Commons and gave a speech prompting the debate of the Boston Port Bill. He declared it impossible for "commerce to be safe whilst it continued in the harbour of Boston," and asserted that "the inhabitants of the Town of Boston deserved punishment." Citing other precedents, North justified punishing the whole town for the sins of the few.[49] Charles Van of the Commons agreed, stating he was "of opinion the town of Boston ought to be knocked about their ears and destroyed… you will never meet with that proper obedience to the laws of this country until you have destroyed the nest of locusts."[50]

The proposed Port Bill would not only close the port, but also move customs to a new port of entry at Plymouth. The tyranny of the bill lay in its qualification for rescindment. "The test of the Bostonians will not be the indemnification of the East India Company alone, it will remain in the breast of the King not to restore the port until peace and obedience shall be observed in the port of Boston." In other words, only when the Ministry was satisfied that the people of Boston were sufficiently pacified would the port be reopened.[51]

Some in Parliament, however, thought the Port Bill too severe. Rose Fuller thought so, warning the Commons that if Boston did not submit, there would be no choice "but to burn their town and knock the people on the head." Fuller predicted that if troops were sent to enforce the bill, the Americans would unite and crush them, and he reminded the Commons that the colonists all had arms and knew how to use them. Despite these few friends in Parliament, the Whig Party would not let their sympathy for America justify the destruction of private property. Lord Chatham, a staunch ally to the colonies, termed the Tea Party a criminal action and showed no interest in lending his name to the opposition. The Boston Port Act unanimously passed both houses and received the King's assent on March 31. It would go into effect on June 1, 1774.[52]

This was not the end of Lord North's diabolical scheme. North thought harsh punishment would force Boston back into line, while sending an important message to other British colonies. So, immediately after the Port Bill passed the Commons, even before the House of Lords or the King had given it their approval, North revealed his grander strategy. On March 28, he proclaimed that "an executive power was wanting in that country [of Massachusetts], and that it was highly necessary to strengthen the magistracy of it", and because power there presently rested with the mobs, he so proposed the Regulating Bill. It called for the stripping of democracy from the populace, effectively rewriting the Massachusetts Charter granted by predecessors of the Crown and giving the governor unparalleled power to appoint his own council, judges, and even jurors. The most radical provision limited town meetings to once a year, and only then to elect assembly officials and make rules for local administration. Any special meeting beyond this would require the governor's approval.[53]

The debate ensued well into the next two months, and American petitions to have a say in the proceedings were ignored. The Whigs, being fundamentally against absolute rule, mounted a heated opposition. "Can this country gain strength by keeping up such a dispute as this?" argued Charles Fox before the Commons, stating that Parliament had no authority to modify a Crown-granted charter. Calling it a crime, he added, "I look upon this measure to be in effect taking away their charter…it begins with a crime and ends with a punishment; but I wish gentlemen would consider whether it is more proper to govern by military force or by management."[54]

Edmund Burke protested against the bill on the grounds that Parliament refused to hear from the aggrieved Americans. "Repeal, Sir, the Act [the remaining tea duty] which gave rise to this disturbance; this will be the remedy to bring peace and quietness and restore authority; but a great black book and a great many red coats will never be able to govern it."[55] Despite the spirited opposition, the bill passed both houses with almost an 80 percent majority, becoming the Massachusetts Governing Act and receiving the King's assent on May 20, 1774.[56]

Lord North was not yet done. Concurrently with the Governing Act, Parliament debated the Administration of Justice Bill, which gave more powers to the governor and allowed him to remove criminal trials to England or another colony, thereby eliminating the right to a fair trial by one's own peers. This bill also passed with an almost 80 percent majority, receiving the King's assent on the same date as the other, May 20.[57] Finally, on June 2, Lord North's fourth and final bill received the royal assent. This was the Quartering Act of 1774, which required Massachusetts to supply and barrack the troops sent there at their own expense, and that the troops were to be stationed in the town proper, or wherever their service was required as determined by the crown officers, thus eliminating Boston's previous claims that the barracks in secluded Castle William met their obligations.[58]

The Boston Port Act stripped the people of their right to trade. It would destroy businesses, skyrocket unemployment, and starve the people. The Massachusetts Governing Act eliminated their democracy and liberty and made their governor a virtual dictator. The Justice Act eliminated their right to a fair trial. The Quartering Act ensured troops would be garrisoned in their very midst. Together these were the Coercive Acts. (Historians a century later would rename them the

Intolerable Acts.)[59] Americans would include among the Coercive Acts the unrelated Quebec Act, passed on the heels of the others. Though the Quebec Act would have little bearing on the immediate crisis, it would eventually alter the shape of the coming war.[60]

The British Ministry had one final coercion up its sleeve. In a twist of irony, Massachusetts had petitioned for Governor Hutchinson's removal, for which Benjamin Franklin had met before the Privy Council. Though their petition was initially rejected, now they would have it. Governor Hutchinson had requested leave to visit England. Meanwhile, Lt. Gov. Andrew Oliver was ailing and, though the news had not yet reached London, had died of a stroke in early March.[61] So the Ministry came up with a brilliant plan. Why not grant Hutchinson his leave and make Lt. Gen. Thomas Gage the new military governor of Massachusetts? Surely, *Governor* Gage could obtain, if necessary, military aid from *General* Gage.[62]

By early April, Gage had sent orders to his deputy in New York, Major General Haldimand, to provide a staff for him at Boston. Gage then arranged for his wife to return to New York, away from the turmoil in Boston. Finally, on April 16, 1774, Gage set sail for Boston aboard the 20-gun warship HMS *Lively.*[63]

England was determined to use force to gain submission from Boston. They believed the other colonies would sit idly by and watch its destruction. But the American colonies would indeed unite, and Boston would not so easily submit.

CHAPTER 3

AN ARMY FROM
ACROSS THE SEA

The Coercive Acts were just the next notch up the precipitous ratchet toward war, certain to antagonize the Americans. Unnecessarily harsh, they fueled the belief that Parliament had an agenda to strip the colonists of their civil liberties. Turbulent Boston was unlikely to give restitution for the tea, even if it was the only way to undo those Coercive Acts. But even if such a direct threat to their freedom would not cause Bostonians to rise up, the economic depression caused by the Port Bill, which would impact every social class from wealthy merchant to lowly dockworker, certainly would.

Americans had learned of the impending Port Bill from letters of Benjamin Franklin and others, but it was not until May 10, 1774, that they learned of its passage. The initial response was one of shock and outrage, with ample cries of despotism sprinkled in.[1] Days after the news arrived, two radical leaders in New York wrote privately to Samuel Adams, announcing a planned meeting there to discuss a new nonimportation agreement. Their letter further proposed that all the principal Committees of Correspondence throughout the colonies meet for a general congress to draft a united redress of grievances, on which Adams agreed.

On May 20, Philadelphia held a large town meeting and became the first to publicly petition for a congress.[2] On May 27, the Virginia House of Burgesses resolved "that an attack, made on one of our sister

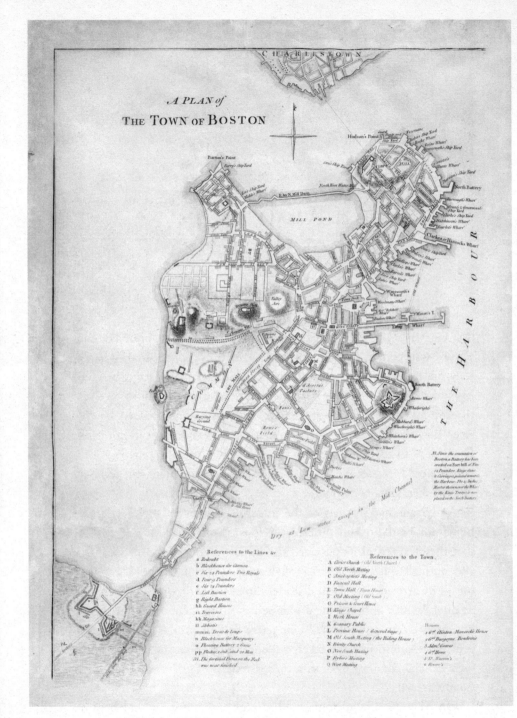

The Town of Boston (1777) by Thomas Hyde Page. Map reproduction courtesy of the Norman B. Leventhal Map Center at the Boston Public Library. Additional details added by the author.

colonies, to compel submission to arbitrary taxes, is an attack made on all British America, and threatens ruin to the rights of all, unless the united wisdom of the whole be applied. And for this purpose it is recommended…to meet in general congress".[3] Meanwhile, other calls for a cessation of trade echoed up and down the Eastern Seaboard.

This was the situation in which Lt. Gen. Thomas Gage found himself as his transport HMS *Lively* sailed into Boston Harbor on May 13, 1774. The warship first took up mooring offshore at Castle William, where Gage met with Gov. Thomas Hutchinson and other officials.[4] Finally, on May 17, he came up to Boston, disembarking at Long Wharf. This was only Gage's second visit to Boston, but now he came as her governor.

Gage took in the view as he walked the gangway down onto the wharf. It was an idyllic spring day, sun shining on the quaint town, the glistening harbor's small waves gently rocking the several naval and transport ships there, which in turn creaked as they pulled on their hemp moorings. The harbor was abustle with longshoremen and carpenters, with fishermen unloading their daily catch. Directly ahead was the custom house, its Doric pillars suggesting it was some kind of Greek temple. Just beyond it lay the redbrick Town House (the Old State House), trimmed in white. And sprawled all around, brick or wooden homes. As one officer later described it, "Boston is large & well built, tho' not a regular laid out town. it has several good streets, the generality of the houses are built of timber & mostly with their gabel ends to the street, & have great yards & gardens to them, this makes the town spread greatly".[5] As Gage looked north, he saw the Charles River and Charlestown Peninsula, with its small hamlet along the riverbank and its vibrant green pastures and hills beyond, dotted with wildflowers and grazing sheep.[6]

Awaiting Gage at the end of Long Wharf were the civil and military authorities, ready to receive him with great pomp and circumstance, joined by throngs of onlookers—ladies in dresses, perhaps with parasols, men in suits, and curious children. Horse-drawn carriages lined the road, having brought in the countryside gentry. The authorities escorted Gage to the Town House, through its white door, and up the stairs to the Provincial Council chamber. There, probably at the balcony window and before the onlookers, his commission was read and his oath of office as governor was administered.

In fact, the townspeople were mostly excited by Gage's arrival, for they so abhorred Thomas Hutchinson that even a military governor was more welcomed there than him. Afterward, Gage attended a large reception banquet at Faneuil Hall, complete with elegant entertainment. He gave "a number of toasts…in which the prosperity of the town of Boston was included," and gave one toast to "Governor Hutchinson, which was received by a general hiss. Such is the detestation in which that tool of tyrants is held among us."[7]

PORTRAIT OF LT. GEN. THOMAS GAGE (C. 1769) BY JOHN SINGLETON COPLEY (1738–1815). YALE CENTER FOR BRITISH ART, PAUL MELLON COLLECTION.

The sixty-two-year-old Hutchinson, the hapless scapegoat who had vainly strove to satisfy the grievances of his people while remaining consistent with his duty, was given before his departure a comfort of sorts for his long service to the colony, receiving warm wishes and sympathies from a large group of merchants, clergy, lawyers, and his Milton estate neighbors. Then on June 1, with one of his sons, Elisha, and his youngest daughter, Peggy, named for her mother who had died giving her birth, Hutchinson boarded the transport *Minerva* for England, never to return to his native country. There he would seek to reverse the Coercive Acts, but the riptide toward war was too strong to break. He would die in England a forgotten expatriate, barred by Massachusetts in 1779 from ever returning.[8]

Looking after his new duties as Massachusetts governor, Thomas Gage found himself quickly inundated. With the upcoming closure of Boston, Gage moved the customs office away to Plymouth. He then moved the rest of the provincial government north to Salem, where he took up residence as well, at the home of Robert Hooper in the district of Danvers.[9]

Meanwhile, June 1, the date the Port of Boston was to be officially closed, was fast approaching. Accordingly, some 119 merchants, traders, and other Bostonians signed an address to the new governor, offering to pay their shares for the restitution of the tea in hopes of preventing the port's closure, despite the public outcry against such offers in light of the Coercive Acts. Gage gave his hearty support, but after several town meetings to effect the result, the obstinate public majority ultimately defeated the measure. Boston would not seek reconciliation on British terms.[10]

Finally, with the closure upon them, the Royal Navy deployed to blockade Boston. Within days, the trauma inflicted by the Port Bill became wholly evident in the small New England town. Less than two weeks later, Boston merchant John Andrews wrote, "Our wharfs are intirely deserted; not a topsail vessel to be seen either there or in the harbour, save the ships of war and transport". However, the Port Bill still allowed the entry of "coaster" transports carrying fuel or victuals, provided their cargo came from elsewhere in America. But as John Andrews described, these were required to undergo an inspection at either Salem or neighboring Marblehead: "The executors of the Act seem to strain points beyond what was ever intended, for they make all the vessels, both with grain and wood, entirely unload at Marblehead before they'll permit 'em to come in here, which…has already greatly enhanced the price".[11]

As Boston learned of the other Coercive Acts and, in particular, of the Massachusetts Governing Act to be effective August 1, the Massachusetts Committee of Correspondence created a subcommittee, chaired by the able Dr. Joseph Warren, which produced a Solemn League and Covenant, a petition by which those who signed were pledging nonimportation of all British goods after October 1. The covenant made clear that those who would not sign would be ostracized. Warren and his colleagues sent the covenant throughout Massachusetts, and it was probably intended for the other colonies too, yet only a few towns ever adopted it.[12]

The Boston radicals did not stop there. On June 7, Gage called the full Massachusetts legislature into session at Salem so that it could consider repayment for the tea. Instead, after other administrative business, the representatives quietly began a plan to call for a continental congress on September 1 in Philadelphia. When Gage learned of the legislature's proceedings, he sent his secretary, Thomas Flucker, to the meeting at the courthouse with a proclamation dissolving the assembly.

But Dr. Joseph Warren, Samuel Adams, and the other Sons of Liberty were ready. Flucker marched into the building and upstairs into the hall leading to the assembly chamber, but found the door blocked. He ordered a messenger there to notify the speaker inside that he *must* be allowed entry to deliver his proclamation. The messenger returned a moment later, stating his instructions were to keep the door fast, that Flucker could not enter.

Incredulous, Flucker tried to get through the barred doorway, but finding himself stuck outside, shouted the proclamation from the stairs to a closed door before him. Inside it, the representatives hastily completed their work. They determined to formally recommend to the towns throughout the province a nonimportation, nonconsumption agreement covering all British goods and selected their delegates for the eventual congress: James Bowdoin (who politely bowed out due to the health of himself and his wife), Thomas Cushing, Samuel Adams, John Adams, and Robert Treat Paine.[13]

Perhaps *Governor* Gage's civil authority could be easily undermined, but *General* Gage's military authority waxed stronger. By mid-June through the first days of July, the first three regiments of troops—the 38th, the 43rd, and the 4th or King's Own Regiment of Foot—began to land in Boston. These were in addition to the 64th Regiment long garrisoned at Castle William.[14] On June 30, Vice Admiral of the Blue Samuel Graves arrived aboard the 50-gun HMS *Preston*, promptly taking command of the fleet from Admiral Montagu, who soon after sailed for England aboard *Captain*.[15] On July 5, the transport *Symmetry* arrived in Boston, carrying a portion of the 5th Regiment commanded by Colonel Hugh, Earl Percy. Lord Percy, along with Lt. Col. Robert Pigot of the 38th, was days later promoted to acting brigadier general in the American service only.[16] On July 22, Stephen Kemble, Gage's brother-in-law, arrived in Salem, having first traveled with Gage's wife from London to New York. Though Kemble was from New Jersey, Gage had secured him a commission in the British Army, and Major Kemble now served as Gage's deputy adjutant general.[17]

Between his many administrative duties and preparing his military, Gage was also amassing evidence against Boston's radical leaders, desiring still to bring to justice those guilty of the Tea Party. His efforts proved unsuccessful, but he still found cause to at least remove the vainglorious merchant John Hancock from his position at the head of a showy honor guard, the Governor's Company of Cadets in Boston, depriving Hancock of his unofficial rank of colonel. Perhaps Gage had been annoyed by a slight from the honor guard shortly after his arrival, when Hancock failed to salute the general as he passed between them on his way to the Town House. Whatever the cause, the remainder of the Cadet Company disbanded in protest, declaring they would never serve until again under Hancock.[18]

Once the Massachusetts Governing Act (the Regulating Act, as the Americans named it) took effect on August 1, Gage moved quickly, calling to elect a new assembly for October. On August 6, he received orders from the home government, listing the thirty-six men selected by the King's Privy Council to serve as the new Governor's Council. Two days

PORTRAIT OF JOHN HANCOCK (C. 1770–1772) BY JOHN SINGLETON
COPLEY (1738–1815). PRIVATE COLLECTION (AN ORIGINAL IS IN THE
MASSACHUSETTS HISTORICAL SOCIETY)/BRIDGEMAN IMAGES.

later, he commissioned those available on short notice, and on August
16, Gage officially commissioned the rest. For the first time, the council
was royally appointed, instead of elected by the popular assembly, and
so thereafter termed the Mandamus Council (that is, a mandated council).[19] Gage also appointed other officials under his newfound authority,
including sheriffs, judges, and as the new lieutenant governor, Thomas
Oliver. Hutchinson had suggested this Oliver because of his last name
alone, believing him to be a relation to the deceased Lt. Gov. Andrew
Oliver, though the two were in fact unrelated.

In response to these late appointments, radical leaders drew forth the mobs. With threats of violence, economic isolation, and ostracism, the new handpicked regime became impotent. In the nether parts of the province, armed mobs utterly refused to allow the courts to open as long as their benches were to be seated by royally appointed judges or their jurors selected by the appointed sheriffs.[20] This turmoil led Brigadier General Lord Percy to declare, when writing to a friend, "The people here are a set of sly, artful, hypocritical rascalls, cruel, & cowards. I must own I cannot but despise them compleately."[21]

Amid all of this, on August 10, John Adams and his cousin Samuel, along with the other three Massachusetts delegates, began their long journey to Philadelphia in anticipation of the Continental Congress, scheduled to convene on September 5.[22]

As the summer of 1774 waned, a tense moment threatened to break the unstable peace. On August 24, Salem illegally called a town meeting, without Gage's permission as required by the new acts. Upon learning this, Gage ordered the 59th Regiment, just then arriving, to send two companies into town center to disperse the meeting. The companies proceeded, but either Gage or their commanders thought better of it, and after going to within a few hundred feet of the meeting, they turned back for their camp. Instead, Gage summoned the Committee of Correspondence and asked if they had called the meeting, to which they admitted they had. Gage then told them they "must abide by the consequences". Accordingly, the sheriff was given arrest warrants, and two were seized that afternoon, though they gave bail and were again released.

The next morning, five others were arrested but refused to give bail, preferring to serve as martyrs in incarceration. While they were held in custody, some three thousand angry inhabitants, all armed with muskets, mustered from the neighboring towns, "with full determination to rescue the Committee if they should be sent to prison, even if they were oblig'd to repel force by force". The militia of nearby Marblehead sent word to the committee that "they were ready to come in at a minute's warning", and with that offer, the seeds of a minuteman force were laid. Hoping to keep the peace, a local magistrate suggested that the governor parole the five prisoners on their honor, but Governor Gage refused, desperate to hold on to any shred of authority he still had.

The five incarcerated committee members were defiant, telling the governor that even if bail was set at a "ninetieth part of a farthing" (a fraction of a penny), "they would not give it". Their cockiness increased with the size of the crowd outside the jail, and they very impertinently retorted to Gage that "if he committed them [then] *he must abide by the consequences*", throwing Gage's words back at him. They also assured the governor that they would not be answerable for what might take place. Gage asked for a day to consider the matter and, on the next day, dropped the prosecution entirely, which one observer noted, "shews a great instance of prudence in him, that seeing them resolute and the people so determinate, he was willing to give up a point rather than push matters to extremities."[23]

Gage continued to find his authority waning as his efforts to enforce the Coercive Acts proved unsuccessful. By the end of the month, he removed himself to Boston, the only place where he could retain his authority, not as governor perhaps, but certainly as general. He took up residence in the traditional governor's residence, the Province House, an elaborate brick three-story mansion centered among a busy row of shops, situated nearly across from Old South Meeting House. Brigadier General Lord Percy also lodged within its walls.[24]

By late August, Gage received still more troops: the 23rd Royal Welch Fusiliers and the rest of the 59th Regiment. This brought his total to six regiments, not counting the garrison at Castle William, plus some sixty artillerymen and eight heavy cannon of the 4th Battalion of Royal Artillery from New York. The open green expanse of Boston Common was soon filled with a sea of white canvas tents interspersed with the red dots that were the soldiers as they moved to and fro. There was little doubt now that Boston was a beleaguered town.[25]

The closure of Boston Harbor also put the longshoremen, rope makers, ship carpenters, and merchants out of business. Without the infusion of trade commerce, the ripple throughout the town's economy quickly drove the town into a deep economic depression. The town's poor, who often survived the harsh winters on the charity of others, were the worst to suffer. But just as Rose Fuller of the House of Commons had predicted, the American colonies would not idly watch as Boston was severed and made desolate. They would unite.

Windham, Connecticut, may have been the first, sending in late June their condolences and moral support, as well as a small flock of sheep for the suffering townspeople. Other New England towns followed suit, then towns throughout the colonies joined in. In August, Baltimore sent the sloop *America*, which was first forced through inspection at Marblehead. She was laden with 3,000 bushels of corn, 20 barrels of rye flour, 2 barrels of salt pork, 20 barrels of bread, and another 1,000 bushels of corn from Annapolis. In September, Quebec City sent wheat, while Essex County in Virginia sent 1,087 bushels of Indian corn specifically intended for the poor, with a promise of four or five hundred more. In November, Providence, Rhode Island, sent both money and sheep, while Philadelphia sent 400 barrels of flour, 5 tons of rod iron, and other supplies. In December, even the Loyalist haven of New York City, "As a token that we have not forgot the poor of your Town", sent some 180 barrels of flour, 9 barrels of salt pork, and 12 firkins of butter.

Donations came from towns both small and large, as near as Concord and as far as South Carolina and Montreal. A few even came in from private individuals. The contributions benefited the poor of both Boston and the neighboring towns, especially Charlestown. To all these, Samuel Adams and the Massachusetts Committee of Correspondence dutifully sent notes of gratitude, in which they further highlighted the injustices toward Boston in hopes of sustaining continental support of their cause.[26]

One of those small towns that made a generous contribution was Brooklyn, Connecticut, at that time a parish of Pomfret, which resolved to donate 130 sheep. Israel Putnam, a fifty-six-year-old staunch Whig and hero of the previous war, herded the flock to Boston. Now a colonel in the Connecticut militia, the round-faced, stocky, impetuous yet charismatic Putnam was so renowned for his former military service that he was welcomed by both colonist and redcoat alike. He was even reported to have held a public debate on politics with his old friend Maj. John Small, a British soldier. Old Put, as his friends called him, stayed several days at the home of his friend Dr. Joseph Warren near Faneuil Hall.[27]

The donations and well wishes brought solace to Boston, but this was the lull before the storm. Gage was in a precarious position, charged with the unenviable task of restoring peace while simultaneously enforcing the controversial parliamentary acts. His decision was to tread carefully yet positively enforce the new laws while removing the ability of the local militia to conduct an armed resistance. And a timely opportunity was about to present itself.

———— •·• ————

Throughout the late summer of 1774, neighboring towns thought it best to remove their towns' gunpowder from the common storage at the Powder House in Cambridge. In late August, William Brattle, a Loyalist and brigadier general in the local militia, sent a message to General Gage warning that the last of the towns had removed their powder, "so that there is now therein the King's powder only," that is, the powder owned by the province, "which shall remain there as a sacred depositum till ordered out by the Captain-General."[28] Gage was certainly within his authority as governor to remove powder belonging to the province, but he feared alarming the countryside. So with this late news from Brattle, he devised a meticulous military maneuver. He called to his headquarters at Province House Lt. Col. George Maddison of the 4th (King's Own) Foot and gave him his secret orders.

Around four thirty on the morning of September 1, with the unsuspecting town still asleep in the predawn darkness, Maddison and some 260 picked men crept from their encampment and made their way to Long Wharf. There they found thirteen longboats waiting, courtesy of the Royal Navy. Once the soldiers fumbled into the rocking boats, their naval rowers pushed off, propelling them across the mouth of the Charles River, past the eastern extent of Charlestown Peninsula, and up the Mystic River.

Easily riding the flooding tide upriver, they passed the backside of the peninsula and reached a landing at Robert Temple's farm.[29] There the boats gracefully fanned out and softly plowed onto the beach, grinding to a halt. After the troops awkwardly climbed out, they formed into a column and silently marched the one mile westward to the Powder House on Quarry Hill, the metal of their shouldered muskets glistening in the dim light.[30]

The Powder House, which still stands today in modern Somerville's Powder House Square, was a gray stone silo with a beehive shingled roof, rising nearly thirty feet above the hill.[31] As the British column reached the magazine, the Sheriff of Middlesex County, Militia Col. David Phips, crept out of the shadows and revealed himself. Phips handed Maddison the keys to the magazine's tall wrought-iron gate, which the regular officer promptly opened. As the sun began to rise around five o'clock, Maddison dispatched a small detachment ahead to Cambridge, their orders to bring away two brass fieldpieces belonging to the province.

The rest of the troops worked quickly. A few slipped inside the magazine's narrow entryway and began passing the 250 half-barrels of gunpowder to those outside, while the rest remained in a long queue, waiting in turn for their half-barrel before carrying it back to the long-boats. Within about an hour, the last of the laden and somewhat dispersed column was trudging back to the Mystic for a swift passage back southward. By noon, the expeditionary force had unloaded their gunpowder at Castle William and was safely back in Boston.[32]

How the colonists first learned of the expedition is unknown, but by late evening, the town was alarmed. Church bells began to toll; messengers streamed from Cambridge to alert nearby towns; and the fire beacons last used in the previous war were lit again, setting off a chain of distant beacons that warned the countryside of an attack.

A frantic but false story quickly spread across the countryside: the Powder House had been robbed and the colonists resisted; British soldiers fired into the crowd, killing six (another "Boston Massacre"); the militia was mustering, and America was at war! Mr. McNeil, a traveler on the road to Boston, later said he "never saw such a Scene before—all along were armed Men rushing forward some on foot some on horseback, at every house Women & Children making Cartridges, running Bullets, making Wallets, baking Biscuit, crying & bemoaning & at the same time animating their Husbands & Sons to fight for their Liberties, tho' not knowing whether they should ever see them again."[33]

By the following morning, September 2, a crowd of farmers and militia approaching near four thousand had gathered on Cambridge Common in response to the alarm. Some were mere spectators, but many were armed, though they had left their pieces "at a little distance".[34] As McNeil continued to travel toward Boston via Cambridge, he found "scarcely left half a dozen Men in a Town, unless old and decrepid, and in one town the Landlord told him…[he] was the *only Man left*" All along the way, McNeil heard the same report: six killed, a battle begun! It was not until within two miles of Cambridge that he began to hear conflicting reports.[35]

When the Cambridge throng learned the rumors of war were false, they turned their attention to the man who had prompted the British raid on the Powder House. William Brattle's letter to Gage had somehow fallen into the hands of radical leaders the night before—a letter that was barely suggestive of Toryism. One story suggested it was by design that Gage had dropped the letter in the street while pulling out a handkerchief, though this is unlikely.

However the leak happened, Brattle's letter was promptly published, and the well-informed crowd flocked toward his nearby Cambridge home on what is now called Tory Row.[36] The incensed mob, their anger aggravated by what was later remembered as the hottest day of the summer, swarmed before his elegant mansion, its gated grounds, gardens, and private mall extending to the Charles River. Whig leaders held the crowd back, but Brattle, seeing the overwhelming disdain now held for him, fled for his life to the refuge of Castle William.[37] With his departure, the throng's attention then turned to the active demonstration against the newly appointed crown officials.

Meanwhile, at about six o'clock that morning, Dr. Joseph Warren was summoned at his home in Boston to come immediately to Cambridge. This was Warren's first opportunity to step out of the shadow of his mentor Samuel Adams, now away in Philadelphia. Warren could probably hear the distant church bells as his informant told him both of the crowd seeking out Brattle and also of an affair at Jonathan Sewall's mansion, where someone inside had foolishly fired a pistol, leading a mob of unruly boys and black slaves to break the windows before dispersing. Fearing "immediate acts of violence", Warren quickly departed for Charlestown Ferry and, presumably taking a horse, made his way to Cambridge Common, meeting up with fellow Whig Dr. Thomas Young along the way.[38]

Back at Tory Row, Lt. Gov. Thomas Oliver had been called on at his house and asked to resign his position as a mandamus councilor, which he did, further offering to renounce his lieutenant governorship. But the crowd told him they did not wish for a better man than him to hold the second office in the government. Strange as this may seem, the Whig leaders had disdain only for the new acts of Parliament, but the royal appointment of Oliver as lieutenant governor was per their beloved colonial charter.[39]

Finding the assembly pacific, Oliver grabbed his horse and galloped toward Boston, crossing paths with Dr. Warren, with whom he briefly conversed before riding on. Once in Boston, Gage listened to Oliver's judgment, and so no soldiers were dispatched.[40]

Back at Cambridge Common, Dr. Warren and Dr. Young arrived to find old, feeble Judge Samuel Danforth addressing the hushed crowd, explaining that though he had "spent the greater part [of his considerable years] in the service of the publick, it was a great mortification to him to find a step lately taken by him so disagreeable to his country", and so he resigned his appointment as a mandamus councilor.[41] Judge Joseph Lee and some other councilors also resigned.[42] And the crowd deemed Col. David Phips immune to punishment for performing his duly appointed duty in surrendering the keys to the Powder House, but compelled him to swear against following any further order under the new parliamentary acts.[43]

However, the peaceful crowd grew inflamed when they saw Customs Commissioner Benjamin Hallowell in an opulent chaise, detested as he was for his long-standing support of Parliament. "...in a few minutes above one hundred & sixty Horsemen were drawn up & proceeded in pursuit of him in full Gallop." As a handful reached him, Hallowell abandoned his chaise, brandishing a pistol, and took to his horse. Kicking the steed into gallop across Cambridge Bridge, he rode toward Roxbury at such speed that his horse finally gave out in exhaustion within sight of Boston Neck. Desperate, Hallowell leaped off his mount and raced toward the finish line on foot, crossing the Neck into the safety of Boston with its British troops.[44]

Meanwhile, militias from distant towns were still on the march. After taking all the accounts he could on the matter, Rev. Ezra Stiles judged "30,000, or near perhaps more than one Third of the effective Men in all New England took Arms & were on actuall March for Boston."[45] Dr.

Benjamin Church Jr., one of Boston's leading Whig leaders, wrote that some twenty thousand from the Connecticut River Valley alone "had risen in one body armed and equipped and had proceeded on their march" toward Cambridge.[46] Gage added, "the whole Country was in Arms, and in Motion, and numerous Bodies of the Conecticut People had made some Marches before the Report was contradict'd."[47]

With the crisis averted, the crowd began to disperse back to their homes by the end of the day. Dr. Warren was very happy with the outcome, but hoped it would be representative of future exertions: "Our all is at stake. We must give up our rights, and boast no more of freedom, or we must oppose immediately."[48]

The Powder House Alarm served as a major transformation from mere political resistance to armed revolution. The significance of the event was not lost on General Gage. Writing to Lord Dartmouth, Secretary of the Colonies, he exclaimed, "Nothing can be done but by forceable Means. Tho' the People are not held in high Estimation by the Troops, yet they are numerous, worked up to a fury, and not a Boston Rabble but the Freeholders and Farmers of the Country."[49] In a second letter, Gage lamented how even the clergy were now involved: "Sedition flows copiously from the Pulpits."[50]

Gage was now a changed man, painfully aware that any future military action might lead to armed conflict. Yet, as if unconsciously desiring to escalate the situation further, he quickly made several decidedly overt military decisions. Within a day or two after the alarm, Gage ordered his engineers to strengthen the Neck's dilapidated brick-and-stone fortifications and two old gates (one for carriages, one for pedestrians), and then to construct new blockhouses in advance of these, and to mount several fieldpieces there. The Boston selectmen met with Gage to inquire: were the Neck fortifications to keep the countryside out, or the town inhabitants in? Gage replied that he was "only about securing the entrance into the Town, that the inhabitants as well as the soldiers may not be expos'd to inroads from the country."[51]

Within seventy-two hours, Gage also sent orders to Maj. Gen. Frederick Haldimand in New York to join him as quickly as possible with all available men. Haldimand had the strange distinction of being Swiss but in British service and was second-in-command under

Gage. Gage further sent orders to Lt. Col. Valentine Jones at Quebec, who was acting as a brigadier general in the American service, ordering him to bring the 10th and 52nd Regiments by sea to Boston, unless Quebec's Governor, Maj. Gen. Guy Carleton, insisted the troops were necessary there.[52]

To prepare for the coming winter and the influx of troops, Gage also ordered barracks to be built on Boston Common. Despite efforts by radical leaders to withhold both wood and carpenters from the British Army, the economic depression induced some laborers to take the employment, though progress was slow. Other troops took up winter quarters in government-procured distilleries and vacant warehouses.[53]

As Gage worried about an uprising, the significance of the Powder Alarm was not lost on the radicals either. Paul Revere began devising a more organized alarm network throughout New England. Dr. Joseph Warren fervently worked to summon a county convention (technically legal, as it was not a *town* meeting) with the intent to create a set of overt resolves that would challenge the legitimacy of Gage's future actions. And delegates to the First Continental Congress were about to create a united set of resolves that would lay the foundation of a national unity such as the continent had never before witnessed.[54]

CHAPTER 4

AN UNSTABLE PEACE

The Massachusetts congressional delegation rode off in style toward Pennsylvania, greeted by the many towns with warm receptions, bells ringing, parades and ceremonies, and private dinners with top local leaders. Everyone was in high anticipation, in particular John Adams, who had never before traveled outside New England.

Though a relative newcomer to political service, the nearly thirty-nine-year-old John Adams (cousin to Samuel) was an experienced lawyer. His greatest victory was the successful defense of British Capt. Thomas Preston and the eight soldiers involved in the Boston Massacre. Despite the efforts of some Boston radicals who had sought severe punishment, Adams won acquittals for all of his defendants except two soldiers, who each received a brand of the letter *M* (for manslaughter) on the brawn of a thumb.[1]

Even with these credentials, Adams doubted his qualification as a delegate among such luminaries as John Jay of New York, John Dickinson of Pennsylvania, or Richard Henry Lee of Virginia.[2] "For my own part," he confided to a friend, "I am at a loss, totally at a loss, what to do when we get there, but I hope to be there taught."[3] In his diary, he confided his deepest worries: "We have not Men, fit for the Times. We are deficient in Genius, in Education, in Travel, in Fortune—in every Thing. I feel unutterable Anxiety."[4]

Despite his trepidation, he had accepted his nomination to the

PORTRAIT OF JOHN ADAMS (1783) BY JOHN SINGLETON COPLEY (1738–
1815). HARVARD UNIVERSITY PORTRAIT COLLECTION, BEQUEST OF
WARD NICHOLAS BOYLSTON TO HARVARD COLLEGE, 1828.

Congress and turned his thoughts to the service before him. Initially, he
had been hopeful of an accommodation with Britain, but as he honed

his political thought, he slowly came to the opinion "that we have nothing to expect from their justice but everything to hope from their fears".[5]

General Gage was fully aware of the proceedings of the Continental Congress, but he vastly underestimated its members. He wrote to Lord Barrington, Secretary at War, that it was a "motley crew" that could only talk and threaten economic warfare, but would be impotent and irrelevant, and so could be ignored. This was especially true of the southern colonies, who "talk very high, but…they can do Nothing, their numerous Slaves in the Bowells of their Country, and the Indians at their Backs, will always keep them quiet". Until radical leaders were "sent Home Prisoners, I fear we shall have no peace".[6]

The Massachusetts delegates traveled at a leisurely pace, taking some three weeks to make their way to Philadelphia, then the largest city on the continent. Upon their arrival on August 29, they settled into Mrs. Sarah Yard's lodging house, conveniently located near the city tavern.[7] There they passed the time for about a week, entertaining with local leaders and discussing the political contest at hand with other arriving delegates.

At last, on September 5, the Congress met in the two-story redbrick, white-trimmed building of Carpenter's Hall, with all of the thirteen colonies represented except the young frontier colony of Georgia. This first day was mostly introductions. On the next day, discussion began with the setting of ground rules for the conclave, including the selection of Peyton Randolph of Virginia as president. One of the two Rutledges from South Carolina, probably the elder, John, reminded the conclave that they had no legal authority and could only recommend measures to their respective colonies. But the most memorable words that day came from Patrick Henry of heavily populated Virginia, who argued that each colony should have an equal vote, not weighted by its population. "The distinctions between Virginians, Pennsylvanians, New Yorkers and New Englanders are no more. I am not a Virginian, but an American." Henry rightly knew it would be crucial to ignore previous intercolony jealousies and form a united front if they were to expect an accommodation from Britain.[8]

When the discussion turned to officially opening the Congress the next day with a prayer, debate over what sort of clergy, from which denomination, threatened to split the convention. John Adams wrote, "we were so divided in religious Sentiments, some Episcopalians, some Quakers, some Aanabaptists, some Presbyterians and some Congregationalists, so that We could not join in the same Act of Worship." But Samuel Adams "arose and said he was no Bigot, and could hear a Prayer from a Gentleman of Piety and Virtue, who was at the same Time a Friend to his Country. He was a Stranger in Phyladelphia, but had heard that Mr. Duché (Dushay they pronounce it) deserved that Character, and therefore he moved that Mr. Duché, an episcopal Clergyman, might be desired, to read Prayers to the Congress, tomorrow Morning."[9] With that, the motion was seconded, and the body adjourned until the next day.

Sometime that same day, the delegates learned the terrible but false news of the "Bombardment of Boston"—the Powder Alarm. With horror and trepidation, they reconvened at Carpenter's Hall the following morning, September 7. Rev. Jacob Duché opened the day, reading "several Prayers, in the established Form" and then read a prescribed Bible passage for that day, Psalm 35: "Plead my cause, O Lord, with them that strive with me: fight against them that fight against me. Take hold of shield and buckler, and stand up for mine help. Draw out also the spear, and stop the way against them that persecute me..." John Adams and the conclave were taken by the relevance of that psalm. "I never saw a greater Effect upon an Audience. It seemed as if Heaven had ordained that Psalm to be read on that Morning."[10] Despite the apparent Whiggish tendencies of Duché, he would a few years later reveal himself to be an ardent Loyalist.[11]

By the next day, the delegates learned the "Bombardment of Boston" was a hoax. According to John Adams, it "made us compleatly miserable for two days, We saw Proofs both of the Sympathy and the Resolution, of the Continent. War! War! War! was the Cry, and it was pronounced in a Tone, which would have done Honour to the Oratory of a Briton or a Roman. If it had proved true, you would have heard the Thunder of an American Congress."[12]

Meanwhile in Boston, Warren sought to capitalize on the public excitement following the Powder Alarm. So he and town leaders throughout Boston's Suffolk County convened their own conclave on September 6 at the house (perhaps the tavern) of Richard Woodward in Dedham. After much debate over their united position on the recent acts of Parliament, Warren was made chair of a committee to draft their resolves.

The county delegates then met again on September 9 in the house of Daniel Vose in Milton. Warren presented his draft, which was read several times, paragraph by paragraph, before it was unanimously adopted. These were the Suffolk Resolves.[13] The convention also drafted a polite but assertive letter of grievances addressed to General Gage, carefully admonishing him for raiding the Powder House but assuring him they had no desire to attack the troops in Boston. Their letter further added "that nothing less than an immediate removal of the ordnance [from Boston Neck], and restoring the entrance into the town to its former state, and an effectual stop of all insults and abuses in the future, can place the inhabitants of this county in that state of peace and tranquility, in which every free subject ought to be."[14]

On about September 11, Dr. Warren, along with Dr. Benjamin Church, it seems, delivered the letter to General Gage. It was likely the first time the two opposing leaders met. Gage heard them out, despite the delegation's extralegal status.[15] After skimming the letter, Gage supposedly replied, "Good God! Gentlemen, make yourselves easy, and I'll be so. You have done all in your power to convince the world and me that you will not submit to the Acts, and I'll make representations home accordingly". But Gage had questions of his own. "What is the reason that the cannon were remov'd from Charlestown?" (Radicals had hid these cannon days earlier.) "And why do the country people go in and out of the town arm'd?"[16] Warren and Gage agreed to answer each other's questions in writing, and so their meeting ended.[17] But when they did reply in the days following, nothing came of it.[18] Despite Warren's best efforts, the fortifications on Boston Neck were "carried on without intermission."[19]

Meanwhile, Warren sent Paul Revere to the Continental Congress, one of his less famous rides, carrying with him the Suffolk Resolves and a copy of the letter to Gage.[20] For the general, his only solace during this turmoil was the arrival, on September 12, of his lovely American-born wife, Margaret Kemble Gage, who had come up by carriage from New York, escorted by two senior British officers.[21]

Portrait of Paul Revere (1768) by John Singleton Copley (1738–1815). Photograph © 2015 Museum of Fine Arts, Boston.

When Revere arrived in Philadelphia, the next morning, September 17, Congress read his dispatches. The Suffolk Resolves proclaimed they safeguarded "the fate of this new world, and of unborn millions", laid out the American right to defend and preserve "civil and religious rights and liberties", called "the late acts of British parliament...gross infractions of those rights", "that no obedience is due...to any part of the acts...but that they be rejected as the attempts of a wicked administration to enslave America." They further resolved "that the inhabitants...use their utmost diligence to acquaint themselves with the art of war as soon as possible" and drill once a week, yet reaffirmed that "we are determined to act merely upon the defensive". They ended by declaring a nonimportation, nonconsumption agreement toward British goods, "until our rights are fully restored to us". That same day, the Congress unanimously voted to endorse the resolves and recommended the other colonies resist likewise.[22]

Back in Boston, a small band of colonists defiantly stole four small, brass 3-pounder cannon from the British encampment. Radicals justified this thievery by arguing the guns belonged to the province, not the Army. The next day, Gage ordered a military detachment to prepare to embark on longboats for Watertown upriver, where the guns were supposedly stockpiled. As the troops began to muster on Boston Common, an alarm spread across the countryside. Though incensed at the robbery, Gage though better of his plan and ordered his troops to stand down, thereby averting a potential crisis.[23]

Meanwhile, Massachusetts militia companies began to "reorganize" as an excuse to reelect officers and thereby purge Loyalists. Additionally, they applied the idea first publicly offered by Marblehead of having militia "ready to come in a minute's warning". By September 21, Worcester County held a convention, voting "to enlist one third of the men of their respective towns, between sixteen and sixty years of age, to be ready to act at a minute's warning". Other militia companies followed suit, and the special division known as the minutemen was born.[24]

With the political storm brewing, Gage wrote at the end of September to Lord Dartmouth, "Had the Measures for regulating this Government been adopted seven Years ago, they would have been easier executed, but the executive Parts of Government have gradually been growing weaker from about that Period, and the People more lawless and seditious".[25] Two weeks later, he added, "The Disease [of political turmoil] was believed to have been confined to the Town of Boston, from whence it might have been eradicated no doubt without a great deal of Trouble, and it might have been the Case some Time ago; but now it's so universal there is no knowing where to apply a Remedy."[26] Gage even wrote his predecessor, Thomas Hutchinson, hinting that "a Suspension of the Execution of the late Acts" might be expedient, a thought Gage later repeated to Lord Dartmouth.[27]

Hutchinson would indeed do his part in London by calling for the repeal of the Coercive Acts—acts he had never condoned. But when the King later read Gage's version to Dartmouth, he wrote to his prime minister, "his idea of suspending the Acts appears to me the most absurd that can be suggested... [If] the mother-country adopts suspending the measures...this must suggest to the colonies a fear" that would only encourage their present violence and mischief. The King was resolute: "we must either master them or totally leave them to themselves and treat them as aliens." That is, Britain would not suspend the Coercive Acts.[28]

His Excellency General Gage also began pressing the home government for more troops. He warned, "they affect to despise our small Numbers, and to overwhelm us with forty or fifty Thousand Men...if you wou'd get the better of America in all your Disputes, you must conquer her, and to do that effectually, to prevent further Bickerings, you should have an Army near twenty Thousand strong composed of Regulars, a large Body of good Irregulars such as the German Huntsmen, picked, Canadians &ca [etc.], and three or four Regiments of light Horse, these exclusive of a good and sufficient Field Artillery."[29]

As autumn progressed, Gage's problems continued to mount. Back on September 1, Gage had ordered a summons for representatives of the towns throughout Massachusetts to convene on October 5 in Salem to elect a new General Court (assembly). However, on September 28, Gage issued a proclamation that, given "the present disordered and unhappy state of the province, it appears to me highly inexpedient that a great and general court should be convened at the time aforesaid", and so excused and discharged all representatives from meeting, and further declared he would not be in Salem. Regardless, some ninety representatives met in Salem on the appointed day. To give the pretense of legality, they gave Gage one day to arrive. When he did not, they reconvened on October 6 and agreed to elect and form a provincial congress, with John Hancock as its president. Their justification was that this extralegal body was duly elected and formed by a meeting convened at the request of the governor, though their argument was untenable. In fact, this formation of the Provincial Congress marked the first true act of treason by the colony as a whole, and likewise its first true act of revolution, as it effectively stripped provincial governing authority from the crown officers and gave it instead to the people.[30]

Meanwhile in Philadelphia, the Continental Congress debated many varied political propositions throughout September. But of all the delegates there, the one most conspicuous was the revered Col. George Washington of Virginia. At more than six foot three, he had a great aura about him, though he was noted for rarely speaking, owing to his uneasiness with his own abilities compared to his formally educated colleagues.[31] Yet he gave considerable reflection and thought to the issues at hand. For instance, late that summer, he had written his friend Bryan Fairfax, referring to the apparent military law forced upon Massachusetts: "what further proofs are wanting to satisfy one of the design's of the Ministry than their own Acts[?]... shall we after this whine & cry for relief, when we have already tried it in vain?, or shall we supinely sit, and see one Provence after another fall a Sacrafice to Despotism? ...I think the Parliament of Great Britain hath no more Right to put their hands into my Pocket, without my consent, than I have to put my hands into your's for money".[32] A few weeks later he forlornly added, "I shall not undertake to say where the Line between Great Britain and the Colonies should be drawn, but I am clearly of opinion that one ought to be drawn; & our Rights clearly ascertaind... the Crisis is arrivd when we must assert our Rights, or Submit to every Imposition that can be heap'd upon us; till custom and use, will make us as tame, & abject Slaves, as the Blacks we Rule over with such arbitrary Sway."[33] Washington was a man of conviction, even if he rarely lent his voice to the debates in Carpenter's Hall.

One of the hottest debates concerned a conservative plan for union introduced by Joseph Galloway, delegate from Pennsylvania. Hoping to restore the once great harmony between the mother country and her colonies, Galloway rejected the proposition that Parliament had no authority over internal colonial affairs, but acknowledged it was unjust to be taxed by a body in which the colonies had no representation.

His alternative was the establishment of a grand council in America, representing all of the colonies. The council, together with a royally appointed president-general, would govern the colonies, subject to approval by Parliament, but would have veto power over bills affecting America. Critics argued that they were still subject to the whims of Parliament. Though the liberal delegates did not know which way to proceed, they were sure a firm union like this would not do.

Meanwhile, Galloway forwarded a copy to his fellow Pennsylvanian Benjamin Franklin in London, asking him to show it to allies in Parliament. Franklin's reply came months later. In it, he questioned Galloway's loyalties, adding, "I cannot but apprehend more mischief than benefit from a closer union. I fear they will drag us after them". Citing the rampant despotism Franklin now clearly saw in England, his eyes opened following the Hutchinson Letters Affair, he added, "I apprehend...that to unite us intimately will only be to corrupt and poison us also."[34]

The Galloway plan seems to have been put to committee for weeks before it was defeated by a vote, six to five, with most references to it later expunged from the minutes. The conservatives lost the initiative in Congress, never to regain it. Galloway would later become a devout Loyalist.[35]

By early October, John Adams was appointed to draft the final resolves of the Continental Congress. On October 14, his proposed Declaration and Resolves was debated and the resolutions made. The declaration noted that Americans were entitled to certain natural liberties irrespective of any sovereign power, entitled to the same rights as all Englishmen, and that the foundation of liberty was participation in government, and thus without representation in Parliament, they were not in fact free. They further resolved that the keeping of a standing army without the consent of the people was illegal. Finally, they acknowledged the King and argued their right to petition him.[36]

The Congress's most important accomplishment was a "Continental Association", a nonimportation, nonconsumption agreement for all British goods, to take effect December 1. Following this, the Congress spent the next week drafting addresses to the people of Britain and of Canada, followed by a petition to the King explaining their protestations and begging for his sovereign interposition. Their petition reaffirmed their "connexion with Great-Britain," and pleaded that the King's indignation "will rather fall on those designing and dangerous men, who [are] daringly interposing themselves between your royal person and your faithful subjects". Finally, Congress made a plan to reconvene in Philadelphia on May 10 of the following year, "unless the redress of grievances, which we have desired, be obtained before that time." Their work done, on October 26, they dissolved the First Continental Congress.[37]

The Congress might have gone to greater lengths, had the delegates not been suspicious of their Massachusetts colleagues. There was a widespread and not entirely unfounded fear that those New Englanders were trying to precipitate open hostilities toward the British. Most delegates from other colonies wanted only to pursue an aggressive political campaign to undo the late acts and reach an accommodation with Britain. It was not yet the time for war, most reasoned, and they would act only in the defensive if necessary.[38]

That night, the delegates gathered for drinks at the City (New) Tavern.[39] They felt accomplished at their great public service, cheerful that their benevolent King would deliver them from the evil Ministry and hopeful that they would not need to reconvene the following year. Moreover, they were proud to be Englishmen. In an era when French King Louis XVI believed his power derived directly from God, the delegates reveled in the spirit of the unwritten, liberty-loving English Constitution. It was the wickedness of the Prime Minister and his parliamentary puppets that the Americans despised. Once their benevolent King intervened, harmony would be restored. (They didn't know the heart of their King, whose benevolent reputation had been saved only because Parliament had taken up the cause of punishing Boston in his stead.) Beer flowed copiously amid the cheers of the confident crowd. Of the many toasts given, "May the sword of the parent never be stained with the blood of her children."[40]

On that same day, the new Provincial Congress of Massachusetts, now in Cambridge, resolved "in consequence of the present unhappy disputes between Great Britain and the Colonies," to form a Committee of Safety as well as a Committee of Supply. The Committee of Safety was authorized, with at least five members present and without the Provincial Congress's approval, to make immediate decisions for the safety and defense of the colony, including ordering up the provincial militia. The Committee of Safety would serve as the de facto executive arm for the extralegal government, in lieu of Governor Gage, whose authority the colonists no longer recognized. The following day, October 27, they resolved that the committee would consist of nine members, three from Boston and six from the countryside. (Two days later, it was expanded to eleven members and ordered to convene in Cambridge.) To represent Boston, the Provincial Congress elected John Hancock (as chairman), Dr. Joseph Warren, and Dr. Benjamin Church Jr. The Provincial Congress also nominated three militiamen as major generals to lead their militia force. Then, on October 28, the Congress appointed Capt. William Heath (soon to be colonel), Warren, and Church "to take care of and lodge in some safe place in the country the warlike stores now in the commissary general's office and that the matter be conducted with the greatest secrecy."[41]

ALLEGED PORTRAIT OF DR. BENJAMIN CHURCH JR. (DATE AND ARTIST UNKNOWN.) THERE IS DOUBT WHETHER THIS IS REALLY DR. CHURCH, BUT IT IS THE ONLY PORTRAIT PURPORTED TO DEPICT HIM. IF AUTHENTIC, IT IS LIKELY A LATER RENDERING OF SOME ORIGINAL PORTRAIT THAT HAS SINCE BEEN DESTROYED. COURTESY OF THE NATIONAL LIBRARY OF MEDICINE.

But such great secrecy would not be kept.

Even his colleagues thought forty-year-old Dr. Church was strange and creepy, though they nevertheless esteemed him as a great Son of Liberty. He had even given a grand oration on the third anniversary of the Boston Massacre, speaking like a true demagogue against the tyranny of the mother country. So the Provincial Congress implicitly trusted him, but this was their fatal flaw. Though it remains unknown exactly how or when Church made the arrangement, soon he would secretly serve the Crown as General Gage's best-placed spy. From his high perch in the upper echelons of the Provincial Congress and the Committee of Safety, he would learn everything of the resistance movement and immediately report it to Gage, either himself or through an intermediary, such as Maj. Stephen Kemble, the head of British intelligence.[42]

Church perhaps smiled smugly as he carefully committed various notes of intelligence to memory, reserved for later transcription when he had enough privacy to conduct his espionage. It is easy to imagine him locked away in his study, skittish that his wife might come in, the drapes pulled closed to guard his covert work; he hunched over a treasonous parchment, carefully penning his secrets by candlelight, sometimes in code, sometimes perhaps in bad French—anything to disguise his authorship. America had its first traitor. And his words would help start a war.

———— • ————

The British troop buildup continued throughout the autumn. On his own initiative, the commander in Newfoundland sent two companies of the 65th Regiment. And at the end of October, General Haldimand at last arrived from New York, bringing with him the 47th plus three companies of the 18th, as well as the bulk of the military stores and probably some artillerymen. Days later, the 10th and 52nd Regiments arrived from Quebec. Gage now estimated his effective force was near three thousand including officers, excluding the Castle William garrison, and by mid-November, he had most of them moved into winter barracks.[43] Gage also reorganized his army into three brigades, one under Lord Percy, another under Robert Pigot, and the third under Lt.

Col. Valentine Jones, who, like the others, was promoted to acting brigadier general in the American service only.[44]

Gage realized this paltry force was no match against an enraged countryside. He wrote to the home government, "This Province and the neighboring ones, particularly Conecticut, are preparing for War; if you will resist and not yield, that Resistance should be effectual at the Beginning. If you think ten Thousand Men sufficient, send Twenty, if one Million is thought enough, give two; you will save both Blood and Treasure in the End. A large Force will terrify, and engage many to join you, a middling one will encourage Resistance, and gain no Friends. The Crisis is indeed an alarming one, & Britain had never more Need of Wisdom, Firmness, and Union than at this Juncture. I sincerely wish a happy End to these Broils."[45] Gage later added, "affairs are at a Crisis, and if you give way it is for ever."[46]

On December 5, the HMS *Asia* arrived from England with some 460 marines plus officers under the command of Maj. John Pitcairn (pronounced *Pit-kAIRn*). The marines were under orders from the Ministry to be placed under direct command of the Army rather than the Royal Navy. This sparked a minor turf battle between Gage and Vice Adm. Samuel Graves, which delayed the landing of the marines until late December.[47]

The marines, along with Gage's nine full regiments and five detached companies, brought his force to near 3,300 rank and file (including artillery but excluding the garrison at the Castle), plus some 330 officers, 3,630 total. On December 12, HMS *Boyne* sailed into harbor with more marines, and the next day, HMS *Glasgow* arrived. But the British leadership was greatly concerned about the large man-of-war HMS *Somerset*, long overdue and feared lost.[48]

As the cool and colorful New England fall turned to a biting, snowy winter, a sort of unstable peace settled on the town. The colonists throughout the Eastern Seaboard planned for the worst, seizing weapons where they could and ordering others from Europe. By December, some forty small cannon were expected by private transport to Rhode Island. Graves put his fleet on alert, but war supplies continued to trickle in.[49] In Boston, the presence of so many troops—intermingled with an oppressed people whose spirit was kept alive by weekly church sermons speaking against tyranny and slavery—led to minor run-ins in the streets and taverns. But nothing of consequence happened…until mid-December.

——•——

The American Dr. Church was now firmly in the service of the British, but Gage was not the only one who had spies. Somehow, intelligence had fallen into the hands of Boston's Whig leaders that the British were planning to send two regiments to seize the mostly undefended Fort William and Mary at Portsmouth, New Hampshire, and take possession of its ample supply of gunpowder and munitions. So on December 13, the Committee of Safety dispatched Paul Revere on another of his less famous rides. The winter weather was horrid and frigid, the muddy ruts along the road now treacherous, frozen furrows.

Other travelers postponed their trips, opting to lodge at the various taverns that dotted the New England roads, keeping warm with the help of both a bright fire and a heady drink. But Revere plowed ahead, driving his poor steed across northern Massachusetts, reaching Portsmouth the same night. Once in town, Revere rode straight for the home of local Whig leader Samuel Cutts, who marveled as he read the intelligence. Cutts then immediately called for the local Committee of Correspondence who, once convened, quickly initiated an alarm of messengers.[50]

By the next afternoon, December 14, some two hundred militia had mustered in Portsmouth, with hundreds more on their way. At their head was the Militia Maj. John Sullivan, one of New Hampshire's delegates to the Continental Congress, only lately returned, later to become a general in the Continental Army. With beating drums and shrilling fifes, Sullivan marched his band of motley-dressed militia in disciplined pageantry toward the river's edge. There they embarked in two large, wooden gondolas and crossed the narrow stretch of the icy Piscataqua River to New Castle Island, where some one hundred fifty more militia joined them from another approach. Together, they marched across the fields and came before the weak defenses of Fort William and Mary, situated on the east side of the island and guarding the main entrance to

Portsmouth Harbor. Its garrison was just six invalid British, including their commander, Capt. John Cochran.[51]

Sullivan yelled to the few British defenders to surrender. They were, after all, outnumbered three hundred fifty to six. But Cochran staunchly refused, yelling it was "on their peril, not to enter."[52]

Sullivan yelled back: he absolutely would enter!

Cochran gave the order, and his five gallant soldiers opened fire, their three 4-pounder cannon belching white smoke with earsplitting thunder. The British managed to get off three harmless cannon shots while Sullivan's men swarmed the fort and scaled its walls, firing a few harmless musket shots in return as they poured inside. Within moments, the Yankees had disarmed the six invalids. No one was killed, and the six British were taken prisoner. Cochran offered his sword in surrender, but Sullivan refused it and returned it to him.[53]

With the fort easily secured, the New Hampshire men gave three huzzahs. But when Sullivan's men began to lower the British flag from its mast, Cochran grew angry. He rushed toward them, brandishing his sword, though the militia quickly beat him back, wounding him slightly and easily restraining him. As a British soldier rushed to the aid of his captain, one overeager militiaman pulled out a pistol, aimed it at the soldier's face…and fired! Nothing happened—the pistol misfired.

Instead of firing again, the militiaman turned his pistol and used the butt end of his gun to beat the British soldier down, wounding him. Had that gun fired, the war might have started then and there. As it was, there were only two wounds suffered by either side. These were the first actual shots fired in what would be the American Revolution, though none of the participants knew it yet.[54]

Before departing, the militia took about one hundred barrels of gunpowder and placed them on the gondolas for transport into the countryside. The following day, hundreds more militia came in from neighboring towns, but Whig leaders held them back. Instead, radicals formed a committee to meet with Gov. John Wentworth to see if he knew of impending troop arrivals, or whether he had requested any. The governor honestly replied he knew of no such designs. That night, the militia began extracting the cache of sixty muskets and got off sixteen of the lighter cannon there, a fraction of the fort's considerable ordnance.

When still more militia arrived the next morning, now upward of a thousand, Gov. John Wentworth was unable to disperse them. Fearing they were determined to dismantle the fortress entirely, he wrote a hasty note back to Gage in Boston.[55]

Late that same day, December 16, Admiral Graves responded by sending the HMS *Scarborough* and the armed schooner *Canceaux*, which weighed anchor immediately. A horrible winter storm and unfavorable winds prevented their fast arrival, but *Canceaux* managed to get to the fort before midnight the next day, while *Scarborough* was delayed for two days. Upon sighting the arrival of the first ship, Sullivan and his militiamen dissolved into the countryside, taking with them sundry small military stores, but leaving behind some fifty-three heavier ordnance, including "a fine train of 42-pounders", too large to quickly transport, having too little time to spike or destroy them.[56]

This was the fourth alarm in months—the Portsmouth Alarm.[57] Yet the intelligence that sparked this raid was false, as General Gage had no plans to seize Fort William and Mary.

HMS *Scarborough* and *Canceaux*, with their twenty-eight combined guns, would remain off Portsmouth for weeks, but the damage was done, and despite Governor Wentworth's best efforts, there was little hope of bringing the guilty to justice.[58] For Gage, the affair was a political blow, proving that American resistance was indeed a poison that had infested the entire continent. The Portsmouth episode would not be the last.

At almost the same time as the Portsmouth Alarm, on December 16, colonists raided unguarded Fort George in Newport, Rhode Island, stealing all of its cannon shot and all but four cannon. Eight days later, colonists stole the cannon belonging to a battery at New London, Connecticut. In Marblehead and Salem, illicit importation of arms and ammunitions grew rampant. At the head of this importation effort was Col. Jeremiah Lee, a prominent member of the Committee of Supply and among the wealthiest men in the province. He leveraged his personal fortune and trade connections to ultimately supply the province with cannon and powder from Spain and Holland. Though in 1774 these efforts had just begun, by the end of the year, Marblehead's smuggling efforts had grown successful enough to prompt Admiral Graves to station there the HMS *Lively*. In another incident, Whigs in Maryland meddled with a shipment of flour, intended for Boston for use by the British. In the end, the shipment was but delayed, yet it marked one of the first acts directly against the British Army. Fortunately for Gage, he had provisions enough for six months.[59]

With all of this bad news, one small relief came to the British on December 19. Though it had been feared lost, the massive 68-gun HMS *Somerset* finally arrived, and while leaky and in need of repairs, she was safe, much to the chagrin of radicals. Accompanying her was the sloop-of-war *Swan*, and together they brought the remaining marines intended for Gage's army.[60]

The arrival of these additional ships and troops finalized Boston's 1774 transition that began in the summertime and stretched to year's end, whereby this quaint New England town was turned from a harbor of tranquility, with just one troop regiment on nearby Castle Island, to a military state, filled with red-coated soldiers, scarlet-coated officers, and blue-coated artillerymen—about 3,600 total—surrounded by six ships of the line, HMS *Somerset, Preston, Boyne, Asia, Glasgow,* and *Mercury,* with 290 total guns, plus various smaller armed sloops and transports.[61] The town of Boston had only about sixteen thousand inhabitants, and now, with the British arrival, about one in five was a professional soldier.[62] Gage needed only to declare martial law to make the picture complete, though he was very wary to do so unless pressed to extremities.

Little did he know that events would soon unfold that would indeed press him to those extremities. Dr. Church was already collecting his treasonous intelligence by which to alert Gage of a weapons cache in nearby Concord, Massachusetts. If Gage dared to seize it, Paul Revere would be ready to ride out and alarm the countryside. For now, an unstable peace remained, but it was slowly waning as each side dug in and prepared for the possibility of open hostilities.

The year was drawing to a close, but there was still one last event of particular consequence, though it did not seem so at the time. In the spring of 1774, while Gage was still on his way from England, Gen. Frederick Haldimand had sent his engineer, Capt. John Montresor, to the remote frontier post of Fort Ticonderoga on Lake Champlain in upstate New York. The ruined fort had been battered apart by British artillery when they had taken it from the French in the last war, more than a decade earlier. Ever since, it was controlled by a small British garrison, consisting mostly of old and invalid soldiers. However, the British success in the last war had left that part of the frontier relatively free from threats, so the fort's importance diminished, and in turn, the funding for its maintenance and repair declined.

It was almost as a minor diversion then that Capt. John Montresor was sent in early 1774 to estimate what repairs were necessary at Fort Ticonderoga. The British engineer reported, "it's ruinous situation is such, that it would require more to repair it than the constructing of a new Fort", adding that most of it was "composed of decayed Wood", its walls and "Outworks are leaning to the Horizon and in many places there are very capital Breaches", and while some barracks were reparable, "those in the Redoubt of Wood are irreparable". His conclusion: "Upon the whole after summing up the Expenses I found them at least equal to the constructing of a New Work". Montresor recommended that new fort be built at Crown Point just up Lake Champlain, which he also surveyed. There stood the heap of ruin that was an old fort, destroyed after an accidental fire in 1773, with just a few structures remaining, garrisoned by a mere dozen or so troops, plus women and children. To rebuild at Crown Point presented two advantages: there would be no need to tear down an old fort, and there was plenty of cut stone in the ruins by which to construct a new work.[63]

In May 1774, General Haldimand, after receiving Montresor's suggestions, wrote to both Lord Dartmouth and General Gage, proposing, under the pretense of rebuilding Fort Crown Point, that they might also augment the garrisons there without raising suspicion. But neither Dartmouth nor Gage saw merit in the idea and the idea seemed abandoned.[64]

It was not until near the end of the year, December 24, with tensions slowly mounting, that Gage received orders from Lord Dartmouth to put both Crown Point and Fort Ticonderoga in a state of defense.[65] But with winter now in full swing, Gage knew such repairs were near impossible until the spring thaw, so he gave no more thought to the order until then.

Ironically, had Gage made immediate plans to strengthen the fort, the events of the coming year would have played out very differently. For, seemingly unimportant and forgotten Fort Ticonderoga would soon become very important.

So ended the last year of peace in British America.

PART 2

Taking Up Arms
(January to Mid-May 1775)

CHAPTER 5

A DISQUIETING THAW

As the first day of 1775 dawned on Boston, calm persevered in the beleaguered town. Still, despite Lieutenant General Gage's small army numbering 3,600, the troops presented many headaches.[1] Perhaps it was too much free time. Perhaps it was too cold a winter. In either case, Gage's greatest problem soon became the erosion of discipline among his men, and cheap rum was the leading cause.

In fact, the first day of the year proved calm precisely because of the rum, since many of the troops were drunk and passed out after a little too much partying the night before. Lt. John Barker noted in his diary, "Nothing remarkable but the drunkenness among the Soldiers, which is now got to a very great pitch, owing to the cheapness of the liquor".[2] Maj. John Pitcairn of the Marines later wrote to his superior, Lord Sandwich, First Lord of the Admiralty, "I have lived almost night and day amongst the men in their barracks for these five or six weeks past, to keep them from that pernicious rum… Depend on it, my Lord, it will destroy more of us than the Yankies will."[3] One drunken on-duty sentry collapsed along the shoreline, and when found the next day, "the tide had washed over him; but as his forehead was much bruised, it is supposed that a fall among the stones on the Beach had seconded the Yanky rum in his death."[4]

With so many soldiers in so small a town, surrounded by an oppressed people, with both sides growing irritated with the other, and each side dabbling in the drink, scuffles were bound to happen.

On the night of January 20, a number of drunken regular officers stumbled out into the snowy streets looking for trouble. They had not far to stagger before they found it in the form of the town house watch, a lawfully appointed group of citizen sentries acting on behalf of the Boston selectmen. A brawl quickly erupted, and the New Boston Watch rushed up, ready to join in, just as an armed guard of regular troops hurried to the scene, its sober officers demonstrating exemplary discipline by taking charge and promptly defusing the affray.[5] Gage was furious and chastised all his officers to be strict with the men, declaring that as the civilian watches "are appointed by Law, the Law will protect them."[6]

This was but one of the many quarrels between the redcoats and the colonists.[7] As tensions increased, the Americans became ever more brazen, regularly taunting the troops as they walked by, jeering at them with slurs such as "lobsters" and "bloody backs". First Lt. Frederick Mackenzie of the 23rd Royal Welch Fusiliers blamed the Americans in his diary: "The towns people encourage this excessive drinking, as when the Soldiers are in a State of intoxication they are frequently induced to desert."[8]

Gage was moderately successful in his crackdown on drinking, but desertion was a growing problem. In one instance at the end of 1774, a soldier from the 10th Regiment attempted to desert across the frozen Charles River at night. However, other sentries saw his attempt by the moonlight and threw him in jail. On Christmas Eve, the soldier received his sentence. Lieutenant Barker put it simply, "A Soldier of the 10th shot for desertion; the only thing done in remembrance of Christ-Mass day."[9] Merry Christmas, indeed! Despite public executions for those that were caught, desertions continued unabated.[10]

Meanwhile, whenever the townspeople were not disrupting army discipline, they were hoarding weapons in preparation for the expected hostilities. It did not take long before a few intrepid Yankees figured these two efforts could complement one another, and so they began inducing soldiers to sell their arms. For any soldier so easily enticed, the penalty was stiff: "A Soldier of the 4th Regiment who was tried a few days ago for disposing of Arms to the towns people, has been found guilty and sentenced to receive 500 lashes."[11]

In one instance, a townsman lacking discretion attempted to

purchase the gun of a soldier in the 47th Regiment. The lowly soldier and his comrades immediately seized the townsman and, borrowing an idea from the Yankees themselves, proceeded to strip him naked, pour burning-hot tar on him, and feather him, "and setting him upon a Truck, in that manner paraded him, in the afternoon, through most parts of the town, to The Neck." Officers of the 47th were aware of what their men were doing but did not intervene. Gage, however, was livid when he learned of it, and though he censured the offending officers, the damage was done, and the people took great offense at it.[12]

Those townspeople who did have weapons began smuggling them out through Boston Neck to stockpile for later use, should war come. When word of this practice filtered to the haughty British officers, they began to gloat, "the more arms the Americans had the greater number our troops would have the honour to take."[13] Hoping to stymie the flow of arms, however, the prudent Gage ordered the Neck Guard to conduct random searches as people crossed in and out of town.

During one such search, the guard discovered a countryman smuggling 13,500 musket cartridges packed with lead shot and powder, plus another four boxes of loose musket balls, about 19,000 balls total, all concealed in a wagon full of candle boxes. The British guard immediately attempted to seize the wagon, but "The countryman struggled hard before he would deliver 'em, and received two or three bad wounds."

Afterward, the man then had the gall to march to Province House and petition to get his ammunition back. When asked what this massive supply was for, he innocently claimed it was for his own private use. The headquarters officers must have laughed before they denied the man's petition, to which the countryman smugly retorted that this was just the last wagon of a large quantity of stores that had been smuggled out for months. In fact, in recent weeks, Bostonian merchant John Andrews had himself seen twenty loads of war supplies covered with dung secretly driven out of the town. However, now that the British were aware of the smuggling, they began enforcing strict searches at the Neck, and soon the outflow petered out.[14]

To combat eroding discipline and prevent the soldiers from growing lethargic in the cramped confines of Boston, in late December Gage had begun sending his troops on exercise marches into the countryside.

The first of these greatly alarmed the people, but slowly they grew accustomed to seeing the soldiers. Even so, the countryside towns appointed scouts to watch the troop movements anytime they left Boston.[15] Gage also instilled discipline with regular shooting practice. For this, the troops would line themselves along the wharves and fire at floating buoys anchored in the harbor. According to Lieutenant Mackenzie, "Premiums are sometimes given for the best Shots, by which means some of our men have become excellent marksmen."[16]

Many soldiers felt it was not their discipline, but that of the townspeople, with which Gage should have been concerned. Instead, Gage's leniency, motivated by his sincere wishes to restore harmony, left many of his men grumbling. For instance, one of Gage's general orders required the town guard "to seize all military Men found engaged in any disturbance, whether Aggressors or not; and to secure them, 'till the matter is enquired into." As Lieutenant Barker wrote in his diary, "[Enquired into] By Whom? By [Yankee] Villains that wou'd not censure one of their own Vagrants, even if He attempted the life of a Soldier; whereas if a Soldier errs in the least, who is more ready to accuse than Tommy?"[17] "Tommy" was just one of several epithets that began circulating among the despondent troops to describe their unaggressive Commander in Chief Thomas Gage. By March, merchant John Andrews had heard many an officer refer to Gage as the "Old Woman".[18]

Though this apparent partiality toward the Bostonians may have earned Gage some resentment from his soldiers, it was precisely what was necessary to keep the unstable peace. Despite the efforts of zealous Americans radicals to paint him as a dictator, he was in fact a fairminded and rather benevolent governor, careful that all his actions remain within the law, careful also not to set a spark to the tinderbox that was his station in Boston.

The mild general cautiously walked the line between his virtues as a Whig in politics, favoring the general notion of pursuit of liberty, and his responsibilities as governor of a troubled town, duty bound to enforce the recent parliamentary acts. For instance, in writing privately to a British officer in New York, he declared his hope for a settlement to the present crisis, "agreeable to the Sentiments and wishes of every Moderate Man, and the real friends of both Countrys."[19] Even Dr.

Joseph Warren thought Gage "a man of honest, upright principles, and one desirous of accommodating the difference between Great Britain and her colonies in a just and honorable way. He did not appear to be desirous of continuing the quarrel in order to make himself necessary, which is too often the case with persons employed in public affairs".[20]

Ironically, Gage very much agreed with Boston radicals that liberty in Massachusetts was threatened by the mounting turmoil, only he saw the source of that threat being the radicals themselves, not Parliament. Indeed, the Loyalists, who constituted perhaps 15 to 20 percent of the white male population, looked to Gage and the Army as peacekeepers, not oppressors. Yet their Whig neighbors, no more than 45 percent of the white male population, were the most vocal and best organized, and so were able to press forward their revolutionary agenda and trump the political will of the Loyalists.[21] (The remainder was largely neutral.)

Far too many histories have dismissed Loyalism simply because fate placed its adherents on the losing side of the great debate, and ignoring them has been an enduring result of the blind patriotic fervor that began during the Revolution. Modern retrospection has given way to a more enlightened and accurate consideration of the Loyalists, and no longer can they be so easily labeled the enemy, for their true character is colored with many shades of gray.

Loyalists comprised all walks of life—they were not merely the haughty rich of the highest social class, fearful of losing their hierarchy in the new order, though plenty fit that description. Rather, some of the wealthiest Massachusetts men—such as Jeremiah Lee of Marblehead and John Hancock of Boston—threw in their lot with the Whigs, not the Loyalists. In truth, Loyalists loved America just as much as the Whigs and, by strict interpretation of the word, were just as much patriots. Governor Hutchinson, for instance, though banished to England, would yearn for the rest of his years for his fair New England birthplace.

While British rule had certainly become oppressive, particularly with the passage of the late acts of Parliament, and taxation without representation was indisputably unjust, Loyalists were not supporters of tyranny, and few generally supported the late oppressive acts. Instead, they desired only a return to the peace that had happily existed before the Stamp Act of 1765. After all, despite the despotism of the English government, the American colonies had risen to prominence in large part *because* of their relationship with the mother country.

Imagine then the circumstance of the peaceful Loyalist, asleep at his home, only to be awoken by an angry mob of radicals as they stormed and invaded his house, determined to force his signature on an agreement to neither import nor consume British goods, which the Loyalist would sign only for fear of tar and feathering or even death. Although the mobs sometimes grew out of control, unleashing their violence *without* orders from the Sons of Liberty, even when yoked, their service was always one of duress.

With such lawlessness—and it was incontrovertibly such—it is no wonder that Loyalists were happy to see the arrival of the British Army as a police force. If these were the methods of the Sons of *Liberty*, where then was this *liberty* to be found? Loyalists were barred from their basic liberty of enjoying a differing political view; barred too from free trade in opposition of the nonimportation, nonconsumption agreement that they had no say in initiating; barred even from representation in the Provincial Congress or Continental Congress. Instead, they lived constantly in fear of their Whiggish neighbors, fearful for their businesses and their resulting ability to care for their families, fearful for the safety of their homes and property, fearful even for their very lives.

This was the ugly but very real side to the American Revolution: the side that shows the Whig patriot not as a virtuous, perfect hero, but as a genuine human—riddled with zealotry, imperfection, and even hypocrisy. In honest retrospection, the American rebel seemed at times to take on the role of villain, turning the British into the victim. The great debate, and the war that followed, was never black and white, and the truth is found somewhere in the middle.

From Gage's perspective as a liberty-loving Whig himself, the crucial aspect of his onerous job was to maintain liberty for the silent majority, the Loyalists and the neutrals. Thus, when he received a petition in January from the coastal towns of Marshfield and Scituate (just south of Boston), in which the townspeople pledged their loyalty to the Crown and requested peacekeeping troops to protect them from their Whiggish neighboring towns, Gage was happy to comply. On January 23, he detached Capt. Nesbit Balfour of the 4th (King's Own) Regiment along with one hundred ten men plus three officers, which set sail down the coast aboard the armed schooner *Diana* and the HMS *Somerset*'s sloop *Britannia*. They arrived in Marshfield two days later, and the people joyously received them. Consequently, the Whig minority there would leave the British unmolested, and preserving the peace proved easy service for the small British detachment.[22]

Though Gage's perception of defending liberty differed from that of the radicals, his policies demonstrated time and again that he was no despot. The local press bristled with attacks on government, yet His Excellency made no attempt at censorship or suppression. Whig leaders gave vehement speeches against tyranny, yet the governor let them be. Militia companies throughout the countryside practiced their art of drilling, often once a week, but the commander in chief did not intervene. Gage even met with civil leaders, whether representatives of illegal committees or not, treating each with respect—hardly the actions of a tyrant. In truth, the people of Massachusetts could not have asked for a more lenient military governor. Had another general been given the station, the American Revolution might have begun much sooner. As it was, Gage allowed even the most extreme of Whigs near total freedom.[23]

Yet, despite his leniency, Gage had a duty to maintain the peace. Recent intelligence informed him a storm was brewing in Salem. So, to avoid a crisis, he decided he would have to send a preemptive strike against the newfound threat.

━━━◆━━━

Since December, General Gage had been aware of a weapons buildup in Salem, so to stymie the flow of illegal weapons imports, he had Admiral Graves send HMS *Lively* to Salem Roads offshore there.[24] But in late February, when Gage received intelligence that at least eight brass field cannon were smuggled into Salem from Holland, he was greatly concerned.[25]

In fact, Salem radicals had acquired between twelve and seventeen cannon, perhaps all 12-pounders. Moreover, they were not new cannon from overseas, but old ships' guns of questionable reliability.

The Americans were therefore modifying these naval guns for use in the field. The wood for their new carriages had been cut, but since they were still awaiting their iron fittings, bracings, and probably carriage axles, the carriages were not yet assembled. For now, the cannon and carriage parts were hidden at Robert Foster's blacksmith shop north of Salem center.[26]

To disarm this new threat, Gage decided to send troops to Salem to confiscate the cannon. However, given the recent alarms, Gage was cautious to maintain secrecy, such that even his own aides-de-camp knew nothing of his plan until it was put into execution. Gage gave his orders to the haughty (though well-liked) Lt. Col. Alexander Leslie, commander of the 64th—the perfect unit to mount a secret operation as they barracked on secluded Castle Island. Furthermore, two of the 64th's companies had been stationed at Salem just months earlier, where they had served on guard duty while Gage had resided there as governor, and so were familiar with the town.[27]

Despite Gage's attempts at secrecy, radical leaders suspected an expedition when they observed a British transport repositioning to Castle Island.[28] So Paul Revere, the de facto head of the loosely organized intelligence for the Sons of Liberty, sent three of his mechanics over on the afternoon of February 25, 1775, to see "what was acting" as he often put it. The mechanics (artisans, longshoremen, or other manual laborers) rowed across the harbor before creeping up the beach toward the Castle, only to be captured and thrown in jail. (There they remained until the coming Monday.) Meanwhile, Revere, wondering what had become of his men, must have met with Dr. Warren and Samuel Adams. But without intelligence, they could raise no alarm.[29]

That night, Lieutenant Colonel Leslie and 120 of his men quietly boarded the transport and set sail just after midnight.[30] At nine o'clock the next morning, Sunday, February 26, the transport dropped anchor at the secluded beach of Homan's Cove on Marblehead Neck. There Leslie waited, ordering his soldiers to remain hidden below deck. As far as any casual observer from shore was concerned, it was just another transport filled with stores, coming in for customs inspection.[31]

It was a cold, wintry day, though the snow had now melted. As the sun climbed high, the British patiently waited until the townspeople were sure to be at afternoon sermon. Then, between two and three o'clock, Leslie gave the order. Suddenly the transport came alive as troops swarmed onto the spar deck while the seamen hoisted the long-boats into position to allow the soldiers to disembark. Once ashore, the troops mustered, probably in line formation. And each carried tools: lanterns, hatchets, pickaxes, spades, handspikes, or coils of rope.

Leslie then faced the men west, making them a column three or four abreast, before ordering them forward, so beginning their four-mile march to Salem center.[32] Finally, Leslie ordered his musicians to flaunt their arrival with a spirited rendition of "Yankee Doodle". But this absurd display did not cost him the element of surprise, for he had already lost it.[33]

Watching the British disembark were Militia Col. Jeremiah Lee and Maj. John Pedrick, who immediately split up, Lee to Marblehead to assemble his militia, Pedrick to his home to grab a horse and warn Salem.[34] For Pedrick, the only road to Salem obliged him to come upon the marching redcoats. He kept cool and sauntered his horse patiently alongside the extended column. Upon reaching Lieutenant Colonel Leslie, with whom he was well acquainted, Pedrick saluted the officer, who kindly returned the gesture. Leslie then looked ahead and, seeing that his 64th and Pedrick were converging toward a small wooden bridge, ordered his men "to file to the right and left and give Major Pedrick the pass." Pedrick expressed his gratitude and sauntered ahead, but once around the bend, he put spurs to his horse and galloped at breakneck speed toward Salem center.[35]

Pedrick and other observers first converged on the home of Militia Col. David Mason before they stormed into the neighboring Salem North Church. Marching down the aisle, Pedrick bellowed, "The Regulars are coming after the guns and are now near Malloon's Mills!" (Just south of the town.)[36] There was a moment of hesitation, then yells, "To arms! To arms!" A dozen men dashed for the door, headed for the blacksmith forge to spirit the cannon into the countryside and out of reach of the troops. As they did, the sexton scurried to the belfry and began vigorously pealing the alarm.[37] Pedrick rushed to Rev. Thomas Barnard and told him to delay the troops until he received word that the cannon were secured. Pedrick then quickly departed and galloped off for Foster's blacksmith forge, situated on the north side of the "North River" (really just a harbor inlet), the two sides linked only by a drawbridge.[38]

Just moments later, Leslie arrived in town at the head of his red-coats. There he halted his column as a few local Loyalists, joyous at his arrival, came to offer assistance. One was John Sargent, brother of William Brown, a mandamus councilor. Perhaps Sargent was the source of Gage's intelligence—at least the local inhabitants thought so. The locals watched as he whispered into the lieutenant colonel's ear. Suddenly, Leslie turned and ordered his men forward at quick time, straight for the North Bridge and the forge beyond. When Sargent saw the disapproving looks from the angered crowd, he grew alarmed, and some say immediately fled for his life, never to return to the town.[39]

With Leslie's column marching quickly toward the drawbridge, a crowd of unarmed townsmen raced ahead to the opposite side and quickly raised the north leaf, stranding Leslie and his column on the south side of the inlet. A few townsmen on the north side climbed the open leaf to straddle its edge, allowing their feet to dangle, while unarmed Militia Capt. John Felt stood on the south side, waiting casually for Leslie to halt his men.[40]

Leslie paused for a moment. Infuriated, he lost his composure, maybe swore, and ordered his first company to fan into line formation. With his troops at the ready, Leslie looked bitterly at Felt, telling him he would be obliged to order his men to fire if the bridge was not let down at once.[41]

"Fire!" Felt exclaimed. "You had better be damn'd than fire! You can have no right to fire without further orders." Felt knew Leslie was bluffing.[42]

The stubborn Leslie huffed before he shouted that this was the King's highway and he would not be prevented from passing over the bridge. Among the growing crowd of spectators, old James Barr yelled back, "It is *not* the King's highway, it is a road built by the owners of the lots on the other side, and no king, country or town has anything to do with it."[43]

"By God! I will not be defeated!" Leslie seethed.

"You must acknowledge, you have already been baffled," Felt calmly replied.

Confounded, Leslie called together his officers for a consultation.[44]

About this time, a militia company from the nearby northern district of Danvers arrived, the first in response to the alarm. They probably crossed the inlet well west of the British and entered the town from that direction. There they crept unnoticed until they got behind a nearby distillery where they remained, ready to spring out in an instant.[45]

As the number of spectators grew, a few zealous men began to jeer. One supposedly taunted, "Soldiers, red jackets, lobster coats, cowards, damnation to your government!" But the cooler heads among the crowd immediately and sharply rebuked the zealous, shouting that nothing should be done to irritate the troops. These cooler heads knew theirs was the position of power. If a war was to begin here, it must begin with the British regulars.[46]

While Leslie's officers continued to huddle, one nonchalantly split off and walked away toward his company. About twenty of his company then casually fixed their bayonets and suddenly darted toward the inlet's shore. The locals also saw their objective: two large gondolas sat beached along the wide mudflat that resulted from the low tide. The townsmen rushed for the gondolas too, beating the soldiers there. Some colonists had hatchets (despite American claims that they were unarmed) and tried desperately to break holes into the wooden boats, even as the British charged in, bayonets first.

Brave, foolish Joseph Whicher tore open his shirt, daring the soldiers to bayonet him. One young soldier, cold and infuriated, pricked Whicher in the chest to give him what he asked, drawing blood. The officers immediately rebuked the impetuous soldier and ordered the rest to fall back. It was futile to fight over the gondolas now, as they were sufficiently scuttled and useless.[47]

At sight of this moment teetering on the edge of violence, Rev. Thomas Barnard approached Leslie and pleaded, "I desire you would not fire on those innocent people."

Leslie asked, "Who are you, sir?"

The minister introduced himself, adding, "My mission is peace."[48]

Leslie assured the minister, "I will go over this bridge before I return to Boston, if I stay here till next autumn."[49]

Felt told Leslie he could stay there as long as he pleased; nobody cared about that.[50]

Leslie sighed as he looked westward toward the sun. The day was growing late: now about half past four, with maybe an hour until sunset. The British commander asked Felt if he had any authority to order the drawbridge lowered, to which Felt replied he perhaps had influence. Leslie told Felt his orders were to cross the bridge and he would do it by all hazards.

Just at that moment, Militia Major Pedrick returned to the inlet's opposite bank. Hearing the exchange, Pedrick yelled a proposal to allow Leslie to cross on "point of honor", and go only a set number of paces beyond, thereby fulfilling his mission, at which time he should then turn and go in peace. Felt considered this, then offered to allow it, provided Leslie not march beyond thirty rods (about five hundred feet) past the bridge, just enough to examine the forge but no farther. Leslie asked for a moment to consult his officers, then promptly returned and accepted the proposal.[51]

As the bridge's north leaf creaked along its hemp cables to its lowered position, Pedrick rode his horse a short distance away, thinking it discourteous to witness Leslie's annoyance after their earlier amicable exchange on the road. Sure enough, as the 64th marched across and explored Foster's blacksmith shop and forge, they found nothing. Leslie then kept to their agreement, re-formed, and marched his men back across the bridge to depart.

When they reached the south edge of town, they passed near the home of a nurse named Sarah Tarrant. She brazenly slid open her window and yelled, "Go home and tell your master he has sent you on a fool's errand, and broken the peace of our Sabbath! What do you think, we were born in the woods, to be frightened by owls?" One of the soldiers, acting without orders, raised his musket in her direction. He was surely instantly admonished, but Sarah defiantly retorted, "Fire if you have the courage! But I doubt it."[52]

As the sullen British marched back to their transport, their musicians played the appropriate tune, "The World's Turned Upside Down", though with empty bravado.[53] Meanwhile, though Salem sent messengers to stand them down, some neighboring towns' militia companies still converged onto the town, fortunately too late to turn the peaceful resolution sour.[54]

So ended the Salem Alarm. The affair might have escalated tensions had it not resolved so peaceably, but it was another political blow for Gage's authority. When Gage learned of the fiasco and that the cannon were old ships' guns that he considered useless, he admitted in a letter to Lord Dartmouth that the mission had been a mistake.[55] The mistake was greater than he realized, for the affair proved to the spirited Americans that they had it in their power to stand down the regulars, even at bayonet point. As another historian later wrote, each side tested the other's resolve, but in these tests, the British continuously failed.[56]

———◆———

Though the Salem Alarm ended without open conflict, given the ever-growing tensions, Dr. Joseph Warren began to think of the safety of his four children at his mother's home in nearby Roxbury, a town situated just beyond Boston Neck's fortifications. Warren also worried for the safety of his new love, Mercy Scollay, presently living with her parents in Boston proper. To ease his mind and free himself to serve the Whig cause to whatever end, he needed to move his loved ones to safety.

Accordingly, by the end of February, Warren arranged to rent a farmhouse from Dr. Elijah Dix in Worcester, some forty miles west of Boston. Mercy agreed ostensibly to accept the role of caretaker of Warren's children there, while he would remain in Boston to carry on his political responsibilities. But secretly, Mercy seems to have accepted Warren's proposal to marry, perhaps with the blessing of her Whiggish father John Scollay, a Boston selectman.[57]

One of Warren's many political responsibilities was the upcoming fifth anniversary of the Boston Massacre, for which he was chosen for the second time as the keynote speaker. Since the actual anniversary in 1775 fell on a Sunday (the Sabbath), the solemn town meeting was scheduled for the following day. Gage was well aware of this town meeting, technically illegal under the late Regulating Act, but he decided not to interfere. The Boston selectmen would argue, as they had successfully done before, the late Act prohibited them from *calling* a town meeting, but as this was merely the *reconvening* of the previous year's *adjourned* meeting, the Regulating Act did not specifically forbid it. Nevertheless, Gage worried about a potential riot and ordered several regiments to be armed and ready in case of alarm.[58]

At about ten o'clock on the morning of March 6, a crowd that may have numbered thousands began to gather at Old South Meeting House to hear Warren speak. Given all that had transpired since the last anniversary speech, this year's was sure to be particularly heated. Dozens of idle regular officers also muscled their way in and took front-row seats, determined to defend the reputation of their service against any insults. The redcoats noticed that many Yankees seemed to expect trouble, "as almost every man had a short stick, or bludgeon, in his hand", and the soldiers suspected many others had concealed weapons.[59]

It was about eleven in the morning when Dr. Warren entered Old South, theatrically wearing a Roman toga atop his typical dress clothes. The room grew hushed as he solemnly walked up to a pulpit decorated with black cloth. With him were Samuel and John Adams, John Hancock, the spy Dr. Benjamin Church, and maybe Paul Revere, as well as the Boston selectmen, including John Scollay. They all took their seats in a reserved pew box near the pulpit.[60]

Warren began, "I mourn over my bleeding country: with them I weep at her distress, and with them deeply resent the many injuries she has received from the hands of cruel and unreasonable men." He then gave a long discourse recounting from the arrival of the first colonists until the present, emphasizing how freedom and liberty had morphed into despotism, pausing to give special focus to the fifth of March, 1770, the Boston Massacre.

As his speech reached the present crisis, the "malice of the Boston Port Bill", and the "mutilation of our charter", he sarcastically commended the presence of the troops as inspiration by which the youth might learn the art of war, assuring his audience, "You will maintain your rights or perish in the generous struggle." To allay the thoughts of some, he proclaimed that independence was not their aim; rather, the province sought with Britain to, "like the oak and the ivy, grow and increase in strength together." But so long as the Acts of Coercion persisted, Massachusetts would follow the recommendations of the Continental

Congress until "the unnatural contest between a parent honoured, and a child beloved" might be peacefully resolved.

As he drew to the end of his oration, he spoke with foreboding. "But if these pacific measures are ineffectual, and it appears that the only way to safety, is through fields of blood, I know you will not turn your faces from your foes, but will, undauntedly, press forward, until tyranny is trodden under foot, and you have fixed your adored goddess Liberty…on the American throne."[61]

Throughout the oration, the British officers gave only a few hisses here and there as the audience enthusiastically applauded. Overall, one officer wrote, it "contained nothing so violent as was expected." Samuel Adams then stepped from his front-pew box and came up to the pulpit, thanking Warren for his oration and reminding the audience they were now *adjourning* the meeting until next year, March the fifth (to of course once again bypass the Regulating Act).

To this, several of the officers hissed. Others yelled, "Oh! fie! Oh! fie!" The New England commoners knew not that high-society derisive interjection and so thought they heard "Oh! fire! Oh! fire!" The meeting instantly erupted in utter pandemonium. Others echoed what they heard, yelling "Fire! Fire!" Women began to cry and so added to the confusion. By sheer dumb luck, at that moment the 43rd Regiment marched by outside, its fifes shrilling and drums beating, causing a few of the Whig leaders to fear they were about to be arrested. With the throng nearly trampling each other to escape the exits, a few of the leaders climbed out of the windows to escape capture. Within moments, everyone had abandoned Old South, with the exception of a few nonplussed British officers. When these British sauntered outside, the crowd soon ascertained the mistake and at length began to disperse in peace.[62]

Planned for later that evening was a solemn procession to mark the anniversary, but Governor Gage, fearing that some riot might yet ensue, beseeched the selectmen to cancel it, and so they did. The night proved quiet and peaceful.[63] Even so, four days later, Gage still harbored fears of a riot. So he issued general orders that his guard was hereafter to march with bayonets affixed to their muskets.[64]

When Warren's oration was published a few days later, several officers took to a coffeehouse balcony, where one, "apparell'd in a black gown with a rusty gray wigg and fox tail hanging to it," delivered a farcical per-version of the oration to a small crowd of "gaping officers. It contain'd the most scurrilous abuse upon the characters of the principal pattriot here, wholly made up of the most vile, profane, blackguard language as ever was express'd." The officers intended to repeat their performance, but once Gage found out, he strictly forbade it. The event gave cause for merchant John Andrews to write, "The officers in general behave more like a parcell of children, of late, than men."[65]

The crisis that might have come from the anniversary of the Boston Massacre had fortunately been averted. In London, meanwhile, a differ-ent storm was brewing.

By autumn 1774, the British government had grown hardened in its position to pacify the American problem. The King and his Tory Party–controlled Parliament saw the Americans as unruly children and thought the Coercive Acts condign punishment, even though the acts were overburdensome and a clear overexertion of Parliament's authority. When the Americans justifiably resisted, the British Ministry wrongly assumed Americans were striving for independence, long before such thoughts had formed in even the most Whiggish colonial minds.[66] This false assumption drove the Ministry to extremes in dealing with the colonies. Rational thought could not prevail, though the minority Whig Party in Parliament would continuously strive for it.

In mid-November 1774, King George III wrote privately on the matter to his Prime Minister, Lord North, "I am not sorry that the line of conduct seems now chalked out...the New England Governments are in a state of rebellion, blows must decide whether they are to be subject to this country or independent."[67] These were the private thoughts of His Majesty on November 30, when he sat in the House of Lords before members of both houses and issued the customary Speech from the Throne that opened the next session of Parliament. In this address, the King did not go so far as to publicly declare Massachusetts in rebellion, but he did reveal his concerns for the growing turmoil there, hinting that if something more was not done soon, other colonies throughout the empire could see weakness in Parliament and likewise become unruly. "And you may depend upon my firm and steadfast resolution to withstand every attempt to weaken or impair the supreme authority of this legislature", the King reaffirmed.[68]

Despite the King's new resolve, Parliament did little before adjourning for the holiday season. As they were on recess, the petition of the First Continental Congress arrived in London, and Benjamin Franklin, along with two other American agents, laid it before Lord Dartmouth, who then laid it before the King. The King actually received it graciously, but decided to lay it before the anti-American Parliament when it reconvened and, in so doing, ensured that no reconciliation might be had from it.[69]

When Parliament reconvened in mid-January 1775, the Whigs immediately mounted a stiff opposition against the late Coercive Acts. In the upper house, Lord Chatham argued in favor of the unwritten English Constitution, reminding the house that "no subject of England shall be taxed but by his own consent."[70] By February 1, Chatham unveiled a sweeping new plan for reconciliation, but the House of Lords rejected it by a vote of almost two to one.[71]

Meanwhile, as the Continental Association's nonimportation agreement met with profound success in America, English merchants, suffering under great financial hardship, began their own campaign to repeal the Coercive Acts. To answer them, on February 10, Lord North introduced another Coercive Act. Called the Restraining Act, it stupidly heaped ruin on the financially depressed New England colonies by limiting all their trade to Britain, Ireland, or the imperial holdings in the West Indies, as well as barring them from fishing off the rich Newfoundland coast. Lord North justified this by saying, "as the Americans had refused to trade with this kingdom, it was but just that we should not suffer them to trade with any nation." When serious debate began days later, Edmund Burke gave valiant opposition, calling the bill "in effect, the Boston Port Bill, but upon infinitely a larger scale." He warned its "evil principles are prolific; this Boston Port Bill begot this New England Bill; this New England Bill will beget a Virginia Bill; again a Carolina Bill, and that will beget a Pennsylvania Bill; till one by one parliament will ruin all its colonies". Nevertheless, the Restraining Act passed with almost an 80 percent majority in both houses, receiving the royal assent on March 30. True to Burke's concerns, North almost immediately proposed a further act restraining trade for most of New Jersey, Pennsylvania, Maryland, Virginia, and South Carolina. This passed as a separate bill, also with strong majority, receiving the royal assent on April 13.[72]

On March 22, Burke gave before the Commons what is generally considered to be his greatest speech on America. Talking for perhaps two hours, Burke declared, "The proposition is peace." He vehemently argued against the Restraining Acts and appealed to the logic of his colleagues: "But when I consider that we have colonies for no purpose but to be serviceable to us, it seems to my poor understanding a little preposterous to make them unserviceable, in order to keep them obedient." Urging reconciliation, he pleaded, "We cannot…persuade them that they are not sprung from a nation in whose veins the blood of freedom circulates… An Englishman is the unfittest person on earth to argue another Englishman into slavery".

Burke then questioned what gains the late Coercive Acts had given the empire. Nothing but further disorder, he concluded. "Let us get an American revenue as we have got an American empire. English privileges have made it all that it is; English privileges will make it all it can be." Despite Burke's passionate imploration, his motion was voted down by more than three to one.[73] The next day an equally impassioned speech was given across the Atlantic by Patrick Henry before the Virginia Convention, which he ended most famously, "I know not what course others may take, but as for me, give me liberty, or give me death!"[74]

The parliamentary debates also turned to sending Gage more troops. In the Commons, Col. James Grant exclaimed of the Americans, "they would never dare to face an English army, as they [are] destitute of every one requisite necessary to constitute good soldiers".[75] The debate in the Lords was much the same. While Lord Camden argued the impracticality of conquering America, the incredulous Earl of Sandwich, First Lord of the Admiralty, called the colonists "raw, undisciplined, cowardly men." Sandwich cynically admitted the colonists were indeed brave, but hoped they would muster together with at least two hundred thousand, "the more the better, the easier would be the conquest… Believe me, my Lords, the very sound of a cannon would carry them off".[76] In the end, the Whigs offered little resistance and the debate was quickly settled, with both houses resolving to send an additional embarkation of troops to America, and to lead them, three major generals.

Though all hopes for an accommodation between Britain and America grew ever more improbable, it was not news of the Restraining Acts or additional troops that was the greatest threat to peace. Instead, it was a secret dispatch already on its way across the Atlantic, sent by Lord Dartmouth, and in it, new orders for General Gage that would have dire consequences.

The American intelligence network was a grassroots, ad hoc entity, consisting of astute volunteers who reported their discoveries to well-connected Whigs, who in turn filtered the information up to top leaders like Samuel Adams and Joseph Warren. The most active node in this network was Paul Revere and his association of mechanics. His thirty or so mechanics met regularly in the Long Room on the second floor of the Green Dragon Tavern in Boston's North End. Revere later related, "We were so carefull that our meetings should be kept Secret; that every time we met, every person swore upon the Bible, that they would not discover any of our transactions, But to Messrs. Hancock, [Samuel] Adams, Doctors Warren, Church, & one or two more." Yet by November 1774, Revere realized their secrecy had been compromised. So they moved their meetings to a more secure location, but still their secrets were leaked to the British. It became a "common opinion, that there was a Traytor" in their midst, but no one yet had reason to suspect that traitor was the eminent Dr. Benjamin Church.[77]

In contrast to the ad hoc colonial network, Gage's intelligence network, under the direction of the able Maj. Stephen Kemble, was organized from the top down. As spring approached New England, the British network began functioning like a well-oiled machine. Gage soon received information from a variety of sources, including unsolicited intelligence from Loyalists and other Friends of Government;

reconnaissance from his officers and men, discovered on their exercise marches into the countryside; and of course his network of paid spies, men such as Dr. Benjamin Church, the nominal Whig who had risen to the highest ranks of the radicals.

The exercise marches were of particular value to the army, not merely as a means of reconnoitering and familiarizing the men with the countryside, but also for the ancillary benefit of desensitizing the country folk to the troops' movements. In this way, when Gage was ready, he could march his troops out on a military objective without raising alarm. Marine Commander Maj. John Pitcairn wrote of these marches: "The people swear at us sometimes… They sometimes do not know what to think of us; for we march into the town where they are all assembled, but we have no orders to do what I wish to do…to seize them all and send them to England." Pitcairn later added, "I am satisfied that one active campaign, a smart action, and burning two or three of their towns, will set everything to rights."[78]

Among the intelligence Gage received, he learned of a growing weapons buildup in Worcester. Fearing he might in time be forced to send troops there to disarm the town, he thought it prudent to gather intelligence on the forty miles of countryside between there and Boston. In late February, Gage selected for this scouting mission two intrepid junior officers, Capt. John Brown of the 52nd and Ens. Henry De Berniere of the 10th. Their instructions: collect whatever intelligence they could and draw sketches of the roads, roadblocks, and places of potential ambush.[79]

Accordingly, on "Thursday", probably February 23, the two officers and Brown's personal servant, John, dressed "like countrymen, in brown clothes and reddish handkerchiefs round our necks", made their way across the icy streets of Boston and descended down to the Charles riverbank. As they awaited the Charlestown ferry, John quietly talked to a British sentry, asking him to pay no attention to his two companions, though the sentry knew Captain Brown well, for they served in the same regiment. The three then boarded the ferry unrecognized, crossed to Charlestown, and walked all the way to Cambridge and just beyond Watertown before fatigue and the cold convinced them to find lodging.

Outside Watertown, they found a Mr. Brewer's Tavern, which they entered and where they sat for dinner. As a black woman took their order, she eyed them suspiciously and questioned where they had come from. The scouts gave a cover story that they were traveling surveyors from abroad, but the waitress remained unconvinced. Nevertheless, she brought them their meals and left them alone. After they had eaten, the incognito officers observed to her, "It is a very fine country".

The black woman sized them up a bit more, then sternly replied, "So it is, and we've got brave fellows to defend it, and if you go up any higher you will find it so."

Brown and De Berniere were taken aback, fearing their identities revealed. They decided it prudent to lodge somewhere else that night. While they gathered their belongings to depart, John went up to the bar to pay the black woman. As he did, he cautiously struck up a conversation. The woman revealed that she had seen Captain Brown in Boston some years ago and so knew him well. John denied this, suggesting she was surely confusing Brown with someone else. But the waitress was certain. She said that she knew their errand was to survey the country, that she had seen a sketch when they shuffled through their papers after having sat down. She advised them to go no farther, but if they did, they were sure to meet trouble. John paid for the dinner and then quickly— though nonchalantly—departed.

Outside, the servant told the two officers what had been said. They huddled together for a moment to discuss. Were they to go back to Boston, they reasoned, their comrades would ridicule them. Instead, they resolved to drive onward.

While they walked another six miles, they encountered an overly inquisitive countryman together with a suspected army deserter, both eager to join them on their hike to Worcester. However, Gage's incognito scouts evaded them by deciding to take a drink at the Golden Ball Tavern in Weston. Inside they found the innkeeper, Isaac Jones, to be most hospitable and not at all inquisitive. They asked for some coffee, to which Jones revealed his true nature, suggesting they could have coffee or even tea, in defiance of the American nonconsumption agreement. The officers were pleasantly surprised to find they were in the company of a Loyalist, and so revealed themselves and resolved to stay there the night. Jones assured them they would be safe, for he had shown his neighbors he was not to be bullied, and they had pretty much learned to leave him alone. Jones also gave them a list of Tory safe houses along their route.

The next two days proved uneventful, and after a night at the Tory safe house of Buckminster's Tavern in Framingham, they arrived in Worcester on Saturday evening. They stayed at a Worcester tavern owned by a relative of Isaac Jones of Weston who proved to be an equally accommodating Loyalist. The next day being a Sunday, the officers remained idle, for local laws restricted traveling on the day of worship. But that night, two gentlemen came inquiring about Brown and De Berniere. The innkeeper sent the gentlemen away but immediately warned his three British patrons of their danger. So Brown and De Berniere decided to leave at daybreak.

The next morning, the British scouts were on their return trip toward Framingham when a horseman galloped up, attentively examined them, then quickly rode off, saying nothing. The horseman split off in the direction of Marlborough, opposite to where they were headed. Though the scouts would not learn of it for two days, a mob had gathered in Marlborough and was anxiously awaiting their arrival. Instead, the scouts returned to Buckminster's Tavern in Framingham. However, this time their stay was not as comfortable.

Just outside the tavern, the local company of militia performed their regular drill. Though the three British scouts slipped inside the tavern unnoticed, the militia "performed their feats before the windows of the room we were in; we did not feel very easy at seeing such a number so near us." Afterward, the militia broke formation and gathered in that very tavern to have a few drinks. With drunk and armed militia in the next room, the British scouts grew especially concerned. Fortunately, the militia eventually dispersed back to their homes without incident, and the British scouts got a restful sleep before heading back toward Weston the next morning.

The next day, a Tuesday, they returned to the friendly Golden Ball Tavern of Isaac Jones in Weston. The following day, De Berniere decided he wanted to return westward, this time along the northern route through Marlborough. Innkeeper Jones tried to warn them that Marlborough was especially violent, but the scouts resolved to press on with their plan. However, to be safe, they opted to send John back to

Boston with all of their notes and sketches thus far. Almost as an ill omen, a major blizzard delayed their departure for hours. Once it had sufficiently abated early that afternoon, they split up and began their respective marches through the bitter cold, De Berniere and Brown heading west, their servant heading east.

They slowly plowed through snow that was at times blinding, their ankles sinking deep into the powder with each step. De Berniere and Brown managed their way through Sudbury before following the road toward Marlborough. On their way, a horseman stopped them to ask many questions, such as who they were, where they came from, where they lived. Finally, the horseman asked pointedly, "Are you with the Army?" The officers told him they were not, but the horseman seemed unconvinced. He asked a few other questions, then galloped off toward Marlborough.

When Brown and De Berniere finally arrived in Marlborough sometime around nine o'clock that night, the townspeople began to pour out of their houses, despite the frigid snowstorm. In particular, a baker inquired where they were going, to which Brown admitted it was to the home of a Mr. Barnes, secretly another trusted friend of the government. Brown and De Berniere arrived unmolested at the Barnes home, where they immediately expressed their fears for both his and their safety.

Barnes told them they could be safe nowhere else, but confessed the town had had a mob waiting for them just two nights before. Barnes then asked whom they had talked to upon entering the town. When the two British scouts told of their encounter with the baker, Barnes was troubled at that news, for the baker was harboring a recent army deserter who could potentially identify the two incognito men. Captain Brown inquired who the deserter was, to which Barnes replied a man surnamed Swain. Brown knew Swain well—the deserter had served as a musician in his same regiment. There was no doubt now: their ruse was up, their true identities known.

Just then, a knock came at the door. Barnes went to see who it was, only to find it was a town doctor, hoping to come for dinner. Barnes was incredulous. They knew each other's politics, and this doctor had not come to Barnes's door in more than two years. So Barnes politely told the doctor he was indisposed with company.

The doctor just huffed as he looked suspiciously around the house.

Seeing Barnes's very young daughter behind the door, the doctor asked her, "Who does your father have with him?"

The daughter innocently answered, "I asked my Pappa, but he told me that it was not my business."

The doctor continued to suspiciously size up Barnes, then abruptly departed. Barnes immediately returned to his guests and warned them of the exchange. The scouts decided they would rest two or three hours and be on the road by midnight. Barnes agreed and ordered his servants to prepare a meal before their journey.

As they were about to sit to eat, one of the servants informed Barnes that a mob was gathering and preparing to storm his house. The officers had not been there but twenty minutes, but now they grabbed some food to go and quickly slipped out the back of the house and into the shadows, braving a snowstorm that grew so fierce that De Berniere thought it "blew as much as ever I [have] see[n] it in my life". Barnes went a short way with them, directing them toward a bypass road that could get them around the mob and safely back toward Boston. Thanking him, the scouts scrambled as fast as they could through the drifts and gusting snow, reaching a dense wood that offered some shelter from both wind and discovery.

While the scout officers stopped for a moment to catch their breath and eat their hastily gathered meal of bread, which they washed down with snow, Barnes returned to his house in time to receive the local Committee of Correspondence and its mob as they swarmed his porch. They demanded entry, bullied their way in, then illegally searched and ransacked the estate, looking for the culprits or at least evidence against them. Barnes assured the mob these were not British scouts but family from his wife's side. The disbelieving mob demanded to know where they had gone, to which Barnes replied Lancaster, a town in the opposite direction from their true course. At this, some of the mob dashed outside and took to horses, riding off on a wild-goose chase.

As De Berniere and Brown made their way through the woods and then along the bypass, a man rushed out of a nearby house, startling them. He yelled, "What do you think will become of you now?" This greatly worried the British officers and they immediately picked up their pace. They quickly plodded past Marlborough and soon reached neighboring Sudbury, still fearful of their pursuers. As they came along the Sudbury road, they saw three or four horsemen waiting, though these equestrians seemed to be unconcerned with their approach. De Berniere and Brown maintained a nonchalant countenance and continued forward, passing by unmolested.

At last, sometime after midnight, the scouts safely returned to the relative security of Isaac Jones's tavern in Weston. The day had been a complete waste: they had marched from Weston to Marlborough and back, through a blinding snowstorm no less, and risked their lives by braving both frigid temperatures and a violent populace. Innkeeper Jones was relieved to see them, and the two officers spent that evening in the deep sort of sleep that only a day of hard fatigue can engender.

The next day, March 1, the two exhausted officers crossed Watertown Bridge and trudged back toward Boston Neck. As they entered the town of Boston, it so happened that General Gage and General Haldimand were inspecting the Neck's fortifications. De Berniere and Brown may not have fooled the country folk, but they approached their superior officers unnoticed, and it was not until they identified themselves that Gage recognized them.[80]

Gage probably gave his fatigued scouts some time to clean up and rest before he debriefed them on their expedition. He must have been content with their intelligence, because he would use them a few weeks later for another mission. Yet Gage was alarmed that the countryside was undeceived by and openly violent toward his two disguised scouts. An expedition to Worcester, he concluded, was too dangerous.

Besides, Worcester was forty miles west. Gage had begun to receive more pressing intelligence regarding a town much closer.

CHAPTER 6

MANY PREPARATIONS

Ever since the (Second) Massachusetts Provincial Congress had reconvened in Cambridge on February 1, selecting Hancock once more as its president, Gage had begun to receive a steady stream of letters of intelligence from one or more sources. The most important letter came on March 9, written in especially bad French. Its author was either half-illiterate or otherwise not fluent in that foreign language and had only chosen it in hopes of masking his identity. Gage sometimes exchanged letters in French with his Swiss deputy Haldimand, and so had little difficulty reading it. He was astounded at its contents.

This godsend explicitly listed the quantity and types of weapons stored in the nearby town of Concord, and more importantly, it told precisely where they were hidden. A few of the statistics, such as a claim of seven tons of powder in one place, seem to have been exaggerated. Yet the hiding places reported, as we now know them, were very accurate. The intelligence reported war stores at the farm of Col. James Barrett, recently recalled to militia service, with more near the entrance to the village, in a white stucco house owned by a man named Whitney. The letter also said that a hundred barrels of flour, enough to feed a militia army, were conspicuously kept at Ebenezer Hubbard's gristmill.

If the author of this damning letter had merely chosen French to hide his identity, he succeeded, for to this day, his identity remains unknown. Might it have been the spy, Dr. Benjamin Church? He certainly had access to the information in the letter, but history may never know.[1]

Whoever the author, Gage's attention was now drawn toward Concord. He summoned Captain Brown and Ensign De Berniere for another scouting mission. Accordingly, on March 20, they departed together with Brown's servant, John. Perhaps they perfected their shoddy disguises, and this time they left prepared, being very well armed. Leaving town via Boston Neck through Roxbury and Brookline, they crossed the Charles River somewhere near Watertown, then made their way through Weston to the Concord Road, which they followed northward, directly toward their objective. Along the way, they noted the many places from which the rebels could mount an ambuscade, fraught as the terrain was with forest-covered hills on their right and lowland to their left, "woody in most places, and very close and commanded by hills frequently."

Upon entering Concord, the three scouts were quite surprised to find the sleepy town heavily defended. They learned the town had fourteen pieces of cannon (ten iron and four brass) and two cohorns (four-and-a-half-inch mortars), though they were mounted so poorly that they could not be elevated. The "iron cannon they kept in a house…their brass they had concealed in some place behind the town, in a wood. They had also a store of flour, fish, salt and rice; and a magazine of powder and cartridges. They fired their morning gun, and mounted a guard of ten men at night." This was no rural village—this was a veritable military post.[2]

The three scouts were to stay that night with Mr. Bliss, a known Loyalist, to whom a woman directed them (for which she was soon chased out of town).[3] There they dined, but midway through dinner, a messenger informed Bliss he had until morning to leave town—or suffer death. De Berniere and Brown revealed their weapons and offered to take him. Bliss heartily agreed and offered to show them a better route along the Lexington Road.

The four set off soon after, passing through Lexington, Menotomy (pronounced *Men-AH-tuh-mee*, now modern Arlington), and Cambridge, before finally arriving at Charlestown, where they took the ferry into Boston. All along the way, the scouts took notes and sketches and observed this path to be much safer for the Army, with much of it open and fewer places to conceal an ambuscade. It was this route that De Berniere and Brown proposed to Gage during their debriefing.[4]

Gage was pleased with the intelligence his scouts had brought. It helped to confirm the reliability of the intelligence written in bad French, as well as the veracity of various other letters that poured in, some of which are now known to be from Dr. Church. Some gave additional information on military supplies and their hiding places, such as one reporting stocks at Worcester, but many gave political insights into the resolves of the Provincial Congress, resolves sometimes so secret they were never committed to the congressional journals.[5]

One such secret resolve, which was straightaway reported to Gage by an informant, perhaps Dr. Church, spoke of the consternation among the people when, on March 30, Lord Percy marched with his 1st Brigade some six miles into the countryside. On that day, "Expresses were sent to every town near: at Watertown… they got 2 pieces of Cannon to the Bridge and loaded 'em but nobody wou'd stay to fire them; at Cambridge they were so alarmed that they pulled up the Bridge."[6] In response to this, the Provincial Congress resolved, "should any body of Troops, with Artillery and baggage, march out of Boston, the Country should Instantly be alarmed, and called together to Oppose their March to the last extremity."[7]

Since the Provincial Congress was an extralegal body of radicals with no official ties to the governor, these letters gave Gage much insight into the group's inner workings. For instance, Gage now understood that if he were to march his troops for a military objective, he had best ensure they pack light, without baggage or artillery, so as not to raise the alarm. When Gage received further intelligence suggesting the Congress was irresolute toward escalating the present crisis, he realized he had time to await orders from the home government and the arrival of more troops.[8]

With this new understanding of the obstacles he faced, Gage sent a letter to Lord Barrington, Secretary at War. "If you yield, I conceive that you have not a spark of Authority remaining over this Country. If you determine on the contrary to Support your Measures, it should be done with as little delay as possible, and as Powerfully as you are able, for it[']s easier to crush Evils in their Infancy than when grown to

Maturity." While Gage did not welcome the possibility of open hostilities, he wanted significantly more manpower if it came to that.[9]

Meanwhile, on April 2, two ships arrived in Marblehead, carrying with them unofficial rumors that a ship was en route to Boston with firm instructions for Gage to take decisive action and arrest the radical leaders. Within days, many Whig leaders and a sizable number of the general populace began hastily packing their belongings and fleeing to the countryside. As John Andrews observed, "we are all in confusion at present, the streets and Neck lin'd with waggons carrying off the effects of the inhabitants, who are either afraid, mad, crazy or infatuated...that they shall be liable to every evil that can be enumerated, if they tarry in town." The customs commissioners moved to slow the exodus by requiring searches of every cask leaving the town, creating a bottleneck that helped to quell the frenzy but did not stop the tide.[10]

Among those who fled were John Hancock and Samuel Adams. Hancock took with him his fiancée, Dorothy "Dolly" Quincy, and his elderly adopted aunt, Lydia Henchman Hancock, departing April 7. Samuel Adams left his family in Boston and joined Hancock three days later. They all took up temporary refuge in the crowded but safe residence of their trusted friend Rev. Jonas Clarke, kin to John Hancock, whose house just north of Lexington Green remains to this day. Meanwhile, in contrast to these and many Whig leaders, John Adams and his family had sometime earlier moved to the safety of his country farm in Braintree.[11]

Gage was unsure what had begun the chaos. Writing to Lord Dartmouth, he said, "I can't learn whether...[the ships] brought [also] Letters to any of the Faction here, but the News threw them into a Consternation".[12] But given the weapons buildup in Concord, as well as this mass hysteria, Gage decided the best way to avoid open conflict was to eliminate the Americans' ability to take up arms. Though he would wait for the expected positive orders from the home government before acting, he nevertheless began devising his plan for a preemptive raid.

———◆———

As Gage began planning for an Expedition to Concord, he applied the lessons of the several recent countryside alarms and, in particular, the need for secrecy to avoid such alarms. His Excellency had already elected to send his force along the northerly route that Captain Brown and Ensign De Berniere had suggested, through Cambridge and Lexington. But to save time and retain the element of surprise, instead of crossing the river at Charlestown Ferry, he decided to send his force across the Back Bay directly to the Cambridge marshes, cutting some four and a half miles off their march.[13]

Such a plan, however, required the assistance of the Royal Navy and the ships' longboats. Ever since the marines arrived in December, there had been an ongoing power struggle between Admiral Graves and General Gage, with about fifty of the four hundred sixty marines the government had promised to Gage still aboard the naval ships. Gage had basically given up on these remaining marines, but it continued to be a point of contention between the two commanders.[14] So with this in mind, on April 5, Gage reluctantly requested that Graves have his boats repaired and ready for an amphibious landing. To Gage's surprise, Graves did not argue; he simply agreed to the request.[15]

In fact, the admiral already had his seamen repairing the warships, particularly the massive 68-gun *Somerset*, which was in such disrepair when she had crossed the Atlantic that her crew had to work two hand pumps nonstop to keep her afloat, though they were able to reduce it to just one upon mooring in Boston Harbor. Though *Somerset* and the slightly larger 68-gun *Boyne* were the largest warships permanently on station in the harbor, their state of disrepair forced Graves to keep the smaller 50-gun *Preston* as his flagship.[16]

So when Gage's request for the longboats was received, Admiral Graves ordered them hauled on deck and the carpenters diverted to work on those repairs. Given the recent work throughout the harbor, Graves must have figured the Yankees would pay no heed to the loud hammering and sawing on those longboats, which the carpenters did in openness before the town. But the suspicious colonists thought the new focus solely on longboats odd, and Gage must have cursed when he saw this wanton lack of discretion.[17]

Paul Revere conferred on this development with Dr. Joseph Warren, now the de facto Whig leader, being the only one left in Boston. Warren feared the redcoats would march to raid the militia war stores in Concord that very Sunday, completely ignoring the Sabbath, just as they had done in Salem. Revere agreed, so Warren wrote a hasty letter explaining their fears. On Saturday, April 8, Revere mounted his horse and galloped for Concord as courier. Jonathan Hosmer was among those in Concord privy to the letter. "We daily expect a Tumult," Hosmer wrote to a friend; "a post…informs them [the town] that the regulars are coming up to Concord the next day, and if they come I believe there will be bloody work."[18]

It was a false alarm—the British did not march that weekend. But the Provincial Committee of Safety would take no chances, so—perhaps at the behest of Dr. Warren or Samuel Adams—the militia in Concord began to spirit the large bulk of their war stores into the countryside.

Gage, of course, was well aware of all going on in Concord, courtesy of his steadfast network of spies. Even Revere's ride to Concord did not go unnoticed. The informant that wrote in execrable French began his latest intelligence, "Last Saturday the 7th [really the 8th] of April: P:—R:—[Paul Revere] toward evening arrived at Concord, carrying a letter that was said to be from Mr. W—n [Warren]."[19]

Because of Dr. Warren's newfound prominence, British officers suddenly took a profound interest in his dealings. Fortunately, residing with the doctor were several trustworthy physician apprentices, including Samuel Adams Jr., son of the Whig leader, and Dr. William Eustis, who, at just shy of twenty-two years, was Warren's most promising apprentice. One evening, Dr. Eustis noticed several officers intently watching the Warren home on Hanover Street and immediately alerted his mentor, prompting Warren to begin carrying a pistol on occasion.[20] With his safety a concern, Warren took some solace knowing his fiancée Mercy Scollay was now at his rented farmhouse in Worcester, while his four children in Roxbury would be there soon.[21]

Meanwhile, to further desensitize the countryside as Gage prepared for his raid on Concord, he began increasing the distance of his troops' exercise marches, especially as the weather grew mild and the snow began to melt. On April 10, two regiments marched all the way to Watertown. According to Lt. Frederick Mackenzie, "As Watertown is farther than the Regiments have usually gone, and they remained out longer, the Country was a good deal alarmed on the Occasion."[22] Though Gage aimed to desensitize the countryside, the troops' marches seemed only to have put the colonists more on edge.

As Gage prepared for an expedition to Concord, intelligence continued to pour in. One letter revealed that the Provincial Congress had debated, but ultimately rejected, a standing army of observation to watch for future troop marches, deciding such a plan would only provoke open hostilities. The same intelligence concluded, "Upon the whole a spirit of irresolution appears through all their transactions."[23] On April 11, further intelligence suggested that many Provincial delegates wanted a recess to consult with their constituents on the growing crisis. The author of this letter was surely Dr. Church, for the author further indicated he had sufficient influence to ensure the debated recess came to pass. The author also suggested, "A sudden blow struck now or…within a fortnight would oversett all their plans [of political resistance]."[24]

If Gage had any doubts after receiving this intelligence as to whether to launch his military expedition into the countryside, he would soon have the final encouragement he needed to give the go-ahead order.

In perfect timing for the gathering political storm around Boston, on April 14, HMS *Nautilus* arrived in the harbor carrying with her the "secret" instructions from Lord Dartmouth, the same "secret" instructions that Bostonians already knew were coming. *Nautilus* moored off Long Wharf, where Army Capt. Oliver De Lancey Jr., quartermaster of the 17th Light Dragoons, disembarked and made for Province House, his gleaming regimental helmet befittingly adorned with a skull and crossbones.[25]

General Gage must have been happy to see that the courier was a De Lancey, a cousin of his wife, and someone Gage knew well. However, true to his duty, Gage postponed all but the most basic of pleasantries and instead immediately looked through the packet of letters De Lancey delivered.

When Gage came across the secret letter from Lord Dartmouth, written back in late January, he found it extraordinarily explicit. "The King's Dignity, & the Honor and Safety of the Empire, require, that...Force should be repelled by Force... It appears that your Object has hitherto been to act upon the Defensive...such Precaution was not necessary...affairs there are now come to a Crisis in which the Government of this Country must act with firmness, and decision."[26]

To ensure Gage would take the resolute part, Dartmouth's letter gave details of a new embarkation of troops to Boston, including three full regiments of infantry and the horse-mounted cavalry unit that was Captain De Lancey's 17th Light Dragoons (he had come ahead of his men to secure horses), plus seven hundred additional marines. Dartmouth was unequivocal that Gage should use these extra men for decisive action: "It is hoped however that this large Reinforcement to your Army will enable you to take a more active & determined part".[27]

As to Gage's previous request for twenty thousand troops, Dartmouth's letter flatly rejected such a proposal. Dartmouth, who undoubtedly echoed the thoughts of the King, explained that such numbers were appropriate only for an "absolute Conquest of the People... you must be aware that such a Force cannot be collected without augmenting our Army in general to a War-Establishment... I am unwilling to believe that matters are as yet come to that Issue." Instead, Dartmouth suggested, "the first & essential step to be taken towards re-establishing Government, would be to arrest and imprison the principal actors & abettors in the Provincial Congress". He hoped it could "perhaps be accomplished without bloodshed; but however that may be I must again repeat that any efforts of the People, unprepared to encounter with a regular force, cannot be very formidable". Finally, Dartmouth assured the general, "It must be understood, however, after all I have said, that this is a matter which must be left to your own Discretion to be executed or not as you shall".[28]

The letter demonstrated the crucial problem of managing a crisis from three thousand miles away—an issue even modern governments struggle with: the politicians were deplorably out of touch with the situation on the ground. This was due in part to the months it took for news to travel across the Atlantic, but also because much of their news was secondhand from newspapers or reports. Only infrequently did British leaders have eyewitnesses to interrogate. And never in this period did any British minister actually travel to America.

So while Lord Dartmouth and even the King were unwilling "to believe that matters are as yet come to that", they were gravely mistaken. Indeed, Gage's request for twenty thousand troops was a hefty one. Surely, he knew there were but just over twelve thousand regular infantry in all of Britain.[29] Yet Gage knew—even if the Ministry could not—that he was in an impossible situation; without such troops, he had no hope of enforcing the Coercive Acts of Parliament. But bureaucracies then were as they are now, and the Ministry was not proactive but reactive, unwilling to commit the resources necessary to pursue the agenda they themselves had instituted, unwilling even to heed the warnings of the very general they had entrusted to command the crisis that was their doing. Their failure was America's gain, for their halfhearted support of the Coercive Acts gave the political and military advantage to the colonies.

Gage might have rolled his eyes when he read Dartmouth's line, "any efforts of the People...cannot be very formidable". The veteran general had grown to somewhat respect the Americans' uncanny ability to muster great numbers at the slightest alarm. He knew too that they could fight, just as they had in the last war. For this reason, Gage took serious note of a letter of intelligence written by an unknown informant that prophetically warned, "The most natural & most eligible mode of attack on the part of the people is that of detached parties of Bushmen who from their adroitness in the habitual use of the Firelock suppose themselves sure of their marks at a distance of 200 [yards]... should the Hostilities unhappily commence, the first opposition would be irregular impetuous & incessant from the numerous Bodys that would swarm to the place of Action, & all actuated by an enthusiasm wild and ungovernable." In other words, the fighting would be brutal, chaotic, irregular warfare.[30]

Regardless of any misgivings the general held, Dartmouth's "secret" instructions made one thing quite clear: the home government expected Gage to take the offensive. To help him do so, Admiral Graves received a letter in the same *Nautilus* packet firmly and almost chidingly ordering him to not only land the remaining fifty marines that Major Pitcairn and General Gage had been expecting, but also to land any additional marines he could spare.[31] And if Gage had any doubts as to the authenticity of the secret instructions Captain De Lancey provided (as they were a copy), the original arrived two days later aboard HMS *Falcon*.[32]

Gage's job was to execute measures, not choose them. And the timing of this "secret" dispatch was impeccable, given his opportunity to raid the Yankee weapons cache west of Boston. Thus, armed with positive instructions to take the offensive, Gage began his final preparations for an Expedition to Concord.

———◦———

Soon after Gage received Dartmouth's letter, Fortune again smiled on his expedition plans. His spies informed him that, whether or not Dr. Church induced the recess, on April 15, the Provincial Congress adjourned for three weeks, not to reconvene until May 10 at Concord. The heads of the rebellion would therefore be scattered away from the object of the expedition.[33]

On the same day, Gage wrote in his general orders, "The Grenadiers and Light Infantry in order to learn Grenadrs. Exercise and new evolutions are to be off all duties 'till further orders." The grenadiers and light infantry were the crème de la crème, the flower of the Army, and this apparent excuse to learn new maneuvers was met with disbelief from colonists and redcoats alike. As Lt. John Barker wrote his in his diary, "This I suppose is by way of a blind. I dare say they have something for them to do."[34]

At midnight of April 15, Admiral Graves again displayed overt indiscretion, ordering his fleet to launch all the recently repaired longboats and lash them to the sterns of the HMS *Somerset*, *Boyne*, and *Asia*. It was quite conspicuous that all three warships now seemed ready for some amphibious assault, doubly so considering that just days earlier the 68-gun *Somerset* had hauled up to a position between Boston and Charlestown, replacing the tiny 8-gun *Canceaux*. From such a position, *Somerset* could block the Charlestown ferry if necessary.[35]

In a town as small as Boston then was, the inhabitants were quick to notice any change in the troops' routine or the preparedness of the longboats. Paul Revere again consulted with Dr. Joseph Warren on these strange developments. The two concluded that perhaps this time the stars had aligned: the British would indeed march out.

The next day was April 16, and though it was Easter Sunday, Revere broke that especially important Sabbath, mounted his steed, and galloped out of town for Lexington to bring the news to John Hancock and Samuel Adams.

As the day stretched on, and once again no British expedition materialized, Revere began to think hard about a more robust and faster alarm network. He spent the rest of Easter with Hancock and Adams in Lexington, then with friends in Cambridge and Charlestown, laying the groundwork for an express system with multiple riders. In Charlestown, he met with Militia Col. William Conant and others to describe his plan.

They agreed to it, but someone astute among them asked how a rider-based alarm should work if Gage first shut up the peninsula of Boston, preventing any rider from galloping off to start the alarm. They quickly devised redundancy to their system: if "the British went out by Water, we would shew two Lanthorns in the North Church Steeple; & if by Land, one, as a Signal". Later, in his famous poem, Henry Wadsworth Longfellow would immortalize their plan quite simply: "One if by land, and two if by sea".[36]

Maybe one of those Charlestown men pointed out the obvious. While Old North's steeple was an ideal location to signal a lantern, for it was then the highest point in Boston, its outspoken Anglican minister was a self-admitted Loyalist. He had become so unpopular that his congregation had stopped his salary and the church was now closed. But Paul Revere assured them he had well-placed friends and would take care of the details.[37]

What Revere did not count on was Gage's cunning. Spies had kept Gage well informed of all of Revere's rides. So as part of the expedition plan, Gage devised a scheme to thwart Revere and his network of alarm riders.

Meanwhile, Gage received intelligence on April 15 describing the Yankee plans to scatter the Concord weapons cache into the countryside.[38] But on April 18, he received the timeliest intelligence of all, its author still unknown, perhaps the wily Dr. Church. It read in part: "The provisions at Concord were not removed last Saturday [April 15]. They are dispersed all over the Town in various places particularly at the North part over the Bridge". The letter gave explicit details on where the supplies were now scattered. Finally, the letter warned of the Provincial Congress's renewed proposal to raise an army of observation from the militia, but that Massachusetts was unwilling to attempt this alone and so had sent couriers to the other New England colonies for a united response.[39]

This was Gage's golden opportunity. If given time, the colonies might unite. On the other hand, if he acted now, perhaps he could prevent their unification and render the proposed provincial army useless for want of supplies. Gage knew what he must do.

And so, as the frigid cold of the New England winter gave way to the mild thaw of spring, General Gage made his fateful decision. He would finally send forth his Expedition to Concord.

CHAPTER 7

THE DIE IS CAST

By noon on April 18, 1775, Gage had in his office Lt. Col. Francis Smith of the 10th Regiment, a fifty-two-year-old dolt to whom Gage was about to entrust his entire expedition. Lieutenant Barker described Smith as "a very fat heavy Man", but as his conduct would show, he was also slow, dim, and without foresight or leadership.[1] His Excellency

PORTRAIT OF LT. COL. FRANCIS SMITH (1764) BY FRANCIS COTES (1726–70). UK NATIONAL ARMY MUSEUM, LONDON/BRIDGEMAN IMAGES.

PORTRAIT OF MAJ. JOHN PITCAIRN (C. 1770S, ARTIST UNKNOWN).
THE LEXINGTON HISTORICAL SOCIETY.

General Gage chose Smith not only because he was the most senior lieutenant colonel, but also because he was a by-the-book sort of officer, and Gage was especially concerned that this expedition be conducted within the law.[2]

To serve as Smith's deputy, Gage selected Maj. John Pitcairn, commander of the marines and the most senior-ranking major in Boston.[3] Due to his congenial and fair treatment of the locals, Americans mostly seemed to respect the fifty-three-year-old Pitcairn. The moderate American Whig Rev. Ezra Stiles, a careful collector of reports on the war and future president of Yale College, described Pitcairn as "a good Man in a bad Cause".[4] In truth, Pitcairn's private sentiments were strongly opposed to the American cause.

It was to these two men that Gage gave his written orders: "you will March with the Corps of Grenadiers and light Infantry, put under your Command, with the utmost expedition and Secrecy to Concord, where you will seize and destroy all the Artillery, Ammunition, Provisions,

Tents, Small Arms, and all Military Stores whatever. But you will take care that the Soldiers do not plunder the Inhabitants, or hurt private property." The orders further described the weapons and stores and how best to destroy them. Gage also gave Smith a map, based perhaps on a sketch from Brown and De Berniere's scouting mission to the town, which annotated exactly where the weapons were hid.[5]

Though Gage left the final preparations to the discretion of Lieutenant Colonel Smith, he required that Smith maintain strict secrecy from even his most senior officers. The officers therefore knew only that they were to march to the countryside, but they knew not where. The rank and file knew nothing of the march whatsoever.

For all of this discretion, that afternoon Bostonians took notice to "an uncommon number of officers" seen "walking up and down the Long Wharf" (where they could discuss the expedition away from prying American ears).[6] Locals immediately transmitted this news to Dr. Joseph Warren, who again began to worry that an expedition might soon be underway.

Just after sunset, soldiers at Boston Neck pulled the gate of the wooden bulwarks wide open, blocking the only land entrance in and out of the town. Out of the gate streamed about twenty mounted soldiers, half of them officers, with Maj. Edward Mitchell at their head. They wore long, dark blue, close-fitting overcoats, had cockades in their hats, were armed with pistols and swords, and kept their horses at a casual saunter. A suspicious Yankee followed, but they "damned him, and told him not to keep near them." Once the patrol passed Roxbury, they made their way northwestward and crossed the Great Bridge across the Charles and into Cambridge. From there they immediately fanned out in different directions.[7]

This was Gage's answer to Paul Revere's alarm system. If Revere or any alarm rider managed to escape Boston once the town was sealed shut, Gage's riders would apprehend them…or worse.

———◆———

Dr. Warren and Revere had been receiving bits of information throughout the day. Shortly after sunset, they also learned of the patrol riders departing via the Neck. Then, as the evening drew late, one townsman reported having seen a light infantryman in a retail shop with his accoutrements on, as if ready for a campaign.[8] Warren was apprehensive, but he had already sent Revere on two false alarms and was wary to do so again.

A long-standing legend claims Warren had acquired a well-placed confidant whom he called upon for intelligence in this darkest hour. Speculation has led to the belief that this spy was none other than the beautiful Mrs. Margaret Kemble Gage, the forty-one-year-old wife of the general. Indeed, Mrs. Gage was divided. She was American born and thus keenly aware of the stakes for her birth nation. But she was also strongly Loyalist, part of English high society, and happily married to the man the King had selected to exact his resolves. Moreover, she would give great comfort to the troops in the coming war and would remain married to her beloved husband until the end of their days. Despite a recurring myth to the contrary, Mrs. Gage was not Warren's informant, and in fact, there was no informant at all.[9]

PORTRAIT OF MARGARET KEMBLE GAGE (C. 1771) BY JOHN
SINGLETON COPLEY (1738–1815). TIMKEN MUSEUM OF ART,
PUTNAM FOUNDATION COLLECTION, SAN DIEGO.

Warren needed no secret spy to deduce the obvious. Every Bostonian Whig was his eyes and ears, and all that transpired was told to him.[10] British officers were in a frenzy. Sailors had come ashore at 2:00 p.m., probably to man the longboats later.[11] A mounted patrol was seen departing Boston (off, some feared, to arrest Hancock and Adams, though that was not the mission).[12] British scouts had reconnoitered Concord just weeks earlier, probably based on information provided by a spy that Warren knew was among the radical leaders (not yet knowing this was Dr. Church). And Concord indeed had something of military value that Gage might seek. Together these facts led to one conclusion: Warren had little doubt of an impending British expedition.

Yet he waited for one more sign.

Late that day, Admiral Graves issued orders to his nearby warships: "The Boats of the Squadron, by desire of the General…ordered to assemble along side the *Boyne* by 8 o'Clock in the Evening". Hours later, the townspeople watched as all the warships' boats repositioned to the *Boyne*, moored off Long Wharf.[13]

This was an unusual event. Why would every tender from every warship line up together, except in preparation for some military action? Warren saw this as a sign and now felt it prudent to act. At near eight o'clock, he summoned a messenger. This was William Dawes Jr., a grand Whig just turned thirty, who had lately proven himself by helping to steal two small cannon from a militia company commanded by a Tory.[14] Warren told Dawes what little information he knew and charged him with warning Samuel Adams and John Hancock in Lexington. But this was the extent of Dawes's mission. Without proof of troop movements, Dr. Warren remained wary about officially raising the alarm.[15]

It was now over an hour past sunset, the moonless night very dark, when the plump Dawes left straight from Warren's house. He rode atop his old, worn saddle horse, its saddlebags filled with meal and drooping from its sides. Dawes himself probably donned his old guise as a farmer or miller, placing a flapped hat upon his head. To the casual observer, he was a countryman on a journey, harmless as a fly.[16]

Dawes casually sauntered his nag over to the Neck, where he found the guards bored with inaction. As they saw him approach, the sergeant of the guard recognized the friendly face and perhaps thought

Portrait of William Dawes Jr. (Date and artist unknown.)
Courtesy of the Evanston History Center.

it unnecessary to search Dawes's saddlebags. The two exchanged a few pleasantries, and the sergeant wished him a safe journey. Moments after Dawes's nag plodded slowly past the Neck and into the dark countryside, an urgent messenger arrived and gave the guard explicit orders: seal off the Neck. No one was to enter or exit the town until further orders. Simultaneously, over at the Charlestown Ferry, seamen rounded up the ferryboats and tied them off alongside HMS *Somerset*.[17]

And so by nine o'clock that night, the town of Boston was entirely sealed off, with Boston Neck secured and the naval fleet deployed so that no one might leave the town.[18] If any dared try, they would likely be shot. Fortunately for the Yankees, Dawes was slowly on his way, carrying with him Dr. Warren's warning to Lexington.

———•———

As Dr. Warren was meeting with Dawes at about eight o'clock on that moonless night, Gage meanwhile had summoned his regimental commanders to Province House. Most of these were lieutenant colonels, since few full colonels actually served with their men. Instead, the rank of full colonel or higher was often a sinecure, a mere honor given to someone who had recruited and equipped enough men to constitute a regiment. More often than not, a regimental colonel simply collected pay from the safety of his home while his men campaigned under command of his regimental deputy, usually a lieutenant colonel.[19]

Once the regimental commanders had all gathered, His Excellency ordered that they send their respective grenadier and light infantry companies to the beach behind Boston Common near the Magazine Guard at exactly 10:00 p.m. They were to bring one day's provisions in their haversacks, but were to leave their knapsacks behind. Most importantly: they were to leave their barracks and proceed to the rendezvous in small parties.[20]

Each regiment of foot comprised ten active companies, eight being the traditional infantry (or battalion) companies. The other two were specialty units, the grenadiers and the light infantry, collectively called the flank companies because when the regiment paraded in line formation, they stood on the extreme right and left, respectively. These flank companies were composed of men handpicked for their physical attributes as well as their skill, and were always kept near full strength, even at the sacrifice of the eight ordinary line or battalion companies. As such, they were considered the crème de la crème of the British foot soldier.

In times past, the grenadiers had been specially designated to carry and throw the large and unwieldy grenades of the early eighteenth century. This function had largely been abandoned, but the tradition of picking the tallest and stoutest men for their special service remained. Steeped in tradition, their uniforms still included a match case on their cartouche box straps, though now ornamental and left empty.

The most obvious accoutrement, however, was their tall bearskin hats, worn to make these tall men seem even taller and more ferocious than they were already.

The light infantry were a recent evolution in the British service and comprised the most athletic men for service as skirmishers and flankers. Given their inherent mission to be nimble runners, their red coats were cut short, hanging to just below the belt line, while other companies' coats tended to fall just above the knee. The light infantry's hats were also distinct, but varied widely between regiments.[21]

Together, the light infantry and the grenadiers, the flank companies, were the best of the regiment's men. As such, they were often detached from their respective regiments and combined for special service. The Expedition to Concord was just such an instance.

If one of the regimental commanders at Province House asked General Gage where their flank companies were to march, Gage replied only that the mission must remain a secret. After leaving the meeting, these regimental officers passed their orders to their respective flank company commanders, typically captains, who began making final preparations for the march.

The rank and file were not apprised of the operation until just before time to muster. They were roused "by the sergeants putting their hands on them and whispering gently to them". The flank company men then dressed quietly, while their battalion company comrades continued to sleep. They were ordered to carry just thirty-six ready-made cartridge rounds of ball and shot.[22] Quietly they gathered their accoutrements, including their haversacks and cartridge boxes, but left their knapsacks behind. They were then "conducted by a back-way out of the barracks, without the knowledge of their comrades, and without the observation of the sentries. They walked through the street with the utmost silence." It was approaching ten o'clock, and only the sound of their boots softly hitting the cobblestone filled the air. In one instance, as a small party of troops noiselessly made their way toward Boston Common, a dog suddenly began to bark at them. Without hesitation, one soldier, his bayonet already affixed, thrust it into the dog. The barking ceased with a gentle whimper as the canine collapsed dead.[23]

As the dark sky slowly gave way to a late moonrise, the parties of troops proceeded to the Charles riverbed beneath the new powder magazine at Back Bay, "the most unfrequented part of the town", south of sparsely populated Barton's Point.[24] The two flank companies of the 23rd Royal Welch Fusiliers were the first to arrive.

At first, only a few other parties came staggering in. Everyone seemed dumbfounded, for not even Lt. Col. Francis Smith had yet arrived. Lieutenant Barker noted, "few but the Commandg. Officers knew what expedition we were going upon."[25] It was obvious what the plan was, however, for lying before them along the shoreline were perhaps ten diverse longboats, ranging from sixteen to thirty feet in length, manned by seamen. The intrepid officers of the 23rd decided to take the initiative, ordering their men to embark in the nearest two boats. As they began to climb in, other flank parties appeared through the darkness that shrouded the Common. Following the example of the 23rd, they too began to embark, just as Lt. Col. Francis Smith and Maj. John Pitcairn arrived on horseback.[26]

With the commanding officers now on the scene, they organized the hushed horde of redcoats into columns by company. The tide was just then flooding, the salt water beginning to flow up the Charles estuary from the harbor, bringing just enough water to the otherwise marshy Back Bay to float the tenders. With the boats bobbing gently in the shallow river's edge, the heads of the columns fanned out as the soldiers awkwardly climbed in from either side.[27]

In all, twenty-one companies were on orders to march: the grenadiers of the 18th; both flank companies (grenadiers and light infantry) of the 4th (King's Own) Regiment; the 5th, 10th, and 23rd Royal Welch Fusiliers; the 38th, 43rd, 47th, 52nd, and 59th; and the Marines, organized to mimic the army regiments. The total expeditionary force consisted of 700 men, officered by about sixty-six regulars, or about 766 total.[28] There was also a handful of volunteers, such as Ens. Jeremy Lister of the 10th, who served for the honor of the regiment in place of another officer feigning illness.[29]

While the soldiers continued to pile into the diverse longboats before them, one Yankee observer cautiously watched from a concealed vantage point on nearby Mount Whoredom (yes, that was what they called it), west of Beacon Hill. With the late moonrise still too low to provide much light, the Yankee could barely make out the British companies trailing down the bluff toward the swelling waters and fanning toward each of the boats, which, once packed to the gunwales, pushed off in turn. That concealed Yankee observer was Dr. Joseph Warren, and he knew at once the implications of what he was witnessing. He had sent Dawes as a precautionary measure, but now his suspicions had proven true. He turned to William Eustis or some other trusted agent there and gave simple but explicit instructions: *summon Paul Revere and meet me at my house!* As the messenger carefully crawled away, Warren took one last look, perhaps peering from a spyglass. He then turned and crept from his hiding place, cautious to remain unseen by the British armed guard on watch that night. With the HMS *Somerset* on his left, creaking against her moorings, he made quickly for his home near Faneuil Hall.[30]

As the doctor headed home, the British coxswains continued to push off each packed boat with care, mindful that their overladen boats would settle to within inches of the waterline. These coxswains, likely midshipmen, often but teens, whispered orders to gruff, stout seamen twice their age. The seamen in turn, with oars wrapped in cloth to muffle their sound, clumsily began to row the near one mile to Phipps's Farm at Lechmere Point, on the Cambridge side of the river. Soon, all the boats were making their way across the Charles. Left behind on the Boston shore were almost half the soldiers, forced to wait for a second trip.[31]

Meanwhile, Revere got the message and rushed the short way from his home in Boston's North End to that of Warren, where he received the doctor's hasty intelligence: William Dawes had been sent to Hancock and Adams in Lexington to give early warning of British activity. But now Warren had confirmed the British were indeed embarking on an expedition, probably, as had long been expected, to seize the stores in Concord (though he may have expressed concern that Hancock and Adams could be ancillary targets).[32]

Revere understood and immediately left for the Old North Church to initiate his alarm signal. After, he would endeavor to slip out of the sealed town and ride to Lexington to warn the Whig leaders.[33] In doing so, he would rouse the countryside and alter the fate of the colonies.

Revere crept quickly from shadow to shadow as he cautiously worked his way toward the large, three-story brick boardinghouse that once stood at the corner of Sheafe and Salem Street, about a block from the Old North Church (officially Christ Church). Its owner was the widow Mrs. Newman, who, though a Whig, was obliged to rent out rooms to British officers so she could feed her family. Revere had come looking for the assistance of her equally Whiggish son, young Robert Newman.

Once Revere reached the house, he was not sure what to do. When he looked through the windows and into the parlors, he was startled to find them full of boisterous regular officers, playing cards and drinking, ignorant of the greater events unfolding that night. But where was Robert Newman? This was Revere's inside man, a sexton of Old North Church before it had closed, who still had keys to its locked doors. Earlier that day, Revere had met with Newman and Militia Capt. John Pulling Jr., a vestryman of the church, as well as a third volunteer, Thomas Bernard. Revere had warned them all to be ready that night. But where were they?

Revere was anxious to get on with his escape from the sealed town and had arranged for use of a boat hidden at a nearby wharf. Yet he knew there was a good chance the roving naval patrol boats might capture him before he safely crossed to Charlestown. If that should happen, and should Dawes be unable to reach Lexington, Revere's lantern signal from atop Old North Church's steeple might be the only way Charlestown would ever learn of the impending expedition, and thus the only warning the countryside might have to raise the alarm.

Otherwise, the British Expedition to Concord would remain a secret until it was too late, the people would be disarmed, and General Gage would score a major political victory against the growing American resistance. The only way to ensure that did not happen was to raise the lanterns atop Old North's steeple, and to do so, Revere *had* to find Robert Newman.

Revere decided to sneak around the back of the Newman House. He hopped over a low iron fence and into the dark backyard. As he pondered what to do next, he noticed a shadowy figure amid the darkness. Suddenly, the figure rushed toward him!

It was Newman! Revere was relieved. Out of the shadows also

appeared Bernard and Pulling. Newman explained: as the officers sat to play cards inside, he had pretended to go to bed, then slipped through an upstairs window and carefully dropped to the ground, where he waited for Revere to arrive.

Revere undoubtedly instructed his trusted friends to light the lanterns in his typically plain style. Perhaps one of them asked how many. Revere replied simply: *two*.

Newman acknowledged, and with that, Revere was off, back over the fence and on to his nearby home. The other three men crept from the backyard and down the street one block to the Old North. Reaching its heavy locked door, Newman pulled from his coat the key and inserted it into the lock. With a click, the bolt slid out of position. Leaving Bernard outside as a guard, Newman and Pulling dashed inside and quickly made their way to a closet where they found the two carefully hidden lanterns Newman had prepared just that day. Each lantern was but a small metal box frame with a windowpane on each of its four faces, with room enough inside for just a small candlestick—they would hardly be beacons, but they would do the job.

Newman and Pulling jury-rigged leather lanyards around their glorified candleholders by which to suspend the fragile things as they climbed to the steeple. These they threw over their necks; then they grabbed a tinderbox each and headed for the long spiral of wooden stairs, 154 of them, and slowly and silently made their way up the tight path to the steeple's apex.[34]

While they trudged up those many stairs, Revere had gone home. He grabbed his warm surtout overcoat, his riding boots, and maybe a tricorne (three-cornered) hat. He then bid good-bye to his second wife, Rachel, and immediately left again, this time sneaking toward the homes of two other friends, Joshua Bentley and Thomas Richardson, who joined him. Together they made their way to the Charles River.[35]

The sky grew brighter, courtesy of a rising moon, and they could just make out before them the softly lit immensity of the 68-gun warship HMS *Somerset*, moored midway between Boston and the opposite shore of Charlestown. With the tide flooding in, she creaked and pulled against her anchor lines like a monster waiting to be unleashed.[36]

One tradition claims that about this time, the three realized they had forgotten to bring some kind of cloth by which to muffle their oars. One of Revere's men went to a nearby house, made a "peculiar signal", and an upper window was softly raised, revealing a woman in her white bedclothes. She and Revere's friend whispered back and forth for a moment, then out the window fluttered a white piece of cloth, which gently floated to the friend's outstretched arms. They found it to be a white wool petticoat, still warm from the woman's body, she having stripped naked for the Cause of Liberty.[37]

As the three proceeded with caution back to the Charles, the great warship *Somerset* rang out its semi-hourly knell: two bells, a pause, two bells, a pause, and one more… It meant half past ten o'clock. *Somerset*'s officer of the deck then announced, "Five bells and all's well!" Little did he know.[38]

———•———

Upon reaching the shoreline, Revere and his two men carefully stepped down the short palisade to the Charles riverbed. From a hiding place beneath a wharf there, they noiselessly dragged out their hidden rowboat and began wrapping the two oars to muffle them.[39] Revere perhaps sat in the boat strapping on his spurs as his two friends then softly pushed the rowboat off the muddy shore before carefully hopping in to man the oars.

The three had left the town unnoticed, but their senses were on high alert as they slowly and gently paddled toward the ominous warship HMS *Somerset* standing before them. As Revere's two companions quietly ferried him across, he looked back at the silhouetted town, backlit by the rising moon. When his eyes came upon the highest point of the skyline, the tall spire of Old North Church, he must have smirked to see two small, dim flickers of light suddenly spring from its northern face, defiantly sending a signal to Charlestown that would raise the alarm even if Revere himself could not slip by *Somerset*.[40]

At that moment, Pulling and Newman were dangling precariously from a ladder out the steeple's open window, each of them stretching to hold out his respective lantern from its leather lanyard hung about his neck. They held out their signals for only a few moments, then quickly pulled in their lamps and blew out the candles. Below them, they saw a detachment of regulars marching on guard through the street. They frantically made their way down the stairs of the tower and deposited their lanterns back in the closet. Then, to avoid the patrol, they climbed a bench near the altar, slid open a window there, and crawled out, plopping to the grounds behind the church. Their mission complete, they made for their homes.[41]

Revere could only hope the dim and momentary signal had indeed been seen in Charlestown. The only sounds were the muffled oars against the oarlocks and gunwales as they traversed with each stroke, the gentle dripping of the water from the oars as they swung over the water, followed by the carefully muted splash as the oars again made contact. But the creaking of *Somerset* lurching against her moorings grew ever more audible with their approach.

Ever since nine o'clock, when the Charlestown ferry was closed for the night, the ferryboats had been tied up alongside *Somerset*. Now they gently bounced off one another with the flooding tide. Private boats had long ago been confiscated as a means to ensure the Port Bill was properly enforced. Thus, Revere's illicit boat was a rare commodity. As Revere's little boat rowed ever closer to the looming warship, he cautiously looked around for the naval longboats on patrol. He found none.[42]

Perhaps *Somerset*'s Capt. Edward Le Cras was apprised of the timeline for the night's expedition and so eagerly paced the quarterdeck of his great warship even as Revere drew near. Perhaps he saw the lanterns from Old North's steeple and ordered his men to be alert. The marines aboard were refused their breaks as they stood guard for boats crossing the Charles. The seamen likely manned the many mobile swivel guns, which they had mounted on the starboard side of the ship, facing Boston. On this night in particular, they were ready to blow out of the water any trespasser that dared cross the river.[43]

This was exactly what most concerned Revere and his two companions. While the vigilant *Somerset* crew kept on the lookout, Revere's two rowers paddled with increasing trepidation on a course that would pass them just east of the mighty ship. With each muffled stroke of their oars, the ominous ship loomed ever closer. The three Yankees began to wonder if they would make it to the Charlestown shore alive, when suddenly they became aware of another obstacle.[44]

Just an hour earlier, the large waning gibbous moon had crested over the horizon. It had risen that night almost behind the town, as seen from *Somerset*, and only now was starting to peak above the diminutive skyline of Boston. It still cast long shadows on the Charles, but in a few moments, the entire river would be awash with moonbeams and the crew of *Somerset* would certainly see the illegal ferry.[45]

Revere's rowboat glided within a couple hundred feet of the menacing man-of-war's hemp anchor lines, which creaked loudly as she tugged hard against the two submerged bower anchors holding her in place against the onrushing tide. The three Americans could see her bowsprit pointed eastward toward the harbor, see too her starboard swivel guns glistening in the moonlight, and the several seamen and marines pacing her spar deck. Revere and his companions were so close that they could hear the flapping of the Navy Jack at the bow, the sheets and lines vibrating in the wind, perhaps even close enough to hear the off-duty men snoring in their hammocks below deck.

Yet, Revere's boat remained undetected. Fortune had smiled upon him, for the moon was not quite behind Revere, but a little off his left, ensuring his crossing could not be seen in silhouette against the blazing moonlight. This, combined with the moon shadows dancing like camouflage across the lightly undulating river, made a confusing pattern for the watchful *Somerset* crew. Somehow, just as the moon climbed higher and the shadows quickly began to evaporate, Revere's boat got around *Somerset*'s downriver anchor cable in time. And once behind that tall sail ship on her port side, the side her crew was doubtlessly ignoring, Revere could hide in her own long shadow almost the rest of the way to the shores of Charlestown.[46]

When Revere reached the safety of the shore, he heard again the warship ring out: two bells, a pause, two bells, a pause, and two more…eleven o'clock. The same officer of the deck then announced, "Six bells and all's well!"[47]

———◆———

Late that evening, all along the dark countryside roads, one could occasionally hear the thuds of hooves beating against the moist ground.

These were the mounted British patrol, now divided in parties that soon took up hidden positions along the road to ambush unsuspecting alarm riders such as Paul Revere. Their cover story was that they were searching for deserters, not an unusual task for officers in the British Army. What *was* unusual was that they wore full accoutrements—swords and pistols, cockades in their hats—and were wrapped in blue overcoats. It looked as if they had ridden to war, not to seek out deserters. What was more, such activity was especially unusual past dark.

When one of these patrol parties made its way past Menotomy, three Provincial Congressmen lodging there took cover and watched them go by.[48] When another party crossed through Lexington to block the way to Concord, three intrepid locals followed, only to be captured and detained soon after. Their friends must have wondered what happened, but sent no one to investigate.[49] When Lexington Militia Sgt. William Munroe heard of these riders, he feared for the safety of Samuel Adams and John Hancock, residing with Rev. Jonas Clarke in town. Munroe's fears seem to have been unfounded, but he made a prudent decision and selected eight to ten men, and together they marched to the Clarke parsonage to stand guard. Another several dozen or so local militia grabbed their arms and headed to Buckman Tavern on the central Lexington Green, to be ready if needed, just in case.[50]

When a party of the mounted British patrol moved on toward Concord through the outskirts of northern Lincoln, a tradition gives that resident Josiah Nelson heard their hooves beating toward his home. He slipped outside wearing nothing but a nightgown, carrying with him a dim lantern, curious to talk firsthand to what he supposed were colonial alarm riders. As he walked the short distance to the road, he yelled out, asking whether they knew if anything was astir. Once they drew near, he was shocked to find they were British riders. The patrol, which now included some Tory guides, took Nelson prisoner. Soon after, the British released Nelson to the Tories' care. These knew him to be an honored citizen, and so in turn released him with an order to go into his house and extinguish the lights, threatening to burn his house over his head if he gave any alarm or showed any light. Yet Nelson was a steadfast Whig, and though he went to his home and extinguished his lanterns as ordered, he then grabbed his horse and rode for nearby Bedford to give the alarm.[51]

Thus, even before Paul Revere's famous ride, the countryside was already keenly aware of some affair unfolding.

———————

Meanwhile in Boston, though they were now adversaries, both Dr. Joseph Warren and Lt. Gen. Thomas Gage each suffered from the same trepidation that night as they waited anxiously for any word of their respective men's missions, that of Revere and Dawes for the former, that of Smith and Pitcairn for the latter. Both political leaders must have conceded they were now helpless, that theirs was a waiting game. At length, each tried with little success to get a few hours of uneasy sleep, for each was expectant that at any moment, they would at last hear of the events unfolding west of Boston.

———————

It was not until about the time Revere crossed the Charles that the first wave of British troops neared the shores of Lechmere Point in Cambridge. With maybe just ten longboats, only a bit over half the expedition crossed on the first ferry. The remainder had to wait for the longboats to return, so their crossing proved tediously long.[52]

Much of the Boston area was then surrounded by extensive marshes and mudflats at low tide, while at high tide the water was but a few feet deep. Consequently, with the flood tide still nearing its crest, the laden longboats ground into the riverbed tens of feet from the shoreline. The rowers then balanced the boats from tipping as the soldiers awkwardly hopped overboard, splashing into the frigid marsh, the icy water up to their knees and instantly rushing into their shoes. (Typically, only the officers had boots, since they purchased their own uniforms, while the soldiers wore cheap leather shoes since the regimental commander outfitted them. Though the soldiers also wore constricting gaiters, these provided no protection from the cold water.) Such was the miserable beginning of their seventeen-mile forced march.[53]

The men sloshed through the marsh and up to the riverbank, careful not to splash water onto their precious gun cartridge boxes, which would soil and ruin their gunpowder. Once reaching more or less solid ground, small parties of light infantry were set as guards to provide security for the detachment. The remainder were permitted to rest as the longboats returned to the Boston shore to collect the second half of the expedition. This welcome respite allowed the men time to pull off their waterlogged shoes and wring out their sodden socks.[54]

It was sometime around eleven o'clock when this first wave landed at Cambridge. As they did, a few mounted Tories materialized from the shadows, ready guides for Smith's expedition. One was a former Militia Captain Beeman, come all the way from Petersham, northwest of Worcester. Another was Samuel Murray of Worcester proper.[55]

On the Boston shore, Lord Percy had come to see the embarkation personally. After he felt satisfied, he started back for his quarters when he came upon a group of townspeople, likely a town watch, who warned, "The British troops have marched, but they will miss their aim."

Percy played dumb. "What aim?"

"Why, the cannon at Concord." Percy was shocked. Even these random townsfolk knew of the profoundly secret expedition. He rushed off to Province House to alert General Gage.[56]

Along the Back Bay, the second wave of British began their slow embarkation, each man climbing in turn into those few longboats just as their comrades had. Also still waiting there were many of the senior officers, a very few of whom were on horseback, including Lieutenant Colonel Smith and Major Pitcairn. For most of the soldiers and officers, however, the march was to be a weary one, much farther than their exercise marches had ever taken them. Moreover, their march was also to be a dangerous one for Paul Revere on his way to alarm the countryside.[57]

Paul Revere climbed up the Charlestown shore and cut through the small town, making his way to the home of Militia Col. William Conant. Upon his arrival, the militia colonel anxiously invited him inside to a room full of uneasy townsmen. They told Revere they had seen the lantern signal, and Revere briefly filled them in on "what was Acting". He then "went to git me a Horse". The Charlestown Whigs had prepared for Revere's possible midnight ride, and so escorted him to the nearby stable of John Larkin, a merchant and local deacon. There Revere was introduced to what he called "a very good Horse", a distant ancestor to the modern Suffolk Punch breed, as one historian reckoned. Larkin family tradition names her Brown Beauty, and this mare was a big, strong, and fast saddle horse, likely the fastest in town.[58]

As a stable boy prepared the horse, Committee of Safety member Richard Devens joined them. He told how he had just come from Lexington that evening, where he met "9 officers of Gages Army, well mounted and Armed going to wards to Concord."[59] Devens warned Revere to be on the lookout. Revere thanked him for the advice as he slipped his foot in the stirrup and sprung up on the saddle. His friends then wished him Godspeed, and with a kick to his grand steed, Revere was off.

Revere quickly rode his mighty mare through the small town and to the hills beyond, riding west of Bunker Hill and then across Charlestown Neck to the mainland, passing a rusty iron cage there displaying the bones of a black slave who had poisoned his master.[60]

It was sometime after eleven o'clock, the night cool but pleasant. Maybe a few traces of snow endured in the shady spots along the road, but the weather had grown mild almost a week earlier, the melting snow having given way to muddy roads and the first green sprouts that were to usher in the springtime.[61] All around, the fresh smells of the winter thaw permeated the air. The moon was now high in the heavens, lighting Revere's way as he splashed his mare at a fast canter across the muddy road westward.

The midnight rider had no sooner ridden onto the mainland than his horse showed a sign of curiosity at something ahead, pricking her ears forward and snorting. Looking ahead, at first Revere saw nothing. Suddenly, a shadow along the roadside moved! Peering closely through the soft moonglow, he saw something ahead beneath a tree—a man on horseback! In the brief moment of hesitation, as Revere wondered whether this might be the patrol he had been warned about, Brown Beauty carried him ever forward. Suddenly, the dark figure turned toward him, and with the moonlight glistening off the figure's metal gorget hanging below his neck, Revere knew him to be a British officer.

The mounted officer, camouflaged as he was in his dark blue surtout, instantly sprang onto the road…as did another rider! "I got near enough to see their holsters and Cockades." The two mounted officers at once kicked into a gallop, straight toward Revere.[62]

Realizing the trap, Revere pulled hard on his mare's reins, rearing the horse on her hind legs and pulling her to a stop. He then swiftly turned her around, even as the mounted officers bore down on him.

Revere hastily kicked his steed into a full gallop, but she needed no prodding—she was spooked enough to anticipate Revere's every intention. As Brown Beauty raced back toward Charlestown, the two officers closed in on her. The hoofbeats of his pursuers continued to grow louder as they drew ever closer. Revere frantically kicked his horse, and somehow the steed found a faster stride yet.

Then one of his pursuers split off, dashing off the road and into the tree line. His lone pursuer struggled to keep up. The best that officer could do was perhaps brandish a pistol and shout at Revere to halt. But Brown Beauty was too fast, and soon she had a considerable lead on the pursuer. The lone mounted officer had no choice but to give up the chase. As Revere smiled at his success and patted his horse, he thought it best to take the longer, northerly route to Lexington via Mystick (now Medford). Revere quickly reached that intersection and turned to take the other road, still at a full gallop, when suddenly, off to his left, breaking from the tree line sprung the second rider.

The second rider galloped across a field to cut off Revere at a bend ahead, and Revere could see that his muddy road was turning him toward his pursuer. The two adversaries were converging, and Revere about to be intercepted. Just as the shadowy British rider came to a roadside fence, expecting to hop it and block Revere's escape: *Splash! Squish!* The British horse ran into an unseen shallow pond of water-covered clay, slowing instantly. As the ensnared rider struggled to free his mired horse, Revere safely galloped by, onward to Lexington.[63]

The unwelcome detour added miles to Revere's ride, but it safely circumnavigated around other roving British patrols. As Revere rode through Medford, he awoke the captain of the minutemen company, Isaac Hall, then "alarmed almost every House" until he got to Lexington.[64] The secret British Expedition to Concord was now anything but secret.

———◆———

Once the entire British force had finally reached the Cambridge shore, sometime around midnight, Lieutenant Colonel Smith formed his men into their proper companies. Being a by-the-book, methodical officer, he next rearranged his companies in order of seniority: first came the light infantry of the expeditionary commander's own 10th regiment, as was traditional, followed by those of each regiment in numerical order, from lowest to highest. The grenadiers then formed in the same order behind. This waste of precious time was not Smith's private obsession, but a source of regimental pride.[65]

It was then well after midnight when, finally, Smith gave the order to march. The British column trudged along the riverbank northward, only to find it painfully obvious why their landing zone was completely devoid of farms and houses—the entire area was one great marsh. They attempted a circuitous path along the very edge of the Charles, but the slippery, pebbled beach proved hardly a better alternative to the thick and sucking mud of the marsh. The men again found their shoes filled with frigid water, but now "they were obliged to wade, halfway up their thighs, through two inlets." The men, shivering cold, eventually found a muddy but firm trail that drew them off the marsh. Here Smith halted his men to await the arrival by longboat of two days' provision, secretly prepared aboard the warships.[66]

This delay cost the expedition still more precious time, time Paul Revere was happy to have as he alerted the countryside of the secret British march.

———◆———

Once in Lexington, Revere came upon a fork in the road, the green space within it forming Lexington Green, where stood the town's meetinghouse. He turned his steed along the northerly fork and, after passing Buckman Tavern, turned again onto the Bedford Road, cantering past a fifty-acre farm on his way to the parsonage of Rev. Jonas Clarke.

The two-story Clarke House, with its simple colonial architecture, was that night crowded with at least ten Clarkes, as well as Samuel Adams, John Hancock, Hancock's fiancée, and his elderly aunt. Adams and Hancock were relegated to the ground floor's parlors-turned-makeshift-bedrooms, while the best chamber upstairs was given to Hancock's two ladies. Inside, all was quiet; all were asleep. Outside, faithful thirty-two-year-old Militia Sgt. William Munroe stood guard with perhaps a dozen Lexington militia.[67]

It was about thirty minutes after midnight when Revere rode up to the Clarke home, his horse cantering loudly into the yard. This annoyed Munroe, who did not know Revere. As the militia guard closed in on the rider, Revere demanded to be admitted into the house. Munroe refused, explaining the family had just retired and had asked not to be disturbed by any noise outside.[68]

"Noise!" Revere retorted. "You'll have a *noise* that will disturb you all! The regulars are on their march, and will soon be among you!"[69]

The two exchanged a few words. Finally, Revere dismounted, pushed past Monroe, and banged loudly on the door. One of the second-floor windows flew open and out popped Reverend Clarke, bathed in soft moonlight, perhaps wearing a long nightcap. Clarke apparently did not know Revere either. He deliberated aloud that given the time of night, he did not like to admit people into his home without first knowing their business. Other faces appeared at the other windows too, when up flew a downstairs window, revealing Hancock and Adams. "Come in, Revere!" Hancock called out. Then he added jokingly, "we're not afraid of *you*."[70]

Inside the home, Clarke hurried downstairs to the parlor as Revere stomped in with his muddy riding boots to give Hancock and Adams his message. While Clarke lit a few oil lanterns, the Whig leaders talked urgently of the unfolding events as Revere knew them. He described the embarkation Dr. Warren had seen and told of the patrols along the approaches from Boston. Revere then asked about William Dawes. Hancock and Adams just looked at each other, dumbfounded. Dawes had never arrived. They feared Dawes might have been captured by the same patrols that nearly seized Revere. No sooner had they come to this conclusion than, a half hour after Revere's arrival, Dawes himself marched into the house.[71]

Not only was Dawes on a slow nag, he had had to ride a circuitous route, longer than Revere's. Dawes traveled west to Brighton, across the Charles to Cambridge, then up to Lexington, a total of about nineteen miles, compared to Revere's thirteen. More significantly, Dawes rode his old nag at an easy pace, for his was not a mission of urgency. He had no reason to race to Lexington as Revere had, for the intelligence at the time of his departure was only that the military was astir, nothing more. Only when Dr. Warren actually saw the British embarking did he send for Revere. There is little evidence that Dawes alarmed any houses along the way, for as far as he knew, there was no alarm to give. Perhaps he was forced to circumnavigate a mounted patrol as well, further delaying his arrival. So when he stepped into the Clarke home and learned of Revere's message, he was just as surprised as Hancock and Adams had been.[72]

The group all decided to walk down the short Bedford Road to Buckman Tavern for refreshments, the two riders likely leading their exhausted horses with them. Sergeant Munroe may have accompanied them, to rouse the several Lexington militia lodged there for the night. As they all refreshed themselves at the bar, they debated how best to proceed. They agreed Dr. Warren's hunch was probably accurate, that the Army's aim was to seize the war stores in Concord. They concluded the town must be warned. Revere and Dawes assented to the undertaking, and after they refreshed their horses, they climbed again into their saddles, though this time a bit slower perhaps, worn as they were from their earlier rides.[73]

About half past one o'clock that morning, now April 19, the two midnight riders set their travel-weary horses into a canter westward toward Concord. As they departed, one of the few Lexington militiamen there trotted over to the town bell that stood on Lexington Green near the meetinghouse. Revere and Dawes had no sooner left Lexington center than the bell's long knell began to echo behind them, signaling the alarm that would rouse and summon the entire Lexington militia company.[74]

———◆———

With Lexington at their backs, Dawes and Revere rode at a fast canter along the moonlit Concord Road. When they approached the first of the houses outlying Lexington, they split off from one another, one taking the left, the other taking the right, riding up to the front doors, yelling to their sleeping inhabitants: "The regulars are coming!" or possibly "Their aim is Concord!" As the sleepy-eyed country folk flung open their windows, Revere rode back to the road, rejoining Dawes, so that they continued side by side onward toward Concord. If those drowsy residents doubted the unusual news, they could hear as confirmation the constant knell of the small, solitary alarm bell just audible from Lexington Green.[75]

All along their path, the midnight riders rode up to each farmhouse in turn: "The regulars are coming!" Maybe instead of *regulars* they said *redcoats*, *Ministerial Troops*, or even *lobsters*. But, contrary to many history books, they did not say "The British are coming!" (Despite the turmoil, the Americans proudly remained and considered *themselves* British.)[76]

Here and there, sleepy colonists, some with nightcaps, others with muskets, popped out of their windows to see what was happening. While the two midnight riders continued westward, each house behind them stirred with commotion as their windows flickered to life with the igniting of candles or oil lamps. In turn, armed men began to filter out of their homes and march back to the rally point: Lexington Green.

As Revere and Dawes beat along the muddy, moonlit road, they suddenly became aware of a horseman halted ahead. They feared the dark figure was a British patrolman, but strangely, the figure did not turn to pursue. So the midnight riders dared to ride a little closer, until they saw in the moonlight that this man was decidedly not a soldier. Coming up to him, they found him to be a young man, just twenty-four, a doctor in those parts named Samuel Prescott.

Prescott had been in Lexington, courting Miss Lydia Mullikan. He had left town only a few minutes before Revere and Dawes had, and was now on his way to his home in Concord. When he had heard the distant alarm bell behind him, he grew suspicious and, upon seeing Revere and Dawes driving toward him, decided to give them his assistance.[77]

Once Revere and Dawes were upon him, Prescott told them that he knew of their errand, for he could deduce it from the commotion in their wake. He offered his aid, adding that the people between here and

Concord knew him well and that his presence "would give more credit" to what Revere and Dawes said.

But Revere warned the young doctor that the road was crawling with British patrols and, further, that he could not vouch for the young man's safety. Yet the congenial doctor did not ask for their protection and eagerly wished to lend a hand. Dawes and Revere sized Prescott up, and Revere, figuring the young man "to be a high Son of Liberty", agreed to let the doctor join them. Revere proposed that, as they might not all make it to Concord before being captured, they must endeavor to alert every house between here and there. The doctor agreed.[78]

With that, the three rode off together for Concord, their horses racing along the country rode, up hills and around densely wooded areas that unfolded to pastures, peeling off in turn for every house they came upon (except for those of known Loyalists), riding up to each, yelling as they knocked on doors or windows, "The regulars are coming!" "Their aim is Concord!" As each house awoke in turn, their owners popping their heads out their windows, the riders repeated their message and urged help in spreading the alarm. The riders then turned their horses and dashed again to the moonlit road, converging together as a trio once more, only to split off for the next batch of homes.

———◆———

On the south boundary and near the eastern tip of the triangular Lexington Green, the small bell continued to knell. Its belfry stood beside the small two-story meetinghouse that also served as the town's church. In front of this building, and just across from Buckman Tavern, forty-five-year-old Militia Capt. John Parker surveyed his militia company as they mustered and fell in to formation. Perhaps as many as one hundred fifty men answered the call, including the "train band" (the main body of militia) and the "alarm men" (the reserve force of aged men and others exempted from turning out except for an alarm).

Once Parker assessed that his full company had turned out, he walked the lines as he told his men the intelligence brought to Lexington by Paul Revere. Someone there suggested they send scouts eastward to find the supposed British column and report back, for no one had yet made visual contact with it. Parker agreed, and two volunteers mounted steeds and rode off.[79]

With that, there was little more Parker could do. So he ordered his men at ease, and they waited.

———•———

Meanwhile, as the three midnight riders continued their mad dash across the countryside, Dawes and Prescott again peeled off to alert a house. As they did, Revere, riding ahead, perceived in the moonlight two mounted patrolmen along the roadside, about a third of a mile ahead, almost identical to his situation earlier. He quickly halted Brown Beauty and quietly called for Dawes and Prescott to come up.[80]

Suddenly, the two horsemen galloped for him! As Revere turned to retreat, from the shadows along either side of a thin trail that intersected the main road there, four more riders emerged, instantly surrounding him. These blue-clad patrolmen unsheathed their swords and brandished their pistols, just as Prescott galloped up.

Prescott tried to race past, beating his horse with the butt end of his riding whip. Revere took the doctor's cue and spurred his mare to follow. But the British quickly responded, moving their horses to block the way. "God damn you! Stop!" yelled one of the officers. "If you go an inch farther, you are a dead man!"[81]

Dawes had hung back a bit, waiting to see what came of Prescott's charge. As he did, the first two patrolmen from down the road, still galloping toward the commotion, spotted him. Without breaking stride, they both flew past the now-surrounded Revere—straight for Dawes. Dawes saw he was about to be intercepted, so he quickly turned his horse and spurred it toward an empty farmhouse nearby. Thinking quickly, he made as much noise as he could, shouting, "Halloo, boys, I've got two of 'em!" Suddenly his pursuers slowed their horses, thinking it imprudent to rush headlong into an ambush.

Dawes's bluff was a success and he raced ahead. No sooner had he escaped than, in the excitement of rushing through the field, his horse spooked and threw him. He landed uninjured, but lost his watch, his horse, and a bit of his pride. Figuring his part in raising the alarm done, he made his way back toward Lexington and then probably to Boston. Days later, he would return to the scene and find his lost watch in the grass.[82]

Back on the road, the four horsemen surrounding Revere and Prescott had planned their ambush just ahead of a gap in a fence where they had earlier removed a pair of bars. Gesturing to the opening and the pasture beyond, one of the patrolmen swore to their two prisoners, "If you do not turn into that pasture, we will blow your brains out!"

The four British then herded the two remaining alarm riders into the fenced pasture, when suddenly, Prescott yelled to Revere, "Put on!"

Prescott immediately kicked his spurs into his horse and wielded the bridle hard left, while Revere did the same and pulled right. Prescott had the advantage of surprise, while Revere must have hesitated for a moment, but in an instant, both were peeling off in opposite directions to the edges of the pasture.

The four British horsemen split to pursue. Surprisingly, no one fired as the young doctor managed to break away with his strong, fresh horse, jumping his steed over a low stone wall and zigzagging it through the woods. His pursuers gave up the chase, and Prescott got away, riding onward to Concord.

Simultaneously, as Revere approached the woods on his side, he decided he would dismount and escape on foot. He gave one last look back and marveled that his two pursuers had given up the chase. Perhaps he smiled at his luck, thinking himself free once more. Just as Brown Beauty reached the woods, six new mounted patrolmen sprung out from the shadows! Revere pulled hard on his reins, attempting to turn his mighty mare, but found himself instantly surrounded yet again.

These six new British quickly closed tight around Revere, their pistols trained. Several jabbed their pistol barrels into his side and chest as one grabbed hold of the bridle and another stripped the reins from his tightly clenched knuckles. They ordered he immediately dismount. Revere saw he had no choice and readily complied.

Among these new six patrolmen was an officer whose name Revere never got, but whom he described later as "One of them who appeared to have the command there, and much of a Gentleman". This mounted officer probably holstered his pistol as he politely asked, "Where did you come from?" Revere answered honestly. "What time did you leave?" Revere told him. The officer was impressed to find Revere had escaped after the quarantine was enforced. "Sir, may I crave your name?"

"Revere."

"What, *Paul* Revere?"

"Yes."

The patrolmen all knew his name, even if they did not know his face. They began to jeer at him, or as Paul himself would write, "the others abused me much".

The kind officer replied, "Do not be afraid, they will not hurt you."

Revere was defiant: "You will miss your aim!"

"We should not, we are after some deserters on the road."

"I know better", Revere retorted. "I know what you are after, and I have alarmed the country all the way up. I know too your boats catched aground. I should have 500 men their [*sic*] soon."

To this, the officer looked surprised. He sized Revere up, trying to detect any hint of his bluffing. Revere was not passive and limp, but confidently responded with cool and calculated assertiveness, almost bordering on belligerence. This sort of bold courage infuriated the patrolmen, but it stood as a classic illustration of Yankee fortitude, an example the British would see plenty more of before the next sundown.

The officer must have known something of the expedition Revere referred to, but as Gage had shrouded it in secrecy, Revere probably knew more. Leaving Revere in the care of the five, the officer abruptly turned and rode to the four others who remained on guard near the fence's opening. Revere watched as the gentleman officer whispered emphatically to another officer, apparently the commander. These five horsemen then swiftly turned and kicked into a full gallop back toward Revere, leaving only the two riders that had chased Dawes still somewhere on the road.[83]

Now ten patrolmen encircled the dismounted Revere, including their commander, Maj. Edward Mitchell. Mitchell was infuriated over the escape of Revere's two companions. He moved his horse close to Revere, unholstered his pistol and placed it directly against Revere's temple, calmly explaining, "I am going to ask you some questions, and if you do not tell the truth, I will blow your brains out."

Revere calmly replied, "I call myself a Man of Truth, and you stopped me on the highway, and made me a prisoner, I know not by what right. But I will tell the truth, for I am not afraid." Mitchell then asked Revere the same questions as the gentleman officer had, and Revere gave much the same answers.

After giving his interrogation, the suspicious Major Mitchell consulted with two of his officers. Mitchell must have known of the expedition, but also did not know its aim. Should he believe this damn rebel? If Revere was right, and Mitchell did nothing, the fate of the entire British expedition might end in ruin.

But by allowing Dr. Prescott to escape, they had already sealed that fate.[84]

At Lechmere Point, the British column remained "halted in a dirty road…waiting for provisions to be brought from the boats…which most of the Men threw away, having carried some with 'em." When timing was critical, here was Lieutenant Colonel Smith dawdling southeast of Cambridge.[85]

Finally, at two o'clock in the morning, with sunrise just three hours away, some four hours wasted, Smith gave the order to march. The column followed a road along the Charles River and soon came upon a wooden bridge that crossed the small Willis Creek. Here Smith again displayed incompetence. Worried the noise of marching over the bridge would alert the neighbors, Smith ordered the men to ford the creek, "wading through…up to our Middles".[86] Once the troops re-formed on the opposite bank, the cold water would collude with their general exhaustion (most had not slept since the night before) in sapping their energy.[87]

The bright moonlight illuminated the path for the long, red column, which marched slightly interspaced to distinguish its twenty-one companies. All was silent but for the hushed, rhythmic march of their boots thudding into the soft, moist ground as the column moved northwestward along the dirt road separating the various pasturelands. Trotting alongside the column on both its flanks were those few officers fortunate enough to have mounts. Pitcairn rode his steed near the vanguard, alongside the light infantry. Also out front, apparently on foot, was Ens. Henry De Berniere, Gage's scout who had mapped the route to Concord.

Halfway down the column marched the grenadiers, easily spotted by their distinctive, towering bearskin hats. And alongside these rode Lieutenant Colonel Smith. Mirroring their progression at some distance off either side of the road, small parties of light infantry traversed the pastures, serving as flankers to protect the main column. The column seemed to sparkle as moonbeams glistened off their muskets and fixed bayonets, which they kept at shoulder arms while on the march.[88]

The British Expedition to Concord was at last fully underway, marching northwestward. But to reach their objective, they first had to pass Lexington. And Capt. John Parker and his militia were there waiting.

—•—

As Major Mitchell consulted in hushed tones with his mounted officers, he eyed Revere with contempt. With Revere's two fellow riders escaped, Mitchell reasoned to his men, their mission to prevent the alarm had already failed. It seemed their duty was now to ride ahead and warn the British column.

After searching Revere for pistols (he had none), Mitchell ordered Revere to remount his horse. But when Revere reached for the reins, Mitchell stripped them away, handing them to an officer. "By God sir, *you* are not to ride with the reins!"

"Let me have the reins," Revere pleaded. "I will not run from him."

Mitchell laughed. "I do not trust you."[89]

The major then yelled toward the moon-shaded woods, and four prisoners appeared. Three were those same volunteers who had at ten o'clock that night ridden from Lexington to watch the patrol, only to be captured by it. The fourth, a one-armed peddler, had been in the wrong place at the wrong time.[90] Major Mitchell ordered them to mount their horses, tied off nearby, and then the British herded their five prisoners to the road, where waited the two other British patrolmen.

The party of eleven mounted sentries then encircled the five mounted prisoners, with Revere given the dubious distinction of being in front, and together the party set off at a "prittie smart" pace toward Lexington.[91]

As they made their way, a gunshot rang out ahead. Mitchell demanded to know what it meant. Revere coolly replied it was to alarm the countryside. They heard too the faint toll of the small bell on Lexington Green.[92]

Halting the party, Major Mitchell ordered all prisoners but Revere to dismount, then he had his soldiers cut their horses' bridles and saddles and shoo them away, before releasing the four prisoners themselves. But when Revere asked if he too could go, Mitchell refused.

Revere and his captors started again for Lexington. When they got "within sight of the Meeting-House," they suddenly heard a volley of gunfire. This "appeared to alarm them very much" and the party halted once more.

Just a moment earlier, one of Captain Parker's scouts had galloped back to Lexington Green. He had ridden as far as Cambridge, but had seen no evidence of a British march. In the scout's opinion, there was no truth in the alarm. Captain Parker considered this, but wondered where his second scout had gone. Finally, the militia captain dismissed his militiamen, still on parade upon the Green, and ordered they be ready to appear again at the beat of a drum. Men who lived nearby went back to their homes. The rest crowded into Buckman Tavern for a bit of cheer.[93] Revere later supposed the volley came from just outside the tavern, probably from Parker's militiamen clearing their guns before going inside.[94]

The countryside was clearly alarmed, Revere's captors quickly reasoned, and they could ride much faster without a prisoner. After further interrogating Revere, Mitchell ordered him to dismount. On Mitchell's orders, the sergeant manning Revere's reins dismounted his small, tired horse as well, then cut its bridle and saddle and shooed it away, taking Revere's Brown Beauty instead. The British then cantered off, leaving Revere alone and horseless on the side of the Concord Road, just outside Lexington. Deacon Larkin's prized horse was never seen again.[95]

There was little more Revere could do to alarm the countryside, so he made his way on foot, cutting across fields and a burying ground, back to the Reverend Clarke home in Lexington.[96]

Though Revere did not yet know it, Dr. Samuel Prescott, eminently familiar with the area since he was a local, had managed to navigate through the pastures and countryside to successfully alarm Concord. Samuel and his older brother, Abel Jr., then rode off to carry the alarm still farther, the former west toward Acton, the latter south toward Sudbury and Framingham.

Meanwhile, after Revere had alerted the Mystick (Medford) minutemen, they too had sent off a rider. It was Martin Herrick, who traveled northward all the way to Salem. And Josiah Nelson, after stumbling onto the British patrol in his nightgown, had alerted nearby Bedford. Each of these alarm riders in turn sparked others, a chain reaction that carried the warning ever deeper into the countryside.[97]

The British expedition made its way past what is now Union Square in Somerville, passing by the home of Samuel Tufts. Tufts had sequestered himself and his black slave in a hut out back of his house, and together they cast musket balls, completely unaware of the troops. His neighbor, the widow Mrs. Rand, had a hog carcass hung in front of her home, slaughtered for her the day before, its blood still draining into a pool below. The poor widow was up all night, fearful someone might steal her valuable meat, when she heard a low rumbling down the road. In just her underclothes, she crept outside to investigate, and hid as the British passed. She then ran to find Tufts, who doubted her until he went to the road and discovered the many foot tracks. Thanking her, Tufts rushed to his barn, bridled his horse, and galloped off to alarm Cambridge.[98]

To make up for lost time, Lieutenant Colonel Smith marched his troops at a "hasty and fatiguing" pace, making their way next through Cambridge.[99] Ahead, two men driving a wagon of fresh milk spotted them, then frantically pulled over and attempted to unhitch their two horses. Lt. Jesse Adair of the Marines, serving as an advance scout, yelled to the mounted Tory guide Samuel Murray to ride ahead and intercept the milkmen. Lt. William Sutherland, a battalion officer of the 38th who had come as a volunteer, followed on foot. The milkmen finally got their two horses unhitched, but just as they mounted, Murray and Sutherland reached them, grabbing the farm horses' bridles while Murray simultaneously blocked their escape with his horse. Major Pitcairn then rode up and ordered the milkmen to dismount their horses, which he gave to Sutherland and Adair, while he forced the milkmen themselves to march with the column, perhaps the first two prisoners of the day.[100]

As the column passed from Cambridge toward the small village of Menotomy (now Arlington), Militia Lt. Solomon Bowman opened his front door and watched them march by. One thirsty soldier broke ranks and went to him, begging for water. Bowman refused and, once they had passed, slipped off to alert his militia company.[101]

At Menotomy's Black Horse Tavern, where the Committees of Safety and Supplies had met in a joint session the day before and were to meet again the next morning, three of the Whig leaders had decided to lodge there for the night. The rumbling in the road roused them, and the tavern landlord, Ethan Wetherby, spirited them out back to lie hidden in the wet mud bristling with the stubble of last year's cornstalks.[102]

At another house, a British officer snuck toward a barn, hoping to find a horse. This homeowner also was awake and rushed outside, shouting, "You are taking an early ride, sir!" The officer retorted, "You had better go to bed and get your sleep while you can!" But he returned to his ranks, horseless.[103]

With the town obviously astir, Smith realized their secrecy was compromised. So he halted his column to give them a momentary rest and ordered that no one was to fire unless fired upon. Smith then summoned all his officers together. Turning to Major Pitcairn, he ordered him to take the lead with six light infantry companies and double-time ahead to Concord to secure the two bridges there, lest the countryside militia be raised and secure them first.

With a salute perhaps, Pitcairn cantered to the front to ready the six companies. To set the pace and lead the detachment, he placed in the van Lieutenant Adair and a small party of perhaps eight men. The mounted volunteers Lt. William Sutherland and the Tory guide Samuel Murray also joined the detachment, as did scout Ensign De Berniere of the 10th. Pitcairn then gave the order, and the lead six companies surged forward at double time.[104]

Once they departed, Smith perceived the distant but audible tolling of church bells accompanied by occasional musket fire. He looked around with trepidation, as did all those soldiers, most of whom were exhausted and generally dejected at their onerous duty. While some of those troops were young, a majority had been in the service for many years, though most of them had little or no combat experience.[105]

Smith then made his most prudent decision of the day, ordering an express courier back to Boston to warn that the secret expedition had now been discovered and to beg General Gage for reinforcements.[106] But the expeditionary commander privately feared that such reinforcements would not arrive in time to provide much aid. The towns were alarmed, the militia would soon muster, and Smith realized he might very well have to fight through a rebellious countryside to complete his mission.

There was no time to rest. He ordered his men to re-form and march out.

———— · ————

When Revere made his way back to Reverend Clarke's parsonage, John Hancock and Samuel Adams must have been surprised to see him. After hearing Revere's story, Clarke and Adams, fearing they might yet be arrested, concluded they should escape to Woburn.[107] Hancock, however, was reluctant. Ever since Revere's earlier departure, he had been polishing and tending his musket. Hancock was eager to fight, fondly recalling his former position as the "colonel" of the Governor's Company of Cadets, a mere honor guard that hardly qualified him as a military man. Samuel Adams gave Hancock a friendly clap on the shoulder and tried to dissuade him, explaining "that is not our business; we belong to the cabinet."

So, Hancock reluctantly conceded to escape with Adams and Clarke, leaving behind his fiancée and aunt, thinking them safer there.[108] It was about half past three o'clock in the morning when the three refugees made their way by carriage to Woburn, escorted by Paul Revere and Hancock's clerk, John Lowell.[109] Sergeant Munroe and some of the militia guards meanwhile went to join their company on the Green.[110]

About this time, tradition gives that Samuel Adams said to Hancock, "It is a fine day!"

"Very pleasant," Hancock replied, noting the mild weather and moonlit sky.

"I mean," Samuel clarified, "this day is a glorious day for America!"[111]

Amid the business of escaping, Hancock had almost forgotten a trunk of papers in an upstairs chamber of Buckman Tavern, which would prove of great value to the British if it fell into their hands. So he asked Revere to fetch it. Revere enlisted Lowell to join him, and the two split off, leaving Hancock, Adams, and Reverend Clarke to make their own way to the home of a Reverend Jones in Woburn, where they soon after arrived in safety.[112]

As Revere and Lowell made their way back to Lexington Green from the west, Pitcairn and the six light infantry companies double-timed to Lexington Green from the east. And waiting at Buckman Tavern, overlooking the Green, were Captain Parker and the bulk of the Lexington militia.

CHAPTER 8

THE RENDING OF AN EMPIRE

While Major Pitcairn's six light infantry companies double-timed through the moonlit western outskirts of Menotomy, his flankers in the adjoining fields struggled to keep up. Pitcairn also deployed several advance scouts, some mounted, at a considerable distance ahead of his column. These scouts would pause at times and take up concealed positions on either side of the road, hoping to surprise any unsuspecting colonial rider that happened by.

One such rider was the second of the two men Captain Parker had earlier dispatched from Lexington to seek this alleged British column. The first had ridden a different route and had reported back that he could find nothing. This one dared to ride farther, all the way toward Menotomy. When he passed a concealed advance party, the British soldiers sprang from their hiding places, trapping Parker's man between themselves and the approaching main column. The advance party forced the Lexington man to dismount, confiscated his horse and gave it to an officer, and ordered the hapless American to march with the other prisoners at the British rear. Consequently, Lexington received no intelligence of the British approach.[1]

A little farther, Pitcairn's advance guard spotted almost a dozen riders swiftly cantering toward them. Much to their surprise, one yelled that day's parole, which meant only one thing: these riders were British! The advance party yelled back the countersign, "Patrole!"[2] This was Major

Mitchell's patrol, which had slipped by Lexington Green unnoticed, perhaps by taking to the pastures. Mitchell reported what Pitcairn already knew: the countryside was alarmed.

Just then, a few musket shots sounded in the distance. Others also noticed the fire beacons burning as alarms off on the horizon.[3] Given the signs, Pitcairn could have ordered his men to load their muskets and be ready—but he did not. He still expected the people would give way.[4]

As the column made their way toward Lexington, the advance guard captured several other country folk. Some were militia; others were mere tradesmen. One "very genteel man" rode toward them in a horse-drawn "Sulky" carriage. He stopped and warned them that six hundred men had gathered at Lexington and awaited their arrival. This was an exaggeration, but because the British thought him a Tory and his intelligence genuine, they permitted him to proceed unmolested.

In fact, he was no Tory. He soon after alerted some converging militia companies to the east, which consequently rounded the British column and got ahead of them.[5] Another man, Simon Winship, was captured two and a half miles from Lexington, "peaceably and unarmed".[6] Still another countryman, driving his wagon full of wood, gave the exaggerated claim that there were "odds of 1000 men in Arms" at Lexington and that they intended to fight.[7]

At this, Pitcairn thought it prudent to heed the warnings. Amid the first hints of daylight around four that morning, he ordered his men to halt there in the road east of Lexington and deploy into firing position, to await the supposed thousand-man Yankee army. But no such army came, and at length, Pitcairn ordered his men to re-form and march out.

As a precaution, volunteer Lieutenant Sutherland rode up ahead about a half mile and took a trail to his left to scout the situation. In the moonlight, he could make out several bands of militia in arms, marching over a hill toward Concord via Lexington. However, he saw no Yankee column advancing. So he spurred his horse forward and galloped up to one straggling militiaman, whom he "mett…in the Teeth". (Did that mean Sutherland punched him in the face?) Sutherland obliged the man to give up his musket and bayonet, "which I believe he would not have done so easily but from Mr. Adair's coming up." As the British column reached Sutherland, this militiaman, Benjamin

Wellington, was released on the promise that he return home. He would do no such thing, and instead took a circuitous route back to Lexington Green to warn the others.[8]

Sutherland then rejoined an advance scouting party that included a sergeant and six or eight men. As they advanced, they were startled to hear several shots fired. Sutherland saw the telltale thick, white smoke "to the right & left of us, but as we heard no Whissing of Balls I Conclude they were to Alarm the body that was there of our Approach". Undeterred, the roaming volunteer Sutherland split from this advance party and instead joined that of Lieutenant Adair, nearer the main column. As they approached with a mile or so of Lexington Green, a stray militiaman upon the right side of the road ahead turned with his musket…and fired!

Flintlock muskets worked by first igniting a priming charge, which then ignited the cartridge in the barrel and in turn fired the ball. However, while this militiaman's musket thundered as its priming charge ignited in its pan ("the Piece flashed in the Pan"), emanating a puff of white smoke, the primary charge never fired, and no ball came whizzing by Lieutenant Sutherland. The thankful lieutenant quickly called Adair to look over, who turned in time to see the white smoke dissipating as the man took off and ran.[9]

Did the gun fail to fire because it was not loaded with an actual charge, or did it misfire? Alternatively, was the colonial an oaf who accidentally discharged his piece, or was he an overzealous belligerent, who attempted to fire on the British and singlehandedly start a war? The answers to these questions are unknown to history, but regardless of his motives, he can perhaps be blamed for the events that happened next.

When Sutherland and Adair related this incident to Major Pitcairn, who was riding back alongside the main column, Pitcairn halted his men once more on that road east of Lexington and this time ordered them to charge their muskets. Pitcairn cannot be blamed for taking such measures. Accident or not, one of his men had just been fired upon— Pitcairn could not risk their safety. But this one colonist, whether by accident or design, had singlehandedly convinced the British column— the same column that had marched all this time with their guns *unloaded*—to only now load their weapons, and so paved the way to bloodshed and war.[10]

Once the men halted, Pitcairn gave his fateful order to charge fire-locks, while his six company commanders gave the multiple specific commands necessary for the men to actually load their muskets in cadence. By command, the men took a paper cartridge holding gun-powder and a ball from their right hip's cartouche boxes, bit off the top, and spit it to the ground. They poured some powder in the flintlock's priming pan, shut the pan, and then rammed the rest of the cartridge (powder, ball, and all) into the top of the musket with a ramrod that sat stowed below the barrel. Once the rammer was restowed, they shoul-dered their arms and were ready.[11]

As the green fields grew more vivid with the fast approaching sunrise, Pitcairn galloped along his column, ordering the men "on no account to Fire, or even attempt it without orders". Then, Pitcairn gave the order and the light infantry again set out at a double-time march, leaving behind a trodden dirt road littered with white paper cartridges.[12]

The British were now less than half a mile from Lexington Green.

———— ·•· ————

Capt. John Parker, commander of the Lexington militia, remained igno-rant of what was happening just down the road. Waiting in Lexington's Buckman Tavern with many of his company, he finally grew impatient and sent Thaddeus Bowman on a horse to reconnoiter eastward. Bowman rode off "pretty rapidly" when "his horse became suddenly frightened, stopped, and refused to go forward." Suddenly, just ahead, two British scouts leaped from opposite sides of the road. Bowman struggled to turn his horse, only to notice the British column in the distance. Finally, with the scouts nearly upon him, Bowman's horse responded, and he galloped off to Lexington and reported to Captain Parker. As he did, Benjamin Wellington, whom the British had released on the condition he return home, arrived and confirmed everything.[13]

With this, Parker and his men swarmed out the tavern and onto Lexington Green. As Parker scanned the Green for his drummer, Paul Revere and John Lowell were racing on foot toward Buckman Tavern in search of Hancock's trunk of papers. History does not record whether Parker saw them.[14] Parker found nineteen-year-old William Diamond, the company's musician, and ordered him to beat his drum.[15] The furious, rattling beat of that rope-tension snare drum quickly summoned the confused militia from their nearby homes. And amid this confusion, Parker endeavored to form his men. Down the road, now plainly in sight, the British column drove ever toward them.

⊷⊷

The sun began its ascent over the horizon about five o'clock that morning of April 19, 1775, bringing a little warmth to an otherwise windy and cool spring day.[16] The red sky and its radiant sunbeams backlit the red-coated British light infantry with terrific splendor as they charged double-time toward the triangular Lexington Green, a sight that must have sent shock and horror into the Lexington men waiting there.

Perhaps the town's small belfry pealed another alarm, but after its last echoes died away, the column of regulars heard only the drumming of William Diamond. Parker urgently formed his militia into two ranks or divisions one man deep, placing them side by side with an interval between them as wide as the divisions themselves, thus forming one gapped line obstructing the Green.[17] But the British approached too quickly. Parker realized he had no more than eighty of his men mustered—barely half his company. Another forty or more spectators, including some armed militiamen (especially the retired reserve), watched from the tavern and houses lining the two streets that formed the Green.[18]

For the British to march to Concord, they should have forked left as they came to the triangular Green, keeping the Green and its meetinghouse upon their right and taking the Concord Road westward. But hard-charging Lieutenant Adair, leading the advance party that set the pace and direction for the main column, saw the mustering of militia and the beating of their drum as a challenge.[19] As if to punctuate this challenge, three shots rang out from Buckman Tavern, meant as alarm shots to summon any remaining militia nearby.

Unwilling to place an armed mob on the British right flank, Adair made a fateful decision. Instead of taking the left fork in the road, he charged his advance party directly toward Parker's militia.[20] Next in column, Captain Parsons followed Adair's lead, ordering his 10th Lights to charge on after, as did Lt. Edward Gould and his 4th.[21]

When William Diamond ceased his drum roll, all became silent but for the rhythmic footfalls as the British plowed toward them. From the British perspective, the militia company stood there as an affront, a challenge to their mighty prestige. Perhaps Adair was that officer Americans later reported as having yelled, "Damn them! We will have them!"[22]

To add menace to the British charge, they began shouting "Huzza! Huzza!" in taunting reply to the militia's defiance, imbuing the soldiers with spirit and fortitude.[23] Though their antagonistic tactics made the British seem ferocious, as Lt. John Barker wrote in his diary, the redcoats were "prepared against an attack[,] tho' without intending to attack them". That is, while the British may have taken a foolishly aggressive posture, they held a genuine desire to avoid bloodshed.[24]

Such foolishness was not limited to the British side. What was Parker thinking to have mustered his men and formed them in battle array?[25] Rev. Jonas Clarke a year later proposed that Parker had not "any design of opposing so superior a force, much less of commencing hostilities; but only with a view to determine what to do, when and where to meet, and to dismiss and disperse."[26] If that was true, Parker was incompetently slow at dismissing his men. Rather, he may have been contemplating a daring protest—one that seemed suicidal only after he saw the oncoming British. According to his own testimony afterward, he had concluded not to "meddle or make with said Regular Troops…unless they should insult us".[27] "Let the troops pass by," he told his men, "and do not molest them, without they being first."[28]

Whatever Parker's justification, both sides saw the others' action as a challenge, resulting in a deadly game of chicken. As the lead British companies surged onto the Green, they fanned into line formation three ranks deep,[29] positioning themselves at the east end of the meetinghouse some 130 feet from Parker's men.[30] Perhaps it was Adair again, mounted on his trusty steed, who called out to the militia: "throw down your Arms & you shall come to no harm".[31]

Only now, as Parker saw the British before him, did he give his men explicit orders: "I immediately ordered our Militia to disperse and not fire."[32] Upon this, some of the militia readily began to fall back, "but, many of them, not so speedily as they might have done".[33] Jonas Parker of the militia refused to retreat and openly avowed he would never run.[34] Others prudently dispersed toward a hedge or wall across from the Green on the north side.[35]

Major Pitcairn, who had been riding alongside the rear of his column, realized what was unfolding. He first ordered his remaining men to take the south fork in the road, as the vanguard should have done.[36] Pitcairn then spurred his horse into a gallop and rode along the Concord Road that hugged the south side of the Green, thus rounding the confrontation, before pulling his horse hard right and positioning himself directly between the two adversaries, while yelling to his men, "Do not fire!" As Pitcairn made himself an obstacle, so too did several of the other horsemen, including Major Mitchell and some of his patrolmen, as did Lieutenant Sutherland.[37]

Pitcairn then yelled to the rebels, something like, "Throw down your arms and disperse!"[38] Some dispersed, though they kept their arms, but too many stubborn Yankees stood their ground.

As Pitcairn's troops continued to huzzah, he repeated to his men, "Do not fire!"[39]

Another officer may have yelled, "Keep your ranks!"[40]

Pitcairn repeated his orders to the militia to disarm and disperse, but they remained steadfast. Finally, Pitcairn, hoping to defuse the situation, gave another order to his men: "Surround and disarm them!"[41]

The front ranks of the British continued to huzzah, even as they cautiously stepped toward the militia. The militia's Captain Parker had already fallen back, but he yelled again to those still in position: "Disperse!" and "Do not fire!" Some Americans stood frozen with fear, but many that remained were pigheaded and itching for a fight. Regardless of Parker's orders, handfuls doggedly remained.

Americans later said they had heard from Pitcairn or some other officer, "Ye villains, ye Rebels, disperse! Damn you, disperse!"[42] One of the mounted officers reportedly yelled, "Lay down your arms! Damn you, why don't you lay down your arms!"[43]

All of this tumult and confusion happened in a matter of seconds. The loud and continuous huzzahs added to the frenzy as British officers yelled contradictory orders—some said *Disperse*, some said *Lay down your arms*—giving the militia cause for confusion. Those few militiamen who actually dispersed retreated to the nearby hedge wall and hopped over. Spectators alongside the Green stood in horror and awe. The frightful huzzahs continued as redcoats and militia shouted orders to one another.[44]

And then...a shot rang out!

Where the shot came from, no one knows to this day. Americans swore they heard a pistol first, suggesting one of the British officers, but the British swore they saw smoke from several fired shots as the militia jumped over the hedge wall, while still other British said they saw smoke pour out of the meetinghouse. Undoubtedly, one or more Americans indeed fired shots from inside the meetinghouse, as they did from the back of Buckman Tavern, but whether any of these were the first shot, or simply shots fired in response to the first, is unknown. One can only speculate, based on the discrepant evidence, but there is a very plausible theory that an American fired first, from the meetinghouse or hedge wall.[45]

Why the shot rang out is another question altogether and equally misunderstood. Perhaps, amid the confusion, someone lost his cool. Equally credible, some zealot deliberately wished to begin a war. A third possibility, just as likely, was that a musket accidentally fired. It was the most inopportune time for such a misfire, but most of the militiamen there carried older muskets they or their fathers had kept as trophies from the Seven Years' War. Misfires and accidents with those archaic guns were all too common.[46]

Regardless of who fired first (whether one shot or more), and whether it was an accident or intentional, it did not matter: the scene devolved into utter pandemonium. Immediately and without orders, a portion of the front British ranks—enraged and confused as they were—fired off a volley, their muskets belching thick white smoke.[47] Their shots instantly killed one, while others fell wounded, several bleeding profusely and soon to expire.

Most of the remaining Americans finally began to fall back, but others stood their ground and fired scattered return shots. Their shots were mostly errant,[48] but two balls grazed the flank of Major Pitcairn's horse, and one slammed into the leg of a private soldier named "Johnson" of the 10th, possibly Thomas Johnston.[49] American Ebenezer Munroe vividly remembered decades later, "The balls flew so thick, I thought there was no chance for escape, and that I might as well fire my gun as stand still and do nothing."[50]

As Paul Revere and John Lowell ran across the far side of the Green with Hancock's trunk of papers,[51] the white smoke of the guns billowed into the space between the belligerents, blinding the combatants as they worked desperately to reload their muskets and shrouding Pitcairn and his officers who desperately yelled to cease fire.

The Americans fired a few more shots as they fell back from the Green, while others whizzed out from the meetinghouse and from behind Buckman Tavern, all without effect.[52] Simultaneously, some of the British replied with another unordered, scattered volley.[53] As they did, the British officers frantically and desperately tried to get their men under control. Major Pitcairn unsheathed his sword and, by slashing and waving it through the air, furiously gestured the cease-fire.[54]

The handful of Americans who stubbornly remained on the Green, upon seeing their dead countrymen and only now heeding their own captain's orders, finally turned and ran in retreat. A few British soldiers immediately broke ranks and charged in pursuit.[55] One soldier ran toward wounded militiaman Jonas Parker (cousin of the captain), who, though writhing in pain on the ground, had his gun in his hand, apparently attempting to reload. The soldier smashed his bayonet through the militiaman's body, and with a literal gut-wrenching twist, disemboweled him on the spot.[56] At the same time, a few light infantry rushed toward the meetinghouse to drive from it the militia snipers there.[57]

Just then, Lieutenant Colonel Smith's main column (the rear light companies and the entire grenadiers) arrived along the Concord Road on the south edge of the Green. There they found Lieutenant Sutherland's horse spooked and carrying him toward some woods, where a hidden militia party fired upon him, missing. The grenadiers fired back, dispersing the militia there.[58]

Smith himself galloped onto the Green, where Sutherland joined him, and Smith looked around for a drummer to sound the cease-fire. As he did, three shots whizzed by his head. Sutherland spotted the billows of smoke emanating from the meetinghouse.[59] Despite those shots, Smith gave positive orders not to storm the houses or the meetinghouse, for, as he later wrote, "I was desirous of puting a stop to all further Slaughter of those deluded People".[60]

But, according to General Gage's official account afterward, "Notwithstanding the Fire from the Meeting House, [Lieutenant] Colonel Smith and major Pitcairn, with the greatest Difficulty, kept the Soldiers from forcing into the Meeting-House and putting all those in it to Death."[61] Good thing they had, for a late story, probably more legend than truth, gives that Joshua Simonds stood ready for them in the meetinghouse's upper gallery, his musket cocked and ready, its muzzle dug into an open cask of powder standing near him, determined to "touch it off" in case the troops entered.[62]

Finally, the British drums began to beat, even as the officers and sergeants barked their orders. But "the Men were so wild they cou'd hear no orders" and it took some time to regain control.[63] At length, the officers succeeded in re-forming the British ranks.

The rest of the Lexington militia licked their wounds and scattered, while spectators cried out in horror, some of them seeing their fathers or sons lying dead on the Green. Seven colonists lay unmoving on the field of battle. Another ten lay wounded and writhing in agony. One of the dead was Caleb Harrington, who, just before the British arrival, had gone with three others into the meetinghouse to resupply his gunpowder. When he haplessly stepped out at the wrong moment, he was gunned down in the crossfire. His other three companions likely were the snipers in that building that tried to pick off officers such as Lieutenant Colonel Smith.[64] Of the wounded militiamen, one was another Harrington named Jonathan, who crawled across the Green to his nearby house and up to his front door, leaving behind him a trail of blood. He tried to stand, revealing a bloody, gushing wound in his breast, but stumbled and fell again. His wailing wife rushed outside and knelt down to hold him as he died in her arms.[65] The final death toll thus became eight.[66] With the British troops finally in order, women and noncombatants poured onto the field to attend the casualties.

Smith called his officers together for a conference. Only now did he reveal to them all the object of their mission: the war stores at Concord.[67]

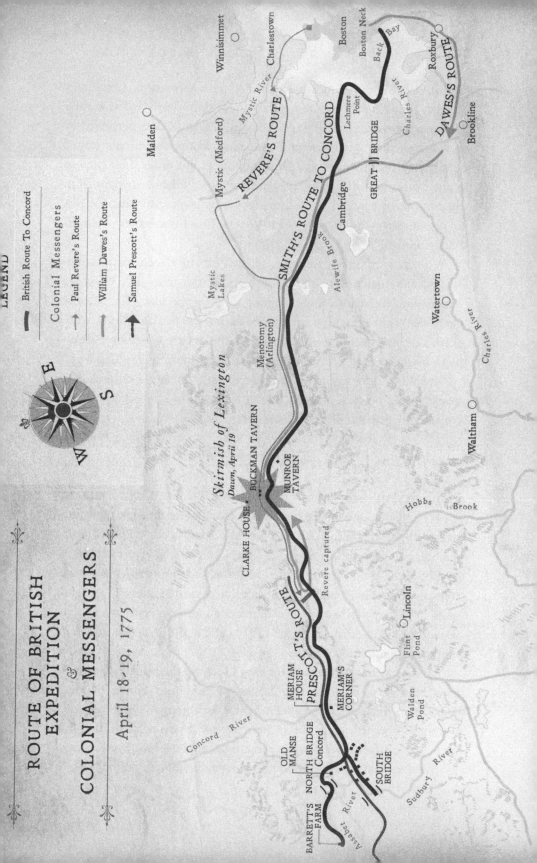

ROUTE OF BRITISH
EXPEDITION
&
COLONIAL MESSENGERS

April 18–19, 1775

LEGEND

British Route To Concord
Colonial Messengers
Paul Revere's Route
William Dawes's Route
Samuel Prescott's Route

N E S W

Malden

Winnisimmet

Mystic River

Charlestown

Boston

Boston Neck

Back Bay

Roxbury

DAWES'S ROUTE

Brookline

Charles River

Mystic (Medford)

REVERE'S ROUTE

Mystic

Lechmere
Point

GREAT BRIDGE

Cambridge

SMITH'S ROUTE TO CONCORD

Alewife Brook

Watertown

Charles River

Mystic
Lakes

Menotomy
(Arlington)

Waltham

Hobbs Brook

Skirmish of Lexington
Dawn, April 19

BUCKMAN TAVERN

CLARKE HOUSE

MUNROE TAVERN

Revere captured

Lincoln

Flint
Pond

Walden
Pond

River

Sudbury River

MERIAM
HOUSE

PRESCOTT'S ROUTE

MERIAM'S
CORNER

OLD
MANSE

NORTH BRIDGE
Concord

SOUTH
BRIDGE

BARRETT'S
FARM

Assabet River

Concord River

Smith next put his troops back into column formation. Once they shifted, the officers ordered a volley fired, doubtlessly to clear their guns, rather than a celebratory volley as the Americans perceived it. The British then left their guns unloaded, as they genuinely hoped to avoid further bloodshed.[68] But the officers did order their men to replenish the top half of their cartouche boxes with cartridges from the bottom section, to be ready for a firefight—just in case. Finally, as one massive thundering voice, they yelled three times: "Huzza! Huzza! Huzza!"[69]

With that, the few companies formed on the Green lurched into motion and marched to the western tip of the triangular Green to reunite with the main column waiting there on the road. The advance guard then split off and reconnoitered ahead, the flankers dispersed to either side, and then the entire main column, a long red ribbon of soldiers, began to stream forward, westward along the Concord Road.

The Skirmish of Lexington had lasted just moments. But news of it would spread quickly, and the British had a lot of countryside left to cross in order to complete their mission.

———— • ————

With a bright morning sun at their backs, the reunited British column made its way along the Concord Road, meandering through the countryside of pastures and scattered woods dotted with the occasional rolling hill. Flankers trod through the terrain on either side of the road to guard the column as it marched in haunting cadence toward Concord. In many places, knee-high rock walls delineated the road from the pastures.[70] On the hills beyond, occasional small militia parties made their way in the same direction as the British, the result of the alarm set in motion by the midnight riders.

For the last mile stretch leading into Concord, the fields to the north grew into steep, wood-covered ledges, the southeast corner of these slopes known as Meriam's Corner, named for the man whose property was there. The British could now hear the town's pealing alarm bell and occasional musket shots.[71] It was perhaps there, at the base of this acclivity, that Lieutenant Sutherland noticed several horsemen on the hills, "I

Suppose…to know our numbers & to make the Cowardly disposition".[72] About this time, two shots rang out. The thunder of the guns immediately attracted Lieutenant Colonel Smith's attention. He scanned the hills and found the telltale white smoke plumes, but as no balls whizzed by, he deduced they were just more alarm shots, fired to warn the people of Concord.[73]

As the long, red column made its way along a bend in the road, streaming northwestward, hugging the base of the slopes to their right, they for the first time laid eyes upon Concord off in the distance. But upon those same ledges on their right guarding the approach into the town, they saw a contingent of maybe one hundred fifty minutemen, all from Concord, Lincoln, and Acton.[74] Pitcairn, still in charge of the light infantry in the vanguard, ordered that they split off from the main body and cautiously take the hill to disperse the Yankees. The "light Infantry…ascended the height in one line, upon which the Yankies quitted it without firing, which they did likewise for one or two more successively."[75]

The lights continued to press the minutemen from one slope to the next, until the colonists at last drew far back to an eastern mound overlooking the town center. The lower slope of this mound was mostly dedicated to a burial ground, but along its south edge stood a small overlook that prominently featured a liberty pole, upon which flew some kind of illegal flag that incensed the British commanders. Perhaps it was the British Union flag, considered then the King's property and not to be used by citizens. Whatever it was, the liberty pole stood not only as a symbol but also as a militia rallying point for the town. From that vantage point, the minutemen could observe all of Concord.[76]

It was about 7:30 a.m. when the British column of grenadiers finally marched into the town proper, the light infantry keeping to the slopes above the road.[77] The people were well aware of their coming, thanks in no small part to Dr. Samuel Prescott, the rider who had accompanied Paul Revere but had escaped capture. So as the British poured into the town, they saw many fearful spectators popping out from all the houses and the central Wright Tavern. Most of these were women, children, and elders too old to join the militia upon the eastern hill. Yet the town still seemed a bit abandoned, with fewer spectators than the British anticipated.

As the grenadiers silently filed into the town center, without music or fanfare, the light infantry continued on the rugged, wooded terrain above. There they saw ahead of them the waiting minutemen, but a deep gully stood between them. The lights had to turn to navigate around it, giving Militia Col. James Barrett, the sixty-five-year-old commander of the minutemen gathered there, a moment to address his men. The colonel, who wore no uniform but instead "an old coat, a flapped hat, and a leather apron",[78] reminded them all of the dangers to which they were exposed and cautioned them not to be careless or needlessly endanger themselves, but to be cool and firm, and most importantly, to not fire unless fired upon.

With that, Barrett thought it prudent to withdraw again and so gave the order. As they did, the lights surpassed the gully and took the Americans' former position on the overlooking eastern slope. Lt. John Barker of the 4th Light Infantry was surprised to see the militia flee once more, writing, "we expected they wou'd have made a stand there, but they did not chuse it." As the Americans silently fled, the light infantry continued their march across the slope to the burial ground. There, Smith and Pitcairn hiked up from the town below, and upon inspecting the liberty pole and its flag, Smith promptly ordered it cut down, thinking it emblematic of sedition.[79]

Smith then summoned Capt. Lawrence Parsons of his own 10th regiment and ordered him to lead six light infantry companies northward, past the North Bridge under a mile away, and onward to Col. James Barrett's Farm about two miles farther to discover and then destroy the war stores known to be held there. Parsons acknowledged the order, selected his companies, and marched them immediately northward. To guide him, he brought Ens. Henry De Berniere, the scout familiar with the area.[80]

Militia Colonel Barrett and his minutemen remained near for a short time, lingering along the road just north of town as an organized body, though Lieutenant Sutherland noted that at least a handful scurried through the adjacent woods.[81] When Barrett saw Parson's six companies starting their march northward, he at once knew their destination was his own farm. Yet he was unwilling to risk his men to prevent the British march. So he gave the order to withdraw once more, this time past North Bridge. There he could keep an eye on the British while safely gathering his militia's strength, hoping to draw together all of the various companies still making their way to Concord.[82]

With his six companies departing, Lieutenant Colonel Smith next ordered maybe two light companies to secure the South Bridge, west of the town center (where modern Main Street crosses the Concord River), to guard that approach into town. The lieutenant colonel then seems to have ordered his remaining two light companies to deploy across the burial hill and provide cover for his troops on the ground below.[83] Aided by his Tory guides and the map provided him from General Gage, Smith next ordered his grenadiers to begin a targeted search for munitions. The grenadiers immediately fanned out to the various homes and businesses, eager to get on with their job so they could get back to Boston and get some sleep.[84]

Just north of the town, as the six light companies approached North Bridge, they found again the minutemen, who withdrew to a hill on the opposite side of the bridge, where gathered a small crowd of women and children, earlier evacuated from Concord. The minutemen sent these evacuees still farther away "at a great distance to the Woods."[85] Then, instead of following the road west toward Barrett's Farm, the minutemen took a northerly fork toward a large hill, atop which were already mustered hundreds of militia, the first of the neighboring towns' companies to arrive in response to the alarm.[86]

Tradition says that hill was Punkatasset Hill, or specifically Hunt Farm on its southern slopes, a commanding position that reached more than three hundred feet at the precipice and stood north of the bridge about a mile. In 1775, with its vantage not obstructed by the many houses and modern woods that now fill the once expansive pastures, the militia could clearly see the North Bridge and the vibrant red dots that were the British. Once the withdrawing minutemen reached this hill, the total force there swelled to three hundred or four hundred men, with additional companies en route.[87] Satisfied his men were out of the way of the British, Colonel Barrett grabbed a horse and rode off to warn his family of the coming redcoats, but was soon back with his men on Punkatasset Hill.[88]

Captain Parsons meanwhile led his British across the North Bridge, but was concerned with the large body of Americans atop Punkatasset

Hill. Once his column was completely across the bridge and at the fork in the road, he halted them and surveyed the situation. He wisely determined to protect his escape path and so ordered the 5th and the 43rd to cover the bridge, which he placed under the command of the 43rd's Capt. Walter Sloane Laurie.[89]

With the bridge secured, instead of marching westward toward his destination, Parsons turned his four remaining light companies onto the northerly road the Americans had taken, following this only about a quarter mile to a rolling hill where Militia Maj. John Buttrick's house stood (near the modern National Park Service Welcome Center). From atop that hill, Parsons could see much of the surrounding area. He thought it prudent to detach the 10th under Lt. Waldron Kelly to cover that hill, and the 4th under Lt. Edward Gould, which took a higher hill slightly west. Satisfied, Parsons turned his remaining two companies, the 38th and the 52nd, and marched back to the fork, taking the westerly road the nearly two miles to Barrett's Farm.[90]

Back in Concord center, as the grenadiers began to scour the town, the citizens reacted with minor acts of civil disobedience. Pitcairn and Smith tried their best, at "all possible pains", to convince the townspeople that the British meant them no injury. If they only opened their doors when required, "not the slightest mischief would be done." Smith found the people "were sulky".[91]

The Concordians had good reason to be sulky. They endured indignity as they watched, upon the hill above, the light infantry saw through the base of their proud liberty pole until it finally came crashing to the ground.

Smith also had reason to be sulky. Some townsman, perhaps a Tory or even a Whig trying to avert an unwarranted search and seizure, informed him "that some cannon had been taken out of the town that day, that others, with some stores, had been carried three days before". Such news robbed Smith of any real success for his mission. As he noted later to Gage, it "prevented our having an opportunity of destroying so much as might have expected at our first setting off."[92]

Smith's new intelligence was a slight understatement. While the Provincial Committee of Safety, sans Dr. Warren, had indeed met for the two days prior and voted to disperse the bulk of their war stores to neighboring towns (select items were to remain hidden in Concord), much of this was not yet done.[93] Rather, it was because of Dr. Samuel Prescott's midnight ride, by which he raised the alarm in town, aided further by the long delays in the British amphibious landing and their delay on Lexington Green, that the Concord militia were able to conceal, secure, or otherwise spirit away a great bulk of the stores just hours before the British arrived.[94] Thus, for all their effort, the British would find very little in that sleepy New England town.

Nevertheless, as some of the soldiers queued to drink from a town well,[95] the rest of the grenadiers went to work, going house to house for the stores as prescribed by the map Lieutenant Colonel Smith carried with him.

One of their chief discoveries was not powder or cannon or even musket balls, but flour. The British found a considerable store of flour in Mr. Ebenezer Hubbard's mill (or malt) house, flour supposed to belong to the province and so intended to feed an army. The grenadiers broke open the boards at one end of the house and rolled the barrels out the wall and into the road. They then busted the barrels into pieces, dumping the flour onto the street. There was so much of this flour that it appeared as if it had snowed.[96]

Other grenadiers proceeded to a storehouse of Militia Capt. Timothy Wheeler, there expecting to find more flour. The grenadiers found the storehouse locked and so prepared to break in the door when Wheeler joined them and offered the key. Inside, they found another large supply of flour barrels and bags, all but two small bags of which belonged to the province. Wheeler's cunning was remarkable, but he could not tell a lie. So he escorted the grenadiers into his storeroom, and when the grenadiers asked him which of it was public property, he turned beside his own two bags and replied, "Gentlemen, I am a miller, and declare to you, that every gill of *this* is mine," at the same time smacking one of those two bags that was indeed his. "Well," the officer in charge replied, taking him at his word, "we do not injure private property". And so the officer ordered his grenadiers out, leaving the whole of the flour untouched.[97]

At the main gristmill, which stood upon a dam that blocked old Mill Brook, the grenadiers found more barrels. They carelessly threw the unbroken casks into the "Mill Pond", that part of the brook swollen behind the mill's dam. The wet flour along the edges of the barrel swelled inside, forming a thick paste that sealed the barrel and made it waterproof. Later, after the British left, the townspeople salvaged the barrels and found a considerable part of the flour inside unspoiled, protected as it was by this outer slurry.[98] In all, about sixty (some say one hundred) barrels of flour were destroyed, although perhaps half of the flour was saved.[99]

Flour was not the only store the grenadiers found. In other hiding places, they discovered small quantities of gunpowder and a considerable number of musket balls, 500 pounds of them, or about 5,500 total shot, kept perhaps in two half-filled quarter barrels. The grenadiers tossed these in the Mill Brook and down water wells.[100]

The greatest find promised to be whatever colonial cannon still resided in the town. At the Jones Tavern, where British intelligence reported several cannon hidden, the grenadiers found the door barred and Mr. Ephraim Jones refusing to open it. Major Pitcairn came over and demanded, with cursing and abusive behavior, that Jones open his tavern. Lieutenant Colonel Smith later reported that someone that day hit Pitcairn—probably it was Jones. This might have been cause for arrest, had the British Army been the devils the Americans thought them to be, but whoever hit Pitcairn, nothing was done about it. In any event, Jones the tavern keeper remained defiant. So Pitcairn ordered the troops to kick in the door, and then Pitcairn led them as they stormed inside, knocking the tavern keeper over in the process. The troops found nothing, so Pitcairn decided to take more aggressive measures. He pulled out one of his two pistols and, at the point of a gun, convinced Jones to show them the way to the hidden cannon. At last, Pitcairn had his way. Jones, not only a barkeep but also a jailer, took the troops to the back of the tavern and out the door to the jail yard beyond. There, concealed under dirt or leaves, lay three large iron 24-pounders, which the grenadiers rendered useless by pounding off their trunnions (pivots). In the prison, Pitcairn found two men, one held for the crime of being a Tory, both of whom he promptly released. Afterward, Pitcairn released Jones and surprised him by ordering breakfast—and paying for it. Other soldiers came too, mostly to buy shots of rum.[101]

Had the grenadiers known where to look, they might have found other cannon, buried under the freshly furrowed dirt of the fields or under piles of manure.[102] But the three 24s were the only cannon they found that day.

Smith obviously thought his work in Concord secure when he decided to send one more light company, the 23rd Welch Fusiliers, up to Captain Parsons at Barrett's Farm. So the 23rd marched to the North Bridge, escorted by a confiscated horse-drawn chaise carrying Capt. John Brown (the scout who had explored the countryside with De Berniere) as well as 1st Lt. William Grant of the Artillery, sent to help oversee the destruction of any cannon at Barrett's Farm.[103]

At the bridge, Captain Laurie stood with his two companies, having waited for near an hour, ever watchful of the gathering militia on the distant northern hill. When the 23rd came marching up from Concord, only to proceed to Barrett's Farm, Laurie probably felt dismayed. But when a messenger arrived from the farm ordering him to send the 5th Lights up as well, he was quite annoyed, yet complied. The American force was swelling even as his was dwindling. He had only his 43rd company at the bridge now, and the 10th and 4th on the nearby hill.[104]

On Punkatasset Hill, Colonel Barrett grew more confident as he watched the 5th Lights march off, figuring his forces now outnumbered the remaining British at least three to one. And so the Yankee commander decided at last to demonstrate boldness. He ordered his men to fall in, and together they descended Punkatasset Hill and began the near one-mile march toward the bridge and the waiting British.[105]

With Barrett's "large Body of Men…[marching] up with the greatest regularity" toward North Bridge, the officers of the 10th Light Infantry on that small knoll governing their approach discussed how to proceed. Ens. Jeremy Lister told acting company commander Lieutenant Kelly that it seemed they were marching "with an intent to attack". Kelly agreed, and so they marched the 10th to the adjacent higher hill to the west, joining the 4th Light Infantry.[106] There all the officers consulted.

The 4th's Lieutenant Barker thought it "seemed as if they were going to cut off the communication with the Bridge".[107] The 4th's acting company commander Lt. Edward Gould and the others agreed and decided, given that they were outnumbered, they should fall back to the North Bridge.[108] Lister objected because they "had to go down a steapish hill, and just in a manner under the Mussels of the Rebels pieces, therefore if they chose to fire upon us[,] which was expected[,] they might have cut us off almost to a Man". But Lister was "over ruild," and so the two companies began descending the hills for the bridge.[109]

Volunteer Lieutenant Sutherland, meanwhile, had given up his horse, and after reconnoitering the area, was on his way with two escorts to the farm. But when he "saw a large body of [militia] men marching almost within Pistol shot of me, it struck me it would be disgracefull to be taken by such Rascals & I made the best of my way for the Bridge".[110]

At the bridge, Captain Laurie thought the Yankees were pursuing his two light infantry companies moving down to him. He turned to his Lt. Alexander Robertson and ordered him to immediately return to Concord center and acquaint Lieutenant Colonel Smith of the situation and beg he send grenadiers for support in case the militia should attack. Robertson mounted a horse, perhaps the one Sutherland had given up, and immediately galloped southward.[111]

As the British advance companies joined those on the North Bridge, the large body of militia drew ever closer...and then halted! The Yankees took position upon a hill near where the advance British companies just vacated. There, Barrett placed his militia behind a small rock wall, and they remained, as Laurie put it, "with Shouldered Arms...looking at us".[112] The two opposing forces now stood within a quarter mile of one another. The colonial militia included the full companies from Bedford, Acton, and Concord, plus the small force from nearby Carlisle, as well as groups or individuals from the farther away Chelmsford, Westford, and Littleton. In all, the colonials were near four hundred fifty strong, greatly outnumbering the three companies of about one hundred British.[113]

———◆———

When Captain Parsons and his men arrived at Barrett's Farm, he begged Mrs. Barrett for victuals and drinks for the men, and offered to pay. She refused payment, retorting, "we are commanded to feed our enemy, if he hunger." Parsons assured her good treatment, but said they must search her house and destroy any public stores, though her personal property was safe. But when they found the eldest Barrett son, a young man, they threatened to arrest him as a rebel until Mrs. Barrett assured them, "he is my son, and not the master of the house." The British ignored the second son, disabled at the time.[114]

When the 23rd and 5th Lights arrived, Parsons had more than one hundred forty men to comb the farm. Yet they found only a few cannon carriages and wooden accessories, which they piled up outside the barn. None could find the supposed four brass cannon or the two large mortars, now concealed in the dirt in freshly plowed furrows. And thanks to the forewarning from her husband, none discovered in the attic the casks of assorted small cannon implements, musket balls, flints, and other items, all concealed under a pile of feathers meant for down pillows, hidden by Mrs. Barrett and her sons just before the British arrival.

Once the redcoats gave up their futile search, they prepared to set aflame the wood accessories piled in front of the barn. Fearing that the fire might also set the barn ablaze, Mrs. Barrett reminded them of their promise to leave her property undamaged. The officers apologized, had the pile moved to the street, and there torched it.[115]

In Concord center, the British there were preparing their own bonfire. In the town's meetinghouse, they found a number of entrenching tools, which they carried into the street and piled near the courthouse, next to a few barrels of wooden trenchers (wood carved plates) and spoons.[116] To add to the wood stack, the soldiers rolled over the three carriages that belonged to the 24-pounder cannon found at the jail yard, along with their associated wooden limbers. They found too about twenty-three extra carriage wheels and a couple of smaller gun carriages and limbers, also thrown onto the pile.[117] Finally, the British added one more inflammable object, sure to also inflame the spectators' spirits: the town's beloved liberty pole.[118]

Ironically, these British also foolishly built their woodpile too near the buildings, but these had no Mrs. Barrett to warn them of their folly. Once they lit the giant stack of tinder, the conflagration grew quickly, until its tall and reaching flames danced onto the courthouse itself. In a remarkable scene of cooperation, despite the constant butting of heads between the British and the Americans, the raging fire quelled for a moment the heated debate between these adversaries and instead brought the two sides together in a bucket brigade, passing water from the nearby Mill Brook all the way to the courthouse. A nearby house also started to catch fire, but after much effort, the brigade made progress, sending gray smoke billowing into the air. With both the courthouse and the neighboring home saved, both sides cheered over their mutual success.[119]

At that moment, north beyond the trees and river on a hill facing the North Bridge, the militia watched with trepidation as billowing smoke rose from their town. Were the British burning Concord? If the Skirmish at Lexington began with one stupid individual firing a shot without orders, here one stupid misinterpretation of events would begin another.[120]

———◆———

Though the militia saw the smoke from Concord and feared the worst, they were unsure what to do about it, because the British blocked their only way across the river. While Lt. Joseph Hosmer, acting as adjutant, reorganized the men (militia companies on the right, minutemen on the left), Colonel Barrett took several of his officers aside for a private council. Among them were his deputy, sixty-year-old Maj. John Buttrick; thirty-year-old Capt. Isaac Davis, commander of the Acton minute company; and Capt. William Smith of the Lincoln minute company.[121]

When the Lincoln men had come in from the east, they brought with them rumors of the Skirmish at Lexington, but they knew nothing of its results.[122] So Barrett's war council held to their doubts and debated what to do. The prevailing opinion was that the Americans must refuse to be the aggressor—a long-standing policy perpetuated by the Committee of Safety and the Provincial Congress. If war was to begin here, the British had to fire the first shots. This was the only way the Americans could be absolved of any wrongdoing or act of rebellion, the only way they could be seen as the victims, rightfully defending their homes against an aggressive, tyrannical force.

With smoke continuing to rise from the town, adjutant Lieutenant Hosmer could wait no more. He stormed over to his senior officers, still debating, and exclaimed, "Will you let them burn the town down?"[123] Barrett and his officers looked at Hosmer and then at their own worried men. The horror and fear on many of their faces was all the senior officers needed to convince them, inexperienced in such great decisions as this. They made their decision. They would take action.

At the North Bridge, British Lieutenant Robertson returned on a fast gallop, accompanied by Capt. Charles Lumm, one of those British patrolmen who had captured Revere earlier. They told Captain Laurie that Lieutenant Colonel Smith would send him two companies of grenadiers,[124] though Smith was a bit lackadaisical in doing so, for as Smith exclaimed to his two messengers, the "3 Compys [presently at the Bridge] must be equal to the defence of the Bridge".[125]

On the hill, Colonel Barrett and Major Buttrick walked the colonial lines and gave the men a few rousing words. Their speeches were stirring but solemn. No one cheered. Upon hearing the plan, the democratically run militia companies, a strange standard to the modern observer, *consented* to the desires of their elected officers, agreeing they would "march into the middle of the town for its defence or die in the attempt".[126] Pleased, Barrett ordered them to load their firearms, but gave strict orders not to fire unless fired upon first, and then to fire as fast as they could.[127]

Simultaneously, Captain Laurie and his fellow British officers saw the commotion of their adversary and watched as they loaded their muskets. At last, one of those inexperienced officers proposed that it would perhaps be wise to cross the North Bridge and position themselves on the opposite side. Lieutenant Barker wrote in his diary that such a maneuver was obvious, "which by the bye he [Laurie] ought to have done at first[,] and then we wou'd have had time to make a good disposition". Barker was too quick to blame others—he, as an officer, was in a position to suggest such a tactic and yet never did so.[128]

On the overlooking hill, the militiamen were loaded and ready. For some reason unknown today, Captain Davis's Acton minute company was given the honor of leading the march—rather than Concord. When offered this prestige, Davis replied, "I haven't a man that is afraid to go."[129] Barrett commanded the whole from the rear of the column while Buttrick executed from the van. The full militia body first turned left face, putting the minutemen in the lead. Then, with great sobriety, without music,[130] cheers, shouts, or marching songs, as if marching to a funeral, the column of militia began to snake first to the north, then around right and onto the road, marching southward in squads, two wide by two deep.[131] British Ensign Lister thought the militia marched with as "much order as the best disciplined Troops".[132]

At the van marched Captain Davis and Major Buttrick. According to tradition, with them was John Robinson of Westford, acting as an aide. Though Robinson was a lieutenant colonel, he had deferred his command to Buttrick since the full of his own Westford company had not yet arrived.[133] As these three officers marched the men around toward the bridge, Buttrick repeated Barrett's orders several times: no one was to fire unless fired upon.

Captain Laurie and his fellow British officers had just made the decision to recross the bridge, but when Laurie saw the militia starting to move, he suddenly felt urgency to get his men across and re-formed. He swiftly turned and ordered them to retreat by divisions (squads), which he hoped would offer protection to his withdrawal. The first to cross was the 43rd, which he ordered to climb over the knee-high rock wall that lined both sides of the road and fan out along the riverbank, thus covering the others as they crossed over.[134] But in the rush and confusion, with the Americans closing in, the British troops were "obliged to form the best way they cou'd as soon as they were over the Bridge".[135]

Simultaneously, British Captain Lumm rode back to Concord to hurry the two companies of grenadiers. Lieutenant Barker complained later that the only reason the reinforcement took so long to come up was because Lieutenant Colonel Smith was "a very fat heavy Man".[136]

It was a short five- or six-minute march from the hills to the bridge, and the militia's silent and rhythmic march—they did not charge—drew them ever closer. Soon, they were practically at the North Bridge and before the British.

As the British finished crossing, the volunteer Lieutenant Sutherland and a few others who brought up the rear decided to buy Laurie some time to get his men organized. Ensign Lister proposed that they destroy the bridge. So they began prying up several planks from the bridge's deck, obviously forgetting or willing to abandon their companies at Barrett's Farm to their fate. In truth, perhaps all of them forgot, in that moment of adrenaline, about the companies at the farm, or perhaps they never meant to remove but a few planks to slow the American advance. Sutherland may have removed that first plank, while Lister and another removed maybe two more. But before they could do further damage, the Americans at last reached the far end of the long bridge itself.[137]

One of the British officers later stated that the Americans halted just shy of the bridge for a moment, perhaps not yet committed to their action.[138] Buttrick reportedly yelled to the British not to tear up the bridge before turning to his own men and asking if they would help him drive the British away.[139] They may have given only a solemn nod. Buttrick then ordered them forward again, but only at a march—still they did not charge.[140]

The four hundred fifty militia lurched silently forward, stepping onto the bridge, driving toward the one hundred soldiers now on the opposite riverbank. Captain Laurie hastily formed his British into a proper column four men wide, with the 4th closest to the bridge, and the 10th right behind, even as the 43rd were still scrambling over the knee-high walls to fan out along the riverbank.

Laurie then ordered the street firing position, probably yelling, "Take care to charge by street firing! Charge!" At this point, the 4th's first platoon (the first three ranks of the column, four men wide, twelve men total) were to reposition themselves for street firing: the front rank of four were to kneel, the next two ranks were to remain standing and interlocked. Once they all fired, they were to all peel off, left and right both, revealing the next platoon, who could move up to keep the same position, advance a bit to move the entire column forward, or keep their position and allow for a slow retreat. This second platoon was to immediately take the same street firing position and fire the next volley, before peeling off themselves and revealing the third. As each platoon peeled off, it rejoined the rear, immediately reloaded and made ready. With a column as long as this one, the detachment could have brought a fresh twelve shooters to the front every few seconds, and with the bottleneck at the bridge, the street firing could have slaughtered the Americans.[141]

Alas, the British had failed to sufficiently practice this evolution, so some of the men did not understand it. Even Lieutenant Barker of the 4th, an officer who should have known better, was ignorant of the mechanics. Unfortunately for the British, the confused Barker and his bewildered men constituted the lead company.[142] At the same time as Laurie got his men into street firing position, the 43rd were still in the way, filing over the knee-high rock wall to fan out alongside the riverbank and provide flanking cover. Apparently, such was the rush and disorder as the Americans came ever closer that the 43rd only moved to the north side of the road, not both sides as Laurie had ordered. Lieutenant Sutherland assisted by begging a portion of the 43rd to follow him over the south wall, but amid the confusion, only three or four soldiers followed him.[143]

Had the 43rd split in half and lined the riverbank on both sides of the road as Laurie ordered, they would have created a devastating cross-fire with an almost constant pouring of musket balls onto the coming Americans. This, coupled with a proper execution of the street firing by the two companies standing in column on the road, would have destroyed the bottlenecked militia. Instead, the 43rd was only half in position on one side, and the 4th stood at the end of the bridge scratching their heads over the order for street firing.

Time was running out. The Americans were halfway across the bridge. To run the militia off, Laurie ordered his 43rd on the north side to fire three warning shots. They did, and the scattered shots smacked harmlessly into the river. But the undaunted Americans kept coming.[144]

The lead platoon of the 4th, standing in that muddled semblance of the street firing position and directly opposite the oncoming Americans, were mostly inexperienced in combat, their eyes wide and darting about in panic.

Then, without orders from Laurie, the British opened fire!

First, a single shot, it seems, then a whole scattered volley.[145] That first shot was what poet Ralph Waldo Emerson, grandson of Concord's Rev. William Emerson, would famously call "the shot heard round the world".[146]

The roaring British muskets spewed forth white smoke between them and their adversaries, while two of their shots aimed true. One smacked into the left cheek of Pvt. Abner Hosmer of Acton, probably kin to Lieutenant Hosmer the adjutant, the ball flying out the back of his neck, spurting blood and brains on his neighbors and instantly felling him. Another shot smashed into the chest of the valiant Captain Davis, the dark red instantly oozing down his body and staining his homespun clothes as he fell into his comrades. Both were dead instantly, their corpses blocking the way, forcing their fellow militia to step over them as if they were fallen logs. Others too were wounded, but as one militiaman later observed, "Thair balls whistled well... Stringe that their wasn't no more killed. But they fired to high [sic]."[147]

Major Buttrick was decisive. Almost simultaneous to the British scattered volley, he raised his own musket and fired as he yelled to his men, "Fire, fellow soldiers, for God's sake, fire!"[148] The cry of "Fire!" rippled down the American column, even as the front ranks, those that could fire "and not Kill our own men", pulled their triggers.[149] The bridge was too tight for many to fire at once, and so the American guns rang out in an irregular and scattered volley, or as Laurie described it, a "general popping from them ensued".[150]

Two British soldiers dropped instantly dead; at least one other fell wounded. Three shots also smacked into Lt. Edward Hull of the 43rd, one through his right breast, and though in critical condition with massive hemorrhaging, he was not dead and his men pulled him to safety. Another shot slammed into the foot of Lieutenant Gould of the 4th, a little above his heel, severely wounding him. Yet another shattered into the arm of Lieutenant Kelly of the 10th.[151]

Scattered shots began to explode from both sides, white smoke was everywhere, and out of that smoke, the Americans kept coming.

The 43rd on the British right flank fired a few scattered crossfire shots from the riverbank. On the British left in the field of Rev. William Emerson (now the Old Manse), Lieutenant Sutherland aimed his light fusil musket and, together with the three soldiers with him, opened fire on the bridge. If their shots wounded any militia, they did not wait to find out. As they desperately attempted to reload, a bullet smashed into Sutherland's right breast, "which turned me half round". Other shots dropped two of the soldiers there, probably just injuring them.[152]

With muskets empty, the 4th Light Infantry's first platoon properly peeled off from its street firing position, but in doing so, now found themselves bottlenecked slightly by the knee-high rock wall on either side of the street, which they had to hop over to get around their own column. The 4th's second platoon, now in the front position, should have then immediately formed into street firing position and fired. But as the men were confused with the street firing maneuver, with the Americans rushing them so, they perhaps thought the first platoon was retreating. Instead of firing in turn, the second platoon peeled off and fell back too—despite the shouts of their officers. Seeing the lead platoons give way sent panic rippling through the British, just as the Americans neared the British side of the bridge. Even as both sides continued to fire scattered shots, suddenly the entire British column broke ranks and began running helter-skelter toward Concord center.[153]

Ensign Lister was more kind in describing the British rout, writing later, "the weight of their fire was such that we was oblig'd to give way then run with the great precipitance".[154] As the British fled, the injured Sutherland managed to join them.[155] In all, four of the eight officers at the bridge were wounded but got off, two soldiers were killed, one soldier was wounded and left behind, and five more rank and file were wounded "and a Running and Hobbling a Bout, Lucking back to see if we [the Americans] was after them."[156]

The Americans indeed "was after them", but they would not get far. For Lieutenant Colonel Smith and the two companies of grenadiers had at last arrived.

———◦◦◦———

The retreating British did not get more than three hundred yards, just past the path leading up to the Old Manse, with the Americans in close pursuit, when the two companies of grenadiers, led by Lt. Col. Francis Smith himself, came into view from around the bend. While about half the pursuing Americans immediately withdrew back across the bridge, taking their dead and wounded with them, many more went straight to the slopes east of the Manse. There they crouched behind a short rock wall, waiting to fire if the British should come closer.

It is strange that so many Yankees fell back across the bridge if they indeed feared their town was burning, but perhaps they had not yet the stomach for battle—and battle was exactly what would have been in store for them had they continued their march forward. As for the half that now crouched on the overlooking slopes, Major Buttrick told his men to hold their fire until he gave the word. Then each was to fire at will, two or three times, before immediately retreating across the bridge.[157]

To the chagrin of Buttrick and his waiting Americans, Smith halted his grenadiers and "Did not Come quite so near as…expected". The fleeing British fell behind this new force for safety. Smith then consulted with his officers while the sergeants re-formed the broken companies, even as the minutemen watched from the slopes above, flintlocks cocked in anticipation for Buttrick's order.[158]

After no more than ten minutes, strangely, Smith decided to turn his five companies and march back for Concord center, leaving the bridge unprotected for the return of Captain Parsons and his four companies at Barrett's Farm. One forgiving theory for his action was that Smith decided he was outnumbered and so withdrew.[159] Still, with all the grenadiers he had in town, it is shameful that he allowed his four companies to remain cut off. Smith was a dolt, neither decisive nor brilliant on the field.

As the British marched away, the Americans on the slopes cautiously followed, though keeping to the wooded acclivity above the road. Meanwhile, those Americans back over the bridge carried their dead and wounded to Major Buttrick's nearby before retaking their former position on the hill overlooking the North Bridge.

So ended the Skirmish of Concord's North Bridge.

In Concord center, the British licked their wounds as they awaited the return of Captain Parsons's four advance companies. Outside the courthouse near the smoldering heap that was the gun carriages, the grenadiers collected horses and chaises for the wounded and bedding by which to bandage the injured or create makeshift gurneys.[160]

Meanwhile, Ensign Lister, as the next senior ranking officer present of the 10th Light Infantry, assumed command from the wounded Lieutenant Kelly and led his men up the slopes over the town to protect the main force. He wrote, "my situation with the remains of the Compy was a most fatigueing one, being detached to watch the Motions of the Rebels, we was kept continually running from hill to hill as they chang'd their position".[161]

———•———

Back at the North Bridge, all was now silent except for the moans of a single soldier of the 4th, wounded but not mortally so, left to his awful fate. His only company were two fellow soldiers that lay dead nearby, the American casualties having already been removed. Half the American forces were a quarter mile west of the bridge in their former position, the rest maneuvering the slopes east of Concord center. This poor soldier lay at the bridge, abandoned.

Perhaps then that poor soldier looked up with thankful joy when he saw one "young fellow" of the country folk, maybe about twenty, walking toward him. This was Ammi White, a private in the Concord militia, his name long protected by old Concord, but now known to history. And he was no savior. This young man was truly excited for the chance to kill a redcoat. Seeing himself alone with a helpless enemy, the fiend seized his opportunity to act upon his disturbing nature and morbid desires. White looked over his shoulder. The Americans on the hill did not see him—or chose to ignore him. Yes, he was indeed alone. Turning back to his helpless victim, he carefully pulled out a hatchet. The redcoat was only wounded. He was trying to stand up.

The bloodthirsty American paused to savor the moment, but "not being under the feelings of humanity," suddenly and swiftly swung his hatchet into the soldier's forehead, instantly dropping the soldier to his knees. Rev. William Emerson watched in horror from his Old Manse nearby. Blood gushed everywhere as White struggled to pull his ax out of the face of the soldier kneeling before him. When at last he dislodged the hatchet, skin came with it, dangling into the soldier's eyes as his body fell to the ground, his brains plainly visible through the broken, mangled face. But the barbarous man was not yet satisfied. He hacked at the soldier's head at least twice more, chopping off the tops of his ears.

Reverend Emerson thought the "poor object lived an hour or two before he expired", though this is hard to imagine. Ammi White probably smirked at his handiwork—he had just killed himself a redcoat. This murderer then made his escape. How it was possible that not one of the Americans on the overlooking hill saw or acted upon this remains a mystery. Sadly, Ammi White was never punished for his war crime, and secrecy surrounded the shameful incident for decades.[162]

When Captain Parsons's men finally returned from Barrett's Farm, upon their march toward North Bridge, they were first surprised to find their guard gone, replaced by a body of militia upon the hill. Though they marched past the watchful militia with trepidation, "they let him [Parsons] pass without firing a single shot, tho they might undoubtedly have cut his [4] Compys off to a Man."[163] As one historian proposed, "It was only because the provincials had not yet made up their minds to war, that they did not block the return of Parsons' companies across the bridge."[164]

Upon traversing the bridge, they quickly noticed the three British dead and the few deck planks taken up.[165] Though they marched in formation, their eyes supposed to be forward, each soldier involuntarily stared a moment upon the mangled corpse of the soldier from the 4th as they passed by: his brain oozing out of his skull, blood everywhere; some say the man was still twitching, some say barely alive. Those that did not know better called it a scalping and denounced the Americans as no better than the "Savages". Though it was technically not a scalping, its gruesome effect on the soldiers was just the same. They were infuriated as they continued their marched back to Concord. When they got the chance, they would whisper of this event to others. Soon, the entire British expeditionary force would know of the "scalping", exaggerated with each retelling, so that when it reached Lister, he heard all the casualties left there had been "afterwards scalp'd their Eyes goug'd their Noses and Ears cut of [sic], such barbarity exercis'd upon the Corps[e] could scarcely be paralelled by the most uncivilised Savages."[166] This one atrocity committed by a wayward Concordian would singlehandedly spark viciousness from both sides before the bloody day was done.

Parsons's advance companies arrived in town center about an hour after the Skirmish of the North Bridge.[167] Lieutenant Colonel Smith then reorganized his men in the same order they had been at the start of their expedition. But this time, Smith expected trouble, so he deployed many more light infantry flankers than before, and they marched farther from the main body. At about noon, they finally set off eastward, back toward Lexington, leaving an angry populace in their wake.[168]

The Expedition to Concord was a dismal failure, though they scoured all of the hiding places as reported by Gage's intelligence. The whole affair was hardly worth what little war stores they found, the lives killed thus far, or the many lives that were about to be sacrificed in the coming hours as the British marched through an enraged countryside. As the British expeditionary force was about to learn, the American Revolutionary War had begun.[169]

CHAPTER 9

A COUNTRYSIDE UNLEASHED

The first mile back toward Lexington was mostly uneventful. The long, red column now marched with the sun high above, the sunbeams glistening off their fixed bayonets, the men weary, hungry, and thirsty. At least two wounded British officers rode ahead in a horse-drawn chaise: Lt. Edward Gould, despite his injured foot, driving it like an ambulance, racing to ferry critically wounded Lt. Edward Hull to Boston. The nasty gunshot wound to Hull's right breast was hemorrhaging profusely.[1]

As the British left Concord, the ridge now stood on their left, while most of the dirt road they traveled was lined with knee-high rock walls, gathered and stacked from the rock-studded pastureland and gentle hills on their right, which was mostly open space, though dotted here and there with sparse, young woods, broken by farms and the occasional apple orchard. The British light infantry felt greater fatigue than the grenadiers, having that morning run ahead to Lexington, then having traveled beyond Concord center to the North Bridge and Barrett's Farm, and now serving as flanking parties off the road, some in the fields south of the column, others along the steep acclivities to the north.

Meanwhile, unbeknownst to the British, the Yankee militia and minuteman companies from Concord's North Bridge had finally, after consultation, decided to press the war. Familiar with all the back ways, they crossed from Concord center, up the slopes that governed its eastern

boundary and down the other side, following a northern path that paralleled the British march but kept the slopes between them. These slopes
fell away at a point near the house of Nathan Meriam, still standing,
where the Bedford Road met the Concord Road, and it was there, at
Meriam's Corner, that the Americans intended to ambush the British.[2]

The tail of the British column had no sooner departed Concord
center than a few independent militia parties from the North Bridge
began firing scattered shots at their rear. The militia mostly sniped from
behind trees and out windows of innocent-looking houses, adopting the
guerrilla-style warfare observed and learned so well during the last war
against the French and Indians. Other scattered Yankee parties, many
of whom were newly arrived to the fight from neighboring towns, also
took their potshots at the British flanks.

Despite many stories to the contrary, the British did not march blindly
and ignorantly as a single column under such galling fire. Rather, the light
infantry deployed far off road to defend the column's flanks by rooting out
and swarming militia snipers. In fact, the light infantry was a rather new
evolution in warfare, also a product of the last war with the French and
Indians, and so fought with the same tactics the militia employed: moving
in numerous but small, independent parties, taking cover behind trees
and rocks, running from one cover to the next.[3] Lieutenant Sutherland,
delirious due to his hemorrhaging right breast, remembered seeing the
lights kill two pursuing militiamen, though two of the British themselves
were also wounded in defending the main column.[4]

The lights performed their job admirably, allowing the main British
column to progress without much harassment or loss for more than a
mile. But as the lights on the British left came to the end of the slopes,
which fell away at Meriam's Corner, they saw two large bodies of militia
coming along a northerly road from Bedford, with a larger third body
farther away. The latter was the main body of colonial militia that had
been at North Bridge and had come around the heights of Concord too
slowly to effect their intended ambush. Of the two nearer bodies, the
leading was the four militia companies of Reading, distantly followed
by the three of Billerica.

Capt. John Brooks, who would be promoted to major for his service
this day, was at the head of these Reading men. As they made their way

southward, one of his men observed, "The British marched down the hill with very slow, but steady step, without music, or a word being spoken that could be heard. Silence reigned on both sides."[5]

In following the slopes' topography back down to ground level, the light infantry necessarily found themselves pressed in close proximity to the main column, very near the road. The Concord-Lexington Road continued eastward past an intersection that defined Meriam's Corner, then grew narrow as it approached a small, wooden bridge, just a few feet in length, that crossed an upstream stretch of the same Mill Brook that wound through Concord.

Modern road construction practically obscures this small crossing, but in that era the narrow bridge caused a bottleneck as it forced even the dispersed British flankers to draw in tight with the main column to cross it. The Reading companies saw this opportunity and rushed forward, taking cover behind Meriam's barn and the farm's nearby walls, a position about three to five hundred feet away from the bridge. And from there the Yankees opened fire.[6]

The first balls whizzed harmlessly by the British lights, totally ineffective at such range. The lights gave a few futile shots in return, defending the main British column as it struggled to speedily cross the narrow bridge. Determined to inflict casualties, the Reading militiamen reloaded as they crept closer to the bridge, taking cover behind rock hedges and trees. At the same time, the two other bodies of militia, those from Billerica, distantly trailed by those from the North Bridge, rushed south along the Bedford Road to join the fight. With the Americans closing in, both opposing adversaries began brisk fire, the most intense shooting of the day thus far. The Americans kept pressing southward between each reload until the lights found their backs against the main column. The grenadiers comprised the bulk of that main body, and now they too halted, midway in crossing the bridge, to give their own volley.[7]

The field between the Meriam House and Mill Brook was quickly shrouded in thick white smoke. Both sides fired briskly and incessantly. The din increased dramatically as the Billerica men joined the Reading men. Severely wounded, Lieutenant Sutherland was probably somewhere in the center of the column on his horse-drawn wagon, laid therein headfirst so that he could only see the fight once his wagon passed it. He saw the Americans "came as close to the road on our flanking partys as they possibly could".[8] To push the Americans back, Ensign Lister led his fatigued 10th Lights in a counterattack away from the main column. As he did, an American musket ball smashed into his right elbow, shattering the joint and instantly disabling his arm, his fusil musket falling from his limp limb. He grabbed his fusil with his good arm and fell back.[9]

Sutherland thought the colonial force thus far engaged was much larger than at North Bridge, and indeed it was. Comprising men from both Reading and Billerica, augmented by another two companies just then arriving from Chelmsford, the force swelled to near 500. When the laggards from the North Bridge at last joined the fight, the total came to somewhere near 900 men.[10] With just under 790, the British were now very much outgunned.[11]

Suddenly, balls began to whiz across Sutherland's wagon from the south. He turned his attention there and found a second small force, probably the lead companies of Sudbury and Framingham, whom he suspected meant to join the first and together attack the British van.[12] As all of these militia companies were bound for Concord center, it was easy for them to divert from their path and find where the fight had now progressed—they needed only follow the thunderous and incessant booms of the musketry. Meriam's Corner marked the beginning of a long and bloody running fight all the way back to Boston.

It is impossible to determine how many casualties each side suffered at the skirmish at Meriam's Corner, just as it is at any point along what is now known as Battle Road. While the Americans kept their cover and perhaps made it through this skirmish unscathed, depending on the account, as few as two or as many as nine or more British died or lay there wounded and incapacitated, with another several wounded but marching off with the column. According to Concordian Amos Barrett, late to the fight as he had come with those from the North Bridge: "When I got thair was a grait many Lay Dead, and the Road was bloody."[13]

Once the entire British column crossed the narrow bridge, they quickly pressed onward. The Americans regrouped and then crossed it themselves, giving scattered shots at the British rear as they pursued.

The Yankees then fanned out as fast as they could to either flank of the British, taking to the fields and woods, trying to get ahead of the British column from where they could take multiple potshots each. All the while, new militiamen poured in from the surrounding areas, some in small parties, some as individuals. One late participant reminisced, "The battle now began, and was carried on with little or no military discipline and order, on the part of the Americans, during the remainder of that day. Each one sought his own place and opportunity".[14]

According to Lister, the battle "then became a general Firing upon us from all Quarters, from behind hedges and Walls[;] we return'd the fire every opportunity".[15] Smith observed, "they began to fire on us from behind the walls, ditches, trees, &c., which, as we marched, increased to a very great degree, and continued without the intermission of five minutes altogether... I can't think but it must have been a preconcerted scheme in them, to attack the King's troops with the first favourable opportunity offered, otherwise, I think they could not, in so short a time...raised such a numerous body".[16] Barker confided to his diary, "the Country was an amazing strong one, full of Hills, Woods, stone Walls &c., which the Rebels did not fail to take advantage of...as we did too upon them but not with the same advantage".[17]

One participant, apparently an officer of the 23rd Welch Fusiliers, complained that most of the soldiers had never been in action. As a result, in the confusion of the running fight, the troops fired back "with too much eagerness, so that at first most of it was thrown away for want of that coolness and Steadiness which distinguishes troops who have been inured to service." The same Welch Fusilier officer added, "The contempt in which they held the Rebels, and perhaps their opinion that they would be sufficiently intimidated by a brisk fire, occasioned this improper conduct; which the Officers did not prevent as they should have done."[18]

Under these conditions, the British managed to plow ahead along the Battle Road. After another mile, they approached the Noah Brooks Tavern, which lay just east of a small wooded mound known as Brooks Hill. It was there that the main forces of Sudbury and Framingham arrived, almost 400 new men, bringing the total force, including those hot on the trail of the British rear, to about 1,300.[19] Some militia positioned behind the sparse young woods on the slopes of Brooks Hill just south of the road, others took cover along the extended stone hedge that lined the south roadside, while many more hopped this and the wall opposite to take cover in the north fields, together hoping to ambush the retreating redcoats with deadly crossfire. But their surprise was ruined. The British lights, deployed again from the main body, swarmed in small parties through the roadside woods and came upon the concealed Americans.

The firefight was instantly sharp. The woods on all sides billowed with white smoke as scattered shots came from both militia and British flankers. The grenadiers on the road gave a volley or two, but the dispersed lights along the roadside fired scattered shots at will. The lights successfully pushed the Americans back and dislodged them, but not before the Yankees gave a few scattered and deadly crossfire shots to the column of grenadiers on the road. Both sides fought fiercely, but the Americans were at last forced to withdraw. Perhaps another eight or more British were killed, with dozens more wounded, one of whom tried to march away with the column, only to collapse along the roadside, where his fleeing comrades left him.[20]

The main column continued its retreat under only scattered and distant potshots, while the pursuing Yankees took to the hills and pastures to get ahead of the column yet again. The eastward road took the fatigued British column past small Tanners Brook, also known as Elm Brook, and then climbed a gentle slope to a broad, flat, and wooded mound, where it turned northward to follow the mound's edge. After traveling only a short distance atop this mound, the road turned again sharply eastward through a wooded area.

Among the militiamen hiding at that sharp curve were Maj. Loammi Baldwin and his three Woburn militia companies, about two hundred fifty men. They had first come onto the main road ahead of the British near the open space of Tanners Brook. But Baldwin knew better than to go head to head with the British, so he opted to move up the road and find a place to take cover. The sharp curve was the perfect opportunity for his ambush. As he and his men sat there waiting, they were joined by militia pursuing from Concord, who had once more cut across the fields to get ahead of the British. When the British turned the sharp curve, the grenadier main body was caught in Baldwin's snare—the Americans immediately fired from behind trees and boulders. This firefight at the Bloody Angle (or Curve), as it has since been called, was the next intense clash. The grenadiers gave a volley from the road, while the light infantry swarmed once more into the deadly woods, braving sniper fire to again dislodge the Americans. But before the British flankers could do their job, the militiamen quickly fired and then retreated eastward, hoping to lay a second ambush.[21]

The beleaguered British pushed their way through the ambush, leaving "many dead and wounded and a few tired."[22] Perhaps eight were left dead there, many more left struggling with agonizing wounds.[23] The British next passed the Hartwell Tavern, which still stands, descended the small mound and soon passed the site of Paul Revere's capture. As they pressed eastward, they were continuously harassed by sporadic, scattered shots from snipers unseen.

The road they followed turned once more, from east to slightly southward to circumnavigate another mound on the British left. There they met with Capt. John Parker and his Lexington militia, now together in full force of about one hundred forty men, concealed upon those northern slopes or across in the fields to the south.[24] As the British moved into Parker's trap, his men let loose with an onslaught of deadly crossfire, this known since as Parker's Revenge. The British received heavy fire and several more casualties, all from hidden militia assailants who fired and then retreated before the weary light infantry flankers could swarm the hill to dislodge them.[25]

The constant work of rooting out concealed Americans from behind hedges and walls was quickly exhausting the light infantry. Now, to add to their exhaustion, they were running short on ammunition. What was worse, they had not even reached Lexington, let alone the many miles that stood between them and Boston. Though the grenadiers had fired less, and so found in their cartouche boxes more ready-made cartridges than the light infantry, even they began to worry that the countryside might soon wipe them all out.

All the British could do was plow forward. They road turned again eastward and around a slope called the Bluff. From there they could see the next mound, Fiske Hill, which they looked upon with utter dread.

Each major mound thus far had been crawling with rabid militia. Sure enough, hidden militia on the Bluff to their left opened up with a new barrage. These were probably Parker's Lexington men, who had fallen back along the opposite side of that slope, ready to send another round or two into the escaping redcoats. The British flankers rushed up the slopes to disperse them, but the militia withdrew ahead of them and headed eastward, continuing to harry the British as they did so.

As the Bluff on the British left dissolved away into a flat valley, the road next took the British slightly northward around Fiske Hill to their right. Hiding there on Fiske Hill was the Cambridge militia, another almost eighty men, and they too opened fire. This, tied with Parker's Lexington men still harrying the British left, produced some of the worst crossfire the British had yet found themselves in. Many of the British, frantically trying to reload, discovered they were down to their last shots. The slopes and trees thundered a hailstorm of lead musket shots all around them—all the woods seemed to be belching forth white smoke. The intense crossfire turned the road into a bloodbath. The "light companies were so fatigued with flanking they were scarce able to act, and a great number of wounded scarce able to go forward, made a great confusion".[26]

Major Pitcairn, who had either daringly remained on his steed or climbed back atop it, raised his sword as he galloped up the boulder-strewn Fiske Hill to lead a charge of his dejected and exhausted light infantry. The lights struggled as heavy fire mowed many of them down, but Pitcairn rode back and forth among them, sword drawn high, weaving his horse between the trees and the constant whizzing balls of the crossfire, commanding and urging the lights forward.

Several Yankees at once recognized Pitcairn as an officer. Hiding behind a pile of wooden rails, they waited for a clear shot through the trees. Then they got it! They sprang out from their hiding place and fired scattered shots. But they were too zealous, for all their shots missed. Pitcairn must have heard the balls whiz by. His horse certainly did. The steed bucked wildly, flinging Pitcairn to the ground before taking off in fright through the crossfire and directly toward Pitcairn's assailants, leaping the rail wall they had hid behind and running off. Pitcairn got up, sore from the fall, but unscathed. The Yankee snipers desperately tried to reload, but the British lights swarmed them, likely slaying one or two by musket ball or bayonet.[27]

Even as the light infantry stormed Fiske Hill, the grenadiers gave their own scattered volleys from the road. Though the Americans "kept the road always lined and a very hot fire on us without intermission; we…returned their fire as hot as we received it".[28] Somewhere along the way, perhaps here, Lieutenant Colonel Smith received a shot in the leg. Whether he dismounted because of this shot, or had done so earlier so as not to be such an easy mark, he walked with his men the rest of the way and was apparently able to do so without much trouble despite his wound.[29] Lieutenant Sutherland, injured and carried helplessly along in a wagon, was around here unseated from his makeshift gurney. He wrote that his "Chair broke down there & my horse was shot thro' the Shoulders." He seems to have ridden the rest of the way on horseback, sitting as low as he could to avoid the deadly crossfire.[30]

About this time, a British soldier fled the skirmish and deserted his comrades to take refuge at a house nearby, possibly the home of Ebenezer Fiske himself. As the soldier approached the home, so did a stray militiaman. When the two spotted each other, they instantly raised their muskets and fired with deadly effect, felling one another instantly on the spot.[31]

The British expeditionary force managed to again drive through the deadly attack and so rounded Fiske Hill. From there they still had more than a mile to even Lexington Green, with about sixteen miles yet to Boston. With the confusion of this latest skirmish, and with a dozen or more left dead or wounded, the men utterly spent, many without ammunition, and many officers wounded, discipline finally gave way, "so that we began to run rather than retreat in order." The orderly march became a terrible rout eastward.[32]

The few able-bodied regular officers remaining attempted to stop this mad rush "and form them two deep, but to no purpose, the confusion increased rather than lessened". At last, the officers pointed their own fusil muskets, bayonets fixed, at their own men, threatening to kill them if they did not heed their orders. At this, the pell-mell retreat finally halted, even under intense musketry, leaving the soldiers caught between a mob of officers brandishing bayonets and swords ahead, and a horde of vicious and deadly militia that continued to envelop them from the rear and the flanks. "Upon this they began to form under a very heavy fire".[33]

The militia horde, now perhaps 1,800 or more, in their browns and their whites of homespun clothes, relentlessly hounded and harried the fewer than 790 redcoats.[34] Embattled Lieutenant Barker bemoaned, "their numbers increasing from all parts, while ours was reducing by deaths, wounds and fatigue, and we were totally surrounded with an incessant fire as it's impossible to conceive, our ammunition was likewise expended".[35] Now each fallen redcoat was left to his own fate. Some dragged themselves up and continued as best they could, only to be captured as the horde engulfed them; others gave up the fight and lay defeated along the roadside. Many others would die of their wounds in the road's red mud mixed with the effusion of blood.

The British column, once re-formed, charged forward at double time under heavy fire and desperate exhaustion toward Lexington. Most of the light infantry had indeed expended their last shots and thus could provide no flanking cover. They pulled in close to the main column, retreating under the protection of the grenadiers who still had a few (but not many) shots left in their cartouche boxes. They must have cursed the order to carry only thirty-six shots per man.

When Lexington Green came into sight, the brokenhearted British prepared for another ambush. The last hill before the Green, Concord Hill, lay on the British left, and from there a small but sizable gaggle of militia gathered to rain down musket balls as the British passed.[36] But the beleaguered troops rushed by, hoping against hope they might flee from their pursuing enemies and make it yet to Boston.

As the desperate British charged along the south road that defined Lexington Green, all was eerily quiet. They feared the worst, yet passed the triangular Green without incident and continued eastward, closely pursued by the relentless militia. But the defeated soldiers hung their heads low as some computed they still had nearly sixteen miles to Boston.

Suddenly: ahead of the British, on the heights commanding both sides of the road, two deafening booms thunder-cracked and echoed across the hills. These were two small but lethal 6-pounder field cannon, which blasted their iron round shot toward the British. Perhaps some of these hopeless redcoats looked up only at this moment to see death head on, hearing the Doppler effect, the increasingly high pitch, as the heavy balls whizzed toward them...and then overhead!

The balls sailed past the retreating British and into the hounding militia horde behind, perhaps ripping to shreds one or two of them and instantly scattering the rest.

As those hopeless British now all raised their bleak and harrowed faces and gazed forward, they beheld a sight both marvelous and awesome. Ahead, in line formation across the entire expanse at the base of those heights: the entire British 1st Brigade (the 4th, 23rd, and 47th) and the entire Marine Battalion—about one thousand fresh British soldiers, plus their officers. Atop two separate heights, maybe two dozen dark-blue-coated artillerymen surrounded their two fieldpieces, which they gracefully and rhythmically worked—almost danced around—as they reloaded. What awe those downtrodden soldiers must have felt, to gaze upon the nearly 1,150 men in total, their brilliant red coats, their prestigious standards flapping in the wind, Brigadier General Lord Percy at their head, *standing* with his men (not mounted on a horse), the thunder as the two cannon roared once more, unleashing two more shot that sailed over the British and into the scattering militia.[37] The British expeditionary force had been routed, mangled, and slaughtered, but for the first time that day, they must have felt victorious. The pursuing militia, however, must have felt loathing as they watched their prey slip from their clutches.[38]

The British were saved! With a shot or two more from the two British 6-pounders, the militia horde fully dispersed, allowing the dogged British expeditionary force to safely pour past the 1st Brigade's lines and take refuge in the fields beyond. They "were so much exhausted with fatigue, that they were obliged to lie down for rest on the ground, their tongues hanging out of their mouths, like those of dogs after a chase."[39]

The British reinforcement had arrived. And the whole tenor of the battle was now about to change.

———◆———

It was the greatest sight many of those men ever beheld. The British reinforcement, which Lieutenant Colonel Smith had sent for before his march into Lexington that dawn, had now arrived. Lieutenant Barker later wrote, "we had flatter'd ever since the morning with expectations of the Brigade coming out, but at this time had given up all hopes of it, as it was so late."[40]

It was now about 2:30 p.m., and the reinforcement was indeed later than planned. The first blunder had occurred when General Gage sent orders to the 1st Brigade to be under arms at 4:00 a.m., but as the brigade major was not in his quarters when the orders arrived, they were left for him on his table and remained unseen. When Smith's courier arrived to request reinforcements at 5:00 a.m., Gage debriefed him and then wasted time inquiring why his 1st Brigade was not already prepared to march. Finally, at 6:00 a.m., Gage issued new orders that the troops muster on Boston Common at 7:30 a.m. Due to a second blunder, the orders for the Marine Battalion were left at Major Pitcairn's quarters with his aides, but Pitcairn was on expedition, and the aides failed to inquire on their immediacy, and so these too were left unseen. Thus, when the 1st Brigade paraded at 7:30 a.m., the marines failed to show, and it took another hour to rectify the mistake. This, plus other delays, caused the reinforcement to not depart from Boston until 8:45 a.m.[41]

The commander of the British reinforcement was Hugh, Earl Percy, and at thirty-two, he was the eldest son of the Duke of Northumberland. Though he appeared sickly, with his thin and bony features, his protruding nose and his body showing signs of degradation from the gout, he had swagger. (Or was that sprightliness in his step from the brandy he kept in his canteen?) He was popular among his troops because they felt greatly honored to serve under a man of such prestigious nobility.[42] Lord Percy had come to the colonies in July of 1774 as the regimental commander (colonel) of the 5th, but had almost immediately been promoted to brigadier general (in the American service only) and given the charge of three regiments—the 1st Brigade.

After he had time to appraise the worsening situation in America, he wrote candidly to a friend, "Our affairs here are in the most Critical Situation imaginable; Nothing less than the total loss or Conquest of the Colonies must be the End of it. Either indeed is disagreable, but one or the other is now absolutely necessary."[43] He had written that letter many months prior to this day, little expecting he would play such a pivotal role in the "disagreable" affair.

Rather than cross the Charles River by boat, Percy's reinforcement marched the longer ground route through Boston Neck and Roxbury to the Great Bridge that crossed to Cambridge, almost an extra four and a half miles.[44] When Percy's advance scouts, some miles ahead, arrived at this bridge, they discovered the rebels had removed the planks. But the Yankees, rather than stealing the planks away, merely left them stacked on the opposite side. Among the British scouts was the engineer Capt. John Montresor, who had gone ahead expressly to investigate the bridge. He had with him four volunteers, whom he sent across on the stringers to collect the planks. Together they were able to quickly rebuild the bridge deck to sufficient strength, and Lord Percy had neither delay nor trouble in getting all his men and their two cannon across the Charles River.[45]

As Percy's reinforcement moved westward from Cambridge to Lexington, "few or no people were to be seen, and the houses were

PORTRAIT OF HUGH (LORD) PERCY, BRIGADIER GENERAL AND EARL (IN 1775), LATER SECOND DUKE OF NORTHUMBERLAND (C. 1788) BY GILBERT STUART (1755–1828). COURTESY OF THE HIGH MUSEUM OF ART, ATLANTA.

in general shut up."[46] The towns were so uncannily quiet that Percy's gut told him that upon their return, "we shall be fired at from those very houses."[47]

Fortunately for Lord Percy, he received timely intelligence from one of Smith's own men. Lt. Edward Gould, slightly wounded, had retreated ahead of the main expeditionary force from Concord, driving the chaise in which he ferried poor Lt. Edward Hull, who suffered from three terrible and life-threatening wounds. After passing Lexington unmolested, Gould and Hull had come upon Percy's reinforcement, marching in column, braced by two strong fifty-man van and rear guards. Percy conferred with Gould and, from the intelligence the young officer provided, the brigadier acted accordingly, deploying many more flankers and probably only then ordering his men to load and ready their muskets.

Percy also sent Lt. Harry Rooke of the 4th Battalion on horseback express back to Boston to inform Gage of the situation. Rooke's ride was Paul Revere's in reverse, with Rooke forced to take detours to avoid the *American* forces. These delays put Rooke in Boston sometime past four o'clock that afternoon. To cover the British return and fend off the defenders of the countryside, if need be, Gage placed his 2nd and 3rd Brigades under arms and ordered to Boston the bulk of the 64th Regiment from Castle William.[48]

Meanwhile, wounded Gould and Hull left Percy and made their way onward toward Boston, only to be captured near Menotomy. As for Percy, armed with his new intelligence, he continued his advance through what he now knew to be hostile territory. When he heard the distant and sporadic musketry ahead, he promptly ordered his men into line formation and his cannon to take up positions on the heights. Then, he waited the few minutes for the retreating British to flee into his open arms.[49]

————•—•————

At about the same time Percy's reinforcement was mustering on Boston Common, anxious Dr. Joseph Warren, undoubtedly awake, received a messenger at his home on Hanover Street. Who this messenger was is unknown. He could have come from outside the town, since by dawn both Boston Neck and Charlestown Ferry were again open for business. Most likely, the messenger was a Bostonian who had observed Percy's reinforcement muster on Boston Common. In any case, the messenger brought rumors of war.

Dr. Warren probably grabbed his fusil musket before giving charge of his patients to his senior resident apprentice, Dr. Eustis, and then mounted his horse and rode at once for Charlestown Ferry.[50] There he encountered the excitable and disconcerted John Adan of Boston. Warren offered his encouragement: "Keep up a brave heart! They have begun it—that either party can do; and we'll end it—that only one can do."[51]

The ferry landed him in Charlestown about eight o'clock that morning, where Warren found the town in confusion and turmoil over the rumors of war to the west. Everywhere he looked, he saw the inhabitants packing their goods and preparing to flee, fearing for their safety once the British returned. Warren navigated the chaotic streets and made his way to meet with local Whigs there. Perhaps one of his stops was the home of militia leader Col. William Conant, for Warren was still uncertain whether Revere had crossed safely the night before.

The doctor spent near two hours in the town talking with various leaders, gathering what information he could. Finally, at close to ten o'clock, he rode off for Menotomy. His destination was the village's Black Horse Tavern, belonging to Mr. Ethan Wetherby, where the Committee of Safety had held a routine meeting the day before. Warren had not attended, but he knew they were due to meet again this morning. Moreover, he knew this morning's meeting would be anything but routine.[52]

Along his path, Warren found all the houses shut up and seemingly deserted. All was hauntingly quiet until he reached Menotomy, where people were hurrying about and discussing the news.[53] He made straight for the tavern.

No record seems to exist of that emergency meeting of the Committee of Safety, but with the Provincial Congress not in session, almost total control and decision-making authority fell to these few men whose special charge was governing the militia.[54] John Hancock, the committee's chairman, was escaping to Woburn, so the members looked to Warren as their acting chairman. Among those at that sub-rosa meeting was committee member and militia leader Col. William Heath.[55] Heath did not stay long, but rode off to Watertown to meet the militia there.[56]

The remainder of the committee discussed what little they knew of the news of day, before talk quickly turned to which side had fired the first shot. It was too early to know the answer to that (and indeed we still do not have it), and yet, though none of them had witnessed the Skirmish of Lexington, everyone there gave much speculation on the matter. Dr. Warren and the other committee members, indeed all of the leading Whigs, were careful to conduct their resistance to British policy in a legally justifiable way. They could only hope then that the British fired first, thus justifying every other action the Americans would take that day as necessary, defensive measures against a tyran-nical government.

While the committee discussed their business, couriers rode to and from Menotomy, bringing in new intelligence and sending out infor-mation to the various but disorganized militia companies streaming in from all directions. One of those was Israel Bissel, who was "Charged to Alarm the Country quite to Connecticut, and all Persons are Desired to furnish him with fresh Horses, as they may be needed."[57]

Sometime after the committee had convened, there was a tense moment in the tavern, and in fact in all of Menotomy, as Percy's rein-forcement approached the village. The people all rushed indoors, and Menotomy instantly became a ghost town as the British marched through. This was the first time Warren had seen the British troops since they had departed from Boston.[58] It would not be his last.

⸻

East of Lexington Green, Lord Percy's reinforcement maintained their line formation across the road and at the base of the heights there, while Lieutenant Colonel Smith's expeditionary force re-formed in safety behind.[59] As for the Americans, without any sort of unified commander, the independent companies only somewhat regrouped as laggards finally rejoined the horde and as detached platoons found one another. But as more Yankees poured in, others departed, seeing themselves as mere volunteers and free to come and go as they pleased. Some left having seen enough blood, others having spent their last bullets, many more feeling they had performed ample service and expecting the fresh troops coming in to fill their places.

The colonial officers could do little to keep their men from departing. Since their own men had elected them to their station, they had very little real authority, particularly if they hoped to retain their men's favor and thus retain their officerships. Because of this independency and volunteerism, knowing the number of militiamen present at any one point is impossible. While perhaps 1,800 militia had engaged the British up to Lexington Green, many now left in droves, particularly upon seeing the strong British reinforcement led by Lord Percy. The American force slowly dwindled now to maybe as few as 1,100.[60]

Even so, all the neighboring hills were alive with small militia parties. They inched to just within firing range of the British, took cover behind trees and rock hedges, and gave an occasional scattered volley without effect. The British held their position and answered the Yankees with their own occasional volley, also without effect.

Lord Percy's job was now to protect Smith's weary detachment and allow the men a brief respite before they marched again eastward. He first ordered Smith's men to fall back farther to the Munroe Tavern, where they could tend to their wounded. Percy then looked to secure his own defensive posture, ordering out strong parties to guard the flanks of his main battle line from the many militia now dotting the hills and pastures. At least three houses on those outskirts of Lexington blocked the battle line and the artillery's clear view of the entire kill zone. The encroaching militia could easily use those nearby houses for cover, so Percy ordered out flanking parties to torch them. Deacon Loring's house was one of those sacrificed. Flankers set fire to its gables, then shattered the windows and threw in their torches. As the blaze quickly spread into a great conflagration, the flankers pulled down the adjacent stone walls, sending puffs of dust into the air to mingle with the massive columns of smoke pouring from the burning home. Lord Percy watched with satisfaction as the flank guards torched the two other homes and perhaps an adjacent barn and shop as well.[61]

As the homes polluted the air with their billowing smoke, British flanking parties darted from cover to cover, firing sporadic scattered shots to keep the encroaching militia at bay. Some of these flankers came from the 23rd Regiment, which seems to have formed the British left and had positioned itself along the gentle hills south of the road. Their adjutant, 1st Lt. Frederick Mackenzie, later wrote, "the Rebels endeavored to gain our flanks, and crept into the covered ground on either side, and as close as they could in front, firing now and then in perfect security. We also advanced a few of our best marksmen who fired at those who shewed themselves."[62]

Whenever the British muskets failed to disperse the clusters of militia, the two 6-pounders roared to life to fire off a ball or two. The greatest throng of militia remained near Lexington Green, having halted there when they gave up pursuit of Smith's expeditionary force. Many of them gathered around the meetinghouse that doubled as the town's church, where some went inside to resupply their powder and balls.

The British fired their cannon several times at this crowd. One ball whizzed not two yards past Maj. Loammi Baldwin of Woburn. He immediately retreated behind the meetinghouse, but had no sooner darted behind it than a second ball smashed through the church itself, flying through the front wall, soaring over its pews, and whizzing out the back side just inches from Baldwin's head, terrorizing him and covering him with splintered debris. He wisely determined to find better cover and so headed north, past the Green, and laid in a meadow where he "heard the balls in the air and saw them strike the ground." In the coming propaganda war, some Americans would cry foul that an artillery shot had crashed through the town's church. But by housing weapon stores, the church was no longer protected under the rules of war.[63]

If some British soldiers wondered why their artillery pieces did not fire more frequently than they had, they soon discovered the answer. Ensign Lister learned that the pieces only had what rounds they could carry in their small carriage side boxes. This was twenty-four rounds apiece, though Lister, unfamiliar with the particulars of artillery, imagined they had but seven. Lt. Col. Samuel Cleaveland, commander of the Royal Artillery in Boston, had prepared a wagon with 140 extra rounds for Percy. However, despite the insistence of the excitable artillery commander, Percy refused it on the grounds that a wagon train would cause him undue delay in his march.[64] There are unconfirmed stories that Gage sent two wagons after Percy, but because they were lightly guarded, the rebels captured them in Menotomy.[65]

As the standoff east of Lexington Green continued, both sides received refreshments. The Americans received theirs on the Green itself, provided by both the neighbors and Buckman Tavern. The British received theirs as they dressed their wounded at William Munroe's Tavern along the road southeast of their main battle line. Left in charge of the tavern was lame John Raymond, who gave to the British whatever they needed. Munroe's Tavern has sometimes been given the misnomer of Percy's headquarters, though the British were hardly there long enough for it to be considered such. In fact, Percy perhaps never set foot in the tavern. Rather, it seems that only Smith and his exhausted expeditionary force gathered on its grounds.[66]

Ensign Lister, wounded near Meriam's Corner, was among the British receiving much-needed medical care. Mr. Simms, surgeon's mate of the 43rd, extracted the ball from Lister's right elbow, "the Ball it having gone through the Bone and lodg'd within the Skin". Mr. Simms bandaged Lister up, but could do nothing for his loss of so much blood. Lister would have to make his way along the march as best he could.[67]

In this brief intermission of the daylong battle, the poisonous news of the "scalping" at Concord's North Bridge transfused to all the troops, even to Lord Percy. Some of the rumors now claimed that the Americans planned to scalp or otherwise mutilate all soldiers left dead or wounded. The British looked upon the Yankees with newfound contempt as rage spread like wildfire across the long line of redcoats.

Finally, after forty-five minutes of dangerous but necessary delays, the time near 3:15 p.m., Lord Percy observed, "it began now to grow pretty late, & we had 15 miles to retire, & only our 36 rounds".[68] Accordingly, he gave a flurry of orders to his various subordinates to make ready the march back to Boston. He ordered the artillerymen to limber their two guns, with which they probably had four horses each.[69] He ordered the 23rd on the south side of the road to form the rear guard. The 23rd immediately sent out flankers and marksmen to line the walls and cover ahead while the main 23rd Battalion moved up the low hills behind them and formed a new line with a better commanding view, there to protect the rest of the British as they formed into one massive column behind.[70]

The vanguard was organized, consisting of the embattled expeditionary force (first the exhausted light infantry, followed by the weary grenadiers), flanked by five companies of the 4th Regiment on the right, "where most danger was to be apprehended", and three companies of the 47th on the left, thus encapsulating the expeditionaries within bodies of fresh troops. The remains of the 4th and 47th served either as flankers or in column directly behind the vanguard. The artillery seems to have marched midway down the column, followed by the marines. Once the column fully formed about half an hour later, the order was given to march, and the column began to move.

The 23rd, still on the heights and serving as the rear guard, fell back from their line formation and formed again in column behind the main body. Together the combined British force of almost 1,900 men departed Lexington, leaving in their wake three smoldering homes with only their brick chimneys still standing.[71]

As the British began their long march eastward, their fifers and drummers started to play that mocking tune "Yankee Doodle"—"by way of contempt", the militia thought. It served only to further incense the Americans. The bloody running battle was far from over.[72]

———— ⋅✦⋅ ————

There was great commotion among the Americans as the British pulled out. One grenadier of the 23rd wrote, "As soon as the rear Guard began to move, the Rebels commenced their fire, having previously crept round under cover, and gained the walls and hedges on both flanks."[73] Ensign De Berniere observed, "the rebels still kept firing on us, but very lightly".[74] Lieutenant Barker thought the first two miles were "pretty quiet", until they "began to pepper us again...but at a rather greater distance."[75]

There was indeed a brief lull in the combat along the Battle Road, but it was not because the Americans had given up. Quite the opposite: they were making their way through pastures and woods, taking long, circuitous paths to gain the advantage ahead of the retreating British.

Most of the Americans attempted to encircle on foot, but some had the benefit of horses. These rode ahead of the column, dismounted, and secured their horse behind some cover, then daringly "crept down near enough to have a Shot; as soon as the Column had passed, they mounted again, and rode round until they got ahead of the Column, and found some convenient place from whence they might fire again."[76]

Fresh American forces were continually coming in, guided by the sounds of the musketry. Soon even the van began taking heavy fire "from all quarters, but particularly from the houses on the roadside, and the Adjacent Stone walls."[77] Lord Percy had deployed very strong flanking parties. Flanking was ordinarily a job reserved for the light infantry, but since the lights had all participated in the expeditionary force and were now spent, platoons were selected from among the main battalion companies to take on this burden. As his column marched along, Percy found these flanking parties "absolutely necessary, as there was not a stone-wall, or house, though before in appearance evacuated, from whence the Rebels did not fire upon us."[78] Just as Percy had anticipated, each apparently empty house was now a bunker for snipers.

The continuous but scattered colonial fire grew ever more effective. Several troops were picked off by enemies unseen, falling dead or wounded along the road. The flanking parties, enraged by an ungallant enemy that fired while in hiding, and remembering the rumors of the scalping, began to storm every house along the way in turn, ready to put to death all inside.

As British casualties mounted, the dead were left along the roadside, but the wounded, fearing a scalping should they be left behind, struggled to stay with the march. Lieutenant Colonel Smith, with his wounded leg, had apparently given up his horse, but now begged a replacement from a marine officer. Dazed Ensign Lister, stumbling along as best he could, exhausted from the earlier work and light-headed from the loss of blood at his shattered elbow, begged of Smith to borrow the same horse, which Smith graciously gave him. Lister was not faring well, but the horse helped. Others nearby eased his burden too. One soldier, who still had in his haversack beef and a small biscuit, generously gave Lister half his meager meal—no more than a mouthful for each of them. A grenadier in Lister's regiment took the ensign's hat, broke ranks from the column, filled it with water at a horse pond, and then rushed it back to Lister. The parched Lister thanked him before gulping down the muddy water from his own hat. Lister's horse carried him along for about two miles, but as the militia parties gathered in increasing numbers around the flanks and the van, balls began to whiz by his head. Suddenly, he felt walking was the safer bet, even in his dire condition. He struggled to dismount and then led the steed along the march. Deadly militia fire continued to rake the column, despite the hard work of the many British flanking parties. So Lister adapted his defense accordingly: "as the Balls came thicker from one side or the other so I went from one side of the Horse to the other for some time".[79]

The roadside crossfire continued to grow ever more ferocious, leading the remaining mounted officers to all prudently give up horses. And in the same manner, all of these horses became walking shields for the wounded, who clung to the saddles and stirrups for support, switching from one side or the other as the intensity of the crossfire shifted. Inevitably, a shot finally hit one of these shield horses, killing it dead on the spot. The heavy beast's corpse instantly collapsed, causing a ripple down the column as the troops attempted to surpass it.

This particular horse had carried one wounded man draped on its back and shielded three other wounded hanging by its side. These all begged Lister to let them join him behind his horse, to which he readily agreed, and soon after he gave it wholly to their use. Others overcrowded the few chaises and wagons that had come with wounded from Concord. Still others piled onto the two horse-drawn artillery carriages and their limbers, clinging to the side boxes to hold on. "It was a very fatiguing march, and not being prepared with any conveyances for our wounded, it required the exertion of everybody to bring them off. The carriages of the guns were so loaded with wounded men that they could scarcely be fired".[80]

The running fight soon approached the sparse village of Menotomy. There the local militia lay in wait, joined with a considerable force of men from distant Danvers, Beverly, and Lynn, and from the nearer Medford and Malden, almost nine hundred men, positioned on the heights just north of the village's center.[81] All were under the command of Col. William Heath, who had returned to the village only a short time earlier. Joining him was Dr. Joseph Warren, who left the committee at Black Horse Tavern and would stay with Heath throughout the coming fight. Heath's force provided the closest semblance to an organized attack by the militia that day, but only in that quarter, for, of the pursuing militia horde and those attempting to harass the British flanks, they were still every one of them their own commander. The British were marching into a trap. Even if Lord Percy knew it, there was little he could do but march his men forward.[82]

With the militia horde closing in, a host still near 1,100 strong, the inexperienced British soldiers carelessly threw their shots away, emboldening the militia to draw closer still. The militia swarmed from all sides, but as Lieutenant Mackenzie observed, "they did not shew themselves openly in a body in any part, except on the road in our rear". Just as the British were coming upon Menotomy, Percy temporarily halted his retreat, ordering the artillery to unlimber and fire on the colonial horde. After the wounded soldiers crawled off the two gun carriages, the dark-blue-coated artillerymen unlimbered and prepared to fire with one of the few remaining shots left in their guns' side boxes. At the same time, the main column's rear guard fired a concerted volley or two into the pursuing militia. The rest of the column could do little but fire scattered shots at the ghostlike snipers along the rock walls, or as Mackenzie explained, "the moment they had fired they lay down out of sight until they had loaded again, or the Column had passed." And sometimes the snipers relocated before firing again, giving the flanking companies tough work as they chased constantly moving, hidden targets.[83]

Once the artillery got their two pieces ready, they both fired their round shot, blasting into the militia horde, perhaps felling a colonial or two while temporarily dispersing the rest. However, it was the ferocious roar of the cannon that was the real weapon—not the shot. Many of the younger men in the militia, those not veterans of the last war, were unaccustomed to the din of battle and easily frightened away.

While the artillerymen quickly re-limbered their cannon and the wounded crawled back on their carriages, the British column, ready to advance once more, saw Colonel Heath's new body of about nine hundred descending from the nearby northern heights. Lord Percy no sooner got his men back into the march than Heath's militia reached the roadside ahead. The British were now surrounded, but Percy had no intention of surrendering. Heath's men took cover behind and inside the houses, took aim on the British vanguard, and opened fire.

———◆———

Here, in the half-mile approach to Menotomy center, the day's bloodiest battle quickly grew into its fiercest as well. From the road ahead, Heath's militia began their deadly onslaught, pouring musket balls into the British vanguard and slowing their march to a crawl as they struggled to counter the attack. In turn, the entire British column began to compress, and the horde of Yankees pursuers seized this opportunity to close in around their prey from the rear. Rev. Ezra Stiles would describe the militia strategy as "*dispersed* tho' *adhering*"—that is, the militiamen were not one body but scattered, yet they kept close on the British. The Yankees soon had the embattled redcoats enveloped in what Percy would call "an incessant fire, wh[ich] like a moving circle surrounded & fol[lowe]d us wherever we went".[84]

One British officer there described Menotomy village as "a number of houses in little groups extending about half a mile". Now every house became its own battleground, with militia swarming into it for cover and firing from the windows. Percy decisively ordered his flankers to storm those houses and kill all inside. The enraged soldiers were only happy to comply, anxious to avenge their justice on what they thought were contemptible Americans who ungallantly assailed them while hiding and who had allegedly scalped their wounded comrades. Driven by their rage, fear, and adrenaline, the intrepid soldiers forced their way toward the first houses, plowing through the heavy fire that erupted from each window even as it picked off several of them. The defending Americans fought with equal rage, spurred on by the tidings of the shots at Lexington and Concord, and their contempt for Percy's burning of homes outside Lexington. The American defenders inside didn't try to flee or hide until the British flankers at last reached the first homes, but the British slaughtered many of the Americans before they could escape.[85] As echoed by several British officers there, Mackenzie wrote, "Those houses would certainly have been burnt had any fire been found in them, or had there been time to kindle any".[86]

When the house-to-house fighting approached the home of Jason Russell (it still stands today), the lame and barely ambulatory fifty-eight-year-old escorted his family into the neighboring woods. There he left them, and he returned to his home, where he hobbled about his porch, stacking a pile of shingles before his front door to serve as a barricade. A neighbor, Ammi Cutter, urged him to flee, but Russell replied, "An Englishman's home is his castle," or so tradition says. The neighbor took his own advice and fled, but encouraged by the old man's spirit, more than a dozen militia joined Russell at his makeshift breastwork.

When the fierce battle at last reached his doorstep, the militiamen fired a volley and then retreated inside. Russell tried to follow, hobbling to go inside quickly, when British flankers opened fire, felling him with two bullets. He was not yet dead, so one of the redcoats plunged his bayonet into Russell's chest, though before the soldier could give that horrible wrench that would ensure Russell's demise, other soldiers thrust their bayonets into the poor old man, finally killing him.

The flankers then stormed inside Russell's home, where a short but vicious melee ensued. The Yankees killed one regular, but the British slaughtered eleven Americans by bayonet (who had no bayonets themselves with which to fight close-quarter combat). The few Yankees who remained fled to the cellar, and the redcoats quickly followed until the first soldier was killed, likely by musket, his corpse tumbling down the stairs. The Americans then yelled that any other that dared to come down would suffer the same fate. So the British gave up the fight, grabbed a few pieces of plunder, and returned to the fight outside.[87]

On the road, the fighting was equally intense. The whole blood-spattered street was one cloud of white gun smoke, which helped provide cover as the British main column slowly pushed through the hail of crossfire, stepping over their dead and wounded and taking heavy casualties as they did so. Even those exhausted light infantry and grenadiers that had marched out with Smith, who now stood in the vanguard protected by the reinforcement, were again under an incessant fire nearly as severe as that on the rear guard. If any of those expeditionary force soldiers still had ammunition left in their cartouche boxes, they ran out of it here in Menotomy. Perhaps some of their neighboring battalion soldiers shared some of their own ammunition.[88]

Though the whole of the British were surrounded in a circle of fire, they slowly pressed on at what must have felt like a snail's pace. Even under such heavy crossfire, the artillery awkwardly fumbled to add to the fight as well, blasting at least one or two rounds into the thick militia biting at the British rear.

Farther along, some of the Danvers militia, darting into a better roadside position from which to harass the British, hurriedly built a barricade of stones and lumber. As these ill-experienced Yankees did so, they quickly found themselves caught between a large British flanking party and the main column. Though the Danvers men had hoped to help pour a crossfire into the main British column, they instead found themselves trapped in one. The British flankers fired viciously into these Danvers men, seven of whom fell dead or dying, with perhaps a dozen more wounded. The British flankers then charged with bayonets, maybe running a few militiamen through, while the lucky rest fled pell-mell from the roadside.[89]

In the heart of this action, Dr. Joseph Warren kept constantly near Colonel Heath, helping to encourage the men as he likely fired his own fusil musket. One colonist told of Warren's service: "he appeared in the field under the united character of the general, the soldier, and the physician; here he was seen animating his countrymen to battle, and fighting by their side; and there he was found administering healing comforts to the wounded".[90]

Though the musketry grew severe from both opponents, Warren was in the thick of it. One British shot whizzed so close by Warren's ear that it struck the pin out of the hair of his earlock, letting his neatly tied hair fall out of place. Heath saw it and looked at Warren to ensure he was okay. The good doctor may have paused for a moment to take a breath, but he remained relentless and undaunted, and likely fired several rounds into the British himself.[91]

Also in the heat of the battle was eighty-one-year-old Samuel Whittemore. As the battle neared his home, he sent his family fleeing and then marched to the road with a musket, two pistols, and a saber. He took position along a stone wall, and as the British came near, he fired all three guns. Legend claims he killed one soldier and wounded two more before the British swarmed him, shot him in the head, beat him with the butt ends of their muskets and bayoneted him several times. Left for dead, he was later attended by Dr. Cotton Tufts, who gave the gloomy prognosis that it was useless to try to save poor Whittemore. Yet Whittemore recovered, not to die until the ripe age of ninety-nine.[92]

The close-quarter street fighting continued as the British tried to break through the ambush. Percy observed that "several of their men…[had] a spirit of enthusiasm…for many of them concealed themselves in houses, & advanced within 10 yds. to fire at me & other officers, tho' they were morally certain of being put to death themselves in an instant."[93] A tradition says that one ball whizzed so close to Lord Percy that it sheared off a button from his scarlet coat.[94]

With the Americans continuing to engulf the British, the pursuing militia horde drew so close to the British heels that militiaman Dr. Eliphalet Downer found himself in close combat with a redcoat. The soldier lunged his bayonet at the doctor's chest, but Downer parried the thrust and wrangled the musket from the redcoat, turned it, and lunged the soldier's own bayonet into him with such force that the blade nearly passed out the other side, felling him on the spot.[95]

The flanking parties meanwhile continued their house-to-house search. At Cooper Tavern, two drunken but armed militiamen, middle-aged brothers-in-law Jason Winship and Jabez Wyman, stood drinking a liquor, beer, and sugar cocktail known as flip.[96] They merrily and obliviously drank away the afternoon, derelict of their duty, when a flanking party stormed in. The bartender and his wife quickly vanished, leaving the drunks to be run through by British bayonets. The British soldiers then barbarously stabbed them multiple times more, before bashing their skulls in and splattering blood and brains on the walls and floor. Afterward, the barkeep Benjamin Cooper found the gruesome corpses and noted more than a hundred bullet holes in the tavern, an example of the ferocity of the fighting throughout the village.[97]

In other houses, flanking parties stormed in but found no one, though they were certain shots had been fired from inside. Lt. Frederick Mackenzie explained, "Some houses were forced open in which no person could be discovered, but when the Column had passed; numbers sallied out from some place in which they had lain concealed, fired at the rear Guard, and augmented the numbers which followed us. If we had had time to set fire to those houses many Rebels must have perished in them".[98]

No house was safe. The British stormed into the house of Deacon Joseph Adams, whom they saw flee from the house as they approached, gutlessly leaving his defenseless wife and children behind. Three soldiers burst into the chamber of his wife, Hannah Adams, where she lay bedridden, recovering from giving birth just over two weeks earlier and scarcely able to walk. She cried out, "For the Lord's sake do not kill me!" One soldier replied, "Damn you!" Another explained to his fellow, "We will not hurt the woman, if she will go out of the house, but we will surely burn it." So Hannah crawled from her bed, having not walked farther than her bedchamber door since giving birth, and two of her daughters, young women, helped to dress her. One of the five Adams children, a nine-year-old boy named Joel, briefly popped his head out from under her bed. The soldiers saw him and told him to come out, to which the boy replied, "You'll kill me if I do." After the soldiers assured the boy they would not, he cautiously crawled out from under the bed and followed the soldiers around as they pilfered his home. Meanwhile, Hannah took her eighteen-day-old newborn and slowly but painfully made her way out the front door, where she took refuge in their small cornhouse (or corncrib) granary just outside. Once the soldiers were satisfied with their loot, they broke up some wooden chairs, lit the pieces by a fire in the hearth, and threw these torches about the home before quickly departing. Drawing on bravery obviously inherited from his mother's side, young Joel acted swiftly, using a pot of his father's home-brewed beer to extinguish the fire before it could spread, thus saving the house.[99]

Outside, the battle waged on. Menotomy was the deadliest skirmish either side fought that day, in large part because it was here that the Americans mustered their greatest numbers. Of an estimated 3,716 militiamen who served at some point throughout the day, probably no more than 2,000 ever gathered at one time. While this difference includes American casualties, mostly it is from the droves of volunteers who returned to their homes after they either had spent their ammo or otherwise given up the fight.[100] In comparison, at about 1,900, the total British force was nearly equal in size, though given that the number included their many casualties and Lieutenant Colonel Smith's depleted expeditionary force, it was maybe just half the effective American strength now.[101] Still, the British inflicted serious casualties on the American force, so much so that Americans would later criticize Lord Percy's tactics in the coming propaganda war.

Fair and less biased retrospection reveals that Percy was absolutely right in storming those houses one at a time. Unfortunately, in the literal fog of war that blanketed the village with thick, white gun smoke, the British officers lost control of their enraged and furious men, and a few of them committed atrocious acts. Indeed, just as we cannot excuse the North Bridge "scalping", which served as the catalyst for this newfound British fury, nor can we excuse the few isolated acts of British barbarism, such as the butchering of the two drunks, which repaid the violence of that American atrocity many times over. But later spins in the propaganda war, as well as biased nineteenth-century claims, would heap unearned atrocities onto the British.[102] For instance, Jason Russell's death was gruesome, but he had fired on the British and so became a lawful target. His death is sad, but it was not an atrocity. In truth, the British soldiers generally fought admirably and honorably, as much as one can expect in a deadly ambush by an enraged countryside.[103] Moreover, Percy's mission was to get his people back to Boston. And swarming the houses to wipe out the snipers was tactically necessary.[104]

That said, the soldiers' plundering of homes cannot be excused as merely isolated incidents. Looting was strictly forbidden by Gage and his officers, and the Americans were justified in their rage over such acts. As Mackenzie observed, "Many houses were plundered by the Soldiers, notwithstanding the efforts of the Officers to prevent it. I have no doubt this inflamed the Rebels, and made many of them follow us farther than they would otherwise have done. By all accounts some Soldiers who staid too long in the houses, were killed in the very act of plundering by those who lay concealed in them."[105]

Lieutenant Barker gave a grimmer opinion in his diary a few days later when he wrote, "Our Soldiers the other day tho' they shew'd no want of courage, yet were so wild and irregular, that there was no keeping 'em in any order; by their eagerness and inattention they kill'd many of our own People; and the plundering was shamefull; many hardly thought of anything else; what was worse they were encouraged by some Officers."[106]

That a few (and it was certainly a very few) officers encouraged the plundering was not only shameful but unforgivable, and could they have been identified, they should have been given a harsh punishment. What was more, looting begot vandalizing and straggling. One wonders how many of the twenty-six British reported missing after the battle were in fact looters who tarried too long and were caught.[107]

Despite the ferocity of the battle, the British at last forced themselves through the massive ambush, leaving the dead and dying strewn across the path, dragging with them about ten prisoners taken in arms, a few of whom would be killed by friendly fire as the militia continued to send scattered shots into the British rear guard. (Other prisoners were apparently later released.)[108]

Though running low on ammunition, the rear guard 23rd Regiment was probably obliged to march backward to fight off the pursuing militia horde, with the regiment's eight companies firing one at a time and then leapfrogging each other back toward the column, thus giving each company time to reload.[109] They covered the rear admirably, but they paid a high toll in casualties, including their regimental commander, Lt. Col. Bery Bernard, shot in the thigh.[110] Mackenzie, adjutant to the 23rd, heard the Yankees call out many times, "King Hancock forever." Given the 23rd's heavy burden and exhausting work to keep the horde at bay, Lord Percy ordered the 23rd to move up one place in the column, making the Battalion of Marines the new rear guard.[111]

The soldiers of the rear guard were not the only ones suffering from extreme fatigue—so too were the flank guards. As the British moved closer to the more populated area of Cambridge, the number of road-side obstructions grew. The Yankee militia took to the pastures and enveloped the rear guard, exerting relentless pressure. Consequently, the British flankers found themselves forced almost against the main column, unable to give wide flanking support.[112]

It took a steady drive on the part of the British, but soon they were through the thick of it. With the Skirmish of Menotomy behind them, the worst fighting of the day was over. But just down the road at Cambridge, the Americans had another ambush waiting. What the Yankees did not know was that Lord Percy had anticipated this next colonial ploy and had adjusted his strategy accordingly. This time, the Americans would be caught off guard.

⎯⎯⎯•⎯⎯⎯

The British marched the path from Menotomy to Cambridge with relative ease, though occasional harassing potshots continued incessantly. Ahead of the British was Watson's Corner, a crossroads about a mile and a half northwest of Cambridge center.[113] There the road forked, its southerly branch heading to town center, its northerly branch bypassing Cambridge and leading to Charlestown. As the British approached Watson's Corner, they found waiting there yet another militia ambush. Some of these were undoubtedly men from Menotomy who had taken to the pastures and woods to circle around the British advance. Most were militia from the lower towns outside Boston: Roxbury, Brookline, Dedham, and Needham, almost nine hundred fresh men. This militia body stood on the northerly path at Watson's Corner, blocking the fork toward Charlestown.[114]

Every Englishman there, be he American or Briton, naturally expected the British column to follow the fork south past Harvard College, across the Great Bridge over the Charles River, and then back to Boston via Roxbury—the standard land route, the one Percy had taken that morning. With this in mind, Colonel Heath had sent the 134-strong Watertown militia ahead to the Great Bridge with orders to again pull up the planks of the deck, barricade the bridge's south end, and take up post to ambush the British when they arrived.[115] The host of militia at Watson's Corner meanwhile had orders to let the British pass, only to then follow the British as they came to the disassembled bridge, thus ensnaring the column in what was sure to be a more devastating ambush than even Menotomy.

Everyone, including Percy's own officers, expected that the British would take the path to the bridge, but Lord Percy was too keen a tactician to fall for the Yankee ploy. He had probably considered as early as his march out to Lexington, when his advance scouts first found the bridge torn up, that it would be disastrous to return the same way. Instead, Percy decided to turn his column and take the fork toward Charlestown, and to plow his way through the nearly nine hundred fresh militia.[116] Lord Percy gave the order, and the British vanguard turned at Watson's Corner, straight for the vast American force. The Yankees were at first stunned by this change in direction…and then they opened fire.

Under assault, Percy halted his men and ordered his artillery to unlimber their guns. The British wounded once more rolled off the gun carriages, and as the bluecoats prepared their two pieces, loading some of the last rounds left in their guns' side boxes, the weary battalion flank guards fired scattered musket volleys to keep the enveloping militia at bay.

With the firefight growing hot again, Maj. Isaac Gardner led several of his Brookline militia to the roadside, where they took cover behind a stack of casks and sniped at the British. But as the flank guards swarmed out, the Brookline men found themselves trapped, and the British mercilessly killed every one of them by ball or bayonet.[117]

Once the British cannon were primed and ready, the flankers took cover and the two 6-pounders thundered to life, belching forth white smoke and orange flame, sending their round shot directly into the throng ahead. The balls blasted toward the fresh militia, perhaps inflicting casualties as they smashed through, persuading the remaining Yankees to instantly disperse. The cannon's roar was mightier than their bite, but in either case, they produced the desired result.[118]

The skirmish was short-lived, but Percy was the clear victor, having outsmarted Yankee ingenuity. Moreover, Percy averted a terrible disaster at the Great Bridge. Though he might not have realized it yet, his keen strategy had saved the British column. The Charlestown route also offered a shorter path back to Boston, shaving about five miles off their return march, or at a standard march rate, saving them almost two hours.[119]

The British drove through the hole made by their cannon and plowed eastward almost unmolested, for none of the Americans had been posted along that route. The militia horde still kept on the British heels, however, among them Colonel Heath and Dr. Warren. Thus, the rear guard was obliged to fire several volleys to keep the militia at bay, which in turn obliged Percy to relieve his rear guard marines with the 47th and later the 4th. Even so, the march to Charlestown was mostly uneventful.[120]

As the British approached Charlestown Common at the end of the mainland, which in turn led to Charlestown Neck, they saw about a mile to the north on Winter Hill the newly arrived militia from Salem, nearly three hundred strong. Their commander, Col. Timothy Pickering, had been reluctant to march to the fight until his men at last implored him. Now he came too late to give battle.[121]

On approaching Charlestown Neck, the thin strip of land that connected Charlestown Peninsula to the mainland, the advantage shifted. Here the militia could not encircle the moving column, which was fortunate for the British, for they had expended nearly all their ammo. By now, the sun had set and twilight was quickly waning. Still, a handful of shots whizzed out of those few houses that lined the final stretch to the Neck, the snipers barely visible in the dim light, illuminated primarily by the orange flame that glowed through the white smoke of their muskets as they fired.

One last innocent was killed here, in this, the most minor of skirmishes that day. A boy, just fourteen, curious and looking out a window as the column passed, lingered too long. The light was nearly gone, and a soldier, fearing the shadowy figure was a sniper, fired his musket and killed the boy, a tragic ending to the daylong battle.[122]

Once the British crossed the Neck, at about seven o'clock that night, they were at last safe. The bloodshed of April 19, 1775, was now over. Percy was modest when he gave his official reports, but the next day, when he wrote home to his father, he would confess, "I had the happiness…of saving them from inevitable destruction".[123]

On Charlestown Peninsula, the triumphant brigadier general formed his men on the northwest side of Bunker Hill to cover the Neck, should the militia dare to cross. He also ordered the artillery to take up position there, but as they were almost out of shot, they must have sent to Boston for more rounds.

The militia, meanwhile, had no intention of crossing into Charlestown. Instead, they decided to take the defensive, just as the British had done. Colonel Heath, with Dr. Warren by his side, took

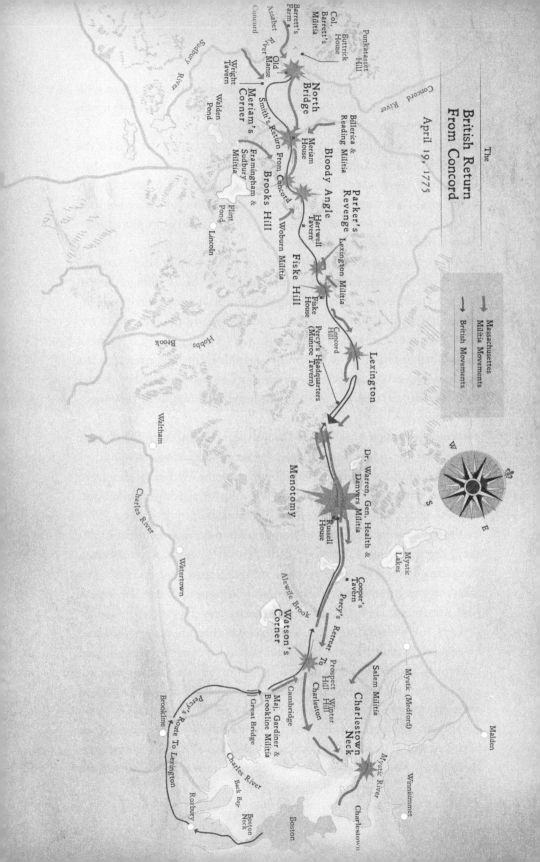

The
British Return
From Concord

April 19, 1775

Massachussettes
Militia Movements

British Movements

Concord
Assabet River
Concord River
Punkatasset Hill
Col. Barrett's Militia
Barrett's Farm
Buttrick House
Old Manse
Sudbury River
North Bridge
Wright Tavern
Meriam's Corner
Walden Pond
Smith's Return From Concord
Billerica & Reading Militia
Meriam House
Bloody Angle
Parker's Revenge
Hartwell Tavern
Lexington Militia
Brooks Hill
Framingham & Sudbury Militia
Woburn Militia
Flint Pond
Lincoln
Fiske Hill
Fiske House
Concord Hill
Percy's Headquarters (Munroe Tavern)
Lexington
Hobbs Brook
Waltham
Charles River
Watertown
Dr. Warren, Gen. Heath & Danvers Militia
Russell House
Menotomy
Cooper's Tavern
Percy's Retreat
Mystic Lakes
Mystic (Medford)
Malden
Watson's Corner
Alewife Brook
Cambridge
Maj. Gardiner & Brookline Militia
Great Bridge
Brookline
Percy's Route To Lexington
Prospect Hill
Charlestown Neck
Salem Militia
Winnisimmet
Mystic River
Charlestown
Back Bay
Charles River
Boston Neck
Boston
Roxbury

command of the loosely organized multitude. He posted a large detachment on Prospect Hill to guard against the British leaving Charlestown. The rest he sent to Cambridge, from whence he sent another large guard across the Great Bridge to Roxbury, to take post outside Boston Neck.[124]

In Charlestown proper, the town's selectmen sent a messenger to Lord Percy at Bunker Hill, offering that if he would agree to not attack the town, they would ensure the safety of the troops and would do all in their power to help them cross the Charles back to Boston. (In other words, the selectmen would do all in their power to get the British out of their town as quickly as possible.) Percy gladly accepted the selectmen's offer. Within moments, the wounded troops and the weary light infantry and grenadiers headed down to Charlestown center. Once there, they found the town itself somewhat abandoned, for many had fled when they had heard the rumors of war to the west.[125]

Earlier that evening, Gage, perhaps in response to Percy's messenger Lieutenant Rooke, had met with Admiral Graves at Province House, eager to discuss the matter of securing the British return. The admiral swiftly sent a courier to HMS *Preston*, his flagship, which hoisted a solid red flag to the main topmast head, then fired a cannon to signal the attention of the other ships' captains. When the captains saw this predetermined signal flag, they immediately ordered all their remaining shipboard marines into longboats, which rowed up the harbor and down the Charles, coming alongside HMS *Somerset* just off Charlestown. The marines all boarded *Somerset*, ready to give aid to Percy's reinforcement when they at last returned. The admiral would later claim credit for being the column's savior, stating, "it was the *Somerset* alone that preserved the detachment from Ruin. The vicinity of that formidable Ship to Charles Town so intimidated its Inhabitants that they (tho' reluctantly) suffered the Kings Troops to come in and pass over to Boston, who would otherwise have been undoubtedly attacked".[126]

Even as his marines were redeploying to the *Somerset*, Admiral Graves urged his counterpart Gage to consider the prudence of the "burning of Charles town and Roxbury, and the seizing of the Heights of Roxbury and Bunkers Hill," but "to this Proposal the General objecting the weakness of his Army" declined. The admiral then suggested that Gage bring up the 64th from Castle William, leaving that fortress to be manned by his sailors. Though Gage did indeed bring up much of the 64th, he still refused to take the offensive, his heart not yet turned to war. Graves proved very vocal when giving his opinion "that we ought to act hostiley from this time forward by burning & laying waste the whole country," but as time would tell, Graves always urged aggressiveness when he did not bear responsibility for the outcome. If the decision were his alone to make, it is doubtful he would have shown the hostility he preached.[127]

Now, with the British safe in Charlestown, the longboats of the Royal Navy made their way to the dark Charlestown wharves, bringing with them fresh troop detachments and ferrying away first the wounded, followed by the exhausted light infantry and grenadiers. From Boston, all one could see in those dark hours before the moonrise was the bobbing of many lanterns across the docks, accompanied by the distant groans of wounded soldiers in agony.[128]

Among the wounded was Ensign Lister, who was feeling faint from both heavy fatigue and loss of blood. Though the ball had been removed from his shattered right elbow, his limp but bandaged arm was swollen and painful. One of his 10th Light Infantry sergeants found him and reported that he could only find twelve of their men and no officer. Lister recalled that Lieutenant Kelly had been shot in the arm at Concord's North Bridge and was probably in as poor condition as him. Lister had no idea what had happened to their company commander, Captain Parsons, but assumed he had been shot along the retreat. So Lister gave charge to the sergeant, offered a few words of advice about command, then told him to do the best he could with the few men they had left.

When Lister then made his way to the wharves, he found by the light of nearby lanterns his Captain Parsons, "who I believe was then in a worse situation than myself", having, depending on the account, either a severe contusion to his knee or a bullet wound to his arm, or both.[129] There, along the docks, Lister also found Lieutenant Sutherland, whose shot to the breast caused him great agony. As Lister wrote, "I believe he was in Violent pain, and did not expect long to survive".[130] Sutherland did survive, as did Parsons, though both were a little the worse for wear.

By nine o'clock that night, Lister was back at his lodgings at a Mr. Miller's house. Despite his wound, he insisted on having some tea, which the missus of the house gladly served him. She, along with a few neighbors gathered there, was eager for his stories. Lister just wanted peace and quiet to enjoy his tea. As he later wrote, "it is beyond the power of Words to express the satisfaction I felt from that Tea, notwithstanding I was interrupted with a Thousand Questions." When asked if he had seen Sutherland, he replied that he had, but that he expected him to soon be dead. Little did Lister know, but among the crowd gathered behind him was Sutherland's wife, who began to faint. Once Lister realized this, he was only half sorry for having said it, because with the attention now on Mrs. Sutherland, he was at last able to enjoy his tea in peace. After he finished, he cut the glove from his swollen, bloody hand and then went to bed. A surgeon came later to change his bandages. Over the next two months, he would be considered for amputation, only to be given a last-minute reprieve by his doctor. He would undergo two excruciating surgeries in an era when the only anesthesia was a swig or two of rum, but finally, after months, he would recover, keeping the arm and apparently regaining some mobility. In December, he would at last return to England, where he was promoted to lieutenant and served as a recruiting officer for the coming war.[131]

By ten o'clock that night, the last of the wounded as well as the expeditionary force were back in Boston. Only Percy's reinforcement still waited for their ferry home. His battle line along the northwest face of Bunker Hill was relieved piecemeal, one detachment at a time, by the 2nd and 3rd Brigades and two hundred men of the 64th from Castle William, all placed under the command of Brig. Gen. Robert Pigot. When the moon finally rose at nearly eleven o'clock, these fresh troops on Bunker Hill began constructing a small flèche (or redan), a V-shaped earthwork with its point facing toward the Neck, built under the able supervision of British engineer Capt. John Montresor. The last incident of the day came when one officer of the 64th strayed too near the Neck and the Americans took him prisoner.[132]

Meanwhile, with the baton passed to the fresh troops, Percy's reinforcement made their way in turn down to Charlestown, there to await their boats. Lt. Frederick Mackenzie and his 23rd, along with the marines, took shelter in the town meetinghouse until the backlog of men at the wharves was finally ferried over. It was not until after midnight that the last of Percy's column landed in the North End of Boston, from which they immediately marched to their barracks.[133]

Of the estimated 3,716 enrolled militia who may have engaged the British that day, the best estimate of the casualties on the American side is forty-nine killed, forty-two wounded, and five missing (taken prisoner, later exchanged), or ninety-six total casualties of war throughout the many skirmishes of the day—a mere 2.6 percent casualty rate.[134] In contrast, of the estimated 766 officers and men of the original expeditionary force, plus the 1,148 officers and men of the reinforcement—a total of about 1,934 counting the patrolmen and artillery—the British suffered sixty-five killed, 181 wounded (some left behind and taken prisoner), and another twenty-six missing and presumably also taken prisoner (including the Tory guide Samuel Murray[135]), for a total loss of 272 men, a devastating 14 percent casualty rate.[136] On both sides, some of the wounded would later die, such as Lt. Edward Hull of the 43rd. The four British light companies that traveled as far as Barrett's Farm had marched more than forty-two miles round trip in less than twenty-four hours, half of which were under sporadic and sometimes heavy fire.[137]

Perhaps the most glaring statistic is that, of the possible 3,716 militia who swarmed to the battle that day, many firing multiple shots each, only 272 balls or so hit their mark. Except for the few that shot men already dead or wounded, more than 90 percent of the Americans that fought that day failed to shoot anyone. Was it because the Yankees were not yet committed to fight, as some histories would have us believe? Or were they terrible marksmen, the inherent inaccuracies of the smoothbore musket notwithstanding?

Lord Percy's triumph at bringing Smith's broken expeditionary force through hell and back was praised by British officers and soldiers alike. Even Lieutenant Mackenzie, not prone to give more than the facts in his diary, wrote, "Lord Percy behaved with great spirit throughout the affair, and at the same time with great coolness."[138] As Lord Percy lodged at Province House with Gage, undoubtedly, Gage kept him up late into the night, anxious to hear every detail.

Percy was humble when he turned in his official report, but when the commander in chief wrote days later to Lord Dartmouth in England, he extolled Percy's actions: "Too much Praise cannot be given Lord Percy for his remarkable Activity and Conduct during the whole Day". A day before Dartmouth would read this letter, Lord Drummond in London would receive the news by another gentleman just come from America. Drummond promptly wrote to Dartmouth, "the retreat by Lord Percy was deemed a piece of masterly officership in bringing off his men with so little loss".[139]

Percy was the only shining example of success in an expedition otherwise marked with dismal failure. Lieutenant Barker wrote in his diary, "from beginning to end was as ill plan'd and ill executed as it was possible to be; had we not idled away three hours on Cambridge Marsh waiting for provisions that were not wanted, we shou'd have had no interruption at Lexington, but by our stay the Country People had got intelligence and time to assemble. We shou'd have reached Concord soon after day break, before they cou'd have heard of us".[140] Barker was mostly right. However, Paul Revere's alarm was extremely effective. Had the British made it to Concord unmolested, they would have still encountered militia upon their return, though not in such great numbers. Certainly, if Lieutenant Colonel Smith had not tarried so long on the Cambridge marsh, both sides would have suffered fewer casualties.

As it was, the fighting retreat was violent and intense. Many of the British, accustomed only to regular combat, were caught off guard by this kind of irregular fighting. Smith lamented, "Notwithstanding the enemy's numbers, they did not make one gallant attempt…though our men were so very much fatigued".[141] Capt. William Evelyn of the 4th was more scathing when he wrote his father, "The rebels…though they are the most absolute cowards on the face of the earth, yet they are just now worked up to such a degree of enthusiasm and madness, that they are easily persuaded the Lord is to assist them in whatever they undertake, and that they must be invincible."[142] But irregular combat was not new to the British, who had learned the ways of Indian fighting in the last war with the French. On this day, the light infantry and flank guards employed guerrilla tactics themselves, similar to that of the militia. Lord Percy almost praised the Americans for their keen strategy when he wrote, "During the whole affair the Rebels attacked us in a very scattered, irregular manner, but with perseverance & resolution, nor did they ever dare to form into a regular body. Indeed, they knew too well what was proper, to do…"[143]

For both sides, it would take several days for the significance of the affair to sink in. Lord Percy may have been among the first of the British to reconsider his opinions of the country folk. When he wrote to Lt. Gen. Edward Harvey, the Army's adjutant general in England, he gave foreboding advice for future conduct with the Americans. "Whoever looks upon them as an irregular mob, will find himself much mistaken. They have men amongst them who know very well what they are about, having been employed as Rangers ag[ain]st the Indians & Canadians, & this country being much covd w. wood, and hilly, is very advantageous for their method of fighting... You may depend upon it, that as the Rebels have now had time to prepare, they are determined to go thro' with it, nor will the insurrection here turn out so despicable as it is perhaps imagined at home. For my part, I never believed, I confess, that they wd have attacked the King's troops, or have had the perseverance I found in them yesterday."[144]

As the British licked their wounds in Boston and fresh troops guarded the only approach into Charlestown, American militia continued to pour in from the most distant towns, gathering on all sides of Boston, brought there by the alarm that William Dawes and Paul Revere first began. Though neither side knew yet what the implications were for that fateful day in April, colonists came toward Boston in droves, setting up camp outside Charlestown, in Cambridge, and outside Boston Neck in Roxbury. If the British had any doubt of the colonial commitment to see it through, they needed only look to the west, where they could gaze upon hundreds of campfires blazing all around the town's western borders. Thousands of militia were there that first night, and thousands more were on their way.

Political resistance had at last given way to a violent struggle in the form of a revolution. The fateful Battle of the Nineteenth of April was over. But the Siege of Boston, and the American Revolutionary War, had just begun.

CHAPTER 10

AN EMBOLDENED PEOPLE

While the running fight of the fateful Nineteenth of April was being waged, Israel Bissel and other couriers rode from Menotomy to spread the alarm. Upon receiving the news, many towns also sent their own couriers in other directions, thus spreading the alarm to the far reaches of the continent.

When the news reached portly, forty-seven-year-old Militia Maj. Gen. Artemas Ward, the top militia officer in all of Massachusetts, he lay bedridden at his home in Shrewsbury, near Worcester. He had reached this high command in part for his service in the French and Indian War, though his battlefield experience was limited. Even so, he would prove to be an able administrator in the present crisis…if only he could get out of bed. Ward cursed his luck that he was again suffering from one of his recurrent flare-ups of "calculus". Perhaps his "calculus" was a gallstone, but more likely it was a bladder stone that he had been unable to pass. Either condition results in an intense abdominal pain. In the colonial era of medicine, removal of such stones often posed more of a health risk than the stones themselves.[1]

Despite his debilitating calculus, Ward nevertheless rode to Cambridge the day after the battle and promptly assumed command. He took up residence at the house of Jonathan Hastings Jr. near Cambridge Common, which for the coming months would serve as the American headquarters for both the Provincial Committee of Safety and the military.[2]

The fifty-year-old Massachusetts Militia Brig. Gen. John Thomas also arrived in Cambridge soon after the battle, and Ward promptly gave him command of the forces amassing in Roxbury. Thomas was a doctor by trade, but the untiring six-foot-tall soldier was also a respected veteran of the last war. And though a strict disciplinarian, Thomas was fair and patient, traits perhaps honed from his deep devotion to family. Thomas's orders were simple: watch Boston Neck and prevent the British from emerging from the town.[3]

When news of the alarm reached the various towns of New Hampshire, they promptly ordered their militia companies to Cambridge by the hundreds. Their spirited response was appreciated, but their companies marched piecemeal, and when they at last reached Cambridge, they found themselves in need of field officers, organization, and regulation.[4]

As news reached central Connecticut the morning after the battle, fifty-seven-year-old farmer and Militia Col. Israel Putnam was out plowing the fields of his farm with a "train," probably of oxen, assisted by his fifteen-year-old son Daniel. The elder Putnam must have been surprised when a mounted messenger galloped up to him to give the excited report. Years later, young Daniel described his father's reaction: "he loitered not, but left *me*, the driver of his team, to unyoke it in the furrow".[5]

Without changing his farm clothes, Colonel Putnam quickly bridled his horse and galloped from his parish of Brooklyn to nearby Lebanon. There he met with Royal Governor Jonathan Trumbull, the only committed pro-Whig royal governor in the entire continent. After hearing the news, Trumbull ordered Putnam to Cambridge, and the stout Putnam eagerly complied. When he rode back home to prepare for the trip, passing Brooklyn Green, he found hundreds of his own militia regiment mustering and awaiting orders. So Putnam arranged with his officers to march the men toward Cambridge.

Putnam then continued home, gathered a few things, and within hours, was riding ahead of his men on the nearly seventy miles to Cambridge, still wearing his dirty farm clothes. Upon his arrival the next day, he learned the details of the fight and accordingly sent dispatches back to Connecticut urging that it send more troops and provisions at once. Putnam then offered his assistance to Major General Ward, who gave him some useful service. But within a week, as the emergency of the Nineteenth of April gave way to more deliberate planning, Connecticut would recall "Old Put" for his advice on a long-term strategy.[6]

It took several days for the news to arrive in the southern colonies, but after it reached George Washington's farmstead of Mount Vernon in Virginia, he reflected on the matter before he wrote, "Unhappy it is though to reflect, that a Brother's Sword has been sheathed in a Brother's breast, and that, the once happy and peaceful plains of America are either to be drenched with Blood, or Inhabited by Slaves. Sad alternative! But can a virtuous Man hesitate in his choice?"[7] It took about three weeks for the news to arrive in the distant and young colony of Georgia, and it took longer still to seep into the American frontier. When the word of the pivotal strife at last reached settlers in the untamed back-country of the Kentucky wilderness, the hunters at one camp there, in honor of those first shots, named their site Lexington, now the modern city of the same name.[8]

Soon, the entire continent was aflame with the talk of war. In Boston, General Gage entrenched and prepared for the worst.

------ ◆ ------

Lt. Gen. Thomas Gage was greatly alarmed when he gazed upon those watch fires burning all around the town of Boston on the night of the fateful nineteenth. As those fires died away with sunrise the next morning, April 20, he saw before him a ragtag siege army comprising country folk numbering in the thousands. They encamped on the mainland across from Charlestown Neck and in Roxbury across from Boston Neck, while many more gathered in Cambridge, which was soon to become the New England Army's headquarters. Seeing so vast a force, Gage and most Bostonians feared the rebels might storm, bombard, or otherwise raze the town, all under their banner of liberty. Rumors began flying that the Yankees vowed "to storm Boston, seize upon and demolish Castle William, fortify Point Alderton, burn all the men of war, and cut off every Tory".[9] (Point Alderton guarded the entrance to Boston Harbor near the waterway Nantasket Roads.)

If such an attack came, Gage knew his little army of 3,200 men and officers could hardly stop such a massive rebel force, which soon exceeded 12,000 (roughly evenly spread among the three American camps).[10] As Rev. William Gordon of Roxbury observed of the Yankee Army, "the people poured down in so amazing a manner from all parts, for scores of miles around, (even the gray-headed came to assist their countrymen,) the General was obliged to set about further fortifying the Town immediately at all points and places."[11]

Gage's first orders were to strengthen the outworks at Boston Neck. Dr. Joseph Warren had always feared those fortifications were built to keep the people in, not to protect the city from a threat without, and now his suspicions were confirmed. For not only did Gage strengthen the Neck against attack from the besieging army, but he also closed off the Neck's gate from all traffic—in or out. Within days, the Neck would have "an *Abbattis* in front of the left Bastion, and across the road is a treple row of chevaux de fries [spiked logs]."[12]

Gage also ordered the closure of Charlestown Ferry, effectively sealing off the peninsular town. Meanwhile, the American siege was almost immediately effective, "So that in the course of two days," Ens. Henry De Berniere lamented, "from a plentiful town, we were reduced to the disagreeable necessity of living on salt provisions, and fairly blocked up in Boston."[13] In contrast, the American forces would have plenty of fresh food throughout the siege.

Also on April 20, the day after the battle, Gage ordered Brig. Gen. Robert Pigot and his men to withdraw from Charlestown Peninsula. His Excellency thought it best to regroup his army in Boston: better there to defend against what Gage thought was an imminent American assault, rather than to try to control both Boston and Charlestown and thereby spread his small and outnumbered army woefully thin. Pigot was no doubt dismayed when he received his orders to withdraw. The night before, his men had constructed a small flèche with its V-shaped salient toward Charlestown Neck. After completing this hasty fortification, the fresh British force had toiled all through the night and into the early morning hours to enclose it into a complete and substantial redoubt from which they could adequately defend against a Yankee attack.

But with his new orders, Pigot was forced to order the redoubt demolished, lest it be used by the rebels. Though much of the original flèche was left intact, the remainder of the redoubt was broken up and left as little more than scattered piles of dirt along the northwest face of Bunker Hill. Finally, with assistance from the Royal Navy's longboats, the British evacuated Charlestown Peninsula around four o'clock that afternoon, thus consolidating British power in Boston.[14]

Adm. Samuel Graves immediately took positive steps to ensure that the British evacuation of Charlestown would not lead to a rebel occupation of the same ground. The admiral ordered Capt. Edward Le Cras of the HMS *Somerset*, whose ship still loomed just south of that town's wharves, to deliver a warning to the selectmen of Charlestown that "if they suffered the Rebels to take possession of their town or erect any works upon the Height", their town would be fired upon and razed to the ground. Given the substantial firepower the Royal Navy now had at its disposal, it was no idle threat, and so Charlestown Peninsula became an understood neutral ground. Meanwhile, to be ready for any rebel attack, Graves also issued orders to all of his ships' captains that they "be kept clear for Action".[15]

Two nights after the battle, on April 21, a party of rebels canoed up to the edges of Castle William to reconnoiter it for a possible attack. The alert sentries could hardly see who was in boats, but when they challenged the rebels with a parole, the Yankees gave as their countersign a scattered musket volley. The sentinels fired back, but the Yankees escaped into the darkness. Admiral Graves responded by placing the massive 64-gun HMS *Asia* and the nimble 6-gun HM schooner *Hope* off Castle Island for its protection.[16]

Meanwhile, Gage was so distressed that an attack would soon commence that he was determined to withdraw even his 110-strong detachment from Marshfield, a small town south of Boston that stood with its neighbor Scituate as rare examples of Loyalism. The detachment had kept the peace by its presence alone, protecting Tories in Marshfield and Scituate from threat of violence from their Whiggish neighboring towns. But now Gage applied to Graves to send a ship there for a British withdrawal. Graves acted with uncommonly quick assistance, ironically sending the armed schooner *Hope* along with two smaller sloops recently impressed. Their orders: to take away not only the British but also all friends of the government. Marshfield and Scituate would be left abandoned to the Whig minority, who surely capitalized on the turn of events by stirring up the spirit of rebellion among those neighbors still on the political fence.[17]

Days after the battle, Gage ordered construction of gun batteries at strategic points in Boston, mostly along the North End and near Boston Neck.[18] Graves offered his assistance in these efforts as well, his new-found cooperation only because of his recent positive orders from the home government to do so. Accordingly, Graves disembarked a number of seamen and some of the few remaining marines directly under his command and ordered they build their own battery on Copp's Hill, designed not only to defend the town from that height but also to protect Graves's fleet. "A Battery was yesterday began on the Hill above Charles Town Ferry, in order to defend the *Somerset* Man-of-War who lays in the Channel from any Battery which might be raised against her on a Hill on the Charles Town side where she cou'd not bring her guns to bear."[19] Graves supplied this with his own ships' cannon, including four large 24-pounders: two from the *Preston*, two from the *Boyne*. Once the structure was completed, the Navy men affectionately dubbed it the Admiral's Battery.[20] Before the end of the siege, many other little batteries would spring up on most of the wharves and hills of Boston.

On the colonial side of the siege, Whig leaders were equally busy. After the late battle, John Hancock and Samuel Adams had escaped to Worcester where they awaited Thomas Cushing and Robert Treat Paine. These were four of the five Massachusetts delegates to the Second Continental Congress, Hancock being the new junior member, taking James Bowdoin's slot from the previous delegation. Once Cushing and Paine arrived, the four would begin their long journey southward to Philadelphia. Their fifth delegate, John Adams, would linger a few days more outside Boston before joining them.[21]

Ironically, the Second Congressional Convention had always been scheduled to reconvene on May 10, unless a redress of grievances was received by then from the King. But the King had given the First Continental Congress's petition over to an anti-American Parliament, which had scoffed at its impositions and refused to consider it. The recent battle resulting from the Expedition to Concord was the nail in the coffin. Only with news of this battle did many of the gathering

congressional delegates from across the thirteen colonies finally conclude that an accommodation with Great Britain was unlikely, though
most still held in their hearts a glimmer of hope that it might somehow
still be achieved.[22]

Before departing for Philadelphia, John Adams decided to see firsthand the results of the late battle. As he wrote many years later in his
autobiography, "A few days after this Event [of April 19th] I rode to
Cambridge where I saw...the New England Army. There was great
Confusion and much distress: Artillery, Arms, Cloathing were wanting
and a sufficient Supply of Provisions not easily obtained. Neither the
officers nor Men however wanted Spirits or Resolution. I rode from
thence to Lexington and along the Scene of Action for many miles and
enquired of the Inhabitants, the Circumstances. These were not calculated to diminish my Ardour in the Cause. They on the Contrary
convinced me that the Die was cast, the Rubicon passed, and as Lord
Mansfield expressed it in Parliament, if We did not defend ourselves they
would kill Us." All that John Adams saw and learned on the Concord
Road was sufficient to convince even him—hardly a man of violence or
aggression—that "the Battle of Lexington on the 19th of April, changed
the Instruments of Warfare from the Penn to the Sword." He rode
for home, prepared to leave for Philadelphia, and "got into a Sulkey
attended by a Servant on horseback and proceeded on the journey." He
met his fellow colleagues before they reached New York, and from there
they "were met by a great Number of Gentlemen in Carriages and on
horseback, and all the Way their Numbers increased till I thought the
whole City was come out to meet Us. The same Ardour was continued
all the Way to Philadelphia."[23]

With the chief Whig leaders of Boston on their way to the
Congress, the able Dr. Joseph Warren was again left in charge of
leading the province through its most trying crisis. During the First
Congress, he had proven himself capable of rising to the challenge,
but times were different now, for an open war had begun, and there
was much to do as the Provincial Congress moved to openly assert
authority over the colony and establish a new system of government
free from Governor Thomas Gage.

The day after the battle, all was in a state of confusion, with the

bulk of everyone's efforts dedicated to burying the dead and tending to the wounded. Meanwhile, Dr. Warren met with various Whig
and militia leaders and tried to make sense of it all. Then, on behalf
of the Committee of Safety, he spent time drafting a circular letter to
be forwarded to the many towns. It proclaimed: "The barbarous mur-
ders committed upon our innocent brethren, on Wednesday, the 19th
instant, have made it absolutely necessary, that we immediately raise
an army to defend our wives and children from the butchering hands
of an inhuman soldiery, who, incensed at the obstacles they met with
in their bloody progress, and enraged at being repulsed from the field
of slaughter, will, without the least doubt, take the first opportunity
in their power, to ravage this devoted country with fire and sword. We
conjure you, therefore, by all that is sacred, that you give assistance in
forming an army. Our all is at stake. Death and devastation are the
certain consequences of delay. Every moment is infinitely precious. An
hour lost may deluge your country in blood, and entail perpetual slavery
upon the few of our posterity who may survive the carnage. We beg and
entreat, as you will answer to your country, to your own consciences,
and above all, as you will answer to GOD himself, that you will hasten
and encourage by all possible means, the enlistment of men to form the
army, and send them forward to head quarters at Cambridge, with that
expedition, which the vast importance and instant urgency of the affair
demands." This was the first blow of the coming propaganda war—the
Second Battle of Lexington and Concord.[24]

On the same day, Warren wrote privately to Gage, "Your Excellency,
I believe, knows very well the part I have taken in public affairs: I ever
scorned disguise. I think I have done my duty: some may think otherwise; but be assured, sir, as far as my influence goes, every thing which
can reasonably be required of us to do shall be done, and every thing
promised shall be religiously performed."[25]

One of the great concerns for the Committee of Safety was the safety
of the noncombatants inside fortified and besieged Boston. The Boston
selectmen at once began to press Gage to allow the exodus of the town's
inhabitants, yet Boston Neck remained sealed, and while Loyalists could
perhaps enter from the countryside (had the Americans along the siege
lines allowed it), none from Boston could leave. Warren's private letter

to Gage pressed for action. It continued, "I should now be very glad to know from you, sir, how many days you desire may be allowed for such as desire to remove to Boston with their effects, and what time you will allow the people in Boston for their removal. When I have received that information, I will repair to congress, and hasten, as far as I am able, the issuing a proclamation."[26]

Giving a rare glimpse into the character and private thoughts of the good doctor, Warren concluded his private letter with a regret of the late, bloody conflict that had ensued. "I have many things which I wish to say to Your Excellency, and most sincerely wish I had broken through the formalities which I thought due to your rank, and freely have told you all I knew or thought of public affairs; and I must ever confess, whatever may be the event, that you generously gave me such opening, as I now think I ought to have embraced: but the true cause of my not doing it was the knowledge I had of the vileness and treachery of many persons around you, who, I supposed, had gained your entire confidence."[27] Gage was indeed surrounded by his remaining mandamus councilors who whispered "vileness and treachery", using their influence to delay Gage in freeing the inhabitants of Boston. As a result, Warren would find himself dealing with the liberation of the Bostonians for the next several weeks.

Meanwhile, sometime during that hectic day following the battle, Paul Revere came upon Dr. Benjamin Church, both apparently on their way to join the Committee of Safety at the Hastings House. Revere had always looked upon Church with suspicion, writing later, "I was a constant & critical observer of him… I never thought Him a man of Principle; and I doubted much in my own mind, wether He was a real Whig." His suspicions were not without merit. Revere and others had long observed that Church kept company and sometimes dined with two questionable men, one a customs commissioner named John Robinson, the other a retired half-pay British officer named Captain Price, though to be fair, these friendships had probably begun long before the present hostilities. On this, Church once justified himself to an intimate friend, claiming, "He kept Company with them on purpose to find out their plans." This was not the only reason to be suspicious of Church, however. As Revere later noted, "Though it was known, that some of the

Liberty Songs, which We composed, were parodized by him, in favor of the British, yet none dare charge him with it." There was also the nagging and ongoing belief that a spy stood among the ranks of the Whigs, since secrets of their past actions were known to have reached General Gage. But while some doubted whether Church was a staunch Whig, no one truly suspected Church of being that spy. Moreover, despite his questionable activities, Church was a strong participant in the Whig movement, often wrote in favor of the Cause, and had even given a spirited third-anniversary oration for the Boston Massacre. Most of the Whig leaders therefore incontrovertibly respected Dr. Church, though Revere thought privately that some Whigs "feared, as well as courted Him." So while Revere remained unconvinced of Church's loyalty and even thought privately that Dr. Warren also "had not the greatest affection for him", Revere kept his suspicions to himself.[28]

These were the thoughts that filled Revere's mind as the two men crossed paths on their way to Hastings House. And then, another thought occurred to Revere. Dr. Warren had fought at Menotomy, Samuel Adams and John Hancock had escaped from Lexington, and Revere himself had helped sound the alarm. But Dr. Church…where was he during the fight? He was the only key Whig leader unaccounted for. Revere determined to find out, and so accosted the creepy doctor.

What Revere said is unknown, but Dr. Church, still wearing the same clothes from the day before, replied by showing Revere "some blood on his stocking, which he said spirted [spurted] on him from a Man who was killed near him, as he was urging the Militia on." Revere was taken aback at this evidence. As he later wrote, "I argued with my self, if a Man will risque his life in a Cause, he must be a Friend to that cause." After much reflection, Revere conceded that his doubts about the doctor must surely be unfounded, and would never distrust or suspect Church again.[29]

It was unfortunate for the Cause that Revere was not less trusting, for Church's story was almost certainly a bold-faced lie. No evidence exists to support Church's claim, and it is especially glaring that not one of the many depositions of the day records him being there, though he was famous enough to have been recognized by many of the participants.

If Church was not at the fight, where did the blood on his stocking come from? A benevolent theory is that it spurted on him when he performed duties as a physician sometime during or after the battle, perhaps helping a wounded militiaman. Even if he had helped a wounded British soldier, such service to the enemy was not treachery, but rather an expectation of a physician, implied in the Hippocratic oath to show compassion for all wounded, be they redcoat or Yankee. Alternatively, perhaps Church planted the blood there to serve as an alibi for whatever treacherous activities he really performed. But these are mere theories, and Church's whereabouts during the battle remain, to this day, a mystery.

Whatever the truth, Church adeptly convinced Revere of no wrongdoing. So the two headed off to join the Committee of Safety in peace, Revere being now engaged "as a Messenger, to do the out of doors business for that committee".[30]

At Hastings House, Dr. Church, being a member of that committee, was among the trusted few who learned of all the American preparations for war. He took careful mental notes, asked deliberate and specific questions, and devised in his mind's eye how he might convey his latest intelligence to the British in Boston, all unbeknownst to Dr. Warren and the others. With Paul Revere now off his trail, this well-placed spy, this not-so-good doctor was now free to continue his treason unabated. And he planned to do just that.

Two days after the daylong battle, April 21, the Committee of Safety was again in session at Hastings House. Though it was not recorded, the committee selected Dr. Joseph Warren as acting chairman, the position vacated because John Hancock had gone to Philadelphia.[31] The committee then spent the bulk of the day dedicated to its greatest concern: the state of its hodgepodge army. This subject undoubtedly interested the spy Dr. Church immensely, and he remained in attendance throughout the day. Since Gen. Artemas Ward was lodging in the same house where the committee convened, he also attended and offered his perspective on the military disposition.

The committee's chief concern regarding its unorganized army was time. Boston's siege army consisted exclusively of volunteer militia companies, which by their nature only served as a temporary response in times of emergency. Thus, as time dragged on with the Siege of Boston, this volunteer force would eventually evaporate away. As predicted by former Governor Thomas Hutchinson, now a refugee in England, "unless fanaticism got the better of self-preservation, they must soon disperse, as it was the season for sowing their Indian corn, the chief subsistence of New England."[32]

Dr. Warren is said to have performed wonders to keep the finicky militia on post.[33] Still, the only long-term means to maintain this army was to enlist and pay them under contracts, thus forming a standing army of observation. So after some debate, the committee proposed to enlist a standing interim army of eight thousand to replace the temporary and volunteer militia force supplied by each town. Additionally, the committee proposed an enlistment contract requiring service until the last day of 1775, though this term would prove daunting to many independent Yankees.[34] Such a far-reaching proposal as this, however, required approval of the committee's parent body, the Provincial Congress, whose delegates were still inbound from across the colony after their adjournment. It would not be until the next day, April 22, that they reconvened. Shortly thereafter, they would take up this proposal of an army of observation.

Later that same evening, near sunset, as Paul Revere returned to Hastings House from his day's duties as their messenger, he found the committee sitting quietly in their parlor room, somber and reflective. Suddenly, Dr. Benjamin Church stood up and declared, "I am determined to go into Boston tomorrow." Everyone just looked at him, dumbfounded.

"Are you serious, Dr. Church?" Warren replied incredulously. "They will hang you if they catch you in Boston!"

Church mulled it over a moment. Of course they would not hang him; he was Gage's best-placed spy. Church obviously wanted an excuse to cross the American and British lines and tell General Gage all there was to know of the American plans to raise and enlist a standing army. Yet Church had not anticipated the siege, and so probably had no arrangement to slip intelligence into the town. He therefore had to make contact with Gage and establish some means of providing future intelligence to the British.

"I am serious, and am determined to go at all adventures," Church replied at last. This resolve made it clear where Church's loyalties lay, but Revere no longer suspected him, and none of the others in that room seem to have ever done so.

Warren and Church went back and forth for a time on the idea, but all Revere gives is that it was "a considerable conversation". We are left to wonder what excuses, what cunning, what deceit Church used on this occasion. Whatever he said, Church at last convinced Warren, and the good doctor remained ignorant of the treacherous doctor's true motives.

So at length, Warren conceded, "If you are determined, let us make some business for you." They agreed that Church would attempt to acquire some much-needed medicine, both for the wounded militia and for their many wounded British prisoners.[35]

Dr. Church planned to go back into Boston the next day, which afforded an unexpected opportunity to carry letters into the sealed town. One who took advantage of this opportunity was Dr. Warren, who wrote again to General Gage, assuring him that the British wounded were well taken care of and offering arrangements to allow for one of Gage's surgeons to inspect and attend the wounded and captured officers.[36] Gage seems to have accepted Warren's generous offer.[37]

In any case, Gage soon learned that his captured wounded were indeed treated both civilly and humanely. Lt. Edward Gould of the 4th, injured at North Bridge and captured ahead of Percy's retreating column somewhere near Menotomy, reported himself that he was "now treated with the greatest humanity, and taken all possible care of by the Provincials at Medford". He seems to have recovered from his wounds.[38] Equally well treated was Lt. Edward Hull of the 43rd, who had "a youthful, fair, and delicate countenance". Hull had been shot three times at North Bridge and remained in critical condition because of the wound to his right breast. The American doctors gave him all the assistance the primitive medical standards of that era could offer, but in the end, there was little they could do but hope and wait.[39]

The Yankee doctors treated both British and American casualties as best they could, though they were woefully unprepared for the many casualties. Their greatest want was of medical supplies. So the young physician apprentice Dr. John Homans, temporarily working under Dr. Warren, also took advantage of Dr. Church's plans to enter Boston. Homans wrote a hasty letter to his physician mentor in Boston, Dr. Joseph Gardner, pleading, "I have not a knife to use, should be much obliged to you for a set of knives."[40]

The next morning, April 22, with these and other personal letters in hand, the British spy Dr. Benjamin Church walked coolly past the American troops in Roxbury and up to the British guard at Boston Neck. America's first great traitor was thus unwittingly handed over to its enemy.[41]

As Church himself would later tell, upon reaching the British guard at Boston Neck, they arrested him and carried him off to General Gage at Province House. There is little doubt he traveled directly to Province House as he claimed, but he was no prisoner. He may have even explicitly asked to have an audience with General Gage. One observer in Boston later recalled that Church was not *marched* from Boston Neck, but carried in a horse-drawn chaise, and when Church and his escort reached Province House, "He got out of the Chaise and went up the steps more like a Man that was acquainted, than a prisoner."[42]

What came of that meeting between Church and Gage is unknown. However, all of the letters Church carried with him, even those of a personal nature, were either confiscated by or, more likely, freely given to General Gage, unbeknownst to their intended recipients.[43] The doctor and the general's meeting undoubtedly discussed the American Army and its troubles, with Church giving as detailed a description as he could remember. Church seems to have also arranged for a scheme to pass future intelligence into the town, which included the use of one of Gage's aides, a Major Cane (who was probably one of Gage's two aides-de-camp).[44]

The traitor and the general talked nearly an hour behind the closed doors of Gage's office in Province House. Once they finished their friendly conversation and eager plans of espionage, Gage escorted Church from his office, the two almost as friends, certainly not as enemies. At least this was the perception of Deacon Caleb Davis, who had been summoned to Province House and was waiting outside Gage's office for nearly half an hour. Davis and Dr. Church apparently knew each other, and when the not-so-good doctor emerged from Gage's office, he was startled and surprised to find Davis there. Davis apparently thought nothing of it at the time, however, and so Church's secret remained safe.[45]

After Church left Province House, according to one observer, he seemed to have complete freedom to go wherever he chose throughout the town, escorted only by Major Cane. In contrast, Church later reported that "He was examined, & then He was sent to Gould's Barracks, & was not suffered to go home but once."[46] The barracks he refers to must have been those of Lt. Edward Gould, the injured officer of the 4th Regiment, now prisoner of the Americans.

With Church making his way freely throughout the town, Paul Revere's wife, Rachel, spotted him. Knowing she could not get herself or their children out of Boston, but learning Dr. Church was free to leave whenever he wished, she gave him a short letter for her husband, along with money to help with her husband's expenses. The letter was simple and sweet: "My Dear[,] by Doctor Church I send a hundred and twenty five pounds and beg you will take the best care of yourself and not attempt coming in to this town again and if I have an opportunity of coming or sending out anything or any of the Children[,] I shall do it[.] pray keep up your spirits and trust your self and us in the hands of a good God[,] who will take care of us[.] [']tis all my dependance for vain is the help of man[.] adieu my Love[,] from your affectionate, R. Revere."

Sweet as the letter may be, Dr. Church readily turned it in to General Gage. It would seem Paul Revere never learned of its existence, not even after the war. As to the £125, Dr. Church's espionage seems to have been at least partly motivated by money, and he likely kept it for himself.[47]

One can only hope that Dr. Church did some good during his trip to Boston, perhaps obtaining the badly needed medicine or medical supplies, as Dr. Warren had hoped. Whatever he did, he would gallivant around town until the next evening, before freely leaving Boston and returning to the Whig leadership in Cambridge. Warren and the others eagerly listened to all Church told them, but it was all lies.

———•———

The Committee of Safety had been in session almost daily, even before the late battle, but it took several days for its parent body, the Provincial Congress, to hastily reconvene, well ahead of its monthlong adjournment. On April 22, as Dr. Church was preparing to depart Boston, the delegates to the Provincial Congress met in Concord. It was a short meeting, and by the same evening, they had adjourned to the Edmund Fowle House in the more strategic location of Watertown.[48]

One of their first actions was administrative. Just as the Committee of Safety found itself suddenly without its chairman due to the departure of John Hancock to Philadelphia, for the same reason the presidency of the Provincial Congress was now open. So on the next day, April 23, the delegates met again at the Fowle House and unanimously elected Dr. Joseph Warren as president pro tempore. Then they turned their attention to the Committee of Safety's resolution to enlist a standing army. They adopted the recommended enlistment terms, but decided to trump their subordinate body with a more substantial call for men, resolving to petition the neighboring New England colonies to help raise an army of 30,000, with Massachusetts committing to provide 13,600.[49]

Such a commitment was more than Massachusetts could readily muster, however, and provincial leaders would soon find themselves struggling with the enlistment effort. Moreover, militiamen served mostly as volunteers, without any long-term obligations, so most were reluctant to commit to a long eight-month enlistment (to the end of the year). The other New England colonies would all adopt similar terms of enlistment and, in consequence, also struggled with their recruitment. Connecticut authorized 6,000 men divided into six massive regiments, but would raise only two full regiments by mid-June. New Hampshire resolved to form an army of 2,000 in three regiments, but would likewise only raise two by mid-June, some 1,300 men. Even tiny Rhode Island, which committed to only 1,500, found it difficult to meet its reasonable quota. It would be many months before the recruitment efforts would prove sufficient.

In the interim, the Massachusetts Provincial Congress pressed its towns to keep their volunteer militia companies in place for as long as they could, or at least until new recruits and enlistments could be had. Even so, the volunteer force began to dwindle away—some from lack of interest in the battle-less siege, others eager to see to their families and to plant their farms. This only made the enlistment effort more critical, with both General Ward and Dr. Warren devoting much of their attention to it. Their only solace was knowing that in an emergency, they could quickly raise the militia and minute companies, again as had been done on April 19.[50]

Interestingly, the enlistment effort spelled the end of the minutemen. Because this on-call specialty corps of militia was invented as a reactionary force to act until the primary militia companies could be mustered, its function became obsolete when the colonies moved to raise a permanent, standing army. The minutemen had fought only once, in the daylong skirmishes of the nineteenth of April, but would never again see battle. Though their distinction remains firmly planted in American memory, they ceased to exist less than a year after they were conceived.[51]

The raising and enlisting of a permanent army and the supply and payment of that army were just two of the major issues burdening the mind of Dr. Joseph Warren. As both acting chairman of the Committee of Safety and president pro tempore of the Provincial Congress, he also found himself inundated with general colonial administration. What consumed Warren the most, however, was his ongoing struggle with General Gage to liberate the helpless Bostonians.

At first, Gage had entirely closed off the town because he feared an attack, especially from the inside. But upon speaking with the town's selectmen, he offered that the women and children could leave, and that their men might do so as well, "upon Condition that the Male Inhabitants within the Town shall on their Part solemnly engage that they will not take up Arms against the King's Troops, within the Town, sho[ul]d an attack be made from without". When Warren learned of this offer, he wrote on April 22 to the town's selectmen and implored them to do as Gage suggested.[52]

Still, Gage remained reluctant. When the selectmen's committee met with him later on April 22, the very day Gage had met with Dr. Church, they pressed the governor on the issue. Gage expressed to the committee his concern "that in case the Troops should be attacked…and the attack should be aided by the inhabitants of the Town, it might issue in very unhappy consequences to the Town". For two days, the two sides jockeyed back and forth, before Gage at last proposed that the selectmen have the townspeople register and turn in all their flintlocks and arms at Faneuil Hall, where the pieces were to remain under guard. At length, the selectmen voted to accept Gage's offer on condition that any Bostonian wishing to leave the town could do so. Gage apparently concurred, so the selectmen arranged to gather the people's arms.[53]

Accordingly, on April 24, the selectmen began their collection. Hundreds gathered outside Faneuil Hall, forming a massive crowd that lined up in all directions, all anxious to relinquish their guns so they might finally escape the besieged town. The selectmen or their agents carefully recorded each owner's name as the pieces were turned in. In this manner, at least in theory, the owners could get their weapons back once the present turmoil had subsided.

Someone in the eager crowd turned in a gun on behalf of Dr. Joseph Warren, perhaps one of his apprentices, such as Dr. William Eustis. While most Bostonians had but one gun or pistol and sometimes a bayonet to turn in, some had several firearms, and a few well-armed Yankees dragged to Faneuil Hall whole cases of guns. Gilbert De Blois held the record, turning in three chests filled with a total of 134 pistols. Thomas Peck was unsure of what to do with two old iron 4-pounder cannon in his store. They had no carriages and had lain there since the last war, but he wrote to Gage inviting the troops to pick them up if they liked. Gage apparently never ordered them hauled off. Indeed, Bostonians were so well armed that the selectmen had to continue their collection until as late as April 26. In all, the inhabitants surrendered near 1,652 guns, 572 pistols, and even 15 of the old Pilgrim-style blunderbuss muskets, plus about 973 bayonets.[54]

Meanwhile, as Dr. Warren waited to see how the situation in Boston played out, he and his colonial leaders undertook their own collection. Gage soon learned that the colonists were forcing his mail riders and messengers to detour to Cambridge and turn over their mail for inspection at Hastings House, where they then waited sometimes two hours for General Ward to read the letters before they were given a pass and released.[55] This infuriated Gage. Not only was he frustrated by the lack of provisions from the countryside, but now he was also prevented from even private communication with the royal governors of the other colonies. Gage would have to depend more on Admiral Graves and the Navy to pass future messages throughout the continent. He would also have to depend on the cunning of spies like Dr. Church to find novel ways to bring him their intelligence, as much of Gage's stream of intelligence was now cut off.

The other grand collection Warren and provincial leaders undertook was the gathering of depositions from the participants in the late battle. Their objective was simple: to convince the world that the British fired first and that the Yankees were victims forced by a brutal soldiery to defend themselves. Once they collected these depositions, they hoped to sail them to England before Gage could send his own account of the daylong battle and, in so doing, score a massive victory in the propaganda war—the Second Battle of Lexington and Concord.

General Gage beat the Yankees to the punch. On April 24, after collecting his own depositions from his officers, he dispatched one Lieutenant Nunn of the Navy as courier to take the first ship he could find back to England. This turned out to be a slow brig transport called *Sukey*, which departed Boston Harbor the same day.[56] There was a moment of panic when Dr. Warren and the other colonial leaders learned of it. By April 25, the Americans had collected twenty depositions signed by almost a hundred participants and eyewitnesses. Two were even given by captured British wounded.[57] The Yankees then scrambled to find a ship to ferry their version of the affair across the Atlantic. It took a day more, but they found Capt. Richard Derby of Salem, who volunteered his fast schooner *Quero*, to be sailed by his son, John Derby.[58] The propaganda race was on.

As the *Quero* made ready to sail, Dr. Warren carefully penned a letter of introduction "To the Inhabitants of Great Britain", which gave "an early, true, and authentick account of this inhuman proceeding" and summarized the accounts given in the depositions. It concluded with an appeal to the citizenry of Britain: "We cannot think that the honour, wisdom, and valour of Britons will suffer them to be longer inactive spectators of measures in which they themselves are so deeply interested; measures…highly incompatible with justice, but still pursued with a specious pretence of easing the Nation of its burden; measures which, if successful, must end in the ruin and slavery of Britain, as well as the persecuted American Colonies."[59] Warren signed this letter as "President pro tem." He then wrote two more letters, one to each of the two London-based agents for Massachusetts, Benjamin Franklin and Arthur Lee. The letter to Franklin asked for his help publishing the depositions and requested that he also put them before the lord mayor and aldermen of the city of London, known to be sympathetic to the American cause.[60]

While the *Quero* crew prepared the schooner for the journey, and Sailing Master William Carlton supervised the placing of the ship in ballast, the Committee of Safety issued instructions to Capt. John Derby that he sail first to Ireland, then cross to Britain and hasten to London, "so he may escape all cruisers". He was then to deliver the package directly to either Benjamin Franklin or his deputy, Arthur Lee. Moreover, Derby was "to keep this order a profound secret from every person on earth." It was not until the night of April 28 or early April 29 that *Quero* finally set sail in ballast, departing from Salem, her destination a secret even to her crew.[61]

Though the *Quero* departed four days after the ungainly 200-ton *Sukey*, the light 60-ton American schooner with its fair curves proved to be a fine, fast ship. It would make England with amazing speed, sailing up to Southampton, where Derby would disembark and ride by land to London. He reached reaching the city on May 28, almost two weeks ahead of Lieutenant Nunn aboard the *Sukey*.[62] The dispatches that Captain Derby brought with him would cause a great sensation throughout Britain.

⎯⎯•⎯⎯

When news of the recent Skirmishes of Lexington and Concord reached New Haven, Connecticut, resident Benedict Arnold was eager to put behind him a variety of failed pursuits for some new adventure, and soon he was marching at the head of a militia company for Cambridge. At thirty-five, Arnold was among the youngest veterans of the French and Indian War. When he was just sixteen, he had run away from his childhood home in Norwich, Connecticut, and enlisted in the militia so he could fight. To his annoyance, his mother and her preacher finally succeeded in dragging him back, but Arnold was an obstinate adventure-seeker, even at that age, and so ran away a second time to rejoin the service. This time he served where his mother's henchmen could not find him, in the frontier surrounding Fort Ticonderoga in upstate New York, a fort that remains to this day, rebuilt to its original splendor.[63]

Fort Ticonderoga was situated on the natural primarily water highway that began in the great harbor of New York, followed up the Hudson River, and crossed a stretch of land to Lake George, which in turn drained via a small, short channel into the south end of Lake Champlain. At that critical channel, Fort Ticonderoga stood guard. The remainder of the water highway followed Lake Champlain northward until it poured into the Richelieu River, which in turn led to the St. Lawrence River and Canada.[64]

The location of Fort Ticonderoga had proved especially important during the French and Indian War. At the beginning of the war, the fort was still controlled by its builders, the French, who had named it Fort Carillon. But in 1758, with the war sweeping across the American frontier and into Canada, the British had mounted a major and bloody offensive to conquer the fort. After battering its walls with heavy cannon, the French garrison finally surrendered it, leaving the British to claim the broken fortress and rechristen it to its present name. The British had eventually won that war, eliminating French military presence in the frontier. However, without the threat of the French, and with the threat of Indians in that area since quelled, Fort Ticonderoga soon fell into utter disrepair. The British had determined that the once strategic fort was no longer of much military value.

But times were changing. A plan was now in the works to reconstruct and make defensible both Fort Ticonderoga and its sister fort farther up Lake Champlain: the ruined heap of former Fort Crown Point. Gage had received orders to do so at the end of 1774, but the winter weather—and his inability to see the new war looming ahead—caused him to postpone issuing an order for the forts' repair until springtime. Moreover, the weak, invalid garrison was as decrepit as its walls and not capable of making extensive repairs. So on March 16, 1775, when Gage finally wrote to Maj. Gen. Guy Carleton, Royal Governor and commanding officer in Quebec, he ordered the latter to send men to first rebuild Fort Crown Point. By April, Carleton had only begun to send a few small parties to augment the mix of invalid and elderly soldiers garrisoning those two posts. It was too little, too late.[65]

Following his service at Fort Ticonderoga, where he had served mostly in garrison, Arnold had begun his post-military career as a druggist, but eventually abandoned that to take up navigation and became a merchant shipmaster, trading horses and livestock, only to end it all in bankruptcy. Though he returned to his roots and tried to pick up the pieces of his apothecary, Arnold still yearned for a life of adventure. He met this need in a limited fashion by serving in the local militia and was granted a captaincy for his service.

But when he learned of the recent Battle of the Nineteenth of April, the opportunity seemed far too alluring, and on April 24, he convinced fifty militia volunteers to march with him to Cambridge. However, Arnold's men lacked ammunition, and New Haven's selectmen were hesitant to offer the town's magazine. Incensed, Arnold demanded the keys to the magazine, threatening to break its gates open if they refused. The selectmen acquiesced. By the next day, Arnold and his men had set off.[66]

Along the road to Cambridge, Captain Arnold encountered Connecticut Col. Samuel H. Parsons, returning from Cambridge to report on the situation. Arnold was eager to hear intelligence of what was ahead for him in Cambridge, and Parsons was glad to give it. Parsons described the flood of volunteers and gave secondhand anecdotes about the recent battle. Parsons also lamented that the Americans had no more than maybe a dozen cannon, all of which were light guns with little range and firepower—hardly enough to threaten the well-armed British and the heavily gunned Royal Navy. Without heavy artillery, Parsons bemoaned, the American siege would ultimately prove useless. When Arnold heard this, he immediately told Parsons that old Fort Ticonderoga had, within its battered and now poorly defended walls, many large cannon and mortars, all of which might easily be taken from the British and hauled to Cambridge for use in the siege. Parsons liked the idea, and the two went their separate ways.[67]

When Parsons arrived in Hartford on perhaps April 27, he met with several trusted friends and together immediately began plotting the capture of Fort Ticonderoga. Without consulting the Connecticut Assembly, they procured money and commissioned two trusted men to promptly head into the frontier of western Connecticut and there raise volunteers for the enterprise. Two days later, April 29, Parsons and his fellow Whigs sent a second party, consisting of Capt. Edward Mott and five handpicked men, to follow and join with the first.[68]

Meanwhile, when Arnold arrived in Cambridge on April 29, he also immediately began plotting to take Fort Ticonderoga. The following day, he met with the Massachusetts Committee of Safety on the issue. Arnold testified, "I have certain information, that there are at Ticonderoga, eighty pieces of heavy cannon; twenty brass guns from four to eighteen pounders; and ten or twelve large mortars… The fort is in a ruinous condition, and has not more than fifty men, at the most. There are large numbers of small arms, and considerable stores, and a sloop of seventy or eighty tons on the lake. The place could not hold out an hour against a vigorous onset [onslaught]."[69]

The idea of taking the fort was not altogether a new idea. In early 1775, the Massachusetts Committee of Safety had secretly commissioned John Brown to scout the frontier and see the disposition of the Canadians, as it was feared they might side with British if war was to come. To help allay these concerns, the First Continental Congress had even invited Canada to send delegates to the Second Continental Congress. It was only now that the Committee of Safety received John Brown's report by courier, which said that the Canadians were on the fence with regard to the war and would not send delegates to the Congress.

Additionally, after Brown had met with the Green Mountain Boys in the uncolonized lands known as the New Hampshire Grants (modern Vermont), he was impelled to report, "One thing I must mention, to be kept as a profound secret. The Fort at Ticonderoga must be seized as soon as possible, should hostilities be committed by the King's Troops. The people on New-Hampshire Grants have engaged to do this business, and in my opinion they are the most proper persons for this job."[70]

So the Massachusetts Committee of Safety now had two recommendations to take Fort Ticonderoga, and yet the committee and Dr. Warren, its chairman, hesitated to make the final metamorphosis from innocent victims of the barbarity of the ministerial troops to the aggressors involved in what would clearly be treason and rebellion. Dr. Warren was also mindful that Fort Ticonderoga was within the boundaries of New York and, equally, that New York was strongly swayed by its large Tory population and so remained uncommitted to the new war now underway. Warren wrote a careful letter to that colony's Committee of Safety on the matter, assuring them, "we would not, even on this emergency, infringe upon the rights of our sister colony of New York; but we have desired…that you may give such orders as are agreeable to you."[71]

Meanwhile, in the town of Salisbury in western Connecticut, the two Connecticut parties joined forces, raised but sixteen volunteers from that poor community, and then marched into Pittsfield in western Massachusetts. It was the night of May 1, and there they happened to meet the Massachusetts agent and scout John Brown, just then returning from Canada. They also met Col. James Easton of the Massachusetts militia, a resident of Pittsfield, and together they all strategized on how best to seek backcountry volunteers for an attack on Fort Ticonderoga. Easton also committed to seek volunteers from among his own militia regiment.[72]

As the Connecticut party gathered its strength and volunteers for an offensive on the fort, Dr. Warren and the Committee of Safety, unaware of the Connecticut party, continued to dwell on Benedict Arnold's identical proposal, hesitant and unsure what course to take, despite the looming showdown with the British. Dr. Warren, it would seem, was still not committed to the war. But that would soon change.

———◆———

While Dr. Warren contemplated the proposal to assail Fort Ticonderoga, he again turned his attention to freeing the Bostonians. Once the Bostonians had given up their weapons, the selectmen, after making arrangements with Gage, sent the Committee of Safety a scheme whereby thirty wagons were to be sent into the town, bringing in any Loyalists and their effects who so desired it. These same wagons, once emptied, would be laden with Bostonians and their effects and sent back out, only to fetch more Loyalists and so continue the exchange.[73] Yet the plan never materialized.

It is supposed that Gage was influenced by his mandamus councilors and prominent Tories to reconsider whether keeping the inhabitants locked in the town was a better strategy. His advisors feared that without the inhabitants as insurance, the massive colonial siege force would surely burn or attack the town.

Had it not been for the urging of his councilors, Gage would still have remained on the fence as to what was best to do. On the one hand, his duty as general and governor to protect the town leaned him in the direction of keeping the people hostage, but on the other, his Whiggish tendencies inclined him to afford the people the same freedoms granted to all Englishmen. That Gage was still swayed toward maintaining the peace is undeniable, for he had it in his authority by the Massachusetts Charter to declare martial law "in time of actual War, Invasion or *Rebellion*"—a point of which Lord Dartmouth had only recently reminded him—and yet he had not done so.[74] Throughout his entire command in Boston, Gage exhibited fair judgment and never once showed a hint of underhanded conniving—except on this occasion. He may have been privately on the fence in this matter, but the persistent urging of his councilors finally got the better of him, at least to some degree.

Instead of outright refusing to let the Bostonians leave, Gage adopted a convoluted permit process by which the townspeople could apply for a pass and quit the town. The arrangement of this scheme was delegated to Col. James Robertson, the barrack master general. The printed passes stated: "No Arms nor Ammunition is allowed to pass." They were then amended by hand with the words "Nor Merchandize." The selectmen argued against this, stating that according to the original oral agreement with General Gage, the people were permitted to remove their "effects", by which he meant *all* effects, be it furniture, money, or whatever. Robertson assured Gage that if the inhabitants departed with all of their personal belongings, they would have no qualms with seeing the town destroyed. So despite the arguments of the selectmen, the British held firm.[75]

Without permission to remove their effects, some Whiggish Bostonians refused to even attempt the enterprise, because they felt obliged to weather the turmoil to protect their property. The merchant John Andrews was one such individual. In what seems to be the last letter he ever got out of the town while the British controlled it, he wrote to his friend, "I find an absolute necessity to be here myself, as the soldiery think they have a license to plunder every one's house and store who leaves the town, of which they have given convincing proofs already… Am necessitated to submit to such living or risque the little all I have in the world…as its said without scruple that those who leave the town, forfeit all the effects they leave behind." Andrews then shrewdly pondered, "Whether they hold it up as *only* a means to detain people or not, I cant say… It has so far avail'd as to influence many to stay, who would otherways have gone."[76] His only solace was that he was able to get his wife out of the town, she "being perfectly willing and desirous of going without me, as her peace of mind depends entirely upon her leaving the town…but am affraid it will be a long time before I shall see her again, if ever."[77]

While many Loyalists appear to have flocked into the town unmolested, only a few handfuls of Bostonians managed to escape with their effects. Many townspeople gave up the endeavor entirely, while most accepted the permit as it was written and fled with little more than the clothes on their backs. No sooner had Gage opened the ways out of Boston, about April 28, than near half of the townspeople poured off the peninsula, either by Charlestown Ferry or by the Neck. This mass exodus shocked the Tories, who moved quickly to press Gage to stymie the outflow. They succeeded, and on about May 1, just days after the town had been opened, suddenly the town was effectively closed once more. According to John Andrews, thousands of people were left stranded in Boston, clamoring for permits to leave, but the approval of new permits dwindled to just two or three a day, "and those with the greatest difficulty." By May 6, all pretenses were at last entirely abandoned, and the British announced that no further permits would be issued. Even most of those Bostonians who held valid permits but had failed to leave promptly were now refused departure. Almost 6,250 civilians were left in the town, more than half of whom desperately wanted to escape. The most obvious result of the exodus was that it left the town even more militaristic, with now one of three inhabitants being a redcoat.[78]

Unexpectedly, amid this latest political struggle, the Whiggish Connecticut Royal Governor Jonathan Trumbull sent a letter to Gage, carried to him by a sort of peace envoy of two men. Trumbull's letter questioned Gage's actions on the nineteenth of April and asked whether the two sides of this political struggle should now be at war. The envoy succeeded in meeting with the general, but Gage waited a few days before sending a polite and explanatory reply back to the Connecticut governor.[79]

The Massachusetts Provincial Congress—and indeed Dr. Warren as well—were extremely annoyed when they learned of this envoy. After all, the Provincial Congress was now acting as the government in place of Gage, and while Trumbull was certainly within his rights to communicate with another royally appointed governor, this act by Trumbull—a Whig and an outspoken supporter of American liberty— seemed to delegitimize all that the extralegal Massachusetts government was attempting to build.[80]

In response, on May 1, the Committee of Safety met with the envoy and read a copy of Trumbull's letter. On the following day, Dr. Warren carefully penned a polite but assertive reply to Governor Trumbull, writing, "We feel the warmest gratitude to you… But you will allow us to express our uneasiness on account of one paragraph in your letter, in which a cessation of hostilities is proposed. We fear that our brethren in Connecticut are not even yet convinced of the cruel designs of Administration against America, nor thoroughly sensible of the miseries to which General Gage's army have reduced this wretched colony."

Warren continued his letter with an admission that he doubted the remaining Bostonians would ever be freed from the town, lamenting, "We have lost the town, and, we greatly fear, the inhabitants of Boston, as we find the general is perpetually making new conditions, and forming the most unreasonable pretences for retarding their removal from that *garrison*." It was because Boston Neck was again sealed shut, the inhabitants firmly trapped, that the good doctor finally conceded the last flickers of hope for peace were now gone.

He concluded his letter with foreboding: "No business but that of war is either done or thought of in this colony…no confidence can possibly be placed in any assurances he can give… Our relief now must arise from driving General Gage, with his troops, out of the country, which, by the blessing of God, we are determined to accomplish, or perish in the attempt; as we think an honorable death far better to meet in the field, whilst fighting for the liberties of all America, far to be preferable to being butchered in our own houses, or to being reduced to ignominious slavery."[81] Trumbull would reply kindly a few days later, pledging firmness and support from his colony.[82]

Warren's correspondence with Trumbull helped to cement a sort of unification of command between the two colonies, something the Second Continental Congress would not achieve for months to come.[83] Moreover, it forced Dr. Warren to cultivate his own position on the crisis, as if in writing the letter, he himself underwent a private transformation from reluctance to acceptance that the natural result of the present strife would only come by donning the gauntlet of war. That same day, another minor event perhaps served to punctuate Warren's convictions.

British Lt. Edward Hull of the 43rd had suffered grievously from his wounds inflicted at the North Bridge, and though he had spent the two weeks since under careful colonial care, the wound to his right breast was proving mortal. When Dr. Warren suspected him to have but hours left to live, he wrote hastily to Gage, offering arrangements to fulfill Hull's final wish to see his regimental adjutant named Miller, probably a lieutenant. It is unknown whether Hull got his final wish before he finally succumbed to his wounds. He died on May 2, and after his body was delivered to Gage, he was buried two days later.[84]

Perhaps it was the combination of the death of Lieutenant Hull and Warren's act of writing to Trumbull that at last crystallized in Dr. Warren's mind the realities of the dire state of affairs. For on this same day, May 2, in an abrupt and dramatic reversal of his position just two days earlier, and without waiting for a reply from New York, Warren led his Committee of Safety to form a subcommittee—really a council of war—to confer on Benedict Arnold's proposal to take Fort Ticonderoga. Suddenly, as if he had been struck with an epiphany, Warren was willing to consider the role as the aggressor.

The council of war consisted of Warren and two others, along with General Ward, and together they quickly agreed to take that first step toward a definite offensive and thereby unquestionably commit treason. That evening, the full committee accepted the subcommittee's conclusions and promptly voted to supply Arnold with gunpowder, balls, flints, horses, and £100 cash for "a certain service approved of by the council of war."[85]

The next day, May 3, the committee called on Arnold and announced their acceptance of his plan. They commissioned him a colonel in the new Massachusetts Army, likely signed by Warren himself. They gave him written orders instructing that he was to be commander of a detachment not to exceed four hundred men, which he was to raise in the western Massachusetts region. He was then to march to Fort Ticonderoga and endeavor to take the fort, where he was then to leave a garrison and bring back to Cambridge the bulk of the artillery.[86] The following day, the newly minted Colonel Arnold left Cambridge, taking with him only a servant, two volunteer officers, and ten horses laden with two hundred pounds of gunpowder, the same of musket balls, and one thousand flints.[87]

As for Arnold's Connecticut militia volunteers, who had marched with him to Cambridge, some of them may have joined with the new enlisted Connecticut men just then arriving company by company. Among the first such companies to arrive were those of the 3rd Connecticut Regiment, commanded by Israel Putnam, who had been freshly promoted to brigadier general of the new Connecticut Army. Putnam served not only as regimental commander but also as company commander of his regiment's 1st Company, which he marched to Cambridge ahead of his other companies. Perhaps he arrived in time to wish Colonel Arnold Godspeed.[88]

Col. Benedict Arnold's orders constituted the first time the Province of Massachusetts initiated a formal military offensive and so the first time the Americans unequivocally became the aggressors, not the helpless victims they portrayed themselves to be in the propaganda war that was just beginning to take shape following the Battle of the Nineteenth of April. In an ironic twist of fate, of all the colonial leaders who might have signed those treasonous orders to seize Fort Ticonderoga, the one who actually signed was the man committing great treason against the colonial cause itself—Dr. Benjamin Church Jr. It is just as ironic that the traitor Dr. Church gave the orders that began the career of the most famous traitor of all. But Arnold was no traitor yet—his treason was still years away. Rather, he was about to become one of America's greatest and most famed war heroes.

CHAPTER 11

THE SPREADING FLAMES OF REBELLION

The current political debate was by no means limited to the provincial leaders. As the public debate heated up, the sensationalistic Massachusetts press was fast at work, eager to stir up readers' passions for liberty. However, publication of incendiary propaganda was not without risk. Isaiah Thomas, editor of the *Massachusetts Spy (Or, American ORACLE of Liberty!)* in Boston, had wisely packed up his press and printing types just two days before the recent Battle of the Nineteenth of April and smuggled them out of the town. He set up shop in Worcester, where he continued to publish his strongly pro-Whig newspaper with the motto "Americans!—Liberty or Death!—Join or Die!"[1]

Benjamin Edes, one of two printers of the *Boston Gazette*, was not as sagacious and so found himself in besieged Boston. He nevertheless escaped by boat at night, much as Paul Revere had, crossing the Charles into Charlestown. Edes made his way to Watertown and there continued printing his news on a battered old press. His partner, John Gill, remained in Boston and was surprisingly left unmolested for months, before he was finally arrested and put in jail, "charged with printing sedition, treason and rebellion."[2]

One of the greatest strokes in the propaganda war came from Ezekiel Russell, printer of the *Salem Gazette*. He issued a famous and dramatic broadside by giving another American account of the recent battle and prominently featuring forty black coffins at the top of the page with the names of the deceased countrymen by each. It was memorably titled, "Bloody Butchery, by the British Troops; or the Runaway Fight of the Regulars". He offered it to New Englanders "either to frame and glass, or otherwise preserve in their houses…as a perpetual memorial".[3]

Yet despite all of this, and despite the looming war, Gage largely tolerated and allowed the freedom of the press, even though most of the articles were scathingly written against him. Instead of evoking censorship, he sought to combat the sensationalism with his own version of the events.

The most obvious means at his disposal to effect his counterattack in the propaganda war was via the few Loyalist newspapers. However, of Boston's two admittedly Loyalist newspapers, the *Boston Post-Boy* shut down just before the battle, while the editor of the *Boston News-Letter* waffled for fear of reciprocity and ultimately failed to publish anything of value to the Loyalist cause before also being shut down in early 1776.[4] Thus, Gage was forced to publish his own broadside, *A Circumstantial Account of an Attack that happened on the 19th April, 1775*, intended to be widely published, partly to combat the American sensationalism and partly to fill the void the Tory papers had left behind.

He sent it to all the continent's royal governors, as well as to many New England printers who in turn dispersed it to the masses. However, his account failed to achieve the desired effect. While pro-Whig accounts gave impassioned appeals to heaven and carefully constructed rhetoric against the unbridled authority of their sovereign, his was a simple and factual account, completely devoid of political comment and wholly unfit to conjure support for Loyalism or even a peaceful resolution to the great debate.[5]

Most Massachusetts Whigs were especially annoyed that *A Circumstantial Account* claimed the Americans had fired first at Lexington (though based on what we know today, this may indeed be the case). For colonial leadership, this was of fundamental importance, the crux of their argument that they were the victims of a barbaric army and a despotic Ministry. Dr. Joseph Warren obtained a copy of *A Circumstantial Account*, and in the margin near where it reported the Americans fired first, he penned in a footnote mark, "✝", then at the bottom added his own note: "✝ the People say the Troops fired first & I believe they did".[6]

Just as Warren was convinced the British fired first, the British were convinced the Americans had done so. Lord Percy was so sure that he wrote to the adjutant general in England, "*they* fired first upon the King's Troops, as they were marching quietly along."[7] Yet neither Warren nor Lord Percy were eyewitnesses to that first action of the battle, and their certainty of how it happened illustrates that both sides were blindly dug in, each convinced that the other was to blame.

In truth, even if Gage had given a wonderful and eloquent argument in his *Circumstantial Account*, it was doomed to failure because he remained steadfast in keeping the remaining inhabitants of Boston penned up in the besieged town—a move that only served to reinforce the Whig argument that the British Army was an instrument of tyranny.

By May 10, with no traction on releasing the remaining inhabitants, the Provincial Congress wrote one last official letter, signed by Dr. Warren, as a polite but stern remonstrance to Gage: "We would not affront your Excellency by the most distant insinuation, that you intended to deceive & disarm the People, by a cruel act of Perfidy... But your Excellency must be sensible, that a Delay of Justice is a denial of it, and extremely oppressive to the People now held in Duress."[8]

Warren took this opportunity to write another letter to the governor, this one private. It was a final plea for cooperation from Gage: "I am very sensible of the Formalities which Gentlemen in your Situation generally think yourselves obliged to observe, but the present state of publick Affairs renders it necessary that you should seriously consider whether you are to sacrifice the Interest of Grt Britain, and the Peace of the Colonies, to mere Form[alitie]s—great Complaints are made respecting the Delays in removing the Inhabitants of Boston, I assure you Sir that this People irritated as they have been, will not with any tolerable Degree of Patience suffer the Agreement made between you and the Inhabitants of Boston to be violated, if you still retain those Sentiments of Humanity which I ever supposed had a very great Influence upon your Conduct, I for the last Time request that you would (without hearkening to the mad Advice of Men who I know have deceived you, and I believe care not if they ruin you, and this Empire) punctually comply with your Agreement with the Inhabitants of the Town of Boston". Warren added an important postscript to the letter: "no Person living knows, or ever will know from me of my writing this".[9]

His Excellency General Gage seems never to have replied, and sadly, Warren wrote to his friend Samuel Adams, away in Philadelphia for the Second Continental Congress, "General Gage, I fear, has trepanned the inhabitants of Boston. He has persuaded them to lay down their arms, promising to let them remove with their effects; but he suffers them to come out but very slowly, contriving every day new excuses for delay." Warren also regretfully informed his friend that his son, Dr. Samuel Adams Jr., an apprentice of Warren, remained trapped in Boston. Warren had tried to secure his safe passage from the town and had even reserved a surgeon's slot in the army for him, but it was all for naught, probably due to the young doctor's famous last name. At last, Warren was unable to leave the surgeon's slot unfilled any longer, and he unhappily expressed this to the senior Samuel Adams. However, another of Warren's apprentices, Dr. William Eustis, did manage to escape the town sometime during this period and would serve alongside the New England Army.[10]

In the end, Rev. William Gordon of Roxbury summed up the whole debacle simply: "The General engaged with the Selectmen of Boston, that if the Town's people would deliver up their arms into their custody, those that chose it should be allowed to go out with their effects. The townsmen complied, and the General forfeited his word, for which there will be an after reckoning, should they ever have it in their power to call him to an account."[11] By mid-May, essentially no more Bostonians would be able to leave the town.[12]

In anticipating the outcome of the struggle to free the remaining inhabitants, the Provincial Congress finally resolved that "general Gage hath…utterly disqualified himself to serve this colony as a governor, and in every other capacity, and that no obedience ought, in future, to be paid by the several towns and districts in this colony, to his writs for calling an assembly, or to his proclamations, or any other of his acts or doings; but that, on the other hand, he ought to be considered and guarded against, as an unnatural and inveterate enemy to this country." If there was any doubt before as to whether Massachusetts was in rebellion, there was no doubt now. When Gage learned of this most treasonous resolve, he forwarded it to the home government, stating simply, "they have set all my Authority aside."[13]

With that resolve, and with the yet secret expedition to take Fort Ticonderoga, the last hope for peace evaporated.

———•———

It was by happenstance that Col. Benedict Arnold's mission to Fort Ticonderoga would not meet its objective until after the Provincial Congress had soundly committed itself to prosecution of the war, resulting in a perceived legitimacy for the enterprise. As Arnold traveled to the westerly extent of the colony, near Stockbridge, Massachusetts, he heard rumors of the parallel Connecticut mission that might snatch from him the glory that he had anticipated and so yearned for.

Fearing his opportunity about to escape his grasp, he issued "beating orders" to his two officers to recruit without him (so called because the recruiting drive in a town was announced by beat of a drum), and then, without a moment's more delay, Arnold rode ahead on horseback with but his servant, eager to meet this Connecticut party. His recruiting officers were to join him once they had drafted the new recruits for his mission.[14]

The Connecticut party was doing its own recruiting, but had found it difficult. When one of their own went to Albany, New York, to raise men, he was sent back empty-handed, the people there telling him "they did not think that we should succeed." At length, the Connecticut party managed to collect about 170 men, including thirty-nine Massachusetts volunteers under Col. James Easton, the rest mostly of the Green Mountain Boys from the New Hampshire Grants (Vermont).[15]

On the evening of May 7, the Connecticut-led force rendezvoused at the then-small backwoods town of Castleton (in modern Vermont). The next morning, May 8, they held a council of war and decided that a party of thirty under Capt. Samuel Herrick would march the next day to the small hamlet of Skenesborough (now Whitehall) in New York, situated at the southern extremity (or "harbor") of Lake Champlain. Skenesborough had been settled by the Maj. Philip Skene, an accomplished British half-pay retired officer and wealthy merchant. He had successfully petitioned in 1764 for a royal patent giving him twenty-nine thousand acres upon which to build his settlement. By 1775, Skenesborough had grown to include a post office, sawmills, ironworks, and a general store. More importantly, it boasted a small schooner named *Katherine*. It was Captain Herrick's mission to capture this schooner and any other boats there, as well as Major Skene himself if possible.[16]

Of the remaining 140 men, the war council elected Col. Ethan Allen of the Green Mountain Boys as their commander, Colonel Easton as their second, and Capt. Seth Warner of the Green Mountain Boys as their third, their ranks commensurate to the numbers of men they had raised.[17] These men were to march out the next morning for Shoreham, a village on the shores of Lake Champlain directly across from Fort Ticonderoga, where they were to wait for Herrick and the boats by which to cross the lake and attack the fort.[18]

Arnold and his servant arrived later that same day, only to find that the war council had broken up and Allen had gone alone in advance to Shoreham to gather extra men and set guards on the roads. When Arnold declared his mission, the party rejoiced at his proof that Massachusetts also desired the capture of the fort, "but were shockingly surprised when Colonel Arnold presumed to contend for the command of those forces that we had raised, who we had assured should go under the command of their own officers". The recruits thought Arnold had gall to declare that he, and only he, had legal right to command, though Arnold cited his orders and commission and gladly revealed these to them. In truth, his argument of legality had some merit, for the Connecticut contingent had not even consulted their assembly. When Arnold strenuously insisted, it "bred such a mutiny among the soldiers which had nearly frustrated our whole design, as our men were for clubbing their firelocks and marching home". (To club one's musket was to turn it upside down as a signal of one's unwillingness to fight.) Arnold promised the men that if he were made their commander, their pay would be the same as though they were under Allen's command. But the men replied, "damn the pay," and that "they would not be commanded by any others but those they engaged with".[19]

Arnold gave up the endeavor until early the next morning, when he left Castleton for Shoreham, hoping to overtake Ethan Allen and convince him to give up his command. When the Connecticut men learned of it, they scrambled to muster themselves and pursue, "for fear he should prevail on Col. Allen to resign the command". They departed with such haste they even left their provisions behind.[20] Arnold and Allen at last met in Shoreham, though no document remains which describes their interaction.

Ethan Allen, at thirty-eight, was as stubborn and vainglorious as Arnold, perhaps more so (if that were possible). Allen exemplified his own quest for great laurels when he wrote, many months later, "The glory of a victory which will be attended with such important consequences, will crown all our fatigues, risks, and labours; to fail of victory will be an eternal disgrace, but to obtain it will elevate us on the wings of fame."[21]

The difference between these two men was that Allen lacked the military competence and natural charisma Arnold had. However, Allen had the support of his men, while Arnold had no men at all, only a piece of paper from the Massachusetts Committee of Safety to cling to. So the conversation on who was to command was no doubt heated. Perhaps Allen thought it wise to add some sense of legality to their mission, or perhaps he simply conceded and chose to placate Arnold. Whatever the case, the two compromised to a joint command.[22]

By midday, the entire colonial force had gathered at Shoreham and waited for sunset. As they did so, they sent a small party under Connecticut Capt. Edward Mott back to Castleton for the provisions they had left behind.[23] Finally, as the sky grew dark sometime after half past seven o'clock, they gathered at Hand's Cove along Lake Champlain and quietly hid among the dense trees, where they could see battered Fort Ticonderoga across the shimmering lake, illuminated by the waxing gibbous moon that shone from almost straight above.[24]

Colonel Allen had managed to recruit still more men that day, and now their numbers were something more than 200, maybe as high at 270, the majority of them Green Mountain Boys.[25] Fort Ticonderoga, on the other hand, was defended by just forty-five men, commanded by Capt. William De la Place of the 26th Regiment.[26] Near half of these were invalids and old men, unfit for service, though the rest were fresh men just arrived from Quebec in two parties, with more on their way, part of a detachment General Carleton was sending to help rebuild the fort. The latest party was led by Lt. Jocelyn Feltham, who held the strange distinction at such a junior rank of being second-in-command at the fort (since there were no other officers present). Two dozen women and children also resided at the fort. This meager garrison was hardly a defense against a surprise attack by veteran frontiersmen.[27]

The Yankees waited at Hand's Cove for many hours, apparently oblivious to the flaw in their plan. It was the job of Captain Herrick's party sent to Skenesborough to bring up the boats intended for crossing the lake, but since that party had not left until midday and the distance was nearly twenty-three miles one way, their mission had been doomed to failure even before it began.[28] As the moon sunk to the horizon around two o'clock in the morning of May 10, the men grew restless.[29] They knew sunrise would soon come, yet they had no choice but to bide their time in the dark woods across from their target, having no way to reach it.

In their moment of desperation, somehow they managed to find two scows or bateaux (flat-bottomed boats, often with a single mast and sail, as these probably had). A tradition claims Capt. Asa Douglas was dispatched to Crown Point to "see if he could not agree with his brother-in-law who lived there, to hire the king's boats, on some stratagem", and in doing so successfully acquired one boat.[30] According to the tradition, Captain Douglas also found a guarded ferry longboat belonging to Major Skene, out near Willow Point across from Crown Point. Douglas and his few companions were able to dupe the ferryman and his two rowers that they needed a ride back to Hand's Cove to pick up a party for a squirrel hunt. The ferryman was suspicious but known to be a bit of a drunk, and Douglas easily enticed him with a jug of rum. Perhaps they rowed both boats together, side by side, southward back to the Shoreham cove. When the ferryman at last discovered the ploy, seeing the eager American backwoodsmen with their muskets hiding in the woods, it was too late—he and his two rowers were made prisoners.[31]

It was near three o'clock in the morning, with the moon now set and the shore shrouded in utter darkness, when the men began boarding the two bateaux for the first crossing. Their senses were high as they carefully and quietly embarked, hoping to retain the element of surprise. About eighty-three men plus Colonels Allen, Arnold, and Easton all managed to pile into the two bateaux, along with a handful of rowers and the Massachusetts agent John Brown. They quietly pushed off and rowed their boats across the mere half-mile stretch of the narrow lake. Upon reaching the opposite shore, the two bateaux gently scraped onto the muddy beach, and the men quietly disembarked before the decrepit fort. The rowers then turned the two bateaux back toward the opposite shore for the next crossing.[32]

By now, the sky was slowly growing bright as dawn was fast approaching. So the two joint commanders, Allen and Arnold, quickly consulted one another and concluded that, rather than waiting for the rest of their men, they would storm the fort immediately.[33]

———— • ————

The Americans quietly rushed around Fort Ticonderoga's broken and rotting walls to the main gate in back, but despite the fort's ruin, they were surprised to find the gate solidly shut. Luckily, the wicket, a small gate just beside the main, was open.[34] Arnold and Allen, both obstinate glory-seekers, vied to be the first to enter the fort, perhaps pushing by each another in the process like two children eager for a prize. The result is unknown, as each says he was first, but probably they both entered the fort side by side.[35]

As the sun began to rise at about half past four o'clock on May 10,[36] the Yankee force poured through the gate behind Allen and Arnold, some giving an "Indian war-whoop" as they did so, catching a lone sentry by surprise.[37] The British sentry "snapped his piece at them; our men, however, immediately rushed forward, seized and confined the sentry, pushed through the covered way, and all got safe upon the parade [ground], while the garrison were sleeping in their beds."[38] Another sentry charged with his bayonet affixed toward a colonial officer standing near Allen, whom the sentry perhaps slightly wounded. Allen reacted immediately, swinging his saber toward the sentry's head. "My first thought was to kill him with my sword; but, in an instant, altered the design and fury of the blow to a slight cut on the side of the head."[39]

Simultaneously, the Americans stormed into the center of the fort's parade ground, immediately formed a hollow square, and gave three loud huzzahs, which woke the fort and brought out the surprised garrison, half undressed.[40] Frazzled and caught off guard, some popped out of their barracks without their muskets, only to dodge or hobble back in and reemerge with pieces in hand. The few women and children who were there with their soldier husbands shrieked with fear as a very short skirmish ensued.

A few ruthless Yankees yelled "No Quarter! No Quarter!" meaning they would slay the British soldiers rather than take them prisoner, but the American officers skillfully prevented their men from such violence.[41] The Americans had the element of surprise, and most of the British soldiers were too decrepit to give much of a fight. Moreover, the Yankees outnumbered the small garrison nearly two to one. It seems not even one shot was fired as the Americans swarmed the feeble garrison still emerging from their barracks.[42]

Lt. Jocelyn Feltham heard the commotion and rushed from his chamber on the upper level of one of the barracks. He was undressed and without breeches, maybe wearing only an undergarment or bedclothes. He knocked on the adjacent door to wake the garrison commander, Capt. William De la Place, then rushed back into his door, putting on his waistcoat and scarlet officer's coat before darting back to De la Place's door, still wearing no breeches. Feltham noticed "rioters on the bastions" as he dashed into his commanding officer's chamber, now open, his commander also struggling to dress.[43]

Down below, the feeble and short-lived melee between British invalids and hardened frontiersmen—hardly much of a fight—was already over. The Americans were now breaking into several chambers below—where they expected the officers to be—but upon finding them empty, they turned their attention toward the upper level. A doorway blocked the stairs up to the officers' chambers, and the Yankees surged toward it and attempted to break it in. Upstairs, Feltham proposed to his commander that he would rush down the stairs and force his way to the men, which De la Place seems to have agreed to.

Just as the half-dressed Feltham popped out of his commander's quarters at the top of the stairs, the Yankees at last broke through and rushed up, with Colonels Allen and Arnold in the lead, swords drawn and pistols in hand. Feltham yelled that they halt, but none could hear him over the tumult. With the mob continuing to thunder up the steps toward him, he put out his hand to gesture that they halt. Allen and Arnold halted just before the half-dressed officer and ordered their own men to silence.[44]

Feltham decided to buy time for his men below, figuring that at any moment, he would hear a volley or two as the British garrison began to slaughter the American invaders.[45] He could not see from his vantage point that the short-lived skirmish was already over. The entire garrison had been captured in less than ten minutes, with no Americans wounded and only a few British slightly so.[46]

Not knowing this, Lieutenant Feltham bode his time. He first demanded by what authority the colonists had entered His Majesty's fort.[47] Ethan Allen would later claim he replied, "In the name of the great Jehovah, and the Continental Congress." Allen observed that it was necessary to refer to a higher power since the authority of Congress was as yet unknown to many.[48]

Feltham next demanded who were their leaders and what was their intent. The colonial officers wore no distinguishing uniforms, so Feltham did not know he was already talking with the men he sought. Allen and Arnold introduced themselves as having a joint command, and Arnold added that he came with instructions from the Massachusetts Congress, which he promptly pulled from his pocket and showed the lieutenant. Not to be trumped by Arnold, Allen then declared his orders were from Connecticut (though he had no written proof of such), and "[We] must have immediate possession of the fort and all the effects of George the third". Feltham paused at those words, but impetuous Allen, having had enough conversation, did not wait for the lieutenant to ponder the situation. Drawing his sword, Allen extended it over Feltham's head, even as some of the colonial mob behind him brought their firelocks to bear. Allen insisted Feltham surrender the fort, "and if it was not comply'd with, or that there was a single gun fired in the fort[,] neither man woman or child should be left alive". With this, Allen proved himself the more brutal and unrefined of the two commanders.[49]

CAPTURE OF FORT TICONDEROGA—ENGRAVING BY JOHNSON, FRY & CO., C. 1866, BASED ON
A PAINTING (BEFORE 1859) BY ALONZO CHAPPEL (1828–1887). IT DOES NOT ACCURATELY
PORTRAY HOW THE SCENE UNFOLDED. CLEMENTS LIBRARY, UNIVERSITY OF MICHIGAN.
(ORIGINAL PAINTING AT THE UNIVERSITY OF MICHIGAN MUSEUM OF ART.)

Colonel Arnold interrupted his co-commander, speaking to Feltham in "a genteel manner", but also insisted that he surrender the fort. Feltham tried to talk around the subject, when at last Arnold realized Feltham was not the commander at all. Arnold must have said so, for his men eagerly pressed to storm the other chamber above, where they now knew the true garrison commander remained hidden. The cooler Arnold prevented it, whereupon Captain De la Place revealed himself, fully dressed in his scarlet coat with all of its accoutrements.

The Americans surged forward, pushed Feltham back into his own quarters, and set a guard of two sentries there. De la Place then asked Arnold and Allen many of the same questions Feltham had. When the commanders began to discuss the terms of surrender, Arnold assured De la Place "he might expect to be treated like a gentleman",[50] but the troops would not parade with arms.[51] At length, De la Place accepted, and the fort now belonged to the colonies.[52]

The short-lived and near bloodless battle to take Fort Ticonderoga was over. But the battle for its command had just begun.

As the rest of the ragtag colonial force crossed Lake Champlain and joined those at Fort Ticonderoga, Benedict Arnold once more demanded command of the men and the fort, again citing his orders from the Massachusetts Committee of Safety. The men were mutinous, finding Arnold's audacity incredible, for "he had not one man there" that he had enlisted himself.

At last, Capt. Edward Mott, who had just himself arrived with the provisions left at Castleton, drew on his extralegal authority as a representative of the Colony of Connecticut and wrote an order to Ethan Allen declaring that Allen must keep the command of the fort and its men.[53] Meanwhile, Colonel Easton and others had had enough of Arnold and drafted a quick letter to be sent by express to the Massachusetts Congress, positively declaring the fort was now in Allen's command and complaining of Arnold's constant difficulties.[54]

Arnold wrote his own express on the matter, stating, "I had agreed with Colonel Allen to issue further orders jointly, until I could raise a sufficient number of men to relieve his people...since which, Colonel Allen, finding he had the ascendancy over his people, positively insisted I should have no command, as I had forbid the soldiers plundering and destroying private property."[55] Though it might seem Arnold was just fuming because he was a colonel without a man to follow him, Allen's men were indeed plundering the private goods of the soldiers and their families, contradictory to the rules of war. As Lieutenant Feltham observed, "the plunder...was most rigidly perform'd as to liquors, provisions &c [etc.] whether belonging to his majesty or private property".[56] Arnold added in his letter, "Colonel Allen is a proper man to head his own wild people, but entirely unacquainted with military service".[57] Benedict Arnold was indeed right on this point as well. Within weeks, Allen's own men would turn on him, and by autumn, he would prove himself a completely incompetent military officer.

As the morning drew on, one of Colonel Allen's first commands was to send Capt. Seth Warner, and fifty of the fresh men recently crossed, to embark aboard one of their two bateaux, row or sail northward down lake, and surprise and secure the ruins of nearby Fort Crown Point. They promptly set off, making their way down the winding, narrow lake. The ruins of old Fort Crown Point were situated on a peninsula that guarded where the lake grew much wider, and when the detachment arrived, they surprised and overwhelmed the meager garrison, commanded by a sergeant and defended by a mere eight men. Ten women and children also resided there. The garrison of Fort Crown Point gave up without a fight.[58]

May 10 proved to be a great day for the American war effort, and it was somewhat apropos that on the same historic day, across the colonies in Philadelphia, the Second Continental Congress was finally convened.[59] As Captain Mott agreeably described the taking of the two forts, "Not one life lost in these noble acquisitions."[60] But it remained unclear just how noble these acquisitions really were. As Arnold explained to the Massachusetts Committee of Safety, "It is impossible to advise you how many cannon are here and at Crown Point, as many of them are buried in the ruins. There is a large number of iron, and some brass, and mortars, &c., lying on the edge of the Lake, which, as the Lake is high, are covered with water."[61]

In all, Ticonderoga had about eighty-six pieces of varying quality. Just as important a discovery was the fort's large war stores, including many artillery implements and tools, carriages, wheels, and hundreds of round shot in the larger 18- and 12-pound varieties, plus thousands of round shot in the smaller 4- and 6-pound varieties—a plethora of artillery ordnance. All that was lacking was gunpowder, because most of the twenty-eight barrels found there were damaged, probably by water.[62] At Crown Point, the first report was of about sixty-one serviceable pieces of artillery, with another fifty-three unfit for service.[63] Of all the artillery between the two forts, the prize pieces were three iron 13-inch mortars. Besides various other mortars and howitzers, some serviceable, some not, there were many brass and iron cannon, including a very large brass 24-pounder, as well as more than a dozen serviceable 18-pounders and nearly as many 12s.[64] But while Arnold made arrangements and laid the groundwork to begin moving these cannon to Cambridge, the plan would soon fall through, and the cannon would mostly remain where they lay for many months to come.[65]

By the next day, May 11, the Fort Ticonderoga prisoners were paraded without their arms and marched southward. In days, they would arrive in Hartford, and there many would remain as prisoners of war.[66] The prisoners from Fort Crown Point were sent soon after.[67]

Also on May 11, Ethan Allen learned that his detachment to the south, the party that had marched to Skenesborough under Capt. Samuel Herrick, had succeeded in taking that small hamlet and the retired officer's prize schooner *Katherine*. However, the schooner was not yet rigged for the spring, and Allen, who knew nothing of seamanship, expected it would take days to do so. (It would take just one.) Allen anxiously planned to bring *Katherine* to Fort Ticonderoga and outfit her with six or eight cannon. As to Herrick's other objective at Skenesborough, Maj. Philip Skene himself, he was not at home, having sometime earlier returned to London. So while the Americans failed to capture their most threatening neighbor in that region, the capture of his schooner *Katherine* would pay out dividends long into the war.[68]

All that remained for the Americans to have total domination of the Lake Champlain region was His Majesty's sloop *Betsey*, known to be longer and better armed than Skene's schooner. *Betsey* had been spotted cruising the north end of the lake, and now that the Americans had a ship of their own, Ethan Allen began plotting to take her.[69]

<hr />

On the same day as the taking of Fort Ticonderoga, the Committee of Safety in Cambridge recognized how encumbered their chairman, Dr. Joseph Warren, was by his many duties, in particular his role as president of the Provincial Congress. The committee apparently selected Dr. Benjamin Church Jr., the well-placed spy in His Majesty's Service, as their new chairman. The chairmanship seemed to ebb and flow to different committee members depending on availability, and Church may not have held the seat permanently. However, even if it was temporary, Dr. Warren must have welcomed this change. Little did Warren and his fellow Whigs suspect that the man now given charge of the committee that wielded the greatest executive power to govern the military, the defenses, and the province itself when the Congress was not in session was the greatest traitor to their cause.[70]

One of Church's first acts seems immediately suspicious to our modern understanding, though it was thought an innocent mistake at the time.

At the Roxbury camp, commanded by Massachusetts Militia Brig. Gen. John Thomas, the number of men had been reduced to between two and three thousand, a result of militiamen going back to their homes and the lackluster success of the ongoing enlistment effort. One anecdote tells that Thomas occasionally marched his men around and around a hill to make his force appear larger than it was. In theory, this might have worked, for the colonists mostly wore homespun clothes of browns and whites, nothing by which to distinguish and count different regiments. But the British were not duped by the ploy.[71]

With the Provincial Congress making strong steps toward open war, Gen. Artemas Ward grew nervous, especially since the colonials' enlistment effort remained incomplete. On this, he consulted his council of war, which included Col. William Heath as representative of General Thomas, the latter opting not to leave his post in Roxbury.[72] The council decided to recommend that the dispersed recruiting officers send whatever men they had so far enlisted to Cambridge at once, instead of waiting to fill their regiments completely.

The decision of the council was given to the Committee of Safety, and Church signed copies of the order, which were sent by couriers to the recruiting commanders in the various towns throughout the province. The order seemed innocent enough: "As we are meditating a Blow against our restless Enemies—We therefore enjoin you…forthwith upon the Receipt of this Order to repair to the Town of Cambridge with the Men inlisted under your command."[73]

The order was intended only for those officers on recruiting service, not those along the siege lines. The questionable conduct by Church was that he sent a copy of this order to Gen. John Thomas in Roxbury. It may have been a mistake, but Thomas read the letter as an explicit order. Yet he was incredulous: if he marched his men to Cambridge, Boston Neck would be left unguarded, allowing the British to freely march out from the town and break the siege.

Thomas was too wise to stand by and allow such a tactical mistake, but he could not complain to Ward, because as Chairman of the Committee of Safety, Dr. Church stood higher in authority. The only higher authority to whom Thomas could then petition was Dr. Joseph Warren, President of the Provincial Congress. Accordingly, Thomas dispatched a courier to find Warren, probably meeting with the Congress at Watertown. When Warren learned of the order, he wrote Thomas a prompt reply:

"I have this moment received your letter, the Contents very much surprised me, as I had been absent from the Committee of Safety all Day I could not at first understand the matter, but upon Enquiry I find the Committee gave Orders that all recruiting Officers should repair to Cambridge with the Men they enlisted, but the sending the Order to your Camp was certainly a very great Error, as it was designed only for those Officers who are in the Country, absent from Camp.

"Your readiness to obey Orders does you great Honor, and your prudence in sending to Head Quarters upon receiving so extraordinary an Order convinces me of your Judgment."[74]

Whether it was indeed a "very great Error"—quite likely the case—or an act of treachery by the secret spy may never be known. One is left to wonder whether Warren later discussed the matter with Dr. Church, or if Warren ever began to suspect his perfidious colleague. The only thing certain was that as Chairman of the Committee of Safety, Dr. Church was now in the best possible position by which to continue his espionage.

Church's promotion to chairman freed Warren to focus on his role as president of the Provincial Congress, but Warren's swift rise to prominence did not go unnoticed by the British and the Tories.[75] As Customs Commissioner Henry Hulton wrote of him, "Since Adams went to Philadelphia, one Warren, a rascally patriot and apothecary of this town, has had the lead in the Provincial Congress."[76] Lieutenant Francis, Lord Rawdon of the 5th Grenadiers, called the "famous Doctor Warren" "the greatest incendiary in all America".[77]

Despite Warren's many burdens, he still found time to look after his family. By May, his children and their belongings were safely removed from his mother's home in Roxbury to the farmhouse he rented from Dr.

Dix in Worcester. There they remained with his fiancée Mercy Scollay, safe from the looming war in Boston. On occasion, Warren allowed his mind to drift to more peaceful and joyous times, which he hoped would return to Massachusetts. Looking to the future with his family, he wrote to Mercy, "am happy in hearing you with the Family are all in Health… Dr. Dix wanted to be informed respecting the sowing some wheat, let the Dr. know I shall acquiesce in his Judgment… I think it will be advisable for him to hire for me ten or twenty Acres more of Land, as I shall keep several Horses and cannot think of being deprived of indulging myself in the Leisure Hours of this one year in the Pleasures of Agriculture."[78]

Unfortunately, Warren would not have the opportunity to enjoy the life of a gentleman farmer, for the war effort would entirely consume him. And while it is unknown, we can only hope that amid all of his responsibilities and burdens, the good doctor found time to ride out to Worcester and see in person his fiancée and four children.

Meanwhile, in the Lake Champlain region, the Americans plotted their next daring raid.

———•———

On the day after the taking of Fort Ticonderoga, Capt. Jonathan Brown (a different man than the Massachusetts agent[79]) and Capt. Eleazer Oswald, Arnold's two recruiting officers, marched into Skenesborough from Stockbridge, Massachusetts, at the head of fifty men, the first of Arnold's recruits. Arnold had apparently sent word back to these men to march southward to Skenesborough rather than Fort Ticonderoga, there to help rig the captured schooner *Katherine*. By the next day, they had completed the rigging, and the men celebrated by joyously rechristening her *Liberty*.

After sending their few prisoners, including Major Skene's family, southeastward to Connecticut, the men boarded their prize schooner and set sail northward toward Fort Ticonderoga, with perhaps a Capt. John Sloan serving as ship's captain. Two days later, May 14, *Liberty* arrived at her destination,[80] where she was immediately outfitted with six swivels and four carriage guns, probably light brass 3-pounders.[81] *Liberty* thus became the first naval vessel of the American colonies, and she arguably marked the foundation of the modern United States Navy.[82]

With *Liberty*, it was now possible for the Americans to capture the King's sloop *Betsey* on the opposite end of Lake Champlain. *Betsey* was believed to have "carried more guns and heavier metal than the schooner." On about May 14, a war council was called on the matter, which included both Benedict Arnold and Ethan Allen, and likely Colonel Easton and Captain Mott. They agreed *Liberty* would set sail at once for the small British post of Fort St. Johns (modern Saint-Jean-sur-Richelieu), situated along the western bank of the Richelieu River, which flows from the north end of the Champlain to the St. Lawrence River. A small handful of bateaux, some of which may have been brought up from Skenesborough, would sail alongside *Liberty* to the same objective. Together they would attempt to take the British sloop, now known to be docked at Fort St. Johns, as well as the fort's meager garrison. But who was to lead such an expedition? Benedict Arnold was anxious to secure his own laurels, and Ethan Allen was anxious to be rid of him. So the council decided to give *Liberty* over to Arnold and his men, owing in part to Arnold's substantial experience in seamanship gained from his otherwise bankrupt profession as a merchant. Ethan Allen and between ninety and one hundred fifty of his own men would follow *Liberty* in four bateaux.[83]

Arnold's selection made him America's first naval commander, and this sort of honor, adventure, and freedom seemed to be just the kind of service one would expect him to revel in. Yet just before he set sail, he sent another letter to the Massachusetts Committee of Safety, lamenting, "I have done every thing in my power, and put up with many insults to preserve peace and serve the publick. I hope soon to be properly released from this troublesome business, that some more proper person may be appointed in my room".[84]

Arnold and his fifty men boarded *Liberty* the next morning, May 15, and with two bateaux aboard, set sail northward down Lake Champlain. Ethan Allen and his men climbed into another four bateaux and followed, but soon found the fast *Liberty*, with her fair curves and fine lines, gliding ahead. She did not get far. The winds turned contrary, and all *Liberty* could make that day was Crown Point.[85]

The next day's winds were no better, and Col. Benedict Arnold, master and commander of *Liberty*, eager to secure his laurels, decided to take thirty of his men and go aboard one of their bateaux to row ahead, leaving *Liberty* with a skeleton crew under Capt. John Sloan.

On the following day, May 17, a fair gale blew in, filling the sails of *Liberty* and allowing her crew to catch Arnold and take them back aboard. They made for Fort St. Johns with fantastic speed, covering near sixty miles in a day, reaching the north side of Isla la Motte, some thirty miles south of Fort St. Johns, before the winds died. They dropped anchor near the opposite shore's Point au Fer, just as the last dim light of the sky faded around eight o'clock.[86] It was here, where Lake Champlain becomes the narrow and windy Richelieu River, that they manned their two bateaux with thirty-five men and quietly rowed northward, again leaving *Liberty* behind with a skeleton crew.[87]

Arnold and his two small bateaux made their way up the circuitous river, guided by a bright and waning gibbous moon that filled the fair-weather sky. All around them were dark, dense trees sprinkled with the occasional flickers of fireflies. The gentle breeze was filled with the sounds of crickets and locusts, accompanied by the light lapping of the water against their bows as they cut their way northward.

Soon the sky began to brighten, the birds began to chirp, and finally, at about sunrise, near half past four o'clock, they came upon a small creek just half a mile south of the fort, where they turned and came to rest along its muddy bank. Arnold ordered one of his men to reconnoiter the fort, and the man promptly hopped out and moved through the thick but sunlit woods northward to the fort. The rest of the men sat waiting in their bateaux, swatting at the "numberless swarms of gnats and muskitoes". There they "waited with impatience for his return." About an hour later, the scout returned, informing Arnold that the small garrison was not on their guard. As the scout hopped back into one of the bateaux, Arnold and his men pushed off. By about six o'clock in the morning of May 18, they laid eyes on their destination.[88]

The two bateaux rowed to within about three hundred yards of the small wooden outpost. As they did, Arnold noted the prize sloop *Betsey* anchored nearby. The two bateaux ground onto the muddy beach, and without delay Arnold and his men clumsily disembarked and split into two prongs: one stormed toward the small wooden fort, the other to the guarded sloop. Arnold led from the front, perhaps driving those that went for the outpost, drawing his sword high above his head, the men eagerly following with their muskets at the ready.

The garrison at Fort St. Johns consisted of a mere sergeant and twelve men, and maybe one camp follower. Because this was a remote fort in deep wilderness, its soldiers were dumbfounded when they unexpectedly found nearly three times their number racing toward them. The seven seamen aboard the sloop were equally astounded. Both the small British garrison and the sloop's crew surrendered at once—neither side gave battle nor fired a shot.[89]

As the Americans searched the fort for war stores, Colonel Arnold interrogated the fort's sergeant in charge. The British noncommissioned officer reported their captain had gone to Montreal and was expected within the hour with a large reinforcement bound for Fort Ticonderoga. Furthermore, from the outpost at nearby Chambly, just ten miles to the north, a company of about forty men was due any minute. Arnold thought it "a mere interposition of Providence that we arrived at so fortunate an hour."[90] Without hesitation, he turned to his men and ordered that they grab what valuable provisions they could, including fourteen stands of arms, and put them aboard the British sloop, along with their fourteen prisoners. They also hastily prepared four of the nine British bateaux they found there, destroying the other five. As his men complied, Arnold boarded the sloop and surveyed his new prize. It was a fine 70-ton sailing vessel, about 60 feet in length, mounted with just two small brass 6-pounder cannon, though the British sergeant reported it was due to be outfitted with more guns once the detachment bound for Fort Ticonderoga stopped there en route.[91] This reminded Arnold that time was of the essence, and he hurried his men along.

Arnold seems to have impressed the seven British seamen to man the sloop. Now, instead of serving the Crown, they would serve the Americans.[92] Within two hours after their arrival, Arnold and his men proudly embarked with their newfound laurels. Fortune smiled on them again as they weighed anchor on their new prize *Betsey*, for as one participant wrote in his journal, "a fine gale arose from the north! we directly hoisted sail and returned in triumph." The new American sloop sailed southward upriver, the flotilla of now six bateaux sailing close behind.[93]

They had not sailed far when *Betsey* came upon the small cluster of four bateaux under the command of Ethan Allen and his men. In fine naval tradition, Arnold fired *Betsey*'s two brass 6s as a salute to Col. Ethan Allen, to which Allen and his men fired a volley of musketry in response. The two sides fired two more such salutes as the two flotillas converged. Allen then came alongside the sloop and, with Arnold's permission, came aboard the fine prize. There they celebrated in the other fine naval tradition, drinking several loyal, healthy toasts (probably of rum) to the Congress.[94]

The foolhardy Allen then proposed that he intended to continue with his men northward to establish a garrison of eighty to one hundred men at Fort St. Johns. Colonel Arnold delicately explained to Allen the intelligence he had gathered from his prisoners, warning, "It appeared to me a wild, impracticable scheme, and provided it could be carried into execution, of no consequence, so long as we are masters of the Lake, and of that I make no doubt, as I am determined to arm the sloop and schooner immediately." However, Arnold's logic could not prevail. What was worse, Allen's men were "in a starving condition". Arnold had the luxury of extra provisions, partly because he had sailed in the spacious *Liberty*, partly because he had collected a little more from their raid on Fort St. Johns. But as the two parties had met some distance north of *Liberty*, Arnold could only redistribute to Allen's men what little he had aboard *Betsey*. The two parties then parted ways, a thankful Allen making his way toward Fort St. Johns and Arnold aboard his prize sloop making his way southward to Isle la Motte and the waiting *Liberty*.[95]

The wind was swift, and within an hour or so, Arnold and his flotilla reached the anchored *Liberty*, where they off-loaded some of their men. Arnold no doubt kept to his new prize, it being the more magnificent sailing vessel. Together the combined flotilla weighed anchor and set sail again, catching the swift wind and riding it into the wider expanse of Lake Champlain to the south.

The next morning at Fort St. Johns, May 19, Ethan Allen and his men were startled when a local frontier trader came to their camp and alerted them that a British reinforcement of around two hundred men under Maj. Charles Preston were on the march from Montreal to attack them. Allen and his men quickly decamped and scurried to their four bateaux.[96] With a swift and favorable wind at their backs, they retreated with full sails southward to rejoin Arnold. Arnold's flotilla reached Crown Point later that same day, while Allen and his four boats arrived maybe the day after. It was perhaps there at Crown Point, before sailing back to Fort Ticonderoga, that they rechristened *Betsey* as the sloop *Enterprise*, the first of a long line of American ships to bear the name.[97]

Within the whole eight-day campaign, British America had formed its first American Navy, comprised of ten or more bateaux, an armed sloop, and a schooner. And with this navy, the Americans now held command of all of Lake Champlain.

On May 20, Quebec Governor and British Maj. Gen. Guy Carleton in Montreal learned of the taking of the two forts and the raid on Fort St. Johns, which, according to his intelligence, had been achieved by "one Dominick Arnold". Carleton promptly wrote of the news to General Gage, but His Excellency already knew of it.[98] For on May 17, when Dr. Joseph Warren first learned the news himself, he wrote of it to Selectman John Scollay in Boston—yet the letter failed to get past the British lines and was instead delivered to General Gage. One is left to wonder if this was a mistake or part of Dr. Warren's design. The spy Dr. Church would also send Gage intelligence on the fort's capture.[99]

Despite the unexpected news, there was little Gage could do about it from besieged Boston. Not even Carleton could do much, because he had few soldiers there in Quebec. Furthermore, Carleton could not rely on the finicky French Canadians or the opportunistic Indians, for as he informed Gage, "I am trying all Ways and Means to animate both the one and the other, whether my Endeavors will meet with Success, I cannot pretend to say".[100]

So the Americans were now masters of Lake Champlain, and with their new and sizable arsenal of artillery, they had the firepower necessary to retain their newfound status. However, getting those cannon to Cambridge where they could do real service was another matter entirely. Until then, the British would remain the masters of Boston.

The American victory in the Lake Champlain region further punctuated what had begun with the Battle of the Nineteenth of April—that the Americans not only *could* fight, but they were also *willing* to fight and even take the offensive. The British now recognized they could no longer be gentle in dealing with the escalating aggression that had started two years earlier in 1773. Nor could they expect to easily squash the growing rebellion that was now sweeping beyond Massachusetts and into the other colonies. Instead, the British realized their only hope in quelling the American insurgency was to bring to bear the full power and aggressive might of the British Army. But the Americans would not give in so easily.

The Revolutionary War—and the fight for British America—had only just begun.

EPILOGUE

The escalation toward war began in earnest in late 1773 with the Destruction of the Tea. Yet the autumn of 1774 was the start of the true political American Revolution, when Massachusetts cast away the authority of its Crown-appointed government and replaced it with a democratically elected Provincial Congress. The spring of 1775 was then the blossoming of that revolution during the Battle of the Nineteenth of April into a genuine though uncommitted Revolutionary War. This advent of hostilities and the immediate aftermath in turn gave way, in the summer of 1775, to a very long Siege of Boston, with each side digging in and preparing for battle.

The New England Army of Observation, drawn from the various colonial militias, would continue to entrench in a semicircle around Boston, while rebel leaders like Dr. Joseph Warren, Gen. Artemas Ward, and Brig. Gen. Israel Putnam would work together to determine just how far they were willing to press the new war militarily. Away in Philadelphia, the Second Continental Congress with representatives from all of the thirteen colonies would likewise debate the measures they would take to press the new war politically. But none would yet press for independence.

The colonies sought only self-determination while remaining under the auspices of the British Empire. Indeed, many Americans yet believed—or hoped—that a peaceful conclusion to the great debate was still attainable, and that their beloved and benevolent King had only been deceived by a treacherous and wicked Ministry and the majority Tories in Parliament—the true enemies of America.

Just as the Americans would entrench around Boston, so too would the British entrench in the town itself, led by Lt. Gen. Thomas Gage and supported by Vice Adm. Samuel Graves and his warships in the harbor. Though the redcoats would receive many fresh reinforcements in the coming months, they would remain greatly outnumbered by the Americans besieging Boston. General Gage's primary strategy would therefore be to strengthen the British defensive positions to deflect any potential American assault while he petitioned the home government for still more troops.

In contrast, the American leaders knew that although they had many more soldiers than the redcoats, they lacked the necessary artillery and gunpowder to force the British from Boston. With Gage's army protected by the many guns of the Royal Navy warships and the newly entrenched field pieces of the Royal Artillery, an American assault with essentially only infantry soldiers was doomed to failure.

To avoid a stalemate, Dr. Warren and the other Americans leaders looked to the west, with its ample supply of heavy artillery at Forts Ticonderoga and Crown Point. But the rebel leaders also looked to the north, where another British force loomed in Canada—one that could swoop in and eliminate all that the Americans had gained. And General Gage looked to his spies. Once aware of the Yankee plans, he would soon prepare an audacious stroke to break the Siege of Boston and cut off the head of the American Rebellion. All now hinged on the next decisions of Dr. Joseph Warren and Lt. Gen. Thomas Gage. Those decisions would determine the fate of America—and would forever alter its history.

ABBREVIATIONS

ADM   Admiralty Records, now part of the UK National Archives
BL   British Library
Carter   Carter, Clarence Edwin, ed. *The Correspondence of General*
                Thomas Gage with the Secretaries of State and with the
                War Office and the Treasury 1763–1775. 2 vols. New
                Haven: Yale University Press, 1931–33.
CHS   Connecticut Historical Society
Clements   Clements Library, University of Michigan, Ann Arbor
Coll.   Collections
Comm.   Committee
Corr.   Correspondence
Fischer   Fischer, David Hackett. *Paul Revere's Ride*. New York:
                Oxford University Press, 1994.
Force   Force, Peter. *American Archives*. 4th ser., 6 vols.
                Washington, DC: M. St. Clair Clarke and Peter Force,
                1837–46.
Hist.   Historical
Huntington   Huntington Library, San Marino, CA
JCC   Ford, Worthington Chauncey, ed. *Journals of the*
                Continental Congress. Vols. 1–4. Washington, DC:
                Government Printing Office, 1904.

JEPCM	Massachusetts Provincial Congress. *Journals of Each Provincial Congress of Massachusetts in 1774 and 1775.* Boston: Dutton and Wentworth, Printers to the state, 1838.
LGFO	Great Britain War Office. *A List of the General and Field Officers…of the Officers in the several Regiments of Horse, Dragoons, and Foot…Artillery…Engineers…Marines…* London: Printed for J. Millan, 1778.
LOC	Library of Congress
Mass.	Massachusetts
MHS	Massachusetts Historical Society
MSS	Manuscripts
NDAR	Clark, William Bell, William James Morgan, and Michael J. Crawford, eds. *Naval Documents of the American Revolution.* 11 vols. Washington, DC: Naval History Division, Dept. of the Navy, 1964.
PBF	Papers of Benjamin Franklin
PGW	Papers of George Washington
PHE	Cobbett, William, John Wright, and Thomas Curson Hansard, eds. *The Parliamentary History of England from the Earliest Period to the Year 1803.* Vols. 16–18. London: T. C. Hansard, 1813.
PRO	Public Records Office, now part of the UK National Archives
Proc.	Proceedings
Pubs.	Publications
NEHGR	*New England Historical and Genealogical Register*
NYPL	New York Public Library
NYHS	New York Historical Society
Soc.	Society
UKNA	United Kingdom's National Archives
WBF	Smyth, Albert Henry, ed. *The Writings of Benjamin Franklin.* 10 vols. New York: Macmillan Co., 1905–7.
WO	War Office, now part of the UK National Archives

Appendix I

Chronology of Key Events

1763	French and Indian War (Seven Years' War) Ends
1767	Townshend Acts (various acts, including tea and other taxes)
Mar 5, 1770	Boston Massacre
Dec 16, 1773	Boston Tea Party
May 13, 1774	Lt. Gen. Thomas Gage Arrives in Boston
Sept 1–2, 1774	Cambridge Powder Alarm
Sept 5-Oct 26, 1774	First Continental Congress
Dec 14, 1774	Portsmouth Alarm
Feb 26, 1775	Salem Alarm
Apr 18, 1775	Paul Revere's Ride; British Expedition to Concord Departs
Apr 19, 1775	Battle of the Nineteenth of April (including the Skirmishes of Lexington and Concord); Revolutionary War Begins; Siege of Boston Begins
May 10, 1775	Taking of Fort Ticonderoga; Second Continental Congress Convenes

APPENDIX 2

THE BRITISH MINISTRY: LORD NORTH'S CABINET (IN 1775)

Prime Minister	Frederick North, Lord North (until Mar 1782)
First Lord of the Treasury	Frederick North, Lord North
Secretaries of State for	
the Northern Department	Henry Howard, 12th Earl of Suffolk
the Southern Department	William Henry Nassau de Zuylestein, 4th Earl of Rochford (until Nov 1775, then Thomas Thynne, 3rd Viscount Weymouth)
the Colonies	William Legge, 2nd Earl of Dartmouth (until Nov 1775, then Lord George Germain)
Secretary at War*	William Barrington, 2nd Viscount Barrington
First Lord of the Admiralty	John Montagu, 4th Earl of Sandwich
Commander in Chief (of the Army)	(vacant from 1769 to 1778, then Lord Jeffery Amherst)
Lord President of the Council	Granville Leveson-Gower, 1st Marquess of Stafford

---

*Subordinate to the Secretaries of State.

Lord Privy Seal   Augustus Fitzroy, 3rd Duke of Grafton
                                    (until Nov 1775, then William Legge,
                                    2nd Earl of Dartmouth)

Lord Chancellor   Henry Bathurst, 2nd Earl Bathurst

Chancellor of the Exchequer   Frederick North, Lord North (succeeding
                                    Charles Townshend, the architect of
                                    the colonial taxes, who died in office
                                    in 1767)

The above Ministry serving under His Majesty, King George III.

APPENDIX 3

ARRIVALS OF BRITISH TROOPS
TO BOSTON IN 1774–1775

On ranks, the regimental colonels (who, despite the title, often held a higher rank) were rarely on campaign with their units and often did little service other than forming and equipping the regiments at their own expense. Rather, the true commander was the deputy of the regiment, generally a lieutenant colonel. Also, for lieutenant colonels and above, it was common to award a brevet rank for a region only (e.g., America, West Indies, India). The officer would be paid per his actual rank and would revert to his official rank when in England. Finally, several promotions occurred late in 1775 though not represented here, per the King's Order, Apr 4, 1776, in Howe's *Orderly Book*, 243–45.

On citations, many names listed throughout this section per evidence in Gage MSS; List of Army Officers, 1 Jan 1775, with additions to 1779, WO, 64/15, UKNA (hereafter just WO, 64/15); and *List of the General and Field Officers...* (1778) (hereafter just *LGFO*). Marines are also in List of Marine Officers, 1777, in ADM, 192/2, UKNA. Fischer, *Paul Revere's Ride*, 308, also has a summary of select names. References to these are not cited here explicitly.

Also relevant to the story given in the chapters, but not listed below: the 7th Royal Fusiliers and the 26th (Cameronian) Regiment of Foot were spread along stations on the Canadian frontier.

Boston Assignments Pre-1774

14th Regiment of Foot

Commanded by Lt. Col. William Dalrymple

Regimental Colonel: Lt. Gen. William Keppel

Arrived: Sept 28, 1768, from Halifax

Departed: circa Apr 1773, to St. Augustine, Florida

Notes: Gage to Lord Hillsborough, Sept 10, 1768, in Carter, 1:195; Gage to Hillsborough, Apr 24, 1770, in ibid., 1:253–55; Gage to Lord Barrington, July 22, 1769, in ibid., 2:517, states they are to stay longer; Gage to Lord Barrington, Apr 7, 1773, in ibid., 2:639, gives they were ordered to Florida; Alden, *General Gage in America*, 163, gives their exact arrival in Boston. Additional recruits for the 14th arrived in Boston in May 1774, probably to be shipped to Florida, and were barracked at Castle William, per undated late May 1775 note in the Frederick Mackenzie MSS Orderly Book, 93, in WO, 36/1, UKNA.

29th Regiment of Foot

Commanded by Lt. Col. Maurice Carr (retired 1772 or 1773);
  succeeded by Lt. Col. Patrick Gordon

Regimental Colonel: Maj. Gen. William Evelyn

Arrived: Sept 28, 1768, from Halifax

Departed: circa Apr 1770, to New York, then to Britain

Notes: Gage to Hillsborough, Apr 24, 1770, in Carter, 1:253–55, gives they were to go to New Jersey, in part due to the Boston Massacre. Gage to Lord Barrington, Apr 7, 1773, in ibid., 2:639, gives they were to be relieved; they are not on Gage's troop list of July 1775, in ibid., 2:690–91; also see Gage to Lord Barrington, July 22, 1769, in ibid., 2:517. Alden, 163, gives their exact arrival in Boston. They return to Canada years later in the Third Embarkation, given below. Gordon and Carr's names provided by the 29th Regiment of Foot, Basset's Company reenactment organization. Gordon was made lieutenant colonel in May 1772, per WO, 64/15.

64th Regiment of Foot

Commanded by Lt. Col. Alexander Leslie

Regimental Colonel: Maj. Gen. John Pomeroy

Arrived: Nov 1768, from Ireland

Departed: circa July 1769, to Halifax

Returned: circa Apr 1773

Departed: Mar 17, 1776 (Evacuation Day), to Halifax

Notes: Gage to Lord Hillsborough, Oct 10, 1768, in Carter, 1:200–201; Gage to Lord
Hillsborough, June 10 and also of July 22, 1769, in ibid., 1:225–28, and 1:228–
31, orders their departure; Gage to Lord Barrington, Oct 30, 1768, in ibid.,
2:489–50; unable to find evidence of their return, but they likely came to replace
the 14th, which was in turn sent to Florida; evidence of the 64th in Boston during
the Tea Party given in the text; Alden, 163, 166.

65th Regiment of Foot

Commanded by Lt. Col. Thomas Bruce

Regimental Colonel: Lt. Gen. Edward Urmston (Urmsten)

Arrived: Nov 1768, from Ireland

Departed: circa July 1769, to Halifax

Notes: Gage to Lord Hillsborough, Oct 10, 1768, in Carter, 1:200–201; Gage to Lord
Hillsborough, June 10 and also of July 22, 1769, in ibid., 1:225–28, and 1:228–
31, orders their departure; Alden, 163, 166.

Embarkation of 1774

4th (King's Own) Regiment of Foot

Commanded by Lt. Col. George Maddison

Regimental Colonel: Lt. Gen. Studholme Hodgson

Arrived: June 14–15, 1774, from Cork, Ireland

Departed: Mar 17, 1776 (Evacuation Day), to Halifax

Notes: Gage to Lord Dartmouth, July 5, 1774, in Carter, 1:358–60; Gage to Lord
Barrington, June 26, 1774, in ibid., 2:648.

5th Regiment of Foot

Commanded by Lt. Col. William Walcott

Regimental Colonel: Colonel (Brig. Gen. in American Service) Hugh,
Earl Percy

Arrived: June 26–July 5, 1774, aboard HM armed transport *Symmetry*
from Kinsale, Ireland

Departed: Mar 17, 1776 (Evacuation Day), to Halifax

Notes: Lord Percy to Rev. Thomas Percy, May 8, 1774, and to the Duke of

Northumberland, July 5 and July 27, 1774, in Bolton, *Letters of Hugh Earl Percy*, 26–30; Gage to Lord Barrington, June 26 and July 6, 1774, in Carter, 2:648–49. Gage suggests that only the 5th was on *Symmetry* in his letter to Lord Dartmouth, July 5, 1774, in ibid., 1:358–60. That Gage says Percy is not yet arrived, while Percy's letter of the same date says he has arrived, suggests Percy arrived later on July 5, after Gage wrote his letter.

38th Regiment of Foot

Commanded by Lt. Col. (Brig. Gen. in American Service) Robert Pigot; succeeded by Lt. Col. William Butler (eff. late 1775, announced Jan 4, 1776)

Regimental Colonel: Lieutenant General Cadwallader, Lord Blayney, died Nov 1775; succeeded by Col. Robert Pigot (eff. Dec 11, 1775, announced Apr 4, 1776)

Arrived: circa June or early July 1774, from Ireland?

Departed: Mar 17, 1776 (Evacuation Day), to Halifax

Notes: Lord Percy to the Duke of Northumberland, July 27, 1774, in Bolton, 27–30, places Pigot there with Percy, so they must have arrived at about the same time. Pigot's promotion: he briefly commands the 55th in late 1775, but after Blayney's death, Colonel Pigot is given the 38th again, per the King's Order, Apr 4, 1776, in Howe, *Orderly Book*, 243–45. On Pigot with the 55th Regiment, see below.

43rd Regiment of Foot

Commanded by Lt. Col. George Clerk (or Clarke)

Regimental Colonel: Lt. Gen. George Cary

Arrived: June 1, 1774, from Cork, Ireland

Departed: Mar 17, 1776 (Evacuation Day), to Halifax

Notes: Gage to Lord Dartmouth, July 5, 1774, in Carter 1:358–60; Gage to Lord Barrington, June 26, 1774, in ibid., 2:648. Commanders' names from references above and Gage's General Orders, June 6, in the Frederick Mackenzie MSS Orderly Book, 100, in WO, 36/1, UKNA. The latter source names Clerk to command the Corps of Light Infantry, detached from the regiments and seemingly now treated as an independent regiment, but it does not mention his successor, so perhaps he also remained in command of the 43rd (see Butler of the 65th below). Some sources name him Clark (Howe to Harvey, June 22 and 24) or Clarke (Gage to Dartmouth, June 25, in Carter, 1:405–6).

1st Battalion Marines (ad hoc)

Commanded by Maj. John Pitcairn (died June 17, 1775, from wounds
at the Battle of Bunker Hill); succeeded by Maj. John Tupper

1st Wave: HMS *Asia*, Dec 5, 1774, from England

2nd Wave: HMS *Boyne*, Dec 12, 1774, from England

3rd Wave: HMS *Somerset*, Dec 19, 1774, from England

Departed: Mar 17, 1776 (Evacuation Day), to Halifax

Notes: Barker, Dec 5, 12, 13, 19, 1774, in *British in Boston*, 10–12; they were probably
evenly spread across the HMS *Asia*, *Boyne*, and *Somerset*; about 460 in all, but on
this, see notes in text; Lord Dartmouth to Gage, Jan 27, 1775, in Carter, 2:179–
83. On Tupper, see 2nd Marines notes below.

Full Regiment Reassignments to Boston in 1774 (from other stations in North America)

10th Regiment of Foot

Commanded by Lt. Col. Francis Smith (promoted to colonel and
made aide-de-camp to the King on Sept 8, 1775)

Regimental Colonel: Lt. Gen. Edward Sandford

Arrived: Nov 1–2, 1774, from Quebec

Departed: Mar 17, 1776 (Evacuation Day), to Halifax

Notes: Gage to Valentine Jones, Sept 4, 1774, in Gage MSS; Gage to Lord Dartmouth,
Nov 2, 1774, in Carter , 1:382–83; Gage to Barrington, Oct 17 and also of Nov
1, 1774, in ibid., 2:656–58 (NB: The "16th" in the first letter should be the
"10th"). Smith's promotion from comparing WO, 64/15, and *LGFO*, v; also see
Howe, *Orderly Book*, 135. He learned of his promotion circa Nov 10, 1775, in
ibid.; it is announced on Nov 11, at which time Howe also gave him the brevet
rank of brigadier general. Other evidence in ibid., hints that as aide-de-camp he
was no longer in command of the 10th Regiment. However, *LGFO*, 64, gives
no successor.

23rd Royal Welch Fusiliers

Commanded by Lt. Col. Bery Bernard

Regimental Colonel: Maj. Gen. William Howe

Arrived: circa Aug 1774, from New York

Departed: Mar 17, 1776 (Evacuation Day), to Halifax

Notes: Gage to Dartmouth, Aug 27, 1774, in Carter, 1:365–58; Gage to Barrington,
     Aug 27, 1774, in Carter, 2:651–52.

47th Regiment of Foot
Commanded by Lt. Col. William Nesbitt
Regimental Colonel: Maj. Gen. Guy Carleton
Arrived: circa Oct 30, 1774, from New York
Departed: Mar 17, 1776 (Evacuation Day), to Halifax
Notes: Gage to Lord Dartmouth, Oct 30, 1774 [No. 17], in Carter, 1:381–82 (NB: Not
     the private letter of Oct 30, but the letter marked No. 17!); Gage to Barrington,
     Oct 17 and also of Nov 1, 1774, in ibid., 2:656–58.

52nd Regiment of Foot
Commanded by Lt. Col. (Brig. Gen. in American Service) Valentine
     Jones
Regimental Colonel: Lt. Gen. John Clavering
Arrived: Nov 1–2, 1774, from Quebec
Departed: Mar 17, 1776 (Evacuation Day), to Halifax
Notes: Gage to Valentine Jones, Sept 4, 1774, in Gage MSS; Gage to Lord Dartmouth,
     Nov 2, 1774, in Carter, 1:382–83; Gage to Barrington, Oct 17 and also Nov 1,
     1774, in ibid., 2:656–58.

59th Regiment of Foot
Commanded by Lt. Col. Ortho Hamilton
Regimental Colonel: Maj. Gen. John Owen
Arrived: circa Aug 1774, from Halifax
Departed: Mar 17, 1776 (Evacuation Day), to Halifax
Notes: Gage to Dartmouth, Aug 27, 1774, in Carter, 1:365–58; Gage to Barrington,
     Aug 27, 1774, in Carter, 2:651–52.

Partial Reassignments to Boston in 1774–1775 (from other stations in North America)

18th Royal Irish Regiment of Foot
Commander unknown; succeeded by Lt. Col. Adam Williamson (eff.
     Dec 9, 1775)

Regimental Colonel: Lt. Gen. Sir John Sebright

Arrived: (3 companies only) circa Oct 30, 1774, under Capt. John Shea (or Shee); (5 companies) July 15, 1775, under Maj. Isaac Hamilton, all from New York

Departed: Mar 17, 1776 (Evacuation Day), to Halifax

Notes: Gage to Lord Dartmouth, Oct 30, 1774 [No. 17], in Carter, 1:381–82 (NB: Not the private letter of Oct 30, but the letter marked No. 17!); Gage to Major Hamilton of the 18th, May 7, 1775, in Gage MSS, orders the remaining five companies there aboard HMS *Asia*; Kemble's diary, July 15, in *Coll. of the NYHS* (1883), 1:48, reports their arrival in Boston. Thus, eight companies came to Boston from New York, while the remaining two were in the backcountry in Illinois, per Gage to Lord Barrington, July 21, 1775, the enclosure giving the list of regiments on station in North America as of July 19, 1775, in Carter, 2:689–91. *British Officers Serving in America, 1754–1774*, 51, names Maj. Isaac Hamilton, but he may not have been with the regiment by mid-1775. Otherwise, *LGFO*, 72, names Robert Hamilton as captain, perhaps given a brevet rank of major, but also names John "Shee" Shea a major as of July 25, 1775. Thus, perhaps Shea replaced Isaac Hamilton as regimental major.

65th Regiment of Foot

Commanded by Lt. Col. Thomas Bruce

Regimental Colonel: Lt. Gen. Edward Urmston (or Urmsten)

Arrived: (2 companies only) circa Oct 1774, from St. John's, Newfoundland; (4 companies) May 6, 1775, under Maj. William Butler, from Halifax

Departed: presumably on Mar 17, 1776 (Evacuation Day), to Halifax

Notes: See the 65th's entry under "Assignments Pre-1774," above. First two companies: Gage to Dartmouth, Oct 17, 1774, in Carter, 1:378–79 (these were borrowed, to be returned in the springtime, but this plan was overcome by the events of Apr 19, 1775, and all seem to have remained in Boston until Evacuation Day). Next four companies: Gage to Major Butler of the 65th, May 7, 1775, in Gage MSS; Gage to Lord Barrington, July 21, 1775, in Carter, 2:689–91. The enclosure of the latter gives the list of regiments on station in North America as of July 19, as follows: six companies at Boston (thus accounted for), three at Halifax, one at St. John's. Gage's General Orders, June 6, in the Frederick Mackenzie MSS Orderly Book, 100, in WO, 36/1, UKNA, says Butler was made deputy commander (under the 43rd's Lieutenant

Colonel Clerk, see above) of the Corps of Light Infantry, which was detached from the regiments and seemingly thereafter treated as an independent regiment, but it does not mention his successor, so Butler perhaps also remained with the 65th.

3rd Battalion, Royal Regiment of Artillery

Commander unknown

Colonel-Commandant unknown

1st Wave: (1 company) circa late July or Aug 1775, from Newfoundland

2nd Wave: (maybe 4 companies plus 2 artillery store ships) circa Nov 9, 1775, from Newfoundland?

Departed: Mar 17, 1776 (Evacuation Day), to Halifax

Notes: French, *First Year*, 726–27, citing, among others, a letter of Lieutenant Colonel Cleaveland, in WO, 55/1537, UKNA. Kemble's diary, Nov 9, in *Coll. of the NYHS* (1883), 1:62, lists four companies of some unnamed artillery battalion arriving Nov 9. French cites an unknown source at NYHS describing one company under a Captain Stehelin and its crossing to Boston. This company is probably one of the four companies and two transports Kemble refers to. Kemble does not give where the four came from, but probably Newfoundland. Duncan, *History of the Royal Regiment*, 1:218–19, gives nothing more.

4th Battalion, Royal Regiment of Artillery

Commanded by Lt. Col. Samuel Cleaveland

Colonel-Commandant: Col. James Pattison

1st Wave: (60 artillerymen and 8 heavy cannon) circa June 1774, from New York

2nd Wave: (perhaps 50 artillerymen, unknown cannon) circa Oct 30, 1774, from New York (5 companies total in Boston by Jan 1775)

Departed: Mar 17, 1776 (Evacuation Day), to Halifax

Notes: Gage to Lord Dartmouth, May 30, 1774, in Carter, 1:355–56; the 2nd Wave came with Haldimand, the war stores, the 47th, and three companies of the 18th, per Gage to Frederick Haldimand, Sept 5, 1774, in Gage MSS and Gage to Lord Dartmouth, Oct 30, 1774 [No. 17], in Carter, 1:381–82 (NB: Not the private letter of Oct 30, but the letter marked No. 17!). Also, Gage's troop list for July 1775, in Carter, 2:690–91. Commanding officers from Duncan, 1:251, 301. Also, *First Year*, 726–27.

First Embarkation of 1775

General notes for this section: Lord Dartmouth to Gage [Secret], Jan 27, 1775, in Carter, 2:179–83, gives the intention of sending this Embarkation, but does not explicitly list the regimental numbers. Gage to Lord Dartmouth, June 25, 1775, in Carter, 1:407–8, gives that the last of the First Embarkation landed on June 19, 1775, but does not say which regiment it was. (They probably arrived days earlier but had sat aboard their ships in the harbor.) A portion of the 63rd and 35th were arrived just before June 17, and participated in the Battle of Bunker Hill. Cf. *First Year*, 727, 734–35.

17th Light Dragoons (cavalry)

Commanded by Lt. Col. Samuel Birch
Regimental Colonel: Maj. Gen. George Preston
Arrived: June 10–15, 1775, from Cork, Ireland
Departed: Mar 17, 1776 (Evacuation Day), to Halifax

Notes: Capt. Oliver De Lancey Jr., quartermaster for the 17th, arrived on Apr 14 aboard HMS *Nautilus*, carrying with him the dispatches that set into motion the Concord Expedition. He arrived ahead of his regiment to secure them horses, which would prove of little use in the coming siege. On this, see Lord Dartmouth to Gage [Secret], Jan 27, 1775, in Carter, 2:179–83. Their arrival, at least in part, in Kemble's diary, June 12, in *Coll. of the NYHS* (1883), 1:43, the remainder reported in Barker, June 15, in *British in Boston*, 59, but Fortescue, *17th Lancers*, 236, claims they began arriving as early as the June 10. Commanders' names per ibid., 29, 33, which also lists the company commanders. Not to be confused with the 17th Regiment of Foot, as given below.

35th Regiment of Foot

Commanded by Lt. Col. Robert Carr
Regimental Colonel: Maj. Gen. Henry Fletcher Campbell
Arrived: circa June 12–13, 1775, from Cork, Ireland
Departed: Mar 17, 1776 (Evacuation Day), to Halifax

Notes: Their arrival, at least in part, in Kemble's diary, June 12, in *Coll. of the NYHS* (1883), 1:43. Gage to Lord Dartmouth, June 25, 1775, in Carter, 1:407–8, says they were all landed by the nineteenth.

49th Regiment of Foot

Commanded by Lt. Col. Sir Henry Calder

Regimental Colonel: Maj. Gen. Alexander Maitland

Arrived: circa June 12–13, 1775, from Cork, Ireland

Departed: Mar 17, 1776 (Evacuation Day), to Halifax

Notes: Their arrival, at least in part, in Kemble's diary, June 12, in *Coll. of the NYHS* (1883), 1:43. Gage to Lord Dartmouth, June 25, 1775, in Carter, 1:407–8, says they were all landed by the nineteenth.

63rd Regiment of Foot

Commanded by Lt. Col. James Patterson

Regimental Colonel: Maj. Gen. Francis Grant

Arrived: June 12–15, 1775, from Cork, Ireland

Departed: Mar 17, 1776 (Evacuation Day), to Halifax

Notes: Their arrival, at least in part, in Kemble's diary, June 12, in *Coll. of the NYHS* (1883), 1:43; the remainder reported in Barker, June 15, in *British in Boston*, 59.

2nd Battalion Marines (ad hoc)

Commanded by Maj. James Short (bedridden since his arrival; Maj. John Tupper acting until June 17; Short died of flux June 23, 1775); succeeded by Maj. William Souter (promoted from captain)

Arrived: May 14–19, 1775, aboard transports *James and William, Francis, Grand Dutchess of Russia, Betsey, Two Brothers*, and *Union*, all from England

Departed: Mar 17, 1776 (Evacuation Day), to Halifax

Notes: Graves to Philip Stephens, May 15, 1775, in Graves, *Conduct* (May 15); Graves, *Conduct* (May 19), this excerpt also in *NDAR*, 1:363; Lord Dartmouth to Gage, Jan 27, 1775, in Carter, 2:179–83; Barker, May 23, in *British in Boston*, 49–50, states they were not all landed until May 23 (see also May 15 in ibid., 47). Two transports arrived May 14, the other four on May 19. Major Short was in command, per Tupper to John Montagu, Lord Sandwich, June 21 and also of June 24, in *NDAR*, 1:731, 745–46, but had the flux and was bedridden, only to die on June 23. Gage to Lord Dartmouth, May 15, in Carter, 1:399–400, gives Tupper was in command with 226 marines and their officers in the two transports that landed May 15 (arrived May 14). Thus, Short was bedridden and Tupper was acting commander since their arrival in Boston. However, after Pitcairn's death on June 17, Tupper was given command of the 1st Battalion (presumably by Major Short). (Cf. Lt. John Clarke's *Narrative* in Drake, *Tea Leaves*, 58–59, which claims a Captain Chudleigh was promoted to major in place of Pitcairn. This contradicts Tupper's June 24 letter.) When Short died days later, Tupper gave the 2nd Battalion to Captain Souter. All this in the two Tupper letters cited. (See 1st Marines above.) The marines were officially reorganized into the 1st and 2nd Battalions by Pitcairn, per Tupper's June 24 letter. This occurred about May 20, the day after the last marines arrived. Strangely, appendix 15 in French, *First Year*, 734–35, suggests Tupper is of the 1st Marines, claiming the marines that arrived first with Pitcairn were brigaded as the 2nd Battalion, while the marines that arrived second with Tupper were brigaded as the 1st Battalion, in contradiction to the other evidence cited here.

Second Embarkation of 1775

General sources for this section: Gage to Lord Dartmouth, July 24, 1775 [Separate], in Carter 1:408–9, which states the last of 2nd Embarkation arrived about July 18 and 19, 1775, while the first arrived June 22, per Gage to Lord Dartmouth, June 25, 1775, in Carter, 1:407–8. All were originally sent to New York, but rerouted to Boston, per Gage to the Officer Commanding the 22nd, 40th, 44th, 45th Regiments, May 30, in Gage MSS. The HM sloop *Mercury* sailed on or shortly after May 30 to reroute the transports, per Graves to Philip Stephens, June 16, 1775, in Graves, *Conduct* (the letter gives Gage asked for a ship on the 29th). See also New York Congress to their Delegates in Philadelphia, June 17, 1775, in Force, 4:2:1017. Cf. French, *First Year*, 727, 734–35.

22nd Regiment of Foot

Commanded by Lt. Col. James Abercrombie (died June 23, 1775,
   from wounds at the Battle of Bunker Hill); succeeded by Lt. Col.
   John Campbell (promoted June 24, 1775)
Regimental Colonel: Lt. Gen. Thomas Gage
Arrived: circa late June–July 19, 1775, from Cork, Ireland
Departed: Mar 17, 1776 (Evacuation Day), to Halifax
Notes: Kemble's diary, July 19, in *Coll. of the NYHS* (1883), 1:49. Commanders'
   names per 22nd's Monthly Return, dated Sept 1, 1774, in Gage MSS. Also,
   Gage's General Orders, June 4, in the Frederick Mackenzie MSS Orderly Book,
   98, WO, 36/1, UKNA. The latter source names Abercrombie to command the

Corps of Grenadiers, detached from the regiments and seemingly now treated as
an independent regiment, but it does not mention a successor, and so he perhaps
also remained in command of the 22nd. He also served as Gage's adjutant general,
per Gage to Richard Rigby, July 8, enclosure, in Carter, 2:687–89.

40th Regiment of Foot
Commanded by Lt. Col. James Grant
Regimental Colonel: Col. Sir Robert Hamilton (promoted to major
   general Sept 1775)
Arrived: circa June 29–July 19, 1775, from Cork, Ireland
Departed: Mar 17, 1776 (Evacuation Day), to Halifax
Notes: Kemble's diary, June 29, July 19, in *Coll. of the NYHS* (1883), 1:45, 49. Grant
   commands per the King's Order, Apr 4, 1776, in Howe, *Orderly Book*, 243–45,
   more on him under the 55th Regiment below. He is the same who talked in the
   House of Commons of the meekness of the Americans in chapter 5.

44th Regiment of Foot
Commander unknown
Regimental Colonel: Gen. James Abercromby
Arrived: circa June 22–28, 1775, aboard transport *Spy*, from Cork,
   Ireland
Departed: Mar 17, 1776 (Evacuation Day), to Halifax
Notes: Gage to Lord Dartmouth, June 25, 1775, in Carter, 1:407–8; also Kemble's
   diary, June 28, in *Coll. of the NYHS* (1883), 1:45. Transport per Williams, June 22,
   in *Discord and Civil War*, 20.

45th Regiment of Foot
Commanded by Lt. Col. Henry Monckton
Regimental Colonel: Lt. Gen. William Haviland
Arrived: circa late June–July 19, 1775, from Cork, Ireland
Departed: Mar 17, 1776 (Evacuation Day), to Halifax
Notes: Kemble's diary, July 19, in *Coll. of the NYHS* (1883), 1:49.

Third Embarkation of 1775 (only a portion sent to Boston)
General source for this section: Washington to Reed, Jan 4, 1776, in
PGW, reports the arrival of the 17th and 55th, but states: "the rest of

the 5 Regiments from Ireland were intended for Hallifax & Quebec; those for the first are arrived there, the others we know not where they are got to." Assuming the 17th and 55th are counted among those five regiments, the others seem to have included the 27th (Enniskillen) Regiment of Foot and 28th Regiment of Foot, as promotions for these are named in the King's Order, Apr 4, 1776, in Howe, *Orderly Book*, 243–45. The final regiment was the 29th Regiment of Foot, sent to Quebec City, per Caldwell [to Murray], June 15, 1776. This was the same unit previously in Boston, prior to 1774, as given above.

17th Regiment of Foot

Commanded by Lt. Col. Charles Mawhood

Regimental Colonel: Lt. Gen. Robert Monckton

Arrived: (4 companies) Nov 8, 1775, aboard HMS *Phoenix*, (6 companies) Dec 30–31, 1775, all from Ireland

Departed: Mar 17, 1776 (Evacuation Day), to Halifax

Notes: Kemble's diary, Nov 8, Dec 30–31, in *Coll. of the NYHS* (1883), 1:61–62; Washington to Reed, Jan 4, 1776, in PGW. Mawhood named in King's Order received Apr 4, 1776, but effective Oct 26, 1775, in Howe, *Orderly Book*, 243–45. HMS *Phoenix* is a fifth-rate 44-gun warship, per the Sept 29, 1775 list in *NDAR*, 2:740–43. Not to be confused with the 17th Light Dragoons, given above.

55th Regiment of Foot

Commander unknown

Regimental Colonel: Col. (Brig. Gen. in American Service) Robert Pigot (eff. late 1775, announced Jan 4, 1776); succeeded by Col. (Brig. Gen. in American Service) James Grant (eff. Dec 11, 1775, announced Apr 4, 1776)

Arrived: (6 companies only) Dec 30–31, 1775 (other 4 companies presumably to Halifax), all from Ireland

Departed: Mar 17, 1776 (Evacuation Day), to Halifax

Notes: Kemble's diary, Dec 30–31, in *Coll. of the NYHS* (1883), 1:62; Washington to Reed, Jan 4, 1776, in PGW. From this latter source: perhaps the remainder of the 55th went to Halifax directly, for they apparently never came to Boston. Pigot's promotion per King's Order, Jan 4, 1776, in Howe, *Orderly Book*, 189. This was temporary: see the 38th Regiment above. The apparent overlap of Pigot's commands is due to the long travel time of the orders across the Atlantic. James Grant came from the 40th Regiment (see above).

APPENDIX 4

TALLIES OF BRITISH TROOPS IN BOSTON IN 1774-1775

To make certain estimates, we must note the makeup of the British Army and establish certain assumptions. First, there were ten companies per regiment (technically twelve: two served as recruiting companies, one in England, one in Ireland). Of these, eight companies were of ordinary infantry, also known as foot guards, and generically called the battalion or line companies. The other two were the flank companies, so called because they took the right- and left-most positions (the flanks) along the regiment when it formed in line formation for parade. These two flank companies were the light infantry (which formed on the left of the regiment during parade) and the grenadiers (which formed on the right). Together they were the flower of the Army, comprised of the best of the men, and often detached from their regiments for special service. In fact, in June 1775, those flank companies of the regiments in Boston were formally detached and formed into a standing Corps of Light Infantry and one of Grenadiers (per Gage's General Orders, June 4, in the Frederick Mackenzie MSS Orderly Book, 98, WO, 36/1, UKNA).

Each full company should have had thirty-nine men, according to 1st Lt. John Clarke of the Marines, in his *An Impartial and Authentic Narrative*. Clarke was a marine stationed in Boston in 1775, so his statistic is thus reliable. These marines, detached for use by Gage alongside his army regiments, were brigaded in the same fashion as the Army. Clarke's statistics and word choice seem to describe the thirty-nine men as the size of any company, be it of the Army or Marines. However, other evidence, presented below, suggests the marine companies were larger. Thus, an assumption is made here: a full *army* company was thirty-nine men, counting all enlisted, be they privates, corporals or sergeants.

Each army company seems to have consisted of about three non-commissioned officers, probably one sergeant and two corporals, thus leaving about thirty-six privates. (The Army did not then have the many other enlisted ranks that are found in the modern British Army.) It is important to note that companies were rarely full, even if all their men were healthy and unwounded, as some "ghost" soldiers were kept on the books to collect pay that would then be used for the company's petty cash and for the comfort of its officers.

Thus, in practice and considering troop estimates sixty days later at Bunker Hill, Army companies in Boston averaged:

Light infantry companies (Army)	30 men avg.
Grenadier companies (Army)	32 men avg.
Battalion companies (Army) (8 per regiment)	27 men avg.

Note the two flank companies (grenadiers and light infantry) were often augmented at the expense of the battalion companies. This gives a total average of 278 men per army regiment, or a total average of 27.8 men per company. (We'll round to 28.) This does not include the surgeons and musicians (unarmed boys who fell dead among the rest, generally two per company, usually able to play both fifes and drums).

Many statistics ignore the officers. Each company was typically commanded by a captain, supported by two subalterns, typically one lieutenant (either first or second lieutenant or the obsolete captain-lieutenant rank, often not differentiated) and one ensign (a rank that no longer exists in the Army). The two elite flank companies, the grenadiers and the light infantry, usually had two lieutenants and no ensigns. Though an unnecessary detail for our simple calculations, Smith and Kiley, *The American Revolutionary War*, 127, state that three companies in each regiment, called field officer companies, had just a lieutenant and ensign, while their commanders were either a major or lieutenant colonel and assigned double duty to the regimental level.

It seems the regimental level had a few unattached officers, as most were drawn from the companies. The regimental staff seems to have not had any additional enlisted. (See Lord Dartmouth to Gage, Aug 2, 1775, in Carter, 2:204.) The regiment's acting commander, a lieutenant colonel who may have also served as a company commander, usually served as the commander in the field. The official regimental commander, a colonel or often a general, rarely deployed with his men, since most colonels and generals held their rank as a form of patronage. (Most never actually led their regiment; many never even traveled to the New World with their men.) The regimental staff also included a major as deputy commander, usually doing double duty as a senior company commander, and at least one subaltern (a lieutenant or ensign) as adjutant, also taken from a company to serve at the staff level. This does not count officers' aides and quartermasters, both of which might be filled by subalterns, also probably counted among the companies. Chaplains and surgeons rounded out the regiment, but as they were noncombatants, we do not include them in our statistics. (See Smith and Kiley, 126–27.)

Thus, for each company, we can expect at least three officers (two subalterns and usually a captain, otherwise a major or lieutenant colonel), while for each full regiment of ten companies, about thirty-one officers (three officers per ten companies, plus perhaps one unattached officer, be it the lieutenant colonel commanding or another, the rest being drawn from the companies).

To summarize, twenty-eight enlisted men per army company at typical strength, thirty-nine at full strength (unusual), with three officers per company. These numbers do not apply to the marines or artillery, treated separately below. With these assumptions in mind, let us turn to the counting of troops.

On November 2, 1774, Gage estimated "a Force of near three Thousand Men exclusive of a Regiment for the Defence of Castle William" (that is, not counting the 64th at Castle William, which, at perhaps twenty-eight men per company, was about 280 strong, plus officers). This three thousand surely included all troops that arrived in 1774, except the artillery (treated below) and the marines, which arrived in December (quote from Gage to Dartmouth, Nov 2, 1774, in Carter,

1:382–83; also appendix 3). To check Gage's numbers, we know by this date there were nine full regiments (of ten companies each), plus three companies of the 18th and two of the 65th, or ninety-five companies total. With at least twenty-eight men per company, this gives just 2,660 men total. The discrepancy with Gage's numbers must be the officers, which is unexpected, since most references to "men" meant the rank and file only, not the officers. Again not counting the 64th or the artillery, the nine full regiments accounted for thirty-one officers apiece, plus three companies of the 18th and two of the 65th, fifteen officers total, plus say two more as detachment commanders for the 18th and 65th, equating to an estimated 296 officers total. We must also count Gage (plus two aides-de-camp per Carter, 2:666–67), Haldimand (plus one aide-de-camp per ibid.) and Kemble (the majors of brigade noted in ibid. belonged to the various regiments). This brings our total to 302 commissioned men. Combining these two estimates together, 302 officers plus 2,660 men gives 2,962 total men, in close agreement with Gage's numbers. Thus, we find that Gage's numbers only make sense when we assume his use of "men" meant officers and men.

On the first arrival of the marines, Lieutenant Barker's diary in *British in Boston* (Dec 5, 12, 13, 1774), 10–11, gives the number of marines as 460; while Gage to Lord Dartmouth, Dec 15, 1774, in Carter, 1:386–88, states that he expected 400, and Kemble's diary (Dec 5, 1774) in *Coll. of the NYHS* (1883), 1:41, estimates 500, as does the newspaper *Massachusetts Spy*, Dec 16, 1774, in *NDAR*, 1:30. Pitcairn estimates 400 as well, but adds that Graves refused to land 50 of the intended marines (including some marine light infantry) until springtime, per Pitcairn to Lord Sandwich, Feb 14 and also of Mar 4, 1775, in Barnes and Owens, *The Private Papers*, 1:57–62. Graves must have landed these by April 19, as he received on April 14 positive orders to do so in the letter Philip Stephens to Graves, Jan 28, which came with the arrival of dispatches on the *Nautilus* in mid-April (letter in Graves, *Conduct*, Apr 14). Thus, Gage probably did have 400 at first, because the remaining fifty were not yet landed. After they were finally landed, Gage seems to have indeed received near 460. It is unclear if this number includes officers or not, but probably not, just as the Second Embarkation of Marines (below) does not. (We will assume the 460 includes only enlisted.) If we assume the same ratio of one officer to sixteen men, as is the case with the Second Embarkation of Marines (below), we should expect twenty-nine officers total.

Our grand total at the turn of the New Year of 1775, sans officers but including marines, was about 3,120 men, not counting the 64th at Castle William, or in round terms, about 3,100. This was about the number of men fit for duty, not counting sick on invalids (cf. *First Year*, 726). The total officers, including those of the marines, added another 331 total. The combined force was then 3,451 redcoats.

Let us turn to the Second Embarkation of Marines. Lord Dartmouth to Gage [Secret], Jan 27, in Carter, 2:179–83, sets the number of marines in the Second Embarkation at 700. An unsigned letter to Admiral Graves and Major Pitcairn, Mar 2, 1775, in ADM, 2/1168, UKNA, also noted in Graves, *Conduct*, Apr 14, states more specifically those that embarked: 600 privates, 25 corporals, 20 sergeants (thus 645 rank and file), 27 subalterns (junior officers), 10 captains, 2 majors (39 officers), plus 20 musicians, 2 adjutants (officers?), 1 surgeon, 2 surgeon's mates, a total of 709 men.

When the troops arrived on May 14 and 19, Pitcairn reshuffled and brigaded them as the Army. Thus they formed into two battalions (the 1st and the 2nd), consisting of ten companies each (two of which were flank companies), just as the Army (Gage to Lord Barrington, July 21, its enclosure, in Carter, 2:689–91, states there were twenty total marine companies). By the time they were brigaded, the marines had suffered some 26 enlisted killed, 6 missing and probably captured if not dead (some captured would be returned during prisoner exchanges), and 38 wounded, perhaps a third of whom we might guess were too wounded to return to duty and thus shipped back to England (Gage's Official Casualty Report, Apr 19, 1775). Thus, of the 460 original marines, their number after April 19 was reduced by 45 to 415 men. With the new arrivals, the marines went from 415 rank and file to 1,060, and given twenty companies, this suggests each company was a whopping fifty-three men strong.

The Royal Artillery, an entirely separate entity from the Army, had five companies at Boston for much of 1775 (Gage to Lord Barrington, July 21, 1775, Enclosure, in Carter, 2:689–91). Which companies were in Boston, however, is uncertain.* French, *First Year*, 726–27, 738, references a return of artillerymen dated October 1, 1775, which French claims is in the Gage MSS, although neither I nor Janet Bloom, a curator at the Clements Library, could find it. As I have been unable to find any other artillery return, even among the UK National Archives, I must concede to using French's figures drawn from this now-lost October 1 return. At that late date, there were six artillery companies in Boston with 214 men, according to French. Thus, five companies should have been about 178 men, or just 36 men per company. Duncan, *History of the Royal Regiment*, 251, says that a full artillery company was much larger, but in their weakened state as they stood in 1771, each company had a mere one captain, one captain-lieutenant, two first lieutenants and two second lieutenants (six officers), two sergeants, two corporals, four bombardiers, eight gunners, fifty-two matrosses (assistant gunners) and two drummers—a company size of seventy-six including men of all ranks. If this 1771 figure is their "weakened state", then the companies as they were in Boston in 1775 were incredibly so. (See also French, *First Year*, 726–27.) Because they were undermanned, the artillery routinely received augmentees from the Army.†

From the end of 1774, we can more easily tally the troops based on their arrivals (listed in appendix 3). (The two official casualty lists noted are for April 19, in Coburn, *Battle of April 19*, 158–59; and for June 17, in Force, 4:2:1097–99.)

	Enlisted	Officers
1774 Arrivals (as detailed above, including detached first arrival of marines, not counting the 64th at Castle William or artillerymen)	3,120	331

---

*There are pay lists and muster rolls for various companies of the 4th Battalion of Royal Artillery in WO, 10/144 and 10/145, UKNA, but determining which men were in Boston becomes almost impossible. A muster roll for Capt. William Johnston's company is one of the few that names where all his company's men were: scattered across the continent from New York to the West Indies. But most pay lists or muster rolls do not list the men's locations and are thus insufficient to determine the number of artillerymen in Boston.

†Various references mention detached infantry assigned to the Artillery: Howe to Lord Richard Howe, June 12, in *Proc. of the Bunker Hill Monument Assoc.* (1907), 112ff.; two undated late May notes in the Frederick Mackenzie MSS Orderly Book, 92 and 94, in WO, 36/1, UKNA; and Gage's General Orders, May 25, in ibid., 95.

	Enlisted	Officers
4th Battalion, Royal Artillery (as detailed above, probably not counted among Gage's troop tally)	178	unk.
TOTAL TROOPS AT THE TURN OF THE NEW YEAR, JAN 1, 1775 (not counting the 64th at Castle William) **3,629**	**3,298**	**331**
Died throughout the winter John Andrews to William Barrell, Jan 9, 1775, in *Proc. of MHS* (1866), 8:393, claims about one hundred, by spring say	–150	unk.
Deserters, say	–100	unk.
TOTAL NUMBER OF TROOPS AS OF APRIL 19, 1775 (not counting the 64th at Castle William) **3,379**	**3,048**	**331**
British Losses of April 19, 1775 (per Gage's Official Casualty List, Apr 19): Missing (presumed captured; officers not counted here, as they were returned in prisoner exchanges)	–26	n/a
Wounded (165 men, 16 officers: Coburn, 158–59) mortally wounded	?	–1
guess one-third of remainder no longer fit for duty	–55	–5
Killed	–64	–1
4 companies of the 65th, arrived May 6, 1775 (as high as 39 men per company, probably closer to 28 per company), plus 3 officers per company, plus say 1 at regimental level	112	13
2nd Battalion of Marines (of the First Embarkation of 1775), arrived May 14–19, 1775: unsigned letter to Graves and Pitcairn, Mar 2, 1775, in ADM, 2/1168, UKNA, states:	645	39
Burgoyne, Clinton, Howe, arrived May 25, 1775 (Carter, 2:687–89, gives them one aide-de-camp each)		6

	Enlisted	Officers
17th Light Dragoons (of the First Embarkation of 1775), arrived between June 10–15, 1775; (per Fortescue, *17th Lancers*, 33) their total (dragoons plus noncommissioned) was	189	19
35th, 49th, 63rd Regiments (of the First Embarkation of 1775) all arrived between June 12–15, 1775 (some of 35th and 49th not landed until June 19), presumably all recruited and sent at full strength (39 men per company, 10 companies per regiment)	1,170	93

TOTAL NUMBER OF TROOPS AS OF JUNE 17, 1775
(not counting the 64th at Castle William)

		Enlisted	Officers
5,513		**5,019**	**494**
British Losses of June 17, 1775 (per Gage's Official Casualty List, June 17):			
Missing		0	0
Wounded (761 men, 70 officers)			
mortally wounded		–23	–2
guess one-third of remainder no longer fit for duty		–246	–23
Killed		–188	–19
New drafts and recruits to augment the regiments already in Boston, arrived June 14–19, 1775;[a] Lord Dartmouth to Gage [Secret], Jan 27, 1775, in Carter, 2:179–83, promises near 500, though Gage to Lord Dartmouth, June 25, 1775, in Carter, 1:407–8, reports receiving probably no officers included in this augmentation		422	0
22nd, 40th, 44th, 45th Regiments (the Second Embarkation of 1775), all arrived between late June and early July, presumably recruited and sent at full strength (39 men per company, 10 companies per regiment)		1,560	124

---

[a]Arrival noted in Gage's General Orders, June 14, in the Frederick Mackenzie MSS Orderly Book, 105, in WO 36/1, UKNA, and Gage to Lord Dartmouth, June 25, 1775, in Carter, 1:407–8.

	Enlisted	Officers
5 companies of the 18th, arrived July 15, 1775 (not fresh recruits, came from New York: as many as 39 men per company, probably closer to 28 per company), plus 3 officers per company	140	15
TOTAL NUMBER OF TROOPS AS OF JULY 15, 1775 (not counting the 64th at Castle William) 7,273	6,684	589
17th Regiment and 6 companies of 55th Regiment (the Third Embarkation of 1775, only this portion sent to Boston) arrived between Nov and end of Dec, presumably recruited and sent at full strength[b] (39 men per company, 10 companies per regiment)	624	50
Royal Artillery, 4 companies (presumably all of the 3rd Battalion), arrived Nov 9, 1775[b]	144	unk.
TOTAL NUMBER OF TROOPS AS OF DEC 31, 1775 (not counting the 64th at Castle William) 8,091	7,452	639

---

[b]For those of the Third Embarkation, we will assume the artillery companies are of the same size as above, while the army regiments are the same size as well, not yet at the new wartime size of 56 men per company, per Lord Dartmouth to Gage, Aug 2, in Carter, 2:204–6, a reasonable assumption, as the 17th had just 10 companies still, not 12. See appendix 3 for the 3rd Battalion of Artillery.

Compare the July 15 estimate to the enclosure with Gage's letter to Lord Barrington of July 21, which provides list and theoretical numbers of men per regiment on station in North America as of July 19, 1775, in Carter, 2:689–91. This theoretical maximum at that date is given as 8,535 men, counting the detached marines and perhaps the officers, but not counting the 64th at Castle William or the artillery-men. My estimate for July 15 above is thus reasonable, at 7,273 total officers and men. (Cf. French, *First Year*, 737–39; Fischer, 309, 313–15.) Also, French, *First Year*, 530n8, estimates about 6,400 British effectives as of October 1, citing evidence in the Clinton MSS, though I have not discovered it. That 6,400 is close to the 6,684 enlisted only reported above, as of July 15.

A final comparison: Howe to Lord Richard Howe, June 12, in *Proc. of the Bunker Hill Monument Assoc.* (1907), 112ff., gives the rank and file as "about 3,400" men, including marines but not including the artillerymen or the infantry detached from regular service to augment the Artillery (a detail I have not calculated here).* Howe's number also excludes the new troops just then arriving in June (the First Embarkation of 1775). Assuming Howe just meant rank and file, the calculations above estimate a slightly higher number of rank and file: 3,482 as of that date.† Howe adds that the newly arriving troops from Ireland (the First Embarkation) "may" give them an additional 1,100 rank and file, in comparison to the 1,359 shown above.

Finally, note the numbers in the table above are likely overestimates, as it becomes difficult to account for all the ill and unfit for duty.

---

*See preceding note †.

†The June 17 enlisted numbers, less the artillerymen at the start of 1775 and the 1,359 of the First Embarkation.

Appendix 5

Key Naval Vessels in 1775 and Early 1776

The following gives detailed statistics for every British ship of significance in the Boston area in 1775. The primary data sources are Rif Winfield's *British Warships in the Age of Sail, 1714–1792* and *Naval Documents of the American Revolution* (*NDAR*). From *NDAR*, I draw upon several ship lists: the "Jan 1775 list" (dated Jan 1, 1775, compiled by Vice Adm. Samuel Graves in *NDAR*, 1:47, republished in Fischer, 310), the "Sept 1775 list" (dated Sept 29, 1775, compiled by the Admiralty Office in London in *NDAR*, 2:742–43), the "Oct 1775 list" (dated Oct 9, 1775, compiled by Vice Admiral Graves, ibid., 2:373–74), the "Jan 1776 list" (dated Jan 27, 1776, compiled by Vice Admiral Graves, ibid., 3:1006–8), and the "May 1776 list" (dated May 4, 1776, compiled by Admiralty Office, ibid., 4:1090–93). These lists are the official rosters of ships in North America.

On crew numbers, listed below is the complement. The actual number aboard varied, either by the granting of passes, or more often the case during this time frame, because some of the men would have been lent to various shore duties, including augmenting various details such as manning Castle William (to free soldiers up for other duty), manning cannon batteries, etc. Thus, the number given does not represent the full number aboard on any given date.

The guns listed are all long guns (that is, long-barreled guns) mounted on trucks (carriages). The "gun deck" is the lowest deck of the ship with long guns. On larger vessels, this is the lower deck; on smaller vessels, this is the upper deck (Winfield, *British Warships*, xiv). Regarding swivel guns (used as antipersonnel weapons), none of the sources list their quantity for the larger vessels, but it is likely that each vessel had a dozen or so, whether listed explicitly or not. Swivels were either ½-pounders or 1-pounders (per Smyth, *Sailor's Word Book*, 670), but for those vessels listed below, for which Winfield explicitly gives the swivels, they are always ½-pounders. Thus, this ½-pounder variety seems to have been the standard.

The ships' dimensions are given as length × breadth × depth in hold. Two lengths are given, separated by a comma. The first is the length of the gun deck; the second is the length of the keel for tonnage (an artificial number that is not the same as the keel length). The breadth given is that used for tonnage, which is actually the breadth at the broadest part of the vessel, outside the planking but inside the wales. Where known, each vessel's draft is also given, in the format: forwards / aft. All measurements are in the Imperial system of feet (') and inches ("). On the tonnage used, it is the builder's measurement ("bm"), a formula used in calculating the carrying capacity of the hull. The equation is bm = $kb \times \frac{1}{2}b \div 94$, where k is keel length for tonnage and b is breadth, both as defined above (Winfield, xiv–xv).

In my references to Winfield, because his listing of ships is hierarchical, I first note the page the ship's information appears on, then the preceding page describing the ship class or establishment group (if any), followed by the still preceding page describing the category of the vessel (e.g., the rate, or description of armed sloops, etc.).

The following vessels are listed in alphabetical order.

HMS *Boyne*

Third-rate ship of the line, *Burford* Class
Under Capt. Broderick Hartwell
68 guns (called a "70 gun" ship):
    Lower (Gun) Deck: 26 × 32-pounders
    Upper (Spar) Deck: 28 × 18-pounders
    Quarterdeck: 12 × 9-pounders
    Forecastle: 2 × 9-pounders
    (some number of swivels, probably 12 or more ½-pounders)

520 men
Dimensions as built:
    162' 0", 134' 6" × 44' 8" × 19' 8", 1426^{87}/$_{94}$ bm;
        draft 11' 4½" / 17' 9"
Launched: May 31, 1766 (Plymouth Dockyard)
Commissioned: Aug 3, 1771
Fate: Broken up at Plymouth in May 1783
Notes: Winfield, 57–58, 27. Though she appears on the various lists as a 70-gun ship
    and was officially called such, in practice she carried only 68 guns, per Winfield,
    57. Departed for England on Dec 5, 1775, per Graves to Philip Stephens, Dec 15,
    in *NDAR*, 3:112.

HMS *Cerberus*

Sixth-rate frigate, *Coventry* Class (a.k.a. Modified *Lowestoffe* Class)
Under Capt. James Chads (1775); Capt. John Simmonds (Aug 1775)
28 guns:
    Upper (Spar) Deck: 24 × 9-pounders
    Quarterdeck: 4 × 3-pounders
    12 × ½-pounder swivel guns (mostly on the quarterdeck)
160 men
Dimensions as built:
    118' 7½", 97' 2⅛" × 33' 10½" × 10' 6", 593^{14}/$_{94}$ bm
Launched: Sept 5, 1758 (East Cowes)
Commissioned: May 1758
Fate: Burnt to prevent capture by the French at Rhode Island on Aug
    5, 1778
Notes: Winfield, 230, 229, 227. According to the Sept 1775 list, the second captain is
    John Symons; Winfield, 230, spells it Simmonds. *Cerberus* had 160 crew on her
    when traveling back to England, per the Sept 1775 list, but by the May 1776 list
    she had 200.

HMS *Chatham*

Fourth-rate ship of the line, Modified 1745 Establishment
Under Capt. John Raynor;
    flagship of Vice Adm. Molyneux Shuldham

50 guns:

> Lower (Gun) Deck: 22 × 24-pounders
> Upper (Spar) Deck: 22 × 12-pounders
> Quarterdeck: 4 × 6-pounders
> Forecastle: 2 × 6-pounders
> (some number of swivels, probably 12 or more ½-pounders)

350 men

Dimensions as later remeasured:

> 147' 0", 122' 2" × 40' 3" × 17' 8", 1052⁴⁰/₉₄ bm

Launched: Apr 25, 1758 (Portsmouth Dockyard)

Commissioned: Feb 1758

Fate: Renamed *Tilbury* on June 29, 1810, broken up at Chatham in
> May 1814

Notes: Winfield, 154, 113. She arrived in Boston Dec 30, 1775 with Graves's recall
> (in Graves, *Conduct*, Dec 30, 1775, reprinted in *NDAR*, 3:300). Winfield reports
> 350 men, in agreement with the Jan 1776 list, but the May 1776 list reports 370.

HM Armed Schooner *Diana*

Schooner (two-masted fore-and-aft rigged)

Under Lt. Thomas Graves

4 guns:

> 4 × 4-pounders (double-fortified)
> 12 × ½-pounder swivel guns (probably throughout the vessel)

30 men

Purchased Dec 29, 1774; was a colonial mercantile vessel

Commissioned: early 1775

Fate: Grounded, abandoned, then destroyed in the Battle of Chelsea
> Creek (a.k.a. the Battle of Noddle's and Hog's Island) on May 27–
> 28, 1775 (seemingly few casualties)

Notes: Winfield, 333, 322. Winfield has it as six guns total, in agreement with the
> Jan 1775 list, which adds that *Diana* was "just purchased intended for an Armed
> Schooner". However, *NDAR*, 1:545–46, provides the "Report of the Massachusetts
> Committee of Safety of the Battle of Noddle's Island," citing the Mass. Archives,
> 146:131, which states she was an "armed Schooner (mounting four 6 pounders
> & 12 Swivels)" (the only claim that they were 6-pounders). Barker, May 28, in
> *British in Boston*, 51, also claims she had just four guns (and only ten swivels; no

indication of the guns' size). *NDAR*, 1:544–45, provides an article from the *New York Journal* of June 8 (also in Force, 4:2:719–20), which claims the provincials *took* "4 double fortified 4 pounders, twelve swivels" from the abandoned schooner, perhaps explaining the disparity. Perhaps one is inclined to think the provincials were only able to *get* four out, as she had run aground and ended up rolling over onto her beam-ends, which might have lodged two more guns on that side into the mud, and thus six total were aboard her. Yet there are no reports that two more guns were found later among the wreckage, despite reports that the Americans continued to explore the wreckage for plunder. Alternatively, one might think to solve the disparity by figuring two guns were removed by her crew as they fled. Yet no such British claim exists. Thus, we must assume though originally outfitted or intended to have six guns, *Diana* had only four. As the vessel was lightly armed, I have assumed the swivel guns were the typical ½-pounders. On deciding among the evidence whether the cannon were 6- or 4-pounders, comparison to the sloop *Spitfire* below, which had 3-pounders, suggests the comparable *Diana* had a small caliber as well, thus 4-pounders. On few casualties: see appendix 17 of French, *First Year*, which gives varied accounts of two to three British killed, a few wounded.

HMS *Eagle*

Third-rate ship of the line, Revived *Intrepid* Class
Under Capt. Henry Duncan
    flagship of Vice Adm. Lord Richard Howe
64 guns:
    Lower (Gun) Deck: 26 × 24-pounders
    Upper (Spar) Deck: 26 × 18-pounders
    Quarterdeck: 10 × 9-pounders
    Forecastle: 2 × 9-pounders
    (some number of swivels, probably 12 or more ½-pounders)
520 men
Dimensions as built:
    159' 8½", 131' 3" × 44' 4" × 19' 0", 1372^{14}/$_{94}$ bm;
        draft 10' 8" / 16' 9½"
Launched: May 12, 1774 (Rotherhithe)
Commissioned: Feb 1776
Fate: Renamed *Buckingham* on Aug 15, 1800, broken up at Chatham
    in Oct 1812

Notes: Winfield, 105, 102–3, 90, 27. Winfield reports 500 men, but the May 1776 list reports 520. She sailed for North America on May 12, 1776, per her journal, reprinted in *NDAR*, 4:1119, arriving off Massachusetts by June 20, 1776, per Howe's letter in ibid., 5:635. She then sailed briefly to Halifax (letter in ibid., 5:966–68), and arrived off Staten Island July 11, 1776 (ship's journal in ibid., 5:1038).

HM Sloop *Falcon*
Sloop-of-war (three-masted "ship sloop"), *Swallow* Class
Under Cmdr. John Linzee
14 guns:
　Upper (Spar) Deck: 14 × 6-pounders
　Quarterdeck: 12 × ½-pounder swivel guns
100 men
Dimensions as built:
　95' 0", 78' 0" × 27' 1½" × 13' 0", 305^{25}/94 bm
Launched: June 15, 1771 (Portsmouth Dockyard)
Commissioned: Jan 1771
Fate: Lost, presumed foundered with all hands in a storm off the American coast on Sept 20, 1779
Notes: Winfield, 280, 273. Winfield, 280, claims Linzee's rank as master and commander, while he is listed as captain on the Sept 1775 list. But then none of the lists give the title of commander to anyone (note that he would have been called "captain" aboard his ship, but his substantive rank would have been lieutenant, as "master and commander" was not made substantive until 1794, per Winfield, xiv). Winfield claims the ship had 14 guns, in agreement with the Sept 1775 list, but the May 1776 list indicates she added two more, making it 16. The Sept 1775 list claims 100 men, while the later lists show more.

HMS *Glasgow*
Sixth-rate frigate, Later *Seaford* Class
Under Capt. William Maltby (1774); Capt. Tyringham Howe (Jan 1775 to Sept 1776)
20 guns:
　Upper (Spar) Deck: 20 × 9-pounders
　(likely 12 × ½-pounder swivel guns, mostly on the quarterdeck)

130 men

Dimensions as built:

109' 4", 91' 2½" × 30' 6" × 9' 7½", 451²⁹/₉₄ bm

Launched: Aug 31, 1757 (Hull)

Commissioned: Mar 1757

Fate: Destroyed in accidental fire in Montego Bay on Jan 6, 1779

Notes: Winfield, 264–65, 224. Winfield, 265, reports that Captain Howe took command Jan 1775, yet Maltby still appears on Graves's 1775 list. (Though the list was dated Jan 1, 1775, it may have been compiled days before.) The note in Winfield that she ran on rocks Dec 10, 1774, but was salved, followed by Captain Howe's taking command days later, suggests a disciplinary action against Maltby. French, *First Year*, 683–84, gives the account of the skirmish between *Glasgow* and two continental vessels, *Cabot* and *Columbus*, though it amounted to nothing. The Jan 1775 list gives her 130 men; the 1776 lists give her more.

HM Sloop *Hunter*

Sloop-of-war (two-masted), *Hunter* Class

Under Capt. Thomas Mackenzie

10 guns:

Upper (Spar) Deck: 10 × 6-pounders (short)

12 × ½-pounder swivel guns (probably throughout the vessel)

80 men

Dimensions as built:

88' 8", 75' 11⅜" × 24' 3" × 7' 0", 223⁶²/₉₄ bm

Launched: Feb 28, 1756 (Rotherhithe)

Commissioned: Apr 1756

Fate: Put out of commission as unfit in 1779, employed as a prison ship at New York until sold there by auction on Dec 27, 1780

Notes: Winfield, 310, 294. Winfield gives her standard crew as 100 men, but 80 are reported on the Sept 1775 list. She is reported with 110 men on the May 1776 list.

HMS *Lively*

Sixth-rate frigate, Later *Gibraltar* Class

Under Capt. Thomas Bishop

20 guns:

Upper (Spar) Deck: 20 × 9-pounders

(likely 12 × ½-pounder swivel guns, mostly on the quarterdeck)

130 men

Dimensions as built:

108' 0", 89' 0¼" × 30' 5¼" × 9' 8", 438^{64}/₉₄ bm

Launched: Aug 10, 1756 (Bursledon)

Commissioned: Aug 1756

Fate: Laid up at Plymouth in Aug 1781, sold there (£405) on Nov 3, 1784

Notes: Winfield, 263, 262, 224. The Jan 1775 list gives her 130 men; the 1776 lists give her more.

HMS *Lizard*

Sixth-rate frigate, Later *Coventry* Class

Under Capt. John Hamilton

28 guns:

Upper (Spar) Deck: 24 × 9-pounders

Quarterdeck: 4 × 3-pounders

12 × ½-pounder swivel guns (mostly on the quarterdeck)

160 men

Dimensions as built:

118' 8½", 97' 2¾" × 33' 11" × 10' 6", 594^{87}/₉₄ bm

Launched: July 4, 1757 (Rotherhithe)

Commissioned: Mar 1757

Fate: A hospital ship in Oct 1799, sold in Sept 1828

Notes: Winfield, 227–28. Winfield reports the standard crew as 200, but on the Sept 1775 list she has but 160, with 28 guns reported. On the Jan 1776 list, she has but 20 guns reported, with 150 crew. Some of these guns must have been kept in Quebec City for the ongoing siege. By the May 1776 list, she is at 28 guns again, with 200 men.

HMS *Preston*

Fourth-rate ship of the line, Modified 1745 Establishment

Under Capt. Jonathan Robinson

flagship of Vice Adm. Samuel Graves

50 guns:

    Lower (Gun) Deck: 22 × 24-pounders

    Upper (Spar) Deck: 22 × 12-pounders

    Quarterdeck: 4 × 6-pounders

    Forecastle: 2 × 6-pounders

    (some number of swivels, probably 12 or more ½-pounders)

320 men

Dimensions as built:

    143' 3", 115' 4" × 41' 3" × 17' 3", $1043^{81}/_{94}$ bm;

        draft 9' 10" / 15' 6"

Launched: Feb 7, 1757 (Deptford Dockyard)

Commissioned: Jan 1757

Fate: Broken up at Woolwich in Jan 1815

Notes: Winfield, 153–54, 113. In Apr 1776, Cmdre. William Hotham came aboard. (The May 1776 list calls him commodore, but Winfield calls him captain and gives the Apr 1776 arrival.) The Jan 1775 list shows just 300 men; 320 comes from the Sept 1775 list, and the 1776 lists give still more.

HMS *Somerset*

Third-rate ship of the line, 1745 Establishment

Under Capt. Edward Le Cras

68 guns:

    Lower (Gun) Deck: 26 × 32-pounders

    Upper (Spar) Deck: 28 × 18-pounders

    Quarterdeck: 12 × 9-pounders

    Forecastle: 2 × 9-pounders

    (some number of swivels, probably 12 or more ½-pounders)

520 men

Dimensions as built:

    160' 0", 131' 4" × 45' 4" × 19' 4", $1435^{62}/_{94}$ bm

Launched: July 18, 1748 (Chatham Dockyard)

Commissioned: Dec 1748

Fate: Wrecked off Cape Cod on Nov 2, 1778 (21 drowned)

Notes: Winfield, 53, 27. She does not appear on the 1776 lists, having been sent back to England.

HM "Sloop" *Spitfire*

Schooner or galley rigged with sails (one or two masts)

Under unknown (likely a master and commander)

6 guns:

    6 × 3-pounders

    (likely 12 × ½-pounder swivel guns, throughout the vessel)

40 men

Purchased

Fate: Unknown

Notes: *Spitfire* is not on any list in *NDAR*. Winfield, 334–35, 322, does list her; however many of the dates reported are clearly wrong. For example, the burning of Falmouth is in 1775, not 1776. Furthermore, Winfield's book reports it as a purchased galley in 1778 but commissioned in 1776, which seems dubious if it was in action in 1775. Perhaps it was a privateer, a hired vessel (Winfield's guess), or even borrowed from a Loyalist. Graves's description in *Conduct* for June 17 states that "The *Preston* manned the *Spitfire* Sloop of Six 3-pounders". This seems to support that *Spitfire* was not under direct control of an independent officer, but under control of the *Preston*, adding to the support that she may not have yet been purchased. Graves's description is therefore the source of the number of guns and size, though Winfield, 334, claims she had eight guns of unknown size. Graves called it a sloop, while Winfield reports it as a purchased galley. *Glasgow*'s journal on the day of Bunker Hill (*NDAR*, 1:701) also names it a sloop. However, the 1775 or 1776 lists seem to suggest it might have been a schooner, for all sloops listed had at least eight guns, while all 6-gun vessels listed were schooners. Winfield, 294, states, "The term 'sloop' applied to all vessels with fewer than 20 guns… it signified the commanding officer was designated 'master and commander'…while he held that command, although he retained the substantive rank of lieutenant, reverting to that designation when he relinquished command." Winfield also reports that the smaller two-masted sloops were "all armed with between 8 and 12 guns." Thus, I can believe this ship is a schooner, just as the *Diana* was a schooner, but per Winfield, 334, "all were fitted for rowing as well as sailing, and were either rigged as either single-masted or two-masted with a fore-and-aft rig." Thus, a galley with such sails would look similar to a schooner, except it would also have the oars necessary to be a galley as well. The fact that it is generically called a sloop seems to confirm it did have sails, but how many masts is unknown. The presence of swivels is assumed, and their number is guessed based on the number and size of those on *Diana*, close in size to *Spitfire*. See

Symmetry notes below, which describe a curiosity about her and *Spitfire* in their use for the coastal attacks that would include the burning of Falmouth.

HM Armed Transport *Symmetry*

Transport (sail ship) of "light draft"

Under Lieutenant Boormasters (or Bourmaster or Bowmaster)

18 guns:

> 18 × 9-pounders
>
> (likely 12 × ½-pounder swivel guns, throughout the vessel)

? men, at least 38 men during the Battle of Bunker Hill

Fate: Deleted from the ship list in 1776

Notes: *Symmetry* is not on any list in *NDAR*, which is typical for transports, as they were often under control of the Army (Winfield, 353, 351). Winfield spells her *Symetry* and claims she had 19 guns. Letter of a British Officer, Boston, July 5, in *Detail and Conduct*, 13–15, gives the guns and her light-draft: "the *Cymetry*, transport, which drew little water and mounted eighteen nine-pounders, could have been towed up Mystic channel…and she could have lain, water-borne, at the lowest ebb tide". *Symmetry* was undoubtedly a ship of sail, despite the note she could be "towed up". I assume the presence of swivel guns. More evidence on *Symmetry* being under the Army: as given in the present text, Gage made *Symmetry* and *Spitfire* available to Admiral Graves for attacking coastal cities such as Falmouth. This suggests they were under the Army, though this could simply be due to Graves's orders, which were to support Gage, and thus perhaps required Gage's permission to take certain ships away from Boston. Graves's *Conduct* for June 17 is the source for the number of men. Kemble's diary, June 29, in *Coll. of the NYHS* (1883), 1:45, lists the *Symmetry* under a Mr. Boormasters. Barker, Oct 16, 1775, in *British in Boston*, 65, calls him Mr. Bourmaster. Williams, Aug 22, in *Discord and Civil Wars*, 28, names him Lieutenant Bowmaster of the Navy, then in charge of a different transport.

Appendix 6

British Cannon Statistics

On statistics of the guns given here, I draw upon the third edition of Muller's *Treatise of Artillery*. In Muller, 6, he gives the caliber (bore size of the muzzle in inches) and diameter of the round shot for typical English guns. We should note also that shot was generally iron ball, and the density of iron is 7.874 g/cm³, from which we can determine the weight of each.

On grapeshot, he writes, "in sea-service 9 is always the number; but by land it is increased to any number or size" (Muller, 200). Manucy's *Artillery Through the Ages*, 69, notes that "grape shot…in the 1700's consisted of a wooden disk at the base of a short wooden rod that served as the core around which the balls stood… In later years grape was made by bagging two or three tiers of balls, each tier separated by an iron disk." (I have seen other evidence that this inter-tier disk need not be present.) We cannot be sure what type of grapeshot was used at any of the battles described in this volume, but I have made an assumption that it is of the three-tiered variety, three balls per tier, thus nine balls per grapeshot. Muller, 12, does not give us much useful information on the dimensions of grapeshot, so we must calculate it, using the assumption of three per tier, nine total. Given three "grapes" per level, if one were to draw a line from one ball's center to the centers of the adjacent two balls, it would form an equilateral triangle with each side $2r$, r being the radius of each grape ball. Note that the grape balls do not touch at the central point of the cannon's bore. (Draw this to convince yourself.) With careful trigonometry, the resulting equation that relates the grape size to cannon caliber is $r = R \div (1 + 1/\cos(30°))$, or more simply, $r = R/2.155$, where R is the effective radius of the cannon, subtracting for windage (that is, R is half the diameter of a round shot, as given), and r is the radius of each grape ball (the diameter of which is $2r$). Windage is the difference between the muzzle caliber and the diameter of a round shot.

Gun	Caliber (in.)	ROUND SHOT Diam. (in.)	Wt. (lb.)	GRAPESHOT (3 per level, 9 total) Diam. (in.) 1 ball	Wt. (lb.) 1 ball	Wt. (lb.) all 9 balls
24-pounder	5.824	5.547	25.422[a]	2.574	2.541	22.871
5½" howitzer[b]	5.500	5.225	21.247	2.425	2.124	19.115
18-pounder	5.292	5.040	19.069	2.339	1.906	17.155
12-pounder	4.623	4.403	12.714	2.043	1.271	11.438
9-pounder	4.200	4.000	9.533	1.856	0.953	8.576
6-pounder	3.668	3.498	6.375	1.623	0.637	5.735
4-pounder	3.204	3.053	4.238	1.417	0.424	3.813
3-pounder	2.913	2.775	3.183	1.288	0.318	2.864

[a]Ironically, 24-pounders actually shot 25-pound shot.
[b]It is assumed here that a 5½" howitzer was indeed 5.50-caliber. Muller's *Treatise of Artillery* gives no details on this size howitzer. Therefore, for the diameter of its shot, I have used the factor of 21/20, typical of all English guns, to determine its windage (per Muller, 40).

In comparison, a typical musket ball was about 0.75 inches in diameter and usually made of lead.

APPENDIX 7

EXPEDITION TO CONCORD: TIMELINE

Let us consider each point in turn. First, the moonrise. U.S. Navy's Sun and Moon Calculator gives a moonrise of 9:37 p.m., a waning gibbous with 90 percent (presumed at moonrise) of the moon's visible disk illuminated. To once again prove this calculator accurate, we can look to both Paul Revere to Jeremy Belknap [circa 1798], and more importantly Jacques Vialle and Darrel Hoff, "The Astronomy of Paul Revere's Ride," *Astronomy*, April 1992, 13–18. The latter source independently calculated the moonrise at 9:36 p.m., and the waning gibbous at just 87 percent by midnight, in close agreement with the U.S. Navy's calculator. Another source, Donald W. Olson and Russell L. Doescher, "Astronomical Computing: Paul Revere's Midnight Ride," *Sky and Telescope*, April 1992, 437–40, gives similar results. Whether the moon was at 87 percent or 90 percent is of little consequence to our historical survey. All sources generally agree on the moonrise time.

Mr. Waters states in Jeremy Belknap's journal, Oct 25, 1775, in *Proc. of MHS* (1860), 4:84–86, that "a party of nine rode out of town with their blue surtouts, and passed through Cambridge just before night". Civil twilight ended just before 7:00 p.m., per the U.S. Navy's calculator, so we can perhaps guess that these men left before then. However, the quantity of nine is dubious. For more, see appendix 9.

Admiral Graves issued orders to have "The [Navy] Boats…assemble along side the *Boyne* by 8 o'Clock in the Evening" (Graves, *Conduct*,

Apr 18, in MHS, this portion republished in *NDAR*, 1:192). *Boyne* seems to have been in Boston Harbor near Long Wharf, but her journals are unclear (in ADM, 51/129, UKNA). This activity, probably between the hour of 7:00 and 8:00 p.m., led Dr. Joseph Warren to suspect something was indeed going to happen that night. He sent for William Dawes, who probably immediately afterward prepared his horse and rode for Lexington.

However, as there is no evidence to support that Dawes alerted the countryside until he arrived at the Rev. Jonas Clarke's parsonage, we might assume he was not in any rush. And why should he be? Dawes's departure, as proposed in the text, was not an errand of urgency, but a warning that something was definitely astir. Dr. Warren had yet to witness anything concrete for which to raise an alarm. Furthermore, as Wheildon, *Curiosities of History*, 36, reports that the Charlestown Ferry was closed by 9:00 p.m., the boats drawn up against HMS *Somerset*, we can surmise that Boston Neck was closed by then too, and thus the town was shut. Therefore, we can then estimate that Dawes left before 9:00 p.m., but probably after 8:00 p.m. once the boats were seen collected at *Boyne*. Let us guess 8:30 p.m.

Mackenzie, Apr 18, in *A British Fusilier*, 50–51, states that the troops were to muster at the embarkation point at exactly 10:00 p.m. Warren seems to have witnessed this embarkation, before urgently summoning Revere at "About 10 o'Clock" (Paul Revere to Jeremy Belknap [circa 1798]). Note Revere says *About*. Mackenzie reported that his flank companies of the 23rd were the first complete companies to arrive, apparently the only ones on time. Warren must have waited a few minute to survey the scene, then sent a messenger (Revere says he was summoned to Warren's house). Warren then rushed to his own house north of Faneuil Hall, a walk that took at least ten minutes. (If he ran, he would have drawn suspicion.) He then arrived at his house by about 10:20 p.m., with Revere arriving from his own nearby home moments later. After a brief discussion, Revere had to stop by North Church; tell his friends to light two lanterns; go home and get his coat, boots, and stirrups; meet two friends who would row him across; and, if tradition holds, go to a nearby house to get a woman's undergarment with which to muffle their oars. (All of this comes from his letter, just cited.) At best, they had their boat ready by 10:45 p.m.

Revere's crossing of the Charles took little time. Its expanse in that era was perhaps 0.3 nautical miles (estimated using modern digital mapping tools), and at a modest three knots for the rowboat to cross, the waterway could have been crossed in just six minutes. Let us give them an extra ten minutes to slow down and creep around the lurching HMS *Somerset* in their path. This puts Revere on the Charlestown shore by 11:00 p.m. and gives him just a few minutes to meet with Col. William Conant and get his horse. By 11:15 p.m., perhaps, he was on his way. (Revere, in the letter just cited, says "about 11 o'Clock". Again, he says *about*.)

Before we continue, let us consider the speed of a horse. Susan E. Harris, *Horse Gaits, Balance and Movement* (New York: Howell Book House, 1993), gives the following average speeds for the four horse gaits: walk: 4 mph (pp. 32–35); trot: 6–8 mph (pp. 35–42); canter: 9–17 mph (not explicitly given, but inferred between a trot and gallop; pp. 42–47); gallop: 18–30 mph (45 mph for a race horse, which none of these were; pp. 47–49).

Using modern digital mapping tools, we can approximate Revere's ride at about 12.5 miles (maybe thirteen, depending on how far he got before he was turned back by the first two mounted patrol). His route was from about the area of the modern USS *Constitution*'s dock, along Warren Street northwestward, becoming Main Street, then Mystic Avenue to High Street (in Medford), following this west where it becomes Medford Street and then joins Massachusetts Avenue (in modern Arlington), which he then took up to Lexington. Unlike Dawes, Revere was on a mission of urgency, trying to raise the alarm. He kept his horse at a canter and sometimes at a gallop, and if the horse was indeed the fastest in Charlestown, as legend supposes, we can suppose the mare averaged perhaps 15 mph, on the high end of a canter. Thus, in about one hour from his departure from Charlestown, he would have arrived in Lexington, 12.5 miles away by the route he took. We can allow a few extra minutes for his alerting the militia captain in Medford and a few other houses along the way. Revere then arrived in Lexington about 12:30 a.m., April 19.

Revere reported that Dawes arrived "about half an Hour" after him, so let us assume "about" 1:00 a.m. Again, no evidence supports that Dawes alerted anyone along the way. However, he was forced to take a more circuitous route, south past the Boston Neck and through Roxbury, west through Brighton, up the Great Bridge across the Charles River, through Cambridge, then up what is essentially the same route Massachusetts Avenue now takes, all the way to Lexington. This total distance is about 16.5 miles (appendix 8). If Dawes kept his horse (admitted to be an old nag) at a typical walking speed of 4 mph, this trip would have taken just past four hours. If we allow that he perhaps had to maneuver or hide to avoid British patrols, that he spent a few minutes chatting with the Boston Neck Guard, and so on, the time easily becomes closer to four and a half or even five hours. As a result, if we calculate back from 1:00 a.m., the time we can suppose he arrived based on Revere's information, we again come to a Boston departure time of about 8:30 p.m.

Revere then reported they had time to refresh themselves, so we can suppose another half hour (1:30 a.m.), which was about the same time the militia alarm was raised on Lexington Green and Captain Parker sent out two scouts (per Rev. Jonas Clarke's *Opening of the War*). Then, from Lexington Green to the present location of Revere's capture site in the Minute Man National Park is about three miles. We know they stopped at many houses to alert the town between the Green and his capture, plus there was an introduction to Dr. Samuel Prescott, but we might guess that even Dawes was now cantering his horse, finally aware of the expedition. So we may estimate that it took them twenty minutes to travel those three miles (1:50 a.m.).

From the events following his capture, per Revere's statement (as cited), we can deduce that he was detained for at least a half hour, or until about 2:20 a.m. If we allow ourselves to acknowledge the source of Elijah Sanderson's [Third] Deposition, Dec 17, 1824, in Phinney, *History of the Battle*, 31–33, dubious because it was given almost fifty years after the fact, it claims that, just before his own release, he was given the time by one of his captors, who reported 2:15 a.m., in close agreement with my estimate. Note that Sanderson and the other three prisoners were released just before Revere, but let us allow ourselves a little longer for the British patrol to have indecision. Thus, Revere's release was at perhaps 2:30 a.m.

We know from Revere's statement also that he was released shortly after a volley of gunfire was heard on Lexington Green. Fischer, 135, makes the supposition that these were the militia unloading their weapons before entering Buckman Tavern, and Revere himself suggests these were fired outside the tavern. Thus, pairing this information with Rev. Jonas Clarke's *Opening of the War*, we might guess that the first scout returned from Cambridge and told Parker there was no British column coming that he could see, at which Parker dismissed his men, though to be ready at the beat of a drum. Dismissed, they unloaded their muskets by firing and then went to grab a beer or rum. (The second scout never returned, because he rode all the way toward Menotomy and was captured by the British.)

Rev. Jonas Clarke's *Opening of the War* says this first rider came back "Between 3 and 4 o'clock", but it seems more likely he came back around 2:30. But is this time possible? Lexington Green to Cambridge, along modern Massachusetts Avenue, is about 8.7 miles, or about 17.4 miles round trip. For an "express rider" as Rev. Jonas Clarke called him, he should have had his horse at least at a fast canter (17 mph), if not a gallop, and so could have easily made it to Cambridge and back in an hour, fitting in nicely with this timeline. (They departed around 1:30 a.m.) In fact, Rev. Jonas Clarke's *Opening of the War* claims the scout checked the roads *from* Cambridge and Charlestown. Where two such roads connected was at Watson's Corner just northwest of Cambridge center, closer to Lexington, thus making this timeline more probable still. Supposing the volley heard by Revere was indeed the militia dispersing, we can estimate this occurred a few minutes before Revere's release (say 2:20 a.m.). Note also that Revere's captors had to ride through Lexington to alert the British column, yet I have seen no deposition describing their second ride through the town, providing even more reason to think Parker had already dismissed his men. (Though it is equally plausible that they rode around the town, through the pastures.)

As for the British, a second account by an unknown author in Mackenzie's diary in *A British Fusilier*, 62–63, reports that the mustering of troops, which was to begin at 10:00 p.m., was delayed: "the whole was not assembled 'till near 11." Mackenzie himself adds, "This was not completed untill 12 o' Clock" (ibid., 51), echoed by Pope (in Murdock, *Late News*, 27). (Cf. the second account in Mackenzie, *Fusilier*, 62, which claims it was near 1:00 a.m.)

After arranging themselves and moving upriver slightly to receive unwanted provisions, the troops were on the move by 2:00 a.m., as Barker (*British in Boston*, 32), Sutherland to Clinton, Apr 26, (in Murdock, *Late News*, 13; cf. the version to Gage, Apr 27, in French, *Informers*, 43), and Pope (in Murdock, *Late News*, 27) all agree.

We are left to guess when (and where) Lieutenant Colonel Smith split off Major Pitcairn and the leading British light infantry to march ahead to Lexington. Before we derive an educated guess, consider Sutherland's April 27 correspondence to Gage, which says that between three and four in the morning the advance light infantry met with Revere's mounted captors, but unfortunately it does not give us *where* they met. (In contrast, Gage's *Circumstantial Account*, which on this point draws from Pitcairn to Gage, Apr 26, claims this happened about 3:00 a.m. within two miles of Lexington. This is an impossible timeline, because it would have required the British troops to stand outside Lexington doing nothing for some two hours.)

Let us tackle the guesswork from two directions: from Pitcairn's point of view and from that of Smith's express rider. Here I make a key assumption. It is logical to conclude that Smith sent his express rider back to Boston at about the same time he split off his front light infantry companies. Smith probably first concerned himself with securing the road ahead, and only then thought about his return to Boston. Thus, Pitcairn was sent first and the express rider was sent second, yet both events were probably nearly simultaneous. *Where* Smith made this decision along the route is important to our guesswork. For this, let us make some approximations based on the source material.

First, we will tackle this question from Pitcairn's point of view. Smith's April 22 letter to Gage states that he split off the light infantry, but makes no mention of Major Mitchell's patrol. Had this patrol, the same mounted men who captured Paul Revere, been the reason for Smith's sending Pitcairn and the lights ahead, surely he would have noted that in his letter. Sutherland's April 27 letter to Gage is not explicit about the split-off, but implies that when they met with Mitchell's patrol, Pitcairn was now in charge.

If we return to Sutherland's statement that they met Mitchell and his men between three and four in the morning, let us average the range he gives and assume about 3:30 a.m. If we then logically assume that Mitchell's patrol set out from west of Lexington just after Revere's release, 2:30 a.m. as shown above, and took its time to carefully make its way unnoticed around Lexington Green, making their way at a cautious pace, not to arouse suspicion, in the interval of this hour they would have arrived near but west of Menotomy (modern Arlington). Thus, the probable area where Mitchell met Pitcairn was west of Menotomy.

Pitcairn and the six light companies were thus split off from Smith's main column ahead of this 3:30 a.m. meeting with the patrol (again as implied by Sutherland to Gage, Apr 27), and so perhaps we can guess they split off somewhere near Menotomy center. As given in the present text, Smith probably split off Pitcairn after noting several inhabitants in Menotomy were aware of their march. Thus, Pitcairn was split off at least at Menotomy center, probably just west of it. (Side note: given Revere's release at 2:30 a.m., it was also at about the time of the patrol's meeting the lead six light companies—that is, 3:30 a.m.—that Revere began escorting Samuel Adams and John Hancock to Woburn.)

As we hone our guesswork, let us now turn to consideration of Smith's express rider. Letter from Boston, July 5, 1775, in *Detail and Conduct of the American War*, 9–10, states "at five o'clock an express from Smith desiring a reinforcement produced an enquiry". Thus, the rider came to Gage at *about* 5:00 a.m., probably just before, because the inquiry began then. As this source calls it an "express", we can assume the messenger was mounted. If he was indeed dispatched where the split off of Pitcairn and the lights occurred, somewhere just west of Menotomy, he had to travel a distance of just over four miles to Cambridge center, then an additional 7.7 miles using the land route across the Charles, through Roxbury, then up to Boston, a total of about twelve miles (appendix 8). If we assume this messenger was indeed on horseback, which would have been prudent, we would hope he tried to canter his horse wherever possible, traveling the distance no quicker than about one hour. If his actual arrival at Province House was, say, 4:45 a.m., this would indicate the rider was not dispatched until no later than 3:45 a.m. However, this rider's journey was through an alerted countryside and he must have halted at times, either to cautiously move his horse through the centers of Cambridge and Roxbury, so as not to alarm their inhabitants, or to avoid any roving militia already on their way. Thus, if we add a half hour to his ride, then his departure was at about 3:15 a.m.

Now, if we indeed believe Smith's express rider was dispatched just after Pitcairn and the advance light infantry, and if we allow at least fifteen minutes for Pitcairn's men to march ahead of the main column and meet Mitchell's patrol (which again we have assumed was at 3:30 a.m.), we find our two conclusions in approximate agreement. Namely, the light infantry and the express rider were both dispatched about 3:15 a.m. (just west of Menotomy). However, when we consider small but time-consuming events such as the lights encountering two country milkmen (see main text), whom their vanguard apprehended, we find ourselves supposing Pitcairn was dispatched a few minutes earlier still, perhaps as early as 3:00 a.m. Let us split the difference and say 3:10 a.m. Unfortunately, all of these are just educated guesses, and without further evidence, we can do no better.

On the British arrival at Lexington Green, we have Robbins's deposition in Force, 4:2:491, which claims "sometime before sunrise" the militia was formed, and the British arrived just moments later. Draper's deposition (ibid., 495) gives "about half an hour before sunrise". Barker, *British in Boston*, 32, puts the time "about 5 o'clock". We can safely guess it was approximately sunrise, essentially 5:00 a.m., but certainly well within civil twilight, bright enough for all the combatants to see one another.

If we subscribe to the sunrise arrival (4:57 a.m., per Navy's Sun and Moon Calculator) of the British at Lexington Green, and if we believe the William Munroe deposition, 1825, in Phinney, *History of the Battle*, 33–35, which states he found near two hundred torn paper musket cartridges (tossed away after loading) left on the road within one hundred rods (0.3 miles) of the Green, we can deduce that the light infantry charged their weapons very shortly before they entered Lexington center, at about 4:30 a.m. (Cf. Lister, *Concord Fight*, 23, who writes, "to the best of my recollection" this happened about 4:00 a.m.)

The skirmish and the reorganization of the British troops afterward might have taken as little as half an hour. Such a time frame is plausible if we assume Smith was still worried about getting his mission accomplished before the militia could muster at Concord. Since none of the sources provide a better estimate of the time, let us assume the British departed Lexington Green at about 5:30 a.m.

The distance they were to travel was barely more than six miles from Lexington Green to Concord center. If we guess about a three-mile-an-hour march, consistent with the speeds kept up by the column thus far (cf. Fischer, 317), this means about two hours of travel time, putting the detachment in Concord about 7:30 a.m. The British report by De Berniere to Gage [circa Apr 19] sets it at between 9:00 and 10:00 a.m., impossibly late in the day, and Gage's *Circumstantial Account* seems to echo De Berniere. However, the depositions of sixteen Americans at Concord (in Force, 4:2:497–98) has the British arriving two hours after sunrise, in close agreement with our estimate.

Adding to this guess, we can estimate that the light infantry arrived at Barrett's Farm, an additional 2.5 miles from Concord center, just under an hour later. If we figure a little time for Smith to issue his orders to those six companies to march there, we can assign 8:30 a.m. as their arrival time at the farm. Along the way, just about 0.7 miles from Concord, was the North Bridge, where they crossed about twenty minutes after their departure from Concord center (near 7:50 a.m.), leaving three companies behind at the bridge and on the heights just west of it.

For the events at Concord, we have to work backward. On the British departure from Concord following their raid, two accounts agree on noon (De Berniere to Gage [circa Apr 19] and the second account in Mackenzie, Apr 19, in *A British Fusilier*, 65). Once the advance party from Barrett's Farm returned to Concord center, we can give Smith a half hour to organize his men for the march. This is supported by Reverend Emerson's diary in Emerson, *Complete Works*, 11:569, though, in the reverend's nonmilitary mind, he saw "by their marches and counter-marches, discovered great fickleness and inconstancy of mind, sometimes advancing, sometimes returning to their former posts; till, at length they quitted the town".

No other evidence supports fickleness on the part of the British, so we can assume Emerson was ignorant of the military movements he saw before him. This half-hour lag brings us to 11:30 a.m. The advance party traveled from Barrett's Farm past the North Bridge and back to Concord center, 2.5 miles total, which took about an hour at a normal march. Thus, they left Barrett's Farm about 10:30 a.m., having spent, based on their guessed arrival, about two hours at the farm.

From this, we can determine when the skirmish occurred at the North Bridge. Barker (in *British in Boston*, 34–35) writes that the light infantry companies were waiting in Concord center, following their retreat from North Bridge, for about an hour before the advance parties from Barrett's Farm finally joined them there. This puts the three light companies from the bridge back in Concord center about 10:30 a.m. The distance from the east end of the North Bridge to Concord center was about 0.7 miles.

However, the first stretch of their withdrawal, from the east edge of the bridge to the present path leading up to the Old Manse, was a running retreat and so only took a few minutes. Then, if we trust Amos Barrett's letter of 1825 (for he was there), the retreating lights consulted with the arriving grenadiers under Lieutenant Colonel Smith for about ten minutes. Figure in some extra time for getting organized, perhaps, and we are up to twenty minutes. The remainder of the distance to town center, 0.5 miles, would have taken about another ten minutes at a normal march. Thus, we have roughly thirty minutes from the retreat from the bridge to the companies' arrival in town center, placing the start of the retreat at about 10:00 a.m.

The skirmish at the bridge took just a few minutes. Note that the militia was first on the overlooking heights. They took a few minutes to maneuver into column formation and come around from the hill to the main road, and from there marched to the bridge, a distance of about a quarter mile, which would have taken another five minutes. Thus, from the start of the militia movements to the British retreat was fifteen minutes or less. This places the start of the militia's movements at about 9:45 a.m., with the Skirmish of North Bridge ending by 10:00 a.m.

Continuing to work backward, the British probably saw the militia loading their weapons and debating the march but minutes earlier, and it was only then that the British considered crossing to the opposite, eastern side of the bridge at, say, 9:40 a.m. Before this, Barker (in *British in Boston*, 33) claims the British and the Americans stared at each other across that small quarter-mile stretch for "a long time very near an hour". In his April 26 letter to Gage, Laurie calls it "a Considerable time", placing the British withdrawal from the heights to the western edge of the bridge, or conversely, the American arrival on the heights after departing Punkatasset Hill at about 8:40 a.m. If we believe our earlier deduced time of 7:50 a.m. for the British arrival at the heights and the bridge, then we have the Americans gathering on Punkatasset Hill for nearly an hour before marching down to these same heights, which is supported by Laurie's letter to Gage. All of this, of course, is logical guesswork.

Using the known departure from Concord center as noon, let us find the times for the skirmishes. For the march back to Lexington, let us use the same average as before of about 3 mph. Even if they double-timed back, which does not appear to be the case, they constantly slowed to give volleys to the harassing militia. The distance from Concord center to Meriam's Corner is about 1.3 miles, placing the fight there at about twenty-six minutes after the hour, or 12:30 p.m. in round terms. The distance to travel to Brooks Hill, the next skirmish, is about 0.9 miles, requiring eighteen minutes. Let us be careful not to compound our rounding errors, so starting with 12:26, this places them at Brooks Hill at 12:44, or 12:45 p.m. in round terms. It is another 0.7 miles to Bloody Curve, requiring fourteen minutes, giving a time of 12:58, or about 1:00 p.m. The stretch to the site of Parker's Revenge is about 1.6 miles, requiring thirty-two minutes, putting us at 1:30 p.m. even. The distance to the north side of Fiske Hill is another 0.6 miles, requiring twelve minutes, putting the time at 1:42, or 1:40 p.m. in round terms.

To check our accuracy, let us consider their arrival time at the point east of Lexington Green midway to Munroe's Tavern, where they met Percy's reinforcement at about 2:30 p.m. per the evidence given below. This point is a distance of about two miles more, requiring forty minutes, which would have, by our series of deductions above, placed them before Percy's reinforcement at about 2:22 p.m., in close agreement with the 2:30 p.m. evidence below. If we figure a few minutes of guesswork error, and possibly a few minutes for the British to be re-formed under heavy fire after they fled pell-mell from Fiske Hill (per De Berniere to Gage [circa 19 April]), we can rectify these last few minutes of difference.

Percy's April 20 letter to Gage gives "about 2 o'clk" as the arrival of the British column into the waiting arms of Percy's 1st Brigade, just east of Lexington Green. But 2:30 p.m. is given by Mackenzie, Apr 19, in *A British Fusilier*, 52 (and for this event Mackenzie himself was there), and the same is given in the second account (ibid., 65). As we have just deduced, the British retreat was at Fiske Hill at about 1:42 p.m., still two miles away from Percy's reinforcement. Thus it is more likely the two forces met near 2:30 p.m., not "about 2" as Percy suggested. However, it was at about 2:00 p.m. (Mackenzie, *A British Fusilier*, 54) when they heard the straggling and distant gunshots. As the reinforcement needed a few minutes to deploy, and perhaps marched a bit farther to take the ideal high ground, they deployed into position at about 2:15 p.m.

On the reinforcement's earlier march, Mackenzie (Apr 19, in *A British Fusilier*, 52–53), says the order was issued "dated at 6 o'Clock" to assemble at 7:30 a.m., but due to a mix-up with the marines, who were not properly informed, the whole was not assembled until 8:30 and did not march until 8:45 a.m. The distance they traveled through Roxbury, Cambridge, and Menotomy before reaching the point east of Lexington Green where they deployed was about 15.8 miles (appendix 8). At our usual figure of about three miles per hour for their march, this distance should have taken about five hours and fifteen minutes, putting them outside Lexington at about 2:00 p.m., in close agreement with the evidence presented above. However, as we have guessed their marching speed, and have not accounted for delays such as when Lord Percy met Lieutenant Gould and gained intelligence, we will defer to the previous conclusion of 2:15 p.m.

Meanwhile, Dr. Warren was seen in Charlestown about 8:00 a.m., according to a Dr. Welch of Charlestown (*Life and Times*, 457). It is reasonable to conclude that Warren's intelligence came from a local who observed the mustering of the reinforcement on Boston Common before 7:30 a.m., so Warren left his home shortly thereafter. (Remember, the British were to be fully mustered by 7:30 a.m., so would have gathered before then.) After a brief time in Charlestown, Warren was observed leaving there at "About ten…riding hastily out of town", per Jacob

Rogers's petition in Frothingham, *Siege of Boston*, 371–72. His hasty ride was for Menotomy, 6.5 miles away, probably arriving in under half an hour, around 10:30 a.m. (The prearranged meeting was for 10:00 a.m., per Committee of Safety to Bigelow, Apr 17, postscript, in *JEPCM*, 516.) All the while, the British reinforcement was still outbound. After traveling 11.5 miles at three miles per hour, given an 8:45 a.m. departure from Boston, the reinforcement reached Menotomy nearly four hours later, at 12:45 p.m. Warren was in Menotomy and watched them march by.

Returning again to the meeting of Smith's expeditionary force and Percy's reinforcement east of Lexington, De Berniere to Gage (circa Apr 19) claims the British departed there after about a half hour of rest, as does Barker, *British in Boston*, 36. Mackenzie, Apr 19, in *A British Fusilier*, 55, claims the British began the march at 3:15 p.m. Mackenzie's times have proven accurate for our study, so we shall use his. (As adjutant of the 23rd Regiment, perhaps he carried a pocket watch.) He claims it took another half hour before he and his rear guard were actually on the move.

Starting at 3:45 p.m., we can deduce the march as before, using 3 mph as the average. The distance from the British position east of Lexington, near the modern Massachusetts Avenue/Woburn Street intersection, to Menotomy (modern Arlington) along Massachusetts Avenue, is about 4.5 miles, a march of about 1.5 hours, giving an arrival there at about 5:15 p.m.—perhaps closer to 5:00 p.m. when the head of the column drew near the town. (Remember, 3:45 p.m. is the time Mackenzie wrote that the rear guard gave up its position and joined the marching column.) It was another 2.2 miles to Watson's Corner (modern Massachusetts Avenue at Rindge Avenue) in Cambridge, just north of Harvard College, and was, in round terms, about a 45-minute march. However, we must account for the heavy fighting through Menotomy. A modest 15 minutes might be appropriate, as the British did keep driving through the chaos of Menotomy. Thus, they came to Watson's Corner about 6:00 p.m.

The remaining distance to the north face of Bunker Hill on Charlestown Peninsula was about 3.3 miles (appendix 8). This gives about 1:06 of marching. This takes about an hour and six minutes of marching. Add a few more minutes before this for the artillery to fire at Watson's Corner and we have about an hour and fifteen minutes to march to Bunker Hill, thus arriving about 7:15 p.m. Percy to Gage, Apr 20, has the British arrived in Charlestown "between 7 & 8", though in his other letters in Bolton, *Letters of Hugh Earl Percy*, 52, 54, he gives 8:00 p.m.

Mackenzie, *A British Fusilier*, 57, our reliable timekeeper, gives about 7:00 p.m. when they crossed the Neck (and thus arrived at the base of Bunker Hill shortly after). De Berniere to Gage (circa Apr 19) also gives "about seven". Barker, *British in Boston*, 36, gives "between 7 and 8". John Andrews to William Barrell, Apr 19, in *Proc. of MHS* (1866), 8:403–5, states the Americans followed them till 7:00 p.m., "by which time they got into Charlestown". According to Mackenzie, *A British Fusilier*, 59, the British remained on the heights for a half hour before the light infantry and grenadiers marched to the town center, about a sixteen-minute walk from the north face of Bunker Hill, probably slower since they were exhausted and no longer pursued, so say twenty minutes at least. Thus, 7:00 p.m. seems likely as the time they began crossing the Neck, 7:15 when they assembled on Bunker Hill's north face, 7:45 when the first companies descended to the town, and about 8:05 when the first regiments reached Charlestown center.

John Andrews to William Barrell, Apr 19, in *Proc. of MHS* (1866), 8:403–5, says the British were bringing over wounded until 10:00 p.m., making their about 8:00 p.m. arrival in the town center reasonable. If 8:00 p.m. seems a little early, with a 7:15 p.m. arrival on the heights, we should remember that Percy had sent Lieutenant Rooke to warn Gage (though we have no idea if Rooke knew Percy was going to turn to Charlestown). In any case, we can expect Gage knew wounded would be on their way and so prepared accordingly. (At least Gage knew by 7:00 p.m. the troops were marching to Charlestown, for John Andrews stated he watched them march there, daylight being still barely sufficient to do so.) To give us further support, the wounded Ensign Lister, in his *Concord Fight*, 33, claimed he was back at his lodgings by 9:00 p.m., and thus, at the latest, he embarked at 8:30 p.m. Perhaps we can guess that by 8:15 p.m. the first longboats were crossing to Boston with wounded.

The remainder of the timeline is murky. Mackenzie, *A British Fusilier*, 59, indicates that after the wounded, light infantry and grenadiers embarked, and new troops came over under General Pigot. Only then did Mackenzie's 23rd Regiment and the marines finally descend Bunker Hill and into the town, not to arrive until near 10:00 p.m. It took another two hours to get the whole 23rd regiment over, and it was "past 12" midnight, per Mackenzie, that his regiment was landed at the North End (hence they departed from Charlestown center about midnight). Mackenzie suggests that his 23rd and the marines were the last of the main force to cross, so we can use his reported time of midnight as the final crossing of any of the troops that night. That is, we may guess that by just after midnight, all of the troops that marched that day were at last back in Boston.

The following summarizes the explanations given above. (Cf. Fischer, 315–17.)

Notional Timeline for April 18–19, 1775

—Apr 18—

6:29 p.m.	Sunset[a]
6:45 p.m.	British patrol departs Boston ("just before night")[b]
6:58 p.m.	End civil twilight[a]
8:30 p.m.	Dawes departs Boston[c]
9:00 p.m.	Charlestown Ferry closed; Boston Neck closed (town sealed shut)
9:37 p.m.	Moonrise (waning gibbous; 90 percent of the moon's visible disk illuminated)[a]
10:00 p.m.	British begin to muster on the Common; Warren calls for Revere
10:20 p.m.	Warren sends Revere on his Midnight Ride
10:45 p.m.	Revere crosses the Charles River
11:00 p.m.	Revere arrives in Charlestown; first wave of British land at Lechmere Point
11:15 p.m.	Revere departs Charlestown

—Apr 19—

12:00 a.m.	Second wave of British land at Lechmere Point
12:30 a.m.	Revere arrives at Reverend Clarke's home in Lexington (his horse canters)
1:00 a.m.	Dawes arrives at Reverend Clarke's home in Lexington (his horse walks)
1:30 a.m.	Dawes and Revere depart to Concord;[b] militia assemble on Lexington Green; 2 scouts sent to Cambridge
1:50 a.m.	Revere captured (approx. 3 miles west of Lexington Green)
2:00 a.m.	British expeditionary force departs Phipps's Farm
2:20 a.m.	First Lexington scout returns; Parker dismisses militia, and they fire a volley
2:30 a.m.	Revere released
3:10 a.m.	Light infantry under Pitcairn split off from the expeditionary force's main column, western outskirts of Menotomy[d]
3:15 a.m.	Smith sends a messenger back to Boston for reinforcements[d]
3:30 a.m.	Revere escorts Samuel Adams and John Hancock to Woburn[d]
3:30 a.m.	Mounted patrol meets Pitcairn's advance light infantry, just west of Menotomy[d]
4:28 a.m.	Begin civil twilight[a]
4:30 a.m.	Pitcairn's light infantry load their weapons outside Lexington
4:45 a.m.	Smith's messenger arrives in Boston
4:57 a.m.	Sunrise[a]
5:00 a.m.	Pitcairn's light infantry arrive in Lexington; Skirmish of Lexington
5:00 a.m.	Gage inquires why his reinforcement is not ready (soon discovers a communications breakdown)
5:30 a.m.	British expeditionary force (rejoined) departs Lexington[d]
6:00 a.m.	Gage issues new orders to send a British reinforcement, to assemble at 7:30 a.m.
7:30 a.m.	British expeditionary force arrives in Concord[d]
7:30 a.m.	British reinforcement assembles on Boston Common; marines do not assemble due to a mistake
7:30 a.m.	Dr. Warren departs his home[d]

7:46 a.m.	Moonset[a]
7:50 a.m.	Light infantry arrive at North Bridge; Americans move to Punkatasset Hill[d]
8:00 a.m.	Dr. Warren crosses Charlestown Ferry with his horse
8:30 a.m.	Advance light infantry arrive at Barrett's Farm[d]
8:30 a.m.	British reinforcement completed with arrival of marines
8:40 a.m.	Americans move to heights over the North Bridge; British withdraw to the North Bridge[c]
8:45 a.m.	British reinforcement departs Boston Common
9:45 a.m.	Americans begin march to the North Bridge[c]
10:00 a.m.	Skirmish of the North Bridge ends; British retreat[c]
10:00 a.m.	Dr. Warren hastily departs Charlestown for Menotomy on horseback; Committee of Safety meeting begins there
10:30 a.m.	Dr. Warren arrives in Menotomy on horseback[c]
10:30 a.m.	British advance light infantry companies from North Bridge arrive in Concord center[c]
10:30 a.m.	Advance light infantry depart Barrett's Farm[c]
11:30 a.m.	Advance light infantry arrive in Concord center[c]
12:00 p.m.	British expeditionary force departs Concord
12:30 p.m.	Skirmish of Meriam's Corner[c]
12:45 p.m.	Skirmish of Brook's Hill[c]
12:45 p.m.	British reinforcement passes Menotomy[c]
1:00 p.m.	Skirmish of Bloody Curve[c]
1:30 p.m.	Skirmish of Parker's Revenge[c]
1:40 p.m.	Skirmish of Fiske Hill[c]
2:15 p.m.	British reinforcement deploys near Munroe's Tavern, east of Lexington Green
2:30 p.m.	British expeditionary force meets Percy's reinforcement
3:15 p.m.	British combined force forms for departure
3:45 p.m.	British combined force departs Lexington for Boston
5:00 p.m.	Skirmish of Menotomy[c]
6:00 p.m.	Skirmish of Watson's Corner in Cambridge[c]
6:30 p.m.	Sunset[a]
7:00 p.m.	End civil twilight[a]
7:00 p.m.	British combined force crosses Charlestown Neck

7:15 p.m.   British combined force assembles on Bunker Hill

7:45 p.m.   Select British regiments descend to Charlestown center

8:05 p.m.   Select British troops gather in Charlestown center[c]

8:15 p.m.   British wounded, followed by light infantry and grenadiers, begin to cross Boston; fresh troops in turn brought to Charlestown[c]

10:00 p.m.   Last of the British expeditionary force and wounded land in Boston

10:41 p.m.   Moonrise (waning gibbous; 83 percent of the moon's visible disk illuminated)[a]

—Apr 20—

past 12:00 a.m.   Last of Percy's British reinforcement land in Boston

---

[a]U.S. Navy's Sun and Moon Data Calculator.
[b]Estimated.
[c]Deduced from evidence, as given above.
[d]A reasoned guess, as given above.

Appendix 8

Expedition to Concord: Land Routes from Boston

The primary land route from Boston to Cambridge was the "Old road to Roxbury", described in *Record of the Streets, Alleys, Places, Etc., in the City of Boston*, 348–49, updated here with modern designations and for clarity. The circuitous Old Road to Roxbury was the earliest road from Boston, beginning south of Boston Common, heading southwestward along the route now designated by Washington Street (crossing what was once Boston Neck), then northwestward on Roxbury Street (at Dudley Square). The road then cut a path through a property that now covers the old road to meet Columbus Avenue, goes northeast a short way on Columbus, then west on Tremont Street (to Brigham Circle), where the street becomes Huntington Avenue.

Following this westerly, the road then follows the modern MBTA Green Line, the street becoming (a different) Washington Street temporarily as it passes underneath Riverway. From there, the road follows Washington Street as it turns sharply northwestward, taking the split that is Harvard Street (in Brookline) and following this past Coolidge Corner, the street eventually becoming Harvard Avenue, which dead-ends on Cambridge Street. The road then follows Cambridge Street northeastward until reaching North Harvard Street, which branches off northward (in North Allston).

Following this as it turns northeastward, the road passes the Harvard Business School off the right, the Harvard Stadium off the left, and crosses the Anderson Memorial Bridge over the Charles River, the site of the former "Great Bridge" (the only bridge near Boston that in 1775 crossed the river), then follows this road, now the J. F. Kennedy Street, to Harvard College until merging with Massachusetts Avenue (in Harvard Square). (For more on the Great Bridge, see ibid., 217.) Measured using modern digital mapping tools, the distance along this route from the south end of Boston Common to the point where J. F. Kennedy Street merges with Massachusetts Avenue is about 7.7 miles.

In contrast, the distance from the northwest of Boston Common to Cambridge center (crossing the Charles by longboat for about a mile, then traveling along the shoreline northeastward and westward over a former bridge at long-ago drained Willis Creek, then following northward along roads no longer extant until turning south and joining Cambridge Street at Inman Square, then approximately following this northwest to Cambridge center, reaching where J. F. Kennedy Street merges with Massachusetts Avenue) is just about 3.3 miles—a savings of 4.4 miles, or more than an hour's march, over the above land route. The path through Cambridge is difficult to rectify with modern maps. (See Pelham's 1777 map, *Boston with Its Environs*.)

The remainder of the route taken by the British on April 19, 1775, follows modern Massachusetts Avenue to Lexington, an additional distance of 8.5 miles to the southeast tip of Lexington Green, or 7.6 miles to Munroe's Tavern, or 8.1 miles to the Woburn Street/ Massachusetts Avenue intersection (where Percy's reinforcement formed in line formation), or 8.8 miles to Rev. Jonas Clarke's home north of Lexington Green.

From Lexington, the approximate route to Concord center following Massachusetts Avenue to Old Massachusetts Avenue, then up Marrett Street and down Nelson Street, cutting across the divide back to Massachusetts Avenue, then following the westward trail through the National Park Service's Minute Man National Historic Park (Virginia Road and Old Bedford Road), passing Meriam's Corner at the split with (the other) Old Bedford Road, then following modern Lexington Road into Concord town center is a distance of 6.8 miles from the southeast tip of Lexington Green to the modern Concord Monument in town center. For completeness, the distance from the Concord Monument to North Bridge is 0.7 miles, and the distance from the monument to Barrett's Farm (via North Bridge), using roads that no longer exist, is 2.5 miles.

Finally, the distance from Watson's Corner (modern Massachusetts Avenue at Rindge Avenue) to the point where modern J. F. Kennedy Street merges with Massachusetts Avenue is about 1.4 miles, and from there, as given above, it is another 7.7 miles to Boston Common, a total of 9.1 miles. For completeness, let us add that the distance from Watson's Corner to the Jason Russell House in Menotomy (modern Arlington) is 2.4 miles.

From Watson's Corner to the Charlestown center, the old path is difficult to derive from the lay of the modern roads. However, it is approximately Summer Street to Washington Street, then down Main Street to what was then Charlestown center, about where Main meets modern City Square Park, a distance of 4.1 miles (or just 3.3 miles from the north face of Bunker Hill). When Percy took this route, he saved about five miles on his return march to Boston.

In total, Lieutenant Colonel Smith's expeditionary force crossed the Charles (about 1 mile) and marched to Concord center via Lexington some 17.6 miles (18.3 miles for those who went on to North Bridge, 20.1 miles for those who went on to Barrett's Farm). They then marched 7.2 miles back from Concord center to just east of Lexington, where they found Lord Percy's reinforcement. Percy had taken the land route from Boston and had marched 15.8 miles. Together, they then marched 10.8 miles back to Charlestown center (City Square Park).

APPENDIX 9

EXPEDITION TO CONCORD: THE BRITISH PATROL

This British patrol is alluded to in Gage's Instructions to Lieutenant Colonel Smith, Apr 18, in Gage MSS, republished in French, *Informers*, 31–32. He says that six of the patrolmen were Maj. Edward Mitchell (5th), commanding; Capt. Charles Cochrane (4th); Capt. Charles Lumm (38th); Lt. Peregrine Francis Thorne (4th); Lt. Thomas Baker (4th); and Lieutenant Hamilton (64th). (*Paul Revere's Ride*, 385–86n28, perhaps drawing from *Informers*, 59n1, and 61n1.) Perhaps Lieutenant Hamilton is Ens. Harry Hamilton of the 64th, listed in *British Officers...Revolution*, 88.

Fischer, 89, supposes there were twenty riders total, half officers, half rank and file, but gives no citation. In contrast, Mr. Waters reported to Jeremy Belknap in Belknap's journal, Oct 25, 1775, in *Proc. of MHS* (1860), 4:77ff. that "a party of nine rode out of town with their blue surtouts". Similarly, the Brown, Sanderson, Loring deposition, Apr 25, in Force, 4:2:489, reported seeing nine officers. (Brown's statement was repeated in Rev. Jonas Clarke's *Opening of the War* and Munroe's deposition, 1825.) However, the most reliable information comes from Paul Revere to Jeremy Belknap [circa 1798].

Revere's 1798 letter and his earlier depositions say that two mounted British were on the road ahead of where he was captured; four others popped out near him on the road and surrounded him; and as he galloped for the woods to escape, another six sprung out there, a total of twelve. (Unlike Fischer, 135, I do not believe the four that first sur-rounded Revere included the two he saw ahead on the road. Instead, I suspect those two galloped past to unsuccessfully pursue William Dawes.) I also suppose the two that had chased Revere earlier outside Charlestown were not among these twelve. Otherwise Revere would have probably said so in his report. Thus, Revere himself encountered at least fourteen different patrolmen that night. Revere's 1798 letter also states of the patrol: "I supposed that after Night, they divided them selves", which need not mean they divided themselves *evenly*. From this, we might guess that Revere encountered only a portion of the total patrol, giving strong support that at least twenty patrolmen were indeed roving about. Thus, while Fischer's statement of twenty riders is uncited, it seems entirely likely and reliable.

APPENDIX 10

EXPEDITION TO CONCORD: THE ARREST OF ADAMS AND HANCOCK

When some of Maj. Edward Mitchell's British patrol passed through Lexington on the evening of April 18, 1775, Solomon Browne, Jonathan Loring, and Elijah Sanderson took note. Sanderson said in his third deposition in Phinney, *History of the Battle*, 31–33 (taken in 1824, almost fifty years after the fact), "we agreed, if we could find the officers, we would return and give information, as the fears were, that their object was, to come back in the night, and seize [John] Hancock and [Samuel] Adams, and carry them into Boston. It had been rumored, that the British officers had threatened, that Hancock and Adams should not stay at Lexington. They had been boarding some time at Parson Clark's." William Munroe's deposition, 1825 (in Phinney, 33–35) corroborates that of Browne and the rest, saying, "Solomon Brown...had seen nine British officers on the road...they were well armed. On learning this, I supposed they had some design upon Hancock and Adams, who were at the house of the Rev. Mr. Clark, and immediately assembled...eight men...to guard the house." This sentiment is echoed in Rev. Jonas Clarke's own *Opening of the War*, where he declares, "it was not without some just grounds supposed, that under cover of the darkness, sudden arrest, if not assassination might be attempted, by these instruments of tyranny!"

Note the people fully understood that the primary objective of the British *column* was the war stores in Concord, not the Whig leaders (per the many depositions of 1775 in Force, 4:2:489ff.), but it seems many in Lexington also thought the objective of the British *patrol* was Hancock and Adams. In fact, William Munroe posted his guard outside the Clarke home for that very reason. Did the British in fact intend to arrest these two famous Whig leaders?

In the secret message of Lord Dartmouth to Gage, Jan 27, received by Gage on April 14 in copy, April 16 in the original (in Carter, 2:179–83), Dartmouth wrote, "it is the Opinion of The King's Servants in which His Majesty concurs, that the first & essential step to be taken towards re-establishing Government, would be to arrest and imprison the principal actors & abettors in the Provincial Congress". Dartmouth, however, left it to Gage's discretion how to proceed. Gage had similar sentiments months earlier when he wrote to Lord Dartmouth, Jan 18, 1775 (in Carter, 1:390, received Feb 20), "it's the opinion of most People, if a respectable Force is seen in the Field, the most obnoxious of the Leaders seized, and a Pardon proclaimed for all other's, that Government will come off Victorious, and with less Opposition than was expected a few Months ago." On June 12, almost two months after the Concord Expedition and days before the Battle of Bunker Hill, Gage issued his *Proclamation* (in Force, 4:2:968–70), written by Gen. John Burgoyne, which famously began, "Whereas, the infatuated multitudes…" The *Proclamation* had in it an offer of peace, and a "gracious pardon to all persons who shall lay down their arms…excepting only from the benefit of such pardon *Samuel Adams* and *John Hancock*, whose offences are too flagitious a nature to admit of any other consideration than that of condign punishment." (Italics changed from original.)

Thus, we see that Gage was encouraged by the home government to arrest the radical leaders, and that he himself had independently concluded such measures were probably prudent. That is, he had both the authority and the desire to make such an arrest. And yet, not a single one of the many contemporary British accounts of the Concord Expedition makes so much as a mention of Hancock or Adams. In fact, there is no British evidence to show an arrest was ever considered in earnest, even if Gage had debated it. So while Hancock and Adams feared their arrest was coming, and thus fled from Boston just weeks ahead of the British march to Concord, the British seem to have never attempted it.

A most conspicuous consideration is that of Dr. Joseph Warren, also a noted top Whig leader. Proponents of the theory that Gage never ordered an arrest of Hancock and Adams are too quick to point to Warren, who remained in Boston unmolested right up to the morning of April 19. But we cannot dismiss the idea of an intended arrest of Hancock and Adams simply on these grounds, because even after Warren became the President of the Provincial Congress, Gage still did not consider the doctor unpardonable when he issued his June 12 *Proclamation*. Thus, for reasons unclear, Gage either did not consider Warren a threat or did not consider him the true head of the radical movement, and so Warren was never at risk of being arrested.

Now, we must admit that it was still *possible* that Gage ordered Major Mitchell or Lieutenant Colonel Smith to keep an eye out for Hancock and Adams. That no written orders exist on the matter means nothing to discourage this theory. For, as given in French's *Informers*, 28–33, Smith's orders must have included additional oral orders, since the written orders (republished in *Informers* as cited) lack practically all of the detail that the first draft of the orders had (also in ibid.), details critical and necessary for the Expedition to Concord. Some of those details were put on a map, alluded to in the official orders, but said map is now lost. Likewise, no orders, written or oral, are known to exist from Gage to Mitchell, and yet the latter clearly had orders to be on patrol. Thus, we cannot firmly rule out the attempted arrest on these grounds either.

On a side note, the present author wholeheartedly disagrees with French's statement (in *Informers*, 33): "if the officers sent in advance [under Major Mitchell] had had that scheme in hand [to make an arrest], surely Smith, who would have had to cooperate with them, would have been informed." Why would Smith have had to cooperate with the mounted patrol? Mitchell could have easily been on detached service.

Fuel was added to the debate in 1888 by two publications, both by the same author. In John Fiske's article "First Year of the Continental Congress," published in the *Atlantic Monthly* for Sept 1888 (Boston: Houghton, Mifflin and Co., 1888) [bound together as v. 62] p. 366, he states: "It was no secret that Gage had been instructed to watch his opportunity to arrest Samuel Adams and his 'willing and ready tool,' that 'terrible desperado,' John Hancock, and send them over to England to be tried for treason." Fiske gave a similar sentiment in a book he was editing, published the same year. Specifically, the comment appears in the article on Samuel Adams, in James Grant Wilson and John Fiske, eds., *Appleton's Cyclopaedia of American Biography* (New York: D. Appleton and Co., 1888), 1:31. That version states: "Toward the end of the following winter Gen. Gage received peremptory orders from the ministry to arrest Samuel Adams and 'his willing and ready tool,' John Hancock, and send them over to London to be tried for high treason. A London newspaper predicted that their heads would soon be exposed on Temple Bar. It was intended to seize them at Lexington on the morning of 19 April, but, forewarned by Paul Revere, they escaped..." In both cases, Fiske gives us no reference to track down his claims or quotes. Nor has modern computer research conducted across many volumes led the present author any closer in discovering Fiske's source, if ever there was one. Yet Fiske's sentiments have been republished by many authors since. Fiske's only evidence seems to be the myth itself, or as he claims, such an attempt was "no secret".

This seems to be the complete evidence known to exist on the matter, and from it, we can draw only one conclusion: there is no evidence to suggest anyone intended to arrest Hancock and Adams, and the plan for their arrest seems likely a rumor become myth. As if in agreement, when the Tory Peter Oliver heard of their escape from Lexington on the morning of April 19, he sneered, "their flight confirmed the observation made by Solomon, vizt the wicked fleeth when no man pursueth." (Quoted from Fischer, 182, citing Peter Oliver's "American Rebellion," in the Hutchinson Papers, British Library.)

We must admit, however, we can never be certain on the matter. Regardless, given how the events of the day worked themselves out, the question ultimately becomes irrelevant. Once the countryside was alarmed, neither Smith nor Mitchell could risk a detour to pursue and arrest the two Whig leaders, even if they did have secondary, oral orders to do so. In the end, the long debate over whether orders were given for the arrest of Hancock and Adams is an academic one and makes no difference to the story of the day.

Appendix II

Expedition to Concord: British Troops Engaged

Lt. Frederick Mackenzie, Adjutant to the Royal Welch Fusiliers and thus responsible for maintaining statics such as these, gives in his diary (Apr 18) in *A British Fusilier*, 50–51, that the following twenty-one companies embarked on the Concord Expedition: grenadiers: 4th, 5th, 10th, 18th, 23rd, 38th, 43rd, 47th, 59th, and 1st and 2nd Marines; light infantry: 4th, 5th, 10th, 23rd, 38th, 43rd, 47th, 59th, and 1st and 2nd Marines. Richard Pope's journal, the original being in the Huntington Library in California, the pertinent excerpt of which is in Murdock's *Late News*, 27, also indicates that the expedition consisted of twenty-one companies. An intercepted British letter of April 28 in Force, 4:2:439–40, also agrees. Allen French was the editor for *A British Fusilier*, but the note on pages 51–52 is apparently by Harold Murdock, and it says that the 18th may not have had a light infantry company, thus explaining the odd number of units.

The marines were organized in the same fashion as the Army, so they also had ten companies, two of which were flank companies (grenadiers and light infantry). At 460 men plus officers (appendix 4), this gave a whopping average of 46 men per company. Many more marines would arrive May 14–19, and together with the original marine force, would be reorganized into two regiments of about equal size, called the 1st and 2nd Marines (appendix 3). This is an important point: the 2nd Marines were not formed until after the Concord Expedition, and so Mackenzie's foregoing list of companies is wrong. As Harold Murdock first noted in *A British Fusilier*, 51–52, it was not the 2nd Marines but the 52nd that marched to Concord, and as proof, the casualties they suffered that day are noted by even Mackenzie himself (in *Fusilier*, 61). Murdock concluded that Mackenzie, perhaps giving this diary entry from memory, knowing there were twenty-one companies, jotted down the 2nd Marines by mistake, forgetting the 52nd. Interestingly, Mackenzie lists the day's casualties by company, but gives no distinction for the marines, suggesting they were just one corps—as indeed they were, since the new marines had not yet arrived. Thus, Mackenzie's list is mistaken. (See also French's *Informers*, 36–38, which notes that Mackenzie duplicated his diary later in life, and perhaps only then made the error.)

Accounting for this mistake, the twenty-one companies that marched to Concord were:

Grenadiers: 4th, 5th, 10th, 18th, 23rd, 38th, 43rd, 47th, 52nd, 59th, and (1st) Marines

Light infantry: 4th, 5th, 10th, 23rd, 38th, 43rd, 47th, 52nd, 59th, and (1st) Marines

As to the number of troops, let us do some math. Mackenzie tells us (*Fusilier*, 62) that his 23rd had 29 grenadiers and 35 light infantry, or 64 total. Having no better information, let us use this 32-man average for all of the other flank companies. (The flank companies were often augmented at the expense of the main battalion companies.) Before doing so, let us note again that the marine companies were swollen to about 46 men per company.

Accordingly, the twenty-one companies on the Expedition to Concord can be estimated as:

19 flank companies from the army, 32 men each (avg.)	608
2 flank companies from the marines, 46 men each (avg.)	
(before the formation of the 2nd Marines)	92
Total Rank and File: Expeditionary Force (est.)	700

These are just the rank and file, not the officers. By drawing upon the assumptions outlined in appendix 4, we can assume a captain was at the head of each company, plus two lieutenants (typically no ensigns for the flank companies). This estimate does not explicitly account for Lt. William Sutherland of the 38th, who came as a volunteer, but he is accounted for in place of Capt. Nesbit Balfour of the 4th, who was on special service in Marshfield, Massachusetts (see chapter 5). The other known military volunteer, Ens. Jeremy Lister, replaced Lt. James Hamilton of the 10th (apparently of the light infantry), and thus does not disrupt our estimate. Perhaps Lt. Jesse Adair of the Marines was a volunteer too, so we will count one extra lieutenant.

For the officers in the expedition, we may estimate the following:

Lieutenant Colonel Smith	1
Major Pitcairn	1
Captains, 1 for each flank company	21
Lieutenants, 2 for each flank company, plus 1	43
Total Officers: Expeditionary Force (est.)	66

The total for the expeditionary force was then 766, not counting noncombatants such as musicians and surgeons, who perhaps raised the total to near 790. Additionally, there were perhaps 20 mounted patrolmen, maybe half of whom were officers (appendix 9). Finally, various Tory scouts accompanied the expedition, though these were few and do not significantly alter our estimate.

Compare this to Harold Murdock's note in French's 1926 edition of Mackenzie's *A British Fusilier* (51–52), which differs from Murdock's own numbers first proposed in his *Nineteenth of April* (47n), published in 1923. Also, compare to Fischer, 313–15, which gives what should be construed as a theoretical upper limit of the expeditionary force at 777 men, unless this also accounts for noncombatants such as musicians. Otherwise, some of these extra men were perhaps "ghosts", kept on the roster to bring in extra cash for company use. Fischer also only counts 62 officers, adding Pitcairn and Smith but not counting the supernumeraries or Mitchell's party. Fischer's numbers seem too high, exceeding the 39 mark for many of the companies listed, despite evidence in appendix 4. But Fischer rightly named his appendix "The Problem of

Numbers," for it is that indeed. Because no clear muster rolls are known for these companies, all any historian can do is give an educated guess.

Lord Percy's reinforcement was his 1st Brigade (consisting of the 4th, 23rd, and 47th) and two "divisions" of marines (per De Berniere to Gage [circa Apr 19]) or "the Battallion of Marines" (per Barker, *British in Boston*, 35). Lister, *Concord Fight*, 30, calls the whole reinforcement "4 Batalians"; thus we can assume the two "divisions" refer to the entire marine force.

Since each regiment had eight battalion companies in addition to their two flank companies (the latter detached and serving in the expeditionary force), we can estimate the size of this reinforcement. First, let us assume the same average of forty-six men per marine battalion company. For the army battalion companies, Mackenzie tells us (in *Fusilier*, 62) that his 23rd had 218 rank and file among its eight companies, or 27.25 men per company, which we will use as the average for every non-marine battalion company. As noted above, it was not unusual to strengthen the flank companies at the expense of those of the battalion, so the latter's smaller average fits with known practices.

Accordingly, the reinforcement can be estimated as:

4th, 8 battalion companies, 27.25 men each (avg.)	218
23rd, 8 battalion companies (given explicitly)	218
47th, 8 battalion companies, 27.25 men each (avg.)	218
Marines, 8 battalion companies, 46 men each (avg.)	368
Total Rank and File: Reinforcement (est.)	1,022

We can then estimate the officers as follows:

Brigade Commander (Brig. Gen. Lord Percy)	1
Lieutenant Colonels or Colonels	
0 for the marines (Pitcairn was highest ranking, already out)	
1 for each of the army regiments	3
Majors	
1 for every colonel or lieutenant colonel	
0 for the marines	
1 for aide-de-camp to Lord Percy	4

Captains

  1 for each company (32 battalion),

  less 3 serving as regimental majors for army only   29

Lieutenants

  1 for each battalion company   32

Ensigns

  1 for each battalion company   32

Total Officers: Reinforcement (est.)	101

We must also account for the two field artillery, both 6-pounders. The two pieces were probably manned by a single artillery company. While we might use the artillerymen numbers in appendix 4, six officers and thirty-six men seem quite high for two pieces and no baggage train of power and ammunition. Instead, let's consider the estimates for artillerymen from Bunker Hill calculations and guess each piece had about ten men, plus the detachment commander and two subordinates per gun. Thus, we can estimate:

2 pieces, 10 men per piece (avg.)	20
Artillery officers	5
Total Artillerymen (est.)	25

Our total then is about 1,148 men in the reinforcement, plus noncombatants such as musicians and surgeons.

On a separate note, there was a small artillery baggage train of possibly two wagons that was sent out independently, guarded by as few as six grenadiers, only to be intercepted by the colonists in Menotomy. (See Murdock's *Nineteenth of April*, 100–101, and cf. Fischer, 243–44, for traditional accounts.) Strange that these supply wagons would be sent with so weak a defense.

To summarize, based on my estimates (excluding noncombatants):

	Enlisted	Officers	Total
Patrol (under Mitchell)	10	10	20
Expeditionary Force (under Smith)	700	66	766
Reinforcement (under Lord Percy)	1,022	101	1,123
(Artillery with reinforcement)	(20)	(5)	(25)
Total Deployed Force (est.)	1,752	182	1,934

APPENDIX 12

EXPEDITION TO CONCORD: ON THE BRITISH LANDING AT CAMBRIDGE

We have no information on the number or sizes of the boats employed in landing the British at Cambridge, but let us make some assumptions.[*] Philip Stephens of the Admiralty to Admiral Graves, Aug 3, 1775, in *NDAR*, 1:1347–51, cites plans to order twenty flat-bottomed boats with a capacity of forty soldiers and sixteen rowers each. If we assume similarly capable boats available on April 18, and allow that some of those that rowed were soldiers meant to disembark, we can guess forty-five soldiers was the average number of men landed by the varied boats, not counting a modest six rowers and one coxswain. (Research beyond the scope of this present volume supports these estimates for the landing before the Battle of Bunker Hill just sixty days later.) Given the estimated 766 men and officers in the expeditionary force (appendix 11), this required seventeen boatloads. The handful of horses that were ferried over perhaps required three or four boatloads more. No cannon were brought over with the expeditionary force, so we need not allocate additional room for these. Mackenzie, Apr 18, in *A British Fusilier*, 51, states that it took two landings, given the few boats present (so each boat conducted up to two boatloads), but his words, "they returned

---

[*]Fischer, 115, claims Mackenzie counted twenty boats, but in fact, Mackenzie, *A British Fusilier*, gives no such number. [John Crozier?] to Dr. Rogers, Apr 23, in Commager and Morris, *The Spirit of 'Seventy-Six*, 77–78, the author of which seems to have played a leading role in organizing the landing, gives us no clue on the number of boats either. He tells us only that the boats came from both the warships and the transports, including his *Empress of Russia* transport.

for the remainder", almost suggest that less than half of the expedition remained to be ferried on the second landing. Let us guess about twenty-one boatloads were required.

Among the vessels in Boston Harbor on April 18 were the third-rates *Boyne* and *Somerset* (five boats each), the fourth-rate *Preston* (four boats), plus at least the two transports *Symmetry* and *Empress of Russia* (say two boats each). This made at least eighteen boats available, nearly enough for the twenty-one boatloads required to ferry the entire expeditionary force in one landing. However, as the reliable Mackenzie tells us it took two landings, we might guess that many of the boats that otherwise might have been employed were still under repair, as such repairs had been underway for some weeks prior, particularly aboard *Somerset*.* We are left to guess how many boats were actually employed, but given that more than one landing was required, it was less than twenty-one boats, and maybe as few as ten boats. Without more concrete evidence, the number of longboats is at best a guess.

Boyne's position is unclear from her journals, in ADM, 51/129, UKNA, but she seems to have been in the harbor near Boston. *Asia* was at King's Roads, per her journals, in ADM, 51/67, UKNA, and probably did not lend her boats. *Lively* and *Glasgow* may have also been near, with three boats each.

APPENDIX 13

EXPEDITION TO CONCORD: ROLE OF THE MARINES AT LEXINGTON

The 10th Light Infantry was given the honor of marching at the head of the British Expeditionary Force on April 18–19 (Lister, *Concord Fight*, 22–23) since the expeditionary commander was Lt. Col. Francis Smith, also of the 10th. What is not clear is whether a similar honor was bestowed on the marines because Maj. John Pitcairn of the Marines was the detachment's deputy commander At the beginning of the British march, at least, given that the marines had less seniority than the numbered army regiments, they probably received no special honors and so marched in the rear. (Likewise, Brig. Gen. Robert Pigot was second-in-command at Bunker Hill, yet his 38th Light Infantry received no distinction as they marched up the Mystic beach.) However, later into the march, when Pitcairn was ordered ahead with six light infantry companies, did this qualify the Marine Light Infantry to march at the head of the advance detachment?

Almost nothing speaks to the role of the marines on April 19. One confounding piece of evidence is the presence of Lt. Jesse Adair of the Marines. Per Sutherland to Gage, Apr 27, Adair was definitely at the head of the advance detachment of six light infantry companies. However, Adair engaged in capturing Yankee prisoners and obtained a horse-drawn chaise that he rode in for a time. These actions make it clear Adair was part of an advance scouting party ahead of even the six light infantry companies, for he could not have done all that he did while officering a company. Still, this evidence does not preclude the Marine Light Infantry from being one of those six companies following Adair, commanded by some other marine officer.

According to Munroe's deposition, 1825, the front "platoon" that marched first onto Lexington Green consisted of eight or nine men. This must have been Adair and his advance party. They that guided the head of the six light infantry companies onto the Green and into the confrontation that began the war. Possibly as many as three light companies actually followed Adair's party onto the Green, but we only know two for sure: the 10th (Lister, *Concord Fight*, 24) followed by the 4th (Barker, *British in Boston*, 32). We know nothing of the Marine Light Infantry during the confrontation, so it seems they were not at the head of the advance detachment of six companies, and perhaps not even among the six.

(Harold Murdock's introduction in *Concord Fight*, 9, proposes that Adair was a volunteer, and Fischer, 189, 324, agrees. Fischer, 324, reports the names of the officers of the Marine Light Infantry, based on evidence in the UK National Archives. Note that, once additional marines arrived in May, Adair would be reassigned to what would be the 2nd Marines, per Major Tupper to Lord Sandwich, June 21, in *NDAR*, 1:731.)

As an interesting aside, Fischer, 324, reports that Lt. William Pitcairn, son of the deputy commander, was among the Marine Light Infantry for this expedition. The younger Pitcairn would play a more memorable role at the Battle of Bunker Hill.

APPENDIX 14

EXPEDITION TO CONCORD: COLONIAL TROOPS ENGAGED

Of the estimated 3,716 militiamen who served at some point throughout the day of April 19, 1775, perhaps no more than 2,000 ever gathered at one time. Many returned to their homes when they ran out of ammunition or otherwise tired of the fight, knowing others were inbound to take their places. Such was the nature of the militia, fighting without a strong central leadership. The enrolled militiamen listed below represent the maximum possible number engaged per company.

Militia Company (by location in battle)	Company Cmdr. (Capt. unless noted)	Enrolled Militiamen	New Arrivals	Running Total	
NORTH BRIDGE					a
Concord	David Brown	52			
	Charles Miles	52			
	George Minot	40?			b
	Nathan Barrett	40?			b
Acton	Isaac Davis	38			
	Joseph Robins	40?			b
	Simon Hunt	40?			b
Bedford	John Moore	51			
	Jonathan Willson	28			c

Militia Company (by location in battle)	Company Cmdr. (Capt. unless noted)	Enrolled Militiamen	New Arrivals	Running Total	
Lincoln	William Smith	62	443	443	
Meriam's Corner					d
Billerica	Lt.? Crosby	12			
	Edward Farmer	35			
	Jonathan Stickney	54			
Chelmsford	Oliver Barron	61			
	Col. Moses Parker	43			
Reading	John Bacheller	61			e
(Maj. John Brooks	Thomas Eaton	63			
commanding)	John Flint	79			
	John Walton	89	497	940	
Brook's Tavern/Hill					d
Framingham	Simon Edget	76			
	Jesse Emes	24			
	Micajah Gleason	49			
Sudbury	Nathaniel Cudworth	40			
	Aaron Haynes	39			
	Isaac Locker	30			
	John Nixon	54			
	Joseph Smith	49			
	Moses Stone	35	396	1,336	
Bloody Angle					d
Woburn	Samuel Belknap	66			
(Maj. Loammi Baldwin	Jonathan Fox	72			
commanding)	Joshua Walker	117	255	1,591	

Militia Company (by location in battle)	Company Cmdr. (Capt. unless noted)	Enrolled Militiamen	New Arrivals	Running Total	
"PARKER'S REVENGE" SITE					f
Lexington	John Parker	144	144	1,735	g
FISKE HILL					f
Cambridge	Samuel Thatcher	77	77	1,812	
MENOTOMY					h
Menotomy	Benjamin Locke	53			i
Medford	Isaac Hall	59			
Malden	Benjamin Blaney	75			
Lynn	Nathaniel Bancroft	38			
	William Farrington	52			
	Rufus Mansfield	46			
	Ezra Newhall	49			
	David Parker	63			
Beverly	Caleb Dodge	32			
	Larkin Thorndike	48			
	Lt. Peter Shaw	42			
Danvers	Samuel Epes	82			
	Samuel Flint	45			
	Israel Hutchinson	53			
	Caleb Lowe	23			
	Jeremiah Page	39			
	Asa Prince	37			
	Edmond Putnam	17			
	John Putnam	35			
Stoneham	(Volunteers)	3			j
Lexington	(Volunteers)	2	893	2,705	j

Militia Company (by location in battle)	Company Cmdr. (Capt. unless noted)	Enrolled Militiamen	New Arrivals	Running Total	
WATSON'S CORNER					h
Brookline	Thomas White	95			
	Col. Thomas Aspinwall	50?			k
	Maj. Isaac Gardner	50?			k
Roxbury	Lemuel Child	35			
	William Draper	50			
	Moses Whiting	55			
Dedham	Eben Battle	66			
	William Bullard	59			
	Daniel Draper	24			
	William Ellis	31			
	David Fairbanks	14			
	Aaron Fuller	67			
	George Gould	17			
	Joseph Guild	59			
Needham	Aaron Smith	70			
	Robert Smith	75			
	Caleb Kingsbery	40			
Charlestown	(Volunteers)[j]	11			
Boston	(Volunteers)[j]	7			
Newton	(Volunteers)[j]	1			
(unknown)	(Volunteers)[j]	1	877	3,582	
GREAT BRIDGE					h
Watertown	Samuel Barnard	134	134	3,716	l

Militia Company (by location in battle)	Company Cmdr. (Capt. unless noted)	Enrolled Militiamen	New Arrivals	Running Total
WINTER HILL		(did not engage British)		m
Salem (incl. Marblehead?)	Col. Timothy Pickering	(300)	(300)	(4,016)

---

[a]Coburn, *Battle of April 19*, 80–81.

[b]Unknown number in this company, guessed at 40 based on average of other companies there.

[c]Lt. Moses Abbott replaced Wilson when he was killed.

[d]Coburn, *Battle of April 19*, 96–97.

[e]Edmund Foster accompanied this company.

[f]Coburn, *Battle of April 19*, 104.

[g]Probably circled back and attacked at the Bluff and Fiske Hill.

[h]Coburn, *Battle of April 19*, 133–35.

[i]Some of these may have gone up to Lexington earlier.

[j]Guess on where they joined the fight.

[k]Unknown number; possibly marched, but did not file for pay.

[l]Probably came up after British turned for Charlestown.

[m]Coburn, *Battle of April 19*, 153–54.

NOTES

CHAPTER 1: DAWN OF AN EPOCH

1. U.S. Navy's Sun and Moon Calculator reports a waxing crescent with 11 percent of the moon's visible disk illuminated. Crescent moons always hug the sunrise or sunset. (On the moon, cf. Drake, *Tea Leaves*, lvx, lxxiii; or Labaree, *The Boston Tea Party*, 144, both without citation.) The Navy website also reports sunset was at 4:13 p.m., and Daylight Savings Time was not yet adopted. That it was rainy: *Dartmouth*'s log in Drake, *Tea Leaves*, lxix.

2. Labaree's *The Boston Tea Party*, 141–45, and *Catalyst for Revolution*, 10 (which reprints a key primary source with subtotals, not all totaled). *Catalyst for Revolution*, 7, notes that the invoiced value includes a tax of three pence per pound by weight; p. 10 notes an 8 percent commission is also included. At 2 grams per tea bag, the 92,616 pounds equates to 21,004,932 tea bags or servings. Some contemporary reports give 342 chests total: two more than here. The higher-priced chests were of smaller size. It is difficult to arrive at an exact estimate of the cost of the tea. One source estimates that £9,659 6s 4d (£9,659.32) in 1773 is worth £1,071,000 in 2013 pounds (on the low end), and by converting with modern exchange rates, is about $1.6 million U.S. dollars (Lawrence H. Officer and Samuel H. Williamson, "Five Ways to Compute the Relative Value of a UK Pound Amount, 1270 to Present," MeasuringWorth, 2014, www.measuringworth.com/ukcompare/). Another approach: use the loose post–Revolutionary War conversion rate of £3 to $10, putting the cost of the tea in Revolutionary War era dollars at $32,197.72. Samuel H. Williamson, "Seven Ways to Compute the Relative Value of a U.S. Dollar Amount, 1774 to Present," MeasuringWorth, 2015, www.measuringworth.com/uscompare/, produces a wide range that begins at $959,000 in 2013 U.S.

dollars. Alternatively, one can consider that the cost in Jan 2015 of a pound of consumer-grade loose-leaf tea starts at about $15 (retail), which at 92,616 pounds by weight, gives $1.39 million. The average of these three approaches gives $1.33 million.

3. For the crowd being in the hundreds, see *Massachusetts Gazette*, Dec 23, 1775, in Drake, *Tea Leaves*, lxviii. But see note 17 below, which indicates that upward of 5,000 were at Old South just before the dumping of the tea.

4. Labaree, *The Boston Tea Party*, 59–71ff. Inventory on p. 67: 18 million pounds, with a plan to sell 11.5 million pounds, leaving a year's worth.

5. Ibid., 331, table I.

6. Labaree, *The Boston Tea Party*, 4. Bohea was grown in the hills, then sent to Canton (now Guangzhou), from which it was bought by Western merchants. Nearly 92 percent of the tea bound for Boston was Bohea (Labaree, *Catalyst for Revolution*, 10).

7. Labaree, *The Boston Tea Party*, 66–77; the actual act is conspicuously not in MacDonald, *Select Charters and Other Documents*, but is in the *Boston Evening-Post*, Oct 25, 1773, front page.

8. Labaree, *The Boston Tea Party*, 96–102.

9. Ibid., 105–114. The six consignees were Richard Clarke with his son Jonathan, Joshua Winslow and business partner Benjamin Faneuil Jr., and the two sons of the governor: Thomas Hutchinson Jr. and Elisha Hutchinson. From Benjamin Carp, *Defiance of the Patriots* (New Haven, CT: Yale University Press, 2010). Kindle edition.

10. Labaree, *The Boston Tea Party*, 126–27.

11. Lavery, *The Ship of the Line*, 1:171.

12. Randolph Cock, "Montagu, John (1718/19–1795)," in *Oxford Dictionary of National Biography*, ed. H. C. G. Matthew and Brian Harrison (Oxford: Oxford University Press, 2004), accessed Oct 17, 2009, www.oxforddnb.com/view /article/19027. His name is sometimes seen as "Montague."

13. The testimony in *Coll. of MHS* (1858), 4:4:386–389, estimates the guard at perhaps twenty-five, unarmed.

14. Labaree, *The Boston Tea Party*, 127–33.

15. Ibid., 133, 150–51. It is unknown if *William*'s tea reached Boston, was sold, or had duties paid.

16. Labaree, *The Boston Tea Party*, 126–45 passim; John Andrews to William Barrell, Dec 18, 1773, in *Proc. of MHS* (1866), 8:325–27; Minutes of the Tea Meetings, 1773, in *Proc. of MHS* (1884), 20:10–17. Especially see ibid., 16, with references to customs collector Richard Harrison; also referenced in Labaree, *The Boston Tea Party*, 137, etc.

17. Carlyle's statement in Drake, *Tea Leaves*, lxxxviii, mentions 7,000; Labaree, *The Boston Tea Party*, 138, estimates "more than 5000", citing more sources.

18. See, for instance, a portion of the speech by Josiah Quincy Jr. in Commager and Morris, *The Spirit of 'Seventy-Six*, 2–3.

19. Minutes of the Tea Meetings, 1773, in *Proc. of MHS* (1884), 20:16–17; John Andrews to William Barrell, Dec 18, 1773, in *Proc. of MHS* (1866), 8:325–27; Labaree, *The Boston Tea Party*, 120, 138–40.

20. U.S. Navy's Sun and Moon Calculator gives sunset as 4:13 p.m., and end of civil twilight as 4:45 p.m., with an 11 percent visible waxing crescent moon.

21. John Andrews to William Barrell, Dec 18, 1773, in *Proc. of MHS* (1866), 8:325–27. Rowe's statement: Drake, *Tea Leaves*, lxx, lxiii. Though Rowe's diary (Dec 16–17, 1773) states he was unwell and at home all night, there is evidence it was tweaked later for political reasons, and Upton, "Proceeding of Ye Body," 294, gives yet another witness stating Rowe said similar words at a meeting a few nights earlier.

22. Minutes of the Tea Meetings, 1773, in *Proc. of MHS* (1884), 20:16–17.

23. Variations exist of this quote, depending on the witness. I use Upton, "Proceeding of Ye Body," 297–98. Compare to John Andrews to William Barrell, Dec 18, 1773, in *Proc. of MHS* (1866), 8:325–27. (Andrews was a latecomer, having ironically been at home drinking tea.) Minutes of the Tea Meetings, 1773, in *Proc. of MHS* (1884), 20:17, says only that the meeting was dissolved, as does Andrews's statement. Labaree, *The Boston Tea Party*, 141, and Carlyle's statement in Drake, *Tea Leaves*, lxxxviii, indicate that Samuel Adams's statement, as if a predefined signal, instigated the Tea Party, but this is debunked by others, including Upton, "Proceeding of Ye Body," 297–98, and the anonymous statement in Drake, *Tea Leaves*, lxx.

24. Upton, "Proceeding of Ye Body," 298, says ten to fifteen minutes from Rotch's news. See note 23.

25. Ibid.; Drake, *Tea Leaves*, civ, lxxii, lxxx.

26. Andrews to Barrell, Dec 18, 1773, in *Proc. of MHS* (1866), 8:325–27.

27. Upton, "Proceeding of Ye Body," 298.

28. Andrews to Barrell, Dec 18, 1773, in *Proc. of MHS* (1866), 8:325–27.

29. Wyeth's 1827 statement in Drake, *Tea Leaves*, lxxi.

30. One hundred sixteen participants are noted per "Participants in the Boston Tea Party," Boston Tea Party Ship Museum, accessed January 6, 2015, www .bostonteapartyship.com/participants-in-the-boston-tea-party.

31. Labaree, *The Boston Tea Party*, 144, believes it was three parties, but statements differ. See, for instance, the newspaper statements in Drake, *Tea Leaves*, lxviii–lxix, and Carlyle's statement, ibid., lxxxviii. That they were so concerned with being caught suggests they split up to do their work as quickly as possible.

32. Statements differ on whether *Beaver* was warped up during the event of the day before or not. Labaree, *The Boston Tea Party*, 144, and Wyeth's 1827 statement in

Drake, *Tea Leaves*, lxxi, suggest the former, while the unnamed Boston paper in Drake, *Tea Leaves*, lxix, suggests that latter. Strangely, however, that same paper claims the first two ships were unloaded before the brig *Beaver*. Why wait to off-load *Beaver* if not because it was being warped alongside the dock? Some statements suggest it was only discovered afterward that *Beaver* had tea onboard, but this is unlikely, as the townspeople had been attempting to persuade the commissioners to send the tea back for weeks. The Boston radicals were well aware of which ships had tea, even if those giving such statements for history writers were not.

33. The stories of the padlock and the rearrangement of goods come from newspaper reports in Drake, *Tea Leaves*, lxviii–lxix, the first being the *Massachusetts Gazette*, Dec 23, 1775, the second an unnamed Boston paper. Which ship had the padlock is uncertain, but it was perhaps not the *Beaver* (Simpson's statement in Drake, *Tea Leaves*, lxxvii–lxviii).

34. Simpson's statement, Drake, *Tea Leaves*, lxxvii–lxxviii. *Bickerstaff's Boston Almanack for 1773* gives high tides at 1:32 p.m. and 2:00 a.m., making a low tide at about 7:46 p.m., about the time of the tea party.

35. Upton, "Proceeding of Ye Body," 298, tells us the radical leaders were the last to leave Old South, but we are unsure if they went to the wharf.

36. Details on Dr. Warren's freemasonry can be found in Cary, *Joseph Warren: Physician, Politician*, 54–59.

37. One can see glimpses into their relationship by consulting the documents in *Libbie & Co., Catalogue of Autographs, Letters*, 223–25, and *Celebration by the Inhabitants of Worcester*, 133 –37. Also see Forman, *Dr. Joseph Warren*. The only reference I have of Dr. Warren being blue-eyed is a recollection many years after, as documented in Frederick Tupper and Helen Tyler Brown, eds., *Grandmother Tyler's Book: The Recollections of Mary Palmer Tyler (Mrs. Royall Tyler) 1775–1866* (New York: G. P. Putnam's Sons, 1925), 43–44, which states: "He was a handsome man and wore a tie wig; he had a fine color in his face and light blue eyes." His hair color is uncertain: the one contemporary painting of him by John Singleton Copley shows his hair powdered white. The many prints of him since his death are originally black and white. The postmortem 1786 painting by John Trumbull, *The Battle of Bunker's Hill*, gives him brown hair. We have no primary sources on where the children all resided between 1773 and early 1775, only that they were at the Roxbury home in early 1775. They likely still spent time with Warren in Boston for various periods.

38. Joseph Warren to Samuel Adams, June 15, 1774, in French, *Life and Times*, 317.

39. Thatcher, *Traits of the Tea Party*, 184–85. Montagu is not mentioned in the Hawkes variation of Hewes's *Memoir*.

40. K. David Milobar, "Haldimand, Sir Frederick (1718–1791)," in *Oxford Dictionary of National Biography*, ed. H. C. G. Matthew and Brian Harrison (Oxford: Oxford

University Press, 2004), accessed Oct 19, 2009, www.oxforddnb.com/view
/article/11899.

41. Lieutenant Colonel Leslie to General Haldimand, Dec 20, 1773, in Scull, *The Montresor Journals*, 532. Leslie's rank and regiment are explicitly given in ibid., 533.

42. Hutchinson's own statement in Commager and Morris, *The Spirit of 'Seventy-Six*, 6–10, citing Hutchinson, *History of the Province*, 3:423–40 passim; Labaree, *The Boston Tea Party*, 146.

43. Troy O. Bickham, "Oliver, Andrew (1706–1774)," in *Oxford Dictionary of National Biography*, ed. H. C. G. Matthew and Brian Harrison (Oxford: Oxford University Press, 2004), accessed Oct 19, 2009, www.oxforddnb.com/view/article/20718.

44. *Pubs. of the Colonial Soc. of Mass.* (1927), 26:349–50. This source indicates that Samuel Adams and his Sons of Liberty appeared in part to protest John Hancock and his Company of Cadets providing an honor guard at the ceremony.

45. Labaree, *The Boston Tea Party*, 115–16.

46. Ibid., 145.

47. Andrews to Barrell, Dec 18, 1773, in *Proc. of MHS* (1866), 8:325–27.

48. Thatcher, *Traits of the Tea Party*, 182–83 ("East Indian" and other quote); Hawkes, *A Retrospect*, 40–41; Drake, *Tea Leaves*, lxxiii.

49. Hawkes, *A Retrospect*, 40–41; Andrews to Barrell, Dec 18, 1773, in *Proc. of MHS* (1866), 8:325–27 (source of the quote). Note that the latter reference claims he was stripped of his clothes, though more likely he was just stripped of his coat if he made his escape, per the version in Hawkes. Italics as in the original.

50. Hawkes, *A Retrospect*, 41; Thatcher, *Traits of the Tea Party*, 183–84.

51. Tide: see note 34.

52. Drake, *Tea Leaves*, lxxxi.

53. Thatcher, *Traits of the Tea Party*, 184.

54. Ibid., 185. Montagu is not mentioned in the Hawkes variation of Hewes's *Memoir*.

55. See note 54.

56. Hawkes, *A Retrospective*, 41 (source of the quote); Thatcher, *Traits of the Tea Party*, 186–87. One crate had been found with tea still inside, and the unscrupulous finder began to sell it off. He was caught and forced to give up his tea and his earnings, while the remaining tea was burned in a bonfire on Boston Common (Thatcher, 187). A few other samples were collected here and there, but not for profit and instead for posterity. The references cited give various examples of this. One sample, collected at Dorchester Neck, is now in possession of MHS. They highlight it on their website at www.masshist.org/object-of-the-month/objects /boston-harbor-a-tea-pot-tonight-2006-02-01 (accessed Oct 20, 2009).

57. What happened to it is unknown, but one statement claims it was later sold by radicals to raise revenue for the coming war.

58. Charlestown (Charleston): Labaree, *The Boston Tea Party*, 152–54; Philadelphia: ibid., 156–60 (did *Polly* have 698 chests, per ibid., 97, or 598, per ibid., 158?); New York: ibid., 154–156 (I have seen no list of the number of chests bound there).

59. Ibid., 164–69. On April 22, 1774, New York followed suit, boarding a small ship newly arrived and dumping her eighteen quarter-chests of privately owned tea. This ship was the *London*, but not the same *London* that in December went to South Carolina (cf. ibid., 152–53).

60. In Franklin to Mass. Assembly Comm. of Corr., Feb 2, 1774, in PBF, 21:075. Benjamin Franklin, learning of the news in London, was shocked at "an Act of violent Injustice on our part", reminding the Mass. Assembly "the India Company however are not our Adversaries". "I am truly concern'd," Franklin added, "as I believe all considerate Men are with you, that there should seem to any a Necessity for carrying Matters to such Extremity, as, in a Dispute about Publick Rights, to destroy private Property". Cf. Franklin to Joseph Galloway, Nov 3, 1773, in PBF, 20:461.

61. Washington to George William Fairfax, 10[–15] June 1774, in PGW.

62. Some offered portions of their personal fortunes to make it so. Ben Franklin first urged, "A speedy Reparation will immediately set us right in the Opinion of all Europe." Franklin to Mass. Assembly Comm. of Corr., Feb 2, 1774, in PBF, 21:075. He wrote again to the Mass. Assembly, "I cannot but hope that the Affair of the Tea will have been considered in the Assembly before this time, and Satisfaction [that is, repayment] proposed if not made; for such a Step will remove much of the Prejudice now entertain'd against us, and put us again on a fair Footing in contending for our old Privileges as Occasion may require." Franklin to Thomas Cushing, Mar 22, 1774, in PBF, 21:152.

63. John Adams's diary, Dec 17, 1773, in PJA.

CHAPTER 2: COERCIVE MEASURES

1. They were Pennsylvania (*WBF*, 10:218); Georgia; New Jersey (ibid., 10:241–242); and Massachusetts (ibid., 10:248).

2. The first news of it comes on Jan 20, 1774, per Labaree, *The Boston Tea Party*, 173. On his fear: *WBF*, 10:245; on Craven St.: ibid., 10:219, or his various letters dated from such; on his doctorate degree: Isaacson, *Benjamin Franklin*, 198. Franklin's London house remains still. More information at www.benjaminfranklinhouse.org.

3. On the Cockpit: Charles Eyre Pascoe, *No. 10, Downing Street, Whitehall: Its History and Associations* (London: Duckworth and Co., 1908), 67–86.

4. *WBF*, 10:266–67; Alden, *General Gage in America*, 199–200. Major General Haldimand was acting commander in chief during Gage's absence.

5. The letter, Benjamin Franklin to Lord Dartmouth, Aug 21, 1773, as well as the reply, the assembly's resolutions, and the assembly's petition to the King, are all in *WBF*, 6:276–81.

6. The letters were believed to be meant for Thomas Whately, a recently deceased member of Parliament with political connections sufficient to influence affairs in the colonies. Once American newspapers published the letters, the London press freely republished them. The London papers then became the battlefield for a gossip war turned witch hunt for the perpetrator, with suspicions on Whately's friend John Temple. This culminated in an unwitnessed duel between Temple and Whately's brother William. Their inaccurate smoothbore pistols both missed their mark, so the two charged each other with swords, whereby Temple severely wounded William Whately. After, as William recovered from his physical wounds, the anger between the two continued. Rumor spread of a second duel to be had, but Franklin's guilt led him to break his silence. Writing to the *Public Advertiser* and the *London Chronicle*, Franklin took full blame. "I alone am the person who obtained and transmitted to Boston the letters in question. Mr. W. [Whately] could not communicate them, because they were never in his possession; and for the same reason, they could not be taken from him by Mr. T. [Temple]." Quote citation: see note 16. The duel story in various sources, including *Franklin before the Privy Council*, 3–5, Isaacson, *Benjamin Franklin*, 271ff., and *WBF*, 10:259–62. Smyth is in error when he refers to William Whately as the deceased. William was the brother and estate executor who engaged in the duel.

7. The thirteen letters are all in *Franklin before the Privy Council*, 19–51.

8. Hutchinson became lieutenant governor mid-1758 and governor in 1771 and so was in leadership for the entire period of the tax riots.

9. Thomas Hutchinson [to Thomas Whately?], Jan 20, 1769, in *Franklin before the Privy Council*, 28–29. Cf. ibid., 62–66, for more on this comment.

10. Andrew Oliver [to Thomas Whately?], May 7, 1767, in *Franklin before the Privy Council*, 31–36.

11. Charles Paxton [to Thomas Whately?], on board His Majesty's ship *Romney*, Boston Harbor, June 20, 1768, ibid., 48.

12. Franklin's own account, in his letter to Thomas Cushing, Feb 15, 1774, in *WBF*, 6:182ff. (quote from 189), also ibid., 10:266, and in PBF, 21:086.

13. Franklin's cryptic explanation is in a private letter to Thomas Cushing, July 7, 1773, in *WBF*, 6:81–85, and PBF, 20:271.

14. Franklin to Thomas Cushing, June 4, 1773, in *WBF*, 6:56–57. The letters were first transmitted along with a letter to Cushing, Dec 2, 1772 (it appears in ibid., 5:448–51, with no mention of the enclosed letters), this according to a later letter to Cushing, Jan 5, 1773, ibid., 6:1–4, where the letters are first mentioned. From the

June 4 letter, Cushing seemed well aware of the stipulation, but none of the earlier letters seem to document Franklin notifying him of such. Perhaps a missing letter attached to the enclosed letters made this stipulation? Wedderburn claims this was the case in his speech, that it was an anonymous letter (see *Franklin before the Privy Council*, 87–88). All of these also in PBF: 20:226, 19:399, and 20:007, respectively.

15. *WBF*, 6:258ff.; ibid., 10:258–63.

16. Benjamin Franklin to the printer of the *Public Advertiser*, Dec 25, 1773, republished in ibid., 6:284, and *Franklin before the Privy Council*, 72–73. The same, verbatim and of the same date, was also sent to the *London Chronicle*, and is in PBF, 20:513.

17. Franklin to Thomas Cushing, Feb 15, 1774, in *WBF*, 6:182ff., or in PBF, 21:086.

18. *Franklin before the Privy Council*, 6–10.

19. Velvet: Dr. Bancroft to William Temple Franklin, [unknown date], in *WBF*, 10:267. Isaacson, *Benjamin Franklin*, 277, says it was blue, without citation.

20. The actual history is missing from the accounts of the speech, but Franklin to Thomas Cushing, Feb 15, 1774, in *WBF*, 6:182ff., says that Wedderburn "bestowed plenty of abuse upon it, mingled with encomium on the governours". The source of the quotes is Wedderburn's speech as cited in n. 35.

21. In Franklin to Isaac Norris, Mar 19, 1759, in PBF, 8:291, Franklin wrote, one year before George III's accession, "it is known here that if the Ministry make a Point of carrying *any thing* in Parliament, they can carry it." (The Ministry comprising the King's ministers and secretaries.)

22. *The Annual Register or a View of the History, Politics, and Literature for the Year 1758*, 4th ed. (London: R. and J. Dodsley, 1764), 1:138–39, gives the debt but no interest for Jan 11, 1758; *The Annual Register or a View of the History, Politics, and Literature for the Year 1763*, 7th ed. (London: J. Dodsley, 1796), 6:187–88, gives the debt and interest as of Jan 5, 1763.

23. Miller, *Origins of the American*, chap. 4; MacDonald, *Select Charters*, 272ff.

24. Ibid., 281ff.; Miller, *Origins of the American*, chap. 5.

25. Ibid., 129–137; Middlekauff, *The Glorious Cause*, 92–98.

26. MacDonald, *Select Charters*, 316–17.

27. Ibid., 322ff. Items including glass, paper, lead, paint, and tea. It was strange that glass, paper, and paint were to be taxed, as these were not major British exports.

28. Miller, *Origins of the American*, 255.

29. It is worth noting that the English political system had fallen into despotism. One reason: many crown offices were little more than sinecures, both in the colonies and in Britain itself. Also, the modern notion of division of government did not then exist, and the holding of multiple offices was not uncommon. (For example, Thomas Hutchinson served not only as Mass. governor but also as a probate court judge, among other offices.)

30. Labaree, *The Boston Tea Party*, 22–23, 31.

31. Alden, *General Gage in America*, 156–66; Miller, *Origins of the American*, 293–95; appendix 3.

32. Middlekauff, *The Glorious Cause*, 210–13.

33. Caldwell and Persinger, *A Source History*, 183.

34. Labaree, *The Boston Tea Party*, 173.

35. All quotes here from Wedderburn's speech. A copy in *Franklin before the Privy Council*, 75ff., is curiously missing several blocks of text, which is partially explained in an editorial note in PBF, 21:037ff. As a result, PBF is best to use. For clarity and conciseness, the quotes given throughout the present text are not in the order in which they appear in the original speech.

36. Ibid.

37. Ibid.

38. *Homo trium literarum* translates to "a man of three letters," the three letters not being physical letters, but wordplay for letters of the written word: *F-U-R*, Latin for "thief." The English equivalent is "a man of five letters," wordplay for *TH-I-E-F*. All quotes from Wedderburn's speech, though not in order (q.v. 35).

39. Dr. Bancroft to William Temple Franklin [unknown date], in *WBF*, 10:267.

40. Wedderburn's speech, see note 35.

41. Alden, *General Gage in America*, 199–200n7.

42. Franklin to Thomas Cushing, Feb 15, 1774, in *WBF*, 6:182f., or in PBF, 21:086.

43. Edward P. Cheyney, *Readings in English History Drawn from the Original Sources* (Boston: Ginn & Co., 1908), 604–5. It is also paraphrased in part in Fleming, *Now We Are Enemies*, 66–67.

44. Alden, *General Gage in America*, 21–31, 62–63 passim. Gage was born sometime in late 1719 or early 1720: ibid., 11.

45. George III to Lord North, Feb 4, 1774, in Fortescue, ed., *The Correspondence of King George*, 3:59.

46. George III to Lord North, Feb 15, 1774, ibid., 3:175.

47. Anecdote in William Knox MSS, X, folder 25, letter 7, p. 13–15 (letter No. 7), at Clements; Thurlow and Wedderburn to Lord Dartmouth, Feb 11, 1774 [Copy], in Gage MSS.

48. Labaree, *The Boston Tea Party*, 175–176.

49. Summary of Lord North's Mar 14, 1774, speech, in *PHE*, 17:1163–67.

50. Debate of Mar 23, 1774, ibid., 17:1178.

51. Lord North's statement in the debate of Mar 23, 1774, ibid. On Plymouth: *Proc. of MHS*, (1899), 2:12:193.

52. Labaree, *The Boston Tea Party*, 187–90; MacDonald, *Select Charters*, 337ff. (the actual bill), which states it passed both the Commons and the Lords "without a division". On the hearings: *PHE*, 17:1189–92. The debates and the bill are also in Force, 4:1:35ff.

53. Debate of Mar 28, 1774, in *PHE*, 17:1192–1193; MacDonald, *Select Charters*, 343ff.

54. Debate of May 2, 1774, in *PHE*, 17:1313.

55. Ibid., 17:1314–15.

56. MacDonald, *Select Charters*, 343ff. (the actual bill). Passed by the House of Commons on May 2 with 239 yeas to 64 nays. Passage by the Lords on May 11 with 92 yeas to 20 nays, with amendments, which the Commons agreed to on May 13. Eleven lords entered a protest against the bill. The debates and the bill are also in Force, 4:1:65ff.

57. Debate of May 6, 1774, in *PHE*, 17:1316–20; other related debates passim. MacDonald, *Select Charters*, 351ff. (the actual bill). Passage by the Commons on May 6 with 127 yeas to 24 nays. Passage by the Lords on May 18 with 43 yeas to 12 nays. Eight lords entered a protest against the bill. Throughout the debate, attendance in each house was small. The debates and the bill are also in Force, 4:1:111ff.

58. MacDonald, *Select Charters*, 355–56. It passed the Commons on May 9 without a division. It passed the Lords on May 26 with a vote of 57 to 16. On June 2, it received the royal assent. The debates and the bill are also in Force, 4:1:165ff.

59. The term "coercive measures" appears frequently among British letters and parliamentary debates of this period. However, the King's parliamentary speech of Oct 26, 1775, in *PHE*, 18:695–97, and Force, 4:6:1–3, is one of the earliest references to explicitly calling these the "coercive acts". In contrast, there seems to be no evidence of the term "intolerable acts" prior to the late 1800s. On this, see J. L. Bell, "No Tolerance for 'Intolerable Acts,'" *Boston 1775* (blog), Apr 27, 2008, accessed Aug 27, 2011, http://boston1775.blogspot.com/2008/04/no-tolerance -for-intolerable-acts.html. Bell also alludes to a modern debate as to which acts were in fact the coercive acts. Such a debate is purely academic, as there was no explicit list. Rather, any parliamentary act circa 1774 onward that was either felt by the colonists as coercive or intended by Parliament to coerce was thus a coercive act. Some have suggested the Quartering Act of 1774 does not qualify, but as it mandated troops to be "stationed where their presence may be necessary and required" (per the actual act, in MacDonald, *Select Charters*, 355–56), thereby preempting Boston's previous solution of barracking the troops in Castle William, it was meant to coerce the Bostonians into a particular action and hence was a coercive act.

60. Much is devoted to the Quebec Act later in the text. It received the royal assent on June 22, 1774. The act is not in MacDonald, but is in Force, 4:1:216–20, which follows transcriptions of all of the parliamentary debates on the subject, beginning at ibid., 169. The Quebec Act was not meant as a coercive act; it was only perceived as such by the Americans.

61. See note 43.

62. Alden, *General Gage in America*, 202.
63. Ibid., 203–4.

CHAPTER 3: AN ARMY FROM ACROSS THE SEA

1. Boston Town Meeting Resolves, in Force, 4:1:331–32 (see notes); Franklin to Cushing, Mar 22, 1774, in PBF, 21:152; Labaree, *The Boston Tea Party*, 218–19, 227ff.
2. Isaac Sears and Alexander McDougall to Samuel Adams and the Mass. Comm. of Corr., May 15, 1774, in the Bancroft transcriptions, NYPL. The whereabouts of the original are unknown, but it is not in the Samuel Adams MSS, NYPL. More on New York's efforts: Labaree, *The Boston Tea Party*, 227ff. Philadelphia's call: ibid., 230–31.
3. Resolve of May 27, in Kennedy, *Journals of the House of Burgesses of Virginia*, 13:xiii–xiv.
4. Gage to Lord Dartmouth, May 19, 1774, in Carter, 1:355.
5. Williams, June 12, 1775, in *Discord and Civil Wars*, 4.
6. The Town House was already being called the State House by some, in defiance of Britain. This began as early as 1773, according to Hutchinson, *History of the Province*, 413n.
7. The quote and much of the detail from Andrews to Barrell, Mar 18, 1774, in *Proc. of MHS* (1866), 8:327–29; Gage to Lord Dartmouth, May 19, 1774, in Carter, 1:355.
8. Bernard Bailyn, *The Ordeal of Thomas Hutchinson* (Cambridge, MA: Belknap Press of Harvard University Press, 1974), 29–30, 273, 278ff., 372–373.
9. Alden, *General Gage in America*, 211–12. Gage to Lord Dartmouth, May 30, 1774, in Carter, 1:355–56, indicates that he planned to move to Salem the following day. Massachusetts had made Danvers a town in June 16, 1757, but the Privy Council denied it that status on Aug 10, 1759. Danvers then conducted itself as a town, but was not officially one until Aug 23, 1775.
10. "Address of Merchants, Traders, and Inhabitants of Boston to Gage," June 1774, in Gage MSS; Alden, *General Gage in America*, 206–7. A similar address by 125 people of Salem is also in the Gage MSS, but gives no offer to repay the tea revenue.
11. Andrews to Barrell, June 12, 1774, in *Proc. of MHS* (1866), 8:329–30. On the requirement to off-load at Marblehead: per the actual bill in MacDonald, *Select Charters*, 337ff., also in Force, 4:1:35ff. Several sources refer to Salem for customs, where the seat of government definitely resided, while others refer to Marblehead (as this letter of John Andrews). Where exactly customs was is unknown, but both towns seem to have played a part, just as Plymouth had a role. Customs may have been in every major port of entry.

12. French, *Life and Times*, 313–14; *Pubs. of the Colonial Soc. of Mass.* (1917), 18:103–122; *Proc. of MHS* (1873), 12:45ff.; Andrews to Barrell, June 12, 1774, in *Proc. of MHS* (1866), 8:329–330; Alden, *General Gage in America*, 207–8. The latter source indicates that Gage denounced the Solemn League, issuing a proclamation that called it illegal and ordering the arrest of those who would circulate it. However, no one dared to enforce Gage's edict. The momentum calling for a Continental Congress soon superseded it.

13. Mass. Representative Resolves for June 17, 1774, as well as Gage's proclamation and the resolutions of the Comm. of Corr., in Force, 4:1:421–23; Alden, *General Gage in America*, 207–208. On Bowdoin: Anson Ely Morse, *The Federalist Party in Massachusetts to the Year 1800* (Princeton, NJ: The University Library, 1909), 22.

14. Appendix 3. Andrews to Barrell, June 12, 1774, in *Proc. of MHS* (1866), 8:330, claims: "Four regiments are already arriv'd, and four more are expected." This is false information; see this book's appendix 3. Perhaps he meant companies, not regiments?

15. Graves, *Conduct* (Mar 6–June 30, 1774), gives nothing on Montagu or the change of command. On Montagu: Neil R. Stout, *The Royal Navy in America, 1760–1775* (Annapolis, MD: Naval Institute Press, 1973), 161, giving no relevant citation, but perhaps the author merely came to the logical conclusion of Montagu's return. *Captain* did not make Graves's ship list in *Conduct*, (July 1, 1774), and it is speculation that Montagu returned on this vessel, which had at least been his flagship in December 1773, during the Tea Party.

16. Lord Percy to Rev. Thomas Percy, May 8, 1774, and to the Duke of Northumberland, July 5, 1774, and also of July 27, 1774, in Bolton, *Letters of Hugh Earl Percy*, 26–30. See also appendix 3.

17. Alden, *General Gage in America*, 44, 74; Kemble's diary, July 18, 1774, entry, with addenda, in *Coll. of the NYHS* (1883), 1:39, which indicates he got to Salem on July 22, after having arrived in New York about July 7. (See the note on ibid. 38, as the diary is not explicit.)

18. Alden, *General Gage in America*, 208–9; Herbert S. Allan, *John Hancock: Patriot in Purple* (New York: Beechhurst Press, 1953), 150–52. Not until after the coming war did they re-form, serving Hancock once he became governor.

19. Though the council had long been selected by the assembly, the governor had the power to veto selections.

20. Lord Dartmouth to Gage, July 3, 1774 [received Aug 6, 1774], in Carter, 2:163–166; Gage to Lord Dartmouth, Aug 27, 1774, ibid., 1:365–68.

21. Percy to Henry Reveley, Aug 8, 1774, in Bolton, *Letters of Hugh Earl Percy*, 30–31.

22. John Adams's diary, Aug 10, 1774, in PJA.

23. John Andrews to William Barrell, Aug 25–27, 1774, in *Proc. of MHS* (1866), 8:346–48.

24. Alden, *General Gage in America*, 211–13. The Province House, a.k.a. the Governor's

House, is depicted on various period maps, such as Price's 1769 *A New Plan of Ye Great Town*. On its description: Nathaniel Hawthorne, *Legends of the Province House* (Boston: James R. Osgood and Co., 1877), 9–10; see the frontispiece for a drawing of it. No longer standing, Province House stood near where Milk Street meets what was then called Marlborough Street, now Washington Street. It featured an arched passage, which gave way to a courtyard, beyond which lay the elegant brick mansion itself, three stories high, surmounted by a cupola, on top of which a gilded Indian stood with a bent bow. Percy lodging there: Lord Drummond [to Lord Dartmouth], Whitehall, [June 9, 1775], in Bolton, *Letters of Hugh Earl Percy*, 53–54n.

25. Appendix 3.

26. The entire collection of donations and the response of the Mass. Comm. of Corr. is in the *Coll. of MHS* (1858) 4:4:1–278 passim, a sample of which is given in Commager and Morris, *The Spirit of 'Seventy-Six*, 31–35. I have not found a reference to South Carolina in the sources cited, but in Gage to Lord Dartmouth, July 20, 1774, in Carter, 1:361–62, Gage reports that South Carolina sent some rice and sheep.

27. *Coll. of MHS* (1858), 4:4:50–52ff., also in Commager and Morris, *The Spirit of 'Seventy-Six*, 33–34, claims 125 sheep; Joseph Warren to Samuel Adams, Aug 15, 1774, in French, *Life and Times*, 339–40 (see the letter's postscript) and ibid., 341, indicate that Putnam actually came with 130 sheep. Also see Livingston, *Israel Putnam: Pioneer*, 175–79. The Aug 15 Warren letter, as cited, also notes that retired British officer and now Virginian Charles Lee had just visited Boston. With all the sheep and a few cattle pouring into Boston, one might wonder where they were kept to pasture. Boston Common had, in times past, been used as a common area for such livestock, hence the name. But now the only thing grazing on the common was the British Army. Still, with Putnam's renowned brazenness, it is easy to imagine he might have marched his bleating sheep into the thick of the British encampment. In the end, most of these sheep were probably kept in private pens throughout the sparsely populated town or in the ample pastures of places like nearby Roxbury. Old Put: friends and seniors called him this, but likely not junior ranking. Location of Warren's home: French, *Life and Times*, 15, 166, gives it was where the American House later stood. This was on Hanover across from where Elm St. dead-ended. Elm was called Wings Lane in Warren's time.

28. Brattle to Gage, Aug 26, 1774, in Force, 4:1:739.

29. *Bickerstaff's Boston Almanack for 1774* gives high tides at 7:56 a.m. and 8:19 p.m., thus low tide was 2:08 p.m.

30. Account of the Expedition, dated Sept 5, 1774, in Force, 4:1:762–64; Andrews to Barrell, Sept 1, 1774, in *Proc. of MHS* (1866), 8:350–51 (which calls the farm that of "Bob Temple"); Fischer, 44–45. Civil twilight began at 4:40 a.m., with sunrise

at 5:09 a.m., per the U.S. Navy's Sun and Moon Calculator website. The Sept 5 account claims the thirteen longboats, but Graves, *Conduct* (Sept 1–2, 1774), makes no mention of the enterprise and refers to the mob that results from the Powder Alarm as responding to the recent acts of Parliament, not the seizure of the powder, as if he were oblivious. However, *Conduct* was written a few years later as an autobiography, so perhaps he had forgotten the details by then. Had it not been for the positive information otherwise, I might have suspected that an army transport was instead employed.

31. It may have featured a lightning rod designed by Benjamin Franklin.

32. Account of the Expedition, dated Sept 5, 1774, in Force, 4:1:762–64; Fischer, 44–45. Sunrise was 5:09 a.m., per U.S. Navy's Sun and Moon Calculator. Civil twilight began at 4:40 a.m. Tide: see note 29. The British were probably successful in taking the two small cannon from Cambridge as well, but I have not seen any positive evidence on this.

33. McNeil gave his eyewitness account to Ezra Stiles, who recorded it in *Literary Diary* (Nov 17, 1774), 1:479–481ff.

34. Andrews to Barrell, Sept 2, 1774, in *Proc. of MHS* (1866), 8:351–53, which estimates that 3,000 formed up, making no mention of spectators. Andrews's letter of Sept 4, 1774, in ibid., 8:354, estimates 4,000, in close agreement with McNeil, who estimated "about Two Thousand & not three—& that the Bystanders were I think a thousand more" in Stiles, Nov 17, 1774, in *Literary Diary*, 1:479–81ff.

35. McNeil's statement, ibid., 1:479–81ff. (source of the final quote); also ibid., 1:477; Johnston, "Building to a Revolution."

36. Story of the handkerchief: Andrews to Barrell, Sept 2, 1774, in *Proc. of MHS* (1866), 8:351–53.

37. Ibid.; Brattle's original letter to Gage: *Boston Gazette*, Sept 5, 1774, p. 2; Brattle's apology: ibid., Sept 12, 1774, 1; Fischer, 47.

38. Warren to Samuel Adams, Sept 4, 1774, in French, *Life and Times,* 355–57; Johnston, "Building to a Revolution."

39. Andrews to Barrell, Sept 3, 1774, in *Proc. of MHS* (1866) 8:353–54; Johnston, "Building to a Revolution"; accounts in Force, 4:1:762–64.

40. Warren later wrote, "Had the troops marched only five miles out of Boston, I doubt whether a man would have been saved of their whole number." Warren to Samuel Adams, Sept 4, 1774, in *Life and Times*, 355–57.

41. Accounts in Force, 4:1:762–64 (quote); Dr. Thomas Young to Samuel Adams, Sept 4, 1774, in Samuel Adams MSS. Danforth previously served as a popularly appointed governor's councilor.

42. Andrews to Barrell, Sept 3, 1774, in *Proc. of MHS* (1866), 8:353–54; accounts in Force, 4:1:762–64. Lee, like Danforth, would remain a justice of the peace.

43. Accounts in Force, 4:1:762–64.

44. Stiles, Nov 17, 1774, in *Literary Diary*, 1:478; accounts in Force, 4:1:762–64.

45. Stiles, Sept 1, 1774, in *Literary Diary*, 1:457.

46. Benjamin Church to Samuel Adams, Sept 4, 1774, in S. Adams MSS; Stiles, Nov 17, 1774, in *Literary Diary*, 1:484–85.

47. Gage to Dartmouth, Sept 25, 1774, in Carter, 1:376–77.

48. Warren to Samuel Adams, Sept 4, 1774, in French, *Life and Times*, 355–77.

49. Gage to Dartmouth, Sept 2, 1774, in Carter, 1:369–72.

50. Gage to Dartmouth, Sept 12, 1774, in Carter, 1:373–75.

51. Alden, *General Gage in America*, 214, has the work begun on Sept 3, without reference, but Andrews to Barrell, Sept 5, 1774, in *Proc. of MHS* (1866), 8:354–55, suggests it began on Sept 5. The Neck's old structures: Drake, *Town of Roxbury*, 70. On the Navy: Letter of Sept 4, in ibid., 8:354. *Canceaux* was hauled up near the Neck until the fortifications could be built: Graves, *Conduct* (Sept 2, 1774). Its gun complement is eight cannon at this point, probably small 4- or 6-pounders, as given in the ships list, Jan 1, 1775, in *NDAR*, 1:47, but it will later swap these out for six carronades, per the Sept 29, 1775 list in ibid., 2:742–43. Gage had planned to send a detachment of troops to Worcester to ensure that the court judges there were properly seated, but given all of the turmoil, he wisely opted to cancel that operation. This from Gage to Dartmouth, Sept 2, 1774, in Carter, 1:369–72.

52. Gage to Haldimand, Sept 5, 1774; Gage to Valentine Jones, Sept 4, 1774; both in Gage MSS. (Q.v. appendix 3.)

53. Boston Selectmen to Gage, Sept 24, 1774, ibid.; Andrews to Barrell, Sept 25, 1774, in *Proc. of MHS* (1866), 8:366–68, which mentions a meeting between Gage and the selectmen on the inducement to prevent the barracks' construction (also in Commager and Morris, *The Spirit of 'Seventy-Six*, 29–30); Capt. William Evelyn to Rev. Dr. Evelyn [his father], Oct 31, 1774, in Scull, *Memoir and Letters*, 38–40.

54. On skirting the ban on town meetings by instead meeting at the county level: Joseph Warren to Samuel Adams, Aug 15, 1774, and to the Comm. of Norwich, Conn., Aug 27, 1774, in French, *Life and Times*, 339–40 and 350–51, respectively. Also see ibid., 341–42ff. On Revere: Fischer, 51–52. The idea of the convention began in August (ibid.), but due to delays that proved advantageous, was to be held after the Powder Alarm. General note on the Powder Alarm: With Samuel and John Adams in Philadelphia, and Dr. Warren at Cambridge during the Alarm, and with Dr. Church apparently there at some point as well, the only major figure unaccounted for was John Hancock. I have been unable to find anything on his whereabouts this day, but he was certainly in the Boston area.

CHAPTER 4: AN UNSTABLE PEACE

1. Robert J. Allison, *The Boston Massacre* (Beverly, MA: Applewood Books/ Commonwealth Editions, 2006), 49–50.

2. John Dickinson did not arrive until Oct 17, 1774, per *JCC*, 1:74.

3. John Adams to James Warren, June 25, 1774, in PJA.

4. Adams's diary, June 25, 1774, in PJA; David McCullough, *John Adams* (New York: Simon and Schuster, 2001), 23.

5. Adams to James Warren, July 17, 1774, in PJA.

6. Gage to Lord Barrington [Private], Aug 27, 1774, in Gage MSS. It is not in Carter.

7. McCullough, *John Adams*, 83; John Adams's diary, Aug 29, 1774, in PJA.

8. Adams's notes in Adams, *Works of John Adams*, 2:366–68; *JCC*, 1:13–27.

9. Adams to Abigail Adams, Sept 16, 1774, in PJA.

10. Ibid.; Psalms 35:1–3, per the Bible, King James Version. Also see Warren, *Genealogy of Warren*, 69–70. Prescribed: the psalm was in a prayer book for that date.

11. Jacob Duché to George Washington, Oct 8, 1777, in PGW.

12. Adams to Abigail Adams, Sept 18, 1774, in PJA.

13. French, *Life and Times*, 360–62, 366. Various references say that it was Woodward Tavern, perhaps the same as his house? The official record in *JCC*, 1:32, gives it as his house. The actual resolves, as cited in note 22. A letter from the Suffolk Delegates to Gage, Sept 9, 1774, in Gage MSS, appears to be a cover letter for the resolves themselves.

14. *JCC*, 1:37–39, gives the undated letter to Gage. (Gage asked to receive the committee on the following Monday, Sept 19, at noon.) The original, in the Gage MSS, also has no date (and so it is filed under the end of 1774).

15. Alden, *General Gage in America*, 218.

16. Andrews to Barrell, Sept 12, 1774, in *Proc. of MHS* (1866), 8:359–60; see note 14 above; French, *Life and Times*, 362–63.

17. Warren agreed to deliver a response the next day (Sept 12, a Monday); Gage, the "following Monday" at noon (maybe the same day, Sept 12, 1774).

18. French, *Life and Times*, 363–65, citing unknown sources (see also note 14). The only remaining exchange I have found on the Neck's fortification is from Peyton Randolph, President of the First Continental Congress, to Gage, Oct 10, 1774 (wrongly filed under Oct 30 in the Gage MSS), and Gage's reply, Oct 20, 1774, ibid.

19. Joseph Warren to Samuel Adams, Sept 29, 1774, in French, *Life and Times*, 381–82.

20. Fischer, 300–301 (which says Revere departed on Sept 11).

21. Alden, *General Gage in America*, 204.

22. The resolves and discussion in *JCC*, 1:31ff.; Revere: Fischer, 300–301. The next day, Sept 18, 1774, Revere rode back to Boston with the reply.

23. Details on the affair are scant; the only excerpt I have found is in Stiles, Sept 28,

1774, in *Literary Diary*, 1:460, a Wednesday, referring to the "Lordsday before last", or Sept 18. The robbery probably then occurred the night of the seventeenth. As of this writing, two of the brass cannon are on display. One, called the Adams, is mounted in the Bunker Hill Monument, at the inside of the top of the obelisk. Another, called the Hancock, is on loan from the Bunker Hill Monument and on display at Minute Man National Park in Concord. Roger Fuller and Dr. Terrie Wallace of the NPS kindly reported to me in private correspondence that the bore of the Hancock was 3⅛" caliber, or in decimal format, 3.125", while the overall length was 46.375", just shy of four feet. Muller, *A Treatise of Artillery*, 6, gives the caliber for a 3-pounder as 2.913" and a 4-pounder as 3.204". Assuming the measurement of the Hancock at 3.125" is accurate, we must assume this is a 3-pounder that has been worn from ample use and thus has an effective caliber that is now slightly greater than when it was first cast. Certainly, it is not a 4-pounder whose caliber has shrank. Muller, 61, says a typical 3-pounder fieldpiece was 3'6" (or 42") long, though unfortunately he does not list the length of a 4-pounder. So let us compare to measurements of naval guns. Naval guns had the same size caliber (a 3-pound ball of iron gives a set diameter ball), but the cannon themselves were constructed slightly differently, depending on the gun. Coggins, *Ships and Seamen*, 152, says that a naval 3-pounder was about 4.5' (54") long, while a naval 4-pounder was about 6' (72") long. The Hancock's length does not match any of these, but as it more closely matches that of a 3-pounder fieldpiece, the Hancock was probably a 3-pounder of nonstandard length. The caliber certainly matches that of a 3-pounder. NB: This incident seems to be distinct from another, late in 1774, in which William Dawes helped steal two more cannon from the British. For scraps of that story, see Holland, *William Dawes and His Ride*, 26ff.

24. Worcester Convention and its resolves in *JEPCM*, 627ff., with this important resolve appearing ibid., 643. Other counties that had conventions, and whose resolves appear in the aforementioned reference, begin on 601. More on the minutemen, and the reorganization of the militia companies: French, *First Year*, chap. 4. (Q.v. note 23.)

25. Gage to Dartmouth, Sept 12, 1774, in Carter, 1:373–75.

26. Gage to Dartmouth, Sept 25, 1774, in Carter, 1:376–77.

27. Gage to Dartmouth [Private], Sept 25, 1774, in Carter, 1:375–76.

28. George III to Lord North, Nov 19, 1774, 3:17 p.m., in Donne, *Correspondence of King George*, 1:216.

29. Gage to Lord Barrington, Oct 3, 1774, in Carter, 2:655–56.

30. *JEPCM*, 3–6, 16. Worcester County was the first to act so defiantly, in early Sept 1774, when the militia there closed the county court by forcing the court officials to abandon their posts. (The court was the lone seat of power of Crown-appointed

officials in the county.) However, this event in Salem is the first such act at the colonial level.

31. Upon his death, he measured 6'3½" "exact" for his coffin, per Tobias Lear, "Circumstantial Account," Dec 15, 1779, Gold Star Collection, Clements. It is transcribed in the Papers of George Washington Exhibits webpage at http://gwpapers.virginia.edu/project/exhibit/mourning/lear.html (accessed Apr 5, 2010), but this portion of the journal is strangely absent from the PGW database. Lear was Washington's personal secretary.

32. Washington to Bryan Fairfax, July 20, 1774, in PGW.

33. Washington to Fairfax, Aug 24, 1774, in PGW.

34. Benjamin Franklin to Joseph Galloway, Feb 25, 1775, in Smyth, *The Sailor's Word Book*, 6:311–12; also in PBF, 21:508.

35. *JCC* (Sept 28, 1774), 1:43–51; Labaree, *The Boston Tea Party*, 252–53; Adams, *Works of John Adams*, 2:386–87ff. I have been unable to find original source material on the vote. The expungement is noted in the congressional *Journals* footnotes, as cited in *JCC*.

36. Adams, *Works of John Adams*, 2:373–75, 535ff., appendix C; *JCC* (Oct 14, 1774), 1:63ff., gives the resolves, more clearly laid out in Commager and Morris, *The Spirit of 'Seventy-Six*, 57–58.

37. Non-importation Association: *JCC*, 1:75–81; addresses to Britain and Quebec: ibid., 1:81–102, 104–13; petition to the King: ibid., 1:115–22; plan to distribute petition to the King: ibid., 1:104; plan to reconvene (Oct 22): ibid., 1:102; Congress breaks up: ibid., 1:122.

38. Alden, *General Gage in America*, 216–17.

39. Washington calls it the New Tavern, per his diary (Oct 26, 1774), in PGW, but John Adams calls it the City Tavern, per his diary entry of the same date, in PJA.

40. Adams's diary, Oct 20, 1774, in Adams, *Works of John Adams*, 2:400, and PJA. His diary notes that many patrons not associated with the Congress joined in, bringing the total party to near one hundred. Perhaps one of these random patrons made the toast, as John would likely have named the delegate if the toast had come from one of them. This toast was actually given at a celebration at the same tavern a few days earlier, but quite possibly repeated here.

41. *JEPCM* (Oct 26, 1774), 31–33ff. (source of the first quote); (Oct 27), 35; (Oct 29), 48; (Oct 28), 41 (source of the final quote). The Provincial Congress first convened in Concord from Oct 11–14, then reconvened in Cambridge on Oct 17, where it would mostly remain for the duration of its existence (ibid., 1). That Hancock was selected chairman: ibid., 505. Captain Heath is our Col. William Heath (see Heath, *Memoirs*, 2–3), whom we will meet later in the text. The three generals are Jedediah Preble, Artemas Ward, and Seth Pomeroy (Oct 27, *JEPCM*, 35). Preble seems to have declined (see Heath, *Memoirs*, 4), probably due to his advanced age. (He was

about sixty-eight.) Pomeroy also would seem to be mostly inactive and was only at Bunker Hill as a volunteer. The war stores were moved to Concord (see later main text).

42. More later in the text. His "Boston Massacre" oration, given on Mar 5, 1773, is in *Orations Delivered at the Request of*, 29ff. More in Walker, *Devil Undone* (11 for his age). Kemble as head of intelligence: Alden, *General Gage in America*, 226, noting only that he was definitely in charge of such by Jan 1775. When he was appointed is unknown.

43. Rear Adm. Molyneux Shuldham in Newfoundland was the commander that sent two companies of 65th by way of the HMS *Rose*, "desiring only that they might be replaced in the Spring." Gage to Dartmouth, Nov 2, 1774, in Carter, 1:382–83, gives Gage's estimation of 3,000 total men (but see appendix 4); Haldimand, 47th and 18th: Gage to Lord Dartmouth, Oct 30, 1774 [No. 17], in Carter, 1:381–82 (NB: Not the private letter of Oct 30, but letter labeled No. 17!). Winter barracks: "leaving the tents standing under the care of a small guard, that they might dry before they were pack'd up, as it had been wet weather for two days." Barker, Nov 15, 1774, in *British in Boston*, 3.

44. Barker, Nov 29, 1774, in *British in Boston*, 9.

45. Gage to Lord Barrington, Nov 2, 1774, in Carter, 2:658–59.

46. Gage to Lord Barrington, Dec 14, 1774, in Carter, 2:663–64.

47. To ensure no jealousies with the British troops, the marines were to be paid and fed by the Army. Graves acquiesced, but it spoiled his private agenda of hoping to supply rations to the marines while taking a profit off the top. Pitcairn wrote privately to a friend, "The admiral can have no reason but to put money in the purser's pocket." The exchange between Gage and Graves is in the form of four letters, Dec 17, 19, 21, and 22, 1774, in *NDAR*, 1:31, 35, 39. Pitcairn's quote from Fischer, 68, citing Pitcairn to Col. John Mackenzie, Dec 10, 1774, in the Mackenzie papers (Additional MSS 39190, BL). See also Barker, Dec 26, 1774, in *British in Boston*, 14–15, which indicates they were still not landed and verifies that Graves wanted to profit by not landing them. I have not seen a source claiming when they did indeed land.

48. Appendix 3; appendix 4. On the fear of *Somerset*, see Mackenzie, Dec 19, in *British in Boston*, 12–13; Gage to Lord Dartmouth, Dec 15, 1774, [No. 20], in Carter, 1:386–88 (NB: There are several letters of Dec 15!).

49. Gage to Lord Dartmouth, Dec 15, 1774 [Separate], in Carter, 1:385–86, says that HMS *Rose* off Rhode Island was put on alert. A letter from Capt. James Wallace (of the HMS *Rose*) to Graves, Dec 12, 1774, in *NDAR*, 1:15, states, "What can be done by the *Rose* shall not be neglected." However, *NDAR* gives nothing more, and I have not determined if the *Rose* was successful in capturing the forty light ordnance.

50. See note 11; Fischer, 52–54.

51. See note 11.

52. Cochran to Wentworth, Dec 14, 1774, in Force, 4:1:1042 (source of the quote).

53. Wentworth to Gage, Dec 16, 1774; Letter to a Gentleman in New York from Portsmouth, Dec 16, 1774; and Letter to a Gentleman in New York from Portsmouth, Dec 17, 1774; all ibid., 4:1:1041–43, also in *NDAR*, 1:27ff.

54. Fischer, 56n30; [Naval] Captain Barkley [of the HMS *Scarborough*] to Graves, Dec 20, 1774, in *NDAR*, 1:38.

55. The number of barrels of powder varies by the report, but most agree about 100. One source already cited (Force, 4:1:1043) says 97. Graves, *Conduct* (Dec 16, 1774), in excerpt in *NDAR*, 1:30, says upward of 100. Letter to a Gentleman in New York from Portsmouth, Dec 17, 1774, in Force, 4:1:1043, gives the unsubstantiated claim of 200 to 220. Finally, after days for the dust to settle, *Essex Gazette*, Dec 20, 1774, in *NDAR*, 1:38, says 106. On the cannon: while Barkley to Graves, ibid., claims 18 pieces were removed, Wentworth twice claims just 16: in his letter to Graves, ibid., 1:37; and a proclamation of Dec 26, in ibid., 1:41. The latter source also gives the number of muskets and military stores.

56. Barkley (of the HMS *Scarborough*) to Graves, Dec 20, 1774, in *NDAR*, 1:38, says there were 53 pieces left unremoved. On the 42-pounders: Letter to a Gentleman in New York from Portsmouth, Dec 17, 1774, in Force, 4:1:1043. On the *Canceaux* and *Scarborough*: their journals in *NDAR*, 1:31 and 1:34, respectively, and Graves, *Conduct*, the pertinent excerpt of which (Dec 16, 1774) in ibid., 1:30. On the ships' delay and the weather: Fischer, 53–57.

57. Four alarms: the Salem Town Meeting Alarm; the Powder Alarm; the Watertown Alarm, when Gage considered going after the stolen brass cannon; and now this alarm.

58. Graves's Jan 1775 list in *NDAR*, 1:47; Wentworth's efforts: his proclamation of Dec 26, 1774, in ibid., 1:41–42.

59. Fort George: *Connecticut Gazette*, Dec 16, 1774, in *NDAR*, 1:30; New London: *Providence Gazette*, Dec 24, 1774, in *NDAR*, 1:40; *Lively* to Salem Roads off Salem and Marblehead: Graves, *Conduct* (Dec 29), this excerpt in *NDAR*, 1:42; Maryland: Gage to Dartmouth, Dec 15, 1774, in Carter, 1:384–85. Jeremiah Lee: see Joseph Gardoqui and Sons to Jeremiah Lee, Feb 15, 1775, in *NDAR*, 1:401, and Elbridge Gerry to Joseph Gardoqui and Sons, July 5, 1775, in ibid., 1:818. Additional details from private correspondence with Judy Anderson, former Jeremiah Lee Mansion Curator (Marblehead, MA), in Apr 2010.

60. Barker, Dec 19, 1774, in *British in Boston*, 12–13, also in *NDAR*, 1:35, along with a pertinent letter from Graves. Remaining marines: of the 460 total marines earmarked for Boston.

61. Graves's list in *NDAR*, 1:47, gives the ships as of Jan 1, 1775. NB: *Boyne* only had 68 guns, per appendix 5. *Swan* was at Rhode Island; *Scarborough* and *Canceaux* remained at New Hampshire. One of the armed transports present was the 18-gun

Symmetry, though transports were typically owned by the Army and thus not on the Naval Lists. The list also includes a schooner, *Diana*, just purchased, being then fitted with six light guns. See also appendix 4.

62. An accurate number of Bostonians is difficult to pinpoint—there was no regular census. However, J. H. Benton Jr., *Early Census Making in Massachusetts: 1643–1765* (Boston: Charles E. Goodspeed, 1905), 74–75 (these pages unnumbered), lists 15,520 total in Boston in 1765. Perhaps, given a smallpox outbreak and new births, the population in 1774 was similar. Cf. Andrews to Barrell, May 6, 1775, in *Proc. of MHS* (1866), 8:405–6, which claims half of Boston left after hostilities began (a nonscientific estimate). A census taken on June 24, 1775, given on a list dated Oct 9, 1775, in the Gage MSS, shows 6,247 Bostonians. We can perhaps trust Barrell and double this number to get about 12,000 before passes were issued in Apr 1775 to leave then besieged Boston, which leaves another 3,000 or so who fled in early Apr 1775 at news that Gage might take the offensive (at the time Adams and Hancock fled).

63. Montresor to Haldimand, May 13, 1774, in Gage MSS; also in French, *Ticonderoga*, 11–12. Garrison: compare Lt. Jocelyn Feltham to Gage, July 11, 1774, enclosure, in ibid., 55, to the Feb 1 return attached to De la Place to Gage, Jan 24, 31–Feb 1, in Gage MSS.

64. French, *Ticonderoga*, 6–15.

65. Lord Dartmouth to Gage, Nov 2, 1774, in Carter, 2:177. Gage acknowledged the receipt in two letters, Gage to Lord Dartmouth, Dec 25 and Dec 26, 1774, both ibid., 1:389.

Chapter 5: A Disquieting Thaw

1. Appendix 4.

2. Barker, Jan 1, 1775, in *British in Boston*, 18.

3. Pitcairn to Lord Sandwich, Mar 4, 1775, in Barnes and Ownes, *The Private Papers*, 1:59–62.

4. Barker, Dec 1, 1774, in *British in Boston*, 9.

5. Andrews to Barrell, Jan 21, 1775, in *Proc. of MHS* (1866), 8:395–96; Barker, Jan 21, 1775, in *British in Boston*, 21–22.

6. See note 5. Mackenzie, Jan 24, 1775, in *A British Fusilier*, 30–31 (source of quote). Over the next few days, a court of inquiry investigated the riot, and at least one of the instigating drunken officers was censured.

7. For another: Andrews to Barrell, Jan 21, 1775, in *Proc. of MHS* (1866), 8:395–96.

8. Mackenzie, Feb 2, 1774, in *A British Fusilier*, 32. He describes his own rank as first lieutenant in a headquarters record book in the Mackenzie MSS (Vol. C, 48), at the Clements.

9. Barker, Dec 17 and 24, 1774, in *British in Boston*, 12, 14. The man shot seems to be the man caught on the night of Dec 17. Barker says that the night before (Dec 16), another man successfully deserted along Boston Neck (by the blockhouse there).

10. When Robert Vaughan of the 52nd was caught in early March deserting via Charlestown Ferry, he too was found guilty and sentenced to execution before the troops. But on the night before his execution, orders were sent to all the men that Vaughan had been given a reprieve. A few days later, Gage announced Vaughan's pardon. Much to Gage's surprise, desertions did not abate. Rather, they immediately increased. Incensed, Gage issued General Orders that, "as he finds his Clemency has had so little effect in bringing the Soldiers to a sense of their duty to their King and Country…this is the last man he will pardon…for desertion." A few days later, an undaunted Vaughan attempted to desert yet again, this time successfully. Mackenzie, Mar 4, 9, 13, 14, 1775, in *A British Fusilier*, 36, 40–41.

11. Mackenzie, Feb 4, 1775, in *A British Fusilier*, 33.

12. Mackenzie, Mar 8, 1775, in *A British Fusilier*, 39–40 (quote); Gage to Lord Dartmouth, Mar 28, 1775, in Carter, 1:394–95.

13. Graves, *Conduct* (Apr 11, 1775).

14. Mackenzie, Mar 18, 1775, in *A British Fusilier*, 42 (which indicates total balls were 19,000); John Andrews to William Barrell, Mar 18, 1775 (the postscript of Monday morning, Mar 20), in *Proc. of MHS* (1866), 8:401. Andrews's letter of Apr 11, 1775, in ibid., 402–3, implies the searches were dramatically increased afterward.

15. Barker, Dec 16, 1774, in *British in Boston*, 11; Mackenzie, Feb 3 and Mar 28, 1775, in *A British Fusilier*, 32–33, 44.

16. Mackenzie, Jan 15, in *A British Fusilier*, 28–29; also noted in Barker, Dec 3, 1774, in *British in Boston*, 9–10. John Andrews to William Barrell, Oct 1, 1774, in *Proc. of MHS* (1866), 8:371–72, gives a story of a colonist mocking the British soldiers' target practice, then showing off his own marksmanship. The story seems woefully exaggerated in favor of the Americans. The colonist reportedly fired one of the soldiers' guns, which were smoothbore muskets and as such were inherently inaccurate. Yet it claims he fired dead accurate, as if he had a rifle, something impossible with a smoothbore.

17. Barker, Nov 15, 1774, in *British in Boston*, 3–4.

18. Andrews to Barrell, Mar 18, 1775 (the postscript of Monday morning, Mar 20), in *Proc. of MHS* (1866), 8:401.

19. Gage to Col. James Robertson, Feb 6, 1775, in Gage MSS. Robertson was barrack master general and still in New York.

20. Joseph Warren to Josiah Quincy Jr., Nov 21, 1774, in French, *Life and Times*, 394–96.

21. Robert M. Calhoon, "Loyalism and Neutrality" in *A Companion to the American Revolution*, Jack P. Greene and J. R. Pole, eds. (Malden, MA: Blackwell Publishing Ltd., 2004), 235. Had the Whigs comprised a more sizable portion of the population, America might have broken the shackles of the empire without the assistance of the French. Also see J. L. Bell, "Estimating Loyalist Strength and Numbers," *Boston 1775* (blog), July 13, 2008, http://boston1775.blogspot.com/2008/07/estimating-loyalist-strength-and.html.

22. Marshfield and Scituate's joint pledge, undated but circa Jan 22, 1775, wrongly filed under Jan 27, 1775 in the Gage MSS English Series; Gage to Lord Dartmouth, Jan 27, 1775, and also of Feb 17, 1775, in Carter, 1:391–93; Mackenzie, Jan 23, 25, 29; Feb 5, 11; Mar 29, 1775, in *A British Fusilier*, 31, 31, 33, 44 (the Jan 23 entry gives exact number of men sent); Frothingham, *Siege of Boston*, 46–47.

23. Murdock, *Nineteenth of April*, 19–21. Weekly drilling was at least called for in the Suffolk Resolves (Resolve #11).

24. Graves, *Conduct* (Dec 29, 1774), in excerpt in *NDAR*, 1:42.

25. Gage to Lord Dartmouth, Mar 4, 1775, in Carter, 1:393–94.

26. Twelve: Gray's Account in *Proc. of the Essex Inst.*, (1856), 1:129–30 (but see note 47); seventeen: Col. David Mason, *Memoir* (by his daughter), in ibid., 131–34; 12-pounders: Charles M. Endicott, "Leslie's Retreat, or the Resistance to British Arms at the North Bridge in Salem," in ibid., 104. Cf. James Duncan Philips, "Why Colonel Leslie Came to Salem," in *Essex Inst. Hist. Coll.*, Oct 1954, 90(4):312–16.

27. On the aides-de-camp's ignorance of the event, see Fischer, 58, citing Thomas Hutchinson Jr. to Elisha Hutchinson, Mar 4, 1775, in the Hutchinson Papers, Egerton MSS, 2659, BL. Gage had two aides-de-camp (Carter, 2:666–67): one was probably Maj. [Maurice?] Cane, the other perhaps Maj. R[obert?] Donkin. Mackenzie, Apr 19, 1775, in *A British Fusilier*, 59, names Lt. Harry Rooke of the 4th Regiment as one of Gage's aides-de-camp, but this seems unlikely given his low rank. Also, ibid., 58n40.

28. One theory posits that Gage's secretary, Thomas Flucker, had passed the news, whether inadvertently or intentionally, to his Whig son-in-law, Boston bookseller Henry Knox. However, such a theory seems unlikely and little evidence supports that Flucker was anything but a staunch Loyalist. Fischer, 58n41, suggests this, but I find it unlikely. Flucker even left with Gage after the latter's recall.

29. Joshua Brackett, Paul Revere, Benjamin Edes, Joseph Ward, Thomas Crafts, and Thomas Chase to the Sons of Liberty in New York, Mar 1, 1775, in Fischer, 382n42. See Fischer's notes on the previous errors in transcribing this letter. Also, Fischer, 58–59. The mechanics were thrown in jail, "lest we should send an express to our brethren at Marblehead and Salem", as Revere put it.

30. Pitcairn to Lord Sandwich, Mar 4, in Barnes and Owens, *The Private Papers*, 1:59–62, states four companies. If we imagine full strength of 39 men each, plus 3

officers each, we have 168 as the max, plus a few extras and Lieutenant Colonel Leslie. If we assume a more modest average per company, say, 30, we have 120 or so men. These assumptions are explained in appendix 4.

31. Endicott, "Leslie's Retreat," in *Proc. of the Essex Inst.* (1856), 1:106ff.; *Essex Gazette*, Feb 28, 1775, in ibid., 1:122–24. Fischer, 59, gives a timeline without reference, and also claims 240 men of the 64th were embarked; I have followed his sources and not found evidence of such.

32. *Essex Gazette*, Feb 28, 1775, in *Proc. of the Essex Inst.* (1856), 1:122–24.

33. Ibid.; Mrs. Story's account in *Proc. of the Essex Inst.* (1856), 1:134–35; "Leslie's Retreat," the second account by Mrs. Story, in *Essex Inst. Hist. Coll.* (1880), 17:190–92.

34. Colonel Lee's role here seems largely traditional, which I learned of in private discourse with Judy Anderson, former Jeremiah Lee Mansion curator (Marblehead, MA), in Feb 2010. That a Marblehead militia company (probably the minutemen) was ready is given in Gavett's account, in *Proc. of the Essex Inst.* (1856), 1:126–28.

35. "Leslie's Retreat," the second account by Mrs. Story, in *Essex Inst. Hist. Coll.* (1880), 17:190–92.

36. Gavett's account in *Proc. of the Essex Inst.* (1856), 1:126–28. The mill is pictured on the map *Plan of the Town of Salem in the Commonwealth of Massachusetts* by Jonathan P. Saunders, 1820, in Clements (4-G-7). No mention of why Colonel Mason was not at church.

37. Mrs. Story's account in *Proc. of the Essex Inst.* (1856), 1:134–35.

38. "Leslie's Retreat," the second account by Mrs. Story, in *Essex Inst. Hist. Coll.* (1880), 17:190–92.

39. *Essex Gazette*, Feb 28, 1775, in *Proc. of the Essex Inst.* (1856) 1:122–24; Endicott, "Leslie's Retreat," in ibid., 109; Gavett's account in ibid., 126–28. On Sargent's flight, Gray's dubious account in ibid., 129–31. Fischer, 60, describes some colonists breaking planks off a bridge ahead of Leslie's column and slowing their march. Fischer gives no source, and I have seen no evidence of it, though I have used the same original source material. Another story has one militia vanguard unit immediately marching off toward the wharves, acting as a decoy and hoping to draw the British in the wrong direction, though this did not work.

40. Gavett's account in *Proc. of the Essex Inst.* (1856), 1:126–28. That they were unarmed, except for one with two pistols peeking out from a cloak: Gray's account in *Proc. of the Essex Inst.* (1856), 1:129–30, and the separate addendum in ibid., 130. But see following text: men had hatchets.

41. Gavett's account in *Proc. of the Essex Inst.* (1856), 1:126–28, which claims Leslie merely bluffed that he might be obliged to fire, versus *Essex Gazette*, Feb 28, 1775, in ibid., 122–24, which says that they fanned out, probably true, but that Leslie ordered his officer to fire before Felt intervened, almost certainly a falsehood.

Leslie was indeed under no orders to start the war and would not have given such an order to his men despite being infuriated. He undoubtedly threatened it, but issuing the order meant it might actually be followed, and though Leslie might have been arrogant, he seems to have been a solid officer. As such, he would never have given such an order on his own accord, with the war not yet begun. In fact, Gage, who always expressed caution, almost certainly gave Leslie explicit verbal orders to follow the law: no plundering and definitely no attacking the town. Despite the biased claims to the contrary, Gavett's is the account to believe. Leslie never ordered his men to fire.

42. Various renditions of this line appear in the sources cited here. I use that of the *Essex Gazette*, Mar 7, 1775, in *Proc. of the Essex Inst.* (1856), 1:124–26.

43. Gavett's account in *Proc. of the Essex Inst.* (1856), 1:126–28; Endicott, "Leslie's Retreat," in ibid., 116.

44. Gavett's account in *Proc. of the Essex Inst.* (1856), 1:126–28 (the source of the entire exchange quoted here).

45. Ibid. Danvers is to the north, but they probably came around to west of town, as there was probably some public bridge west. One way to confirm this would be to discover where the distillery was that they hid behind, belonging to a Colonel (or Major?) Sprague. Unfortunately, I have been unable to verify its whereabouts. Traditional claims from members active on the Salem Hist. Soc. website forum suggest the distillery was at the intersection of modern Federal and North Streets, south of where the drawbridge was, but this remains unverified.

46. Ibid. Another claim is that one townsman noticed the troops, standing in formation, shivering in the cold. He then jeered, "I should think you were all fiddlers, you shake so." However, statements such as these come from dubious source material, which I deem secondary source material: accounts taken years or decades later, based on memories of old men whose eager retellings were sure to be flavored. This particular claim comes from Abijah Northey's memories of what he heard his father relate. It is in ibid., 130–31.

47. Gavett's account in *Proc. of the Essex Inst.* (1856), 1:126–28; *Essex Gazette*, Feb 28, 1775, in ibid., 122–24. Was it two gondolas or three? The sources cited say two, but Gray's account in ibid., 129–30, says three (and perhaps Fischer, 62, draws on this; he does not report his source). Gray was just shy of ten years old at the time and gave his account many years later, and so it must be used selectively. *Bickerstaff's Boston Almanack for 1775* (close enough to Salem for our needs) gives high tides at 9:21 a.m. and 9:45 p.m., and thus low tide was 3:33 p.m., about the time of the incident with the longboats.

48. The exact words here are uncertain, as they are recorded by eyewitness Gray, years later (note 47). However, all of the other, more reliable sources cited throughout this section indicate that some similar exchange took place, only they give no

words to the parties, and thus, while the words are uncertain, the principle of the quotes given here can be trusted.

49. Gavett's account in *Proc. of the Essex Inst.* (1856), 1:126–28.

50. *Essex Gazette*, Feb 28, 1775, in *Proc. of the Essex Inst.* (1856), 1:122–24.

51. Gavett's account in *Proc. of the Essex Inst.* (1856), 1:126–28; *Essex Gazette*, Feb 28, 1775, in ibid., 122–24; "Leslie's Retreat," the second of the two accounts by Mrs. Story in *Essex Inst. Hist. Coll.* (1880), 17:190–92. Sunset was 5:31 p.m. per the U.S. Navy's Sun and Moon Calculator.

52. Ibid.

53. Mrs. Story's account in *Proc. of the Essex Inst.* (1856), 1:134–35.

54. Requesting the militia companies stand down: "but the alarm flew like lightning…so that great numbers were in arms, and soon on the march before our messengers arrived." *Essex Gazette*, Feb 28, 1775, in *Proc. of the Essex Inst.* (1856), 1:122–24.

55. Gage to Lord Dartmouth, Mar 4, in Carter, 1:393–94.

56. That historian is Fischer, on 64.

57. Dr. John Warren (Joseph's youngest brother) lived in Salem and may have witnessed Leslie's debacle. See chap. 1, n. 37, for more. Also see Forman, *Dr. Joseph Warren*.

58. Mackenzie, Mar 6, 1775, in *A British Fusilier*, 37–38, indicates this was the case; that selectmen argued adjournments versus calling new meetings: Gage to Lord Dartmouth, Aug 27, 1774, in Carter, 1:365–68.

59. Mackenzie, Mar 6, in *A British Fusilier*, 36–39.

60. Ibid. Mackenzie, *A British Fusilier*, 37n3, refutes the claim that Warren came in via a ladder (as does Barker's diary, cited below). That original claim is in French, *Life and Times*, 429. Toga: "A Spectator," in *Rivington's Gazette*, Mar 16, 1775, in Moore, *Diary of the American Revolution*, 1:34–35 (which also debunks the ladder story).

61. The "Boston Massacre" oration of Mar 6, 1775, in *Orations Delivered at the Request of…Boston…*, 57ff.

62. Mackenzie, Mar 6, in *A British Fusilier*, 36–39. Barker, Mar 6, in *British in Boston*, 25–26, claims Hancock made the thank-you speech. As Mackenzie seems more impartial, I prefer his account over Barker's. An unsubstantiated story from Everett, *Joseph Warren*, 112, says an officer near the pulpit held up his hand to reveal "several pistol bullets on the open palm. Warren observed the action, and, without discontinuing his discourse, dropped a white handkerchief upon the officer's hand." Everett's material is completely unsourced, but he seems to have relied on both letters and interviews to write his biography. However, as this anecdote is not supported by any known contemporary source, I omit it from the present text.

63. Mackenzie, Mar 7, in *A British Fusilier*, 39; Barker, Mar 6, in *British in Boston*, 25–26.

64. Mackenzie, Mar 10, in *A British Fusilier*, 40.

65. Andrews to Barrell, Mar 18, in *Proc. of MHS* (1866), 8:399–401. It is unclear if John Andrews meant this scene happened on March 8 or 15, giving us only that it happened "Last Wednesday, the day the oration was publish'd".

66. Save one perhaps: Samuel Adams.

67. George III to Lord North, Nov 18, 1774, in Donne, *Correspondence of George III*, 1:214–15.

68. PHE, 18:33–34.

69. William Bollan, Benjamin Franklin, and Arthur Lee to the Speaker of the Assembly of Pennsylvania, Dec 24, 1774, in PBF, 21:398. From this, the date of the arrival of the petition is uncertain, but within a day or two of Dec 24.

70. PHE, 18:149–60. The Lords voted 68–18 against Chatham's motion: ibid., 18:168.

71. Chatham's sweeping new plan: in exchange for the Americans making voluntary grants toward their own support and for explicit recognition of its theoretical supremacy, Parliament would withdraw all troops from America, repeal the late Coercive Acts, and give up all attempts at internal taxation. Chatham's proposal: ibid., 18:198ff., the vote against, 61–32, is on ibid., 18:215. Prime Minister Lord North soon followed with his own limited reconciliation plan, and though it passed, it failed to arrive in America in time to have any consequence. North's proposal: ibid., 18:319ff.; its passage in committee by a vote of 274–88, ibid., 18:338, with its adoption by the House on ibid., 358; North's actual resolution appears in MacDonald, *Select Charters*, 367–68. Also, Labaree, *The Boston Tea Party*, 263–64.

72. The introduction of the New England Bill: PHE, 18:298–300ff.; Johnstone: ibid., 18:301; bill carried (261 to 85): ibid., 18:305; debate on the New England Bill: ibid., 18:379ff. Burke: ibid., 18:389–90; bill's approval to be engrossed by the Commons (215 to 61): ibid., 18:392; introduction of the Southern Colonies Bill: ibid., 18:411ff.; passage of a joint New England/southern colonies bill in the Lords (73 to 21): ibid. (Mar 21), 18:457 (followed by the protest of 16 Lords); the actual text of the New England Bill (the southern bill not given): MacDonald, *Select Charters*, 368ff.; the actual text of the bill for the southern colonies: *Proceedings in the North Atlantic Coast Fisheries Arbitration before...the Hague*, 12 vols. (Washington, DC: Government Printing Office, 1912), 5:908ff.

73. PHE, 18:478–538; portions also in Commager and Morris, *The Spirit of 'Seventy-Six*, 233–38, from which I draw all of these quotes. The vote against (270 to 78): PHE, 18:540.

74. The speech is in Moses Coit Tyler, *Patrick Henry* (Boston: Houghton, Mifflin and Co., 1899), 140ff.

75. PHE (Feb 2, 18:226–27) only hints at Grant's speech, while the *London Evening Post* (Feb 18, 1775, p. 3) gives the probably near-verbatim words spoken by

Grant, as quoted in the text, though I corrected the tense ("were" appears where I placed "[are]"). It seems Grant's assertion as quoted was twisted with each retelling, and once it reached America, it became the incendiary claim that Americans could not fight, and that Grant thought he could march from one end of the continent to the other with a mere 5,000 men. Although some wrongly attribute this quote to Lord Jeffery Amherst, all historians seem to repeat it, yet none seem to know where it came from. Having found no evidence that Grant ever uttered a word about a "march from one end of the continent", I suspect it was twisted sometime after. (In private correspondence, J. L. Bell, author of the blog *Boston 1775*, concludes the same.) See, for instance, the Letter from Weathersfield, Apr 23, in *New-York Gazette*, May 1, 1775, p. 2, which in the postscript asks: "Query, Will Col. Grant believe now that New-England Men dare look Regulars in the Face?" This is clearly in response to the quote given from the *London Evening Post*, but no mention is made of the marching across the continent. The earliest reference I have found to the "marching" reference is in William Alexander Duer, *The Life of William Alexander, Earl of Stirling, Major-General in the Army of the United States During the Revolution* (published for the New Jersey Hist. Soc. by Wiley & Putnam, 1847), 2:162n, citing the manuscript diary of Lord Stirling, which I have not located. The version of the twisted words I give are from William S. Stryker, *The Battles of Trenton and Princeton* (Boston: Houghton, Mifflin and Company, 1898), 48n1. (NB: William Alexander, Lord Stirling was not the one who heard the original words in the Commons, because he was in New Jersey by February.) I conducted extensive searches across the newspaper databases Archive of Americana and British Newspapers, 1600–1900, both provided by Cengage Learning's Gale Infotrac, and have found no other clues to this mystery.

76. Lord Sandwich's quotes of Mar 16, 1775: PHE, 18:446–48. The debate on augmenting naval forces ibid., 18:305 (Feb 13, 1775); on land forces, ibid., 18:316 (Feb 15).

77. Paul Revere to Jeremy Belknap [circa 1798]; Fischer, 79–80.

78. Pitcairn to Lord Sandwich, Feb 14 and also of Mar 4, 1775, in Barnes and Owens, *The Private Papers*, 1:57–59 and 1:59–62, respectively. The second also says that Gage had a meeting with some "Great Whigs" and told them he would burn any town to the ground if they killed even one soldier. That such a meeting happened is likely, probably in response to the Salem Alarm, but this exchange as Pitcairn presents it is doubtful, given what we know of Gage. Furthermore, Pitcairn could not have known of the exchange except secondhand. Despite the supposed quotes Pitcairn attributes to Gage, what he reports was probably camp rumor.

79. Gage's Instructions to Brown and De Berniere, Feb 22, 1775, in Force, 4:1:1263.

80. The entire story, including any quotes, from De Berniere's narrative in ibid.,

4:1:1263–68, also in *Coll. of MHS* (1816), 2:4:204ff. De Berniere hardly uses quotation marks, but seems to quote some of the participants. So I have liberally added quotation marks to suggest that the words in his narrative are what was spoken, though in doing so, I have been forced to correct the tenses and pronouns in a few select cases. It is my hope that this adds to the clarity of the story rather than detracts from it. Some minutia from Fischer, 81–84.

Chapter 6: Many Preparations

1. The original intelligence, Mar 9, 1775 [written in French], is in the Gage MSS, but without a translation. It appears transcribed but not translated in French, *General Gage's Informers*, 11–13, with a synopsis following. Thank you to Vicky Lee Chan for her machine-assisted translation of the letter. Also see *JEPCM*, 77, 84.

2. Cohorns or Coehorns were brass 4½" mortars, firing 12-pound shells, per Smyth, *The Sailor's Word Book*.

3. Before they got far, the woman ran back to them, crying. She told the scouts that unless she left the town immediately, the townspeople were going to tar and feather her for directing Tories in their road. It seems the discovered British officers did nothing to help her, but instead continued on to the Bliss home.

4. The entire story, including any quotes, comes from De Berniere's narrative in *Coll. of MHS* (1816), 2:4:214–15. Menotomy sometimes pronounced *Mee-NOT-oh-mee*.

5. All of these are detailed in French, *General Gage's Informers*, 15ff. The originals are all in the Gage MSS.

6. Barker, Mar 30, 1775, in *British in Boston*, 27.

7. Intelligence, Apr 3, 1775, in Gage MSS (NB: There are two intelligence documents with this date). Also, a summary of this intelligence—along with the summary of letters of Mar 30 and Apr 9, packed together under the date "circa April 10" in the Gage MSS—gives an important added note in describing Percy's march to Watertown. Cf. *JEPCM*, 112, which gives nothing of the resolve that the intelligence of Apr 3 provides.

8. Further intel: Intelligence, Apr 9, 1775, in Gage MSS, in piecemeal in French, *Informers*, 18–21.

9. Gage to Lord Barrington, Mar 28, 1775, in Carter, 2:671–72.

10. Gage to Lord Dartmouth, Apr 22, 1775, ibid., 1:396–97; Barker, Apr 3, 1775, in *British in Boston*, 28; Andrews to Barrell, Apr 11, 1775, in *Proc. of MHS* (1866), 8:402–3 (source of the quote); Fischer, 75.

11. Fischer, 108.

12. Gage to Lord Dartmouth, Apr 22, 1775, in Carter, 1:396–97. Percy had a theory: "Things now every day begin to grow more & more serious; A Vessel is arrived by

accident here that has brought us a Newspaper in which we have the joint Address of the two Houses of Parliament to His Majesty; this has convinced the Rebels (for we may now legally call them so) that there is no hopes for them but by submitting to Parliament". Percy to Rev. Thomas Percy, Apr 8, 1775, in Bolton, *The Private Papers*, 48–49. Percy refers to a joint address from both houses given on Feb 9 at St. James's Palace, the details of which are in Force, 4:1:1540–90, while the final revision of the address is in PHE, 18:297–98.

13. Appendix 8.

14. The biggest driver was the admiral's ego and desire to profit from his station. The marine commander, Pitcairn, grew frustrated with the admiral and wrote privately to his trusted personal acquaintance, Lord Sandwich, who also just so happened to be the First Lord of the Admiralty. Meanwhile, Gage seems to have given up on the matter. Yet, unable to leave things be, Graves exacerbated the situation in early March when he demanded that Pitcairn embark some of his marines back aboard the warships. Pitcairn politely refused. As he explained to Lord Sandwich, "I should do it with the utmost pleasure, if it was in my power, but I was absolutely under the command of General Gage and could order nothing but as he directed me". Graves swore and threatened he would court-martial Pitcairn, but the refined Pitcairn took the idle threat in stride, for he truly respected his superior officer, not because he was Samuel Graves, but for the dignity of the rank he bore. In writing to Lord Sandwich, Pitcairn added, "It is needless for me to tell your Lordship how he talked to me and what [vulgarities?] he said; but be assured that nothing he says or does shall make me deviate from the rules of politeness and the respect due to an admiral and commander of a squadron." When Pitcairn mentioned the episode to his immediate commander, Gage, the latter was quite surprised at the admiral's behavior. Pitcairn to Lord Sandwich, Feb 14 and Mar 4, 1775, in Barnes and Owens, *The Private Letters*, 1:57–62 (both quotes from the latter); Pitcairn to Gage, Mar 5, 1775, in Gage MSS; appendix 4.

15. Revere to Belknap [circa 1798]; Gage to Graves, Apr 5, and the reply (same date), both in *NDAR*, 1:168–69.

16. Appendix 5. The 64-gun HMS *Asia* was another candidate as a capital ship, but would frequently be dispatched elsewhere. The "70-gun" *Boyne* (she carried just 68 guns) was two inches longer than *Somerset*. Of note, when the repairs made it necessary to off-load *Somerset*'s heavy stores and cannon, Graves must have found it somewhat humiliating to beg of his rival for the use of two of the Army's transports, which Gage politely lent him. See Graves, *Conduct* (Mar 31) and Graves to Philip Stephens, Apr 11, 1775 in *Conduct* (Apr 11).

17. Revere to Belknap [circa 1798]; Gage to Graves, Apr 5, and the reply (same date), both in *NDAR*, 1:168–69.

18. Fischer, 87.

19. Intelligence, Apr 15, 1775 [written in French], in Gage MSS. The translation of this portion only can be found in Alden, *General Gage in America*, 227.

20. About this time, Warren and Eustis overheard some British regulars insulting the rebels. Warren is said to have turned to Eustis and said, "These fellows say we won't fight: by Heavens, I hope I shall die up to my knees in blood!" Another anecdote tells that sometime in early spring, Warren was walking near Boston Neck, which featured within its new fortifications a brand-new gallows. One of three officers there recognized him and yelled, "Go on, Warren: you will soon come to the gallows." Warren defiantly turned and stomped over to the officers, demanding who said it. None would reply. French, *Life and Times*, 451–52. On the apprentices: Cary, *Joseph Warren: Physician, Politician, Patriot*, 31.

21. It is assumed that Mercy was his fiancée by now. On Apr 10, Dr. Warren wrote to his landlord, Dr. Elijah Dix, asking for a couple of wagons to go to his mother's Roxbury home to fetch his children. Warren hoped they would arrive no later than "next Thursday Night", Apr 20. See chap. 1, n. 37 for details of citation. Also see Forman, *Dr. Joseph Warren*.

22. Mackenzie, Apr 7 and 10, 1775, in *A British Fusilier*, 45–47. On the weather: Apr 5, 1775, ibid., 9.

23. Intelligence, Apr 9, 1775, in Gage MSS, in piecemeal in French, *Informers*, 18–21.

24. Intelligence, Apr 11, 1775, in Gage MSS, in piecemeal in French, *Informers*, 21–22.

25. Alden, *General Gage in America*, 233. Fischer, 75–76n28, gives some interesting additional info on the 17th Light Dragoons, but his claim that they fought at Bunker Hill is incorrect. That De Lancey was quartermaster: *Boston Gazette*, Apr 17, 1775, in *NDAR*, 1:188. The uniform of a 17th Dragoon soldier is depicted in Smith and Kiley, *Illustrated Encyclopedia*, 150; an officer is depicted in Mollo, *Uniforms*, plate 91.

26. Lord Dartmouth to Gage [Secret], Jan 27, 1775, in Carter, 2:179–83.

27. Ibid.; appendix 3.

28. All quotes here, not necessarily in the order they appear in the original, from Dartmouth's letter in ibid.

29. Total of troops in Britain: Piers Mackesy, *The War for America, 1775–1783* (Cambridge, MA: Harvard University Press, 1964), 524.

30. The quote is from the Intelligence enclosed with the letter from Gage to Lord Dartmouth, Mar 4, 1775. (I have replaced "yards" over the obvious error of "rods" in the original, as not even rifles had a range of 200 rods, or 1,100 yards, and most New Englanders had only smoothbores.) The letter is included in Carter, 1:393–94, but not the enclosure. I have not seen the original enclosure, probably in the UKNA, but a transcription is in the Bancroft transcriptions, "England and America," vol. 13, *Jan–Aug 1775*, NYPL. Intelligence, Feb 24, 1775, in Gage

MSS, seems to be the first two pages of this much longer document. Gage is not the author of the words quoted here (contrary to some sources). Instead, the words belong to the unknown author of the Intelligence, which Gage merely forwarded, calling it a "Paper of Intelligence of the Machinations and Projects of these People." Ironically, the letter was endorsed as received by Lord Dartmouth on Apr 19. Prophetic indeed!

31. Philip Stephens to Graves, Jan 28, 1775, in Graves, *Conduct* (Apr 14). This letter came with the arrival of dispatches on the *Nautilus*. Perhaps only now did Gage have about 460 marines under his command. (On the dispute between Gage and Graves on these marines: note 14.) See also appendix 3.

32. Alden, *General Gage in America*, 233, 239–40; Graves, *Conduct* (Apr 16), this portion in *NDAR*, 1:187–88.

33. *JEPCM* (Apr 15, 1775), 146.

34. Barker, Apr 15, 1775, in *British in Boston*, 29; Mackenzie, Apr 16, in *A British Fusilier*, 50.

35. Revere to Belknap [circa 1798]. Graves to Philip Stephens, Apr 11, 1775, in Graves, *Conduct* (Apr 11), shows he ordered the *Somerset* to replace the *Canceaux*, which had in turn previously replaced *Lively*. *Somerset*'s journal in ADM, 51/906, UKNA, says she warped up on Apr 14. *Boyne*'s position is unclear from her journals in ADM, 51/129, UKNA, but she seems to have been in the harbor near Long Wharf. *Asia* was at King's Roads, per her journals, in ADM, 51/67, UKNA. King's Roads is now President Roads, north of Massachusetts's Long Island.

36. Revere to Belknap [circa 1798]. The poem is of course Henry Wadsworth Longfellow, "Paul Revere's Ride," originally in the *Atlantic Monthly*, Jan 1861. Also, Fischer, 88, 99.

37. Fischer, 99.

38. Intelligence, Apr 15, 1775 [written in French], in Gage MSS.

39. Intelligence, Apr 18, 1775, in Gage MSS, given piecemeal in French, *Informers*, 25–28. Though this letter refers to Dr. Church in the third person, it still may be of his authorship.

CHAPTER 7: THE DIE IS CAST

1. Barker, Apr 19, 1775, in *British in Boston*, 34; cf. additional account in Mackenzie, Apr 18, 1775, in *A British Fusilier*, 63.

2. Mackenzie, Apr 18, 1775, in *A British Fusilier*, 52, see also the note.

3. Ibid.

4. Stiles, Aug 21, 1775, in *Literary Diary*, 1:604.

5. Gage's Instructions to Smith, Apr 18, 1775, in Gage MSS, republished in French,

Informers, 31–32. Cf. the draft orders, together with the one given, also in Gage MSS and French, *Informers*, 29–30.

6.   Mr. Waters's statement in Belknap's journal, Oct 25, 1775, in *Proc. of MHS* (1860), 4:84–86.

7.   Appendix 9. On the patrol's route: appendix 8. I suppose they did not fan out until Cambridge, perhaps at Watson's Corner.

8.   Mr. Waters's statement in Belknap's journal, Oct 25, 1775, in *Proc. of MHS* (1860), 4:84–86; Fischer, 93–94.

9.   The entire debate is treated in full in Alden, *General Gage in America*, 247–50. Writing to a friend, Mrs. Gage summarized her private turmoil by quoting Shakespeare's *King John* (from Scene 1, spoken by Blanche of Spain): "The Sun's o'ercast with blood: fair day, adieu! Which is the side that I must go withal? I am with both; each army hath a hand, And in their rage,—I having hold of both,—They whirl asunder, and dismember me... Whoever wins, on that side shall I lose, Assured loss, before the match be played." Mrs. Gage had also reportedly lamented to a friend that she hoped her husband would never be the instrument of sacrificing the lives of her countrymen: Hutchinson, *Diary and Letters*, 1:497–98. Her support to the troops is after Bunker Hill (more later). The legend is that Warren "got intelligence of their whole design; which was to seize Adams and Hancock, who were at Lexington, and burn the stores at Concord." This from Mr. Waters's statement in Belknap's journal, Oct 25, in *Proc. of MHS* (1860), 4:84–86. It may simply have been a rumored story that spread as part of Warren's legend through the military camp in Cambridge (where Belknap was collecting his statements, soon after the Battle of Bunker Hill). Clearly, if the secret well-placed informant existed, the supplied intelligence would have been reliable. But since there was no order to seize Adams and Hancock, the legend of *any* secret informant seems dubious. I have published on this subject at *Journal of the American Revolution* as well (http://allthingsliberty.com/2014/04/dr-joseph-warrens-informant/).

10.   Warren needed no informant, for even the townspeople deduced the same: see text at note 56.

11.   Mackenzie, Apr 18, 1775, in *A British Fusilier*, 52.

12.   Though Gage's "secret" instructions from Lord Dartmouth did encourage the arrest of the Whig leaders, Gage seems to have never given such an order. See appendix 10.

13.   Graves, *Conduct* (Apr 18, 1775), this portion in *NDAR*, 1:192. *Boyne*'s exact position is unclear from her journals, in ADM 51/129, UKNA.

14.   For scraps to that story, see Holland, *William Dawes*, 26ff.

15.   There is no evidence that Dawes (or Revere) carried written intelligence, probably just oral (see note 33). Also, appendix 7.

16. See note 17.

17. Holland, *William Dawes*, 10, 18–19, 35. Charlestown Ferry's boats secured: Wheildon, *Curiosities of History*, 36. The ferry was routinely shut each night, but the new barricade at Boston Neck seems never to have been. If it was, why is there no record of this concern by the Americans? And why did Revere only lately devise the plan of the lanterns from North Church? Rather, the Neck was probably closed that night for this special circumstance.

18. Appendix 7.

19. See note 20. Most of these regimental colonels and their deputies are listed in appendix 3.

20. Mackenzie, Apr 18, 1775, in *A British Fusilier*, 50–51.

21. Noting the obvious advantage of shorter coats, Maj. Gen. John Burgoyne would later order all of his men to cut their coats to such length. More on selecting the flank companies: Spring, *With Zeal*, 60.

22. Letter from a Private Soldier in the Light Infantry, Aug 20, 1775, in Margaret Wheel Willard, ed., *Letters on the American Revolution* (Boston: Houghton Mifflin Co., 1925), 197–200. This letter is generally unreliable in its specific details, but agrees on the 36 rounds, which is what the 1st Brigade carried, per Percy to Gage, Apr 20, 1775. Quote: see note 23.

23. Mr. Waters's statement in Belknap's journal, Oct 25, in *Proc. of MHS* (1860), 4:84–86, source of all the quotes given in this paragraph.

24. Ibid.; appendix 7.

25. Barker, Apr 19, 1775, in *British in Boston*, 31ff.

26. Mackenzie, Apr 18, 1775, in *A British Fusilier*, 50–51. Longboats: appendix 12. Horses: see note 57.

27. Revere to Belknap [circa 1798] calls it a young flood tide. On the tide, *Bickerstaff's Boston Almanack for 1775* has the high tide on Apr 19 as 2:39 a.m., while Donald W. Olson and Russell L. Doescher, "Astronomical Computing: Paul Revere's Midnight Ride," *Sky and Telescope*, April 1992, 437–40, gives it as 1:26 a.m., using modern calculators.

28. Appendix 11.

29. Lister, *Concord Fight*, 21–23. As the embarkation continued, Capt. Lawrence Parsons of the 10th Light Infantry noted his subaltern Hamilton had not shown up, even after having been repeatedly sent for, reportedly too ill for duty. Parsons reported this absence to Smith, the regimental commander for the 10th. Ens. Jeremy Lister, also of the 10th, thought this would be a stain on Smith's expedition, to have one of his own regiment's officers derelict of duty. So Lister volunteered in Hamilton's stead, though Smith wished him to return to his barracks and "not go into danger for others particularly Hamilton[,] whose Illness was suppos'd by everybody to be feign'd". Since it was customary for the

detachment commander's own troops to march at the head of the expedition, Lister thought it would be a disgrace if the expedition's lead company didn't have its full complement of officers. Using this argument, Lister begged permission, for the honor of the regiment, to march in place of Hamilton. At this, Smith relented. A day or so later, it was found that Hamilton had indeed faked his illness to avoid duty.

30. Everett, *Life of Joseph Warren*, 120. Everett's material is completely unsourced: he relied on a host of period letters and on various interviews decades after the fact, though is generally very reliable. It is the present author's theory that Dawes was sent first without a clear message, as a preemptive measure, and only after Warren confirmed the rumors himself did he send Revere. The information Revere supposedly reported (see note 33) is too explicit to have been given without observing the embarkation, which did not muster until 10:00 p.m. Furthermore, Revere says he was summoned "about" 10:00 p.m., in Revere to Belknap [circa 1798], reaffirming the plausibility that Warren first observed the embarkation. The same gives the two met at Warren's house. Who summoned Revere is unknown. This theory is discussed and supported more fully in appendix 7.

31. [John Crozier?] to Dr. Rogers, Apr 23, in Commager and Morris, *The Spirit of 'Seventy-Six*, 77–78; Mr. Waters's statement in Belknap's journal, Oct 25, in *Proc. of MHS* (1860), 4:84–86. The Charles was once much broader, but has since been made narrow by landfill. Fischer, 115, claims the British longboats were strapped together to not get lost as they crossed the Charles on that still moonless early night, but gives no source. This is unlikely. The warship crews were used to operating at open sea, where the sky was darker still, and thus would not need to strap themselves together in this manner. Moreover, it was not completely dark that night: there was still some glow from Boston. Note that the Yankee observer could make out what was going on. I discussed this point in private correspondence with John Harland (author of *Seamanship in the Age of Sail*), May 23, 2010, and he agreed.

32. Some historians have doubted Warren's grasp of the situation, assuming he thought the whole expedition was for Hancock and Adams alone. I doubt this.

33. As noted above, there is no evidence that Revere or Dawes carried written intelligence; it may have just been oral. Fischer, 97, latched on to the statement of Clarke, *Opening of the War*, 3, which gives, "we received intelligence, by express, from the Honorable Joseph Warren, Esq.; at Boston, 'that a large body of the king's troops (supposed to be a brigade of about 12, or 1,500) were embarked in boats from Boston, and gone over to land on Lechmere's Point (so-called) in Cambridge: And that it was shrewdly suspected, that they were ordered to seize and destroy the stores, belonging to the colony, then deposited at Concord'". Fischer deduced from this that there was written intelligence, and these were the words. However, I

do not agree, as the statement itself is written in past tense. At least, this supposed quote was not copied from any written message. Rather, this statement sounds like Clarke's attempt to recreate the scene. Clarke, remember, was indeed at his house when Revere delivered the message. It is *possible* Revere delivered a written message, but Revere was well aware of the facts and needed no parchment. Moreover, no such letter has ever been found, though most other critical documents associated with that day still exist. Clarke's statement "we received intelligence" need not mean written intelligence. While such a letter may have existed, the present author believes there never was a letter, and Revere delivered his message orally, and this is what Clarke attempted to record in his *Opening of the War*, though he did so from memory, perhaps a year later. Revere to Belknap [circa 1798] gives us nothing more, but perhaps this is more proof, for Revere gives ample detail, yet mentions no written message. The only evidence I have ever found of a written message was the dubious statement, given fifty years after the fact, by Sgt. William Munroe, his 1825 deposition in Phinney, *History of the Battle*, 33–35. As Munroe probably never joined Revere and the Whig leaders inside the Clarke home, but remained outside on guard, and as Munroe gave this statement as an old man, fond of his part in the Revolution, one immediately considers his statement suspect. That no single piece of evidence supports Munroe's claim gives us further reason to rule out his statement on this matter entirely. On a separate note, see Fischer, 387–88n17, which discusses the rumor of a third messenger sent out that night.

34. The entire section drawn from Fischer, 99–101, the Newman information of which is cited from the rare Robert Newman Sheets (which I have not seen), in *Robert Newman: His Life and Letters in Celebration of the Bicentennial of His Showing of Two Lanterns in Christ Church, Boston, Apr 18, 1775* (Denver: Newman Family Society, 1975). Much is debated on who hung the lanterns: see Fischer, 388–89n28.

35. Revere to Belknap [circa 1798]; Goss, *Life of Colonel Paul Revere*, 1:188–90n3.

36. Appendix 7. It is presumed *Somerset* had all her guns back aboard (as noted previously, citing Graves, *Conduct* for Mar 31 and Graves to Philip Stephens, Apr 11, in *Conduct*).

37. Goss, *Life of Colonel Paul Revere*, 1:188–90n3. The tradition does not explicitly call it a petticoat, but it was an undergarment, and as such implies she was naked, or nearly, so after stripping it off.

38. Danton, *Theory and Practice of Seamanship*, 282–83. Thanks to Fischer, 104, for this clever bit of literary visualization.

39. Goss, *Life of Colonel Paul Revere*, 1:188–90n3. Goss gives a quaint but doubtless fictional tradition which gives that Revere, having forgotten his spurs for his horse ride, noticed his dog had followed him to the shore and wrote a note to his wife Rachel, tied it to his dog's collar, and sent the canine home. The

faithful dog returned moments later with the spurs in its mouth. This is cute, but highly doubtful. After all, did Revere forget his spurs but remember a quill, ink, and parchment?

40. The timeline is uncertain, and Revere never tells us more about the signals, nor whether he saw them. They did not become the famous icons they are now until perhaps Longfellow wrote of them in his poem (previously cited).

41. Fischer, 103. We are left to wonder what happened to Thomas Bernard, watching for the patrol out front.

42. Charlestown Ferry's boats: see note 17. On the weather: see note 61 below.

43. Details of *Somerset* come from Admiral Graves's 1775 ship list in *NDAR*, 1:47.

44. Revere to Belknap [circa 1798].

45. U.S. Navy's Sun and Moon Calculator gives the moonrise as 9:37 p.m., and on that night it was a waning gibbous with 90 percent of the moon's visible disk illuminated. It is in strong agreement with Revere to Belknap [circa 1798], and helps to corroborate the accuracy of the calculator in giving moon and sun information for dates of antiquity. See also appendix 7.

46. Olson and Doescher, "Astronomical Computing: Paul Revere's Midnight Ride," 437–40. Graves to Philip Stephens, June 16, in Graves, *Conduct* (June 16), gives: "The *Somerset* has hitherto been of very great use at the Ferry between Boston and Charlestown, but…especially as she could be moved only by warping, and that on a flood tide". This comment led me to consider how the *Somerset* was anchored there between the two towns, as a single anchor line from the bow might have allowed her keel to drag in the low water, thus causing her further damage. The *Somerset*'s journal, Apr 19, in *NDAR*, 1:199, gives she was "Moored between Boston and Charlestown". Mooring, by definition, requires she had two anchors down (Smyth, *Sailor's Word Book*, 484), but this could have been a bow-and-stern anchor, or two bower anchors. Revere to Belknap [circa 1798] states of *Somerset*, "It was then young flood, the Ship was winding…" Winding or wending (per Smyth, *Sailor's Word Book*, 727) is defined as "Turning as a ship does to the tide." With these clues, and after extensive private correspondence with the gracious John Harland, author of *Seamanship in the Age of Sail*, we have concluded that *Somerset* must have been moored with two bower anchors, the standard anchorage, as illustrated in his book on the top left of p. 257 ("Maintaining a clear Hawse"). In that figure, up would be east toward Boston Harbor, and the ship in position 1 (the far left of the image) is how *Somerset* probably was when Revere passed her bow (Revere passing along the top of that figure from right to left). One is left to wonder if *Somerset*'s ever increasing leakiness, as given later in the text, was partly because she at times dragged on the riverbed at ebb tide, even though she was approximately pinned in location with her two bower anchors.

47. Danton, *Theory and Practice of Seamanship*, 282–83; appendix 7.

48. See note 102.

49. Elijah Sanderson's [Third] Deposition, Dec 17, 1824, in Phinney, *History of the Battle*, 31–33, and his two earlier depositions in Force, 4:2:489.

50. William Munroe's deposition, Mar 7, 1825, in Phinney, *History of the Battle*, 33–35, which must not be too relied on, as it was given fifty years after the fact; Clarke, *Opening of the War*. Appendix 10.

51. Hurd, *History of Middlesex County, Massachusetts*, 2:619. I have seen no contemporary evidence to support the story at all. But most legends have a grain of truth, and this one probably is true in at least that it was Nelson that alarmed Bedford. The undoubtedly mythical part of the tradition claims one of those patrolmen slashed his sword across Nelson's head, dropping him and causing him to bleed profusely. In truth, such an event likely never happened, for the patrol was cautious and careful not to rile the people, and no other examples exist to support such brutality. Furthermore, Gage had given all his officers explicit orders not to attack or plunder.

52. Appendix 12.

53. Barker, Apr 19, in *British in Boston*, 31ff.; Mackenzie, Apr 18, in *A British Fusilier*, 50–51. Officers accoutered themselves at their own expense and so often wore a quality boot, but the rank and file were accoutered by the regiment's colonel, who always found ways to cut his costs at the men's expense.

54. Barker, Apr 19, in *British in Boston*, 31ff.; Mackenzie, Apr 18, in *A British Fusilier*, 50–51. Tide: see note 27.

55. Beeman: Mr. Waters's statement in Belknap's journal, Oct 25, 1775, in *Proc. of MHS* (1860), 4:84–86; Shattuck, *History of the Town of Concord*, 107. Murray is introduced later in the text. Also, appendix 7.

56. Stedman, *History of the Origin*, 1:119. This incident seems to imply there was no curfew in the town, even though it had been sealed off. However, equally plausible, there was indeed a curfew, and these were gathered members of one or more legally appointed town watch parties. Clearly, if the townspeople guessed the objective of the British march, then Dr. Warren needed no secret informant to deduce it (see text above note 10).

57. Evidence for Smith and Pitcairn on horseback comes with the presentation of the Skirmish at Lexington, q.v. (cf. Mackenzie, *A British Fusilier*, 63n).

58. Revere to Belknap [circa 1798]; Fischer, 106–7, 389nn38–39, give a thorough discussion on the horse. Some say it was named Brown Betty. Larkin was deacon at the First Congregational Church, Charlestown. Regardless, I will use this name to help clearly delineate which horse I am referring to, as a method of clarity.

59. Revere to Belknap [circa 1798] says Devens saw ten mounted, while Revere's Deposition Draft, circa May 1775, in MHS, says he saw nine (from which I

quote). Devens on the Comm.: Revere to Belknap [circa 1798], and *JEPCM* (Feb 9), 89. See also French, *Concord*, 85–86.

60. This was Mark, a black slave, the remains serving as a morbid greeting into Charlestown. Mark's accomplice was burned at the stake. Revere to Belknap [circa 1798], but details from Fischer, 10.

61. Mackenzie, Apr 5, in *A British Fusilier*, 45, gives that it snowed, but by the ninth, in ibid. 46, it had grown mild.

62. Paul Revere's Deposition Draft, circa May 1775, in MHS.

63. This entire episode is a literary retelling to the few scant lines of the incident provided in Revere to Belknap [circa 1798], with some details from Revere's Deposition Draft, circa May 1775, both in MHS.

64. Revere to Belknap [circa 1798]; Fischer, 140.

65. That the 10th was in the first position: see Lister, *Concord Fight*, 21–23. Fischer, 117, hints at the order, but does not mention the marines. Where were the marines? The second position, since Pitcairn was the deputy commander? Or at the end of the column? It is unknown, but see appendix 13. Also, appendix 7.

66. The second account in Mackenzie, Apr 19, in *A British Fusilier*, 62–63.

67. Fischer, 108–9.

68. Appendix 7.

69. Traditional, given in Phinney, *History of the Battle*,16–17. The words Phinney ascribes to Revere are impossible, as Revere would *not* have called them "British troops."

70. Also traditional, in Phinney, *History of the Battle*, 17; Fischer, 109–10.

71. Revere to Belknap [circa 1798]; Fischer, 110–12. Once again, as noted previously, there is no evidence either couriers had written intelligence, it may have just been oral.

72. See appendix 7, where considerable detail is given on this subject. Cf. Holland, *William Dawes and His Ride*, 14.

73. Fischer, 110–12; Revere to Belknap [circa 1798]; Munroe's deposition, 1825.

74. Revere to Belknap [circa 1798]. On the bell: see note 75.

75. Rev. William Gordon to a Gentleman in England, May 17, in Force, 4:2:625–31, gives "the bells have been rung to give the alarm; but let not the sound of bells lead you to think of a ring of bells like what you hear in England; for they are only small-sized bells (one in a parish), just sufficient to notify to the people the time for attending worship, etc."

76. Of the many alarm riders that night, not one of them said, "The British are coming." To do so would have been as nonsensical as a modern American citizen announcing of an approaching police squad, "The Americans are coming!" The Americans colonists were, after all, very much British, and proudly so, even with all of the turmoil. This pride did not diminish with the marching of these troops through the

countryside. For, as most Americans thought, these were troops sent by a wayward Ministry, a Ministry that had deceived their benevolent and beloved King George III, of whom they were still proud to be subjects. In fact, they were resisting the late parliamentary acts precisely because they strongly believed they should be treated as natural born Englishmen, not just as colonists.

77. Fischer, 129.

78. This entire following section, including quotes, from the sources given in note 96, except as cited.

79. Gordon to a Gentleman in England, May 17; Clarke, *Opening of the War*. The latter reports 130 militia first mustered.

80. Revere to Belknap [circa 1798] states 100 rods, or 550 yards (0.31 miles).

81. For all unreferenced quotes throughout this section, see note 96.

82. Holland, *William Dawes and His Ride*, 14–15.

83. Fischer, 134 (and especially 392n18), supposes Revere was trying to steer the patrol away from Lexington (and away from Hancock and Adams), supposing they were in search of the two Whig leaders and hoping to arrest them. This theory is plausible, but the evidence Fischer provided is thin. Furthermore, if this was Revere's plan, he failed miserably, for they immediately set off for Lexington afterward. Moreover, Fischer's theory assumes the British patrol was indeed seeking the Whig leaders, and no evidence supports this. Fischer gives unwarranted credence to Elijah Sanderson's [Third] Deposition, Dec 17, 1824, in Phinney, *History of the Battle*, 31–33, to support his theory, though Fischer rightly notes that the Americans *feared* the British patrol were seeking the Whig leaders. This might be motive for Revere to make such a ploy, but the evidence that he did so is weak. See appendix 10.

84. See note 96.

85. Barker, Apr 19, in *British in Boston*, 31–32; appendix 7. Also, the second account in Mackenzie, Apr 19, in *A British Fusilier*, 62–63. It is strange that the British delayed their expedition for these supplies considering that ever since Apr 7, the men had orders to march with one day's provisions. This per Mackenzie, Apr 7, in ibid., 45–46. Maybe these are the provisions they already had, per Barker.

86. Barker, Apr 19, in *British in Boston*, 31ff.; Coburn, *Battle of April 19*, 48. Coburn details the entire march throughout each village and town, with anecdotes in each. See appendix 7.

87. Fischer, 123–24.

88. Sutherland to Gage, Apr 27; on flankers and De Berniere: De Berniere to Gage [circa Apr 19].

89. For all unreferenced quotes throughout this section, see note 96.

90. The three were Elijah Sanderson, Jonathan Loring, and Solomon Brown; the one-armed peddler was named Allen. Elijah Sanderson's [Third] Deposition, Dec 17, 1824, in Phinney, *History of the Battle*, 31–33. As this source is fifty years after the

fact, his specific details are not trustworthy. His two earlier depositions, the first signed also by Loring and Brown, appear in Force, 4:2:489. Also, Clarke, *Opening of the War*.

91. Twelve British mounted patrol, 5 prisoners. See appendix 9. Sanderson's horse was not swift enough, so one officer slapped it on its hind with his "hanger" (sword belt), keeping it moving, per Elijah Sanderson's [Third] Deposition, Dec 17, 1824, in Phinney, *History of the Battle*, 31–33. I have generally ignored statements such as this, fifty years after the fact, but perhaps we can accept this specific incident, as it happened to Sanderson himself, and he seems to gain nothing by exaggerating it.

92. Perhaps here we can once again use the fifty-year-old info of Elijah Sanderson's [Third] Deposition, Dec 17, 1824, in Phinney, *History of the Battle*, 31–33, as it is supported by the evidence in note 75.

93. Gordon to a Gentleman in England, May 17; Clarke, *Opening of the War*; Munroe's deposition, 1825, in Phinney, *History of the Battle*, 33–35; the deposition of 34 participants, in Force, 4:2:492. In placing these two events together, I suggest that Clarke's *Opening of the War* is incorrect in that the first scout returned at about 2:30 a.m., not "Between 3 and 4" as Clarke proclaims. See appendix 7 for support on this claim.

94. Revere's Deposition Draft, circa May 1775. Fischer, 135, supports this supposition.

95. Fischer, 136–37, gives more detail on Brown Beauty.

96. This entire section is drawn from Revere to Belknap [circa 1798]; Revere's Deposition Draft, circa May 1775; and occasionally drawing for clarity from (but discounting any discrepancy in) Revere's Deposition Draft [Corrected Copy], circa May 1775. All three are in MHS.

97. Emerson's diary in Emerson, *Complete Works*, 11:567–68, also in Commager and Morris, *The Spirit of 'Seventy-Six*, 84–85; Fischer, "The Alarm" in *Paul Revere's Ride*, 138–48 (see the map on 146). Fischer, 287, gives the fates of Dawes and both Prescotts.

98. Coburn, *Battle of April 19*, 50–51.

99. The second account in Mackenzie, Apr 19, in *A British Fusilier*, 62–63.

100. Thomas Robins and David Harrington were the milkmen driving a wagon of fresh milk from Lexington to Boston. Coburn, *Battle of April 19*, 51; Fischer 125. I suppose this is the same story described in Sutherland to Gage, Apr 27, and draw extra details from it. However, the various accounts of prisoners taken are difficult to reconcile, particularly when one considers the American and British evidence against each other. Cf. Fischer, 127, which supposes Sutherland was not mounted until near 4:00 a.m., when he took Asahel Porter and Josiah Richardson, the story described in Coburn, *Battle of April 19*, 57–58. This seems unlikely, since Sutherland describes the event that gave him a horse as occurring well before Mitchell and the British patrol came up, while Coburn gives Porter and Richardson

were not captured until near the Lexington line, thus just before the battle, well after Mitchell's arrival. NB: Fischer, 127, claims that the Murray that served as a Tory guide was Daniel Murray (brother to Samuel), but gives no reference. Daniel seems to not have been involved that day, but Samuel definitely was. More on Murray: chap. 9, n. 135. Adair was for a time in a chaise after this event, but must have been in a horse shortly thereafter (more on this: chap. 8, n. 31).

101. Coburn, *Battle of April 19*, 54–55.

102. Coburn, *Battle of April 19*, 52–54. The three Whigs were Col. Azor Orne (Comm. of Safety), Elbridge Gerry, and Col. Jeremiah Lee (Comm. of Supply). Lee would die a few weeks later thanks to a fever caught in this episode. Fischer, 391n23, warns this section of Coburn is strongly biased against Elbridge Gerry, as it was used as an anti-election weapon when Gerry ran as Massachusetts governor. See also French, *Concord*, 85–86. Dr. Warren did not attend the meeting of Apr 18.

103. Coburn, *Battle of April 19*, 56.

104. Gage, *Circumstantial Account*; Sutherland to Gage, Apr 27; De Berniere to Gage [circa Apr 19]; appendix 7. Adair: appendix 13.

105. Hagist, "How Old Were Redcoats? Age and Experience of British Soldiers in America."

106. Appendix 7; Letter from Boston, July 5, 1775, in *Detail and Conduct of the American War*, 9–10.

107. Revere to Belknap [circa 1798]. Appendix 10.

108. Later that day, Hancock would send for both his ladies, as well as a fine salmon he had planned to eat for dinner. Madam Scott's statement in *NEHGR* (1854), 8:187–88; Munroe's deposition, 1825.

109. Fischer, 179; appendix 7.

110. Munroe's deposition, 1825. Perhaps a few stayed to guard those remaining at the house.

111. This earliest version of the quotation is from John Eliot, *A Biographical Dictionary* (Salem, MA: Cushing and Appleton; Boston: Edward Oliver, 1809), 10, which states the exchange happened "after the day dawned". Eliot would have known Samuel Adams personally, and may have confirmed the story. A slightly different version is in Gordon, *History of the Rise*, 1:311. Modern histories, like Fischer, 183, in considering the first shots were at dawn and the dialogue was also at dawn, put the two together and report the dialogue was Samuel Adams responding to having heard the first shots as they escaped Lexington. And yet, all three of Paul Revere's statements, including his two depositions given immediately afterward, give a timeline that confirms Adams and Hancock were well on their way to Woburn about 1.5 hours before dawn, since Revere himself went with these men at least part of the way (the earlier depositions say 2 miles, the 1798 letter suggests all the way) and still had time to go all the way back to collect the papers at Buckman Tavern,

just as the British were arriving (at dawn). Hence, if this traditional commentary from Adams indeed occurred upon departing Lexington or on the way to Woburn, it was before the first shots were fired. Alternatively, if the commentary was said at Woburn (likely, since they were there by dawn and this matches the Eliot timeline), then Adams and Hancock were well beyond where they could have heard those first shots. In either case, the traditional commentary was not said in response to having heard the first shots.

112. Revere to Belknap [circa 1798], etc. See note 111.

Chapter 8: The Rending of an Empire

1. Phinney, *History of the Battle*, 18–19; Clarke, *Opening of the War*; Munroe's deposition, 1825.
2. Mackenzie, Apr 19, in *A British Fusilier*, 51, gives it. I have seen it in another contemporary source, but the reference is lost. The exchange here is assumed.
3. Sutherland to Gage, Apr 27; Lister, *Concord Fight*, 23; Pitcairn to Gage, Apr 26.
4. Pitcairn to Gage, Apr 26.
5. Sutherland to Gage, Apr 27.
6. Winship's deposition in Force, 4:2:490. It is difficult to reconcile the incidents of how each prisoner was taken as reported by the British with those reported by the Americans.
7. Sutherland to Gage, Apr 27.
8. Ibid. Wellington: Murdock, *Late News*, 16n; Phinney, *History of the Battle*, 19.
9. This whole section comes from Sutherland to Gage, Apr 27. Cf. Reverend Gordon to a Gentleman in England, May 17.
10. Lister, *Concord Fight*, 23; Pitcairn to Gage, Apr 26. Also, Simon Winship's deposition in Force, 4:2:490.
11. *New Manual and Platoon Exercise.* The debris of 200 paper cartridges is noted in Munroe's deposition, 1825, almost the exact number we should expect from six companies of thirty-two men each (or five companies of thirty-two men plus the marine company of forty-six men). See appendix 11; appendix 13.
12. Pitcairn to Gage, Apr 26; appendix 7.
13. Phinney, *History of the Battle*, 19; Clarke, *Opening of the War*; Munroe's deposition, 1825. Was Parker in the tavern or the meetinghouse? Phinney, 18, says the former, 19 says the latter. Most sources say the tavern. (Where else could an annoyed Yankee sit to take the edge off? Cf. Coburn, *Battle of April 19*, 62.) Sutherland to Clinton, Apr 26, or to Gage, Apr 27, gives nothing of the Bowman episode, so probably he knew nothing of it. Apparently, Sutherland was no longer in the most advance position.
14. Revere to Belknap [circa 1798].
15. Coburn, *Battle of April 19*, 59, 62 (which gives his age and date of death), and his

Muster Rolls appendix p. 5; Sylvanus Wood's deposition, 1826, in Dawson, *Battles*, 22–23, also in Commager and Morris, *The Spirit of 'Seventy-Six*, 82–83.

16. Rev. John Marrett's diary, Apr 19, in Samuel Dunster, *Henry Dunster and His Descendants* (Central Falls, RI: E. L. Freeman & Co., 1876), 84, which calls it cold, not cool. Belknap's entry for the day calls it "fair, cool wind", per the note in Murdock, *Nineteenth of April*, 55. Cf. the weather as noted in Mackenzie, Apr 5, 9, in *A British Fusilier*, 45, 46.

17. Munroe's deposition, 1825; De Berniere to Gage [circa Apr 19]. Cf. Sylvanus Wood's deposition, 1826, in Dawson, *Battles*, 22–23, which gives: "formed us in single file…the whole number was thirty-eight, and no more."

18. Gordon to a Gentleman in England, May 17; captured British Lieutenant Gould's deposition in Force, 4:2:500–501. The former source reports sixty or seventy Lexington militia now mustered. Coburn, *Battle of April 19*, 166–68, reports seventy-seven of the 144 total Lexington militia were present. The Lexington Hist. Soc. website, http://lhsoc.weebly.com/frequently-asked-questions1.html (published on July 24, 2009; accessed on Apr 5, 2010), gives a slightly different list of participants, some eighty men, as identified by local historian Bill Poole and the reenactment company calling themselves the Lexington Minute Man Company, out of 146 total.

19. Munroe's deposition, 1825, claims the front "platoon" consisted of eight or nine men. How can this be? If we assume the three-rank system (French, *Concord*, 137) is applied here, then as given in appendix 11, the 10th and the 4th companies were about thirty-two total, or about eleven wide by three deep. Perhaps Munroe's memory was lacking when he gave that deposition fifty years after the fact? Or, perhaps this front "platoon" was Adair's advance party, eight or nine strong (probably the case). Also see appendix 13.

20. Sutherland to Gage, Apr 27.

21. Lister, *Concord Fight*, 24; Barker, Apr 19, in *British in Boston*, 32.

22. Sanderson's [Second or Lone] deposition, Force, 4:2:489.

23. Clarke, *Opening of the War*, Robbins's deposition, Force 4:2:491, and Draper's deposition in ibid., 495, all claim the British huzzahed as they charged onto the Green, not once they fanned out, as Willard's deposition, Force 4:2:489–90, suggests. Captured British Lieutenant Gould's deposition, in Force, 4:2:500–501, suggests the huzzahs continued throughout.

24. Barker, Apr 19, in *British in Boston*, 32; echoed in Smith to Gage, Apr 22.

25. Murdock, *Nineteenth of April*, asks the same question on 23ff., where he muses whether or not Samuel Adams, known to be an instigator of violence, ordered Parker to stand there and provoke the British.

26. Clarke, *Opening of the War*.

27. Parker's deposition, Force, 4:2:491.

28. Revere's Deposition Draft, circa May 1775, at MHS. Old men that thought fifty years later of that order; in the 1825 depositions, in Phinney, *History of the Battle*, 31ff., remembered it as "Stand your ground! Don't fire unless fired upon! But if they want to have a war let it begin here!" This line is of course completely out of character with the real Parker. See Coburn, *Battle of April 19*, 32 and the note.

29. French, *Concord*, 137.

30. Munroe's deposition, 1825; Draper's deposition, Force, 4:2:495. Willard's deposition, Force, 4:2:489–90, gives eight rods (132 feet).

31. Sutherland to Gage, Apr 27. Adair was for a time in a chaise, per this source (French, *Informers*, 45). One can imagine Adair taking to a chaise, only to later be chastised for it by Pitcairn, for he could hardly set the pace in such a vehicle. Moreover, based on the evidence used in the following text, we are given no reports of a British officer in a chaise on Lexington Green. Perhaps Adair was one of those on a horse by then. The details remain murky.

32. Parker's deposition, Force, 4:2:491.

33. Clarke, *Opening of the War*.

34. Munroe's deposition, 1825.

35. Pitcairn to Gage, Apr 26. Cf. Smith to Gage, Apr 22, which suggests the hedge wall is on the left, though perhaps Smith meant only the militia dispersed to the left (to the south).

36. This is implied, as the grenadiers come up shortly after and remain on the road south of the Green. Though I tell elsewhere in these notes how Amos Doolittle's drawings are not to be trusted in regards to the position of troops, I must here admit that Doolittle too shows the bulk of the troops continuing on the road, in his engraving *Plate I: The Battle of Lexington, April 19, 1775*.

37. Pitcairn to Gage, Apr 26; Sutherland to Gage, Apr 27; Willard's deposition, Force, 4:2:489–90.

38. De Berniere to Gage [circa Apr 19].

39. Pitcairn to Gage, Apr 26.

40. Sutherland to Gage, Apr 27.

41. Pitcairn to Gage, Apr 26; Sutherland to Gage, Apr 27; De Berniere to Gage [circa Apr 19].

42. Clarke, *Opening of the War*.

43. Willard's deposition, Force, 4:2:489–90. Plenty of variations on these lines in the various depositions (see surrounding pages of ibid.).

44. Fessenden's deposition in Force, 4:2:495–96, gives that they continued to huzzah until shots were fired. This is seconded by captured British Lieutenant Gould's deposition in Force, 4:2:500–501.

45. Munroe's deposition, 1825, admits that the Americans did fire shots from the tavern, though he denies these happened before the British fired first. Clarke, *Opening of the*

War, denies that men fired from the meetinghouse, "unless after the dispersion of our men", which proves he really did not know. Captured British Lieutenant Gould's deposition, in Force, 4:2:500–501, gives it best (perhaps under duress): "which party fired first, I cannot exactly say". The second account in Mackenzie's diary, Apr 19, in *A British Fusilier*, 62ff., gives: "Shots were immediately fired; but from which side could not be ascertained, each party imputing it to the other." However, several reliable British sources say the Americans fired first, while early American sources deny this. The personal theory of the present author is that some perhaps solitary American indeed fired first, without orders, likely from the sidelines. Consider the evidence. First, the American claims that the British fired first (the American depositions in Force, 4:2:486–501) also falsely suggest the Americans never fired at all (a few hint of it, but most ignore the Americans fired). Only the late American depositions, 1825, in Phinney, *History of the Battle*, 31ff., explicitly admit the Americans indeed fired (e.g., Munroe's deposition, 1825), something always known from British accounts. Such a glaring omission or falsity places the reliability of those early depositions in question. Second, those first depositions were all taken days after the battle in an explicit attempt to paint the Americans as innocent victims, and were intended as propaganda for newspapers. Thus, given the agenda, how can we trust those early American depositions on such a crucial question? Yes, they were sworn depositions, but perhaps that is why they merely omit discussing the Americans firing. Certainly, the Americans had the most to gain from claiming the British had fired first. In contrast, the British accounts, all for private use and written shortly after the battle, seem to generally accept their role in the day's later affairs (see note 145), even accepting that the they themselves (the British) were responsible at Concord. Why were they truthful about Concord but not about Lexington? They had nothing to gain by lying to their personal diaries or to Gage. Thus, the British accounts are more believable, and three such accounts (Pitcairn to Gage, Apr 26; Sutherland to Gage, Apr 27; Lister, *Concord Fight*, 24), all generally accurate in other known details, claim the Americans fired first, though they disagree on where exactly the first shot came from. Third, dozens of Lexington men testified under oath that some British officers ordered their men to fire, but there is far too much stronger evidence against this, including the British sources themselves—which, while perhaps having the potential for bias, were again accurate for the rest of the day's events. What those Lexington men probably heard, over the din of the skirmish, was the British officers telling their men to NOT fire. So the Lexington men probably were not lying, they were just mistaken. But it again brings us to doubt the American claims. Fourth, the early American depositions describe only the actions of the militia company on the Green (they did not shoot first), and give us nothing about what some American spectator on the sidelines may have done to provoke the skirmish. Indeed, I agree with the American statements that "they" (those on the Green) did not shoot first. Finally, we must admit that some of the Lexington militia had been hanging out in the tavern, some drinking while awaiting the rumored British march. Thus, we cannot rule out that alcohol may have been a factor. In contrast, the British soldiers, while lacking combat experience, were not all young and untrained as so often is said, and therefore likely to follow orders (see Hagist, "How Old Were Redcoats?"). I expand on my theory, which is only a theory and can never be proven, in my article "Who Shot First? The Americans!" *Journal of the American Revolution*, Apr 16, 2014, http://allthingsliberty.com/2014/04/who-shot-first-the-americans/. Also, see the debate in French, *Informers*, 47ff., with all of the British evidence presented. Cf. Gordon to a Gentleman in England, May 17; Fischer, 194; French, *Concord*, 111ff.

46. Those muskets, even if kept in pristine condition (likely for those drilling regularly), were prone to misfire by virtue of their imperfect design.

47. Some dubious claims give that the Yankees thought the shots were only powder and no balls, used only as intimidation—they were of course wrong. Sylvanus Wood's late deposition, 1826, in Dawson, *Battles*, 22–23, gives that he still thought this was the case, even fifty years after the fact. This sentiment echoed in Shattuck, *History of the Town of Concord*, 104. However, I have found no contemporary evidence to support this was the fear at the time.

48. Almost all of the early American depositions obstinately deny that the Americans shot at all. This is absurd, as Pitcairn's horse was wounded, as was a soldier in the 10th. Later depositions, such as Munroe's of 1825, finally admit that indeed the Americans did fire, though Munroe still insisted the British fired first.

49. Lister, *Concord Fight*, 24; Pitcairn to Gage, Apr 26; and referenced in all the other British accounts. Fischer, 403n47, explains that no Johnson was on the muster roll for the 10th, but a Thomas Johnston was listed as transferred from another company of the 10th to the light infantry, effective Apr 24. He cites the 10th Muster Roll, WO, 12/2750, PRO, now part of the UKNA.

50. Ebenezer Munroe's deposition, 1825, in Phinney, *History of the Battle*, 36–37.

51. Revere to Belknap [circa 1798].

52. Pitcairn to Gage, Apr 26; Rev. Gordon to a Gentleman in England, May 17; Munroe's deposition, 1825.

53. Munroe's deposition, 1825, at least gives a second fire, but from which "platoon" he is not specific. However, Robbins's deposition, in Force, 4:2:491, for instance, says just one volley. Spectator Benjamin Tidd's deposition, in ibid., 492, says "fired a volley or two", and that of spectators Mean and Harrington, in ibid., 494–95, gives "several volleys".

54. Clarke, *Opening of the War*; Munroe's deposition, 1825; and various other depositions in Force, 4:2:490ff. All of these misunderstandingly claim Pitcairn was gesturing to fire, not cease fire. Stiles, Aug 21, in *Literary Diary*, 1:605, states secondhand information that Pitcairn "struck his staff or Sword downwards with all

Earnestness as the signal to forbear or cease firing." Fessenden's firsthand deposition (Force, 4:2:495–96) states "he brandished his sword over his head three times".

55. Barker, Apr 19, in *British in Boston* 32.

56. Munroe's deposition, 1825.

57. De Berniere to Gage [circa Apr 19].

58. Sutherland to Gage, Apr 27.

59. Ibid.

60. Smith to Maj. R. Donkin, Oct 8, in French, *Informers*, 62, original in Gage MSS. Maj. R[obert?] Donkin is, according to a letter signed by him of Sept 15 and dated Boston (also in Gage MSS), an aide-de-camp, probably to Gage. *LGFO*, 98, names Robert Donkin, later of the 44th Regiment.

61. Gage, *Circumstantial Account*, footnote.

62. Ebenezer Munroe's deposition, 1825, in Phinney, *History of the Battle*, 36–37.

63. Barker, Apr 19, in *British in Boston*, 32.

64. Phinney, *History of the Battle*, 21.

65. Charles Hudson, *History of the Town of Lexington, Middlesex County, Massachusetts* … (Boston: Houghton Mifflin Company, 1913), 1:153. Phinney, *History of the Battle*, 21, says he was killed on the field.

66. Clarke, *Opening of the War*. Another of the dead was Asahel Porter, captured earlier by the British column, who attempted to escape during the fighting.

67. Barker, Apr 19, in *British in Boston*, 32. Cf. the second account in Mackenzie, Apr 19, in *A British Fusilier*, 62ff., which tells that Smith's officers attempted to dissuade him of the expedition. This is unsubstantiated, and given the many other problems of the Lexington portion of this second account, as described in ibid., 65n1, it is dubious.

68. Note until they heard the alarm at Lexington Green, the light infantry had marched the entire expedition with guns unloaded. The grenadiers only loaded after they had balls whizzing by, per Gage, *Circumstantial Account*, footnote. The grenadiers' first fire was at Lexington Green (see present text: Sutherland's wayward horse was saved by them). It is logical to presume, as the British were genuinely attempting to avoid bloodshed, and as their men had just shown themselves out of control, that they emptied their muskets not as a show of celebration, but as a prudent measure to avoid further bloodshed as they proceeded farther into an enraged countryside. There are no reports of the British reloading their muskets on Lexington Green.

69. Clarke, *Opening of the War*; Sutherland to Gage, Apr 27.

70. The product of residents clearing their farms of boulders that had littered their land.

71. Smith to Gage, Apr 22.

72. Sutherland to Gage, Apr 27. Perhaps two of these fired the warning guns that Smith saw, as noted below.

73. Smith to Maj. R. Donkin, Oct 8, in French, *Informers*, 62, original in Gage MSS.

74. Clarke, *Opening of the War*, gives 150–200, but he was not there. Amos Barrett's Letter of 1825 gives they were 150 before sunrise (but possibly more at this point, two hours later), and that they were minutemen. Emerson's diary in Emerson, *Complete Works*, 11:568, gives where they were from.

75. See note 76.

76. Barker, Apr 19, in *British in Boston*, 32. The falling back of the militia is supported in the depositions in Force, 4:2:497–501. It would be interesting to know what flag they flew! In private correspondence with Mr. Peter Ansoff (July 2010), former president of the North American Vexillological Association, he provided a suitable argument *against* the tradition that there was a "Sons of Liberty" flag of red and white stripes at the time, if ever. Instead, the Concord flag may have been a British union flag or red ensign. In that era, such flags were considered the King's property—not for use by private citizens—so to use one would be to express defiance.

77. Appendix 7.

78. Fischer, 209.

79. Barker, Apr 19, in *British in Boston*, 32. These general events are supported by the depositions in Force, 4:2:497–501. These American depositions, however, suggest that the militia withdrew only after they saw the British detachment headed for North Bridge. This is unlikely, as Barker talks of the cutting down of the Liberty Pole as if he was there, and yet he went to North Bridge as well. The only way Barker could have witnessed both was if they occurred in the order given in the present text. Thus, the American depositions are either unclear or false: they did not give way merely because they anticipated the British going northward; they fled again before the redcoats. One must assume they lingered then somewhere north of town until they saw the British indeed marching for the North Bridge. Amos Doolittle's *Plate II: A View of the Town of Concord* engraving shows Pitcairn and Smith at the burial ground. Amos Barrett's Letter of 1825 suggests they departed with fife and drum, and the British also played theirs, together making "grand Musick". But no other statement supports this, and Barrett's was written fifty years after the fact. Instead, the British were still very much on alert and wary of bringing more militia to obstruct them or endanger them, and so undoubtedly they remained silent until their return to Lexington, as given later in the text.

80. De Berniere to Gage [circa Apr 19]; etc.

81. Sutherland to Gage, Apr 27.

82. Barrett's deposition, in Force, 4:2:499. See note 79.

83. There were ten light infantry total. Six were sent to the North Bridge, and as we shall see in the text, a seventh was sent for their support soon after. Remember too that Smith had previously ordered Pitcairn to march ahead with six light infantry

companies to take the *bridges*, plural, per his orders from Gage (Orders in French, *Informers*, 31–32). So now Smith must have sent at least one, but no more than three, the number of light infantry companies unaccounted for, to the South Bridge. I have seen no contemporary account of the number sent, but we can suppose Smith kept at least one light company with him beside the one he would later send to the North Bridge. As there were no stores to seek out at the South Bridge, we might guess he sent few there. Mackenzie's map in *British Fusilier*, facing 78, shows what appears to be two companies at the South Bridge. One might guess these were the 47th and 59th, two of the three lights not accounted for in our text, while the marines, being the largest company, were quite likely kept as the flankers over the town, also supported by Mackenzie's map. Furthermore, if we read between the lines of Gould's deposition, Force, 4:2:500–501, where he says that once the light infantry were on the hill, those detached to the bridges "were ordered down", it suggests those lights that were not sent (or immediately sent) to the bridges remained on the hill, thus as a guard.

84. On the map in Smith's hands, see French, *Informers*, 33.

85. Laurie to Gage, Apr 26.

86. Sutherland to Gage, Apr 27.

87. French, *Informers*, 99; Gould's deposition in Force, 4:2:500–501. Tradition gives also that this hill was one of perhaps several predetermined rally points for a militia alarm.

88. Ripley, *History of the Fight*, 19.

89. Laurie to Gage, Apr 26.

90. Multiple sources name the 4th, 43rd, and 10th, but the only source to name these and the 52nd, is Lister, *Concord Fight*, 25, who also mentions Kelly. The distance of the second detachment is given in Barker, Apr 19, in *British in Boston*, 33, and repeated in Sutherland to Gage, Apr 27. The 38th is named in ibid., as is its commander, Captain Boyd. Laurie to Gage, Apr 26 names the 5th, and thus we account for all six companies. See French, *Informers*, 85ff., for more. Gould's deposition, in Force, 4:2:500–501, confirms his command. French, *Informers*, 88n4, gives the first names of the commanders of the 38th and 52nd: Capt. St. Lawrence Boyd of the former, Capt. William Browne of the latter, not to be confused with Capt. John Brown, also of the 52nd (see note 103). Lister, 25, notes the 4th and the 10th were positioned "to Command the road he had to go". That is, the two hills commanded the westerly road to Barrett's Farm, though they also commanded the northerly road to Punkatasset Hill.

91. Smith to Gage, Apr 22.

92. Ibid.

93. *JEPCM*, 515ff.

94. Clarke, *Opening of the War*.

95. French, *Concord*, 180, gives that it was at Elisha Jones's house, across from the Old Manse, but this was based on traditions of the town tied to misunderstood information. It was not until new evidence in the Gage MSS was discovered, as outlined in French, *Informers*, that proves such a tradition is false: for the troops near the bridge were on the west side of the Concord River, not on the east side by Jones's home. Instead, the tradition probably has some merit, and I suppose that soldiers did indeed line up for water at some well, being famished and dehydrated from the long march, but this well could have been any of the number of wells in the town, as most homes had them. It is doubtful any troops lined up at Elisha Jones's house, however, as his home was out of the way from any of the British positions that day.

96. Ripley, *History of the Fight*, 19; Amos Barrett's Letter of 1825, note.

97. Ripley, *History of the Fight*, 19; Abiel Holmes, *American Annals* (Cambridge, MA: W. Hilliard, 1805), 2:326n2, also in French, *Concord*, 177. The Holmes version predates the Ripley version—a good reason to use it perhaps, being closer to contemporary, while Ripley gives no source. However, the Holmes versions seems a bit of fictional dramatization.

98. Ripley, *History of the Fight*, 19–20.

99. Gordon to a Gentleman in England, May 17, gives sixty barrels, as does Emerson's diary in Emerson, *Complete Works*, 11:568; Barker, *British in Boston*, 33, gives "about 100 barrels of flour".

100. Gordon to a Gentleman in England, May 17; with extra details from Smith to Gage, Apr 22, and Barker, *British in Boston*, 33. A musket ball was about ¾" (1.905 cm) diameter, at a volume of 3.62 cm^3 each. Most were made of lead, which weighs about 11.34 g/cm^3, giving each ball a weight of about 41.0 g. Now, 500 total pounds of balls, or 226,796.185 total grams, equates to about 5,525 balls. Not counting spacing between the balls, together they made a volume of almost exactly 20,000 cm^3, or about 20 liters, or 5.28 gallons. If we arbitrarily figure in a 10 percent increase for spacing, we have, in round terms, about 6 gallons or 22 liters. All of these could have fit into a single quarter barrel called a firkin (≈41 liters), but that one barrel would have weighed 500 pounds! Perhaps they were distributed to at least two separate quarter barrels?

101. Marquis De Chastellux, *Travels in North America in the Years 1780–81–82* (London: G. G. J. and J. Robinson, 1787, 2nd ed.), 2:218–221; French, *Concord*,174–76. One contemporary heard a rumor that Pitcairn crowed over their discovery, declaring these three pieces alone made the whole expedition worth it (hardly!). Gordon to a Gentleman in England, May 17 is the "contemporary" I speak of, but he wrongly gives that there were just two 24s, while the Draft Instructions of Gage to Smith, Apr 18, in Gage MSS, republished in French, *Informers*, 29ff., states there were expected to be three 24s there in the prison yard. Smith to Gage, Apr 22, also confirms there were three pieces, though does not give their size. (Gordon

claims the two 24s are the only cannon found.) By knocking off the trunnions, the cannon were rendered unmountable and unaimable.

102. Ripley, *History of the Fight*, 13–14.

103. Laurie to Gage, Apr 26. Capt. John Brown of the 52nd traveled with De Berniere through the countryside: note 90. Grant: also in Sutherland to Gage, Apr 27; name from *LGFO*, 203.

104. Laurie to Gage, Apr 26.

105. Lister, *Concord Fight*, 25.

106. Ibid.

107. Barker, *British in Boston*, 33.

108. The actual company commander for the 10th was Parsons, while that of the 4th was apparently Capt. Nesbit Balfour (Fischer, 322). Balfour was on special assignment with a detachment to Marshfield, near Plymouth. Fischer, 402n34, which claims Balfour was indeed at the bridge, was based on Fischer's logical assumption, not knowing of Marshfield. Gould's own deposition, in Force, 4:2:500–501, confirms his command.

109. Lister, *Concord Fight*, 25–26. Lister erroneously wrote the 23rd, an obvious error here corrected.

110. Sutherland to Gage, Apr 27.

111. Laurie to Gage, Apr 26. French, *Informers*, 101–4, gives a convincing theory that Sutherland was in the Manse field during the skirmish, along with two others, and that these three are who is depicted in Amos Doolittle's engraving *Plate III: The Engagement at the North Bridge in Concord*. In that engraving, the three are depicted without horses. While we know Sutherland was mounted at the first encounter at Lexington, here he was perhaps not. Maybe he donated his horse to this urgent messenger. In any case, it seems that Robertson returned with Smith's response rather quickly, certainly well before the grenadiers could march up; hence Robertson was certainly not on foot. Robertson's name from Lister, *Concord Fight*, 26.

112. Laurie to Gage, Apr 26.

113. French, *Concord*, 184. Coburn, *Battle of April 19*, 80–81 (and appendix 14), with his valuable work with the muster rolls, gives 443 total men (if we arbitrarily assign a reasonable forty men per company to those companies whose size is unknown). Also, Robinson, Spring, Bancroft, Adams's deposition and Gould's deposition, in Force, 4:2:500–501. On the British, if we go back to our estimates in appendix 11, each company was about 32 men each, or 96 men, plus the 8 officers (see note 156), or 104 men. On the wall: Barker, *British in Boston*, 33.

114. See note 115 below.

115. Most of this section, especially Mrs. Barrett's quotes from Ripley, *History of the Fight*, 20–21. On the cannon at the farm: Gage's Instructions to Smith [Draft],

in Gage MSS, republished in French, *Informers*, 29–31. Also, Emerson's diary in Emerson, *Complete Works*, 11:568. On 140 troops: four companies times thirty-two men plus three officers per company, plus Parsons, Grant the artilleryman, De Berniere, about 143 total (see appendix 11). Additional sources: French, *Concord*, 179–80; De Berniere to Gage [circa Apr 19].

116. Amos Barrett's Letter of 1825; Shattuck, *History of the Town of Concord*, 107.

117. Gordon to a Gentleman in England, May 17; with extra details from Smith to Gage, Apr 22, and Barker, *British in Boston*, 33. As given in note 101, Gordon was wrong in that there was only two 24s. It is thus conjecture, but he is probably also wrong that there were just two 24-pounder carriages.

118. Ripley, *History of the Fight*, 20.

119. Martha Moulton's (of Concord) Petition, Feb 4, 1776, in Frothingham, *Siege*, 369–70. It is generally believed by modern historians that the British did not intentionally set fire to the courthouse, as Martha's petition implies, nor did Pitcairn and other officers sit and sneer before she finally convinced them to begin a bucket brigade. Such action was contrary to the morals of the real-life British officers there, who deplored the idea of wanton destruction of private property as much as the Yankees did. Furthermore, they had positive orders from Gage to protect private property. And, as we have seen in his dealing with Graves, Pitcairn was an upstanding military officer. Rather, Moulton was looking for compensation for her service (she received £3), and her petition is flavored accordingly.

120. Depositions in Force, 4:2:497–501.

121. French, *Concord*, 183–88; Coburn, *Battle of April 19*, 169, 173, 177; Shattuck, *History of the Town of Concord*, 111.

122. French, *Concord*, 185–86; Emerson's diary in Emerson, *Complete Works*, 11:569.

123. Shattuck, *History of the Town of Concord*, 111.

124. Laurie to Gage, Apr 26.

125. Lister, *Concord Fight*, 26. Also, Sutherland to Gage, Apr 27.

126. Ripley, *History of the Fight*, 23, attributes this to Davis and Buttrick, Shattuck, *History of the Town of Concord*, 111, makes it more general.

127. Amos Barrett's Letter of 1825; James Barrett's deposition in Force, 4:2:499.

128. We can perhaps forgive the other officers of their inexperience, but if Barker was wise enough to know what was proper and yet never acted upon it, then Barker is as much to blame as any other.

129. Solomon Smith's dubious [First] Deposition, 1835, for instance, echoed by others, all of which are published in Adams, *Address Delivered at Acton*, 45–46, also in Adams, *Letter to Lemuel Shattuck*, 16–17 (which is no letter at all, but a booklet). On some of the theories why Davis marched first, see French, *Concord*, 188n1. One theory is that only the Acton men had bayonets, though I have seen no evidence to support this.

130. A late but unsubstantiated and dubious claim gives that a single Acton fifer and drummer near the van shrilled and beat the song "The White Cockade" as they marched. (More likely, the nonaggressive militia silently marched like regular soldiers down the hill, keeping their muskets unprovokingly at their sides.) This claim comes from Charles Handley's deposition, 1835, in Adams, *Address Delivered at Acton*, 46–47, also in Adams, *Letter to Lemuel Shattuck*, 18–19, and is the only statement of its kind. That it was made sixty years after the event makes it utterly dubious. No contemporary source supports this claim, and it is strange that so many historians report it as fact. See D. Michael Ryan, "White Cockade: A Jacobite Air at the North Bridge?" accessed Dec 4, 2009, http://lincolnminutemen .org/history/articles/ryan_white_cockade.html.

131. French, *Concord*, 187–90; Amos Barrett's Letter of 1825. Barrett says they "marched 2 Deep", while Sutherland to Gage, Apr 27, says they marched in "Divisions" (see French, *Informers*, 89n2). Shattuck, *History of the Town of Concord*, 111, calls this motion wheeling about, but to wheel is to pivot on one end of the line. They probably did a left face then marched in column with the head going north for a moment before turning to the right, 180°, onto the northerly road that led from Punkatasset back to the bridge, and there, meeting the westerly road that came from Barrett's Farm, turned left (east), and so headed for the bridge.

132. Lister, *Concord Fight*, 27.

133. French, *Concord*, 189–90.

134. Laurie to Gage, Apr 26. Strangely, French in his *Informers*, 101, supposes the British could not possibly fan out in line formation across the road because of the wall. This wall was, like most in Concord that still exist today, only knee-high or so. So while a line formation would have been broken slightly with the wall cutting the line twice, on either side of the road, there is no reason they could not have formed in line formation. Whatever French's logic, perhaps this is why, on 102, he supposes that the 43rd never did form up along the riverbank. It is true that Laurie's letter only says this was his intent, to line the riverbank, but if French's logic is correct, that the 43rd never moved there, then they blocked the way out front. Yet this cannot be, for the 43rd was the closest to the bridge and thus the first to cross. They could not have remained in front to block the retreat of the other two companies across the bridge. And yet their Lieutenant Hull is mortally wounded here, and thus he at least, if not his company, was nearer the bridge. This is best explained if we assume the 43rd did indeed take up the north side riverbank, and thus it was most likely they who fired the warning shots. We also know the 4th was the lead platoon on the road, blocking the bridge, from Laurie's letter and Barker's *British in Boston*, so the 43rd were not still on the road, between the two small rock walls, where Hull could be hit. Furthermore, we know from Sutherland to Gage, Apr 27, that only he and a few others went to the south of the road. Thus, we can logically conclude that,

where Laurie tells in his letter that his intent was for the 43rd to line the riverbank, this was done, but out of confusion, only on the north side.

135. Barker, *British in Boston*, 34.

136. Ibid. One wonders if Smith marched up with the men instead of riding up on his steed. On Lumm: Sutherland to Gage, Apr 27.

137. Sutherland to Gage, Apr 27; Lister, *Concord Fight*, 26–27. Lister makes it sound as if they were fired upon even as they removed the planks, in stark contrast to other statements. Amos Barrett's Letter of 1825 suggests the Americans only stormed the bridge *because* the British were removing planks, also in stark contrast to other evidence.

138. Barker, *British in Boston*, 34, which gives they "halted and fronted filling the road from the top to the bottom."

139. Amos Barrett's Letter of 1825 suggests Buttrick says this earlier, before the march, which is impossible, as it is out of sequence with the events. Ripley, *History of the Fight*, 26–27, gives that Buttrick yelled something like this while on the march.

140. Ripley, *History of the Fight*, 27, suggests a quicker pace, though I have seen no contemporary evidence to support it.

141. On street firing: Lister, *Concord Fight*, 27, says so explicitly. See also French, *Informers*, 101ff., and his *Concord*, 194ff., which explains the maneuver thoroughly, drawing from Pickering, *Easy Plan of Discipline*, 119ff. (the source for the command I give as a possible quote for Laurie). French, *Informers*, 102–103, supposes that, from Laurie to Gage, Apr 26, Laurie meant to retreat in the street firing mode away from the bridge. I disagree. Laurie's line, "I determined to repass the Bridge...retreating by Divisions" seems to the present author to describe only Laurie's design to maneuver his men back to the opposite side. His letter then goes on to suggest he was making a defensive stand. In fact, no British account suggests they were attempting to make an orderly retreat, nor should they have. Theirs was the responsibility to secure the bridge in order to protect the return of the four advance companies. Instead, Laurie was hoping to hold his ground using the street firing method. He never intended to retreat.

142. Barker, *British in Boston*, 34. Barker states the three companies got behind one another, in contradiction with Laurie to Gage, Apr 26, which gives the 43rd were on the north side of the road, giving covering fire (note 134). Barker was in the lead company, thus in the confusion, so we can forgive his mistake. See also French, *Informers*, 101–104.

143. Sutherland to Clinton, Apr 26, gives the clearer account, vice to Gage, Apr 27.

144. Amos Barrett's Letter of 1825; depositions in Force, 4:2:497–501. Some historians suggest the militia were not yet on the bridge, yet Amos Barrett clearly tells us he heard the balls hit the water off to his side. What is perplexing is: he says they hit on the right of him. Who was on the right to shoot them? It would have been unwise

to use any of the front line defenders of the 4th to fire such shots, as it took too long for them to reload. The warning shots must have been on Barrett's left (remember, he gave his statement perhaps around the 50th anniversary, like so many others). If so, these would have been fired from the 43rd on the north side of the road. Historians have usually felt the militia were not yet on the bridge when the firing began, because of Amos Doolittle's engraving *Plate III: The Engagement at the North Bridge in Concord*, but that was based on a drawing made sometime late summer by an artist who did not witness the event—he merely conducted interviews. The terrain in those engravings is accurate, but the exact troop positions cannot be trusted. See further notes for another example where I choose not to trust Doolittle.

145. Laurie to Gage, Apr 26, supposes one of his men shot first ("afterwards killed", perhaps immediately after, as in one of those killed by the American volley), "tho' Mr. Southerland has since assured me, that the Country people fired first." Barker, *British in Boston*, 34, states "The fire soon began from a dropping shot on our side," whatever a "dropping shot" means. Historians love to quote this line, but none seem to have made sense of the terminology. Smith to Gage, Apr 22, reports a British soldier shot first, then an American volley, followed by that of the British. Lieutenant Gould's deposition, in Force, 4:2:500–501, gives the British gave the first fire. Amos Barrett's Letter of 1825 and the American depositions give no such first shot, but give three shots fired (only Barrett suggests they were warning shots), followed by a British volley, then the American volley. Emerson's diary in Emerson, *Complete Works*, 11:569, claims there were three "volleys" before the Americans fired: possibly the three or so warning shots, then the single shot, then the actual volley. All of these then agree that the British fired first, though Barker (as cited) says the volley from each side occurred almost simultaneously, which they no doubt did. Lister, *Concord Fight*, is unclear, but it almost sounds as if he says the Americans fired first. The only definite disagreement is from Sutherland to Gage, Apr 27, as well as his similar letter to Clinton, Apr 26, which claim the Americans fired "3 or 4 Shot…which our People returned" in the Gage version, similar in the Clinton. Sutherland was by this time in the Manse field, as he says himself, and as he is the only one to claim the Americans fired first, one has to wonder if— with his back turned, running into position—he simply supposed and convinced himself that those three or four shots were from the Americans, though in fact those were the warning shots from the British. Gage, taking into account all of the information from his officers, reported generically in his *Circumstantial Account* that the Americans fired on the troops, which is true, but it almost implies that the Americans fired first, without any shot first from the British. Then again, Gage is not explicit. The truth is of course uncertain, but each contemporary probably reported the truth as they saw or supposed they saw it. But in all the confusion, there was bound to be error in their testimonies. If they had been all in agreement,

it would perhaps signal a concerted conspiracy. The version as it is laid out in the text is the present author's supposition on this uncertain matter.

146. Ralph Waldo Emerson, "Concord Hymn," 1836.

147. Amos Barrett's Letter of 1825 (the quote); Shattuck, *History of the Town of Concord*, 112, gives generic locations (head and body) where the shots hit; Fischer, 406n40, gives that the bodies were exhumed in 1851 and gives this precise location of the shot to Hosmer.

148. Ripley, *History of the Fight*, 27.

149. Amos Barrett's Letter of 1825. Ripple of "Fire!": French, *Concord*, 191, citing Thaddeus Blood's letter in *Boston Advertiser*, Apr 20, 1886.

150. Laurie to Gage, Apr 26.

151. Lister, *Concord Fight*, 27–28; Mackenzie, Apr 19, in *A British Fusilier*, 61. Lister states four men of the 4th were killed, but Gage's official *Circumstantial Account* gives three (two at the onset, one left wounded and about to die a horrendous fate, as given below). More on Hull: *Proc. of MHS* (1878), 16:155–58; more on Gould: Evelyn to Reverend Dr. Evelyn, Apr 23, in Scull, *Memoir and Letters*, 53–55, and Gould's deposition in Force, 4:2:500–501.

152. Laurie to Gage, Apr 26; Sutherland to Gage, Apr 27. In the latter, Sutherland claims the two near him were killed, in contradiction to the information in note 151 above. The two men must have just been injured and hobbled off, as it is more likely the two killed outright were among the 4th, standing there in the deadliest position at the end of the bridge, not these two off in the field a little away from the fight.

153. Lister, *Concord Fight*, 27–28; Laurie to Gage, Apr 26; Sutherland to Gage, Apr 27; French, *Informers*, 101–4. Barker, *British in Boston*, 34, gives the next platoon, who should have fired, failed to do so because "there being nobody to support the front Compy. The others not firing the whole were forced to quit the Bridge". In other words, perhaps they began to peel off with the first platoon. (But remember, Barker himself was confused of the maneuver, so perhaps here we should not rely on his testimony much.)

154. Lister, *Concord Fight*, 27.

155. Sutherland to Gage, Apr 27. Sutherland thought two of his soldiers were "dead on the Spot", but then how did they get back to the bridge, where only three bodies were found? (More on this: see French, *Informers*, 109–10.) Perhaps we can excuse Sutherland: he was seriously wounded, losing blood, and much of his remaining details are incorrect or misleading.

156. Barker, *British in Boston*, 35, says four out of eight officers. French, *Informers*, 104n2, rightly considers there should have been nine officers (three to a company, see appendix 4), but Parsons of the 10th was ahead at Barrett's Farm, though we can count in his stead Sutherland the volunteer. However, what French does not

remember is that the 4th was missing their Captain Balfour, on special assignment to Marshfield. (See previous text, which draws on Mackenzie's *A British Fusilier*. French edited *Fusilier* years before *Informers*: thus he knew but forgot this detail.) Hence, Barker's number is correct: there were eight officers at the bridge, not nine. Barker also notes a wounded sergeant and "several Men", but Gage's *Circumstantial Account* explicitly lists, besides the three killed (two killed straightaway, one about to die) and four officers wounded, one sergeant and four privates, which I sum together in the text to call the five soldiers. The casualty toll given in Amos Barrett's Letter of 1825 gives eight to ten wounded, counting the four officers, and so generally agrees. (Ibid. is the source of the quote.) The eight officers were: 4th: Lieutenant Gould, Lieutenant Barker; 10th: Lieutenant Kelly, Ensign Lister; 43rd: Captain Laurie, Lieutenant Robertson, Lieutenant Hull; volunteer Lieutenant Sutherland of a 38th battalion company.

157. Laurie to Gage, Apr 26; Barker, *British in Boston*, 34; Amos Barrett's Letter of 1825 (which gives only 200 ascended the hill across from the Manse, or about half). Mackenzie's map (facing p. 78 of *A British Fusilier*) gives, it is supposed by French, *Informers*, 83, the location at which the fleeing British met up with the grenadiers, marked by four slashes on the road. I have no reason to doubt this interpretation. Lister, *Concord Fight*, 28, gives one was the 47th and suggests they were the only one, but Laurie to Gage, Apr 26, gives he was to receive two, though does not say if two was indeed how many he received. Gage, *Circumstantial Account*, gives there were indeed two.

158. Amos Barrett's Letter of 1825.

159. Fischer, 216, advances this theory.

160. Many sources give this. On the bedding: Ripley, *History of the Fight*, 29, for instance.

161. Lister, *Concord Fight*, 28.

162. Emerson's statement in Gordon to a Gentleman in England, May 17. French, *Informers*, 105–9 (especially see 106 for the deposition from the Gage MSS). Cf. the false deposition in Shattuck, *History of the Town of Concord*, 350, though perhaps this is not a deliberate lie but a mistake, as it suggests they buried two soldiers, making no mention of the third, the "scalped" soldier. On the "scalping", Emerson's statement gives: "as to his being scalped and having his ears cut off, there was nothing in it. The poor object lived an hour or two before he expired." It seems hard to imagine the soldier survived this attack, and perhaps what is meant is that he survived an hour or so since his wounds before this event occurred. But while Emerson did not think the ears were cut off, he likely did not go see the corpse up close, and too many British reports from those coming back from Barrett's Farm confirm the ear tops gone. On Ammi White, and late musings on the matter, see the brief discussion in Fischer, 406–407n49. Murdock, *Nineteenth of April*, 71–77,

goes into more detail on the subject. And for another discussion, see J. L. Bell, "British Corpses at the North Bridge," *Boston 1775* (blog), May 14, 2013, accessed Jan 25, 2015, http://boston1775.blogspot.com/2013/05/british-corpses-at-north-bridge.html, and the two posts following (newer). Bell also notes there may have been more than three dead at Concord's North Bridge.

163. Lister, *Concord Fight*, 29.

164. French, *Informers*, 84.

165. De Berniere to Gage [circa Apr 19].

166. See note 162. Lister's quote from *Concord Fight*, 27.

167. Barker, *British in Boston*, 35.

168. De Berniere to Gage [circa Apr 19]. See appendix 7.

169. Lexington claims the war began there, while Concord claims it was at North Bridge. It is hard to argue with town pride, so I choose no side.

Chapter 9: A Country Unleashed

1. Murdock, *Nineteenth of April*, 28–29. On Hull and Gould, see chap. 8.

2. Emerson's diary in Emerson, *Complete Works*, 11:569.

3. Barker, *British in Boston*, 35. Some evidence of the light's technique is in Lister, *Concord Fight*, 29–30.

4. Sutherland to Gage, Apr 27.

5. Edmund Foster to Daniel Shattuck, Mar 10, 1825 (the quote; but see note 6); Brooks's statement [c. 1825?], in Sumner, *History of East Boston*, 355–56n2. Years later, Brooks would be a Massachusetts governor.

6. Foster to Shattuck, Mar 10, 1825; Brooks's statement in Sumner, *History of East Boston*, 355–56n2. Foster claims the British fired first, but as described in the bibliography, information provided by old men in 1825 will not trump contemporary information. Unfortunately, no contemporary evidence exists. Lister, *Concord Fight*, 29 (the closest to contemporary, but written in late 1782), claims the Americans fired first here. To give corroboration, Brooks's statement agrees. Brooks claims they were 20 to 30 rods (330 to 500 feet) away, in agreement with Lister's claims that they fired from too far at first. Did Brooks know of the earlier skirmishes, or did he act on his own volition, contrary to the Whig policy to let the British begin the war?

7. Lister, *Concord Fight*, 29–30; Foster to Shattuck, Mar 10, 1825; Brooks's statement in Sumner, *History of East Boston*, 355–56n2.

8. Sutherland to Clinton, Apr 26, is clearer in this case. I suppose, unlike French, *Informers*, 94, that Sutherland was drawn on a carriage lying headfirst. Thus, when he says the major attack was to *his* right, this is the British left, and vice versa.

9. Lister, *Concord Fight*, 29–30.

10. Appendix 14. The numbers given are the possible maximum, or the total militia enrolled, and do not account for those that did not attend, who were sick, etc. Coburn, *Battle of April 19*, 96–97, gives 1,534 as the possible high, but includes those that arrived at Brook's Hill and Bloody Curve, and in any case, his total seems in error given the breakdown he provides.

11. Appendix 11: 786 or so, including Mitchell's patrolmen.

12. Sutherland to Gage, Apr 27; French, *Informers*, 94. The bulk of the Sudbury and Framingham men would not join the fight until the next major intersection.

13. Amos Barrett's Letter of 1825. Foster to Shattuck, Mar 10, 1825, only gives two British dead and does not recall any American losses, while Brooks's statement in Sumner, *History of East Boston*, 355–56n2, claims nine casualties total.

14. Edmund Foster to Daniel Shattuck, Mar 10, 1825.

15. Lister, *Concord Fight*, 29–30.

16. Smith to Gage, Apr 22.

17. Barker, *British in Boston*, 35.

18. The second account in Mackenzie, Apr 19, in *A British Fusilier*, 65–66.

19. Appendix 14; Coburn, *Battle of April 19*, 96–97.

20. Edmund Foster to Daniel Shattuck, Mar 10, 1825. Fischer, 408–9n69, gives plenty of details on the lay of the land, etc.

21. Loammi Baldwin's journal, Apr 19, in Hurd, *History of Middlesex County, Massachusetts*, 1:447.

22. Ibid.

23. Coburn, *Battle of April 19*, 100.

24. Across on the field: Fischer, 410n84.

25. Appendix 14; Coburn, *Battle of April 19*, 104.

26. De Berniere to Gage [circa Apr 19]; appendix 14; Coburn, *Battle of April 19*, 104.

27. Edmund Foster to Daniel Shattuck, Mar 10, 1825 (which suggests, unsupported, that Pitcairn's arm was broken). It says this rider was with the troops "rising and passing over Fiske's hill", so with the light infantry. As to the horse, the militia soon caught it, and some stories (Coburn, *Battle of April 19*, 107n1) say it had a pair of pistols belonging to Pitcairn that were sold at auction. The purchaser later offered the pistols to George Washington, but after he declined, they were given to Israel Putnam, who would carry them throughout the war. They are today at the Lexington Hist. Soc. (Hancock-Clarke House), and a picture of them are in Fischer, 231. But recent research suggests the crest on them belongs to the family of Capt. William Crosbie, an officer of the 38th Grenadiers there that day. Thus, the story of the pistols is in doubt, though they could have been given to Pitcairn to pay some debt (gambling?). Regardless, the officer on the horse is likely Pitcairn, not Crosbie. First, there is no indication that captains on the march had horses (though some junior ranking advance scouts did). But even if Crosbie acquired

one later, it is also unlikely he would have been storming the woods with the light infantry. He was, after all, a grenadier, and his place was with his company on the road. See J. L. Bell, "Where Those Pistols Really Came From," *Boston 1775* (blog), Mar 18, 2009, accessed Jan 26, 2015, http://boston1775.blogspot.com/2009/03 /where-those-pistols-really-came-from.html.

28. De Berniere to Gage [circa Apr 19].

29. The second account in Mackenzie, Apr 19, in *A British Fusilier*, 65–66; De Berniere to Gage [circa Apr 19].When exactly he was shot is unclear, but about at Fiske Hill seems likely, based on the context of the first source. Murdock, *Nineteenth of April*, 51–52, supposes the same. See further discussion on this in Fischer, 410n84.

30. Sutherland to Gage, Apr 27. It is unclear exactly when this occurred, but he claims he rode all the way from Lexington back to Charlestown after this event. As there seems to have been few casualties once the British force had their rest on the east side of Lexington Green, this last skirmish before reaching the Green seems the most probable point at which this event occurred.

31. Foster to Shattuck, Mar 10, 1825.

32. De Berniere to Gage [circa Apr 19]. Sixteen miles assumes the land route back to Boston, see appendix 8.

33. Ibid.

34. Appendix 14. To know how many militia were at any given point is almost impossible. We can guess that many that had so far joined the fight continued to harry the British rear, but as given in the text, many did not stay with the fight all day long. On the British numbers, see appendix 11. Seven hundred ninety comes from the original 766 plus the twenty mounted patrol that had now joined up with them. Of course, the actual numbers for both parties were now less due to casualties left behind along the running battle.

35. Barker, *British in Boston*, 35.

36. Coburn, *Battle of April 19*, 108–9. The militia were probably from Fiske Hill and the like, circling back to get ahead of the column once more.

37. That Percy was probably horseless: see an extract from a letter of Percy's mother to Percy, 1770, in Bolton, *Letters of Hugh Earl Percy*, 21. Murdock, *Nineteenth of April*, 87, doubts Smith was still on horseback, as Doolittle engraved in his *Plate IV: A View of the South Part of Lexington*, given his leg injury. The engraving also depicts Percy on horseback. (Cf. Lister, *Concord Fight*, 31, which claims Smith was walking but took a horse from a marine officer, apparently sometime after the retreat from Lexington.) See Ron Aylor, "British Regimental Drums & Colours," Mar 23, 2003, accessed May 22, 2010, www.fifedrum.org/crfd/drums.htm, which depicts most of the standards present.

38. On the numbers present, see appendix 11. The troop disposition is unknown. (Cf. Fischer, 245, which disagrees with his own map on p. 252, where it makes explicit

positions for the troops without reference. I suspect he drew their positions from a misinterpretation of Sutherland to Gage, Apr 27, which gives a similar relative position of the men as they marched in column back toward Boston.) Mackenzie, *A British Fusilier*, 54–55, gives us small hints of the disposition, and tells us that his 23rd's left was blocked somewhat by a "Morassy ground" (echoed by Richard Pope, see Murdock, *Late News*, 31). From this, we might guess that the 23rd was south of the road, along the shallow heights there, their left somewhat near the modern day Upper Vine Brook and its surrounding marsh. The same source claims the line formation was not as regular as it might have been due to the topography and the rock hedges. The second account in Mackenzie, *A British Fusilier*, 66–67, tells us little more. Doolittle's *Plate IV: A View of the South Part of Lexington* shows the troops in column formation, still on the road, when they met with Smith, despite evidence to the contrary, proof once more that Doolittle's drawings are not reliable for positions. Doolittle's accuracy of the troops is dubious, as his engravings, based on the sketches by Ralph Earl, were made based on walking the land and taking interviews months after the fact. On this: Murdock, *Nineteenth of April*, 87–88.

39. Stedman, *History of the Origin*, 1:118.

40. Barker, *British in Boston*, 35–36.

41. Appendix 7; Mackenzie, Apr 19, in *A British Fusilier*, 52–53; Letter from Boston, July 5, 1775, in *Detail and Conduct of the American War*, 9–10. About that same time, an unconfirmed tradition gives that a Boston schoolmaster, hearing the rumors of fighting, boarded up the school and declared, "War's begun and school's done," then quietly departed to join his militia company. This from French, *Concord*, 228. Had it not been for the first blunder, the British reinforcement may have departed shortly after Smith's messenger arrived at five o'clock, joining up with Smith just outside of Concord center. But even with the first, had the second not occurred, the reinforcement would have passed Lexington just after half past noon, and would have met the retreating expeditionary force somewhere west of Fiske Hill or near the site of Parker's Revenge. See appendix 7. The first supposition: if the British departed at about 5:00 a.m., it would have taken about 7:40 hours (at 3 mph) to travel the about 23 miles (see appendix 8) through Roxbury, Cambridge, Menotomy, Lexington to Concord, placing them in Concord at about just after half past noon. Smith's force departed about noon, so the two would have met about midway between Concord and Meriam's Corner. The second supposition: as given in appendix 8, the distance the reinforcement actually traveled to east of Lexington Green, about 15.8 miles, would have taken about 5:15 hours (at 3 mph). Had they departed at 7:30, they would have been east of Lexington Green about 12:45, just as Smith's force was leaving Brooks Hill. The two would have then met midway between Brooks Hill and the position Percy ultimately took up east of Lexington Green, at a point somewhere between Parker's Revenge site and Fiske Hill's north face.

42. Percy to Duke of Northumberland [his father], July 27, 1774, in Bolton, *Letters of Hugh Earl Percy*, 27–30; and see 81. Brandy in his canteen: Letter from a Private Soldier in the Light Infantry, Aug 20, 1775, in Margaret Wheel Willard, ed., *Letters on the American Revolution* (Boston: Houghton Mifflin Co., 1925), 197–200.

43. Percy to Rev. Thomas Percy, Oct 27, 1774, in Bolton, *Letters of Hugh Earl Percy*, 40–41. The recipient may be distantly related, see Bolton, *Letters of Hugh Earl Percy*, 25n. On his promotion, etc., see previous text.

44. Appendix 8.

45. Scull, *Journals of Montresor*, 120. Cf. French, *Concord*, 230.

46. Mackenzie, *A British Fusilier*, 52–53.

47. Stedman, *History of the Origin*, 1:117n.

48. Gould and Percy: Evelyn to Reverend Dr. Evelyn, Apr 23, in Scull, *Memoir and Letters*, 53–55, and Percy to Gage, Apr 20 [Draft], in Bolton, *Letters of Hugh Earl Percy*, 51n. Hull: see previous text and *Proc. of MHS* (1878), 16:155–58. (More on him later.) Rooke: Mackenzie, *A British Fusilier*, 59, which names him one of Gage's aides-de-camp, but this seems unlikely given his rank.

49. Mackenzie, *A British Fusilier*, 52–53. Gould and Hull: see note 48 and Murdock, *Nineteenth of April*, 28–29.

50. It is supposition here that he took his horse across the ferry. We only know he was on horseback after he left Charlestown. It is also supposition that he took his fusil: see note 90 for the argument.

51. French, *Life and Times*, 456–57, citing an unknown "Manuscript letter of Mr. [John R.] Adan."

52. Appendix 7; French, *Life and Times*, 457–59; *JEPCM*, 515–16. Black Horse Tavern no longer stands, but according to private correspondence between myself and Ms. Doreen Stevens of the Arlington Hist. Soc., it stood on a site at modern Massachusetts Avenue, between the streets of Foster and Tufts.

53. French, *Life and Times*, 456–57, gives three interesting but unlikely incidents Warren experienced along the way, as given by an unknown manuscript of a Dr. Welch of Charlestown. In two of the stories, Warren supposedly encountered straggling soldiers of Percy's reinforcement, and in the other, he attempted to circumnavigate the reinforcement itself, as he was making his way to Menotomy. Now, if we are to believe he did indeed leave at 10:00 a.m. from Charlestown on horseback, to travel from Charlestown to Watson's Corner and then on to Menotomy was about 6.5 miles, and had he kept his horse at a modest four-mile-an-hour walk, he would have arrived in Menotomy about 11:30 a.m. Meanwhile, the British reinforcement had not left until 8:45 a.m. and had to travel 9.1 miles to reach Watson's Corner, the first point where Warren could have met Percy's reinforcement. At our usual three-mile-an-hour march, Percy would not have been at Watson's Corner until about 11:45. By this time, Warren should have

already been ahead of Watson's Corner, in Menotomy 1.4 miles up the road. More likely, Warren was not leisurely riding his horse to Menotomy, but was cantering if not galloping, "riding hastily out of town" as one source gives (see appendix 7), covering the distance in less than half an hour, reaching Menotomy by 10:30 a.m. (The meeting was to begin at 10 a.m.) In any case, he was well ahead of the column, not behind it, and thus could not have experienced the three incidents Welch so nostalgically gave. Unfortunately, because the Welch source is now unknown, we are unable to give it more scrutiny as to its reliability. It was instead probably not until two hours after Warren arrived in Menotomy that he saw the British reinforcement pass by. See appendix 7 for timeline details and appendix 8 for distance calculations. Houses shut up: Mackenzie, *A British Fusilier*, 52–53.

54. *JEPCM*, 515ff., gives nothing of their meeting, but Heath, *Memoirs*, 7, claims they did meet.

55. Many sources call Heath a general already, but his promotion is confounding. *JEPCM*, 65 (Dec 8, 1774), gives that he was chosen as general (along with John Thomas), and ibid., 90 (Feb 9, 1775), shows the Provincial Congress resolved to appoint him general, but the journal continues to call him colonel through Apr 18 (ibid., 515ff.) and beyond, to at least May 18 (ibid., 240). And yet, John Hancock to the Comm. of Safety, Apr 24, calls Heath a general (ibid., 527–28). Then, on June 17, the Provincial Congress resolved to reconsider Heath as brigadier general, as "he has not yet received his commission" (ibid., 350). (But see the confounding resolution of June 16, ibid., 347. Is the reference to him here as "Mr." indicative of something more?) Perhaps he refused the first attempt to promote him, and the journals fail to record this. As given in the text later, he is eventually promoted to major general in the Mass. service, but it was short lived. By late July, the Continental Army was forming, and he would be put back to the lower grade of brigadier in the Continentals (see following text). Heath, *Memoirs*, 3–4, in contrast, claims he was indeed promoted on Feb 9, citing the evidence already given, but ignoring the further evidence above. See also French, *First Year*, 753–54.

56. Heath, *Memoirs*, 7; French, *Life and Times*, 458.

57. Elias Boudinot, *Journal or Historical Recollections of American Events During the Revolutionary War* (Philadelphia: Frederick Bourquin, 1894), 1–2, also in Commager and Morris, *The Spirit of 'Seventy-Six*, 90–92. A copy, Joseph Palmer to Capt. Philip Mortimer, Watertown, Wednesday Morn: Near 10 oClock [Apr 19, 75], without the timekeeping as Bissell reached various towns (unlike in the sources above), is in the Gold Star Collection of the Clements. It is odd that Joseph Palmer of the Comm. of Safety signed this document from Watertown, while the Comm. of Safety seems to have met in Menotomy, given the evidence presented in the text. (Some of that evidence is traditional, to be sure, but *JEPCM*, 515–

Notes | 421

16, gives explicitly a plan to reconvene at Black Horse Tavern in Menotomy at 10:00 a.m. on the 19th.) If the Boudinot source is an accurate transcription of the original journal, the whereabouts of which are unknown, then perhaps Palmer was indeed at Menotomy, but then he traveled to nearby Watertown specifically to find the trusted Mr. Bissel and from there set him on his ride.

58. Appendix 7.

59. Mackenzie, *A British Fusilier*, 54–55.

60. Appendix 14. No more than about 2,000 ever engaged the British (see following text).

61. *Plate IV: A View of the South Part of Lexington* depicts three houses burnt; the American depositions in Force, 4:2:497–98, give that three houses, one barn and one shop were burned; and Gordon to a Gentleman in England, May 17, gives that in fact two shops were burned, one of which was adjoined to one of the houses. Also see Murdock, *Nineteenth of April*, 89–92. Mackenzie, *A British Fusilier*, 56, clearly states after leaving Lexington, no other homes were burned, though he thought there should have been, had there been time.

62. Mackenzie, *A British Fusilier*, 54–55.

63. Ibid.; Murdock, *Nineteenth of April*, 89–90; Loammi Baldwin's journal, Apr 19, in Hurd, *History of Middlesex County, Massachusetts*, 1:447.

64. Extract of [Lt.] Colonel Cleaveland's letter in Scull, *Memoir and Letters*, 98ff.; Lister, *Concord Fight*, 30, where Lister adds, "had we had plenty of that commodity [of cannon shot] they would have been of the greatest use to us".

65. French, *Concord*, 230, claims Percy left his baggage train to repair the bridge, despite the evidence in the extract of Cleaveland's letter in Scull, *Memoir and Letters*, 98ff., which tells of the wagon he had prepared being refused, and also the evidence, as given above, of Montresor repairing the bridge. Fischer, 243–44, subscribes to the wagons being sent separately, and gives the various traditional but dubious accounts. Murdock, *Nineteenth of April*, 100–101, gives more on it.

66. Ripley, *History of the Fight*, 35–36, which unfortunately paraphrases this valuable part of the lost letter from Foster to Shattuck, Mar 10, 1825, though he otherwise quotes the letter in full; also Munroe's deposition, 1825. Murdock, *Nineteenth of April*, 114–18, thoroughly discusses, and in the opinion of the present author, satisfactorily debunks the claim that the lame man was gunned down in cold blood as the British departed, though he clearly died that day, perhaps, as he was a militiaman, in battle. Reading Munroe's deposition carefully, he never claims the lame man was gunned down outside the tavern, and his deposition supports the theory provided by Murdock. Murdock also debunks calling the tavern "Percy's headquarters."

67. Lister, *Concord Fight*, 30–31. Simms is named in Sutherland to Gage, Apr 27.

68. Appendix 7; Percy to Gage, Apr 20. Per appendix 8, the route, through Roxbury, was 15.8 miles.

69. Four horses for a 6-pounder: Spring, *With Zeal*, 195, citing Burgoyne.

70. Mackenzie, *A British Fusilier*, 55.

71. De Berniere to Gage [circa Apr 19]; Sutherland to Gage, Apr 27 (source of the quote, which also gives the flanking positions); appendix 11. Query: was the protection of these flankers around the beleaguered expeditionary force what some (e.g. Stedman, *History of the Origin*,1:118; "English Account of the Battles…from 'The Historical Record of the 52nd Regiment,'" in Scull, *Memoir and Letters*, 57) would describe as Percy's "square" formation around them?

72. Gordon to a Gentleman in England, May 17. This was probably the first time the British played music since departing Boston, despite late 1825 claims to the contrary (see chap. 8, n. 79).

73. Second account in Mackenzie, *A British Fusilier*, 67.

74. De Berniere to Gage [circa Apr 19].

75. Barker, *British in Boston*, 36.

76. Second account in Mackenzie, *A British Fusilier*, 67. A similar story exists of an old man on a white horse, the "white horseman," often retold, but it seems more legend than truth. For an account of the white horseman, see Henry Smith Chapman, *History of Winchester, Massachusetts* (Winchester, MA: Published by the Town, 1936), 104–5, available in the database Heritage Quest Online.

77. Mackenzie, *A British Fusilier*, 56.

78. Percy to Gage, Apr 20.

79. Lister, *Concord Fight*,31–32.

80. Ibid. 32; Hunter, *Journal*, 9. It should be noted here that almost all of Hunter's remembrances of Apr 19 are incorrect, as evidenced by sources used throughout this volume. This remembrance is plausible, however, and so given here.

81. Appendix 14; Coburn, *Battle of April 19*, 133–35.

82. Barker, *British in Boston*, 36–37; Heath, *Memoirs*, 7–8; Heath's note in *Proc. of MHS* (1860), 4:294.

83. Both quotes from Mackenzie, *A British Fusilier*, 56–57.

84. Stiles, May 12, in *Literary Diary*, 1:552; Percy to Gen. Harvey, Apr 20.

85. De Berniere to Gage [circa Apr 19].

86. Mackenzie, *A British Fusilier*, 56; echoed by Barker, *British in Boston*, 36. See also Murdock, *Nineteenth of April*, 104ff.

87. Coburn, *Battle of April 19*, 138–40, which claims the twelve men dead (Russell and eleven others) included the "seven men from Danvers", which was probably a separate incident nearby. See text below and note 89. Murdock, *Nineteenth of April*, 129–31, claims Russell was aided by Essex militia, but gives no more on the discussion. Later that day, after the fight had moved on, Russell's wife and children returned and found him dead at their doorstep, pierced multiple times.

88. Mackenzie, *A British Fusilier*, 57.

89. Foster to Shattuck, Mar 10, 1825, who states he did not witness it, but received word of it on good authority. He claims eight (not seven) Danvers men died. Also, Daniel P. King, *An Address Commemorative of Seven Young Men of Danvers...* (Salem, MA: W. & S. B. Ives, 1835), 12–13 (which also gives the claim that three or four were in fact murdered after surrendering: dubious because it was not reported until 1835). Also, Fischer, 256. Some (e.g., French, *Concord*, 248) suppose this event and that of Jason Russell are linked, and are one in the same, which *may* be true, but seems not.

90. French, *Life and Times*, 462, citing the eulogy of Perez Morton. There is no proof Warren carried his fusil on this day (as he did at Bunker Hill: e.g., Swett, *History of the Bunker Hill Battle*, 25). But given that he was in the heart of danger, that others thought he did great service (*Life and Times* as cited), and that he later used his fusil at Bunker Hill (proving he was willing to fight), it seems highly likely he was in the Menotomy fight with a weapon as well. Conversely, it is rather difficult to imagine he was merely standing there defenseless while others around him did the work, which is much out of his character as found of his service later at Bunker Hill, not to mention incredibly dangerous. Finally, read again the quote cited in the main text. It claims he fought with the men, and served as a soldier. If true, he had a gun.

91. Heath's note in *Proc. of MHS* (1860), 4:294. Cf. Heath, *Memoirs*, 7–8.

92. Coburn, *Battle of April 19*, 141–42; Murdock, *Nineteenth of April*, 127; *Columbian Centinel*, Feb 6, 1793, p. 3. Fischer, 257.

93. Percy to General Harvey, Apr 20.

94. I have not found primary sources for this, but it is in all the secondary sources, such as French, *Concord*, 248.

95. Heath's note in *Proc. of MHS* (1860), 4:294, and Heath, *Memoirs*, 7–8 (which clarifies who died—the soldier, but makes it sound as if Downer fought at Watson's Corner, not Menotomy on the "plain," as the first source gives). The Plain, according to Ms. Doreen Stevens of the Arlington Hist. Soc., is "in general the gently sloping lands of Arlington Center and East Arlington, which flattens toward Alewife Brook and the Charles River. This relatively flat land is in contrast to the hillier terrain between Lexington Center and Concord, which continues into current-day Arlington until nearly Arlington Center, the junction of Pleasant Street/Route 60 and Massachusetts Avenue."

96. Eggs as an ingredient were not added until the late 1800s, and beer was eventually removed as an ingredient.

97. Murdock, *Nineteenth of April*, 125–29; the Coopers' 1775 deposition in Shattuck, *History of the Town of Concord*, 351.

98. Mackenzie, *A British Fusilier*, 57–58.

99. Hannah Adams's 1775 deposition in Shattuck, *History of the Town of Concord*,

350–51, leaves one to wonder how she could have left her four other children in the house with the soldiers. Though I generally ignore late evidence, it is only with such that we can make sense of Hannah's deposition. The relevant late evidence is outlined in Murdock, *Nineteenth of April*, 121–25.

100. Totals from appendix 14 (not counting the Salem men); Coburn, *Battle of April 19*, 159, gives 3,733. He spent considerable time poring over the muster rolls. Mackenzie, *A British Fusilier*, 60, guessed about 4,000 total, and he was quite right, particularly when we add in the about 300 Salem men. Perhaps this point lends to his credibility as an unbiased primary source. Too many of the British contemporary sources grossly overestimated the Americans, especially Sutherland to Gage, Apr 27.

101. Compare appendix 11 with the casualties noted in appendix 4.

102. Murdock, *Nineteenth of April*, 105–12, gives a thorough discussion on this subject. That Fischer, 414n69, calls Murdock an Anglophile for his honest consideration of the atrocities seems, to the present author, unwarranted.

103. Rev. William Gordon of Roxbury, not an eyewitness, later wrote, "The people say that the soldiers are worse than the Indians; in short, they have given the Country such an early specimen of their brutality as will make the inhabitants dread submission to the power of the British Ministry, and determine them to fight desperately rather than have such cruel masters to lord it over them." This ignores the British perspective, the "scalping", and the tactics necessary, but makes for good propaganda. From Gordon to a Gentleman in England, May 17.

104. One unearned atrocity: of the seven Danvers men, caught between the flankers and the main body, a story gives that three or four were actually surrendering before the British gutted them—a claim that is surely false, instead steeped in postwar propaganda. They would have had only seconds to surrender in this quick action. It seems dubious. Propagandists also seized on the story of bedridden Hannah Adams with her baby, forced to flee her home. This one is debatable, but her home was just as likely to become a sniper haven as all the others already were. Consider too that the British did not harm her or her children. See note 89.

105. Mackenzie, *A British Fusilier*, 58.

106. Barker, Apr 25, in *British in Boston*, 39.

107. Gage's Official Casualty Report, Apr 19, 1775, in Coburn, *Battle of April 19*, 158–59.

108. Mackenzie, *A British Fusilier*, 58. Mackenzie gives just one or two "more" killed, but only five prisoners are reported in the end (see present text around note 134).

109. Fischer, 251, supposes this, and I agree.

110. Gage's Official Casualty Report, Apr 19, 1775, in Coburn, *Battle of April 19*, 158–59; Mackenzie, *A British Fusilier*, 61. The 23rd did not suffer the worst: this distinction went to the Marines, followed by the 4th.

111. Mackenzie, *A British Fusilier*, 56–57.

112. Ibid.

113. Now at the modern and nondescript intersection of Massachusetts Avenue and Rindge Avenue.

114. Appendix 14; Heath, *Memoirs*, 7–8 (who adds Dorchester to the list). We must not count the Watertown men, 134, who should have been at the Great Bridge. They probably came up to give battle once the British turned off the road to Cambridge though.

115. Heath, *Memoirs*, 7; appendix 14.

116. Percy to Gage, Apr 20 [Draft], in Bolton, *Letters of Hugh Earl Percy*, 51.

117. Heath, *Memoirs*, 8; Foster to Shattuck, Mar 10, 1825.

118. Percy to Gage, Apr 20 [Draft], in Bolton, *Letters of Hugh Earl Percy*, 51.

119. Appendix 8; Percy to Gage, Apr 20 [Draft], in Bolton, *Letters of Hugh Earl Percy*, 51.

120. Mackenzie, *Fusilier*, 56–57.

121. Coburn, *Battle of April 19*, 153–54; Heath, *Memoirs*, 8–9; appendix 14. Pickering's conduct was under scrutiny because he had not come sooner. See Fischer, 260, 414n74.

122. Percy to Gage, Apr 20; Mackenzie, *Fusilier*, 58. Little of the boy is known, but the origin is a petition of Jacob Rogers, in Frothingham, *Siege of Boston*, 371–72. Murdock, *Nineteenth of April*, 120–21 gives little more on the boy. Coburn, *Battle of April 19*, 154, gives a bit more, calling him Edward Barber, son of a sea captain named William. In appendix 7, we note that civil twilight ended at 7 p.m., just as the British were coming up on the Neck.

123. Percy to Duke of Northumberland [his father], Apr 20, in Bolton, *Letters of Hugh Earl Percy*, 54–55; appendix 7.

124. Heath, *Memoirs*, 9.

125. De Berniere to Gage [circa Apr 19]; Mackenzie, *A British Fusilier*, 59.

126. Graves, *Conduct* (Apr 19), this portion published in part in *NDAR*, 1:193; HMS *Preston*'s journal, Apr 19, in ibid., 1:195. See Philip Stephens to Graves, Jan 28, 1775, in Graves, *Conduct* (Apr 14), which gives that Graves had just, days earlier, received positive orders to give up as many marines as he could spare (thus he was not being generous here, he was following orders from the home government). More on Graves later.

127. Graves, *Conduct* (Apr 19), in part in *NDAR*, 1:193. As *Conduct* was completed over a year later, one wonders if some of this was just flavored telling by Graves, given the later events in Boston.

128. Mackenzie, *A British Fusilier*, 59; appendix 7.

129. The list in Mackenzie, *A British Fusilier*, 61, lists Parsons as "Arm.—Contusion", but Lister, *Concord Fight*, 33, gives "a contusion on his knee" and says nothing

of his arm. Which was it? His arm, his knee, or both? Or does Mackenzie tell us he was wounded in the arm (by gunshot) and also had a contusion? The answer is unknown.

130. Lister, *Concord Fight*, 33.

131. Ibid., 34–35ff.

132. De Berniere to Gage [circa Apr 19].

133. Strangely, the flèche is not on any of the contemporary Bunker Hill maps, though it was still there during the Battle. Its construction is hinted at in John Andrews to William Barrell, Apr 19, in *Proc. of MHS* (1866), 8:403–405, and Barker, *British in Boston*, 36–37. The details of the crossing, and the timeline are in Mackenzie, *British Fusilier*, 59, expanded upon in appendix 7.

134. Coburn, *Battle of April 19*, 156–57, 159; appendix 14. Present historians are indebted to this author for his considerable time spent with the muster rolls while conducting his research. On the prisoner exchange: it was June 6, more on this later (also noted in Clarke, *Opening of the War*).

135. "Murray" was considered significant enough to be noted by name in the hasty letter of a surgeon [Dr.] "J H" to Dr. Jos[eph] Gardner, Apr 22 (see chap. 10, n. 40). This was Samuel Murray, the Tory guide from Worcester, son of Mandamus Councilor Col. John Murray, as noted in *JEPCM* (Apr 28), 166, and "Letter from Weathersfield, Apr 23", in *New-York Gazette*, May 1, 1775, p. 2. Daniel Murray was Samuel's brother, but despite some secondary claims (e.g., Fischer, 127), he seems to have not been a guide that day. Thank you to John L. Bell, author of the blog *Boston 1775*, for his private correspondence in helping me sort this out.

136. Gage's Official Casualty Report, Apr 19, 1775, in Coburn, *Battle of April 19*, 158–59. Note there are slight variations: De Berniere to Gage [circa Apr 19] lists 273 casualties; Mackenzie, *A British Fusilier*, 61, reports 274. Both give slightly different mixes of dead versus wounded, some of which can be explained by the eventual deaths of some wounded. The exact number is probably of little importance, as they all generally agree. Cf. Richard Pope, in Murdock, *Late News*, 31, which fails to give the missing, but reports a total 271 killed and wounded. One outlier is Gage to Lord Dartmouth, n.d., in Bolton, *Letters of Hugh Earl Percy*, 53n, which gives 62 killed, 157 wounded, 24 missing (without a breakdown by rank), a total of 243—a number much lower than any other. This letter is *not* in the Gage MSS, nor in Carter. The quote it gives on Percy resembles that of Gage to Lord Barrington, Apr 22, in Carter, 2:673–74, which in turn claims to have enclosed a casualty list, but the reported enclosure is not in Gage MSS, nor Carter. It is not worth tracking down among the British archives, however, as the list in Coburn, *Battle of April 19*, is official.

137. Appendix 8.

138. Mackenzie, *A British Fusilier*, 59.

139. Gage's quote: Gage to Lord Dartmouth, Apr 22, in Carter, 1:396–97, endorsed received on June 10; Drummond's quote and mention that Percy lodged at Province House in Lord Drummond [to Lord Dartmouth], Whitehall, [June 9], in Bolton, *Letters of Hugh Earl Percy*, 53–54n.

140. Barker, *British in Boston*, 37.

141. Smith to Gage, Apr 22.

142. Evelyn to Reverend Dr. Evelyn, Apr 23, in Scull, *Memoir and Letters*, 53–55.

143. Percy to Harvey, Apr 20. The last word of the quote is "so", replaced here with an ellipsis for clarity.

144. Ibid.

Chapter 10: An Emboldened People

1. Martyn, *The Life of Artemas Ward*, 27, 127, refers to the calculus, as do many other sources, but on ibid. 89 he calls it a bladder stone, without reference, probably an assumption. "Calculus" must mean either renal calculus (kidney or bladder stones) or gallstones. I have found no definitive original source to clarify what form of calculus it was. Ward apparently suffered frequently from it, causing debilitating pain. In old medicine, stones were simply endured. It was even an explicit prohibition of the original Hippocratic oath to not attempt procedures on stones, as they should be left to "specialists." The procedures at this time were considered quite risky. Because Ward's problem is chronic, it is perhaps more likely that it was a gallstone, as kidney or bladder stones tend to pass, though in some cases can become lodged. We cannot be certain. In either case, the symptoms are similar.

2. Martyn, *The Life of Artemas Ward*, 89–90. Documents of the Comm. of Safety from Apr 20 onward are dated Cambridge, likely meaning the Hastings House. They are in *JEPCM*, 518ff. Revere to Belknap [circa 1798], explicitly tells they were at Hastings House when Church determined to go to Boston, which, as Revere notes, was the Friday after: Apr 21.

3. Thomas's rank was probably brigadier general, but I have found no explicit proof. He was promoted to colonel on his last promotion, promoted at the same time as Col. William Heath, who definitely later became brigadier. His selection to "general" (which must mean brigadier) is in *JEPCM* (Dec 8, 1774), 65, and (Feb 9, 1775), 90. See notes on Heath's convoluted promotion in chap. 9, n. 55. Thomas's exact arrival and taking command is unclear. He was born in 1724, but when is unknown, so he was either 50 or 51. More on Thomas in Lockhart, *The Whites of Their Eyes*, 144ff.

4. French, *First Year*, 80–82.

5. Daniel Putnam to Bunker Hill Assoc., Aug 1825, in *Coll. of CHS* (1860), 1:231.

6. Livingston, *Israel Putnam: Pioneer*, 192–95; French, *First Year*, 83–85.

7. Washington to George William Fairfax, May 31, in PGW.

8. Bancroft, *History of the United States from the Discovery*, 4:168. On the time it took, I rely on the illustration in Fischer, 272.

9. Graves, *Conduct* (Apr 22).

10. Barker, Apr 24, in *British in Boston*, 38, claims ten or twelve thousand, while Stiles, Apr 21, in *Literary Diary*, 1:537, gives "yesterday there were assembled 16 or seventeen Thousd Provincials of which 7000 were at Cambridge, 4000 at Charlest° & 4000 at Roxbury." The numbers are difficult to pinpoint, and the American force was constantly growing and shrinking on the whims of its volunteer force. It was probably at its peak days after Apr 19. On the British force: appendix 4, counting artillerymen and latest casualties.

11. Gordon to a Gentleman in England, May 17.

12. Barker, Apr 24, in *British in Boston*, 38.

13. De Berniere to Gage [circa Apr 19].

14. Mackenzie, Apr 20, in *A British Fusilier*, 69. The detachment of the 64th presumably went back to Castle William straightaway.

15. Graves, *Conduct* (Apr 20).

16. Graves to Philip Stephens, Apr 22, in Graves, *Conduct*. Also, Graves's Jan List, in *NDAR*, 1:47. *Asia*'s journal in ADM 51/67, UKNA, reports she took up this new position on Apr 23. By early May, *Asia* was sailing to New York.

17. Gage to Graves, Apr 20, and the reply of the same date, in *NDAR*, 1:201–2. Marshfield: see chap. 5; 110 men (not counting officers): Mackenzie, Jan 23, in *A British Fusilier*, 31.

18. Barker, Apr 24, in *British in Boston*, 38.

19. Ibid.

20. Graves, *Conduct* (Apr 22).

21. *JCC* (May 10), 2:11 gives the delegates; John Hancock to the Comm. of Safety, Apr 24, in *JEPCM*, 527–28, gives they were in Worcester as of this date, detained for two days.

22. *JCC* (Oct 22, 1774), 1:102.

23. Quotes from Adams's *Autobiography*, part 1, "John Adams" through 1776, sheet 18 of 53 [electronic edition] p. 3, in PJA. A similar quote is Adams, *The Works of John Adams*, 4:8. It comes from a conversation between Adams and Jonathan Sewall in 1774, where the latter attempted to assert the rights of Parliament, to which Adams replied, "that I knew Great Britain was determined on her system, and that very determination determined me on mine; that he knew I had been constant and uniform in opposition to all her measures; that the die was now cast; I had passed the Rubicon; swim or sink, live or die, survive or perish with my country, was my unalterable determination."

24. *JEPCM* (Apr 20), 518, also in French, *Life and Times*, 466. I have corrected one use of "county" to be "country," and one "meet" to be "met," both probably mistakes in *JEPCM*, not in Frothingham.

25. Warren to Gage, Apr 20, in French, *Life and Times*, 467, also in Force, 4:2:370–71.

26. Ibid.

27. Ibid.

28. Revere to Belknap [circa 1798].

29. Ibid.

30. Ibid.

31. Warren signs this as chairman: Warren to the Boston Selectmen, Apr 22, in Gage MSS, also in *JEPCM*, 521.

32. I have been unable to find the original source. I quote French, *Life and Times*, 502–3.

33. Ibid.

34. *JEPCM* (Comm. of Safety Journals, Apr 21), 519–20.

35. Revere to Belknap [circa 1798], which gives the whole story.

36. Warren to Gage, Apr 21, in Gage MSS.

37. Evelyn to Reverend Dr. Evelyn, Apr 23, in Scull, *Memoir and Letters*, 53–55, claims Gould was attended by a surgeon, implying it may have been a British surgeon, under the arrangements proposed by Warren.

38. Gould's deposition, Apr 25, in Force, 4:2:500–501; Evelyn to Reverend Dr. Evelyn, Apr 23, in Scull, *Memoir and Letters*, 53–55.

39. *Proc. of MHS* (1878), 16:155–58. Note that while Rev. Dr. David McClure visited Hull, he seems to have not been Hull's physician. Per Williams, Apr 20, in *Discord*, 15, Hull was guarded by three deserters from his own regiment, one of whom threatened to shoot him in his bed for having previously brought him to a court-martial. NB: This is secondhand, as Williams was not in Boston until June. More on Hull in main text below.

40. [Dr.] "J H" to Dr. Jos[eph] Gardner, Apr 22. This letter ended up in the Gage MSS. "J H" might refer to Dr. Jonathan Hunt (see Swett, 50), a physician who later served at Bunker Hill. More likely, it was recent Harvard graduate and physician apprentice John Homans, whose mentor was Dr. Joseph Gardner. This evidence was provided courtesy of Dr. Sam Forman, in private correspondence (Jan 2010). Forman is the author of *Dr. Joseph Warren*. Forman's deduction makes sense: if an apprentice required surgical tools, he would have asked for them from his mentor, and Forman was able to verify that Homans was indeed an apprentice to Gardner.

41. Besides those of Warren and "J H" as noted, there is one other in the Gage MSS of Edm. Quincy to Dolly, Apr 22, which states explicitly that Dr. Church was its bearer.

42. Revere to Belknap [circa 1798]. It is almost certain that Revere did not learn of this

opinion until the final revelation of Church's treachery, and such an opinion may in fact be flavored by that final outcome.

43. The letters in note 41 are all now in the Gage MSS. They all appear to be the originals, not copies.

44. Cane's role: evidence later in the present text. Who was Cane is uncertain. A Lt. Col. Maurice Cane appears on the List of Army Officers, 1 Jan 1775, with additions to 1779, WO, 64/15, UKNA, but this Cane belongs to the 6th Regiment of Foot, not on station in Boston.

45. Revere to Belknap [circa 1798]. According to Revere, Caleb Davis did not give this anecdote until after the final revelation of Church's treachery.

46. Ibid.

47. Rachel Revere to Paul Revere [circa Apr 22 or 23, 1775], in Gage MSS (filed between April and May).

48. *JEPCM*, 147.

49. *JEPCM* (Apr 23), 148–49.

50. French, *First Year*, 67ff. French goes into exhaustive detail of the enlistment process by colony throughout his book, particularly chap. 4–7.

51. On their birth in Sept 1774, see chap. 4.

52. Warren to the Boston Selectmen, Apr 22, in Gage MSS, also in *JEPCM*, 521, and Force, 4:2:374. Perhaps this letter also crossed the British lines by way of Dr. Church.

53. Selectmen to Dr. Warren, Apr 23, and the enclosures, in Force, 4:2:374–77.

54. The complete list is in the *Twenty-Ninth Report: Boston Records: Miscellaneous Papers*, this volume titled *A Volume of Records Relating to the Early History of Boston, Containing Miscellaneous Papers* (Boston: Municipal Printing Office, 1900), 321ff. Cf. *JEPCM* (Apr 28), 526, which is the source for the quantity of bayonets. Also, Thomas Peck to Gage, Apr 24, in Gage MSS. His cannon do not appear on the list just cited.

55. In Gage MSS, there are at least four depositions of this kind. Three are dated Apr 24, one of which is that of a Mr. John Noble, from which I draw, while a fourth is dated Apr 26. They all basically give the same point.

56. Robert S. Rantoul, "The Cruise of the 'Quero': How We Carried the News to the King," in *Essex Inst. Hist. Coll.* (1900), 36:13–14; Dartmouth to Gage, July 1, in Carter, 2:199–202; *Proc. of MHS* (1876), 14:350. *Sukey* commanded by one Captain Brown, per *London Chronicle*, May 30–June 1, 1775, Issue 2883, p. 2.

57. Depositions in Force, 4:2:489ff. They are all dated Apr 23–25.

58. *JEPCM* (Apr 26), 159; Rantoul, "Cruise of the 'Quero,'" 36:3–4ff. (see the note).

59. Dr. Warren to the Inhabitants of Great Britain, Apr 26, in Force, 4:2:487–88.

60. Dr. Warren to Benjamin Franklin, Apr 26, in Force, 4:2:488. The letter Warren to Arthur Lee, Apr 27, is in French, *Life and Times*, 471.

61. *JEPCM* (Apr 27), 159, or 523, without the postscript; Rantoul, "Cruise of the 'Quero,'" 36:3ff.; ibid., 19; Hutchinson, May 29, in *Diary and Letters*, 1:455.

62. Hutchinson, May 29, in *Diary and Letters*, 1:455; Rantoul, "Cruise of the 'Quero,'" 36:11–13.

63. Sparks, *Life and Treason of Benedict Arnold*, 3–11.

64. The Richelieu River was sometimes called the Sorel River, particularly the length beyond St. Johns.

65. Gage to Carleton, Mar 16; Feltham to Gage, June 11 (in French, *Ticonderoga*, 42ff.). In Gage to De la Place, Mar 8, Gage warned Fort Ticonderoga to be on guard. All three documents in Gage MSS. The engineer Montresor had recommended rebuilding Crown Point: see chap. 4.

66. Agreement of Apr 24, in Force, 4:2:383–84, which says 50 men; Sparks, *Life and Treason of Benedict Arnold*, 8–13, which says 60 men.

67. Parsons to Capt. Joseph Trumbull, June 2, in *Coll. of CHS* (1860), 1:181–84.

68. Ibid.; Mott's journal in *Coll. of CHS* (1860), 1:165–68. Noah Phelps and Bernard Romans were the first party, sent to Salisbury, CT, there to raise men. Edward Mott and five others were sent a day later to overtake and join them.

69. Arnold to Mass. Comm. of Safety, Apr 30, in *JEPCM*, 695, also 529.

70. John Brown to Mass. Comm. of Corr., Montreal, Mar 29, in Force, 4:2:243–45. It is unknown when the letter arrived, and it is supposition here that it reached Cambridge by Apr 30, when Arnold was giving his plan.

71. Warren to New York Comm. of Safety, Apr 30, in *JEPCM*, 695.

72. Mott's journal in *Coll. of CHS* (1860), 1:167–69ff.

73. Letters between Boston Comm. and the Mass. Comm. of Safety, in Force, 4:2:391 (Apr 25) and 424–25 (Apr 27).

74. Lord Dartmouth to Gage, Jan 27 [Secret], in Carter, 2:179–83. He would declare it a month later, see text below.

75. French, *First Year*, 122–28, and appendix 11. French apparently was unsure who Col. James Robertson was, but he is listed as the barrack master general in Gage to Richard Rigby, July 8, in Carter, 2:687–89 (see the enclosure). Also see the letters between Boston Comm. and the Comm. of Safety, in Force, 4:2:424–25 (Apr 27), 449–50 (Apr 30), 461 (May 1).

76. John Andrews to William Barrell, June 1, in *Proc. of MHS* (1866), 8:406–408. Italics as in the original.

77. John Andrews to William Barrell, May 6, in *Proc. of MHS* (1866), 8:405–406.

78. Ibid. (see the postscript). The same claims half of Boston left. Also, letters between Boston Comm. and the Comm. of Safety, in Force, 4:2:424–25 (Apr 27), 449–50 (Apr 30), 461 (May 1), imply a timeline for the passes: probably Apr 28–30 was the main exodus. A census taken on June 24, given on a list dated Oct 9, 1775, in the Gage MSS, gives 6,247 Bostonians.

79. Trumbull's letter (Apr 28), in Force, 4:2:433–34; Gage's reply (May 3), in ibid., 4:2:482–83. It is unclear if the envoy met with the Provincial Congress before or after they met with Gage. Lockhart, *The Whites of their Eyes*, 99, suggests these two envoys were staunch Tories, sent to Boston to allow the Whigs in Connecticut to easily move in support of Massachusetts.

80. Provincial Congress to the Connecticut Delegation, May 2, in *JEPCM*, 179–80.

81. Warren to Governor Trumbull, May 2, in French, *Life and Times*, 475–76, also in Force, 4:2:473–74, and *JEPCM*, 532–33. Underlining as in the original, per the first source.

82. Trumbull to the Mass. Congress, May 4, in *JEPCM*, 196n. A further reply by Mass. Congress, May 5, in ibid., 193–94. Was Trumbull's envoy really just a political tactic, in case the rebellion was squashed and Trumbull had to again make peace with the British government? Possibly.

83. I refer here to the ordering of a Continental Army under a single commander in chief. But it could also be argued that unification was not truly achieved until enlistments were required for the full duration of the war, which was not implemented until late 1776 and only began to yield real results in 1777.

84. Warren to Gage, Apr 30, in Gage MSS; *Proc. of MHS* (1878), 16:155–58; Barker, May 4, in *British in Boston*, 42. Mackenzie, Apr 19, in *A British Fusilier*, 61, reports Hull died May 2, while Barker, as cited, reports he was buried on the fourth.

85. *JEPCM* (Comm. of Safety), 530–31; affirmed by the Mass. Congress in ibid., 185. Ibid. gives this event occurred before the Comm. of Safety *reading* of Warren's letter to Trumbull, but Warren still could have *written* the letter earlier. In any event, Warren had met with Trumbull's envoy the day before, so he at least had a sense of what he was going to write, even if he had not yet done so. Thus, there is little doubt the Trumbull incident had some influence in Warren's decision on Arnold's mission. Dr. Sam Forman, my trusted colleague and author of Warren's latest biography, notes that John Hancock was already pressing Warren to attack Boston, citing Hancock to the Comm. of Safety, Apr 24 Evening (which urges an attack against Boston; in ibid., 170). Dr. Forman also notes that the supplies given to Arnold for his expedition ultimately proved unnecessary, and so might have made a bigger difference to the Americans in the coming Battle of Bunker Hill had they not been given to Arnold.

86. *JEPCM*, 534, gives the orders. The whereabouts of the original commission is unknown. However, a blank commission that fell into Gage's possession and is now at the end of the Gage MSS was signed by Dr. Warren. Perhaps then, Warren also signed Arnold's.

87. *JEPCM*, 530–31, gives the supplies.

88. Livingston, *Israel Putnam: Pioneer*, 196; Daniel Putnam to Bunker Hill Assoc., Aug 1825, in *Coll. of CHS* (1860), 1:232.

CHAPTER 11: THE SPREADING FLAMES OF REBELLION

1. Isaiah Thomas, *The History of Printing in America* 2v. (2nd ed., original printed in 1810) 1:168–69, republished in *Transactions and Coll. of the American Antiquarian Soc.* (Worcester, MA: Printed for the Society, 1874) v. 5–6.

2. Boardman, *Peter Edes: Pioneer Printer*, 8; Peter Edes's diary, Aug 4, in ibid., 99.

3. It was issued circa May 5. A copy is in MHS, and a digital version is on their website, www.masshist.org/revolution/doc-viewer.php?item_id=467 (accessed Jan 22, 2010). On the author: Fischer, 273.

4. Gale/Cengage Learning's Archive of Americana online database shows the *Boston News-Letter* (a.k.a. *Massachusetts Gazette*) went from a weekly four-page publication to an erratic two-page paper that waffled until the British Evacuation, issuing its last paper on Feb 29, 1776. The *Boston Post-Boy* (a.k.a. *Massachusetts Gazette* too) published on Apr 10, 1775, but missed its regular Monday issue on Apr 17, never to publish again. Also see Fischer, 277–79.

5. In the Gage MSS are the letters, all identical, addressed to the 13 other royal governors, dated Apr 29. (This dates the *A Circumstantial Account* broadside, as these letters are but a cover page for a copy of such.) The cover letter to Trumbull with the entire *Account* is in Force, 4:2:434–36. The *Account* is also in *JEPCM*, 180ff. (notes) and 679ff. Since the *Account* was not available until Apr 29, it was *not* completed in time to be sent with Nunn aboard the *Sukey* to London.

6. One of the copies of *A Circumstantial Account* at MHS was originally in the Warren MSS. The copy was pulled from the Warren MSS and put into a Broadside file, and the ownership of it was forgotten in the process. However, in the Warren MSS is a note stating that a copy was removed from there, and that it had a note in the margin. Of the copies of the *Account* presently at MHS, only one had such a note in the margin, and thus the one quoted here must be that of Dr. Warren. Furthermore, having examined every Warren letter at both MHS and Clements, I am convinced the handwriting on this *Account* is his. The footnote mark is in the left margin next to the line "them who had jumped over a Wall, then fired four or five". MHS has conveniently placed an image of this exact copy, with the footnote visible, on their website. It is at www.masshist.org/revolution/doc-viewer.php?item_id=498 (accessed Jan 22, 2010). Warren to Arthur Lee, May 16, in French, *Life and Times*, 488–90, reiterates his opinion that British fired first.

7. Percy to Harvey, Apr 20, in Bolton, *Letters of Hugh Earl Percy*, 52–53.

8. *JEPCM* (May 10), 212–13, an original in Gage MSS.

9. Warren to Gage [Private], May 10, in Gage MSS.

10. Warren to Samuel Adams, May 14, in French, *Life and Times*, 483–85. *JEPCM* (May 8), 203, gives the order to appoint surgeons, thus Warren kept open a slot for six days.

11. Rev. William Gordon to a Gentleman in England, May 17, in Force, 4:2:631.

12. See Gage's short take on the debacle in his letter to Lord Dartmouth, May 13, in Carter, 1:397–99. Some would continue to receive passes, but very few. Probably most of these were Tories, granted permission to sail away to more peaceful provinces such as Nova Scotia or Quebec. On this, see the two updates to a census of the town on a list dated Oct 9, 1775, filed under Oct 8, in the Gage MSS.

13. *JEPCM* (May 5), 192–93; Gage to Lord Dartmouth, May 13, in Carter, 1:397–99.

14. Thomas Allen to Maj. Gen. Seth Pomeroy, May 9, in Rev. David Dudley Field, *A History of the Town of Pittsfield, in Berkshire County, Mass* (Hartford, CT: Press of Case, Tiffany, and Burnham, 1844), 75–76; Sparks, *Life and Treason of Benedict Arnold*, 15.

15. Mott's journal in *Coll. of CHS* (1860), 1:168–70. Thirty-nine gives the combined total. Jericho must be Jericho Valley, now part of Williamstown, MA.

16. The name *Katherine* comes courtesy of private conversation with Ms. Carol Greenough, Director of the Skenesborough Museum in Whitehall, NY (Jan 26, 1775). Its length and tonnage are unknown. Allen supposed the sloop was "about twice as big as the Schooner", per Allen to Trumbull, May 12, in *Coll. of CHS* (1860), 1:178–79. On the settlement: Nelson, *Benedict Arnold's Navy*, 23–24.

17. Allen, *Narrative*, 9, calls Seth Warner a colonel, but as it was written four years after, it must refer to his later rank. Warner was a captain, per Allen to Trumbull, May 12, in *Coll. of CHS* (1860), 1:178–79; Mott to the Mass. Congress, May 11, in Force, 4:2:557–60; and Feltham to Gage, June 11, the enclosure in French, *Ticonderoga*, 51. (As given later, Warner was soon made lieutenant colonel.)

18. Mott's journal in *Coll. of CHS* (1860), 1:170–71; Mott to the Mass. Congress, May 11, in Force, 4:2:557–60.

19. Ibid.

20. Mott's journal in *Coll. of CHS* (1860), 1:171–72.

21. Allen to Gen. Richard Montgomery, Sept 20, in Force, 4:3:754.

22. Once a controversial topic, it has long since been settled, and is described at length in French, *Ticonderoga*, 28ff., 85–87, and in Feltham to Gage, June 11, in ibid., 42ff.

23. Mott's journal in *Coll. of CHS* (1860), 1:171–72.

24. U.S. Navy's Sun and Moon Calculator. Fort Ticonderoga is not in their database, so the coordinates 43° 50' N 73° 23' W are used (but for simplicity, one could use Albany, NY). On May 9, sunset was 7:05 p.m., end of civil twilight was 7:38 p.m., and the moon was a waxing gibbous with 68 percent of its disc illuminated, with its lunar transit near end of twilight, 7:46 p.m.

25. Each account is different; see French, *Ticonderoga*, 79–81.

26. "De la Place" or "Delaplace"? Contemporaries often use "Delaplace," such as Feltham to Gage, June 11, as transcribed in French, *Ticonderoga*, 42ff. (I did not

examine the original). The copy of Gage to Lord Dartmouth, May 17, as it appears (in copy) in Gage MSS, gives "Delaplace," but the transcription of the original, in Carter, 1:400, gives "De la place." Yet the copy of Gage to De la Place, Mar 8, in Gage MSS, names him "De la Place." So while French, *Ticonderoga*, 10n2, claims he found two signatures of the captain for each variation, in my own research in the Gage MSS, I have only found his name as "De la Place" in each of the five letters and three returns authored by him or his secretary. Thus, while secondary sources have apparently settled on "Delaplace," "De la Place" seems to be proper.

27. Feltham to Gage, June 11, in French, *Ticonderoga*, 42ff. and esp. the enclosure in ibid., 55. A return enclosed in Captain De la Place to Gage, Jan 31, (the return dated Feb 1), in Gage MSS, gives the Fort Ticonderoga garrison as twenty rank and file, plus him as the lone officer, with a sergeant and a drummer (twenty-three total). De la Place to Gage, Apr 19, in Gage MSS (NB there are two such letters), reports a Major Dunbar, three matrosses and nine men (thirteen total) came in on Apr 18, which Feltham's letter confirms. However, Dunbar then left, for Feltham's letter does not give him among those captured, nor does any other source. Instead, Feltham's letter reports the following were captured: thirty-five rank and file, one captain, one lieutenant, one sergeant, one drummer, one artillery conductor, one artillery corporal, three matrosses, one commissary, a total of forty-five souls. Now Feltham reported he brought ten men himself (eleven total), thus between his men and the original (twenty-three) plus Dunbar (thirteen), a total of forty-seven, we find that Dunbar must have left earlier with one other, probably a rank-and-file man. Perhaps he went back to Quebec to fetch additional men, as Feltham's letter implies more men may have been expected with a Lieutenant Wadman. Dunbar is shortly after captured, however, according to Gage to Carleton, May 20, in Gage MSS.

28. Mott to the Mass. Congress, May 11, in Force, 4:2:557–60, or Mott's journal in *Coll. of CHS* (1860), 1:170. At almost 23 miles away, assuming they were marching at an average 3 miles per hour, it would have taken them near eight hours just to get there. And with the Skenesborough party not originally supposed to depart until the day after the Castleton war council in the afternoon, thus late on May 9, it is strange that this party was intended to bring boats from there back to Shoreham on the same night of May 9–10, in time for the crossing to take the fort, a forty-six-mile round-trip.

29. U.S. Navy's Sun and Moon Calculator. Moonset was 2:22 a.m. See note 24.

30. Mott's journal in *Coll. of CHS* (1860), 1:170.

31. Lucius E. Chittenden, *The Capture of Ticonderoga*, in *Proc. of the Vermont Hist. Soc.* (Montpelier, VT: Tuttle & Co, Oct 8, 1872), 41–42; J. Smith, 1:133–34. The original source for the tradition seems to be Rev. Josiah F. Goodhue, *History of the Town of Shoreham, Vermont*, (Middlebury, VT: A. H. Copeland, 1861), 13–14.

32. Easton and Brown's participation: Allen to Mass. Congress, May 11, in Force, 4:2:556. Douglas may have also been there: ibid., 4:2:1250. There are various claims of the total that crossed (French, *Ticonderoga*, 80–81), but tradition has settled on 83, per Allen, *Narrative*, 6, roughly agreed to by Brown's Statement, May 20, Force, 4:2:623–24, and Easton's Statement, May 18, Force, 4:2:624–25.

33. U.S. Navy's Sun and Moon Calculator (see note 24). Dawn was 4:33 a.m.; civil twilight began at 4:01 a.m.

34. Allen, *Narrative*, 6 references it (amid his likely fictional harangue to his men), as does Brown's statement in Force, 4:2:623–24. See the layout in Lossing, *Pictorial Field-Book*, 1:118, which gives the fort as it stood in 1758.

35. Arnold to Mass. Comm. of Safety, May 11, ibid., 4:2:557, and "Veritas" in Force, 4:2:1086–87, give Arnold was first (though the latter also says Allen and Arnold together led the men to the gate). The author "Veritas" was likely Benedict Arnold himself, as noted in French, *Ticonderoga*, 88–90. Allen, *Narrative*, 7–8, gives the same story of "Veritas," but here Allen takes the credit as first. Yet Allen to Albany Comm., May 11, in Force, 4:2:606, in typical fashion, contradicts his own *Narrative*, giving "Colonel Arnold entered the fortress with me side by side." Allen's *Narrative* seems too often filled with exaggeration to be trusted, particularly when other contemporary accounts give differing statements.

36. Most statements agree it was dawn: Allen, *Narrative*, 6; "Veritas" (Force, 4:2:1086–87); Brown (Force, 4:2:623–24), Allen to Mass. Congress, May 11, (Force, 4:2:556), etc. Also, French, *Ticonderoga*, 82.

37. Brown's Statement, May 20, in Force, 4:2:623–24.

38. Easton's Statement, May 18, in Force, 4:2:624–25. Cf. Allen to Albany Comm., May 11, in Force 4:2:606, which claims the sentries fled. Allen, in his *Narrative*, 7–8, gives a slightly different account.

39. Allen, *Narrative*, 8; strongly supported by Lt. Jocelyn Feltham to Gage, June 11. Because of noted contradictions in Allen's *Narrative* (in note 38 and especially note 35), where Allen's *Narrative* flatly contradicts other statements and even himself, and because it seems a bit too much the hero story that Allen always sought to make of himself, it was tempting to dismiss this statement from the present volume. Only then did I discover that Feltham's letter gives strong support for it. French, *Ticonderoga*, 83, missed this point. I say perhaps the officer near Allen was slightly injured only because other evidence, given below, says no American was injured.

40. Easton's Statement, May 18, and Brown's Statement, May 20, both in Force, 4:2:623–25. Brown says nothing of the huzzahs.

41. Feltham to Gage, June 11.

42. Hand-to-hand: evidenced by the lack of anyone seriously wounded and none killed, and that Feltham was waiting to hear a volley. (See later main text.)

43. Lt. Jocelyn Feltham to Gage, June 11.

44. Ibid.

45. Ibid.

46. Brown's Statement, May 20, in Force, 4:2:623–24.

47. Feltham to Gage, June 11.

48. Allen, *Narrative*, 8. Though his *Narrative* has been exaggerated and unreliable, it is just this sort of haughty reply that we might expect from the glory-seeking Allen, and so might be quite true. In any event, he or Arnold replied *something* to Feltham's question.

49. Feltham to Gage, June 11. Allen, *Narrative*, 8, agrees with the sword incident.

50. "Veritas" (probably Arnold), in Force, 4:2:1086–87.

51. Lt. Jocelyn Feltham to Gage, June 11; Allen, *Narrative*, 9.

52. Lt. Jocelyn Feltham to Gage, June 11.

53. Mott to the Mass. Congress, May 11, in Force, 4:2:557–60.

54. Easton, Mott, et al. to Mass. Congress, May 10, in Force, 4:2:556.

55. Arnold to Mass. Comm. of Safety, May 11, in Force, 4:2:557.

56. Lt. Jocelyn Feltham to Gage, June 11.

57. Arnold to Mass. Comm. of Safety, May 11, in Force, 4:2:557.

58. Allen, *Narrative*, 9–10, gives the general idea, but claims 100 men, or about half the men there. As that source has proven unreliable in its details, as noted above, it is best to use the fifty men cited in Arnold to Mass. Comm. of Safety, May 11, in Force, 4:2:557. (NB: The letter Arnold refers to dated May 10 was never received by the Mass. Congress, and its contents are therefore lost, per *JEPCM*, 698.) Also see Allen to Trumbull, May 12, in *Coll. of CHS* (1860), 1:178–79. On the garrison there: Feltham to Gage, June 11, the enclosure in French, *Ticonderoga*, 55. Note the word choice: north was down lake, while south was up lake!

59. *JCC* (May 10), 2:11.

60. Mott to the Mass. Congress, May 11, in Force, 4:2:557–60.

61. Arnold to Mass. Comm. of Safety, May 11, in Force ,4:2:557.

62. Enclosure to Arnold to Mass. Comm. of Safety, May 19, in Force ,4:2:645–46.

63. Arnold to Mass. Comm. of Safety, May 14, in Force, 4:2:584–85. Cf. enclosure to Arnold to Mass. Comm. of Safety, May 19, in Force, 4:2:645–46, which gives 111, not 114 total.

64. Enclosure to Knox to Washington, Dec 17, 1775, in PGW. Cf. enclosure noted in last note.

65. For instance: Arnold to Mass. Comm. of Safety, May 14, in Force, 4:2:584–85.

66. Feltham to Gage, June 11; French, *Ticonderoga*, 61ff.

67. Clearly, they did not march together. From Allen to Trumbull, May 12, in *Coll. of CHS* (1860), 1:178–79, Allen still has no idea if Warner had taken Crown Point.

68. Allen to Trumbull, May 12, in ibid., wrongly states they had also captured Skene.

Arnold to Mass. Comm. of Safety, May 14, in Force, 4:2:584–85, also claims Skene was captured, as does Dr. Joseph Warren to John Scollay, May 17, which is enclosed as an attachment to Gage to Lord Dartmouth, May 17, in the Gage MSS (attachment not in Carter, 1:400). In fact, they had captured Skene's son, Andrew (Nelson, *Benedict Arnold's Navy*, 23). Maj. Philip Skene was in London, petitioning to be made the first lieutenant governor of the Fort Crown Point and Fort Ticonderoga region. Gage and the Ministry knew his petition was coming: Lord Dartmouth to Gage, Aug 26, 1773, in Carter, 2:158, and the reply of Dec 1, 1773, in Carter, 1:354. Instead, Philip Skene was not captured until he returned circa August, just off Philadelphia's coast (see Gage to Lord Dartmouth, Aug 20, 1775 [Secret], in Carter, 1:412–13; the story detailed in full in Nelson, *Benedict Arnold's Navy*, 23–24). He is examined by a committee of the 2nd Continental Congress: *JCC* (June 8), 2:82.

69. Ethan Allen to Governor Trumbull, May 12, in *Coll. of CHS* (1860), 1:178–79; Allen, *Narrative*, 10. The name *Betsey*: De la Place to Gage, Apr 19, in Gage MSS (NB: There are two such letters), which gives her master is a Captain Friend.

70. There is no explicit Resolve electing him, but on May 10, he took over the duties as such, and signed many documents thereafter as chairman. See *JEPCM*, 541, 543, 548. However, a letter Comm. of Safety to Moses Gill [of the Comm. of Supplies], May 14, in French, *Life and Times*, 482–83, is signed again by Warren as chairman. Another reference, in ibid., 500–501, claims Warren again signed as chairman on June 4 (the quote there is incomplete and difficult to trace to the original). Neither of these two references in Frothingham appears in *JEPCM*. Perhaps Warren and Church alternated, depending on their availability. Neither signed as "acting chairman." At least once when Church was in Philadelphia (see below), Benjamin White signed as chairman: *JEPCM* (June 18), 571. As there are no clear appointments of any chairman after Warren, it suggests a nebulous command structure.

71. Gordon, *History*, 1:339. This author ascribes the impossibly low number of 700 to the Roxbury camp. Barker, May 9, in *British in Boston*, 44, gives the number, which agrees with Stiles's 4,000 at the start of the siege (Stiles, Apr 21, in *Literary Diary*, 1:537), and shows the British were not duped.

72. Judge Prescott's account in *Proc. of MHS* (1876), 14:73.

73. Martyn, *The Life of Artemas Ward*, 102–3; the order also in *JEPCM* (May 10), 541.

74. Martyn, *The Life of Artemas Ward*, 103–4. Was it just a mistake? Maybe. The letter was addressed "To General Thomas of Plymouth", but Thomas was indeed of Plymouth County. French, *Informers*, 161–62n2, suspects it was indeed a mistake.

75. An interesting quote often wrongly attributed to Warren appears in a Mar 7, 1774 letter of a Tory pamphleteer. It reads: "One of our most bawling demagogues and voluminous writers is a crazy Doctor, whom some years ago they were going to

banish out of Town, for professing himself an Atheist." The original source is a Tory writer under the pen name "Sagittarius," and it appears in John Mein, ed., *Sagittarius's Letters and Political Speculations: Extracted from the Public Ledger* (Boston: Printed by Order of the Boston Selectmen, 1775), 9. It is often quoted in many secondary sources, often without reference, almost always without the crucial end of the sentence. It is from the end of the sentence that we can draw our conclusions. Warren was never known to be at risk of banishment nor ever known to be an atheist. He seems to have been just as religious as most average Bostonians. Though French, *Life and Times*, 157, is one of the many secondary sources that quote this without the crucial ending, he does note the Tory may have been referring to Dr. Thomas Young. From private correspondence with Sam Forman (cited above), Dr. Young was accused (not professing himself) of being an atheist, and Samuel Adams helped defend him. Ultimately, following repeated death threats, Dr. Young did leave Boston, late in 1774.

76. Letter of Henry Hulton, June 20, in Hulton, *Letters of a Loyalist Lady*, 97–100. An excerpt appears in Commager and Morris, *The Spirit of 'Seventy-Six*, 136–37, wrongly attributed to his sister, Anne Hulton, the author of most of the letters in Hulton's *Letters of a Loyalist Lady*.

77. Lord Rawdon to Earl Huntingdon, June 20, in *Report on the Manuscripts of the Late Reginald Rawdon Hastings*, 3:154–55, also in Commager and Morris, *The Spirit of 'Seventy-Six*, 130–31.

78. Warren to Mercy Scollay, May 10. The original is lost. But it can be largely reconstructed by comparing Item 5445 in *Libbie & Co., Catalogue of Autographs, Letters*, 224, and the "Fourth Letter" in *Celebration by the Inhabitants of Worcester*, 136. Also see the details cited in chap. 1, n. 37.

79. Brown's Statement, May 20, in Force, 4:2:623–24, certainly gives no indication the two men were the same. In fact, that statement and other references to this Brown always call him John, not Jonathan, and call him a mister and an esquire, not a captain. Arnold to Mass. Comm. of Safety, May 19, in Force, 4:2:645–46, deliberately calls him "Jonathan" and a captain.

80. Oswald's journal, May "11" (really 12), May "13" (really 14), in *NDAR*, 1:312, 327, citing the original in the *New England Chronicle* (a.k.a. *Essex Gazette*), June 1, 1775. Oswald's dates must be used with caution. The second entry as cited gives May 13, Sunday. But that Sunday was May 14, throwing into question all of the other dates. To pinpoint the error, let us consider Arnold to Mass. Comm. of Safety, May 19, in Force, 4:2:645–46, which explicitly gives that they arrived 30 miles south of St. Johns on May 17. Oswald's journal, May 16, in *NDAR*, 1:344, gives the same event. Thus, Oswald is accurate in what day of the week he gives (Sunday, etc.), when he gives one, but incorrect in what day of the month he gives (14th, etc.). In his May 11 entry, he does not give a day name, but given that the

error seems perpetuated throughout the beginning of the journal, we might safely guess that the May 11 entry was really for a departure from Skenesborough on May 12, and that his May 13 entry for his arrival at Fort Ticonderoga was really May 14. Captain Sloan: Oswald's journal, May "15" (really 16), in *NDAR*, 1:340; the name is also referenced in a payroll statement in the U.S. Archives, reproduced in Morton's *Birth of the United States Navy* cited below.

81. Arnold's Regimental Memorandum Book, May 14, in *Bulletin of the Fort Ticonderoga Museum* (Summer 1981), 14:71.

82. Sparks, *Life and Treason of Benedict Arnold*, 15, 18; Arnold to Mass. Comm. of Safety, May 14 and May 19, in Force, 4:2:584–85, 645–46. It is quite clear from these letters that Arnold sent his men to Skenesborough to fetch the schooner. What is not clear is when he gave this order. Did they come first to Fort Ticonderoga? If so, when? Given the distances and the timeline, with the recruits coming from Stockbridge far to the south, it seems most likely Arnold sent an express back to his traveling recruiting officers, redirecting them to Skenesborough. Another element is unclear: what happened to Capt. Samuel Herrick? Did Arnold send his men to Skenesborough to take command? Did Herrick and his men get absorbed into the crew of the schooner? The answers to these questions remain unknown. Perhaps Herrick and his men brought the bateaux that were perhaps found at Skenesborough (they suddenly appear without explanation in the original source material; see below). Cf. Doris Begor Morton, *Birth of the United States Navy* (Whitehall, NY: The Whitehall Independent, orig. 1982, 2nd. ed. 2007) pamphlet, which unfortunately lacks citations, graciously provided me by Ms. Carol Greenough, Director of the Skenesborough Museum in Whitehall, NY. It claims Herrick's men joined with those of Arnold. This is also the source of Skene's family, corroborated by Gage to Lord Dartmouth, May 17 [Separate], in Carter, 1:400, a copy of which is also in the Gage MSS and includes the attachment Dr. Joseph Warren to John Scollay, May 17, reaffirming the details (but see note 68).

83. Arnold to Mass. Comm. of Safety, May 14 and also of May 19, in Force, 4:2:584–85 and 645–46; Allen, *Narrative*, 10 (source of the quote). Arnold's experience in seamanship: Sparks, *Life and Treason of Benedict Arnold*, 8–9. On the bateaux, see note 82, perhaps brought in by Captain Herrick. Arnold to Mass. Comm., May 19, reports Allen had 150 men, but Oswald's journal, "Thursday" May 18, in *NDAR*, 1:358, reports four bateaux and 90 men. Allen's own account gives us nothing more.

84. Arnold to Mass. Comm. of Safety, May 14, in Force, 4:2:584–85.

85. Arnold to Mass. Comm. of Safety, May 19, in Force, 4:2:645–46; Allen, *Narrative*, 10; Oswald's journal, May "14" (really 15), in *NDAR*, 1:330 (see note 80). Cf. Extract of a Letter from Crown Point, May 19, in *NDAR*, 1:367, which claims they departed May 14.

86. U.S. Navy's Sun and Moon Calculator, using 44° 52' N 73° 20' W for Isle La Motte, VT. Sunset was 7:17 p.m.; end of civil twilight was 7:52 p.m.

87. Oswald's journal, May "15" (really 16), May "16" (really 17), in *NDAR*, 1:340, 344 (see note 80); Arnold's Regimental Memorandum Book, undated May 16–18 entry, in *Bulletin of the Fort Ticonderoga Museum* (Summer 1981), 14:71–72; Arnold to Mass. Comm. of Safety, May 19, in Force, 4:2:645–46.

88. Arnold to Mass. Comm. of Safety, May 19, in Force, 4:2:645–46; Oswald's journal, "Thursday" May 18, in *NDAR*, 1:358 (source of the quote). U.S. Navy's Sun and Moon Calculator (see note 86). On the 17th, the waning gibbous had 92 percent of its visible disk illuminated. Sunrise on the 18th was 4:21 a.m., while the moon did not set until 7:29 a.m., assuring them a bright path throughout their night journey.

89. Arnold to Mass. Comm. of Safety, May 19, in Force, 4:2:645–46; Oswald's journal, "Thursday" May 18, in *NDAR*, 1:358, which reports fourteen prisoners total.

90. Arnold to Mass. Comm. of Safety, May 19, in Force, 4:2:645–46.

91. Ibid. Using the builder's measure (bm) equation for tonnage presented in appendix 5, and assuming the length of the keel for tonnage (k) is about 82 percent of the length of the gun deck (l), and assuming a breadth (b) of 28 percent the length (l), on par with other ships cited in that appendix, we can calculate that, in order for the ship to be 70 tons, it must be about 60' in length (l) and 17' in breadth (b).

92. Allen, *Narrative*, 10–11, and Oswald's journal, "Thursday" May 18, in *NDAR*, 1:358, for example, do not count them among the prisoners taken. Arnold to Mass. Comm. of Safety, May 19, in Force 4:2:645–46, gives there are seven, but says not if they were impressed.

93. Arnold to Mass. Comm. of Safety, May 19, in Force, 4:2:645–46; Oswald's journal, "Thursday" May 18, in *NDAR*, 1:358. Extract of a Letter from Crown Point, May 19, in ibid. 1:367, seems to parallel Arnold's May 19 letter, almost as if the author is the same. However, Extract of a Letter from Crown Point reports five bateaux destroyed, five taken, in contrast with Arnold.

94. Allen, *Narrative*, 10–11, which suggests he met Arnold after he had come back to *Liberty*, but then contradicts himself by saying he was within miles of St. Johns. Arnold to Mass. Comm. of Safety, May 19, in Force, 4:2:645–46, claims he came upon Allen 5 leagues, or 17 miles, south of St. Johns, and thus before they returned to *Liberty*. Oswald's journal, "Thursday" May 18, in *NDAR*,1:358, gives it was six miles south of St. Johns. Thus, the last three accounts agree it was before they came to *Liberty*, though they disagree on how far along.

95. Arnold to Mass. Comm. of Safety, May 19, in Force, 4:2:645–46; Oswald's journal, "Thursday" May 18, in *NDAR*, 1:358.

96. Oswald's journal, "Thursday" May 18, in *NDAR* 1:358; Carleton to Gage, May 31,

in Gage MSS. Arnold to Mass. Comm. of Safety, May 19, in Force, 4:2:645–46, warns of an expected detachment.

97. Oswald's journal in *NDAR*, 1:513 (this entry strangely marked May 23 in ibid. but "Saturday, [May] 19" in the original in *New England Chronicle*, a.k.a. *Essex Gazette*, June 1, 1775, p. 3). Also, Nelson, *Benedict Arnold's Navy*, 53.

98. Carleton to Gage, May 31. Gage has already written of the news to Carleton, May 20, but his letter was not yet received in Montreal. Both letters are in the Gage MSS.

99. Mass. Congress learns of Taking of Fort Ticonderoga: *JEPCM* (May 17), 233. Mass. Congress learns of taking of St. Johns, etc.: Warren to Comm. of Safety, May 25, in French, *Life and Times*, 494, original in Mass. Archives, SC1/ser. 45X, Mass. Archives Coll. 193:241. Mass. Congress responds on that latest victory: *JEPCM* (May 27), 263. Gage learns of the taking of Fort Ticonderoga the same day the Mass. Congress did (May 17): Dr. Joseph Warren to John Scollay, May 17, intercepted by the British and attached to Gage to Lord Dartmouth, May 17, in the Gage MSS (this attachment not in Carter, 1:400). Church also reported the taking of the fort: Intelligence, May 24, in Gage MSS (more on this in French, *Informers*, 147ff.).

100. Carleton to Gage, May 31. In Carleton to Gage, June 4, Carleton adds that one Indian tribe had now pledged its support. However, the Indians ultimately do little. Instead, they mostly remain on the sidelines for the 1775 campaigns, despite British attempts to rouse them. (Both letters in Gage MSS.)

BIBLIOGRAPHY

On endnotes in this volume: Any letter, diary entry, etc., given without a year, should be assumed to be of the year 1775, unless context clues suggest otherwise.

On sources: Letters are cited in the format of author to recipient, place, date, in source. I only include place when it provides clarity. Likewise, personal diaries and journals are cited in the format author's journal, date of entry, in source. However, if the letter or journal is one I cite frequently, I generally do not give its source in the endnotes, but instead list those key letters or journals explicitly here in the bibliography, and only here include its full citation. But even in these cases, I sometimes also specify the source in the endnotes when it provides clarity, particularly in lengthy letters and journal entries.

On style: For all quotes of original written documents, which are the majority of those in this volume, I have retained all spelling and grammar errors and have mostly left the abbreviations and punctuation as in the original, except where necessary for clarity. However, I have at times slightly modified quotes first uttered as spoken words that were later recorded in letters, correcting punctuation and misspellings only in these instances, and only for clarity. In doing so, I have on very rare instances found it necessary to correct the tenses and pronoun choices of some of the words used. In these rare cases, or in any other departure from the original, I have described my changes in the related endnotes.

Lastly, I employ the "logical quotation" style. That is, I have carefully transcribed all written quotations such that any punctuation included within the quotation was there in the original. (So, a quotation ending with a comma inside the quotation marks, such as "quotation," indicates the comma was in the original, while one with the comma outside the quotation marks, such as "quotation", indicates there was no comma in the original, usually because I ended my quote mid-sentence of the original.) While I generally follow the Chicago Manual of Style (CMOS), this quotation style is from the Council of Science Editors (CSE) Scientific Style and Format. The only exception to logical quotations is in adding punctuation (per CMOS) to article names in full citations, as listed in this bibliography.

ARCHIVES

Citations to the Evans Collection refer to the massive microform collection available at most research libraries, also online in the Archive of Americana database by Readex.

Adams Family Papers. Digital Edition. Massachusetts Historical Society, Boston. www.masshist.org/digitaladams/.

Adams Papers. Digital Edition. Massachusetts Historical Society, Boston. www.masshist.org/publications/apde/. Formerly titled *Founding Families: Digital Editions of the Papers of the Winthrops and the Adamses.* Note: I rely on the Founding Families database for any letter between John Adams and a recipient other than his wife, Abigail. However, for letters between these two, as well as his diary and autobiography, I have always consulted the Adams Family Papers database, as it of a far better design and usability. Most of the original of these documents are held at MHS.

Clinton, Henry. Papers. University of Michigan William L. Clements Library.

Franklin, Benjamin. Papers. Yale University. www.franklinpapers.org.

Gage, Thomas. Papers. University of Michigan William L. Clements Library.

Scollay, Mercy. Papers. Cambridge Historical Society, Cambridge, MA.

Sparks, Jared. Papers. Harvard University Archives.

Thomas, John. Papers. Massachusetts Historical Society, Boston.

Warren, John Collins. Papers. Massachusetts Historical Society, Boston.

Washington, George. Papers. University of Virginia. http://rotunda
.upress.virginia.edu/founders/GEWN.html. Note: As of this
writing, one can gain free access via the Mount Vernon website.
Many of the originals in the George Washington MSS at LOC
at http://lcweb2.loc.gov/ammem/gwhtml/gwhome.html.

PRIMARY SOURCES
Almanacs (and Calculators)

George, Daniel, ed. *George's Cambridge Almanack, or, The Essex Calendar
for the Year of Our Lord 1776*. 1775. Evans Microfilm, 14062.
Reprinted with Joseph Warren Memorial. Salem, MA: E.
Russell, 1775. Evans Microfilm, 14063. No other years seem
to exist for this almanac.

Gleason, Ezra, ed. *Bickerstaff's New England Almanack for the Year of
Our Lord 1776*. Newburyport, MA: Mycall and Tinges. Evans
Microfilm, 14066.

Thomas, Isaiah, ed. *Thomas's Boston Almanack for the Year of Our Lord
1775*. Boston: Isaiah Thomas, 1774. Evans Microfilm, 42711.
No other years seem to exist for this almanac.

U.S. Navy's Sun and Moon Calculator website. http://aa.usno.navy.mil
/data/docs/RS_OneDay.php. Note: All times given throughout
this volume are in Eastern Standard Time.

West, Benjamin, ed. *Bickerstaff's Boston Almanack*. Boston: 1772–74.
Evans Microfilm, 12613, 12074, 13763. No other years seem
to exist for this almanac.

Books and Articles (of Primary Source Material and Letters)

Adams, John. *Familiar Letters of John Adams and His Wife Abigail Adams,
During the Revolution*. Edited by Charles Francis Adams. New
York: Hurd and Houghton: 1876.

———. *The Works of John Adams, Second President of the United States.*

Edited by Charles Francis Adams. 10 vols. Boston: Little, Brown and Co., 1850–56.

Adams, John, Samuel Adams, and James Warren. *Warren-Adams Letters.* Vol. 1, *1743–1777.* Cambridge, MA: Massachusetts Historical Society, 1917.

Barnes, George Reginald, and John H. Owen, eds. *The Private Papers of John, Earl of Sandwich, First Lord of the Admiralty: 1771–1782.* 4 vols. London: Naval Records Society, 1932–38.

Bolton, Charles Knowles, ed. *Letters of Hugh Earl Percy from Boston and New York 1774–1776.* Boston: Charles E. Goodspeed, 1902.

Burnett, Edmund C., ed. *Letters of the Members of the Continental Congress.* Vol. 1, *Aug 29, 1774–July 4, 1776.* Washington, DC: Carnegie Institution, 1921.

Carter, Clarence Edwin, ed. *The Correspondence of General Thomas Gage with the Secretaries of State and with the War Office and the Treasury 1763–1775.* New Haven: Yale University Press, 1931–33.

Clark, William Bell, William James Morgan, and Michael J. Crawford, eds. *Naval Documents of the American Revolution.* 11 vols. Washington, DC: Naval History Division, Dept. of the Navy, 1964.

Clarke, Rev. Jonas. *Opening of the War.* See Letters.

Cobbett, William, John Wright, and Thomas Curson Hansard, eds. *The Parliamentary History of England from the Earliest Period to the Year 1803.* Vols. 16–18. London: T. C. Hansard, 1813.

Commager, Henry Steele, and Richard B. Morris, eds. *The Spirit of 'Seventy-Six.* Edison, NJ: Castle Books, 2002. First published 1958 by Harper Collins.

Dawson, Henry B., ed. *The Historical Magazine.* Morrisania, NY: Dawson, various dates.

Donne, William Bodham, ed. *The Correspondence of King George the Third with Lord North from 1768 to 1783.* 2 vols. London: John Murray, 1867.

Force, Peter. *American Archives.* 4th ser., 6 vols. Washington, DC: M. St. Clair Clarke and Peter Force, 1837–46.

Ford, Worthington Chauncey, ed. *British Officers Serving in America, 1754–1774.* Boston: David Clapp & Son, 1894.

———. *British Officers Serving in the American Revolution, 1774–1783*. Brooklyn, NY: Historical Printing Club, 1897.

———. *Journals of the Continental Congress*. Vols. 1–4. Washington, DC: Government Printing Office, 1904.

———. *The Writings of George Washington*. Vol. 3, *1775–1776*. New York: G. P. Putnam's Sons, 1889.

Fortescue, John William, ed. *The Correspondence of King George the Third from 1760 to December 1783*. Vol. 3, *July 1773—Dec 1777*. London: Macmillan and Co., 1927–28.

Fortescue, John William. *A History of the 17th Lancers*. See Secondary Sources.

Great Britain War Office. *A List of the General and Field Officers… of the Officers in the several Regiments of Horse, Dragoons, and Foot…Artillery…Engineers…Marines…* London: Printed for J. Millan, 1778. Later editions titled *A List of the Officers of the Army and of the Corps of Royal Marines*.

Hulton, Anne. *Letters of a Loyalist Lady*. Edited by Harold Murdock and "C. M. T." Cambridge, MA: Harvard University Press, 1927.

Kennedy, John Pendelton, ed. *Journals of the House of Burgesses of Virginia*. Vol. 13, *1773–1779*. Richmond, VA: 1905.

Massachusetts Provincial Congress. *The Journals of Each Provincial Congress of Massachusetts in 1774 and 1775*. Boston: Dutton and Wentworth, Printers to the State, 1838.

Murdock, Harold. *Late News of the Excursion and Ravages of the King's Troops on the Nineteenth of April, 1775*. Cambridge, MA: Press at Harvard College for the Club of Odd Volumes, 1927.

Scull, Gideon Delaplaine, ed. *Memoir and Letters of William Glanville Evelyn*. Oxford: James Parker and Co., 1879.

———. *The Montresor Journals*. In *Collections of the New-York Historical Society for the year 1881*. Publication Fund Series. Vol. 14. New York: NY Historical Society, 1882.

Smyth, Albert Henry, ed. *The Writings of Benjamin Franklin*. 10 vols. New York: Macmillan Co., 1905–7.

Sparks, Jared, ed. *The Writings of George Washington*. Vol. 3. Boston: American Stationers' Company, 1837.

Upton, L. F. S. "Proceeding of Ye Body Respecting the Tea." *William and Mary Quarterly*, 3rd ser., 22, no. 2 (April 1965): 287–300. Provides a widely accepted eyewitness account.

Walpole, Horace. *Horace Walpole's England as His Letters Picture It.* Edited by Alfred Bishop Mason. Boston: Houghton Mifflin Company, 1930.

Wortley, E. Stuart, ed. *A Prime Minister and His Son.* New York: E. P. Dutton and Company, 1925.

Collections and Proceedings of Societies and Archives

A partial list, various volumes of each as cited throughout the endnotes:

Bunker Hill Monument Association. *Proceedings of the Bunker Hill Monument Association at the Annual Meeting.* Boston: Published by the Association, June 17, 1907.

Colonial Society of Massachusetts. *Publications of the Colonial Society of Massachusetts.* Boston: Colonial Soc. of Mass., various volumes, as cited.

Connecticut Historical Society. *Collections of the Connecticut Historical Society.* Vol. 1. Hartford, CT: Printed for the Society, 1860.

Historical Manuscripts Commission (Britain). *Report on the Manuscripts of Mrs. Stopford-Sackville.* 2 vols. London: Historical Manuscripts Commission, 1904.

———. *Report on the Manuscripts of the Late Reginald Rawdon Hastings, Esq., of the Manor House, Ashby de la Zouche.* 4 vols. London: Historical Manuscripts Commission, 1928–47.

Massachusetts Historical Society. *Collections of the Massachusetts Historical Society.* Boston: Mass. Hist. Soc., various volumes, as cited.

———. *Proceedings of the Massachusetts Historical Society.* Boston: Massachusetts Hist. Soc., various volumes, as cited.

New England Historic Genealogical Society. *New England Historical and Genealogical Register.* Boston: Samuel G. Drake, various volumes, as cited.

Peabody Essex Museum (formerly the Essex Institute). *Essex Institute Historical Collections.* Salem, MA: Essex Institute, various volumes, as cited.

————. *Proceedings of the Essex Institute*. Salem, MA: Essex Institute, various volumes, as cited.

Journals, Diaries, and Autobiographies (Personal)

Selected journals and diaries frequently referenced. Ships' journals (logs) are not listed here, but are as cited throughout the endnotes.

Adams, John. See Archives, PJA.

Allen, Ethan. *Narrative of Ethan Allen*. Bedford, MA: Applewood Books, 1989. Originally published in 1779.

Barker, John. *The British in Boston—The Diary of Lt. John Barker*. Edited by Elizabeth Ellery Dana. Cambridge, MA: Harvard University Press, 1924. Originally published in part in *Atlantic Monthly* of 1877.

Emerson, Ralph Waldo. *The Complete Works of Ralph Waldo Emerson*. Vol. 11, *Miscellanies*. Boston: Houghton, Mifflin, and Co., 1904. (Source of an excerpt of the diary of Concord's Rev. William Emerson in 567–69.)

Farnsworth, Amos. "Amos Farnsworth Journal." In *Proceedings of the Massachusetts Historical Society*, 2nd ser., vol. 12, *1896–1899*, 78–102. Boston: Massachusetts Historical Society, 1899.

Franklin, Benjamin: See Archives, PBF.

Heath, William. *Memoirs of Major-General William Heath By Himself*. Edited by William Abbatt. New York: William Abbatt, 1901.

Howe, William. *General Sir William Howe's Orderly Book at Charlestown, Boston and Halifax, June 17, 1775 to 1776, 26 May*. Edited by Benjamin Franklin Stevens. London: Benjamin Franklin Stevens, 1890.

Hunter, Martin. *The Journal of Gen. Sir Martin Hunter*. Edinburgh: Edinburgh Press, 1894. Note: The book is very rare. A copy is at the Huntington Library, CA.

Hutchinson, Thomas. *The Diary and Letters of His Excellency Thomas Hutchinson*. Vol. 1. Compiled by Peter Orlando Hutchinson. Boston: Houghton, Mifflin, and Co., 1884.

Graves, Samuel. "The Conduct of Vice Admiral Samuel Graves, Considered during the Period That He Held the Command

of His Majesty's Naval Force, in North America, 1774–1776."
[Edited by George Gefferina?] Circa Dec 11, 1776, to Dec
1, 1777. Original in British Library, Ad. 14.038 and 14.039;
a transcription in MHS, selections in *NDAR*. Note: Editor
appears to be George Gefferina, Graves's flag secretary while in
Boston (see *NDAR*, 2:1025), for in the introduction it is twice
signed G. G., and many letters throughout, especially in the
appendixes, are signed "G. Gefferina, by order of the Admiral".
Though Gefferina was the editor, much of this work was
probably dictated by Graves himself.

Kemble, Stephen. "Kemble's Journals, 1773–1789." In *Collections of the
New-York Historical Society for the year 1883*, 1–247. Publication
Fund Series. Vol. 16. New York: New-York Historical Society,
1884. It is sometimes referred to as *The Kemble Papers*. Vol. 1:
1773–1789.

Lister, Jeremy. *Concord Fight: Being so much of the Narrative of Ensign
Jeremy Lister of the 10th Regiment of Foot as pertains to his
services on the 19th of April, 1775, and to his experiences in
Boston during the early months of the Siege*. Edited by Harold
Murdock. Cambridge, MA: Harvard University Press, 1931. It
was written in 1782.

Mackenzie, Frederick. *A British Fusilier in Revolutionary Boston*.
Edited by Allen French. Cambridge, MA: Harvard University
Press, 1926. Note: This publication only includes the diary
from Jan 5 to Apr 30, 1775. Sadly, many volumes are
missing, including those covering May 1, 1775 to Sept 3,
1776. Though I did not use it, a two-volume set of all of
Mackenzie's extant diary volumes, from 1775 through 1781,
including the one published in *A British Fusilier*, is available
in *Diary of Frederick Mackenzie*. Cambridge, MA: Harvard
University Press, 1930.

Mott, Edward. "Journal of Capt. Edward Mott." In *Collections of the
Connecticut Historical Society*, vol. 1, 163–174. Hartford, CT:
Printed for the Society, 1860.

Newell, Timothy. "A Journal Kept During the Time that Boston was
Shut Up in 1775–6." In *Collections of the Massachusetts Historical*

Society, 4th ser., vol. 1, 261–76. Boston: Massachusetts Historical Society, 1852.

Pope, Richard. "Journal of an Officer of the 47th Regiment of Foot, after 1783." In Orderly Books of the American Revolution. Huntington Library, Santa Marino, CA. Note: A photostat has been reported as being at NY Public Library, but does not appear in their catalog. It remains unconfirmed whether Pope was an officer or a camp follower. The Apr 19, 1775, entry also in Murdock, *Late News*.

Rowe, John. *Letters and Diary of John Rowe, Boston Merchant, 1759–1762, 1764–1779*. Edited by Anne Rowe Cunningham. Boston: W. B. Clarke Company, 1903.

Stiles, Ezra. *Literary Diary of Ezra Stiles, D.D., LL.D.* Edited by Franklin Bowditch Dexter. Vol. 1. New York: Charles Scribner's Sons, 1901.

Thacher, James. *A Military Journal during the American Revolutionary War from 1775 to 1783*. 2nd ed. Boston: Cottons & Barnard, 1827.

Warren, Dr. John. In Warren, *Genealogy of Warren*. See Secondary Sources.

Washington, George. See Archives, PGW.

Williams, Lt. Richard. *Discord and Civil Wars; being a portion of the Journal kept by Lieutenant Williams of His Majesty's Twenty-Third Regiment while stationed in British North America during the time of the Revolution*. [Buffalo, NY?]: Easy Hill Press for the Salisbury Club of Buffalo, 1954.

Letters (and Reports)

These are only the *key letters* frequently drawn upon in the endnotes, for which I have used shorthand notation, listing their source information here only. The endnotes throughout this volume cite many other letters not listed here. Note that many of the sources for these items are in other volumes listed in the sections above. See the start of this bibliography for more details.

On the various depositions cited for the Battle of the Nineteenth of April, the first and earliest are all in Force, *American Archives*,

4:2:486–501. Depositions, taken days later, mostly regarding the supposed "scalping", are in Shattuck, *A History of the Town of Concord*, 350–51. (For discussion of these depositions, see Frank Warren Coburn, *Fiction and Truth About the Battle of Lexington Common, April 19, 1775*. Lexington: F. L. Coburn & Co., 1918.) Finally, the later 1825 depositions, unreliable as they were given fifty years later for the battle's anniversary, are in Phinney, *History of the Battle at Lexington*, 31ff.; while still more from 1835 are in Adams, *Address Delivered at Acton*, 43ff.

Clarke, Jonas. *Opening of the War of the Revolution: A Brief Narrative of the Principal Transactions of that Day*. Lexington, MA: Lexington Historical Society, 1901. (First written for a sermon on April 19, 1776, the original at the Lexington Historical Society.)

Barrett, Amos. Amos Barrett Letter of 1825. Edited by his great-grandson, Henry True. Originally published in True, Henry. *Journal and Letters of Rev. Henry True, of Hampstead, New Hampshire...* Marion, OH: Printed for the Author, 1900. Republished in Swayne, Josephine Latham, ed., *The Story of Concord Told by Concord Writers*, 49–52. Boston: E. F. Worcester Press, 1906. The former revises the language; the latter preserves it as in the original.

De Berniere, Henry. Ens. Henry De Berniere to Lieutenant General Gage [circa Apr 19, 1775]. In *Coll. of MHS*, 2nd ser., vol. 4, 215–18. Boston: 1816.

Feltham, Jocelyn. Lt. Jocelyn Feltham to Lt. Gen. Thomas Gage, June 11, 1775. In French, *Taking of Ticonderoga*, 42–55; original in Gage MSS.

Foster, Edmund. Edmund Foster to Daniel Shattuck, Mar 10, 1825. In Ripley, *A History of the Fight at Concord*, 32–37. Note: The whereabouts of the original are unknown. I have sought to avoid 1825 information, and generally quote it only when it can be corroborated by contemporary information, but for the fight from Concord back to Boston, few contemporary accounts mention more than a plain, generic note that it was a running fight all the way.

Gage, Thomas. *A Circumstantial Account of an Attack that happened on the 19th April, 1775.* Boston: John Howe, 1775. In MHS. Also transcribed in Force, *American Archives,* 2:435–36.

———. Lt. Gen. Thomas Gage to Lord Barrington, Apr 22, 1775. In Carter, *Correspondence of General Thomas Gage,* 2:673–74. (NB: Two letters here of same date.)

———. Lt. Gen. Thomas Gage to Lord Dartmouth, Apr 22, 1775. In Carter, *Correspondence of General Thomas Gage,* 1:396–97.

———. Lt. Gen. Thomas Gage's Official Casualty Report on the Expedition to Concord, Apr 19, 1775. In Coburn, *Battle of April 19, 1775,* 158–59. Variations exist, such as that in *Coll. of MHS* (1816), 2:4:218–19; Mackenzie, *A British Fusilier,* 61, or Richard Pope's narrative in Murdock, *Late News,* 31.

Gordon, William. Rev. William Gordon to a Gentleman in England, May 17, 1775. In Force, *American Archives,* 4:2:625–31.

Laurie, Walter Sloane. Capt. Walter Sloane Laurie to Lt. Gen. Thomas Gage, Apr 26, 1775. In French, *General Gage's Informers,* 95–98.

Munroe, William. Deposition, Mar 7, 1825. In Phinney, *History of the Battle at Lexington,* 33–35. NB: Use with caution, as it is given fifty years after the event.

Percy. Lord Percy to Lt. Gen. Thomas Gage, Apr 20, 1775. In Bolton, *Letters of Hugh Earl Percy,* 49–51.

———. Lord Percy to Lt. Gen. Thomas Gage, Apr 20, 1775 [Draft]. In Bolton, *Letters of Hugh Earl Percy,* 51n.

———. Lord Percy to Lt. Gen. Edward Harvey [the Adjutant General], Apr 20, 1775. In Bolton, *Letters of Hugh Earl Percy,* 52–53.

Pitcairn, John. Maj. John Pitcairn to Lt. Gen. Thomas Gage, Apr 26, 1775. In French, *General Gage's Informers,* 52–54. Original in Gage MSS, Clements Library.

Revere, Paul. Deposition Draft, circa May 1775. In MHS.

———. Deposition Draft [Corrected Copy], circa May 1775. In MHS.

———. Paul Revere to Jeremy Belknap [circa 1798]. In MHS. Printed in many places, including *Proc. of MHS* (1878), 16:371–76. Note: All three Revere letters are published together in Edmund S. Morgan, ed., *Paul Revere's Three Accounts of His Famous Ride.* 4th ed. Boston: Mass. Hist. Soc., 2000, a booklet available from MHS.

Smith, Francis. Lt. Col. Francis Smith to Lt. Gen. Thomas Gage, Apr 22, 1775. In *Proc. of MHS* (1876), 14:350–51n.

Sutherland, William. Lt. William Sutherland to Maj. Gen. Henry Clinton, Apr 26, 1775. In Murdock, *Late News*, 13ff. Original in Clinton MSS, Clements Library.

———. Lt. William Sutherland to Lt. Gen. Thomas Gage, Apr 27, 1775. In French, *General Gage's Informers*, 42ff., continues on 58ff., continues again on 85ff., concludes on 111ff. Original in Gage MSS, Clements Library.

Manuals (of Military Discipline)

Muller, John. *A Treatise of Artillery*. 3rd ed. London: Printed for John Millan, 1780. Available in Eighteenth Century Collections Online, Gale Cengage.

A New Manual and Platoon Exercise: With an Explanation. Dublin: Boulter Gribrson, 1764. Also known as *Manual of Arms*.

Pickering, Timothy, Jr. *An Easy Plan for Discipline of a Militia*. Salem, MA: Samuel and Ebenezer Hall, 1775. Available in Eighteenth Century Collections Online, Gale Cengage.

Maps and Sketches

Boston

Montresor, Capt. John. *[Plan of the Neck and fortifications]*. "Delivd. to H.E. Gl. Gage, June 30th. 1775." 1775.

Page, Thomas Hyde, and John Montresor. *Boston, its Environs and Harbour, with the Rebels Works Raised against that Town in 1775*. Faden, William, 1778.

Pelham, Henry. *A plan of Boston in New England with its Environs*. 1777.

Price, William. *A new plan of ye great town of Boston in New England in America, with the many additional buildings, & new streets, to the year 1769*. 1769.

Concord

Blaisdell, H. W. *Centennial Map of Concord, 1775–1875*. Concord, MA: J. H. Bufford's Lithography, 1875.

Sketches

Doolittle, Amos, four engravings, 1775, from etchings by Ralph Earl, 1775. Original prints exist in the Connecticut Historical Society, Hartford, CT. They have been reproduced in many volumes, including:

Plate I: The Battle of Lexington, April 19, 1775
    in Murdock, *The Nineteenth of April, 1775*, facing p. 4.
    in French, *Day of Concord and Lexington*, facing p. 134.
Plate II: A View of the Town of Concord
    in Murdock, *The Nineteenth of April, 1775*, facing p. 50.
    in French, *Day of Concord and Lexington*, facing p. 152.
Plate III: The Engagement at the North Bridge in Concord
    in Murdock, *The Nineteenth of April, 1775*, facing p. 68.
    in French, *Day of Concord and Lexington*, facing p. 190.
Plate IV: A View of the South Part of Lexington
    in Murdock, *The Nineteenth of April, 1775*, facing p. 42.
    in French, *Day of Concord and Lexington*, facing p. 232.

Newspapers
A partial list:

Boston Commercial Gazette
Boston Gazette
Boston New-Letter (*Massachusetts Gazette*)
Boston Post Boy (*Massachusetts Gazette*)
Columbian Centinel (of Boston)
London Chronicle
London Evening Post
Massachusetts Spy
New England Chronicle (*Essex Gazette*)
New London Gazette (of Connecticut)
New York Journal (*General Advertiser*)
New-York Gazette
Rhode-Island American
Rivington's *New York Gazetteer*

SECONDARY SOURCES

Adams, Josiah. *An Address Delivered at Acton, July 21, 1835, Being the First Centennial Anniversary of the Organization of that Town.* Boston: J. T. Buckingham, 1835. Note: This rare book is available in select libraries, including the Clements. The depositions in it are all republished in *Letter to Lemuel Shattuck.*

———. *Letter to Lemuel Shattuck, of Boston, from Josiah Adams, of Framingham: in Vindication of the Claims of Capt. Isaac Davis, of Acton, to His Just Share in the Honors of the Concord Fight.* Boston: Damrell & Moore, 1850. (No letter at all, but a small booklet.)

Alden, John Richard. *General Gage in America.* Baton Rouge: Louisiana State University Press, 1948.

———. "Why the March to Concord?" *American Historical Review* 49, no. 3 (1994): 446–54.

The Analectic Magazine. Vol. 11, *January–June 1818.* Philadelphia: Moses Thomas, 1818.

Arnold, Howard Payson. *The Memoir of Jonathan Mason Warren, M.D.* Boston: 1886.

Arnold, Isaac Newton. *The Life of Benedict Arnold: His Patriotism and His Treason.* Chicago: Jansen, McClurg & Co., 1880.

Bailyn, Bernard. *The Ideological Origins of the American Revolution.* Enl. ed. Cambridge, MA: The Belknap Press of Harvard University Press: 1992.

Bakeless, John Edwin. *Turncoats, Traitors, and Heroes.* New York: Da Capo Press, 1998. First published 1959, 1960 by Lippincott.

Bancroft, George. *History of the United States from the Discovery of the Continent.* 6 vols. New York: D. Appleton and Co., 1895–96. Author's last revision.

Belcher, Henry. *The First American Civil War: The First Period 1775–1778.* 2 vols. London: MacMillan and Co, Ltd, 1911.

Boardman, Samuel Lane, ed. *Peter Edes: Pioneer Printer in Maine: A Biography.* Bangor, ME: Printed for the De Burians, 1901. Includes Ede's diary.

Bond, Henry, and Horatio Gates Jones. *Genealogies of the families and descendants of the early settlers of Watertown, Massachusetts, including Waltham and Weston...* 2nd ed. Vol. 1. Boston: New England Hist. Gen. Soc., 1860.

Boston Record Commissioners. *Twenty-Eighth Report of the Record Commissioners, Boston Marriages. 1700–1751.* Boston: Municipal Printing Office,1898.

Boston Street Laying-Out Department. *A Record of the Streets, Alleys, Places, Etc., in the City of Boston.* Boston: City of Boston Printing Office, 1910.

Brown, Rebecca Warren. *Stories about General Warren in Relation to the Fifth of March Massacre and the Battle of Bunker Hill by a Lady of Boston.* Boston: James Loring, 1835.

Caldwell, Howard Walter, and Clark Edmund Persinger. *A Source History of the United States: From Discovery (1492) to End of Reconstruction (1877)...* Chicago: Ainsworth and Co., 1909.

Cary, John H. *Joseph Warren: Physician, Politician, Patriot.* Urbana: University of Illinois Press, 1961.

Celebration by the Inhabitants of Worcester, Mass., of the Centennial Anniversary of the Declaration of Independence, July 4, 1876: To Which are Added Historical and Chronological Notes. [Edited by Benjamin F. Thomas?] Worcester, MA: 1876.

Coburn, Frank Warren. *The Battle of April 19, 1775, in Lexington, Concord, Lincoln, Arlington, Cambridge, Somerville and Charlestown, Massachusetts.* 2nd ed. Boston: Wright & Potter Printing Co., 1922.

Coggins, Jack. *Ships and Seamen of the American Revolution.* Harrisburg, PA: Stackpole Books, 1969.

Danton, Graham. *The Theory and Practice of Seamanship.* 11th ed. New York: Routledge, 1996.

Dawson, Henry B. *Battles of the United States.* 2 vols. New York: Johnson, Fry, and Company, 1858.

The Detail and Conduct of the American War, under Generals Gage, Howe, Burgoyne, and Vice Admiral Lord Howe. 3rd ed. London: Richardson and Urquhart, 1780.

Drake, Francis S. *Tea Leaves: Being a Collection of Letters and Documents...* Boston: A. O. Crane, 1884.

———. *The Town of Roxbury: Its Memorable Persons and Places, Its History and Antiquities...* Boston: Municipal Printing Office, 1908.

Duncan, Francis. *History of the Royal Regiment of Artillery*. 3rd ed., 2 vols. London: John Murray, 1879.

Everett, Alexander. *Life of Joseph Warren*. Edited by Jared Sparks. New York: Harper and Bros., 1856. Republished in Wilson, James Grant, and John Fiske, eds. *Appleton's Cyclopaedia of American Biography*, 10:91. New York: D. Appleton and Co., 1888. (10:101 of the 1902 ed.) The pages cited in the present text correspond to Sparks's compilation.

Fischer, David Hackett. *Paul Revere's Ride*. New York: Oxford University Press, 1994.

Fleming, Thomas J. *Now We Are Enemies: The Story of Bunker Hill*. New York: St. Martin's Press, 1960. Note: My limited use of this source is with caution, as it is entirely unreferenced.

Forman, Samuel A. *Dr. Joseph Warren: The Boston Tea Party, Bunker Hill, and the Birth of American Liberty*. Gretna, LA: Pelican Publishing Co., 2011.

Fortescue, John William, ed. *The Correspondence of King George the Third*. See Primary Sources: Books.

Fortescue, John William. *A History of the 17th Lancers (Duke of Cambridge's Own)*. London: Macmillan and Co., 1895.

———. *Franklin before the Privy Council, White Hall Chapel, London, 1774…* Philadelphia: John M. Butler, 1860.

French, Allen. "The British Expedition to Concord, Massachusetts, in 1775." *Journal of the American Military History Foundation* 1, no. 1 (Spring 1937):1–17.

———. *The Day of Concord and Lexington*. Boston: Little, Brown and Company, 1925.

———. *The First Year of the American Revolution*. Boston: Houghton Mifflin, 1934.

———. *General Gage's Informers*. Ann Arbor: University of Michigan Press, 1932.

———. *Life and Times of Joseph Warren*. Boston: Little, Brown, & Co., 1865.

———. *The Siege of Boston*. New York: The Macmillan Company, 1911.

———. *The Taking of Ticonderoga in 1775: The British Story*. Cambridge, MA: Harvard University Press, 1928.

Frothingham, Richard. *History of the Siege of Boston.* 3rd ed. Boston: Little, Brown, and Company, 1872.

Gordon, William. *The History of the Rise, Progress and Establishment of the Independence of the United States...* 3rd. ed., 3 vols. New York: Printed for Samuel Campbell by John Woods, 1801.

Goss, Elbridge Henry. *The Life of Colonel Paul Revere.* 2 vols. Boston: Joseph George Cupples, 1891.

Greene, Jack P., and Richard M. Jellison. "The Currency Act of 1764 in Imperial-Colonial Relations, 1764–1776." *William and Mary Quarterly*, 3rd ser., 18, no. 4 (October 1961): 485–518.

Greenleaf, Jonathan. *A Genealogy of the Greenleaf Family.* New York: Edward O Jenkins, 1854.

Hagist, Don N. "How Old Were Redcoats? Age and Experience of British Soldiers in America." *Journal of the American Revolution*, May 21, 2014. Accessed January 21, 2015. http://allthingsliberty .com/2014/05/how-old-were-redcoats-age-and-experience-of -british-soldiers-in-america/.

Harland, John. *Seamanship in the Age of Sail: An Account of the Shiphandling of the Sailing of Man-of-War 1600–1860, Based on Contemporary Sources.* London, 1984. Reprinted with illustrations by Mark Myers. Annapolis, MD: Naval Institute Press, 1985.

Hawkes, James. *A Retrospect of the Boston Tea-Party: A Memoir of George R. T. Hewes.* New York: S. S. Bliss, 1834.

Holland, Henry W. *William Dawes and His Ride with Paul Revere: An Essay.* Boston: John Wilson and Son, 1878.

Hurd, Duane Hamilton, ed. *History of Middlesex County, Massachusetts.* 3 vols. Philadelphia: J. W. Lewis & Co., 1890. Includes Loammi Baldwin's journal.

Hutchinson, Thomas. *The History of the Province of Massachusetts Bay: from 1749 to 1774, Comprising a Detailed Narrative of the Origin and Early Stages of the American Revolution.* Edited by John Hutchinson. London: John Murray, 1828.

Isaacson, Walter. *Benjamin Franklin: An American Life.* New York: Simon & Shuster, 2003.

Johnston, Patrick. "Building a Revolution: The Powder Alarm and

Popular Mobilization of the New England Countryside, 1774–1775." *Historical Journal of Massachusetts* 37, no. 1 (Spring 2009): 123–40.

Labaree, Benjamin Woods. *The Boston Tea Party*. 1966. Reprint, New York: Oxford University Press, 1970.

———. *Catalyst for Revolution: The Boston Tea Party 1773*. Massachusetts: Bicentennial Commission, 1973.

Lavery, Brian. *The Ship of the Line*. 2 vols. Annapolis, MD: Naval Institute Press, 2003–4.

Leffingwell, E. H. *Catalogue of Autographs, Letters and Historical Documents, Collected by the Late Prof. E. H. Leffingwell, of New Haven, Conn.* Compiled by John S. H. Frogg. 2 vols. Boston: C. F. Libbie & Co., 1891. Note: "To be sold by auction Tuesday January 6th, 1891 and following days", though in the copy held at the American Antiquarian Society (the copy I used), a handwritten note states "and Tuesday, March 17th". The auction was in Boston, by C. F. Libbie & Co., Auctioneers, Boston, Mass. The catalogue is dated 1891.

Livingston, William Farrand. *Israel Putnam: Pioneer, Ranger, and Major-General, 1718–1790*. New York: G. P. Putnam's Sons, 1901.

Lockhart, Paul. *The Whites of their Eyes*. New York: Harper Collins, 2011.

Lossing, Benson. *American Historical Record and Repertory of Notes and Queries*. 3 vols. Philadelphia: Chase & Town, 1872–74.

———. *The Pictorial Field-Book of the Revolution*. 2 vols. New York: Harper & Bros., 1851–52.

MacDonald, William. *Select Charters and Other Documents Illustrative of American History, 1606–1775*. New York: Macmillan Co., 1899.

Manucy, Albert C. *Artillery Through the Ages: A Short Illustrated History of Cannon, Emphasizing Types Used in America*. 1949. Reprint, Washington, DC: U.S. Government Printing Office, 1962.

Martyn, Charles. *The Life of Artemas Ward*. New York: Artemas Ward, 1921.

May, W. E. *The Boats of Men-of-War*. Annapolis, MD: Naval Maritime Museum, 1974. Reprinted with additions by Simon Stephens. Annapolis, MD: Naval Institute Press, 1999.

Middlekauff, Robert. *The Glorious Cause: The American Revolution, 1763–1789*. 2nd ed. New York: Oxford University Press, 2005.

Miller, John C. *Origins of the American Revolution*. Boston: Little, Brown and Co, 1943.

Mollo, John. *Uniforms of the American Revolution in color*. Illustrations by Malcolm McGregor. New York: Macmillan Publishing Co., Inc., 1975.

Moore, Frank. *Diary of the American Revolution from Newspapers and Original Documents*. 2 vols. New York: Charles Scribner, 1860.

Motte, Ellis L. et al., eds. *The Manifesto Church: Records of the Church in Brattle Square, Boston, 1699–1872*. Boston: The Benevolent Fraternity of Churches, 1902.

Murdock, Harold. *The Nineteenth of April, 1775*. Boston: Houghton Mifflin Company, 1923.

Nelson, James L. *Benedict Arnold's Navy: The Ragtag Fleet that Lost the Battle of Lake Champlain but Won the American Revolution*. Camden, ME: McGraw-Hill Professional, 2006.

Nicolas, Paul Harris. *Historical Record of the Royal Marine Forces*. 2 vols. London: Thomas and William Boone, 1845.

Orations Delivered at the Request of the Inhabitants of the Town of Boston to Commemorate the Evening of the Fifth of March, 1770... Boston: Peter Edes, 1785. Note: This rare volume is in the Evans microfiche, No. 18997, available at most research libraries.

Perrin, William G. *British Flags, Their Early History, and Their Development at Sea*. London: Cambridge University Press, 1922.

Phinney, Elias. *History of the Battle at Lexington, on the Morning of the 19th April, 1775*. Boston: Phelps and Farnham, 1825.

Ripley, Ezra. *A History of the Fight at Concord, on the 19th of April, 1775...* Concord, MA: Allen & Atwill, 1827.

Sabine, Lorenzo. *American Loyalists...* Boston: Charles C. Little and James Brown, 1847.

Selig, Robert A. "Artillery." AmericanRevolution.org. Accessed November 7, 2008. www.americanrevolution.org/artillery.html.

Shattuck, Lemuel. *A History of the Town of Concord...* Boston: Russell, Odiorne, and Co., 1835.

Smith, Digby, and Kevin K. Kiley. *An Illustrated Encyclopedia of Uniforms from 1775–1783: The American Revolutionary War*. London: Lorenz Books, 2008.

Smyth, W. H. *The Sailor's Word Book: An Alphabetical Digest of Nautical Terms*. London: Blackie and Son, 1867.

Sparks, Jared. *Life and Treason of Benedict Arnold*. Boston: Hilliard, Gray, and Co., 1835.

Spring, Matthew H. *With Zeal and with Bayonets Only: The British Army on Campaign in North America, 1775–1783*. Norman: University of Oklahoma Press, 2008.

Stedman, Charles. *The History of the Origin, Progress, and Termination of the American War*. 2 vols. London: Printed for the Author, 1794.

Sumner, William Hyslop. *History of East Boston*. Boston: William H. Piper & Co., 1869.

Swett, Samuel. *The History of the Bunker Hill Battle, With a Plan*. 2nd ed. Boston: Munroe and Francis, 1826.

Thatcher, Benjamin Bussey. *Traits of the Tea Party; Being a Memoir of George R. T. Hewes…* New York: Harper & Bros., 1835.

Truax, Rhoda. *The Doctors Warren of Boston: First Family of Surgery*. Boston: Houghton Mifflin Company, 1968.

Tsu, Sun. *The Art of War*. Translated by Thomas Cleary. Boston: Shambhala Publications, 1988.

Walker, Jeffrey B. *The Devil Undone: The Life and Poetry of Benjamin Church, 1734–1778*. New York: Arno Press; 1982. Originally presented as the author's doctoral thesis at Pennsylvania State University, 1977.

Warren, Edward. *The Life of John Warren, M.D.* Boston: Noyes, Holmes, and Company, 1874.

———. *The Life of John Collins Warren, M.D.* 2 vols. Boston: Ticknor and Fields, 1860.

———. *Watertown's Military History*. Boston: David Clapp & Son, Printers, 1907.

Warren, John Collins. *A Genealogy of Warren with Some Historical Sketches*. Boston: Printed by John Wilson and Son, 1854.

Weems, Mason L. *A History of the Life and Death, Virtues and Exploits of General George Washington*. J. B. Lippincott, 1918. Mount Vernon Edition. Note: To be used with caution, as it has many legends purported as fact.

Wheildon, William W. *Curiosities of History: Boston...1630–1880*. 2nd ed. Boston: Lee and Shepard, 1880.

Wilson, Timothy. *Flags at Sea*. Rev. ed. Annapolis, MD: Naval Institute Press, 1999.

Windsor, Justin, ed. *The Memorial History of Boston...1630–1880*. 4 vols. Boston: James R. Osgood and Company, 1881–82.

Winfield, Rif. *British Warships in the Age of Sail, 1714–1792: Design, Construction, Careers and Fates*. Barnsley, South Yorkshire, UK: Seaforth Publishing, 2007.

Wood, Gordon S. *The Radicalism of the American Revolution*. New York: Vintage Books, 1993. First published 1991 by Alfred A. Knopf, Inc.

INDEX

ABOUT THE AUTHOR

Derek W. Beck has always had a passion for military history, which inspired him to start his career in the U.S. Air Force. He has served as an officer on active duty in science roles and in space operations. In 2005 he earned a master of science degree at the Massachusetts Institute of Technology (MIT), where he also fell in love with Boston's revolutionary past. To more fully pursue writing, he later transitioned to  the Air Force Reserves, though he still remains quite active, presently holding the rank of major. When not working on future history books, Derek is a frequent contributor to the online *Journal of the American Revolution*. You can follow or connect with him through his website at www.derekbeck.com.

PHOTO BY MISSY WASHINGTON/i102fly

STATEN RIVER

Farm

Mount Pigot

Mount Pisgah

Bunkers Hill

Cobble Hill

Ploid Hill

CAMBRIDGE

Redoubt

Redoubt

CHARLES RIVER

BROOKLYN

GLASS

Lechmere Point

Phipps Farm

MYSTICK RIVER

Floating Battery

Charlestown Point

CHARLESTOWN

Winisimmit

NODDLES ISLAND

Williams House

HOG

Bartons Point

Hudson's Pt

North Battery

Mill Dam

Mill Pond

Wharf

South Battery

Bird Island

GOVERNORS ISLA

Brindley's Meadow

Muddy River

Barrys Hill

Rebels

Newtoun Mill

ROXBURY

Lines

Tan Yard

Roxbury
Burying ground

Roxbury Hill

Floating Battery

Windmill Point

Dorchester

Dorchester Flatts
Hard Mud

61⁄2

61⁄2

61⁄4 Upper Middle S.W.

Seven Feet Channel

Feet

61⁄2

DORCHESTER NECK

Dorchester
Point

CASTLE ISLAND

Muscle Bank

THOMPSONS ISLAND

DORCHESTER

CH

Engraved & Published by Wm FADEN, Charing Cross; as the Act directs, 1st Octr. 1778.